Introduction to Psalms
The Genres of the Religious Lyric of Israel
Gunkel/Begrich

Introduction to Psalms

The Genres of the Religious Lyric of Israel

by
Hermann Gunkel

completed by
Joachim Begrich

translated by
James D. Nogalski

WIPF & STOCK · Eugene, Oregon

Wipf and Stock Publishers
199 W 8th Ave, Suite 3
Eugene, OR 97401

Introduction to Psalms
The Genres of the Religious Lyric of Israel
By Gunkel, Hermann and Begrich, Joachim
Copyright © 1998 Mercer University Press
and Vandenhoeck & Ruprecht All rights reserved.
Softcover ISBN-13: 978-1-5326-9016-7
Hardcover ISBN-13: 978-1-5326-9017-4
Publication date 2/5/2020
Previously published by Mercer University, 1998

Contents

Foreword

Hermann Gunkel died 11 March 1932 without being able to complete his great work on Psalms. While he was still living, the great suffering of his last years forced him to give up one section of his *Introduction to Psalms* after another, until finally when I last saw him at Christmas, 1931, he placed the entire work in my hands.

He worked on the second half of his *Introduction to Psalms* as long as it was possible. Chapter 7 (the Individual Thanksgiving Song) and chapter 10 (Wisdom Poetry) are his work, apart from several redactional changes and abbreviations required with respect to the whole. He wanted to complete §9 (Prophetic Elements in the Psalms) himself even until the very end, but he was only able to complete sections 1-18. In places where he was unable to do the work himself, he aided his student with advice and help. Such is the case especially for chapter 6, whose completion he lived to see, and whose rendering he approved (even those places which deviated from his own ideas). Nevertheless, the informed reader will frequently recognize the hand of the master in this chapter.

It goes without saying that, in the chapters which fell to me, I have relied on the collections and notes of my revered teacher as far as possible. His plan for chapter 6 was available to me in detail, as was the broad outline of chapter 9. In chapter 6, an abundance of illustrative passages, arranged by section numbers, as well as bibliographic references stood at my disposal. In chapter 9, I had several short notes and textual references from which the goal of the chapter was clear. In chapter 14, I had a list of his interpretations of the musical terms of the psalm superscriptions. In the remaining chapters, I was on my own. I bear sole responsibility for the thought process and the presentations of the sections I reworked.

The reader may perhaps be afraid that the lengthy chronological distance between the introduction and the commentary (and the change in the person presenting it) may damage the unity of the entire work. Without attacking this critique, I believe I can say that the unity has generally been preserved. I have nowhere felt required to deviate from the standpoint of my teacher's method. Therefore, it was my task to take over the chapters he began (apart from some necessary abbreviations), and finish them. He was satisfied with this process in chapter 6.

By contrast, I must ask for patience in those sections which refer to details in the commentary. It is not very easy to present them when it has become clear during the course of the work that many things should perhaps appropriately be arranged somewhat differently. As Hermann Gunkel wished, dialogue with pertinent literature which has appeared since the commentary was finished is only undertaken to the degree that it does not burden the connection between the commentary and the introduction. I believe this sacrifice for the sake of the unity of the work offers no real harm. I have also found it necessary to deviate in isolated points from premises suggested in the commentary and in the first half of the introduction. These deviations are noted explicitly in the affected passages.

In conclusion, I would make several unrelated comments. I could not take account of Walter G. Kunstmann's work (*Die babylonische Gebetsbeschwörung*, Leipziger semitistische Studien, n.s. 2 [Leipzig, 1932]) in §6. On the one hand, the religiohistorical and the psychological aspects do not appear adequate. On the other hand, it does not in the least disturb the correctness of the study undertaken in §6. It addresses specific types of individual Babylonian prayers, for which I am grateful. However, in doing so, it overlooks the fact that these types stand in a comprehensive genre context. For example, the song of innocence, the psalm of confession, and the song of confidence only represent subcategories of the individual complaint song. In order to guard against misunderstandings like those in Kunstmann (p. 2), I would also like to take this opportunity to note that the Babylonian quotations have been checked against the original text in the vast majority of cases. The translations make it possible for the reader, even one who is not proficient in Akkadian, to examine the material which is scattered in inscriptional works and which can be quite fragmentary.

Citations of psalms basically cite the translation of the commentary. Deviations from this translation occur only in isolated cases where necessary.

At the request of the publisher, the illustrative texts are provided in footnotes under the text beginning on p. 124. Publisher and author hope this change will serve the legibility and readability of the whole. The reader of the work is indebted to my wife for the subject index at the end.

Completing this work on Psalms has filled me with joy and gratitude that my venerable teacher Hermann Gunkel entrusted it to me. As far as it was within my power, I have attempted to justify his trust. I hope my work brings honor to his work. May the completed work deepen and challenge the love for Old Testament psalmody in our days.

Leipzig, July 1933   *Joachim Begrich*

Translator's Preface

Amazingly, this seminal work remained untranslated for sixty-five years. I am grateful to the editors of Mercer University Press for correcting this oversight, and for allowing me the opportunity to undertake this translation. I have attempted to render the German faithfully, but in readable English. This often required shortening sentences, rearranging word order, breaking paragraphs, changing from passive to active constructions, and specifying antecedents. I have followed Gunkel/Begrich's numbering system for the individual sections of the chapters which should facilitate comparing the translation to the original. A complete index of scripture references is included. I am grateful to Melanie Greer Nogalski for her help in compiling this index.

The *Introduction to Psalms* by Gunkel/Begrich is a historic work that deserves to be available to English readers because it has so greatly influenced the study of Psalms in the latter half of this century. Many of the genre categories delineated here have stood the test of time. However, like any work, this volume also contains dated material that must be evaluated critically. For example, Gunkel's presuppositions about the development of Israelite religion have not fared as well as his delineation of genre categories, but these presuppositions greatly affect his argumentation for dating genre developments and individual psalms. Like many in his time, Gunkel presumes Israelite religion began as a primitive religion, climaxed in the works of the great prophets, and then degenerated into a legalistic religion overly influenced by the law. Needless to say, this paradigm can no longer be deemed adequate.

Gunkel's translations of biblical texts should also be evaluated. He worked during a time in the history of the discipline which more readily assumed textual corruptions than would be the case after the finding of the Dead Sea Scrolls in 1948. Sometimes, Gunkel's interpretation hinges upon textual emendations he has accepted in his commentary. For this reason, I have attempted to translate his translations faithfully (rather than utilize a standard English translation). I have attempted to follow his practice of indicating reconstructed texts where he has noted them.

Despite these and other shortcomings, this work has no equal. Its comprehensive nature, careful systematic argumentation, and its eye for detail will quickly show why Gunkel remains one of the giants in Old Testament studies. Even though this work contains dated material, it also frequently anticipates questions that still plague the discipline.

Those reading Gunkel for the first time may be surprised to learn that he is hardly a detached observer of Psalms, despite his scientific approach. His style can quickly change from descriptive prose to lofty, almost poetic, images which unabashedly convey his great admiration for the giftedness of Israelite poets.

In conclusion, I would echo the words of Begrich in his foreword: May my work bring honor to their work.

Lombard, Illinois, February 1998   *James D. Nogalski*

§1 The Genres of the Psalms

1. The Psalter is perhaps the most frequently interpreted and most beloved book of the Old Testament. Nevertheless, for historical understanding, it creates extraordinary *difficulties* that still have not been thoroughly considered, despite all sincere efforts. For the scholarly observer it is apparent that the basis of these difficulties should be precisely identified. Only then may one hope to proceed a step further in overcoming them.

These difficulties derive primarily from the particular *manner of speech* of Hebrew Poetry. Ancient Israel was greatly gifted in the power of its outlook and in the depth of its perception, but it was less gifted than the Greeks in the logic of its thought. Typically, in the poetry of Israel, Hebrew versification incorporates very short sentences which often consist of only two or three words. However, these short sentences are very frequently placed next to one another without any description of their logical relationship. The Hebrew would say: "The LORD is my shepherd. I shall not want." The Greek would have expressed that the second sentence was a result of the first. The Hebrew omits a "therefore." Thus, the poetry of Israel is sometimes comparable to a glockenspiel. The individual tones resound powerfully and magnificently, but each reverberates by itself so that only the one who is knowledgeable is able to hear the melody which the tones form according to the intention of the artist. Understanding these creations may not have been as difficult in the time they were composed, when so much of what was not explicitly expressed by the poet could be easily supplemented. But to those of us born later, their internal connection is not immediately clear.

In addition one may add that all poetry, and especially that of the Psalms, by nature prefers an *indeterminate means of expression*. Everyday prose, especially scholarly prose, wants to describe things as precisely as possible, but it is the way of poetry to circumvent the general reality and only state the essential. To write poetry means to simplify, to accentuate, to emphasize, and to intimate. Thus, the poet of the complaint song (this genre and others will be expressly treated in the following chapters) speaks about his many enemies without ever specifying the type of enemy. We ask: Are they opponents of his religion, his people, his person? And if they are personal antagonists, why do they threaten him? What do they have against him? All too often we experience nothing from the text itself concerning these questions, or at least nothing satisfying. As a result, it is extremely difficult for us to gain a clear picture of the fate of the author. Or, the author is content to speak in all kinds of allusions and images. The enemies have trapped him in a snare as the hunter does with a wild beast. What have they done to him? He is sure they have done something. He is stuck in the mire; torrents of water overcome him. Certainly these are images, but for what purpose? In his time, all of this was easy to understand because then everyone knew the presuppositions and the formal language of the poetry. Today's expositors, however, make all kinds of suggestions in these cases, sometimes very unfortunately, without ever being able to attain complete certainty.

Further, the explanation is complicated by the inundating *passion* of the Israelite character which actually seeks the most extreme overstatement rather than shy away from it. The highest praise for a modern researcher, with his/her sense of reality, is discipline and tranquility of spirit. Exegetical sobriety is the highest praise for the philological biblical interpreter. Yet the modern researcher or the philological interpreter often stands dumb-founded and helpless before the overflow of the hot-blooded Hebrew, and sometimes grasps for the most unusual outlets in order to gain some tolerable meaning for such words. The Israelite poet can protest that he was dead and delivered from the underworld. Still, he wants to call for universal judgment against his personal enemies and wish his king, the lord of poor little Judah, victory and lordship over all nations. For the modern person, who would never speak in such terms, this kind of hyperbole appears completely impossible.

Further, consider the particular difficulties which grow out of the *use of "tenses"* in Hebrew poetry. Hebrew sentence formation, particularly in Hebrew poetry, is somewhat primitive, and the tenses are extraordinarily ambiguous. Thus, it can happen that even today the commentators sometimes waver over whether a poem should be conceptualized as a complaint about present need or as a thanksgiving for a fortunate deliverance (cf. Ps 41; 116; Isa 38:10-20).

In addition, *the psalms are often not very long*. Yet, it is characteristic of Israel's intellectual manner that its poets sometimes aim for the deepest and finest reactions in the narrowest realm. Often, the shorter the poems, the more beautiful and impressive they are. But, for that reason, they are also more difficult for us to understand today. Longer poetic works would be easier to interpret because the individual passages could be explained in view of other passages.

In addition, the individual songs *lack almost any credible tradition* about the poet, or the reasons and times when the songs originated. If only those entrusted with the task of collecting these jewels had cared more about those who came later and had left behind reliable indicators for understanding and dating the individual songs. Instead, we are left almost completely in the dark concerning the transmission, and must fill the gaps by our own work. Cf. § 12.

Further, our work on the psalms is grievously disturbed by the condition of *our texts*. There can be little doubt that one finds the text of the psalter in a particularly dismal condition. All too frequently, none of the lines can be translated with certainty, and even using current methods we remain in the dark in our understanding of the entire poem.

And now in closing, an important observation can be made. No *internal ordering principle for the individual psalms has been transmitted for the whole*. To be sure, some-times related psalms stand together in the collection of the psalter: "complaints of the individual" (Pss 5–7; 54–57; 61–64; 69–71; 140–143); "hymns" (65f [95–100]; 103–105; 134–136; 145–150); "thanksgiving psalms" (40f); "royal psalms" (20f); "communal complaints" (79f); "wisdom speeches" (127:1f, 3-5); alphabetic psalms (111f); those treating the fate of Israel (74–83); those containing narratives (105f); those with eschato-logical contents (46–48). More commonly, however, no internal relationship can be discovered between neighboring psalms, particularly in the following groups: 15–20; 22–24; 28–30; 31–37; 41–46; 48–51; 71–75; 76–79; 80–82; 83–87; 88–95; 100–102; 108–110. In these groups, not one individual psalm coincides in genre with its neighbor. Even the so-called pilgrimage psalms (120–134) are comprised almost exclusively of different genres. Thus no certainty exists in questionable cases, whether a psalm should be understood with its neighbor. The following chapters will deal with the genres that have been named above in quotation marks. What Goethe says in *Westöstlichen Divan*

(*"Segenspfänder"*) about the inscription goes for the individual psalm as well: It "has nothing behind it. It stands alone, and must tell you everything." However, there is an unbreakable principle of scholarship that nothing can be understood outside of its context. Accordingly, the *particular task of psalm studies should be to rediscover the relationships between the individual songs* that did not occur with the transmission, or that occurred only in part. Once we have coordinated the psalms that belong together internally, we can hope to achieve a precise understanding of the poem by means of a thoroughgoing comparison. Then with the help of meaningful analogous passages we can hope to resolve many of the individual difficulties.

2. The primary preliminary task will be *to provide an overview of the entire material transmitted to us*. The reason is self-evident. It cannot be satisfactory simply to observe the poetry of the biblical psalter. Rather, one must ask whether there are psalms or psalm-like poetry outside the psalter. Only when we have incorporated this poetry into the observation is a real understanding of the poetry possible, including that of the psalter. One of the main reasons why current Psalms research offers such a confused and fuzzy picture is that no one has earnestly undertaken this foundational step. But if someone researching the past wants to obtain the true picture of what happened, that researcher first has to disregard the context in which the items came to us more or less accidentally. Rather, the researcher's goal is to observe things in the contexts in which they were originally found. However, in so doing, it should be irrelevant initially whether these songs are found inside the canon or outside the canon, or even whether they are found within Israel or outside Israel. These things are irrelevant if they really demonstrate internal relationship with the psalms. Only during the investigation can one ascertain how highly to evaluate these poems to be compared outside the Bible.

We have these items, in part and in whole. The *authors of the narrative books* were quite aware of the delightful effect made by the river of beautiful verse when it interrupted the footpath of prose. Thus the authors inserted songs at certain points and placed them in the mouths of the heroes of their narratives. Here (as in what follows) we mention several examples without striving to be exhaustive. The entire material in question will then be placed under the individual genres. The following have been preserved for us: Moses' "Song of the Sea" (Exod 15), the thanksgiving songs of Hanna (1 Sam 2), of David (2 Sam 22, which reprises Ps 18), of Jonah (Jonah 2), and of Hezekiah (Isa 38:9ff). In addition, one can note the placement of psalm elements in Chronicles (1 Chr 16:8ff). Also, in the Apocrypha we read the songs of Tobit (Tob 13) and of Judith (Jdt 16). Even in the New Testament, we read the hymns of Mary and Zacharias (Luke 1:46ff, 67ff).

The book of Job, as evidenced by its overall tone, did not grow from the soil of the psalmic poetry. Nevertheless, the poet drew heavily from psalmic poetry in places. When the poet wants to present Job's immense pain, or when he wants to let Job protest his innocence, he knew of no better means than to have him take up "complaint songs" and "songs of innocence" as they also appear in the psalter (cf. Job 10; 13:23–14:22; 16:6–17:9; 19:7ff, etc.). When the poet wants to praise the majestic sovereignty of God, he sang "hymns" which are comparable in tone and in form to those of the psalter (cf. Job 5:9ff; 9:3-13; 12:13ff; 26:5ff; 36:26ff; 38:4ff; etc.).

Prophetic books especially contain many psalm-like elements. Indeed, the prophecy of Israel originally had nothing to do with religious lyric, but at a certain stage of its development, prophecy took hold of the poetry of psalms as well as other literary genres.

It did so in order to be able to express itself fully, and simultaneously to influence a people, with prophecy, who were in large measure receptive to poetry. When the prophet wanted to provide the most moving expression to the complaint of the people's desire for deliverance, then the prophet reached for a "complaint song" like the community tended to sing elsewhere, and like those which can also be found in the psalter (cf. Jer 14:1-6, 7-9, 19-22; Isa 63:11ff; Mic 7:7ff). Or the prophet composed a song in the tone of the "hymns" that Israel would sing at the point it was freed from crisis to celebrate the Jubilee festival to its God (cf. Isa 12; 25:1ff; 26:1ff; 42:10-12; 49:13; 52:9f; etc.). Jeremiah in particular, derided and persecuted, often close to death, would pour out his pain and his hope in moving songs that are similar to the "complaints of the individual" in the psalter (Jer 11:18-20; 12:1-6; 15:15-21; 17:12-18; etc.). See W. Baumgartner, *Klagelieder des Jeremia*, 1917. Concerning the prophet's lyrical practice, cf. my introductions to Hans Schmidt, *Die großen Propheten,*[2] pp. lviiiff.

In addition, one can include chapters 3 and 5 from the book of *Lamentations*, both "complaint songs" that should be placed in line with those of the psalter. By contrast, chapters 1; 2; and 4 derive from "corpse songs" and are not classified among the psalms.

Further, the *apocrypha* offers us particularly rich material. The collections of speeches in Jesus ben Sirach contains a great deal of lyric (cf. W. Baumgartner, "Die literarischen Gattungen in der Weisheit des Jesus Sirach," *ZAW* 34 [1914]: 169ff). In addition to the songs of Tobit and Judith that we already mentioned, the following also come into view: the prayer of Azariah, and the song of praise of the three men in the fiery furnace—both in the additions to the Greek version of Daniel; the prayer of Manasseh; and the lyric elements in the books of Baruch, 1 Maccabees, 4 Ezra, as well as the Apocalypse of Baruch, etc. Indeed we possess a completely different collection of Psalms from this time, the so-called Psalms of Solomon, written in the first century BCE. These elements have not been satisfactorily taken into account in the research of the biblical psalms. This fact is especially true with respect to dating, where it is hardly mentioned. In this regard, it should be clear from the outset that those who argue that several, or many, of the psalms are Maccabbean are obligated to compare them with the poems mentioned here, which certainly stem from a later time.

This poetry is also continued in the *early Christian* period. Psalm-like witnesses are also found here and there in the New Testament. In addition to Luke 1:46ff, 67ff, see also Rev 4:11; 5:9ff; 11:17f; 15:3f; 19:6f. Even the Psalms of Solomon, which was composed by gnostic Christian of Jewish origin in the second century A.D., shows the influence of the ancient forms (cf. Pss.. Sol 5; 16:11ff; 18; 25; 29).

However, we cannot remain just in the cabinets of Israelite convention. Rather, we must also peruse the lyric of other nations of antiquity to see whether we perceive something similar. For decades we have recognized the extraordinarily rich cultic poetry of the *Babylonians and Assyrians*, from which many specimens demonstrate a relationship to the biblical psalms that is more than superficial. It has long been recognized, but has not been satisfactorily taken to heart in Psalms research. Cf. H. Zimmern, *Babylonische Hymnen und Gebete*, 1905; vol. 2: *Auswahl*, 1911; M. Jastrow, *Religion Babyloniens und Assyriens*, vol 1, 1905, pp. 393ff; vol 2., 1912, pp. 1ff; E. Ebeling and H. Greßmann, *Altorientalische Texte und Bilder*[2], 1926, vol. 1, pp. 241ff; J. Böllenrücher, *Gebete und Hymnen an Nergal*, 1904; J. Hehn, *Hymnen und Gebete an Marduk*, in *Beiträgen zur Assyriologie*, vol. 3, 1907; E. G. Perry, *Hymnen und Gebeten an Sin* 1907; St. Langdon,

Sumerian and Babylonian Psalms, 1909; A. Schollmeyer, *Sumerisch-babylonische Hymnen und Gebete an Šamaš*, 1912; J. Pindert, *Hymnen und Gebete an Nebo*, 1920; W. Schrank, *Babylonische Sühnriten*, 1908; R. Kittel, *Psalmen*,[3, 4] 1922, pp. xxiiff; Fr. Stummer, *Sumerisch-akkadische Parallelen zum Aufbau alttestamentlicher Psalmen*, 1922.

In addition, it has recently been shown that at times the cultic poetry of *Egypt* blossomed as magnificently as the Hebrew cultic poetry. Cf. A. Erman, *Ägyptische Religion*, 1909[2], pp. 79ff; *Ägyptische Literatur in der 'Kultur der Gegenwart, '* part I, section 7, 1906, pp. 28ff; *Literatur der Ägypter*, 1923; H. Ranke and H. Greßmann, *Altorientalische Texte und Bilder,*[2] vol. 1, 1926, pp. 12ff; Gr. Roeder, *Urkunden zur Religion des alten Ägypten*, 2nd printing, 1923; Gunkel, *Reden und Aufsätze*, 1913, pp. 136f, 141ff.

Finding these ancient oriental poems has been the most significant event of the entire nineteenth century, or at least it should have been, especially since they precede the biblical poetry by centuries and in some cases by millennia.

If we observe the psalms in the context which our generation has demonstrated with other contexts, then a comprehensive religious type of poetry has now appeared for us in place of a single biblical book. We also possess an abundance of exemplars of this type of poetry outside the psalter. We can also trace these exemplars in and outside Israel from the third millennium until the time of the origin of Christianity, where they are then gradually superseded by the poetry of the early church and the synagogue. As a result, however, the goal of our work has simultaneously shifted. Now our task is not just to explain a particular psalm or the book of the psalter—even though that is precisely what so many have done. Without paying attention to the larger contexts, the complete success of the previous work has not been achieved. Rather, *the final goal must be to describe the entire type of poetry and its history*, which certainly traveled a very circuitous path.

It should still be added that in the comprehensive reckoning we have also taken account of *the world of the prose prayers* inside and outside Israel since the biblical psalms are mostly, though not exclusively, prayers. We have taken prose prayers into account when they are expressly communicated, or when they are mentioned in the narrative, or elsewhere. Cf. Hans Schmidt, "Gebet," *RGG* (note also that bibliography), especially Heiler, *Gebet*[4], 1921.

3. After all the material has become so much more complicated and more difficult, the challenge is raised *to bring light and order* onto that which is new *in this diverse material*, and to demonstrate its internal arrangement. How should that proceed? Since it concerns literary witnesses, the *genres* of this type of poetry must be substantiated. Accordingly, *genre research* in the Psalms is nonnegotiable, not something one can execute or ignore according to preference. Rather, it is *the foundational work* without which there can be no certainty in the remainder. It is the firm ground from which everything else must ascend.

Already there have been relatively frequent attempts to divide the psalms by genres, although admittedly without recognizing the significance of the task. Thus, Hupfeld[2]-Riehm (*Psalmen*, vol. 1, pp. 3ff) arranged all the material according to praise, thanksgiving, complaint, petition, and didactic songs. As a result, several genres were correctly designated according to their essential content, even though his execution remained stuck in the categories of Dogmatics. Similar beginnings are also found in Ed. Reuß (*Geschichte der heiligen Schriften des Alten Testaments*, pp. 148ff, §126 [cf. Also pp. 597ff, §479f]) and in Fr. Buhl, (*RE*, vol. 4[3], pp. 626ff). These correctly recognized the chief genres, without a meticulous classification and without really making significant impressions upon their contemporaries. Fr. Baethgen's suggestion (*Psalmen*³, p. iv), is much weaker. He differentiates between songs that are happy, sad, and contented. This differentiation rests upon rather sparse observation that cannot lead further. Also, E. Kautzsch (*Heilige Schrift des ATs*³, vol. 2, p. 106), who mentions dividing according to "odes, hymns, songs, and elegies," does not conceive the material for the correct purpose. How can Hebrew poetry be divided according to precepts which arose in Hellenistic writings? Likewise, Ed. König claims (*Hermeneutik des ATs*, 1916, p. 95) that the division of Old Testament genres must be conducted "only according to recognized stylistic norms of the general history of literature." However, this claim should be rejected since Israelite literature often concerns images that can scarcely be entrusted to the current literary historian. Recently, König suggests (*Psalmen*, 1926, pp. 33ff) dividing the ancient Hebrew poems according to their relationship to the activities of the soul and according to their contents: (1) narratives, (2) descriptions, (3) argumentation, (4) celebratory contemplations, and (5) statements that should influence the will. This division is far too general to suit the particularity of the psalms, and consequently his own commentary does not follow it. C. Steuernagel (*Einleitung in das AT*, pp. 729ff) goes another direction. He thinks differentiating according to "types of piety" highlights "the differences between the religiosity of the prophets and the people of the preexilic period, the specifically Deuteronomistic piety, the priestly religiosity of the postexilic temple cult, and the religiosity of the scribes, of the wisdom teacher, and of one interested in eschatology." These observations are certainly valuable, but do not constitute the central point. Literary material should be arranged primarily according to its own regulations—regulations derived from the history of literature. It is certainly true that Hebrew lyric traversed various periods of piety, and was in turn influenced by them. However, this fact cannot be placed at the beginning of the investigation.

Now, even if all of these efforts have not attained the goal, they have, in the meantime, still normalized certain genre designations for the researchers themselves. One can mention the names "songs of confession, songs of vengeance, and royal songs." For example, by relying upon a more precise literary historical observation of the objects, Bertholet distinguishes between "morning and evening songs, illness songs, songs of complaint about personal antagonism, songs about estrangement from Zion, songs of personal trust in YHWH, personal protestation of innocence, and again, personal confessions" (*Kulturgeschichte Israels*, p. 244). From this and similar enumerations, it becomes apparent that differentiating the genres belongs to the nature of the material. So much so, that even those for whom the meaning of the content did not arise (or arose only partially from this differentiation) are nevertheless forced to build the entire explanation upon it. Thus, even that which follows is by no means concerned with saying something completely new. Rather, that which follows systematically compiles certain self-evident observations that until now have not been satisfactorily appreciated. Subsequently, attempts it to explain the Psalms based upon that compilation. Such considerations were generally undertaken without great scientific rigor and without specialized understanding. To be sure, to this point, the result of such considerations has been that the contemporary researcher was virtually assured that classifying the psalms was not possible at all, or, at least, not yet achieved (e.g., cf., Steuernagel, *Einleitung in das AT*, p. 728).

With this state of the research, it is even more necessary that one proceed as cautiously as possible. The division that we attempt, should not be arbitrarily instituted. Rather, it should derive from *the character of the material itself*. The researcher should strive to overhear the innate, natural division of this type of poetry. It requires a *basic observation concerning the original essence of this poetry, whereby it falls seamlessly into various genres.*

4. Those to whom the literary history of Israel has been entrusted have no doubt where one should attempt this fundamental observation. The literary witness of the natural times and environments can be distinguished from those of more developed nations. Those literary witnesses of more developed nations are only conceivable on paper, but these witnesses arise in the *real life of persons and have their setting therein*. In real life women sing the victory song to those returning, triumphant armies. In real life some of the professional mourners strike up the moving dirge over the one who has passed away. The prophet raises his thundering voice above the gathered community, perhaps in the outer court of the sanctuary. These examples could be multiplied greatly (cf. "Israelitische Literaturgeschichte" in the "Kultur der Gegenwart" vol. 1, part 7 [1906[1], pp. 58ff; 1923[2], pp. 60ff). One can see from these examples that *the genres of an ancient writing must be differentiated by the various events of life from which they developed* (cf. "Reden und Aufsätze," 1913, p. 33).

So where would the poetry of Psalms have had its "setting in life?" Judaism would have performed the poetry in its cult, as even the name of the psalter, *těhillim* (meaning hymns), demonstrates. The Babylonian psalms belong with certain worship celebrations (cf., e.g., E. Balla, *Das Ich der Psalmen*, 1912, p. 88); O. Weber, *Literatur der Babylon und Assur*, 1907, p. 119). Even now, the biblical Psalms are used by the synagogue and the Christian church in the original text, in translations, and in paraphrase. Thus, we may dare to presume that they also arose in the cult of Israel originally.

This supposition is then immediately confirmed by an observation that no observant reader of the psalter can deny, specifically the *formal nature* of many, though not all, of these poems. How remarkably similar they are; often so much so, that we can scarcely distinguish one from another. Relatedly, the purely personal retreats into the background, that which appears only once by an individual poet. We really encounter very few specific details in these songs. So many of the poets content themselves with very general references and suggestions. (We mentioned this already: see p. 1.) To a certain extent, this type of poetry, as we have seen, could be descriptive of all lyric, but not entirely. In his dirge, David mentions Saul and Jonathan by name, so why do the Psalms not mention the name of one person who lived at the time of the poet? The explanation for this highly noteworthy manifestation can only be found in the fact that the original substance of these songs should not be regarded as the outpouring of the most personal piety. However, if they belong to the worship service, then it is understandable that they speak so generally. Their oldest origins are cultic formulas, or at least they derive from such. One can see that we are on the right path with this conclusion by the fact that the Babylonian poems demonstrate the same formality, only in greater measure. As we have already mentioned, this revelation can be explained from the same cause as the Babylonian poetry, namely, by its purpose in the worship service. (Cf. M. Jastrow, *Die Religion des Babylon und Assur*, vol. 2, pp. 10f, 61f, 116; O. Weber, *Literatur der Babylon und Assur*, 1907, p. 116.)

Now please do not misunderstand this idea, as though it belies, or does not sufficiently value, the appearance of creativity in the psalms (contra M. Löhr, *Psalmen-*

studien, pp. 2ff). Rather, stating this idea by no means excludes the fact that now and then one finds various deviations from the usual form, even very personal chords of the heart. Sometimes, these deviations are quite notable. However, in these deviations we perceive a particularly high religious and poetic power which elevates itself beyond the pattern. We only gain the means for measuring the individual poet's independence and the singularity of the poet's creation when we have first recognized the dominant norm in the poet's time. However, Baethgen is generally believed to be incorrect when he states that "the singers of the psalms have not composed according to a particular pattern" (cited by A. Bertholet, in E. Kautzsch[4]/Bertholet, *Heilige Schrift des AT*, vol. 2, p. 114). This sentence stems from a time in which there was (and is) no specific genre research. One only needs to observe the very similar linguistic forms of the hymns (§2) in order to recognize the superficiality of Baethgen's judgment.

5. Now perhaps to the modern researcher an adjoining matter appears to be that one should proceed from the notes about the performance of the psalms contained in certain psalm superscriptions and other traditions (as R. Kittel, "Psalmen," *RE*, vol. 16[3], p. 190, and A. Bertholet, *Biblische Theologie*, vol 2, 1911, pp. 67ff have attempted). It seems at first that here we possess a solid foundation. But that is only how it appears, because this tradition is attested much too late and certainly includes secondary elements. It is impossible to begin the research of the evangelical church song with the affirmation that in the 19th century, "A Mighty Fortress Is Our God" was sung at the Reformation festival, or that "Jesus, My Confidence" was sung at funerals. These later usages prove nothing about the origin of the poem. And the fact that the psalm superscriptions by no means authenticate the oldest performance can be recognized using Ps 30. In Ps 30, an individual "song of thanksgiving" (§7) has been used at the temple consecration, apparently at a time much later than the time of its origin. So, if one wishes to research the type of a literary branch, one may not begin with its last tributary. Rather, one must begin at its origins.

If we are to make any progress, we must immerse ourselves in the *oldest worship service*. We must particularly observe those places in the worship service where words were spoken or songs were sung. Since time immemorial, Israel's worship service, like that of any other people of antiquity, consisted of all kinds of actions that one undertakes for the divinity or in its name (cf W. Robertson Smith/R. Stube, *Religion der Semiten*, p. 19). We mention several here, especially those that must concern us in that which follows. For example, the community gathers itself on the holy day in order to present a large sacrifice to their God. The community marches through the sanctuary in a dance that had been transmitted from antiquity. Or the community gathers at the holy places in times of calamity—an enemy threat, famine, or pestilence—to fast before YHWH, and to ask him to overturn the judgment. For that purpose, there are a plethora of ceremonies of a private nature: the one who confesses appears at the sanctuary in order to find expiation and deliverance from his calamity; or the person who has been delivered from a life threatening situation (like illness) presents a thanksgiving offering to the God who delivered him, an offering which he had vowed during the calamity. We possess a wealth of material concerning the holy actions from clues in the law, the narrative books, the psalms themselves, and elsewhere. In the following treatment of the particular psalm genres, our task will be to gather together details about these actions.

Now, we frequently hear that in antiquity such celebrations were accompanied with *holy speeches*. These speeches should clarify and reinforce the celebrations. (Cf. H.

Ranke, *RGG²*, vol. 1, col. 100f; Fr. Heiler, *Gebet²⁻⁵*, 1920–1923, pp. 71f, 75f; Fr. Pfister, "Kultus," in Pauly/Kroll, *RE der klassischen Altertumwissenschaft*, vol. 11/2, col. 2157; P. Stengel, *Die griechischen Kultusaltertümer,³* pp. 78ff, for other literature). From the secular arena, one can compare the speeches belonging to the worship activity to the "work song" which was sung while certain physical work was performed. It also occasionally appears in the Old Testament (see Sir 38:25; cf. K. Bücher, *Arbeit und Rhythmus⁵*, 1919; Erich Schmidt, "Anfänge der Literatur" in *Kultur der Gegenwart*, part I, section 7, pp. 6-7). More closely related is the incantation which also belongs very frequently with a specific undertaking. In the Old Testament we have an excellent example of such in Elisha's victory spell (1 Kgs 13:15ff): The young king must shoot an arrow through the open window toward the east while the holy hands of the man of God rest on the king's hands and convey their divine power to them. At that point, the prophet speaks the oath:

> An arrow of YHWH's victory;
>> An arrow of victory over Syria!

In addition, there is the "song of the well" (Num 21:17), perhaps once sung at the digging of a well for conjuring up the well water:

> Spring up, O well! Sing to it!
>> The well, sunk by the leaders,
> The nobles of the people bore it,
> With the scepter, with their staffs!

Jeremiah also had his curse against Babylon be read by a disciple who then sunk it in the Euphrates while simultaneously speaking:

> Thus shall Babylon sink,
>> And not be raised again (Jer 51:59ff).

When blessing, it had been the habit of the one speaking the words of blessing to lay hands on the one being blessed (Gen 48:17ff).

In the *arena of the Israelite worship service*, there is an impressive example of this type of connection between the speech and action of the priestly blessing whose execution we know from Lev 9:22f; Sir 50:20. At the end of the worship service the priest raised hands over the entire community and spoke the blessing to them, whose wording has been conveyed in Num 6:24ff:

> May YHWH bless you and keep you!
> May YHWH let his face shine upon you,
>> And be gracious to you!
> May YHWH turn 'his eyes'[1] on you and give you peace!

If a corpse is found murdered in the country and the perpetrator is unknown, then an elder of the closest town should break the neck of a young cow to signify their innocence in the matter. They should wash their hands and say: "Our hands have not poured out this blood; our eyes have not seen it," etc. (Deut 21:7). Or whoever delivers the fruit basket with the first fruits or the proscribed tithe to the sanctuary must speak a formula which

---

[1]Text: "his face"; better *ʿēnāv* ("his eyes"), cf. S. Mowinckel, *Psalmenstudien*, vol. 5 (1924) p. 22n.1. Text changes here and following will be marked by single quotes (' ').

the law proscribes with the action (Deut 26:5ff, 13ff). Similarly, during the proceedings against a wife suspected of adultery, the priest should speak a specific curse, which is conveyed literally in the law. At that point, the words are written down, and the writing is placed in water and given (to the woman) to drink (Num 5:19ff). Or one is reminded of Samuel's anointing of Saul, during which the seer poured the oil flask over Saul's head while proclaiming to him: "YHWH has hereby anointed you as prince over his people" (1 Sam 10:1, LXX). Isa 6:6f suggests a worship service celebration. The prophet is absolved of his sins when one of the seraphim hovering before God touches him on the lips with a burning ember, and says:

> Since, this has touched your lips,
>> your guilt is taken away, and your sins atoned.

In a real life worship service, the priest would undertake a similar action and would speak the pardoning formula. Such divine actions are even repeated in the calls of Jeremiah and Ezekiel, where the divine actions are seen in the vision and accompanied by speeches (Jer 1:9f; Ezek 2:9ff). After all of this, we can imagine that Israel's worship service was once very full of these cultic speeches. One gains this impression even more strongly from the Babylonian worship service (cf. H. Zimmern, *Beiträge zur Kenntnis der babylonischen Religion*, 1896–1901, pp. 29-33, 35, 45-51, 101, 107, 111, 125, 127, 129, 133, 137, 139, etc). Such mergers of the holy speech with the holy action are found everywhere on earth where there was a cult in the ancient sense (for the Indian religion, cf. De la Saussaye, *Religionsgeschichte*, vol. 2, pp. 7f; for the Greek religion, ibid, p. 300). The last venerable remnant of this combination appears in the Christian church, where *verbum* and *signum* stand together.

6. This point is repeated everywhere. One does not owe the form of such speeches to the inspiration of the moment. Rather, they contain fixed forms and have been transmitted from generation to generation. In antiquity, those speeches tend to be *arranged by a rhythm* upon which one places particular value or with which one hopes to achieve a particular effect. Incantations, oaths, and oracles exhibit poetic form the world over. (Cf Fr. Küchler, *Abhandlungen, Baudissin überreicht*, p. 297.) The same was often true in Israel as demonstrated by the previously noted examples. Those cult speeches were even more certainly poetic when they were to be spoken collectively by a larger group, the entire congregation or a sanctified choir. Certainly, in ancient times it might be enough to indulge in a simple, unstructured "call." Examples of such calls include: the ancient Roman "*Triumpe*" which the Arvales struck up as a cult dance; and the "*Axie Taure*" in the Greek worship of Dionysius (cf. E. Schmidt, *Anfänge der Literatur*, pp. 7ff); and the Hebrew "hallelujah" which will be addressed later (§2, ¶10). However, in more civilized cultures, such calls waned, remaining active only as the poetic refrain of the masses. A moderately artistic singing arose instead, since a larger group of people could only express itself in a relatively orderly fashion using this form.

Two songs of summons serve as excellent examples of these ancient cult songs. When these songs were raised defiantly in the morning in order to call the people into battle, then one swore these words to God:

> Arise, YHWH, so that your enemies scatter
>> and those despising you flee before you.

But when they sat down in the evening to rest, then one sang:

Sit down, [2]YHWH
    in the camp[3] of the family of Israel (Num 10:35f).

The action in another poem of summons (Ps 24:7ff) is unattested, but still easy to amplify. Here, it celebrates the entry of God into his sanctuary which he had left for a while. When the procession, with the symbol in its midst, reached the venerable gates, one sang this song:

> Raise your heads, O gates;
> Raise yourself, O ancient doors,
> For the majestic king enters.

(Cf. further in the Psalms commentary.)

In the last three mentioned examples, one encounters the classification of a cult poem: both speech and action belong together closely. Every time that the action transpires, the speech is delivered. And when the song is sung, the action is performed.

We possess the precise description of the execution of such a poem in Exod 15:20 which concerns a song that is sung by dancing women while beating the drum. A woman leads the holy dance and sings the words. The song is the well-known "Song of the Sea."

Only a few places in the Old Testament specifically express speech and action together. However, we can create a picture of the ancient cult song of Israel when we understand that certain observations should be taken together that are scattered across various passages. Situations involving such songs are occasionally described in the law and in the narrative books. In several poems of the psalter, the accompanying action still shines through. Additionally, one finds imitations of older songs in the prophets, or allusions to them, in the prophets and Job. If cultic actions are portrayed in our transmission, then we must ask whether, and what, one would have sung with them. And if songs are given to us, then we should figure out the actions to which they would have belonged. One example is chosen here as a preliminary illustration of the method. This is one example from the larger material that we have acquired that will be treated comprehensively in the following.

Here and there in the law, the "thanksgiving offering" is mentioned. We therefore connect that thanksgiving song in the psalter with the "thanksgiving offering," which carries the same name (*tōdā*), and often speaks of the sacrifices that are offered alongside. We learn the more precise place of the "thanksgiving song" in the cult from allusions in the psalms in question which mention something about the celebratory action of raising the "cup of salvation" (Ps 116:13), or which presuppose the celebrating community dancing around the altar (Ps 118:27). The prophet also mentions these celebrations of the grateful ones in the sanctuary where a familiar formula of the thanksgiving song is conveyed that also appears in the psalter (cf. Jer 33:11). The personal situation of a person who voiced one such "thanksgiving song" at the "thanksgiving offering" is portrayed for us in Job 33:19ff., which we then relate to numerous allusions in our psalms. By gathering these and other references together, it is finally possible to draw a lively picture of the action belonging to these songs.

---

[2]*šĕbà.*
[3]*bĕrib'oth?*

We already spoke of the cult setting of the *holy dance* (see above, p. 11, regarding Exod 15:20). 2 Sam 6:5 mentions the same thing, except without the song sung at the time. Ps 149 demonstrates that this dance was still operating in the time of the psalmists. According to v. 3, this song was apparently to be performed while dancing. More precisely, it concerns a sword dance as we may deduce from v. 6 (cf. the commentary), and just such a dance, in full armor, is described in Jdt 15:13.

One is reminded of the *festival procession* for the dedication of the walls in Neh 12:27ff. Ps 48:13 presupposes the same kind of holy parade around the city as the related action. Ps 42:5 has a procession to the sanctuary in view:

> For I once went
> > to the 'tent of the God'
> with the sound of rejoicing and thanksgiving
> > to the noise of the pilgrims.

Psalm 68:25f describes it:

> See the procession of YHWH,
> Your procession into the sanctuary, my god, my king.
> The singers in front, the string players behind,
> > the women beating drums in the middle.

The prophet also recalls such processions:

> The song shall be (I)[4] as in the night of the festival dedication,
> And gladness of heart as *the devotee to the sound of the flute*,
> At the coming to the mountain of YHWH, to the rock of Israel (Isa 30:29).

The last line was taken from a pilgrimage song. We conclude that from another poem where the prophet presents how the heathen will at some point convert to YHWH. In order to make the point clearly, he calls the pilgrimage to mind which they will then undertake, and pronounces in advance the pilgrimage song that they will sing at the time:

> Come, let us go to the mountain of YHWH,
> > to the house of the God of Jacob (Isa 2:3).

In Ps 24:7ff we find a poem that was performed at the entrance of the temple of YHWH. Others that belong to the same location include Ps 100 and 95:1-7. Cf. Ps 100:4:

> Enter into its gates with thanksgiving,
> > into his courtyards with praise!

The same situation is found in the thanksgiving psalm of Ps 118:19:

> Now, open for me the gates of righteousness,
> > That I may enter and thank YHWH.

And even here we possess a prophetic imitation of such songs:

> Open the doors,
> > That a righteous people may enter,
> > > Who keep faithfulness (Isa 26:2).

---

[4]The Roman numeral in parentheses indicates the number of Hebrew words omitted. Cf. the commentary.

The previously mentioned passage (Isa 30:29) also speaks of the unending joy which one celebrated by singing on the night before the festival. It is easy enough to conceptualize that they sang at "vigils" like we sing *Christmas carols*." How better could one shorten the long night than by singing? And about what else could one sing at holy festivals besides the honor of YHWH?

(I) Bless YHWH, all servants of YHWH,
   who stand in YHWH's temple in the nights (Ps 134:1).

But enough of the details. These will be multiplied strikingly in the following sections. The examples mentioned already suffice to show that, even in the psalms, we find an abundance of clues to their worship service setting. There are of course other songs (they even form the majority in the psalter) which provide nothing, or almost nothing, in the way of such clues. By and large, they are of a more personal nature and stem from the religious life of the pious individual. It would appear to us to be a grave mistake if one were to overlook all this purely personal material and to explain the psalms wholesale as "cult songs" (as S. Mowinckel has done in his "Psalm Studies." On the contrary, we must pay special attention to that which deviates from the typical worship genre of the time because of its particular significance for the religion (note especially the commentary). However, one can expect from the outset, based on the general path of the history of religion, that the "cult poems" are older while the "spiritual songs"—as we call the poems that really demonstrate the personal life—represent a later developmental stage. Accordingly, we have also maintained that the occasional hints to worship service practices in "spiritual poems" were leftovers of the old style. We will speak later about such practices. A. Bertholet (*Kulturgeschichte Israels*, 1920, p. 244n.13) expresses a different opinion, specifically that such hints result from secondary borrowing. However, this opinion overlooks the larger context of the history of religion. Indeed, we know from elsewhere that the religion in ancient time had its climax in the worship service, and we know that a noncultic piety, indeed one that is hostile to the cult, could only appear at a later stage. Accordingly, we can accept that, even in Israel, *the pious individual did not sing the first psalms* in order to pour out his most personal thoughts before God. Rather, the *priests composed* these psalms and preserved them at the sanctuary in order to use them at appropriate occasions. We think that the following detailed portrayal will offer impressive documentation for this comprehensive outlook.

Accordingly, we will begin our investigation of the psalms with the cultic songs. However, if one desires to classify these songs according to their internal nature, then that can only be done according to the *actions to which they belong*. The same thing is true of the Babylonian cultic poetry whose arrangement according to genres is still in its early stages, as is frequently noted here in passing. Nevertheless, this work also promises a bountiful profit in the area of the history of religion and philology. Hopefully, we will not have to wait too much longer for this.[5]

---

[5]In the meantime Fr. Stummer (*Sumerisch-akkadische Parallelen zum Aufbau alttestamentlicher Psalmen*, 1922) has begun this work, and has really taken up, or newly situated, an abundance of literary historical observations about the Babylonian and biblical area. At the same time, he has advanced a plethora of erroneous beliefs and hasty conclusions. The work suffers above all from the fact that it begins too early with the comparison of the Babylonian and biblical literature, before

7. I have dedicated myself to this work since I recognized its significance for Psalms research, and have advocated cooperation in a series of publications. In "Ausgewählten Psalmen" (1904, ⁴1917), I stated the genre of every psalm treated. I have attempted to place the meaning of the individual song in this context, and have presented the main genres using their most evident example. I sketched the history of this type of poetry in broad strokes in my *Israelitischen Literaturgeschichte* (*Kultur der Gegenwart*, vol. 1/7, ¹pp. 62ff, 88f; ²pp. 64ff, 90f), which I considered to be a program of future literary research, and again in the article "Psalmen" (*RGG*¹). Alongside these works, I have laid out the fundamental questions in the following essays: "Die Psalmen" and "Die Grundprobleme der israelitischen Literaturgeschichte" (*Reden und Aufsätze*, 1913, pp. 29ff; 92ff), "Ältere und neuere Psalmenforschung" (*Christliche Welt* 30 [1916]: col. 142ff), "Formen der Hymnen" (*Theologische Rundschau* 20 [1917]: 265ff), and "Frommigkeit der Psalmen" (*Christliche Welt* 36 [1922], cols. 2ff, 18ff, 79ff, 94ff, 105ff). I have also presented particularly meaningful examples in the following: "Danklieder im Psalter" (*Zeitschrift für die Missionskunde und Religionswissenschaft* 34 [1919], 177ff, 211ff), "Michaschluß" (*Zeitschrift für Semetistik* 2 [1924]: 145ff, "Jesaja 33" (*ZAW* 42 [1924]: 177ff), "Lieder in der Kindheitsgeschichte Jesu bei Lukas" (*Festgabe für Harnack*, 1921, pp. 43ff), "Psalm 149" (*Oriental Studies Dedicated to Paul Haupt*, 1926, pp. 46ff), etc. Finally, I conducted the entire program in my *Psalmenkommentar* (1926).

For many years, these efforts have exercised no noticeable influence upon the scientific enterprise. Yet no fundamental objection has been raised to them, apart from the

---

both have been completely investigated according to their own genres to some degree. It seems obvious that one can only really compare two things with one another if one has first recognized both as individual manifestations. Thus, only after one has studied the Babylonian and biblical lyric by themselves can a more comprehensive comparison of the two be fruitfully attempted. Only then can such a comparison combine genres recognized as the same. Stummer has not yet satisfactorily conducted the genre research, though he recognizes it to some degree and gleans all kinds of details from it. However, Stummer puts forth the incredible theory that the religious lyric of Israel arose from a single Babylonian model. On the whole, in his comparison he has only concerned himself with formal similarities. All too often he overlooks the situations of the performance and the content of the poem, whereby he often travels back and forth between genres and frequently combines entirely different material. Stummer then attempted to expand his earlier writing in a later publication (*Journal of the Society of Oriental Research* 8 [1924]: 123ff), including Egyptian material without changing his position. Stummer has made all kinds of correct observations in details, even though he has missed the proper path in our opinion. Nevertheless, one may welcome the fact that work on the history of genres has now essentially moved into Assyriology. The extent to which this work can someday provide valuable contributions to biblical research is immediately clear from the fact that the cultic performance form from that discipline is evidenced in the text itself while in the psalms it must first be explored painstakingly. First, the task must be to investigate each of the two literatures in which the occasional reference to similarities and differences would be permissible. Once that happens, the time will come to conduct a comprehensive comparison of the two literatures and then to write the history of the entire type of poetry. During this work, I would have a request for the Assyriologists that hopefully finds a friendly reception, a request that also holds true for Old Testament colleagues. The request is this: do not unnecessarily change the cultic expressions we found that took so much contemplation. Otherwise, a great confusion may result for the one who is not as close to the research.

occasional remarks.[6] But the representatives of the older school have opposed all of this for a long time now in an almost completely united front in a silent refusal. Now it has again become apparent to me how little effect all of these publications have had upon readers, since many recensions have declared my commentary to the Psalms (which presupposes this research) to be "incomplete." They do so because it does not explain the principles.

In the last several years genre research has finally found friends. W. Staerk ("Lyrik" in *Schriften des Alten Testaments*, vol. 3/1, [1]1911, [2]1920) has treated the entire psalter in this manner for the first time. One must give him his due even if one cannot read his assignation of entire genres and his arrangement of individual songs without objection, and even if one cannot share his hope that, in the second edition, he has brought these investigations "to a certain conclusion." Following him, R. Kittel (in his *Psalmen-Kommentar*, [1, 2]1914, [3, 4]1922) decided to walk in the new path, although without adding anything remarkably new. More valuable are several smaller works in the same vein: E. Balla, *Das Ich der Psalmen*, 1912; H. Greßmann, "Die literarische Analyse des Deuterojesaja," *ZAW* 34 (1914): 254ff; W. Baumgartner, "Die literarischen Gattungen in der Weisheit des Jesus Sirach," *ZAW* 34 (1914): 161ff, and "Die Klagegedichte des Jeremia," 1917; H. Schmidt, "Die religiöse lyrik im Alten Testament," in *Religionsgeschichtliche Volksbücher*, 1912; J. Begrich, "Der Psalm des Hiskia," 1926. M. Löhr (*Psalmenstudien*, 1922) fundamentally recognized genre research. Naturally, I agree completely with his remark that, in genre research, he is not "able to see the key that unequivocally opens every door for understanding the psalm poetry of the Old Testament" (p. 4). Cf. my *Psalmenkommentar*, pp. xf. Even A. Bertholet, in increasing measure, welcomes this whole type of research. He is, however, of the opinion that "by recognizing the legitimation and the challenging effects of this viewpoint . . . one should be under no illusion regarding the boundaries of this type of approach" (E. Kautzsch[4]=Bertholet, "Heilige Schrift des Alten Testaments," vol. 2, p. 114). To be sure, like all other types of research, genre research has its limits which are tied to the nature of the task. However, it is unclear whether these limits lie where Bertholet seeks them. Namely he believes that one should never employ genre research in "spiritual poetry" (cf. below, p. 20). One cannot make a confident statement on this question until a comprehensive and precise investigation has been presented. For that reason, I believe a decision on this question should call upon the judgment of the reader after that reader becomes immersed in the following paragraphs. Finally, S. Mowinckel (*Psalmenstudien*, vol. 1 [1921]; 2 [1922]; 3 [1923]; 4 [1923]; 5 [1924]; 6 [1924]) also stands on the ground floor of this research, although he seeks to continue the research largely independently.

8. Accordingly, we must accomplish the following tasks.

First, the *genres* of the psalms must be delineated. One should not take this task too lightly by quickly grouping selected psalms together where one believes a certain similarity can be seen, and then grouping them into a presumed unit under a speedily invented name. Rather, one may only speak of a "genre" when one first meets very specific, strictly observed stipulations.

---

[6]The objection of Ed. König, recently made in *Psalmen*, p. 37, remains so superficial that it may be bypassed here.

First, according to that mentioned above, one may only assemble together those poems which as a group belong to a specific *occasion in the worship service*, or at least derive from one. We must present this cultic occasion as precisely as possible, utilizing the allusions created from the numerous sources for this purpose. Examples of this work are already given above, pages 11ff.

Further, those songs belonging together must naturally indicate a common treasury of *thoughts and moods*. These are the ones which were provided by their life setting (*Sitz im Leben*), or which could be easily attached to it. We must also present this shared intellectual material of the individual genre.

A third factor of the genre that is absolutely necessary is that all of the individual pieces belonging to the genre should indeed be associated relatively clearly by their common "language related to the form." Here is the place where the researcher cannot manage without certain aesthetic considerations. Now "form" is indeed a concept, taken here in its broadest sense, that is generally not easy to recognize for many people. Goethe, whom no one would deny the right to judge this fact, says: "Everyone sees the material before them, but only someone who has something to do with it sees the contents, and the *form* is a *secret* to most." This is true, especially if one believes the meaning of forms was not established in the cradle. Rather, people must achieve the meaning by much work and self-education. So many recent Old Testament researchers of aesthetic research harbor a mistrust that is all too frequently materially unfounded. They are accustomed to maintaining from the outset that every aesthetic observation or argumentation is subjective. They shove it to the side as "unscientific," or they rather inartistically contrast the bare "word" to the content as something of lesser value (A. Bertholet, *Kulturgeschichte Israels*, p. 232). Or, they confuse the "form" with the "pattern" or the "manner" (K. Budde, *Das Lied Moses*, p. 8). However, without this form investigation, genre research in the area of Old Testament is impossible for this reason. The language of form carried a greater significance in ancient times than is the case today, because it was determined by the custom, even authorial custom, more than the more developed present time. For our purposes, however, this investigation of form is particularly important because it provides extraordinarily clear signals of the genre—if we only understand how to observe. However, in order to forestall any misunderstanding (cf. A. Bertholet, *Israelitische Kulturgeschichte*, p. 232), it should be expressly accented that a literary-historical inspection concerns itself not only with the form, but also just as much with *the content* of the poem. Also, we would like to affirm for the benefit of those resisting, that the following will treat such simple form observations that they will provide no one with serious difficulty (cf. my essay "Formen der Hymnen"). We will therefore place particular value on specific *sentence forms* that constantly repeat in the genres, as for example, in other areas where the *vav* consecutive with the imperfect is characteristic of the narrative and the imperfect or *vav* consecutive with the perfect are characteristic for the prediction. The simpler the observations are, the more impressive they will be, or so we hope. Also, the *preferred vocabulary* of the individual genres will be investigated alongside. At a later point, specialized lexicons for the genres will need to be compiled.

If the three demands designated above are followed strictly, then it will be possible to keep the subjectivity in check which R. Kittel (1, 2, p. xli n.1) still presupposes as unavoidable and even Bertholet (*Kulturgeschichte Israels*, p. 245n.13) presupposes as self-evident. It will then be possible to trace the rules according to which the Psalms have grown. W. Staerk's (*Lyrik*[2]) blunders into the assignation of genres may be charged to the fact that he has not met these challenges consistently enough. For example, he summarily placed all kinds of psalms under the name "procession hymns" which together presupposed a procession, but which have very different forms and are by no means "hymns." Likewise, the group labeled "spiritual poetry" is disputable. On the other hand, he separated elements that belong together, for example, the wisdom psalms 1; 91; 112; 128. Similar arguments may be brought concerning Bertholet's (*Kulturgeschichte Israels*, p. 244) classification of "spiritual songs" (cf. above, p. 13) which are determined by very different situations: prayer time ("morning and evening songs," the situation of the one praying (illness psalms, thanksgiving songs, etc.), or the content of the poem (songs of personal trust, etc.). The same can be said of Bertholet's specification of "cultic poetry" (p. 245), where, for example, he places the vigils (Ps 134) beside the hymns, even though the form of Ps 134:1 is a hymn. Moreover, Pss 120–134 are called "Pilgrimage songs" according to the Hebrew superscription, even though each psalm belongs to very different genres. S. Mowinckel (*Psalmenstudien*, vol. 2, 3ff) does the same when he associates very different types under the name "throne installation songs" by neglecting the necessary investigations of forms. G. Beer's comprehensive overview of the psalter (*Kurze Übersicht über den Inhalt der Alttestamentlichen Schriften*) suffers from the same shortcoming. In this work Beer coordinates many psalms properly (under the influence of genre research). On the other hand, because Beer appears to know nothing of the laws of form, he very often overlooks the contexts. Beer's main mistakes are two: he sometimes is not so much led by the attitude of the entire psalm as he is led by one or more sentences (Pss 102; 61; 63; 41); and (especially) he does not pay satisfactory attention to the "mixed poems" and "liturgies" which consist of different pieces. In the future, progress toward better recognition will depend upon whether researchers learn to employ greater precision.

Further, within the genres themselves we differentiate the *motifs*, the smaller components into which the individual poem falls. Even here we are not treating self-discovered, arbitrary differentiations. Rather, we are treating those paragraphs provided by the meaning itself, and which are designated by the form. The beginning of the poem, the "introduction," is generally the easiest to recognize because, in ancient and in recent time, it is the place that the force of the form tends to be placed most heavily. The beginning of the genre as such is thus the most clearly recognizable part. In English, the fairy tale is recognizable by its four first words, "once upon a time;" or the sermon can be recognized in the first moment by its address, something like "beloved in the Lord" or "dear friend;" or the letter by the heading, "dear sir" or "dear friend." The same is true for Hebrew psalm genres where the majority are already made clear from the first three words. Observations of this type are generally so easy to gather, and so convincing, that one cannot help but wonder how they escaped previous researchers. However, if the introduction has been placed by a later hand (as in Ps 144:12ff), or for other reasons is not present (e.g., §2 ¶17), then determining the genre sometimes creates tremendous difficulties. In addition to the introduction, one must pay special attention to the "conclusion," which very frequently corresponds to the form.

The third venue one must consider is the "main element" in the middle, which again we divide into its individual components. Even these "motifs" tend to follow more or less clear rules according to their form and content. By contrast, one must note expressly that the order of these components generally follows the preference of the poet so that the arrangement is very frequently the weakness of a Hebrew literary work. G. Jacob (*Altarabischen Beduinenleben,* [2]1897, p. xxii) says the same thing about the poetry of the Arabs: "In all of the pre-Islamic poetry, affectations dominate . . . ; it arises in affectation, and we are not justified within this poetry in seeking to place an overemphasis upon logically divided, serenely arranged understanding, that indicates a cultured people." Now the poetry of Israel, particularly the later poetry, stands high above the ancient Arabian poetry in intellectual content and the rule of logic. However, one should be warned against observing it with all too modern eyes, thereby placing the logical connection above the power of perception that dominates here. It is no different in ancient Egypt, where A. Erman has noted the lack of a good order in the poetry (cf. *Literatur der Ägypter,* p. 13). One would therefore make a critical error if one sought something like a Greek "chorus" in the poetry of Israel, and not being able to find such, renounced all further research into the form. It thus appears to me to be a gross error that Fr. Stummer has begun his comparison of the Babylonian and Hebrew poetry by comparing the arrangement, even if he has seen something proper in so doing. He begins with a fundamental presupposition, namely, that the style as such will include "strict ordering and clear arrangement." However, the fundamental presupposition with which he begins is only a bias that does not hold up for ancient oriental poetry without some qualification.

Our task in the individual work will be to collect *those elements of various psalms which contain the same motif in the same genre.* We can hope that this process will place in our hand a new and far-reaching means to understand difficult texts and to fix that which is corrupt. At the same time, by observing the motifs we acquire the natural sections of meaning. The researcher is thereby placed in the position of recognizing the arrangement of the poem which the author himself desired, and of judging the attempts to this point of putting the poem into strophes. In doing so, as the explication will demonstrate in detail, several of these assumptions can be confirmed by this new procedure, while even more will actually be refuted.

Further, it is self-evident that all attempts of joining several psalms into one, dividing a single psalm, or removing larger and smaller additions, can only hope to succeed if one has most carefully researched the normal linguistic form of the genres in question. Otherwise it could happen that one would declare certain sentences as secondary, when they are indispensable to the genre, or that one could manufacture poems that are impossible in Hebrew. One finds horrendous examples of such processes in abundance in C. A. Briggs (*Psalms,* vol. 1, 1906/1907; vol. 2, 1909).

More important than all of this, however, is that by grouping the entire material by genres and motifs, we achieve firm standards that enable us to arrange the entire myriad *world of piety* expressed in the psalms according to their own disposition. We will find that the genres correspond to *religious types* that one can legitimately recognize (cf. "Frommigkeit der Psalmen" *Christliche Welt,* vol. 36, 1922, col. 2ff). So from this point, all "biblical-theological" or, better, "religiohistorical" investigations treating the psalms that do not wish to get lost in generalities must be based upon genre research.

While we have stressed that in the future we hope this research will play a very significant role in the investigation of all Hebrew literature, we must also reiterate that this research can in no way solve every problem. Rather, much more still remains to be done that cannot be treated in this context (cf. my *Psalmenkommentar,* pp. xf.).

In the following undertaking, we place particular value on those genres which appear most frequently in the psalms. There were certain worship occasions that occurred so often in life, and which represented so rich an opportunity to sing, that not just one song, but a whole series of these songs arose, and were also transmitted to us. These are the celebrations and events that we named earlier (8f): *the celebration of sacrifice and the lamentation of the community, the act of confession and the thanksgiving offering of the pious individual*. The *chief genres* of the psalms arose from these events: the "hymn" (§2), the "communal complaint song" (§4), the "complaint" and "song of thanksgiving" of the individual (§6, 7). The evidence that these genres belong with the named situations will be offered in the following. The reader will probably do well to proceed first from these larger genres and to begin with the simplest songs while reading the commentary. For the hymn one could select, Pss 150; 148; 147; 145; for the communal complaint song, Pss 79; 83; 80; 44; for the complaint song of the individual, Pss 13; 54; 88; 3; for the individual thanksgiving song, Jonah 2; Ps 30; 66:13ff. The "songs of YHWH's enthronement" are connected to the hymns in §3 because they are related in many respects. In §5, the royal psalms are added to the entire group of §2-4 that treat the piety of the people.

Further, one must treat the *history of the genres*. In the earliest time, the individual poems were extraordinarily short corresponding to the receptivity of that ancient generation. In later times, the poems grew considerably (cf. "Reden und Aufsätze," pp. 33f, and "Israelitische Literaturgeschichte," pp. 53f). In earliest times the individual was proportionally less forthcoming with his personal piety. In later times, the individual was empowered by the genres available at the time and attempted to express something personal with them. Here is the place where the creative power and the religion of the individual poet should be addressed. Also, this careful treatment of the personal character of the poetry must be one of the most important tasks, especially with the explication of the individual poem. In so doing we do not therefore deviate from Löhr as he curiously assumes (*Psalmenstudien*, p. 4). Rather, we agree with him completely. One cannot, however, go to the personal character too prematurely. How can one measure the height of a mountain if one does not possess the measure of the ground above which it stretches? And how can one appreciate the significance of an Israelite poet, if one has not first investigated the genres from which he begins? However, even that relatively undeveloped antiquity is dependent upon the constraints of the situation in a very different way, even in literary things, as we are able to show (cf. above, p. 16). One of the main reasons why genre research has been slow to take hold among many current researchers is the fact that many of them (a notable example in A. Bertholet, *Theologische Rundschau* 10 [1907]: pp. 150f.) have not been able to discover this character of antiquity and the challenges to our research stemming from it.

When the great individual poets appear in history, the genres themselves experience *all kinds of changes*. The most important of these changes to occur is the *mixture of genres* (§11) whereas the oldest genres were pure and simple. They were concerned with their established setting in the worship service and had a specific effect in view, even one that was presumed by them. They were produced in a traditional circle of thought and in strictly marked forms. Even then, to enliven the cult, one tended to use the *antiphonal chorus* of different voices (cf., e.g., Ps 24:7ff). "Liturgies" were formed at a later time in which selections from various genres were spoken by these changing voices. So, the lamenting voice of the people in its great need might ring until the divine oracle, perhaps proclaimed by the priest, delivered the comforting answer (cf. §4, ¶14). In this artistic form of the liturgy, one had a wonderful means that never failed to achieve its goal of presenting the manifold voices of a people that had become more wealthy and realized the most shocking consequences. Even the prophets have made use of this form and thus created their majestic poems (cf. my introduction to Hans Schmidt, "Die großen Propheten,"[2] pp. lixf, and the essays about *the conclusion of Micah* [*Zeitschrift für Semitistik* 2 (1924): 145ff] and *Isaiah 33* [*ZAW* 42 (1924): 177ff]. The psalmists have also gone the same way. Several of the most moving psalms present such liturgies in which different genres stand side by side. Simultaneously, particular "mixtures" occur. First, individual selections were taken up from other genres. These can occur when the spiritual contents of related elements are mutually attracted to one another, such as the hymn and the song of thanksgiving which both share the mood of rejoicing (§2, ¶54; §7, ¶8). Next, this mixture can occur when very diverse elements are intentionally placed next to one another in order to accentuate a striking affect, as when the wailing song of lamentation takes up components of the rejoicing hymn (§4, ¶12; §6, ¶28; §2, ¶55, 56) which was already very common in Babylonian poetry (§2, ¶36). At the close of the whole develop-ment, these mixtures had grown so much that here and there a complete formlessness occurred. A notable example is Ps 119. Even this relatively frequent appearance of mixed witnesses in the psalter has greatly hindered genre research to this point since, to the casual observer to whom this first jumps out, it can easily appear as if Hebrew poetry possesses no genres at all (cf., e.g., E. Kautzsch, *Die Poesie und die poetischen Bücher des AT*, p. 14). Likewise, one may counsel anyone interested in becoming immersed in genre research, not to begin with those mixed psalms. Rather, one should only pursue these psalms after the pure genres have become completely clear from one's own contemplation.

At the same time, the *various time periods* through which psalmody traveled brought their own intellectual influences. Thus, here, but only here, is the place where C. Steuernagel's challenge should be undertaken, namely that the period of piety must be brought into consideration (cf. above, p. 6). Prophecy, many of whose practitioners were psalmists, particularly influenced the period (cf. §9). Thus, the pious poets took up genres that were fashioned by the prophets. Like these prophets, they proclaimed something of the will of God (Ps 50, for example) and predicted the future (Ps 82). The most significant effect of the prophets, however, was this: the psalmists learned from the prophet's exalted models to evaluate the external worship service as inferior. In so doing, psalmody experi-enced a decisive change. Originally, psalmody arose from the cult and was closely bound to it, but now turned its back on it. Pious individuals had learned to sing songs in which they disregarded every external action. These songs were no longer designated for public worship. At the same time, the massive individualism of the prophets returned: the indi-vidual appeared before God alone. Thus arose spiritual poetry, the particular treasure of the psalter. Still, one cannot overlook the fact that the forms of the genres in which the change occurred, as a rule, remained the same, particularly the individual complaint and the individual thanksgiving song.

In contrast to this presentation, S. Mowinckel (*Psalmenstudien*, vol. 1, pp. 137ff) denies the availability of a spiritual poetry at all in the psalter. He maintains his position is a consistent extension of mine, but in the history of research not everything that is logically consistent is actually correct. It appears to me that his whole perspective includes a massive overstatement that extends beyond the bounds of what is correct. Evidence for this belief, which can only be conducted from the state of the text itself, will be brought in §2, ¶44; §6; and §7. Still, it should be noted here that Mowinckel's fundamental error appears to consist of undervaluing the spiritual heights of the psalmist, and Israel's spiritual life in general. He conceives of the psalmist in particular as too primitive.

Later psalmody changed in that perceptive reflection increasingly replaced the sorrow and solemnity of the older poetry. In so doing, the *wisdom psalm* (§10) entered the picture. Originally, the wisdom psalm had nothing to do with psalmody, and its life setting was in an entirely different location. In Israel, wisdom was originally proclaimed by the old men in the gate or in the market. Even in the psalter, these reflections are preserved in particular psalms, or they have penetrated the lyrical genres and finally completely disintegrated them.

The question with which research has occupied itself to this point is with *assigning a date* to the psalms. One can tell from the position that we generally give it in the investigation that we do not consider this problem to be the most important. Understanding a written work appears far more important to us as the proper and final task behind which all "criticism" should constantly take a back seat in significance. Likewise, we ask the reader to suspend, for now, the questions of dating and literary criticism during the foundational investigation of the genres. If these questions are mixed too early with such a different type of research, then all of the effort is in vain. Nevertheless, we will endeavor to give these problems their due as well, at the end of the discussion of every specific genre, and summarily at the conclusion of the whole (§12). Even the manner by which dating currently tends to be undertaken needs a fundamental revaluation. Thus, the reasons for the customary suppositions of the time should be evaluated once again. Above all, genre research provides new means for resolving these questions. It expands the scientific material by referencing related poems outside of the psalter, the canon, and even the people of Israel itself. Using genres creates new relationships between the individual psalms and often provides a new understanding. All of this affects the assignation of time. In particular, genre research provides new standards for differentiating the new from the old within the psalms, and finally a vast internal history of the entire poetry can be recognized. Particularly in these parts of our work, we hope for an understanding reader who is prepared to renounce long settled and comfortable prejudices.

At the close of the history of psalmody, collections of psalms were formed from which our "psalter" emerged (§13). Of course, this process very seldom comes into play for understanding the individual songs, as one would expect from the collection of songs. When the psalter arose, *public worship* again took hold of the songs. They were performed in the temple as "hymns." We have made comments about the specific use in the superscriptions of the Hebrew and Greek text, as well as with the rabbis (for an overview of the rabbis, see Staerk,[2] pp. 6ff).

Finally, we point to the fact that a work as comprehensive as the one described above naturally cannot be completed in a single stroke. We must be satisfied to begin the work. Later generations who can still find enough to do in this area, may take it up, utilize it from every angle, and take it to completion.

§2 Hymns

Ausgewählte Psalmen,[4] 1917, index "Hymnen." — *RGG*, "Psalmen," 3, 12. — "Formen der Hymnen," *Theologische Rundschau* 20 (1917): 265ff. — "Die Lieder in der Kindheits-geschichte Jesu bei Lukas," *Festgabe für A. von Harnack*, 1921, pp. 43ff. — "Psalm 149," *Oriental Studies Dedicated to Paul Haupt*, 1926, pp. 46ff. — E. Balla, *Das Ich der Psalmen*, 1912, pp. 34ff., 48-49, 50, 59ff., 90ff. — W. Staerk, *Lyrik in den "Schriften des AT*," vol. 3, part 1,[2] 1920, pp. 6ff. — H. Greßmann, *ZAW* 34 (1914): 283ff. — W. Baumgartner, *ZAW* 34 (1914): 169ff.

1. We begin with the genre which is easiest to recognize, and simultaneously, the genre in which the foundational thoughts of pious poetry were generally expressed. In the psalter, we possess the following hymns: Pss 8; 19; 29; 33; 65; 67; 68; 96; 98; 100; 103; 104; 105; 111; 113; 114; 117; 135; 136; 145; 146; 147; 148; 149; 150. In addition, one should include the related "Zion songs" (see below, ¶52): Pss 46; 48; 76; 84; 87; 122; and also the comparable "enthronement songs" (see §3): Pss 47; 93; 97; 99; and the "thanksgiving songs of Israel" (cf. ¶41): Pss 124; 129. Hymns and hymn-like elements are also found in "liturgies" and "mixed poems" (cf. §11): Pss 9:6-13, 16f; 12:7-9; 24:1f; 36:6-10; 75:2, 5-11; 81:2-6; 89:2f, 6-19; 90:1, 2, 4; 95:1-7; 106:1-3; 115:3-8, 16-18; 134:1f; 139:1-18; Isa 63:7; Mic 7:18ff. In the acrostic poem of 119, the following verses contain hymns or hymn-like elements: 4, 7a, 12a, 13, 14, 39c, 54, 62, 64a, 64b, 68a, 72, 75a, 86a, 89, 90, 91, 96, 103, 105, 129a, 130, 137, 138, 140, 142, 144a, 151, 152, 156a, 160, 164, 171, 172. In addition, hymnic elements in the *individual complaint song* (§6, ¶28) appear in: Pss 5:12f; 7:18; 11:4-7; 13:6; 16:7, 9b, 10; 22:4-6, 23ff; 25:8-10; 26:12b; 27:6; 28:6f; 31:8f, 20, 22; 35:9f, 27, 28; 36:6-10; 40:17; 43:4; 51:17; 52:11; 54:8f; 57:8-12; 59:17; 61:9; 63:4-6; 69:31, 35ff; 71:8, 15f, 18b, 19, 22f; 77:14-21; 86:5, 8-10, 12f, 15; 102:13-23, 26-29; 109:30f; 140:14. Compare also Jer 11:20; 16:19; 17:12f; 20:13; Lam 3:22f, 25; 5:19; Tob 3:2, 11; Wis 9:1-3; Pr Man 15; Pss. Sol. 5:1. See also the *communal complaints* (§4, ¶¶4, 12): Pss 44:2-4; 74:12-17; 79:13; 80:2, 9-12; 106:1-3; 1 Kgs 8:23; Isa 37:16; 63:7; Jer 14:8; 32:17-22; Hab 1:12f; Lam 5:19; Neh 1:5; 9:6-15; Dan 9:4; Pr Azar 1:3-5; Add Esth 3:2-4; 1 Macc 4:30; 2 Macc 1:24f; 3 Macc 2:1ff; 6:2; Pss. Sol. 17:1-3; 4 Ezra 8:20-23; 2 Apoc. Bar. 21:4-17; 48:2-10. See also the royal lament (§5, ¶6): Ps 144:1f. In the *thanksgiving songs of the individual* (§7, ¶¶3, 7, 8) one finds hymnic elements: Pss 9:2f 18:2f, 32-49, 50f; 22:23ff; 30:2, 5f, 13; 32:11; 34:2-4; 35:27f; 40:5; 66:1-12, 20; 92:2-9, 16; 106:1; 107:1, 8f, 15f, 21f, 31f, 33-42; 116:1; 118:1-4, 21, 24, 28f; 136:1-3; 138:1f, 4-6; Isa 38:18-20; Jer 33:11; 1 Chr 16:34; 2 Chr 20:21; Dan 2:20-22; cf. Sir 51:1, 12 (1ff); Pss. Sol. 16:5. Hymns and elements related to this genre also appear in the *narrative books*: Exod 15:1-18, 21; Deut 32:3f, 43: 33:26-29; Judg 5:3-5; 2 Sam 2:1-10. The also appear in the prophets: Isa 6:3; 12:1f, 3-6; 25:1, 5, 9; 26:1-6; 30:18d; 40:12-17, 22-24, 26, 28f; 41:13; 42:5, 10-12; 43:1, 14, 15, 16f; 44:2, 6, 23, 24-28; 45:6f, 11, 15, 18; 46:10f; 47:4; 48:12, 17, 20; 49:5, 7, 13; 51:15, 22; 52:9f; 57:15; 61:10f; 63:7; Jer 2:6; 5:22, 24; 10:6f, 10, 12-16; 31:7, 35; 33:2; 51:10, 15f; Joel 2:21, 23; Amos 4:13; 5:8; 9:5f; Nah 1; Hab 1:12f; 3:18f; Zeph 3:14f; Zech 2:14; 9:9; 12:1. In Job, one finds: 5:9-16; 9:4-12; 11:10f; 12:13-25; 25:2f; 26:5-14; 34:18-30; 36:22–37:13; 38f. In Daniel, one finds:

2:20-23; 3:28, 33; 4:31f, 34; 6:27f. In the Chronicler's works, one finds: 1 Chr 16:8-36; 29:10-12; 2 Chr 6:14f; 20:21; Ezra 3:10f; Neh 1:5; 9:5, 6-15, 32. In the apocrypha, one finds: 1 Macc 4:30; 3 Ezra 4:59f; Tob 13:1-7, 8-16; Jdt 9:12; 13:14, 17; 16; Pr Man 1-7; Pr Azar 3-5; Song of Praise of the three men (Pr Azar 29-68); Wis 11:20–12:2; Sir 10:14-18; 15:9f 16:18f, 26ff; 17:29f; 18:1-7; 35:13; 39:14b-35; 42:15–43:33; 45:26; 50:22. See also, Pss. Sol. 2:33-37; 3:1f; 5:1f, 9-11, 19; 6:6; 8:24, 34; 10:5-8; 17:1-3; 18:1-4, 10-12; Luke 1:46f, 49-55, 68-75; Odes Sol. 16:11-20. We will also compare the prose texts with similar contents (cf. ¶¶14, 19-21). Readers not yet comfortable with genre research would do well to familiarize themselves first with the indicators of the genre according to the following sections. Then, readers can process the entire psalms mentioned above, while saving the shorter and shortest hymnic elements until the end.

I. The Linguistic Form

2. We begin with the *linguistic form*, since it is particularly clear in hymns, especially with the beginning of the poems, where the genres are usually most clearly recognized (cf. §1, ¶8).

Normally, hymns begin with a pronounced "introduction." The most frequently appearing form of this introduction is the call to rejoice and sing using a plural imperative, such as *halĕlu*, ("praise"): Pss 113:1; 117:1; 135:1, 3; 148:1-4; 150:1-5; Jer 31:7; (Pss 22:24; 148:7; Jer 20:13); *zammĕru* ("play"): Pss 33:2; 66:2; 105:2; 135:3; (Pss 9:12; 30:5; 47:7; 68:5; 98:4,5; 135:3; 147:7; Isa 12:5); *hōdū* ("give thanks, praise"): Pss 33:2; 105:1; 106:1; 107:1; 118:1; 136:1-3; Jer 33:11; Sir 51 (1ff); (Pss 30:5; 97:12; 100:4; 118:29; 136:26: Isa 12:4); *širū* ("sing"): Pss 33:3; 96:1, 2; 98:1; 105:2; 149:1; Exod 15:21; Isa 42:10; (Ps 68:5, 33; Jer 20:13) (relatively frequently, in the form *širū šir hādāš* ["sing a new song"]: Pss 33:3; 96:1; 98:1; 149:1; Isa 42:10; cf. Pss. Sol. 3:1; Jdt 16:14); *harî'ū* ("rejoice"): Pss 47:2; 66:1; 81:2; 100:1; Isa 44:23; Zeph 3:14; (Ps 98:4, 6); *bārĕhū* ("bless"): Pss 96:2; 134:1, 2; (Pss 66:8; 100:4; 103:20-22; 135:19, 20; Sir 39:35; 45:26; 50:22); *ranĕnū, ronnū,* and *harnînū* ("rejoice"): Pss 33:1; 81:2; (Deut 32:43; Isa 44:23; 49:13; 52:9; Jer 31:7; Pss 32:11; 98:4). This same introductory form is not infrequently repeated at the beginning of new parts and at the conclusion of the poem (cf. §1, ¶8). In the aforementioned, examples of such are enumerated in parentheses. These imperatives appear extraordinarily frequently in the hymns, some 200 times. This phenomenon, so frequently attested, can certainly not be explained on the basis of the literary dependence of one poem on another. Rather, a given manner of speech here forms the basis of the style of the hymn. It has been the usual custom to tend to explain the similarities of various passages as the dependency of one writer on another. Thus, at this point, those who do so should learn a fact fundamental to the literary history of Israel, namely that there were fixed linguistic forms in Hebrew literature, and therefore also patterned genres.

3. Another form is closely related, but *never stands as the first word of the hymn.* Thus, it should be seen as changed from the original manner of speech, whereby the summons is issued in the third person plural of the jussive. Examples include: *yōdū* ("Let them give thanks, praise"): Pss 67:4,6; 99:3; 138:4; 140:14; 145:10; *yĕhalĕlū* ("Let them praise"): Pss 22:7; 69:35; 148:5, 13; 149:3; *yāronnū,* and *yĕrannĕnū* ("Let them rejoice"): Pss 5:12; 35:27; 67:5; 96:12; 98:8; 145:7; 149:5; Isa 42:11; *yiśmĕhū* ("Let them be glad, rejoice"): Pss 5:12; 35:27; 40:17; 67:5; 68:4; 96:11; 97:1; *yōmĕrū* ("Let them say"): Pss

35:27; 40:17; 107:2; 118:3,4; 145:6,11; *yaggîdū* ("Let them announce"): Pss 22:32; 145:4; Isa 42:12; *yāgîlū* ("Let them be happy"): Ps 149:2, etc. In all there are around sixty cases.

4. Yet another form is the *cohortative, or the first person plural imperfect*: *nārî'ā, nāria'* ("Let us exult"): Ps 95:1,2; *něranněnā, něrannēn* ("Let us rejoice:"): 95:1; Isa 38:20; *nāgîlā* ("Let us rejoice"): Ps 118:24; Isa 25:9; *niśměhā* ("Let us be glad"): Ps 118:24; Isa 25:9; *něsappěrā, něsappēr* ("Let us tell"): Ps 79:13; Jer 51:10; *nôdeh* ("Let us thank, praise"): Ps 79:13; *něbārēk* ("Let us bless"): Ps 115:18; *nikrě'ā* ("Let us bow down"): Ps 95:6; *něqadděmā pānāyv* ("Let us bow down before his face"): Ps 95:2, etc. In all, there are around seventy cases.

5. The main words which are accented through their position in the hymn are expressions which designate the fundamental mood of the type of poem, such as "rejoice," "exult," "be happy," or the like. Or the words concern more the form of the performance, such as "sing," "play," "strike the drum" (Ps 81:3), "blow the horn" (Ps 81:4). The instruments played during the singing of the song are particularly preferred: Pss 33:2f; 43:4; 57:9; 71:22; 81:3f; 92:4; 98:5f; 108:3; 144:9; 147:7; 149:3; 150:3-5; Jdt 16:2; Sir 39:15. Also, the movements performed by those singing are mentioned: "Enter before him in his gate" (Ps 100:2,4); "Fall down before YHWH" (Ps 29:2); "clap your hands" (Ps 47:2); "Raise your hands" (Ps 134:2); in Ps 149:5ff a weapon dance is described (cf. the commentary; for the form of the infinitive with *lě*, see ¶8 below). Or, the main words presuppose more the meaning of the poem: "rejoice," "thank," "Give honor and praise: (Pss 29:1; 96:7); "exalt" (Ps 99:5,9); "Call out his name" (Ps 105:1; Isa 12:4; Jdt 16:1; "Seek his countenance" (Ps 105:4); "Proclaim" (Ps 9:12; Isa 48:20); etc.

6. It is easy to recognize how to explain these forms. The common foundational form of all these sentences is that of a summons to a group. Thus, we learn that *these hymns were performed* by holy choirs. A choir summons itself in the cohortative ("Let us sing"). In the imperative ("Sing") and the jussive ("Let them sing") the summons is issued to the choir by someone else, apparently the lead singer. The fact that the last explanation is correct is proven by the hymns of Miriam and Judith. They begin with these imperatives, and their form of performance is described explicitly: both singers address the choir of the people to whom they sing the words of the song (Exod 15:20; Jdt 15:12ff). Even the later Jewish-Christian worship service used these summonses from the one praying to the congregation: "praise YHWH," "pray" (cf. Fr. Heiler, *Gebet*,[2-5] p. 441).

7. The *persons who should perform the poem* are very frequently mentioned specifically. The situation of the performance, and thereby the origin of the style, stands out very clearly when the temple choir (Pss 118:2-4; 135:19f) "that stands in the temple of YHWH" (Pss 134:1; 135:2) is thereby addressed. In other places those singing are called "the servants of YHWH" (Pss 113:1; 134:1; 135:1), "sons of Jacob" (Ps 105:6), or "the sons of Zion" (Ps 149:2; Joel 2:23). They receive all kinds of names of honor: YHWH's pious ones (Pss 30:5; 145:10; 149:5), "the righteous" (Pss 32:11; 33:1; 68:4; 140:14), "upright ones" (Ps 33:1), "upright in heart" (32:11), "those fearing YHWH" (Ps 22:24; Pss. Sol. 2:33), "those who love his name" (Ps 5:12), "those who love his salvation" (Ps 40:17), "those who praise him" (Sir 43:30), "those who seek him" (Pss 22:27; 40:17; 105:3), "those who hide themselves in him" (Ps 5:12), "those who love Jerusalem (Isa 66:10). In certain contexts the "waste places of Jerusalem" (Isa 52:9) or "the land" (Joel 2:21) are summoned. However, it was not sufficient for the poet, who was inspired and delighted by his immeasurable God, that only Israel should praise him. Thus, the poet

casts his view to the distance and calls all beings of the earth and heaven to join in the song: "all the world" (Pss 33:8; 66:1, 4; 96:1, 9; 98:4; 100:1), "the earth" (Ps 97:1); "the many islands" (Ps 97:1); "the ends of the earth" (Ps 67:8), "all the inhabitants of the world" (Ps 33:8), "all flesh" (Ps 145:1), "all that breathes" (Ps 150:6), "the families of the nations" (Pss 22:28; 96:7), all "peoples and nations" (Pss 47:2; 66:8; 67:4, 5, 6; 117:1; 148:11; Deut 32:43), "the kingdoms of the earth" (Ps 68:33), all "kings and princes" (Pss 138:4; 148:11), even the "enemies of YHWH" (Ps 66:3). Further, "all creation" (Ps 145:10; Tob 3:11) loves to proclaim the hymn: heaven and earth, the sea and its fullness, field and trees (Ps 96:11f), heaven and the depths of the earth, mountain and forest (Isa 44:23), even the sons of God and the angels (Pss 29:1; 103:20-22; 148:2), and even the dead (Ps 22:30, cf. the commentary). Further examples of these summons include: Pss 22:28-32; 69:35; 98:7f; Isa 42:10f; 49:13; Joel 2:21f; Tob 8:16. Sometimes the entire poem is even filled with them: cf. Ps 148 and the Song of Praise of the Three Men (Addition to Daniel 1:33-64 = Pr Azar 29-68). The forceful choir that fills all creation roars to the honor of YHWH. This glorification of the God of Israel as the one to be praised by all powers of the earth and of the heavens has its counterpart in the predictions of the prophets, especially Deutero-Isaiah, where all the beings of the world will one day fall at the feet of YHWH. We may certainly accept that the hymns of the later period were even kindled by this prophetic model. However, this kind of hymnic praise did not originate with the prophets. Rather, this kind of praise already appeared in the earliest time, as shown by Ps 29:1. Also, the two types of speaking, even if related must be clearly differentiated from one another: the prophets speak of the future, the psalmists of the present.

8. The *number of summonses* in the hymns corresponds to the throng of beings called who should sing God's praise. In the simplest form, the poet is satisfied with one such address: "sing," "praise," "rejoice," or something similar: Exod 15:1,21; Pss 98:1; 104:1; 111:1; 148:7; Jer 33:11; Jdt 16:14. The poet can also combine two summonses according to the practice of Hebrew poetry: Pss 47:2; 75:10; 103:1f; 117:1; 147:7, 12; 149:5; Isa 25:1; 61:10; Jer 20:13; Joel 2:21, 23; Zech 2:14; 9:9. It is, however, quite normal, particularly in later times, to use a whole series of these expressions : Pss 29:1f; 33:1-3; 34:2-4; 66:1-4; 67:4-6; 68:4f; 81:2-4; 95:1f; 96:1-3, 7-12; 98:4-8; 100:1-3, 4; 103:1f; 105:1-5; 108:2-4; 113:1-3; 135:19ff; 145:1f, 4-7, 10-12; 149:1-3; Isa 12:4-6; Jer 31:7; Zeph 3:14; Jdt 16:2. Just as the Gothic artist never tired of endlessly repeating the pinnacle, the characteristic form of his style, so the same form is continually changed in this "expanded introduction." This is also a sign of the overwhelming enthusiasm of the Hebrew poet. Even this continual repetition is certainly evidence for us that we have found the characteristic form for the hymn in this introductory formula. The impression is still more impressive, however, as well as the strength of the power of the evidence, when, in celebratory monotony, the introduction uses the same word in a row: Pss 47:7; 96:1, 2; 103:20-22; 135:19-20; 136:1-3; 148:1-5; 150; and especially the Song of the Three Young Men (Pr Azar 29ff). Ps 149:5ff contains another form of the expansion, where several more specific references are added to the summons to rejoice, finally with the infinitive and *lĕ* (cf. 149:7ff; see ¶5).

9. We have already enumerated several *singular* entities listed among the beings who are called to praise God. Other examples, particularly collectives, include the following: "Israel" (Ps 149:2; Zeph 3:14; cf. also 68:35a; "the seed of Jacob" (Ps 22:24), "seed of Israel" (Ps 22:24), "seed of Abraham (105:6), "Jerusalem" (Ps 147:12), "daughter of Jeru-

salem" (Zech 9:9; Zeph 3:14), "Zion" (Ps 147:12; Isa 54:1), "daughter of Zion" (Zeph 3:14; Zech 2:14; 9:9), "inhabitant of Zion" (Isa 12:6), "the land" (Joel 2:21), etc. Therein the leading word appears in the singular with the *imperative* or *jussive*, "sing" or "Let him/her/it sing."

10. In the final analysis, all of these forms mentioned in the introduction go back to the basic form "sing," from which these variations occur. As one became tired of always speaking in the second person of the imperative, one seized on these new forms. There-fore, it is not just being clever to accept that the "hallelujah" is the original cell of the singing of the hymn. "Hallelujah" is preserved as subscription or superscription in Pss 104–106; 111–113; 115–117; 135; 146–150 (in the Greek translation only as superscrip-tion). It was originally voiced by all the people at the end of the song of praise (cf. ¶44), as evidenced in Ps 106:48; 3 Macc 7:13; 1 Chr 16:36 (Ezra 3:11). We hear elsewhere that ancient religions knew a similar kind of rejoicing to God where the entire people joined in heartily as a carryover from the earliest cultic customs (e.g., cf. A. Erman, *Ägyptische Religion*,[2] p. 61). These "calls" are the oldest forms and at the same time a nucleus of the poetry. They also tend to remain in place as a refrain sung by the masses when a higher civilization produced an ordered song (cf. E. Schmidt, "Anfänge der Literatur" in *Kultur der Gegenwart*, vol. 1/7, pp. 8-13; and Fr. Heiler, *Gebet*,[2-5] pp. 47, 58). Even though it is first attested in a much later time, the Israelite "hallelujah" is also to be seen as the original cell of the hymn that preserved the birthmark of its origin in its common beginning "honor," "praise," "sing," "rejoice to YHWH" (cf. *RGG* article "hallelujah").

11. Beside this introductory form that summons a group to sing stands another form in which an "I" calls himself to sing. In other words, beside the choral song we also find the song of the individual singer (cf. ¶44). We can imagine that one entrusted such a solo to a particularly beautiful and trained voice.

A poem of this type begins with the *cohortative* or the *first person singular imperfect*. We find the same form in Babylonian while the plural does not seem to appear: "I will praise the camp of the gods" (J. Böllenrücher, *Gebete und Hymnen an Nergal*, p. 13; Jas-trow, *Die Religion Babylon und Assur*, vol. 1, pp. 172, 176, 180, 199; Fr. Stummer, *Su-merischen-akkadischen Parallelen*, pp. 18ff). Thereby one finds a fundamental difference between Babylonian and Israelite hymnic poetry (cf. Fr. Stummer, ibid., p. 26). See also §4 ¶5. The beginning "I will sing" also appears in Homer's hymn to Aphrodite (Allen-Sikes, *Homeric Hymns*, p. 244), Heracles (p. 254), Zeus (p. 277), and Gaia (p. 296).

The leading words that introduce the individual hymn are generally the same as those beginning the hymnic choral song. Those occurring most frequently are: *'ôdeh* ("I will thank, praise") Pss 8:18; 9:2; 18:50; 28:7; 30:13; 43:4; 52:11; 54:8; 71:22; 86:12; 108:4; 109:30; 111:1; 118:21, 28; 119:7; 138:1, 2; 139:14; Isa 12:1; 25:1; Sir 51:1; Luke 10:21; Matt 11:25; *'ăzammĕrāh, 'ăzammēr* "I will play"): Pss 7:18; 9:3; 27:6; 57:8, 10; 61:9; 71:22; 75:10; 104:33; 108:2, 4; 138:1; 146:2; Jdt 5:3; *'āšîrāh* and *'āšîr* (*"I will sing"*): *Pss 13:6; 27:6;* 57:8, 10; 59:17; 89:2; 104:33; 108:2; Exod 15:1; Jdt 5:3; *'ăalĕlāh* ("I will praise"): Pss 22:23; 69:31; 109:30; 145:2; 146:2; Sir 51:1,12; *'ăbarĕkāh* and *'ăbarĕk* ("I will bless"): Pss 16:7; 26:12; 34:2; 63:5; 145:1,2; Sir 51:12; *'ărômēm* ("I will raise up"): Pss 18:2; 30:2; 118:28; 145:1; Isa 25:1; *'ăsappĕrāh* ("I will tell"): Pss 9:2; 22:23; Sir 42:15; 51:1. We count around 100 examples of such forms.

This introductory form, just as with the plural, is found at the paragraphs and the conclusions of the poems. Also there are "expanded introductions" that were already introduced in the list mentioned above. These kinds of repetition also appear in Babylonian Hymns (cf. Fr. Stummer, *Sumerischen-akkadischen Parallelen*, pp. 19f, 23.

12. In liturgical poetry (cf. §11) the plural and singular introductory forms alternate with one another to the pleasure of the lively Hebrew spirit which loves the oscillation (cf. Pss 8; 75). For the type of performance, cf. ¶44. In later poems, they stand side by side (Pss 9; 145; Tob 13).

When *the poet* calls *his soul or his mouth* to praise God, it is an impressive mixture of self-summons and calling of others. This call sometimes happens in the *vocative* and in the *imperative*: *bārĕkî nafšî* or *halĕlî nafšî* ("bless" or "praise my soul"; cf. Pss 103:1f; 104:1; 146:1; cf. also Pss. Sol. 3:2. Only one time in the morning song (¶44) does the deviation appear ("wake up my soul" in Ps 57:9). Usually, the call comes in the *jussive*: *tāgîl* (Ps 35:9), *tāgēl* (Isa 61:10), *tāśîś* (Ps 35:9), *tithallēl* (Ps 34:5) with the subject *nafšî* ("let my soul rejoice, be happy, praise"); *yāgel libbî* ("let my heart rejoice," Ps 13:6); *yĕzammēr "kĕbēdî"* ("let my liver play," Ps 30:13 [see the commentary]); *yĕdabbēr* (Ps 145:21), *yagg îd* (Ps 51:17), *yĕsappēr* (Ps 71:15), *yĕhallēl* (Ps 63:6), *yimmālē'* (Ps 71:8), with the subject *pî* ("let my mouth speak, proclaim, tell, praise, be full [of God's] praise); *tehgeh* (Ps 35:28; 71:24), *tĕrannēn* (Ps 51:16), *ta'an* (Ps 119:172), with the subject *lĕšōnî* ("Let my tongue rejoice, sing"); *yĕśabbĕhū* (Ps 63:4), *tĕrannēnnāh* (Ps 71:23), *tabba'nāh* (Ps 119:171), with the subject *śĕfātay* ("let my lips praise, rejoice, utter praise"); *tāgēlnāh* (Ps 51:10), *tō'marnāh* (Ps 35:10), with the subject *'ṣmōtay* ("let my bones rejoice, speak").

13. All of these introductions have something in common, namely, they contain a praise to YHWH in some form. Less frequently, they contain a *description of the rejoicing* which does not make such a passionately moving impression as the summons. Rather, it gives a more peaceful, calm, or even occasionally confident and grand impression. Thus 1 Sam 2:1 ("my heart rejoices, my horn is exalted, my mouth opens wide, and I rejoice"); Sir 51:12 ("I thank"); Luke 1:46f ("my soul exalts, my spirit rejoices"). Or it appears in plural: Ps 75:2 ("we thank"); Ps 68:4 ("the righteous rejoice, are glad"); 68:27f. ("in choirs, 'they praise' YHWH"); Ps 19:2 ("the heavens tell"). The more typical form would have been, e.g., "Let the heavens tell." Other examples are: "my heart is steadfast" (Ps 57:8); "I thank you and praise you" (Dan 2:23; cf. 4:34); I praise you seven times a day (Ps 119:164); "I rise at midnight to praise you" (119:62). Even this form appears at times in "expanded" form (cf. 1 Sam 2:1; Pss 68:4; 75:2). There are also somewhat less colorful phrases: "O, how I love your law" (Ps 119:97); "I love your command above 'all' " (119:27). A freer form (cf. ¶29) bears the word: "Your statutes are my songs" (119:54).

14. Alongside the active introductory formulas mentioned in the preceding, a passive formula also exists: *bārūk* ("blessed is"). Deviations include: *yĕhî mĕbôrāk* (Ps 113:2), *mĕhullāl* (Ps 113:3) ("be praised"). This formula appears very frequently at the beginning of the prayers of thanksgiving (§7, ¶3) which are found in prose before Gen 14:20; 24:27; Exod 18:10; 1 Sam 25:32, 39; 2 Sam 18:28; 1 Kgs 1:48; 5:21; 8:15, 56; 10:9; Ruth 4:14; Ezra 7:27; 1 Chr 29:10; 2 Chr 6:4; especially in the apocrypha (εὐλογητός) Tob 3:11; 8:5, 15-17; 11:13, 16; 13:1; Jdt 13:17; 1 Macc 4:30; 2 Macc 1:17; 15:34; 3 Macc 7:23; 3 Ezra 4:40, 60; 8:25; Jub 25:12. It is seldom an introduction in the psalms (Pss 113:2, 3; 144:1) and only later does it become common: Dan 3:28 (*bĕrîk*), cf. 2:20; Pr Azar 3; Song of the Three Young Men 29-33; Tob 13:1; Luke 1:68. By contrast, this form appears frequently in the psalms in new paragraphs and in the conclusion: Pss 18:47; 28:6; 31:22;

41:14; 66:20; 68:20, 36; 72:18f; 89:53; 106:48; 113:2f; 119:12; 124:6; 135:21; 1 Chr 16:36; Pss. Sol. 2:37; 5:19; 6:6; 8:24, 34.

All of these introductory formulas may be traced back to three original formulas: "sing to YHWH," "I will sing to YHWH," and "blessed be YHWH."

15. It belongs to the nature of the material that *any substantive* will be added to the verbal forms. The substantive stands in the accusative, dative, nominative, or vocative and designates the *subject of praise*. These substantives are also worthy of attention since we thereby experience something of the content of the hymn. Cf., e.g., Ps 105, which contains a narrative from holy history. However, by using these substantives in the introduction, it declares that a narrative of this type should be understood as *a proclamation of the majestic deeds* of God. Naturally, the fact that the word YHWH stands in the first position among these substantives (or in any form for that matter) is indispensable here. It is the most important thing that the hymnic poet can say: his song will concern just this God. Thus, the introduction will say: "sing to YHWH;" "rejoice to YHWH;" "I will praise YHWH; etc."Cf. Pss 7:18; 26:12; 27:6; 33:1; 35:2; 35:9; 66:1; 81:2; 95:1; 96:1; 103:1; 104:1; 109:30; 136:1; 146:1; 147:7,12; 148:1; 149:1; Exod 15:1; Isa 42:10; Jer 20:13; Hab 3:18; etc. Or, all kinds of poetic deviations occur: "The Most High" (Pss 7:18; 9:3; 92:2); *'ēl* ("God", 19:2; 150:1); "the God of Jacob" (81:2); "Holy One of Israel" (71:22); "Creator and King" of Israel (149:2); "our God" (66:8; Deut 32:3; our King: 47:7); "'YHWH' our protection" (81:2); "the rock of our salvation" (95:1); "my rock" (144:1); "my God" (30:13; 104:33); "the God of my salvation" (Hab 3:18; Sir 51:1); "my God, you are king" (145:1); "the king YHWH" (98:6); "God of heaven" (136:26); "King of heaven" (Dan 4:34; Tob 13:7); "God of gods" (Pss 136:26); "Lord of Lords" (136:3; cf. especially, Sir 51:1ff). Very frequently the "name" of YHWH is mentioned as the subject of praise (*šēm, zēker*). Cf. Pss: 7:18; 9:3; 22:23; 29:2; 30:5; 34:4; 54:8; 61:9; 66:4; 68:5; 69:31; 86:12; 92:2; 96:2; 99:3; 100:4; 103:1; 105:3; 113:1; 135:1; 138:2; 145:1f, 21; 140:14; 148:5, 13; Deut 32:3; Isa 25:1; Dan 2:20; Sir 39:35; 51:1, 12; Pr Azar 3; Song of Three Young Men 29, etc. Or the qualities and deeds of YHWH are accented in this form: his "praise" (*tĕhillāh* in Pss 35:28; 51:17; 71:8; 145:21; Isa 42:10); "his praiseworthy deeds" (*tĕhillôt*, 63:7); his "renown" (96:3); "the glorious majesty of his splendor," (145:5); "the majesty of his name" (66:2) and "of his kingdom" (145:11); "the fullness of his greatness" (150:2); his "salvation" (13:6; 35:9; 71:15; 96:2; Isa 25:9); his "protection" (Ps 59:17); his "faithfulness" (71:22; 89:2); "grace and faithfulness" (92:3); his "grace" (31:8; 59:17); his "graces" (89:2; Isa 63:7); his "righteousness" (Pss 22:32; 35:28; 71:15, 16, 19, 24); "goodness and righteousness" (145:7); his "arm" (71:18); his "strength," *gĕbûrāh* (71:18; 145:11); his "works," *ma'ăśîm* (145:4, 10; Sir 42:15); "deeds," *'ălîlôtāyw* (Pss 9:12; 105:1); YHWH's "acts," *mif'ălôt yhwh*, (66:5); "powerful deeds," *gebûrôt* (145:4, 12; 150:2); the "works of his hands" (92:5); his "mighty deeds," *gĕdullôt* (145:6); "miracles," *niflā'ôt* (9:2; 75:2; 96:3; 105:2, 6; 145:5); the "power of his terrible deeds," *nôrā'ôt* (145:6); his "signs and the judgments of his mouth," (105:5, etc.). Thus, this compilation expands the whole fullness of the majesty of God before us which had filled the heart of the poet with bliss and respect.

In the simplest introductions only one word is mentioned: Pss 98:1; 111:1; 117:1; 134:1; 150; Exod 15:1,20. In the more extensive introductions, several express the enthusiasm of the poet: Pss 66:1-4; 92:2f; 95:1; 104:33; 136:1-3; 145:1; 146:2; Isa 25:1; 61:10; etc. The Babylonian hymn recognizes similar substantives as the subject of the praise: the name, the divinity, power, strength, greatness, the majesty of the God (cf. Fr. Stummer, *Sumerischen-akkadischen Parallelen*, pp. 18ff, 23f).

16. Now, on to the *looser forms of the introduction*. These stand as poetic deviations, usually in the second half-line: "Praise YHWH, o my soul, and do not forget *all his good deeds*" (Ps 103:2); "Praise his holy name, let the heart of the one who seeks YHWH be glad" (105:3); "Rejoice over YHWH, you righteous ones; praise becomes the upright" (33:1); "I will bless YHWH always, his praise will constant be in my mouth" (34:2). These kinds of sentences also occasionally begin the poem: "Praise is befitting for you" (65:2); "It is good to thank YHWH, for . . . " (92:2-5). A similar introduction appears in a Babylonian hymn (cf. H. Zimmern, *Babylonische Hymnen und Gebete*, p. 16; cf. Fr. Stummer, *Sumerischen-akkadischen Parallelen*, pp. 26ff). The introduction "I know that . . . " is very peculiar (cf. ¶25).

17. Very few hymns are entirely *without an introduction*. These few hymns begin with a powerful sentence of a form that appears in the "main part" of the hymns (cf ¶25), as in the rhetorical question (Pss 8:2; cf. 84:2; cf. ¶31). Or, these hymns begin with a particularly emphatic statement (Pss 114:1f; 19:8ff; 139:1; Nah 1:2; Dan 4:31; cf. Also the beginning of Ps 90). Such words may also stand at the beginning of paragraphs and conclusions (cf. Ps 104:31). The hymn of the seraphim (Isa 6:3) contains only two sentences that are typical for the main part. Hymnic elements in "mixed poetry" (§11) frequently lack the introduction (cf. Pss 24:1f; 36:6ff; Deut 33:26ff; cf. Isa 40:12). The thanksgiving song of Israel (¶41; see Pss 67; 124; 129), which is related to the hymn, as well as the eschatological hymn (¶51; see Ps 68) begin with the great matter for which one is thankful and over which one rejoices. The enthronement songs, likewise influenced by the hymn, (Pss 93; 97; 99; not 47) have the beginning that is characteristic of that genre: *yhwh mālak* ("YHWH has become king"; cf. §3, ¶1). The Zion songs, which are similar to hymns (Pss 46; 48; 76; 84; 87; see ¶¶26, 52) begin immediately with the praise of YHWH and Zion, in other words with the main part. The highly unusual Zion song (Ps 122) begins in a highly unusual manner by maintaining a personal style.

Several hymns consist exclusively, or almost exclusively, of expanded introductions (Ps 150; Song of the Three Men; Ps 148).

18. Usually, the *main part* follows the introduction of the poem. We designate the "main part" as that part of the whole which remains after one separates the introduction and conclusion. The Hebrew hymn loves to add a sentence beginning with "for, that" (*kî*, Aramaic *dî*) to the introductory words. This sentence establishes the rationale for the summons and thus provides the particular content of the song of praise. This phenomenon appears so frequently that it furnishes one of the most certain and most easily recognizable characteristics of the hymn. The oldest example of this element is the song of Miriam: "Sing to YHWH, for he is highly exalted" (Exod 15:21). Other examples include: Ps 135:3: "Praise 'YHWH' for 'he' is good. Sing to his name for it is lovely"; Ps 13:6: "I will sing to YHWH, for he has dealt well with me"; Ps 52:11: "I will give thanks to you forever, for you have done it." Additional cases include: Pss 5:13; 9:5, 13; 22:25, 29, 32; 28:6; 30:2, 6; 31:22; 33:4, 9; 47:3, 8; 54:8, 9; 57:11; 59:17; 63:4; 66:10; 67:5; 69:36; 71:15, 24; 81:5; 86:13; 89:3; 92:5; 95:3, 7; 96:4, 5; 98:1, 9; 100:3, 5; 106:1; 107:1; 109:31; 116:1f; 117:2; 118:1-4, 21, 29; 135:4, 14; 136; 138:2, 4, 5, 6; 139:14 (with the form *'al kî*); 147:13; 148:5, 13; 149:4; Deut 32:43; Isa 12:1, 2, 5, 6; 14:29; 25:1, 10; 44:23; 49:13; 52:9; 54:1; 56:10; 61:10; 66:12; Jer 20:13; 33:11; Hos 9:1; Joel 2:21, 23; Zech 2:14; Dan 2:20, 23;

1 Macc 4:30; Jdt 16:3, 15-17; Tob 8:16, 17; 11:14; 13:2, 16; Pr Man 15; Pr Azar 1:4; Song of the Three Men 66-68; Sir 51:1 (1ff); Pss. Sol. 2:33; 3:2; 5:2; Luke 10:21; Matt 11:25. All together, there are around 100 examples. This is also a place where those inexperienced in investigations of style can learn to see.

W. Baumgartner brought to my attention, that in the history of the genre this type of rationale or object sentence originally *further explicated* the introduction, especially the subject of the praise mentioned in ¶15. The result of this sentence is that what now appears to us as the "main part" is really only an expansion of one part of the "introduction," which represents the oldest part of the hymn.

19. Another transition from the introduction to the main part also arose as an expansion of the "introduction." It consists of the addition of *bywords praising* the name of God in the form of the *apposition*. Compare: "Praised are you, Lord, God of our fathers" (Pr Azar 1:3); and especially: "I will lift you up, YHWH, my strength, 'I,' my rock, my fortress, 'my sanctuary,' my God, my refuge to which I flee, and the horn of my salvation" (Ps 18:2). These attributes appear very seldom in this position in Hebrew (although admittedly they are more frequent in Babylonian, cf. Fr. Stummer, *Sumerischen-akkadischen Parallelen*, p. 22). In order to anticipate this fact, they sometimes stand in the main part of the hymn: Pss 65:6; 89:8; Deut 33:29; Job 9:5ff; particularly in the hymnic expansion of the "call" to prayer, specifically of complaint songs (cf. §4, ¶¶4, 12; §6, ¶¶10, 28): Jer 14:8; 16:19; 17:12f; 32:18f; Hab 1:12f; Neh 1:5; 9:32; Dan 9:4; Jdt 9:12; 2 Macc 1:24; 3 Macc 2:2; 6:2, 9; Add Esth 3:2; Pr Man 1; and in the introduction of the prophetic oracle by the formula: "thus said YHWH" (*kōh 'āmar yhwh*): Isa 43:16f; 44:6; 45:11; 48:17; 49:7.

20. Sometimes a *relative sentence* takes this position: "I will bless YHWH, who has counseled me" (Ps 16:7); "I will rejoice and be glad to you who has seen my affliction" (Ps 31:8); cf. further 66:20; 124:6. These relative sentences prefer to follow the formula, "blessed be YHWH (*bārūk yhwh*), cf. ¶14). Cf. Pss 66:20; 124:6, and especially in the prose prayers of Gen 24:27: "blessed be YHWH, the God of my father Abraham, who has not forsaken his lovingkindness and his truth toward my Lord." Further examples include: Exod 18:10; 1 Sam 25:32,39; 2 Sam 18:28; 1 Kgs 1:48; 5:21; 8:15, 56; 10:9; Ruth 4:14; Ezra 7:27; Dan 3:28; Tob 11:16; 3 Ezra 4:60. One can find the same type of hymnic relative sentences in other places: Pss 46:9; 71:19; 135:8; 136:23; 1 Kgs 8:24; Jer 5:22; 32:20; Job 34:19; Neh 9:7; Pr Man 4; 4 Ezra 8:21-23.

21. Nevertheless, these two transitions from the introduction to the main part seldom occur. More frequently, one will find a participle added to the divine name which is reflected by a relative sentence in English. One can compare: "Sing to YHWH, who lives in Zion" (*yôšeb*, Ps 9:12); "Thank the Lord of Lords, who alone does great wonders" (Ps 136:3f); "Blessed be YHWH, my rock, who teaches my hands war" (144:1). Further examples include 18:48, 49; 66:9; 68:5, 34; 103:3-5; 114:8; 135:21; 136:5-7; 147:8, 9, 14-17; Jdt 13:17; Sir 45:25; 50:22. One can particularly recognize that these participles following the introduction are a characteristic piece of the hymn from the fact that several often stand next to one another (cf. ¶8 regarding the accumulation of the signals of the genre). Here also, the particular cause of the accumulation is the enthusiasm of the poet for his God. His heart is so full of everything God does, so full of all the grace that God pours out so bountifully, that the poet cannot do enough to tell all of this. One example, where one can learn to recognize the character of this aspect is Ps 103:1-5: "Bless YHWH, o my

soul, all that is 'in me' *bless* his holy name. . . . Who forgave all your sins, and who healed all your suffering, who delivered your life from the grave, ' ' who crowned you with grace and compassion, who satisfies 'you' 'bountifully' with goodness, so that your youth is renewed like an eagle." Another example is Ps 147:7-9: "Sing to YHWH with thanksgiving, play to our God on the zither, who has covered the heavens with clouds, who prepares rain for the earth, who makes grass sprout on the mountains, 'and vegetation for man's steer,' 'who' gives the cow its food, and the young ravens that which they cry." Other examples include: Pss 18:48f; 66:9; 136:4-7; 147:14-17. It is part of the nature of the material that these participles usually carry a more specific determination, the article, a suffix, or a genitive (cf. Fr. Stummer, *Sumerischen-akkadischen Parallelen*, pp. 65ff), although at times they also stand without any such determination (cf. Pss 33:7; 113:7; 135:7; 147:9; Amos 5:8; Mic 7:18; etc.). These kinds of hymnic participles are found not too far removed from the divine name in other places as well (just as the attributes treated in ¶19). To this group belongs: Pss 33:5, 7, 15; 46:10; 65:7, 8; 66:6f; 104:2b-4, 32; 135:7; 146:6; Isa 40:26; Jer 2:6; 5:24; Amos 4:13; 5:8; 9:5f; Zech 12:1; Job 5:9ff; 9:5ff; 12:17, 19-24; 26:7-9; 34:18. They are found in the hymn especially after rhetorical questions (cf. ¶31): Pss 18:33-35; 35:10; 89:8; 113:5-9; Exod 15:11; Isa 40:22f; Mic 7:18 (cf. also Exod 15:11; Deut 33:26). Further, they appear in prayers, especially prose prayers, in hymnically expanded "summonses:" Ps 80:2; 1 Kgs 8:23; Isa 37:16; Jer 11:20; 14:8; 32:18; Dan 9:4; Neh 1:5; 9:32; Pr Man 2f. They appear in the prophets after the introductory formulas, "Thus said YHWH," *kōh 'āmar yhwh*, (Isa 42:5; 43:1, 14, 16f; 44:2, 6, 24-28; 45:11, 18; 48:17; 49:5, 7; 57:15; Jer 31:35; 33:2) and "utterance of YHWH," *nĕum yhwh* (Zech 12:1). They appear after "divine self-presentations," *'ănî* or *'ānōkî yhwh* (Isa 41:13; 44:24-28; 45:6f, 19; 48:17; 51:15. In these cases also, the accumulation of participles is favored (cf. Pss 18:33-35; 65:7f; 66:6f; 136:16f; Isa 40:22f; 41:13; 43:16f; 44:24-28; 45:6f; 48:17; Jer 10:12; Amos 4:13; 5:8; 9:5f; Zech 12:1; Job 5:9-13; 9:5-10; 12:17, 19-24; 26:7-9; Pr Man 2f (cf. H. Greßmann, *ZAW* 34 [1914]: 284ff). In the above mentioned examples, Pss 103:1-5; 147:7-9, one can recognize how much these participles were perceived by the poets as a distinguishing speech characteristic of the hymn. There, the poet occasionally deviates from the characteristic participial style, but then returns to it again. The entire poem of Ps 104 is dominated by this stylistic form where the characteristic participle stands in the first part, not far removed from the introduction: "the one who stretches out the heavens like a tent curtain, who lays his balcony's beam in the water, who makes the clouds into his chariot, who rides on the wings of the storm; who uses the wind as his messengers" (104:2b-4a). From this point, the individual parts begin with participles (104:5, 10, 13, 19, cf. the commentary) so as to conclude with other constructions. However, with each new paragraph the poet again reflects the typical speech characteristic. It is similar in Ps 136, in which these same participles introduce the main element (136:4-6) and each new part (7, 10, 13, 16). Compare also Ps 107:40. Hymnic pieces also begin with participles elsewhere and very frequently and then continue with the tense of the portrayal: Pss 66:7; 68:34; 147:18, 20; Job 5:14f; 12:18; 26:10ff; 39:20; Isa 40:22ff; Jer 10:13; Amos 5:8; 9:5f; or the narrative: Pss 18:35ff, 49; 66:6,9-12; 104:6ff; Isa 43:17; 45:18.

22. This style using the attribute, the relative sentence, and participles is also very common in *Babylonian* (cf. J. Hehn, *Hymnen und Gebete an Marduk*, pp. 288f, 312f, 321, 325f, 330, 336, 348, etc. Cf. M. Jastrow, *Religion Babyloniens und Assurs*, vol 1, pp. 449,

450, 536, 547, etc; H. Zimmern, *Babylonische Hymnen und Gebete*, vol. 1, pp. 7, 10, 11, 14, 15, 17, 19, 24; vol. 2, pp. 8, 17f, 18f, 23; A. Ungnad, *Die Religion der Babylonier und Assyrer*, pp. 176, 179, etc.; J. Böllenrücher, *Gebete und Hymnen an Nergal*, pp. 45, 50; O. Weber, *Literatur der Babylonier und Assyrer*, p. 123. Compare also E. Balle, *Ich der Psalmen*, p. 91, and Fr. Stummer, *Sumerischen-akkadischen Parallelen*, pp. 11ff, 62ff.). As an example, one can take the expanded introduction of the lament by H. Zimmern, p. 15:

Mighty, glorious,	ruler of Eridu
majestic, exalted one,	firstborn of Nudimmud
Marduk, the wise one,	who makes Egurra rejoice!
Lord of Esagil,	Helper of Babylon,
who loves Ezida,	who keeps life unharmed
prince of Emachtila,	who allows health to prosper!

Likewise, *Egyptian hymns* usually consist purely of combined divine predicates. "They begin with the name of the one being praised, to whom eventually flows yet another address like 'blessed be you' or 'honor to you.' Then, names, pure adjectives, substantives, participles, and relative sentences follow, actually as synonyms to this divine predicate. These elements portray the character of the one being praised or they recall his deeds" (A. Erman, *Literatur der Ägypter*, p. 13). As an example, cf. the poem in A. Erman, *Ägyptische Religion*,[2] p. 61:

Blessed be you, Osiris, son of Nut, you who carry horns and lean on your arrows. To whom the crown and joy before the nine gods was given, whose power Atum made in the hearts of men, gods, and the transfigured ones. To whom lordship was given in Heliopolis; whose being is great in Busiris, feared in the two holy places. The one who is great in power in Rosetta, a lord of might in Ehnas, a lord of power in Tenent. Greatly loved on the earth, with good remembrance in the divine palace. . . . The one before whom the great powers fear, before whom the nobles rise from their mats. Before whom Shu excited fear, and whose power created Tesnet. The one before whom upper Egypt and Lower Egypt bow down, because his fear is so large and his might is so powerful.

For further examples, see G. Roeder, *Urkunden zur Religion des alten Ägypten*, pp. 5, 6, 7, 8, 9, 10, 14, 22f, 27, 31, 49, 52, etc.

This predicative style is also well known in Greek, where participial constructions and relative sentences appear beside the "nominal summons" (cf. E. Norden, *Agnostos Theos*, pp. 141ff, 166ff, 201ff). Similar styles appear in syncretistic Hellenistic hymns of entreaty (A. Dietrich, *Abraras*, p. 139), in the Koran (Sure, 87), in the Jewish Shema, etc.

We may conclude from the frequency of this type of speech in Hebrew hymns, and from their particular meaning that appears within them, that they belong to the oldest components of this poetry. We receive confirmation for this supposition from the material just cited. This manner of praising the gods arose in Babylon and Egypt long before Israel, and from there penetrated even to this point.

23. In Israelite hymns, it is rather uncommon to see the main part follow the introduction *without any connection*, and then it is to be seen as a late deviation (cf. Pss 104:1; 105:7; 113:4; 115; Isa 42:13; Hab 3:19; Zeph 3:15; Zech 9:9).

24. The *main person* of the hymn is of course YHWH himself. YHWH is normally addressed in the *third person*. These hymns are thus actually not "prayers" in the proper sense, in which the "appeal" (in vocative) and the address in the verb are much more characteristic (cf. §4, ¶4; §6, ¶10). The third person is utilized consistently throughout the en-

tire hymn: Pss 24:1f, 29; 33:1-21; 46; 47; 81:2-6; 95:1-7; 96; 98; 100; 103; 105; 111; 113; 117; 134; 146; 147; 148; 149; 150; 1 Sam 2:1-10; Isa 6:3; 12:4-6; 61:10f; Hab 3:18f. Very seldom does the second person dominate the entire poem: Pss 8; 65; 139:1-18; Isa 25:1-5; cf also Ps 90. The mixture of second and third person is more frequent: Pss 9:6-13; 48; 66:1-12; 67; 68; 76; 77:14; 84; 89:2, 3, 6-19; 92; 97; 99; 104; 135; 145; Exod 15; Mic 7:18-20; cf. Dan 2:20-23; as well as Ps 18:32ff. This alternation also occurs occasionally in Babylonian (cf. Fr. Stummer, *Sumerischen-akkadischen Parallelen*, pp. 19f, 23, 38). According to Fr. Heiler (*Gebet*,[2-5] pp. 167f), this alternation also appears in Egyptian, Vedic, and Mexican poetry. Heiler maintains the second person is original; but for the Hebrew this would be decidedly incorrect. The situation as presented shows it is far more certain to deduce that the most original form of the hymn spoke of YHWH in the third person. Later, the second person also appeared under the influence of prayers. Being more personal, it more forcefully expresses the direct piety. The hymn also begins in third person in Babylonian, only then to go over to address here and there (cf. Fr. Stummer, p. 23). As in the "he" psalms, however, the ever repeating and ever recurring YHWH, accented in honor and remembrance, expresses the enthusiasm of the poet. A particularly clear example of this is found in Ps 146:7c, 8ab, 9a: "YHWH frees the prisoners, YHWH makes the blind to see, YHWH raises up those who have been humiliated; YHWH protects the foreigners." So also in the "you" parts, the "you" is accumulated. Cf. Ps 89:10-12: "You remain Lord of the swelling sea; 'by the' roaring of its waves, you bring them to rest. You scattered Rahab like a carcass, you scattered your enemies with a strong arm. The heavens belong to you, and the earth belongs to you. You have established the world and that which fills it." Cf. Ps. 74:13-17; 1 Chr 29:11f. The same appears in Babylonian (P. Jenken, *KB*, vol. 2, pp. 118f; Fr. Stummer, *Sumerischen-akkadischen Parallelen*, pp. 48ff), as well as in Greek and Latin hymns (cf. E. Norden, *Agnostos Theos*, p. 149). In Babylonian, the God sings the hymn about himself in "I" style (H. Zimmern, *Babylonische Hymnen und Gebete*, vol. 1, p. 22; vol. 2, p. 9; cf. M. Jastrow, *Die Religion Babylon und Assur*, vol. 1, pp. 458, 460ff, 538ff; E. Norden, pp. 207f). This happened in Babylonian, but it must have also have been a practice at one time in Israelite hymns, as demonstrated by the echoes of this kind of hymn in the great divine speech of Job at the end of the book (Job 38f) and in the self-praise of Wisdom (Sir 24:1-22, etc.; ¶26; cf. W. Baumgartner, *ZAW* 34 [1914]: 172f). In the Old Testament, one does not find these "I" hymns to YHWH. The reason is easy to recognize. A priest, dressed as God, would have performed these kinds of songs, and the YHWH religion would not have produced this type of dress where a person would be dressed as God. They saw their God in such elevated terms, that they would have perceived his representation by a person as a devaluation.

25. The *main part*, that is, the particular foundation, of the hymns often contains only short sentences *that state something particularly praiseworthy about God when the poet's heart delights in God's greatness*. The fact that these sentences are very short is explained by Hebrew meter, which forces the meaning to be compressed into bi-cola or cola. The hymn consists from the accumulation of these kinds of sentences of accolade. Therefore, its contents are characterized with expressions like, "YHWH's wonder, plans, or the like" (Pss 9:2; 26:7; 40:6; 75:2; 96:3; 139:18; Sir 18:4; etc.). Here and there these sentences are introduced by something sounding like a confession, "I know it well, *yāda'tî* (Pss 119:75,152; 135:5; 1 Chr 29:17; 4 Ezra 7:132). It lies in the nature of the material that *YHWH's name is the subject* in most of these sentences. It is thus not a type of speech but

a reality that the hymn, among other things, praises (*hizkîr*), sings (*zimmēr*), and rejoices (*hillēl*) over YHWH's name.

Next, there are statements that treat YHWH's *qualities* and thus usually take the *form of the nominal sentence*: YHWH is compassionate and gracious, patient and full of favor" (Ps 103:8); YHWH is right in all his ways and gracious in all his deeds (Ps 145:17); "YHWH is a great king, an 'I' king over all gods" (Ps 95:3); "Thus, YHWH 'was' a fortress for the oppressed, a refuge in hours 'of need' (Ps 9:10). Other examples include: Pss 11:5, 7; 22:4; 25:8; 33:5, 20; 34:19; 40:17; 46:2, 6, 8, 12; 47:3; 48:2; 68:6, 20, 36; 76:2; 77:15; 84:12; 86:5, 10, 15; 89:18; 92:9, 16; 93:4; 95:7; 96:4; 97:9; 99:1, 5, 9; 100:5; 102:13; 105:7; 111:4; 113:4; 115:3; 119:68, 137, 151; 135:3, 5; 145:3, 8, 9, 18; 147:5; Exod 15:3; Deut 33:27; 1 Sam 2:3; Isa 6:3; Jer 10:10; Hab 3:19; Nah 1:2, 3, 7; Job 36:22, 26; Lam 3:25; Dan 6:27; 2 Macc 1:25; Jdt 16:14; Pr Azar 4; Pr Man 7; Add Esth 3:4; Pss. Sol. 18:1-4.

26. a deviation of this type of speech occurs when YHWH's *qualities, limbs* (more or less metaphorically), *works, endowments*, or anything else belonging to him becomes the subject of the sentence. Examples include: YHWH's "hand is strong" (Ps 89:14); and "his right hand" "is exalted" (89:14), "full of righteousness" (48:11), "majestic in power" (Exod 15:6); YHWH's "words are pure words" (12:7); "His word" "is purified" (18:31; cf. 119:140), "is upright" (33:4); "endures forever" (119:89; 4 Ezra 8:22); "His 'speech' remains forever" (119:90). For this praise of the divine word, cf. the Babylonian hymn in H. Zimmern (*Babylonische Hymnen und Gebete*, vol. 2, pp. 21f = a. Ungnad, *Die Religion der Babylonier und Assyrer*, pp. 212ff). And thus the hymn treats YHWH's eye and eyes (Pss 11:4; 33:18; 34:16; 66:7; Jer 32:19; Job 34:21; 4 Ezra 8:20); his face (Ps 34:17); his name and memory (Pss 8:2; 76:2; 102:13; 111:9; 113:3; 135:3, 13; 148:13; Isa 12:4; Jer 10:6; Luke 1:49); his way and his ways (Pss 18:31; 25:10; 77:14; Deut 32:4; Nah 1:3b; Dan 4:34; Pr Azar 4); his actions and his works (Pss 33:4; 66:3; 86:8; 92:6; 104:24; 111:2, 3, 7; 139:14; Deut 32:4; Pr Azar 4); his judgment (Pss 36:7; 105:7; 119:7f, 39, 54, 151); his council and his thoughts (33:11; 92:6 [139:17]); his dominion (145:13); his kingdom (103:19; 145:13; Dan 3:33; 4:31; 6:27; Pss. Sol. 17:3); his throne (Pss 11:4; 93:2; Lam 5:19; 4 Ezra 8:21); his majesty and power (Pss 68:35); his power (Pss. Sol. 17:3); his majesty and splendor (Pss 8:2; 113:4; 138:5; 148:13; Isa 6:3; 4 Ezra 8:21); his praise (Pss 48:11; 111:10); his greatness (145:3); his indignation (Nah 1:6); his mercies (Pss 119:156; 145:9; Pss. Sol. 2:33; Luke 1:50); his favor, grace, and faithfulness (Pss 31:20; 36:6, 8; 57:11; 63:4; 86:13; 89:3, 15; 100:5; 103:11, 17; 108:5; 117:2; 118:1-4, 29; 119:90; 136; Jer 33:11; Lam 3:22f); his righteousness (Pss 36:7; 111:3; 119:142); his understanding (Ps 147:5); his wisdom (Job 11:8f); his fear (Ps 111:10); his law and commandment (Ps 119:72, 98, 142); his laws, commands, ordinances, and speeches, etc. (Pss 111:7f; 119:39, 54, 86, 103, 137, 143, 151; 4 Ezra 8:23); his testimonies (Pss 93:5; 119:129, 144); his words (Ps 12:7); his signs and wonders (Dan 3:33). Reference to YHWH's *voice* also belongs here with the hymn: "YHWH's voice over the waters, YHWH's voice with power, YHWH's voice with majesty. YHWH's voice smatters cedars," etc. Likewise, the praise song about the *law*, which should of course be considered much later (19:8ff): "YHWH's law is spotless." "YHWH's decree is certain." "YHWH's commands are right." "YHWH's commandment is pure." "YHWH's word is healing." "YHWH's laws are truth." As they have been presented by us in the preceding and in that which follows, these assertions have the goal of portraying the form-language of the hymns. They do so

in order that when the reader comes upon it, the reader might recognize the individual passage as "hymnic" in nature. At the same time, the *contents* of the hymns are thus expanded, which will be presented further in Part III of this chapter (below, p. 47).

In addition, there are songs which also praise God's sanctuary along with God. We call these particular songs "Zion Songs" (cf. ¶¶17, 52) since they also differ somewhat from the usual form of the hymn. Here, Zion (or something similar) is of course frequently the subject of the sentences (cf. Pss 46:6; 48:3, 12; 76:3; 84:2; 122:3; cf. Isa 26:1; Jer 17:12).

One also finds *hymns to wisdom*, particularly in the wisdom literature, but these will not be treated since they do not appear in the psalter. Cf. Prov 3:13-20; 8:6-21, 22-36; Job 11:8f; 28; Sir 1; 24; Baruch 3:9ff; Wis 6:12ff; 11:20 (cf 3 Ezra 4:33-40).

Songs of praise to the heroes and the fathers have a certain relationship with hymns in 1 Maccabees and Sir 44:1–50:52, but of course with the fundamental difference that "hymns" concern God and the divine while the former concern human beings. The glorification of Judas Maccabeus (1 Macc 3:3-9) and Simon (14:6-25) are, by form, a historical narrative and a portrayal of the fate of that time. The well-known "Praise of the Fathers" in Sir 44:1ff contains much related to the hymn in form: there is a hymnic introduction at the beginning (44:1; cf. Also 45:26; 50:22); then attributes presented comparably to the way they appear in the hymn, ¶19 (44:3-6; 46:1), particularly participles, ¶21 (45:1; 46:13; 48:5-10; 49:9, 13; and 50:4) and relative sentences, ¶20 (47:13; 49:10, 12; 50:1-3), and also rhetorical questions, ¶31 (46:2-4; 47:14; 48:4; 49:11; 50:5), and a "wish for a blessing," ¶32 (48:11). These hymn-like forms should here be considered as ornaments added secondarily to the narrative.

27. Those sentences describing YHWH's *regular or repeated* action form the transition from YHWH's qualities to his historical deeds. The verbs stand in *participles, imperfects, or perfects.* Examples include: "YHWH looks down from heaven, and looks on all the human children. From his dwelling he looks out upon all the inhabitants of the earth" (Ps 33:13f); "YHWH makes the rich and the poor; he also brings low and raises up. He raises the oppressed from the dust; he raises the poor from the mud so that they sit among princes, and assigns them an honored place" (1 Sam 2:6-8); "YHWH frees the captives, YHWH makes the blind to see; YHWH raises those who have been bowed down. YHWH protects the aliens; he helps the orphans and widows. YHWH loves the righteous, but leads the Godless into error" (Ps 146:7c, 8a, b, 9a, b, 8c, 9c). Other examples include: Pss 5:13; 9:9; 11:4-6; 12:8; 25:8f; 29:3, 5, 6, 8, 10; 33:5-7, 10; 34:19, 20, 21, 23; 35:10, 27; 36:7; 68:7, 20, 36; 84:12; 87:2; 89:10; 90:3, 5; 97:10; 103:6, 9, 10, 13, 14; 111:5; 115:3; 119:68; 135:6, 14; 138:6; 139:14; 145:14, 16, 19, 20; 146:10; 147:6, 11, 18; 148:14; Deut 32:4; 1 Sam 2:9,10; Isa 40:28f; 45:15; Jer 10:6; Nah 1:3, 4, 8, 9; Job 12:14ff; 34:20f, 24-26; 36:27-32; 37:3-7, 11, 13; Lam 5:19; Neh 9:6; Dan 2:21f; 6:27f; 2 Macc 1:25; Sir 10:14-18; 4 Ezra 8:20, 23; Apoc. Bar. 21:6ff; 48:2ff.

28. In addition, YHWH's *past deeds* appear in *perfect or narrative imperfect*, as is typical in poetry, although it was only recently recognized by the grammars (cf. B. Stade, *Reden und Abhandlungen*, 1907, p. 69; H. Bauer, *Die Tempora im Semitischen*, Beiträge zr Assyrologie 8, 1910; H. Bauer/P. Leander, *Historische Grammatik der hebräischen Sprache*, §36h; Gesenius[29]/G. Bergssträßer, part II, §7b and h). These deeds are also portrayed with the imperfect plus *vav* consecutive. Examples include: "for he spoke, then it happened; he commanded, and it stood there" (Ps 33:9); "You have founded the earth

and all that fills it. You created north and south" (89:12f); "*Yah* chose Jacob; he 'desired' Israel for his own" (135:4). In the oldest style, this was treated in short allusion, as in the song of Miriam (Exod 15:21): "Sing to YHWH, for he is exalted. He cast horse and rider into the sea." "You commanded your testimonies in righteousness" (Ps 119:138); "You commanded your testimonies" (119:4). However, later times preferred more detailed narratives. Cf. Ps 104:6-9: "Once, 'it held' the deep covered like a garment, the waters stood on the mountains. They fled before your rebuke. They were terrified at the sound of your thundering voice. 'Going up' to the mountains they sank to the valley at the place you established. You fixed a boundary which they could not overstep, so that they could never again cover the earth." Thus, the later "Song of Moses" (Exod 15:1-8), which uses the older song of Miriam as its beginning and expands the poem, adds detailed portrayals of the event of the Sea of Reeds and the subsequent wilderness wandering (15:8-10, 13-17). And in this way, several poems are transmitted to us in the psalter. In their basic form, they are nothing more than additional poetic narratives of holy history, to which a hymnic introduction has been placed at the front (Pss 105; 106). Ps 114 also belongs to this category. Its poet experiences the past as present and takes up the hymn form in the concluding verses (7f). Further examples of short allusions to events include: Pss 16:7; 22:25; 24:2; 28:6; 31:22; 52:11; 54:9; 59:17; 66:20; 86:13; 92:5; 95:5; 100:3; 102:26; 103:19; 111:4, 6, 9; 119:138; 147:13; 1 Sam 2:8c; Jer 20:13; 32:17; Hab 3:19; Job 9:13; Tob 8:6; 11:14; Pr Azar 5; Add Esth 3:3; Apoc. Bar. 21:4. For longer narratives: Pss 31:8f; 44:3f; 66:10-12; 71:19f; 74:13-17; 77:16-21; 80:9-12; 89:11-13; 99:6-8; 104; 135:9-12; 148:5f; Deut 33:27f; Judg 5:4f; Jer 32:20-22; Job 26:10-13; Neh 9:9-25; Jdt 16:3-13. These YHWH deeds refer to the great mythic events in the world (¶50), the salvation history of Israel and the singer's own experience (¶54), as will later be treated more precisely. a particular case is Ps 139:13ff, where the marvelous creation of the poet himself is described. Sometimes this kind of narrative is unfolded by the controlling participial and relative clauses (e.g., 104:5-9; 135:8f, 10-12). Here the transition from hymn into the narrative can be seen particularly clearly. In addition, as we will treat in ¶51, there are also sentences that concern YHWH's actions in the future (cf. Pss 9:6-11, 13, 16, 17; 46:5, 6, 10; 48:9; 68:2, 7, 10, 11, 18, 19, 22; 69:36f; 75:8f; 76:4, 9, 10; 86:9; 93:1, 4; 96:10, 13; 98:2f, 9; 99:4; 102:14, 16-18, 20-23; 147:2; 149:4; Deut 32:43; Isa 12:1, 5; 44:23; 49:13; 61:10; Jer 16:19; Joel 2:21, 23; Mic 7:19, 20; Zeph 3:15; Zech 2:14; Tob 13:5; Luke 1:51-54, 68b, 69).

29. Of course, the hymn does not always behave with complete regularity. Sometimes, identically formed sentences of the kinds described stand side by side, not infrequently in sublime monotony. Cf., for example, the "expanded introductions" (¶8) where participial clauses (¶21) or sentences where YHWH is the subject (¶27), or cases like Pss 29; 67; etc. Often, however, the different forms alternate. For example, the attributive style alternates with the independent sentences (cf. e.g., Pss 146; 147; etc. The same happens in Babylonian (cf. Fr. Stummer, *Sumerischen-akkadischen Parallelen*, pp. 62ff).

In between these forms, freer forms also appear in order to enliven the style. Several of these are mentioned here. Occasionally, for the sake of variation, the poet deviates from the pattern in which "YHWH" functions as the subject of sentences praising God, by opting for a passive construction instead. So, instead of the usual manner of speech, "YHWH's word created the heavens," he chooses instead the expression, "the heavens are created by YHWH's word" (Ps 33:6). Other examples include: Ps 76:6f; Exod 15:8. Or, YHWH's mercy is described indirectly. Cf. e.g., 1 Sam 2:4,5: "The hero's bow breaks, still the feeble gird themselves with power," etc. Here, the stricter form stands right alongside: "YHWH kills and makes alive," etc. (6-8). Both stand next to one another in v. 9: "He protects the feet of his faithful, but the Godless come into darkness." The first is the typical form of speech, while the second is the deviation. Cf. also Ps 113:9; Job 5:11ff; 12:25. Similarly, Ps 65:10-12 describes how YHWH is the one who blesses the land in the old manner, but then 13f cease using YHWH as the subject and present the results of this blessing. Another example of such indirect praise is Ps 36:8b,9. Further cases of the freer form are as follows: "The whole earth is full of his honor (Isa 6:3; cf. Pss 119:64); "The gate lights your words" (Ps 119:130); "The sum of your words is truth" (119:160). These freer forms are especially preferred in the more detailed narratives and portrayals, even in those that treat the future (cf. Pss 46:5a, 7a; 48:5-7; 68:2, 3, 9; 76:9; 77:17-21; 80:10-12; 104:6-8, 10b, 11, 12, 13b, 16-18, 20-23, 24c, 25, 26-28; 114; Deut 33:28; Judg 5:4f; Nah 1:4f; Job 9:13; Jdt 16:4f, 7ff; etc.).

Especially in later poems, a further exposition follows the main sentence with *lě* and an infinitive: "He made known the power of his deeds to his people, to bestow the inheritance of nations to them (Ps 111:6). Other examples include: 33:18f; 102:21ff; 104:14f; 113:7f; 149:7-9; Job 5:11; Pss. Sol. 2:34f, 36; 5:9; 7:10; Luke 1:54, 72, 74f (cf. *Festschrift für a. v. Harnack zum 70. Geburtstag*, pp. 50f).

Hymns also preferred to name the essence and qualities belonging to YHWH: "The kingdom is YHWH's (Ps 22:29); "The earth belongs to YHWH" (24:1). Other examples include: 36:10; 74:16; 89:12, 14; 95:4f; 100:3 (cf. the commentary); 115:16; 1 Sam 2:8c; Job 12:13, 16; 25:2; Dan 2:20; 1 Chr 29:11. The conclusion of the Lord's Prayer, "for yours is the kingdom and the power and glory" (Matt 6:13) takes this form. The same occurs in Babylonian (cf. Fr. Stummer, *Sumerischen-akkadischen Parallelen*, p. 52). The first part of the very late and subjective hymn, 139:1-12, is full of freer forms, while the second part speaks in familiar forms.

30. Frequently, all kinds of *portrayals of rejoicing, trust, or fear* stand in the main part of the hymn. They are comparable to those which occasionally appear in the introduction (cf. ¶13). Examples include: "Tabor and Hermon rejoice at your name" (Ps 89:13); Morning and evening (65:9); the cities of Zion and Judah (48:12; 97:8); Israel (89:17); the righteous (68:4); all people (76:11); "from the rising and setting" (75:7); everything is glad and rejoices. "Our soul boasts about you" (Pss. Sol. 17:1). "The occupants of the temple praise him" (Ps 84:5); "The heavenly host praises him" (Pr Man 15); "'In the' heavens, they praise his wonderful deeds" (Ps 89:6); "With my lips, I tell of the ordinances of your mouth" (119:13); "One pays the vow to you; to you all flesh 'brings' the matters of sin" (65:2f); "Our soul looks forward to YHWH" (33:20); "We hope on God, our savior" (Ps 17:3); "We trust in his holy name" (Ps 33:21). "All eyes wait on you" (145:15; 104:27). "The whole earth is afraid before YHWH" (33:8; 65:9; Sir 16:18f), trembles (68:9), and is terrified (Jer 10:10); "The host of heaven falls down before him" (Neh 9:6); "Even your enemies must extol you" (66:3). Also here comes the enumeration of the one praised (Pss 75:7; 89:6).

These descriptions of rejoicing and honor also appear in Babylonian relatively frequently (cf. H. Zimmern, *Babylonische Hymnen und Gebete*, p. 12: ["The Igigi bow down before his countenance, the Annunnaki kiss the ground]," 14, 15, vols. 2, 4, 5, 24, 26; a. Ungnad, *Die Religion der Babylonier und Assyrer*, pp. 173f, 192, 194, 218. The same is true for Egyptian in G. Roeder, *Urkunden zur Religion des alten Ägypten*, pp. 1, 2, 3, 5, 6, 7, 8, 10, etc.; and the same for the Rigveda (cf. Fr. Heiler, *Gebet²*, p. 172).

31. Further, the enthusiasm for the majesty of God flows in many *rhetorical questions*: "How majestic is your name!" (Ps 8:2, 10); "How precious is your grace!" (36:8); "How awesome are your deeds!" (66:3); "Who can stand before you!" (76:8); "Who is a God greater than our God!" (77:14); "YHWH, how great are your works, how powerfully deep are your thoughts! (92:6); "Who can speak YHWH's powerful deeds, or proclaim all his splendor!" (106:2). Other examples: Pss 18:32; 31:20; 35:10; 71:19; 84:2; 89:7, 9; 104:24; 113:5; 119:103; 139:7,17; 144:3; Exod 15:11; Isa 40:12-14, 18, 25; 43:13; Jer 10:7; 49:19; Mic 7:18; Nah 1:6; Job 9:4, 12; 11:8, 10; 25:3; 34:29; 36:22, 23; 38f; Dan 3:33; Sir 17:29; 18:4f; 43:31; Wis 11:21; 12:12; Pss. Sol. 17:2. Often, the hymnic participles described in ¶21 follow these questions (cf. Pss 18:32ff; 35:10ff; 89:7f; 113:6ff; Exod 15:11; Mic 7:18). These rhetorical questions also appear in the Babylonian hymn (cf. M. Jastrow, *Die Religion Babylon und Assur*, vol. 1, pp. 475, 479, 496f, 499, 509, 533, 539, 540, 543; J. Hehn. *Hymnen und Gebete an Marduk*, pp. 326, 333; H. Zimmern, *Babylonische Hymnen und Gebete*, vol. 1, pp. 10, 11, 12, 20, vol. 2, pp. 6, 7f, 9, 24, 26; a. Ungnad, *Die Religion der Babylonier und Assyrer*, p. 175; Fr. Stummer, *Sumerischen-akkadischen Parallelen*, pp. 57ff; and *JBL* 45 (1926): 181f; Fr. Heiler, *Gebet,²⁻⁵* pp. 170f.

Now and then, *negative sentences* appear instead of these participles: "No one is holy like YHWH, there is no rock like our God (1 Sam 2:2). These occasionally also contain attributes: "No one is 'like' Jeshrun's God, who comes from the heavens to help you, and for 'your' praise in the clouds" (Deut 33:26). Other examples include: Ps 86:8; 1 Kgs 8:23; Jer 10:6; Dan 4:32; Add Esth 3:4. For Babylonian examples, see M. Jastrow, *Die Religion Babylon und Assur*, vol. 1, p. 434; P. Jensen, *KB* 6/2, pp. 28f, 94f, 98f; Fr. Stummer, *Sumerischen-akkadischen Parallelen*, p. 38; cf. further, Fr. Heiler, *Gebet,²⁻⁵* p. 171. Pss 119:96 has a less rigid form: "I have seen an end 'to all;' your commandment reaches very wide."

32. An indirect way of praising God is the *blessing* introduced with *'ašrê* ("blessed is the one who . . . "). The hymn praises the pious one and the people who may call such a God their own. Examples include: "Blessed is the people whose God is YHWH, the nation whom he chose" (Ps 33:12); "Blessed is the one whom you choose and allow to live so that he lives in your courts" (65:5). Even here, divine attributes may follow: "Blessed is the one whose help is the God of Jacob, whose hope is on YHWH, his God, who made heaven and earth, the sea and everything in it, who keeps faithfulness forever, who creates justice for the oppressed and gives breath to the hungry" (146:5-7). Other examples include: Pss 40:5; 84:5, 6, 13; 89:16; 106:3; Deut 33:29; Isa 30:18d; also cf. Ps 144:15.

There are similar examples in Greek. Cf. Homer's Hymn to Gaia 7ff (Allen-Sikes, eds., *Homeric Hymns*, ¶30, 3:7ff, pp. 296f). This type of blessing speech contrasts with the woe speech which Judith (16:18) pronounces over YHWH's and Israel's enemies (cf. Jer 17:13).

33. Or, the hymn contrasts *other beings* with the God whose majesty he proclaims, and demonstrates with all power that no praise, no honor, no trust can be granted them alongside YHWH. "All the gods of the heathen are nothing, but YHWH created the heavens" (Ps 96:5). The heathens' gods are only silver and gold, the work of man's hands. They have a mouth, but cannot speak; they have eyes but cannot see; they have ears but cannot hear. There is also no 'breath in their nose.' Those who make them, whoever trusts them,

will be the same" (Ps 135:15-18). Other examples include: Jer 10:3-5, 8f, 14f; Dan 4:32; cf. also Pss 97:7; 115:4-7; Isa 40:19f; Jer 16:19f; 51:17f. And as with the gods, so also the kings and their hosts are no cause. The combination of the two entities is explained by the deification of the kings at that time. "Do not rely on princes, on a man in whom is no help. His breath departs. He returns to dust. In that day, his thoughts perish." Pss 146:3f. Cf. 33:16f; Isa 40:23f; Pss. Sol. 17:2. Other such contrasts, or similar ones, include: Pss 8:5; 40:5; 44:4; 92:7; 102:26f; 103:14-16; 144:3f; 147:10; Isa 38:18; Dan 4:32.

34. We have just now encountered a *warning speech*: "Do not rely on princes" (Ps 146:3). Even a serious and emphatic way of speaking like this occasionally appears in the hymn, again as an indirect form of the praise of YHWH: "Let no defiant speech, no presumptuous word, come out of your mouth" (1 Sam 2:5). Other examples include: Pss 75:5f; 76:12; Isa 26:4; cf. Pss 46:9,11; 66:5; Nah 1:9. On the whole, however, such warnings are foreign to the hymn and may have entered under the influence of prophecy or wisdom poetry (§10, ¶5).

35. *Wishes for* YHWH also occur only in isolated cases in the hymn: "Let YHWH's renown be eternal. Let YHWH be glad in his works" (Pss 104:31; see also 113:2; 57:6, 12; 108:6; 18:47; 40:17; 35:27). To express these wishes for YHWH is perhaps originally the meaning of the expression "to bless YHWH." However, the more developed religion allowed this type of speech to fall away in its vast respect before YHWH. These kinds of wishes are common in Babylonian (cf. M. Jastrow, *Die Religion Babylon und Assur*, vol. 1, pp. 429, 501, 503, 521, 543f). The same is true in Egyptian and even among the primitive peoples (cf. Fr. Heiler, *Gebet*,[2-5] p. 170).

36. Now, concerning the *internal arrangement of the hymns*. Genre-historical research may not allow the assignation of the sections of the poems according to the subjective taste of the individual researcher, as has occurred until now. Rather, genre-historical research has the task of seeking *certain, objectively occurring markers* which result from the disposition desired by the poet (cf. §1, ¶8, p. 18). One such marker, to which we previously alluded (¶¶2, 11), is the fact that the new sections are rather often designated repetition of the introductory formulas (Pss 66:5,8; 95:6; 96:7; 98:4; 100:4; 139:14; 145:4, 10; 147:7, 12; 148:7; 149:5; Jdt 16:14. In the Song of the Three Young Men 34 and 66 the paragraphs are also accented very clearly by new introductory formulas. So the hymn soars triumphantly in the heights, carried by two, or sometime three, wings. Elsewhere, in the middle, the Hebrew poets love to repeat the beginning (Pss 18:32; 116:10; §4, ¶14; §6, ¶28; §11). In other cases, a smaller pause is made in those places where the middle element begins after the introduction (Pss 29:3; 104:2b; 105:7; 113:4; 146:3). Sometimes, as we noted (¶18), the "for" stands at this point (cf. Pss 33:4; 96:4; 100:5). In the midst of the "main element" one should acknowledge paragraphs in those places where a new form begins, whether it be in the "blessing" (¶32; cf. Pss 65:5; 146:5), the participle (¶21; cf. 65:7; 135:7), the sentence where YHWH is the subject (¶25; cf. 103:6; 135:13; 146:7c), or another, particularly powerful sentence (¶17; cf. 104; 31). The form of the rhetorical question (¶31) sometimes begins the whole psalm (8:2; 84:2 [106:2]), the main element (92:6), or a new section (31:20; 139:7, 17; 144:3). This last example occurs especially when the rhetorical question introduces a participle that belongs to it (18:32ff; 35:10; 113:5-9; Exod 15:11; Mic 7:18). Here and there the entire poem is dominated by participles reappearing everywhere that a new section begins (Pss 104:2b, 5, 10, 13, 19; 136:4, 7, 10, 13, 16; cf ¶21). Elsewhere, the beginning of a new element is designated by the be-

ginning of a new motif. Thus, 65:10 starts with the portrayal of the fruitful rain. Ps 103:14 starts with observations about human failure and the eternal nature of divine grace. Here and there, the conclusions are expressly accented by refrains (67:4, 6; 99:5, 9). On the basis of this and other reliable observations, one may explore the question whether the poet thought about regular strophes, or whether these are not found, as is generally the case.

Even the *conclusion* of the whole frequently manifests the forms of the introduction, as we already noted in ¶¶2 and 11. Examples include: Pss 65:9; 67:4, 6, 8 (cf text notes); 68:33, 35; 75:10; 97:12; 103:20-22; 104:35; 114:7; 135:19; 136:26; 145:21; Tob 13:7; Sir 39:35. At times, the hymn concludes with an "expanded introduction" (¶8) in order to express the whole with flair (cf. Pss 68:35ff; 75:10; 103:20-22; 135:19-21. It is particularly beautiful when the introduction ends with the same introduction with which it began, thus rounding off the poem as a unit (cf. Ps 8:10). In Ps 148:14, the song at the end is designated as a *tehilla*. Or, the poem concludes with the thought that there really could be a lot more to say (Ps 139:18; Sir 43:27ff). Or, the final word forms a "contribution formula," with which the singer lays his creation before the throne of God, hoping the words of his mouth are pleasing to God (Ps 19:15), hoping his meditation will be sweet to God (104:34). Elsewhere the poet adds yet another wish or petition: "May you show mercy on us, YHWH, as we hope in you" (Ps 33:22); "Let the wicked disappear from the earth" (104:35; Jdt 5:31); "If only you, God, would kill the wicked" (Ps 139:19). Likewise, at the end of the "thanksgiving song of Israel" (¶41): "May those hating Zion be put to shame" (Ps 129:5ff); and the "thanksgiving song of the individual" (40:12; 138:7f; etc.; cf ¶¶7, 8). An accumulation of wishes appears in the conclusion to Ps 104 (cf. 104:31-35), while wishes and petitions conclude Ps 139 (cf. 19f, 23f). In 19:8ff, a personal application that contains a petition (14f) is added to the glorification of the law. Thus, the mixed poem of Ps 36, whose center and main component is a hymn (36:6-10), contains a petition for the preservation of divine grace immediately before the conclusion 36:(11f). Sometimes, these petitions may have been added later (Ps 29:11; 1 Sam 2:10b). The eschatological hymns (¶51) also know these kinds of petitions. They hope to fulfill the predictions (9:18-20; 69:29-32). In Babylonian and Egyptian, this combination of hymn and petition is very typical (E. Balla, *Ich der Psalmen*, p. 92; a. Ungnad, *Die Religion der Babylonier und Assyrer*, pp. 167, 168c, 171f, 175, 177, 198, 201f; G. Roeder, *Urkunden zur Religion des alten Ägypten*, 2, 11, 14, 25f, 27, 48f, 54, 55, 56, 58, 65, 70, etc.), although fairly rare in the hymns of Israel (¶46). The Babylonian and biblical poems come very close to one another when the petition concluding the Babylonian hymn is very short (cf. H. Zimmern, *Babylonisches Neujahrsfest*, pp. 4f, 6 [top]; cf. Also Fr. Heiler, *Gebet*,[2-5] p. 173). Where the hymn contains no concluding formula, it concludes at least with a powerful word (Pss 29:10; 47:10; 48:15; 89:19; 111:10c; 146:10; Exod 15:18; 1 Sam 2:10) that forcefully represents YHWH's greatness, and often closes with the expression "in eternity" (cf. the commentary to Ps 15:5 for this last point). Ps 89:19 and 1 Sam 2:10 conclude with a thought about the king. Pss 65 and 113 lack any conclusion.

The overall picture demonstrates a rich treasury of forms, but at the same time a great strictness of form. All of the deviations constantly revolve around just a few basic forms that remain constant throughout the literary history of Israel.

37. The Hebrew language developed particular names for only the most favored genres, since the people only become cognizant of these forms as particular entities. It is notable that the song of praise belongs to the expressly named genres. It appears extraordi-

narily frequently, and had a powerful significance in the worship service. More common are designations like *šîr* (Pss 40:4; 46:1; 149:1; 2 Sam 6:5 (1 Chr 13:8); Isa 26:1; 30:29; Sir 39:15; 47:9; 50:18); *šîrâ* Exod 15:1; Ps 18:1); *mizmōr* (Sir 47:9 [*tōdâ*, Ps 100:4]); *rinnâ* (2 Chr 20:22; cf. Sir 50:19). The most common and apparently the most characteristic expression is *tĕhillâ*, "to praise, a praise, a song of praise (cf. Pss 22:26; 33:1; 34:2; 35:28; 40:4; 65:2; 66:8; 71:8; 100:4; 106:12; 119:71; 145:1, 21; 147:1; 148:14; 149:1; 2 Chr 20:22; Sir 15:9f). The leading word belonging to that expression is *hillēl*, "sing a hymn" (cf. 1 Chr 16:4; 23:5, 30; 25:3; 2 Chr 5:13; Ezra 3:10; Sir 47:8,10; etc). In addition, other words include words like *hizkîr hōdâ* (1 Chr 16:4; 23:30; 25:3; Ezra 3:10; etc).

II. The Manner of Performance

38. We first gain a dynamic view of the hymn when we recognize the *manner of its performance*, and fortunately we are rather well informed concerning this performance. The most important thing we would like to say about the performance of hymns is that hymns originally belong to the *holy places*. Cf. the allusions in Pss 65:2; 76:2; 84:3, 5; 87:7; 95:2, 6; 100:2, 4; 134:1; 135:2; 138:2; Isa 38:20; 2 Macc 3:30. The particular place of the singing of the hymn is the sanctuary (Sir 47:8-10), YHWH's outer courts (Pss 84:3; 100:4; 135:2), or "before YHWH's face" (95:2; 100:2). One struck up these songs to come rejoicing to God (cf. Ps 95:2f). One did not just tend to this holy custom with the advent of the Zion temple. "Tabor and Hermon also shout his name" (Ps 89:13), and Ps 81:2-6b preserves a hymn stemming from the "house of Joseph" (i.e. Northern Israel). The same is true for Ps 89:2, 3, 4-19 and Ps 29. And everywhere one finds the singing of hymns together with *sacrifice and festivals*. Amos 5:21-23 speaks in the same breath of festivals, grain and whole offerings, noisy songs (*šîr*) and the plucking of harps. The old legend already describes one such celebration of Israel where a huge ecstatic rejoicing breaks out with the sacrifice and the holy meal. This blaring singing resounded loudly in the stillness of the mountains and echoed like a battle cry (Exod 32). The Canaanites already knew about such jubilatory singing. In Shechem, the wine harvest festival was called the feast of rejoicing (*hillūlîm*, Judg 9:27). At the time, this custom was practiced in the entire orient. Even the Babylonians (cf. Meißner, *Babylon und Assur*, vol. 1, p. 332; M. Jastrow, *Die Religion Babylon und Assur*, vol. 1, p. 551; H. Zimmern, *Babylonische Hymnen und Gebete*, pp. 9ff) and the Egyptians possess, as we have seen, an abundance of these festival hymns which agree in many ways with the formal language of Israel (cf. ¶¶11, 22, 24, 31). This custom also existed throughout the entire history of Israel. Even in the latest time period, and precisely in this time, the sanctuary of Jerusalem resounded with those singing on every festival day (Sir 47;10). Concerning the wild, passionate hymn singing among other nations, see Fr. Heiler, *Gebet*,[2-5] pp. 159, 165f.

39. Let us briefly visualize an *Israelite festival* in order to understand the festival hymn. On these days, the people come together from near and far to the holy places, but a festival day is a real day of joy. The harvest has been brought in. The country again has grain and wine. It is well known that the great recurring festivals of ancient Israel, were harvest festivals with the exception of the *passah*. How could the people not rejoice and thank its gracious God? So everyone is gathered at the sanctuary in their best clothes and in the happiest mood. They all show off their prettiest jewelry, and it is also the day in which the priests officiate in their festive garments. There, the drunken eyes in the crowd of those appearing see the greatness of Israel in the ancient time, insofar as the king's

sanctuary is concerned, and the splendor of the ruler's house. There, a rich, multifaceted worldly urge develops among the powerful mass of lighthearted people, by far the majority of whom are only seen on such days. The same thing happens in the Catholic church, where the "fair" becomes the market, as well as among the ancient Arabs (cf. J. Wellhausen, *Reste arabischen Heidentums*, 2nd ed., reprint, 1927, pp. 87n.3 and 88ff; and G. Jacob, *Altarabisches Beduinenleben*, 1897, pp. 147f). The main events, however, are the multifaceted holy actions in which the laity participates in their own way. They present gifts to God, which they have vowed to present during the preceding year. In all of this worship activity, as in the meaningful images which fill every great sanctuary, the heart very delightfully perceives the nearness of YHWH. Those attending the festival "see God" (cf. Ps 11:7). Then, it continues with the exorbitant eating and drinking. Indeed, in ancient times, the danger was all too real that the celebration would end in serious riots (cf. e.g., Exod 32:6; 1 Sam 1:13; Isa 28:7f).

When Israel was still young, these folk festivals certainly possessed important significance for the growth of the nation, just as the plays did for Hellenism. Later, when the Jews were so widely scattered, the fstivals became the particular center for the Jews, just as today the pilgrimage to Mecca unites the wide variety of the peoples of Islam. The individual Jew otherwise might live among a foreign people who did not understand him and who mocked his most sacred things. Yet, here that person perceives that he is not alone, but belongs to a large people of YHWH. Zion is the mother of all of them (Ps 87:5). And when he must again return into the foreign land, then he can think with longing about the beautiful festival: "I remember it once again" (Ps 42:5). If Judaism did not possess these festivals at the same place as a unifying bond, they would have perhaps been spiritually scattered as well.

40. From time immemorial, Israel was a people who was poetically gifted to a high measure and receptive to poetry. From that, one understands that among all these festivals the *hymn* held a prominent, even decisive, position

In the Old Testament, then, we also hear of a whole series of sacred celebrations that were undertaken at these festivals. The hymn was sung at these festivals.

The pious one enters the lavish gates after a happily *completed pilgrimage* (Ps 122). Already in the previous night, "since one would consecrate the festival days before" (Sir 47:10), the song of jubilation (Isa 30:29) resounds with an expression of the "preceding joy," with the image of the rejoicing heart that is generally comparable to our beautiful Christmas songs. In the early morning, "the sanctuary" then "rejoices" (Sir 47:10). The hymn already begins with the rising of the sun, in order to greet the light. On the following day, the *entry of the community* into the sanctuary occurs with loud hymn singing: over and over, when a multitude enters the outer courts through the holy gates (Ps 100:4), leading with their gifts (Ps 96:8), it falls down, bows, and kneels (Ps 95:6), and greets God with rejoicing (Ps 95:1f). Examples of songs which would have been sung with the entry into the sanctuary are Ps 95:1-7 and 100. The prophet, who knew this kind of singing, had previously composed the hymn (Isa 26:1-6; cf. Jer 51:10). The hymn belongs, above all, to the *sacrifice itself*, even though there are rather few allusions to the sacrifice in the psalter. However, from Amos 5:21-23 we may deduce such hymns of sacrifice existed. From the perspective of antiquity, it was indeed self-evident that the God could no more lack the song at the sacrifice than the king could lack the feast at the festival (cf. §5, ¶3). Allusions to this kind of hymn singing with the sacrifice do appear in 1 Chr 23:31; 2 Chr 23:18; 29:27f; 1 Macc 4:52ff; 2 Mac 1:30. Naturally, one would have also sung at the *sacrificial meal*. Amos 6:5 rages fiercely at this type of song from the luxuriant revelers, in which they perhaps compete with David. Even those songs would have been hymns. The situation in which psalms would have been performed at the festival meal is still mentioned in 3 Macc 6:35.

The highpoint of the festival is the common *procession through the sanctuary*. Ps 68:25f describes one such festival march: "the singers at the front, the musicians behind, 'in the midst of' the young women beating tambourines. The procession begins at the entrance where the participants wash themselves with water from the basins standing there (Ps 26:6), bind themselves together with ropes in order to follow the artistic figures of the lead dancers (118:27). Thus, they will march around the altar in the middle, by which they will stop at last, in order to attach the ropes to the horns themselves (118:27). Ps 42:5 speaks of such a processional as the highlight of the festival: "that I once led the way 'to the tent of God,' to YHWH's house, with the sound of joy and thanksgiving, 'the noise' of the pilgrims." Here and there we hear of the festival procession moving along in *dance step* (cf. Pss 42:5; 87:7; 149:3; 150:4), that is then elsewhere reported as a kind of holy dance (Exod 15:20; Judg 21:21; 2 Sam 6:5,14; Jdt 15:12f; 3 Macc 6:32, 35). The extent to which such a procession was valued as the most important celebration of the entire festival can be deduced from the fact that the name *ḥāg* ("dance, festival") derives from it. Illustrations of the worshiping dance can be found in H. Guthe, pp. 178, 542; Br. Meißner, *Babylon und Assur*, vol. 1, p. 261, illustration 72; H. Greßmann, *Altorientalische Texte und Bilder*, vol. 2, illustrations, 456, 457, 554.

The *end of the festival celebration* in a later time is vividly described in Sir 50: appearing from behind the curtain of the holy of holies on the great day of atonement, the high priest, in his magnificent festal vestments, surrounded by his sons, stands high above on the walk around the altar, casts the offering into the fire, and pours out the wine of the drink offering. Then, celebratory temple music rings out: the priests blow their horns, and all of the laity bow down before the most high. "Then the singers let their voices be heard and ring out the jubilation of their favorite music, and the whole laity rejoice in prayer before the merciful one" (18f). From this account one can tell that music and song tended to conclude the worship service of the great Day of Atonement. Only the priestly blessing came afterward. In this part, first the priests appear with the blowing of the horns, then the singers appeared with their musical accompaniment, until finally a general choir broke out. Both times, it concerns a hymn (root *šîr, rnn*). 2 Chr 29:26ff has a similar account.

Elsewhere, *special festivals* are occasionally mentioned at which the hymn would be sung. Hos 9:1 speaks of the jubilation of Israel and the rejoicing at the autumn festival. This jubilation would certainly have broken out in hymns. And the young girls who annually "dance" from the vineyard to the silo would naturally have also sung. There they held a YHWH festival to honor their God, that is, they would have sung YHWH hymns (Judg 21:19,21). Here we can thus deduce hymns at the autumn festival (cf. also Isa 62:9). In Ps 67, we possess a thanksgiving song after a bountiful harvest.

In later time, the *passover festival* must have had particular significance. It is no accident that the hymns are mentioned repeatedly in the exodus story. Accordingly, we may consider Ps 114; Exod 15; and perhaps Ps 81:2-6 as passover hymns. Echoes appear in Pss 66:6; 77:16ff; 78:43-53; 105:24-38; 106:8-12; 111:9; 135:8f; 136:10-16; Isa 43:16f (cf. ¶50).

On certain days (cf. commentary to Ps 132) one might also consider the sanctuary in particular, and thereby the "Zion songs" would have been performed in Jerusalem (¶¶17, 26, 52). According to a very acceptable supposition of S. Mowinckel, the *enthronement songs* belong to the New Year's festival (cf. §3, ¶¶8, 9).

41. In addition, *other specific occasions* come into play, especially national festivals that are embellished by the singing of hymns. Already according to the legend of the sea of reeds, *Miriam* celebrated a victory song with the women of Israel after the destruction of the Egyptians, and thereby voiced the famous hymn (Exod 15:20f). King *David* led the YHWH-ark with praise songs (*šîrîm*) while dancing to the sound of instruments on Zion (2 Sam 6:5).

We hear about such celebrations especially frequently even in later times. The *prophets* envision a *future* victory festival and deliverance festival when they compose the "eschatological hymns" (cf. ¶51). Ps 48:13ff presupposes a procession around the walls of Jerusalem to celebrate the future deliverance of the city. Ps 68:27f describes a worship celebration where the choirs are arranged according to tribal territories. Ps 149 presupposes a victory festival in which the returning warriors, with swords in their hand, will perform a weapon dance. The same type of festival is valid for Judith which is celebrated by the men of Israel in full armor (Jdt 15:13). The eschatological hymns were sung on certain days for those currently living. These hymns were performed so that the congregation which almost succumbs to the misery of this time, can experience the jubilation of the end time in advance. This is particularly apparent in Pss 48; 68; and 149, and also holds true for the eschatological enthronement psalms (cf. §3, ¶9), particularly Ps 47.

When *Nehemiah* had rebuilt the wall of Jerusalem, he instituted a great festival of consecration. The Jewish proceedings made its way around the city in two "thanksgiving choirs," in order to meet in the house of God. The joyous jubilation resounded widely over the countryside (Neh 12:28ff). Also, when Nehemiah proclaimed the forgiveness of debts, the people show their gratitude by singing a hymn (Neh 5:13). The Chronicler cannot think about any important or celebratory action without sacred music (Ezra 3:10f; Neh 12:27ff; 1 Chr 15:16ff; 29:20; 2 Chr 5:12f; 20:21, 26, 28; 23:13; 29:27). And also in the Maccabean period and later, there is singing with every turn of fate and significant deliverance. The hymn rings out: with the return after a victory (1 Macc 4:24; cf. 2 Chr 20:28); when entering a conquered city (1 Macc 13:47; 2 Macc 10:38) and the recaptured fortress of Jerusalem (1 Macc 13:51); with the reconsecration of the sanctuary (1 Macc 4:54ff; 2 Macc 10:7); with the deliverance of the temple from an attack (2 Mac 3:30f); with a joyful message (3 Ezra 4:62); with a just retaliation (2 Macc 12:41); or elsewhere when divine help comes (3 Macc 2:20; 5:35; 6:32; 7:13, 16, 19); and also with the reading of the law by Ezra (Neh 9:5).

So the celebration of Judith is described very similarly to the festival of Miriam, where the choir of Jewish women sang their hymn (Jdt 15:12ff; cf. 2 Chr 20:26). Also, one storms into the battle with the hymn as a battle cry (2 Chr 20:21). One also greets with a hymn a divine sign that promises victory (2 Macc 11:9).

The "thanksgiving songs of Israel" are related to the hymns. These thanksgiving songs were performed at the great public thanksgiving celebrations, when once again a difficult crisis was fortunately weathered with the help of God (cf. ¶50). One may deduce from the eschatological song of Isa 12, that the act completed in the worship service was the creation of the water (cf. Isa 12:3). We possess samples of these communal thanksgiving songs in Pss 124 and 129:1-4. Other songs of this type belong to the harvest thanksgiving festival, wherein one should count Ps 67 (cf. ¶40). These thanksgiving songs and hymns merge into one another in Pss 65:2-9; 66:8-12; 67; 75.

42. In the large sanctuaries, especially in the temple of Jerusalem, particularly in the later time, hymns were also sung outside of the festival days and nights (1 Chr 9:33). "They rejoice over your name all day long," says a song from the Northern Kingdom (Ps 89:17). "They praise you always" says Ps 84:5, which also stems from the royal period. The hymn refers to the daily sacrifice (Sir 47:8). Ps 96:2 sings, "Proclaim his salvation day by day" (cf. also 68:20). According to 1 Chr 23:30, singing would have occurred in the morning and in the evening with the whole offering (2 Chr 23:18; 29:27), on the sabbath, new moon, and at the festivals. We hear about hymns of "the servants of YHWH" who stand *at night* with raised hands in YHWH's temple (Ps 134:1). Perhaps Ps 8 also presumes a performance at night.

43. Here and there in the preceding we have already mentioned *bodily movements* which accompany the singing of hymns: with dancing and processionals, lifting of hands (cf. also Ps 63:5; Neh 8:6), numerous types of prostrations (cf. Pss 29:2; 95:6; 96:9; 99:5, 9; 138:2; Neh 8:6; 1 Chr 29:20; 2 Chr 29:28ff; 1 Macc 4:55). In addition, one finds the clapping of hands (Pss 47:2; 98:8), an expression of enthusiasm but also a means of accentuating the beat of the melody. One also finds the act of standing when one had previously laid down (cf. Neh 9:5). We can deduce from Pss 29:2 and 96:9 that the hymn singers wore beautiful clothes and expensive jewelry. We can also experience it from Ezra 3:10; 1 Chr 15:27; 2 Chr 5:12; 20:21.

Jdt 15:12f, 1 Macc 13:51, and 2 Macc 10:7 (cf. 3 Macc 7:16) narrate that the people's choir was decorated with greens and flowers at the processional dance. We hear of the weapon dance with swords swinging in Jdt 15:13, whereby Ps 149:6 becomes understandable (cf. ¶41).

The *musical instruments* played during the hymn are frequently listed (cf. ¶5; and 2 Sam 6:5; Neh 12:27; etc.). The instruments to which the individual sings his song are the zither, harp (Ps 57:9), and the "ten stringed" *harp* (Ps 92:4). For dancing, the kettle drum is used (Exod 15:20; 2 Sam 6:5; Pss 149:3; 150:4; Jer 31:4). Where the text speaks of kettle drums, one thinks of a circle dance (Pss 68:26; 81:3). Frequently, the instruments are mentioned at the same time (cf. 2 Sam 6:5; Neh 12:27; 1 Chr 15:16ff; 2 Chr 5:12f; 20:28; 29:26f; Pss 81:3f; 98:5f; 150:3-5). Together, these strike a forceful sound. Even the sound of the singers would be as loud as possible. The singing of the seraphim in Isaiah sounds so loud that the heavenly palace shakes from it (Isa 6:4). And the "hallelujah" (cf. ¶10) must be roared out like the surging of the sea (cf. Ps 98:7). The entire festive noise (*tĕrū'â*) was called *hāmôn* (noise, din) (Ps 42:5; cf. Amos 5:23), and was comparable to the monstrous din of a battle (Exod 32:17; Lam 2:7). It resounds far across the countryside (Ezra 3:13; Neh 12:43). So it corresponds to the Israelite religion (cf. ¶46).

44. Finally, concerning the *persons* who voice the hymn. From the forms of the introduction (cf. ¶¶6, 11), we saw that there were two *types of performance*. The hymn was either sung by a choir or by an individual. The choral hymn and the individual hymn can scarcely be distinguished by content. The individual hardly says more than that which the choir sings. The individual song is usually distinguished only by its form, which is particularly clear in the "introduction." *Choral hymns* can more or less clearly be seen in the following: Pss 33; 65:2-9; 66:1-12; 67; 68; 81:1-6; 95:1-7; 96; 98; 100; 105; 113; 117;

124; 135; 136; 147; 148; 149; 150; Exod 15:21; Jdt 16; Dan 1:29ff. One can seldom recognize in individual cases the degree to which the choral songs are employed by trained, sacred choirs or by groups of the people. Sometimes, even the individual singer would have sung such a communal song (cf. the song of Judith and Ps 135, where an "I" appears). In later times, the temple song would have been in the hand of a particular, large guild to which the Levites belonged (cf. Ezra 2:41; Neh 7:23; 12:27; 1 Chr 15:16-21, 25; 16:4ff). When the hymn was entrusted to these "singers," then the people at least participated at the end when they called out "amen" (Neh 8:6; 1 Chr 16:36) and voiced the "hallelujah" (Ezra 3:11; 1 Chr 16:36; cf. ¶10). Or, following the artful choral song there was perhaps a less embellished one from the laity (Sir 50:18f). Here and there we hear of several choirs. The voices of the people, priests, Levites, and proselytes alternate (Pss 135:19f; 118:2-4; cf. 150:3-5; 33:1-3). Ps 68:27f portrays choirs of the individual tribes of Israel. These choirs are called *maqhēlôt* or *miqrā'îm* (cf. also Ps 26:12). Pss 134:1f; Sir 45:26; and 50:22 are priestly hymns (cf. Also 1 Macc 1:30). If a more extensive poem should be sung by the people, then *every individual line* would be spoken in advance by the lead singer (cf. Exod 15:1; Jdt 16:1). Or, the crowd sings a half-line as the recurring refrain while the lead singer recites the particular poem (cf. Pss 136; 118:1-4; Sir 51 (vss 1-16). In the Song of the Three Men, this inspirational form is imitated. In Isaiah's vision, the seraphim sing the half line of the short hymn to one another in constant repetition (cf. Isa 6:3). Alternating choirs are presupposed in Pss 19:3; 65:14c.

Hymns of individual singers would be the following: Pss 65:10-14; 89:1-19; 103; 104; 111; 139; 146; Exod 15:1-18; 1 Sam 2:1-10; Dan 2:20-23; 4:31f,34; Sir 42:15ff; cf. Isa 63:7. The original hymn of the individual would certainly have been recited in a worship service. The singer appears "in the circle of the pious and of the community" (Ps 111:1, see Ps 149:1; Pss. Sol. 5:1, cf. also Ps 26:7). Later, the hymn was forced into smaller circles, where it was frequently voiced with the thanksgiving offering (cf. ¶54). The hymn finally becomes a purely private expression of personal piety and a pious artistic exercise. However, even in this case, one can seldom recognize the individual with certainty. Still, we can see clearly how the pious one will pour forth joy in a beautiful song of the springtime (Ps 65:10-14), or will pour out his thankfully trembling heart following recovery from a severe illness (Ps 103). We can see how, in very personal tone, he introduces his deep contemplations about the relationship between God and himself (Ps 139:1-18), or how, in the latest times, he sings about the law *in his own house* (119:54).

Thus, at the end of the entire development, hymns (both that were transmitted or submitted for the occasion) or hymnic speeches were sung or spoken in the following: in the early morning (Pss 57:9; 59:17; 92:3; 108:3); at night (92:3; 119:62; Job 35:10; Pss. Sol. 3:1f; 6:4); or even seven times during the day (Ps 119:164); after mealtime (Deut 8:10; Sir 35:13); after great deliverance or a happy change of fortune (cf. the situation of Hanna, as well as Ezra 7:27f; Dan 2:20-23; 3:28; 4:31f, 34; 6:27f; Tob 3:11; 8:15ff; 10:13; 11:13, 16; 12:6, 17, 20, 22; 3 Ezra 4:59f); Susanna (the addition to Daniel) 63; Jub. 25:12. From the outset, the alphabetic hymns were intended only for a written record (9; 111; 145). Even from this picture, one can see that the singing of hymns finally became an exercise of the Jewish *household*. The general belief of Mowinckel that psalmody did not contain the "outpouring of the heart of private persons" (cf. §1 ¶8, p. 20), is not confirmed in this instance. Psalms like Ps 103, with its pathos stirring the depths of the soul, and Ps 139, with its devout and astounded immersion in the secret of God, can surely only be conceived as the outpouring of an individual praying alone. And it is not very easy to perceive how one could doubt that even for a moment.

There are also hymns that would have been performed by the choir and the individual at the same time, or at least that carry the form of such alternating singing. The middle section of Ps 8:4-9 manifests the voice of an individual, while the beginning and the restated conclusion appears to be the refrain of a choir. Still, it is also possible that this poem is not determined by a particular performance, but only imitates those forms. We may also accept this alternation of voices in Pss 65 and 66. Ps 145 and Tob 13 contain both types of speech. Ps 9 mixes them together inorganically. Cf. also ¶12.

45. On the whole, we achieve a very dynamic picture of the performance of hymns. Still, one should notice that the transmitted hymns seldom speak about the manifold celebrations to which they belong. However, similar statements were spoken repeatedly on very diverse occasions. As a result, it is not advisable to speak of individual worship occasions in which one would have sung the hymn, with the exception of very specific cases that are particularly clear (in contrast to W. Staerk,[2] p. 8, and R. Kittel,[3,4] p. xxxv).

III. The Religion of the Hymns

46. Everything we have said in the preceding sections about the festivals and the performance of the hymns should be summarized in order to understand the *religion of the hymns* therein, because *Israel primarily expressed the spiritual content of its festivals* using this *form of the hymn.*

The hymn was the highpoint of the most beautiful and most profound days of Israel during which Israel made known the majesty, greatness, and grace of its God with full delight and in deepest humility. As a result, the fundamental moods of this poetry are *enthusiasm, adoration, reverence, praise, and exaltation.* The entire forceful echo of all these moods confronts us powerfully in the "introductions" (¶¶2ff). Of course, these are the dominant moods of the Israelite religion generally, but they appear in this position with immeasurable potency. The Babylonian and Egyptian songs certainly sing with exalted words about the greatness of the gods ruling the world. It is not only the common words (cf. ¶¶11, 15, 16, 19, 22, 24, 29, 30, 31, 35, 36), but also the content of these songs (cf. the commentary to Pss 29:1; 65:2ff; E. Balla, pp. 92f; and the following paragraphs) that make it apparent that Israel occasionally learned from them. Thus, it is no accident that the beautiful hymn to the sun of the reformer king Amenophis IV clearly agrees with the well-known Ps 104 (cf. further, ¶¶47-50). However, it remains characteristic of Israelite religion and a sign of its particular majesty that the fundamental moods are so dominant here: my first feeling is praise and thanksgiving!

In Babylonian and Egyptian poetry the petition was very frequently attached to the song of praise, making the petition appear to be that which the one praying really had in mind (cf. §4, ¶12; and H. Zimmern, *Babylonische Hymnen und Gebete*, vol 1. pp. 10, 14, 15, 16, 18f; vol. 2, pp. 5, 8, 9, 18, 20; P. Jensen, *KB*, vol. 6/2, pp. 50ff, 90ff, 108ff, 140ff). The Israelite psalms also know the moaning and the demands of human necessity all too well (cf. §4, ¶6). The connection between praise and petition appears in the prose prayers and laments frequently enough (cf. ¶55; §4, ¶¶12, 13; §6, ¶¶10, 28). Even in Israel by reading between the lines in one instance, we can perhaps hear the childlike belief that God might gladly hear (Ps 104:34) just as the king rejoices at the celebratory meal when the songs ring out to honor him. It is all the more significant that the *hymns of the psalter very seldom have a petition attached* (cf. ¶36). Whoever appears before YHWH in order to praise him should think of YHWH and YHWH's majesty, not of himself and his own wishes! Thus, in contrast to the foreign religions, one finds a *disinterested piety* here. Israel's hymns meet the deepest and most honorable need of all true religion, to worship in the dust that which is beyond us.

As a result, the Hebrew hymn has tremendous *objectivity* in regard to that which is human. For example, when it describes how God directs his power over humans, and how God is inclined to make the rich poor and the poor rich (cf. ¶49), then the heart is not filled with mourning over the transitory nature of everything earthly. Rather it is filled with rejoicing about the greatness of God. The hymnic poet does not look at things from the standpoint of human beings, for whom the waves toss and turn. Rather, the poet speaks of the things of God, which can support and exalt according to God's pleasure.

For this reason, the hymn does not avoid portraying the *imposing side of YHWH*. Rather, it sometimes even accents this aspect forcefully. One thinks especially of the powerful thunder psalm of Ps 29, which depicts how everything trembles, reels, and shatters in wild shrieks before the terrifying voice of YHWH! Even this is material for praising and honoring, for it glorifies the God who is so imposing! The Babylonians had already felt similarly in their hymns where they sang now and then of the horrible characteristics of the gods, apparently with trembling respect: "The lord, who is incomparable in his rage, the lord, whose attack overthrows the strong, who is the one who does not speak of his terror." (P. Jensen, *KB*, vol. 6/2, pp. 73ff, 99, 115, etc.). The mood in Ps 90:3, 4c, 5, 6 is different. It describes the short life span inflicted by God over humanity with sublime mourning.

Naturally, the singing of praises to God also has great value for the singers. Religious thought becomes stronger if it is powerfully expressed. The individual is then carried away by the general enthusiasm. Therefore, these hymns, in which the entire people participate loudly, can be great experiences for the individual (cf. ¶39). However, one seldom considers the subjective side of the matter, if at all. One sings the hymn *for God only*.

Such a hymn of Israel produced the most beautiful blooms. The Babylonian and Egyptian praise songs for the most part contain lifeless divine predicates strung together one after the other (cf. ¶22): "Endless and confusing, the more so, since the poet did not even take the time to arrange them in a clear order." (A. Erman, *Literatur der Ägypter*, pp. 13f). The same holds true for ancient Indian poetry (cf. Fr. Heiler, *Gebet*,[2-5] p. 167). Even the biblical hymns, considered both artistically and religiously, are not equally valuable throughout. The psalter contains its share of dull praise songs (cf. ¶66). However, alongside these, there are more than a few that tower above the majority of the ancient oriental poetry, in that they are distinguished by their inner, personal life and especially by their majestic power (cf. examples in ¶47). These witnesses show us that Israel produced the loftiest examples. Specifically, it raised the personal quality of the traditional genre, and infused it with Israel's own life.

These hymns reveal to us, in marvelous impressiveness, how powerful the people's *enthusiasm* for YHWH had been. No word about its God is too great for Israel when it is celebrating. Not just the celebrating community (as it is often called) should praise him. Rather, all peoples, all beings, all areas of nature must participate if his praise is to sound worthy (cf. ¶7). A chorale had to resound, and fill the heavens and earth! Thus, the celebrants sing and play loudly (cf. ¶43). Such praise is the highest obligation of the pious ones (Ps 81:5), and a most beautiful privilege. The heavens are YHWH's heavens—God reserved them for himself—but he loaned the earth to the children of humanity. The dead do not praise YHWH—his praise does not ring out in the silence of the underworld. However, we who live on earth who are able to sing want to praise him in all eternity (Ps 115:16-18)! The *praise of YHWH* is thus an *essential piece of religion*. Enthusiasm for God is a foundation of piety.

This mood, particularly the enthusiasm toward God, is foreign to the perception of later times, including ours. One understands this withdrawal of Israel from its God, if one remembers that the Israelite religion was not completely monotheistic from the beginning, but elevated itself to monotheism slowly. All the huge predicates of divinity, which appear as self-evident to us with their highest "absolute" completion, were then something relatively new in Israel. And as they were first composed with enthusiasm, so they continually inspire the heart of the pious to enthusiasm: "YHWH created the heavens and the earth." "YHWH looks down from heaven on the inhabitants of the earth" (Ps 33:13f). At that time, such ideas were not overly commonly presumed with the concept of God itself. Rather, it was the unparalleled majesty of the God of Israel that attributed the rule of the world to him.

47. The preceding discussion demonstrates that the object of religion appears in the hymn, YHWH's own characteristics and deeds. At the same time, in order to understand the specifics, one must bear in mind that the *basic mood is awe and enthusiasm*. Thus one can also say of the hymn: "Take off your shoes! The land you enter is a holy land!"

Now we provide an overview of that which we hear in the hymn concerning YHWH.

The hymn sketches a powerful image of a God who is eternal (Pss 9:8; 10:16; 29:10; 66:7; 90:1, 2, 4; 92:9; 93:2; 102:13, 26-28; 103:17; 104:31; 135:13; 145:13; 146:10; Isa 40:28; Hab 1:12; Lam 5:19; Dan 3:33; 4:31; 6:27; etc.), holy and awesome (Pss 89:19; 96:4; 99:5, 9; 105:3; 111:9; 1 Sam 2:2; Isa 6:3; 12:6; 57:15), highly exalted over all the world (Pss 46:11; 97:9; 99:2; 113:4; Isa 40:15; 57:15), majestic and magnificent (Pss 8:2; 56:6, 12; 66:2; 96:6; 104:31; 108:6; 111:3; 113:4; 145:5; 148:13). This God is powerful beyond measure (Pss 115:3; 135:6; 1 Sam 2:4; Dan 4:31f), great in works and deeds (Pss 77:13; 92:6; 104:24; 111:2; 135:5; 145:3; 150:2), unending in his knowledge (Pss 40:6; 104:24; 139:17; 1 Sam 2:3; Job 9:4), and incomparably wonderful (Pss 77:12; 139:14; Isa 25:1; Job 5:9; 9:16; Dan 3:33; 6:28). In addition, God is just, good, and compassionate (cf. ¶49).

We mention here several of the most exalted sentences as examples: "YHWH, "you remain God forever; and you have been from before; before the mountains were born, before the earth and the world were brought forth. For a thousand years are like yesterday when 'they are past'" (Ps 90:2c, 1b, 2ab, 4ab). "You founded the earth before time, the heavens are the work of your hands. These will pass away, but you remain. They all fall away like a garment. You change them like a robe, but you remain the same, and your years have no end" (Ps 102:26-28). "O YHWH, how many are your works. The earth is full of your creatures" (Ps 104:2ac). "He spoke, and it happened. He commanded and it stood there" (33:9). "They all wait on you, so that you offer food at the right time. You give it to them, they harvest it. You open your hand, and they are satisfied with goodness. You hide your face, they cower. You take their breath, and they expire and turn back to their dust" (Ps 104:27-29). "His favor is over his pious ones as high as the heavens are above the earth. Let our sins be as far from us as the sunrise is from the sunset. YHWH has compassion on his pious ones as a father has compassion on his children" (Ps 103:11-13). "YHWH, your grace is 'like' the heavens, your truth reaches to the clouds. Your righteousness is like the mountain of God; your ruling 'like' the great flood. You help humans and animals. Your grace is so precious" (Ps 36:6-8). "Lebanon does not suffice to burn, nor its beasts do not suffice for a sacrifice" (Isa 40:16). "Lord, you are the one enthroned forever, whose magnificence is exalted, whose chamber is in the air, whose throne is undescribable, whose majesty is incomprehensible, before whom the host of angels stand with trembling, whose choir turns into fire and storm, whose word remains firm, whose orders are valid, whose commands are powerful, whose calling is feared, whose sight withers the earth, whose threatening look melts the mountains, whose truth remains . . . " (4 Ezra 8:20-23).

But where does one begin, and where does one stop? "There is still so much and we are not yet at the end" (Sir 43:27). All in all he is a divine image of particular majesty! And the hymnic poets are entirely correct when they praise God as *incomparable*. Among the gods, there are none who are similar in holiness, power, wisdom, and grace: "Who is like you among the gods, YHWH? Cf. Exod 15:11; 1 Sam 2:2; Pss 18:32; 35:10; 71:19; 77:14; 86:8; 89:7, 9; 113:5; Jer 10:6f; cf. ¶31. He is "the king (God) of the gods" (Ps 95:3; Deut 10:17; 136:2). The impression of the incomparability of the God does appear in Babylonian materials (e.g., among others, in the hymn to Sin in Jastrow, *Die Religion Babylon und Assur*, vol. 1, p. 438, which says ""among the gods you have no brothers, none is like you." See further, pp. 446, 475, 496, 501. See also H. Zimmern, *Babylonische Hymnen und Gebete*, vol. 1, pp. 12, 24; vol. 2, pp. 5, 24; A. Ungnad, *Religion der Babylonier und Assyrer*, pp. 197, 204; Fr. Stummer, *Sumerischen-akkadischen Parallelen*, pp. 58f; Fr. Heiler, *Gebet*,[2-5] p. 171. However, for modern readers it is entirely clear how much more proper this judgment is for YHWH than for the Babylonian divinity.

There is another expression of the same thought which emphasizes that YHWH creates his great works *alone*, and is *alone* God (cf. Pss 72:18; 83:19; 86:10; 136:4; Deut 32:12; 1 Kgs 8:39; 2 Kgs 19:15,19; Isa 2:11; 37:16, 20; 44:24; Neh 9:6; 2 Macc 1:24f; 7:37; Sir 18:1). The same idiom is relatively common in Babylonian (Fr. Stummer, *JBL* 45 [1926]: 183f.).

The counterpart of this enthusiasm for YHWH is that the Israelite religion looks with contempt upon everything earthly and human, which would stand beside YHWH or oppose him. Israelite religion also heaps disdain upon the other gods, YHWH's rivals (cf. ¶33). The mocking of heathen gods is a component of the hymn, which is also a particularly Israelite characteristic.

48. *Recurring themes* of hymns are as follows: first, YHWH's *exalted dwelling and his rule in heaven*. In the fact that he dwells at the highest point of the world, one makes clear that he himself is "the highest:" YHWH established his throne in the heavens, and his majesty reigns over everything" (Ps 103:19). At the same time, it provides an impressive image of his omniscience. He looks down on the earth from his heavenly throne, from which the whole world lies at his feet. He sees everything that happens below with his peering eyes. (Cf. Pss 11:4; 14:2; 33:13f; 53:3; 66:7; 113:5f; 138:6; cf. further Pss 29:10; 68:34, 35b; 80:15; 92:9; 93:4; 102:20; 115:3, 16; Amos 9:6; Isa 40:22; 57:15; Pr Azar 31f; 4 Ezra 8:20.) This image of the gods dwelling in heaven is also well known in Babylonian hymns (M. Jastrow, *Religion Babyloniens und Assyriens*, vol. 1, p. 218; vol. 2, 801; *Babylonische Hymnen und Gebete*, vol. 2, p. 5) and Egyptian hymns (A. Erman,

Ägyptische Religion,[2] p. 79; G. Roeder, *Urkunden der Religion des alten Ägypten,* pp. 5, 6, 8, 9, 10, 14, 47, 54, etc.).

Characteristically Hebrew is YHWH's *appearance in storm and weather, in fire and earthquake, with thunder and lightning.* It is ancient Israelite poetic material that already appears in the Song of Deborah (Judg 5:4f), and which originated from revelation on the volcano at Sinai (cf. the commentary to Ps 18:8-15). It is found in hymns in the description of the coming of YHWH in the final time (Ps 97:2-5). Ps 29 is an ancient song about the thunder as the voice of YHWH. Later echoes include Job 37:2-5; Pss 68:34; 135:7; Jer 10:13; Nah 1:3-6. Thoughts about YHWH's anger play a significant role in these psalms as well. The hymn praises the God who can be so terrifyingly angry (cf. Nah 1:2, 6; Jer 10:10; etc.).

Elsewhere, it is not uncommon to find *mythological observations about nature.* Light is YHWH's coat; the clouds his chariot; wind and flames his messengers (Ps 104:2-4). He marches over the high places of the earth (Amos 4:13). If the earth quakes, it is because YHWH looked at it. If the mountains smoke, it is because YHWH touched them (Ps 104:32). Cf. also Jer 10:10; Amos 9:5; Nah 1:5. When the change of seasons causes life and death to enter the world, the reason is that YHWH has inhaled and exhaled his life-protecting breath (Ps 104:29f). The Hebrew poet signifies the "harmony of the spheres" as the song that the heavens sing to honor YHWH. He also portrays the sun as a clever runner who keeps his tent in the sea (Ps 19:1-7, cf. the commentary).

Still, this type of immediate connection between the divinity and world events are more or less poetic allusions. It is more common that the realities of nature are YHWH's creation that come to being at his calling, not living expressions of the divinity: "He commanded and it stood fast" (Ps 33:9). In so doing, his glance does not so much linger on the every event of nature, but on the conspicuous, those events that were unexplainable in antiquity. These were viewed with awe as particular acts of the divinity. Also, it generally makes no difference in antiquity's observation of the world whether the events belong to our concept of "preservation" or to the actual "creation." Every new event appears as a new creation. YHWH changes darkness into morning, and darkens the day to night (Amos 5:8). He arranges the stars at daybreak (Job 9:7, 9), and he calls the stars by name (Isa 40:26; Ps 147:4). Snow and ice, and especially the rain, come from him (Pss 147:8, 16f; 65:10-12; Job 5:10). He causes the earth to quake (Ps 104:32; Job 9:6; Nah 1:5; Sir 16:18f. He pours the water down on the earth (Amos 5:8; 9:6) and stills the roaring of the rushing flood (Pss 65:8; 89:10). In summary, he does great things that are not required and miracles that cannot be counted (Job 9:10). Compare Egyptian hymns in this regard in G. Roeder, *Urkunden der Religion des alten Ägypten,* pp. 7, 8, 22, 62ff; A. Erman, *Ägyptische Religion,* pp. 74, 79; and many Babylonian hymns A. Ungnad, *Religion der Babylonier und Assyrer,* pp. 173, 190. The apex of this connection is the "supernatural" observation of nature in a particular sense that is found in the majestic hymns of the book of Job (26:5ff; 36:27ff; 37:2ff; 38f) as well as in the famous creation hymn of Ps 104. In the latter poem, the religion of Israel also manifests a powerful *optimism* whereby the world is good and God is its gracious and wise creator. This optimism does not erroneously believe that creation contains no wicked entities striving against the almighty (Pss 104:35; 139:19ff; cf. also Sir 39:16ff; 42:15ff).

Not until the latest time does the hymn look more deeply to see a divine miracle in the *everyday* event of the development of a child in the mother's womb (Ps 139:13ff). It is also not until this time that the hymn *speaks of law* (for examples, see ¶¶13, 26, 28, 29).

49. At the same time, the hymn treats the subject of YHWH's *dominion over humanity.* (Cf. the Egyptian statements on this subject in G. Roeder, *Urkunden zur Religion des alten Ägypten,* pp. 48, 50; and the Babylonian material in M. Jastrow, *Die Religion Babylon und Assur,* vol. 1, pp. 429, 432, 535, 536; in A. Ungnad, *Religion der Babylonier und Assyrer,* pp. 176f, 187ff, 196 = H. Zimmern, *Babylonische Hymnen und Gebete,* vol. 2, pp. 24ff, and *Babylonische Neujahrsfest,* p. 6.) Here, with utter respect and marvel, pious observation also ascribes to God everything great and significant that happens in the world: divine omnipotence is seen in everything so that it can overthrow or exalt according to its pleasure. The hymn loves to describe both sides of the divine act in sharp contrast: "YHWH kills and brings to life, he takes down to Sheol and leads up; YHWH makes the poor and the rich; he humbles and exalts (1 Sam 2:6f; cf. also 4f; Pss 75:8; 107:33ff; 113:7f; 146:9; 147:6; Job 5:11ff; 12:17ff; 36:5ff; Dan 2:21; Sir 10:14ff; 39:22f [11:4-6, 11-13]). These portrayals of God's dominion are constantly held in rather general terms (Pss 107:33ff; 113:7ff). In so doing, a fundamentally despotic concept of God is presupposed. This concept grew out of the governmental relationships under which the poets lived, and which they considered natural. But even this image of an unlimited and high power, who operated and ruled with both grace and favor, filled the pious ones of that time with awe and deepest respect (¶46).

Sometimes moral thoughts of righteous retribution also appear (cf. Pss 11:5ff; 33:5; 66:7; 89:15; 92:10ff; 97:2,10; 98:9; 99:4; 103:6; 111:3; 145:20; 146:9; 147:6). This retribution is of course not considered as just a peaceful, regularly considered act. Rather, it is considered as an affectual action of the wrathful, or loving and graceful, God. The idea of a "double retribution" within the psalter generally belongs more to reflection, thus the wisdom poetry (cf. §10, ¶¶1, 2). The inexhaustible *love and faithfulness* of God toward his people Israel and toward the pious is even more dominant in the hymn (Pss 33:18f; 34:16, 20, 22; 68:36; 97:10; 100:3; 103:8-13; 117:2; 135:3f; 147:13f; 148:14; Jer 14:8; Mic 7:18; Nah 1:3, 7f). He blesses them with everything good and delivers them from all danger. His compassion is near to all *the suffering and the weak* (Pss 34:19; 68:6f; 103:6; 107:41; 113:7ff; 145:14, 19; 146:7-9; 147:3, 6; 1 Sam 2:8; Job 5:11) in their distress, but also to *the sinners* who will turn to him (Pss 65:4; 103:9; Sir 17:29). His compassion is even near to all creation (Pss 33:5; 36:6-10; 136:25; 145:8f, 15f; 147:9; Job 38:39ff) which is completely directed toward him and his grace (Pss 65:3f; 104:27f). Thus, in nature, YHWH's *moral majesty* appears along with the exalted character of YHWH. Babylonian counterparts appear relatively seldom (see M. Jastrow, *Die Religion Babylon und Assur,* vol. 1, pp. 429, 435, 448, 449, 501, 533). The same is true in other religions (Fr. Heiler, *Gebet,*[2-5] p. 170). Just as it honors the king when he kindly sits down with the poor and indigent, so YHWH is given highest praise because he does not overlook the need of his creation. Also, by praising divine compassion, the poets have found words of enduring depth and beauty (cf. Pss 30:6; 34:19; 36:6-10; 103:8-13; 104:27f; 108:5). Here we may recognize the prophetic influence (cf. especially Ps 103).

50. The hymn also glorifies the *past deeds of YHWH.* Babylonian (cf. Jastrow, *Die Religion Babylon und Assur,* vol. 1, pp. 464f, 477f, 479; Ungnad, *Religion der Babylonier und Assyrer,* 172ff = P. Jensen, *KB,* vol. 6/2, pp. 108ff, 114f) and Egyptian (A. Erman, *Literatur der Ägypter,* pp. 61, 73f; Roeder, *Urkunden der Religion des alten Ägypten,* pp.

xf, xxi, 2, 3, 8, 23ff, 47) poetry of this type often alludes to *mythic elements*. The same is true for Mexican and Vedic poetry (Fr. Heiler, *Gebet*,[2-5] pp. 169f).The religion of Israel tended toward monotheism from the oldest period forward, and increasingly expressed this tendency more clearly. We now know that the religion of Israel vehemently resisted mythology in general. However, this hostile attitude was not as sharply formed in the ancient time, so that the poets in particular insisted upon using this marvelous material with its powerful outline and flaming disposition. As a result, one can understand how even the Israelite hymn can contain occasional mythic allusions. We already noted traces of the mythological observation of nature (cf. ¶48). Here, however, more or less explicit allusions to *mythical narratives* appear. The myth of the *overthrow of the chaos dragon* is mentioned frequently. This dragon once contested YHWH for power over the earth until God defeated him and established the present world order. This battle with the chaos dragon is comparable to the battle in which Marduk defeated Tiamat. For a long time it must have been seen as YHWH's greatest act. It is no wonder that it repeatedly appears in the hymns (cf. Pss 74:12-17; 89:11-13; Job 26:12f; Sir 43:23; cf. Ps 104:25). In later times the mythic material becomes ever more pale. The primal roaring waters that are afraid of God appear in place of the arrogant, disgracefully wounded monster (Pss 104:5-9; cf. 65:7f; Pr Man 3; and Pss 46:4; 93:3f). One hymnic passage (Ps 90:1f; cf. also Job 38:8ff) recalls another creation narrative where the earth writhed and bore the mountains while the deity watched.

All of these places speak of the creation. That is no accident since thoughts about the act of creation, which represent the *omnipotence of God*, is one of the main topics of hymns, even among other nations. Examples occur in hymns to Marduk (J. Hehn, *Beiträge zur Assyriologie* 5, pp. 280ff), to Ašur (M. Jastrow, *Die Religion Babylon und Assur*, vol. 1, p. 520), and to Nebo (M. Jastrow, *Die Religion Babylon und Assur*, vol. 1, pp. 511f), etc. In addition, examples may be found in Egyptian hymns (cf. A. Erman, *Ägyptische Religion*,[2] pp. 74, 79ff; G. Roeder, *Urkunden der Religion des alten Ägypten*, pp. 5, 6, 7, 8, 10, 54, etc.). The same is true for Indian hymns (Fr. Heiler, *gebet*,[2-5] p. 171).

Creation ideas also appear in Israelite hymns frequently: Pss 8:4-9; 19:1-7; 24:2; 33:6f,9; 65:7; 74:13-17; 89:11-13; 90:2; 95:4f; 96:5; 102:26; 104; 136:5-9; 146:6; 148:5f; 1 Sam 2:8; Isa 37:16; 40:22,28; 42:5; 44:24; 45:18; Jer 10:12; 31:35; 32:17; 33:2; Amos 4:13; 5:8; 9:6; Zech 12:1; Job 9:8f; 26:7-13; 37:2ff; 38:4ff; Neh 9:6; Add Esth 3:3f; Sir 42:15ff; Pss. Sol. 18:10ff; Odes Sol. 16:11ff; cf. also Ps 139:13ff. These thoughts are favored on the one hand because they present a fruitful religious idea; namely, that the creator is the rightful owner and lord of his creation (Pss 24:1f; 74:16f; 89:12f; 95:5; 1 Sam 2:8; Isa 37:16). On the other hand, these thoughts simultaneously provide the poet with the opportunity of portraying the manifold fullness of that which God created using colorful images (cf. above all Pss 19:1-7; 104; Job 37:2ff; 38f Sir 42:15ff). As a result, the poets connect the aesthetic enthusiasm for the beauty and unity of the world with the religious feelings of reverence and worship. These *portrayals of nature* are characterized by their sense of reality, their delightful richness of color, but at the same time their majestic simplicity.

It is well known that the Egyptians already possessed similar material in the song to the sun of Amenophis (cf. ¶46). Cf. Fr. Heiler, *Gebet*,[2-5] pp. 185ff, 392, for general information about nature hymns. See the commentary to Ps 104:10f, 14, 27 concerning Babylonian portrayals of nature. One can see, when viewed as a whole, that these presentations of natural events were undertaken as a substitution of the older myths. When these myths lost their power over the hearts of people the hymnic poets turned to the presentation of the beings of nature. It is a sign of later, thoroughgoing subjectification of the hymn when even the creation thoughts are related to the individual. In Ps 139:13-15, the poet praises God who marvelously made him, even with the aside that the psalmist is completely in God's power.

The sacred legend is another substitution for the myth. We have a series of hymns which praise the God who led his people in the past. The material they used was taken mostly from the existing narrative books. They did not, however, draw from the material strictly from the more realistic reports of the historical narrative, but from the more poetic, fabulous, and legendary components (cf. Exod 15; Pss 105; 114). Additionally, we find numerous allusions to those types of narratives (cf. Pss 8:3; 22:5f; 44:2-4; 66:6; 77:16-21; 80:9-12; 99:6-8; 103:7f; 111:4, 6, 9; 119:138; 135:8-12; 136:10ff; 147:19; Deut 33:27f; Isa 41:9; 43:16f; Jer 32:20ff; Neh 9:7ff). We thus see how the particularly great idea preserved by the prophets renewed and exalted later ones. Namely, the history of Israel is a cohabitation of YHWH with his people. The appearance of the sacred legend in the hymn is then a particularly Israelite manifestation that has no counterpart in Babylonian and Egyptian literature. Excluding the influx of prophetic eschatology into the hymn (cf. ¶51), this manifestation of the narrative is the most characteristic difference between the biblical hymns and those of the foreign lands. The consistent theme of these allusions is the Passover story (cf. ¶40). This narrative operated as the most significant narrative of the past. The festival in which the most enthusiastic hymns resounded would have been the Passover.

In addition, the conquest of Canaan by Israel was praised (Pss 44:3f; 80:10; 111:6; 135:12; 136:21f). The oldest form in which one recalls these narratives was perhaps the brief allusions that are often only recognizable to the expert (cf. Pss 8:3; 65:8; 105:14f; 111:9; 114:8; 136:23f; Isa 43:16f), which were then later unfurled into extensive narratives. Ps 114 stands at a later stage in which the hymnic attire completely fell away. Cf. §8 concerning the origin of the narrative material.

It is very remarkable that all of these allusions only treat the *very oldest* history of Israel. At the time, only this history possessed the sacred character that made it worthy to be named in the hymn to God. If something later, or even in the present, had to be recalled, it was mentioned only in very general terms (cf. Pss 136:23f; 147:13, perhaps 148:14a). This was true of the New Year's festival hymns. One can also document similar patterns for the "thanksgiving songs of Israel," which may have been performed at special thanksgiving festivals (¶41) by comparing Pss 65:2-9; 66:9-12; 67:2,7; 124:6f; 129:1-4. It was apparently different for those hymns that were sung at victory celebrations (¶41). We can develop a picture from the songs containing the sagas of Miriam (Exod 15:20) and Judith that shows how these hymns would have looked. We can recognize that these songs permitted the poets to present that which had just been experienced. God's actions that had just happened could also be presented in the "eschatological hymns" (¶51) which sometimes imitate these victory hymns.

51. Just as the hymn speaks of YHWH's present and past, it also speaks about his future. The heart of the pious rejoices when it thinks of the time to come when the Lord will be seen in his true greatness and when he will take the throne of the world.

Periodically, the poems rely on these wonderful hopes. Individual sentences are inserted that take up this topic in praise of YHWH (cf. Pss 69:36f; 86:9; 96:10-13; 102:14-23; 147:2; Jer 16:19; cf. ¶28). In our opinion, these passages stem from a time when the prophetic proclamation influenced the hymn (cf. ¶63; §9). The original hymn of Israel would not have contained these predictions since they are not typically found in Babylonian and Egyptian poetry.

While these occasional references are relatively infrequent, another connection between the hymn and the prediction are even more frequent. In this instance, it becomes indisputable that the hymn singer borrows from the prophetic material.

The prophets' powerful spirit pushes toward the final time and loves to paint the final condition graphically (cf. my introduction to H. Schmidt, *Große Propheten*,[2] pp. li and liii, lviif). They eagerly present the powerful jubilation into which Israel will break forth when the great YHWH battle will take place and Zion will be redeemed. Or, they demand this rejoicing immediately (cf. Isa 9:2; 24:14; 30:29; 52:7ff; 65:18; 66:5; Jer 31:4, 7; 33:11; Nah 2:1; Zeph 3:14f; Tob 13:6). This type of rejoicing about the future is very vividly described in Ps 68:27. In order to fashion jubilation about that majestic future in the hearts of their contemporaries, they even compose the song that one will sing "on that day" (Isa 12:1; 25:9; 26:1; 27:2) when "they see what he has done with them" (Tob 13:6). Or, the prophet breaks into jubilation when his soul is full from the vastness of everything which YHWH had promised to do. He rejoices so that the normal person can finally understand when the great things finally happen (Isa 30:18d; Mic 7:18ff; Hab 3:18; Pss 12:7-9; 75:10). These songs of rejoicing are particularly common in Deutero-Isaiah: Isa 42:10-12; 44:23; 45:15; 48:20; 49:13; 52:9f; 54:1; also Deut 32:43; Isa 12:1f, 3-6; 25:1-5, 9; 26:1-6; 27:2; 61:10f; Jer 31:7; 51:10; Joel 2:21, 23; Zech 2:14; 9:9; Tob 13; and Luke 1:46f, 49-55, 68-75. Take Isa 12:4-6 as example:

> On that day you will say: Give thanks to YHWH. Call on his name. Make his deeds known among the nations. Proclaim that his name is exalted. Play *songs* to YHWH, for he has done something great. Let this be made known in all the earth. Rejoice and be glad, she who inhabits Zion, for the holy one is great in your midst.

The observant person will immediately recognize from this example that this kind of poem has taken the well-known *form of a hymn*. There are expanded introductions (cf. ¶8 with its succeeding "then" ["that"], or ¶18). The eschatological hope differentiates the *content* of this kind of poem from typical hymns. We call the resulting deviation "eschatological hymns."

One easily understands that speaking this way would have been particular impressive. By this poetry, the people of that day would have been powerfully transported from the suffering of its present into the majestic future. Instead of its concerns, the people would taste the rejoicing of the end time. One conceives that the psalmists have borrowed this wonderful type of poetry from the prophets for the sake of its effect. One also conceives that the priests, who were obligated to shape the worship service, did not want to lose the most important element of the religion of the time, but provided a place for this element in the cult instead. The particular days on which these poems would have been performed will remain unknown. Thus, we find "eschatological hymns" among the Psalms, including Pss 68; 98; 149; as well as 9:6-13, 16, 17; 75:2, 5-11).

52. Another deviation among the other hymns is the "Zion song," which we already mentioned(cf ¶¶17, 26) and whose specific treatment we have saved until now. It is not

uncommon in the hymn that the poet will take the opportunity to speak of word of praise concerning the sanctuary of God, earthly or heavenly, (cf. Pss 29:9; 68:16f; 93:5; 96:6; cf. 78:68f; Jer 17:12). In several of these poems this praise of the holy place appears especially strong, meaning that we call these poems "Zion songs" (Pss 84; 87; 122), according to Ps 137:3. One can also compare Jer 17:12f where God and sanctuary are addressed and magnified simultaneously in the introduction to a complaint song. Egyptian literature also contains songs that praise the sanctuary (A. Erman, *Literatur der Ägypter*, pp. 337ff, 363ff). These "Zion Songs" (cf. ¶26) also deviate slightly in form from the typical hymn, since they tend to lack the introduction (¶17). Also, the *address* to the holy place is characteristic of the Zion songs (Pss 87:3; 122:2f,6ff), especially when the poet breaks into blessings for the holy place (cf. Pss 84:5f; 122:6ff; Jer 31:23). One may well imagine that this kind of poem was sung at particular occasions that celebrated Jerusalem's majesty (cf. ¶40). The content of Ps 132 is the endowment of the sanctuary, and simultaneously that of the king's palace, but has no hymnic forms. However, it should be compared to the "Zion songs."

This type of poetry and those like it are also filled with prophetic contents, which is how we understand Pss 46, 48, 76. The prophets also proceeded the psalmists in the deviation of the genre, since one may already find these praises of the transformed Jerusalem in the prophets (Isa 26:1; 27:2-5; Jer 31:23; cf. Isa 61:10f). It is not hard to understand why songs of the praise of the sanctuary contain eschatological contents. Jerusalem played an important role in the future promises since the time of Isaiah. Jerusalem is the place where these events will occur by which YHWH will be proven as lord of all nations. It is *here* that every poem resounds triumphantly. Here, kings are seized with terror (48:7), and *here* YHWH breaks 'quivers and' bows (Ps 76:4).

Recently, S. Mowinckel (*Psalmenstudien*, vol. 2, 1922) and Hans Schmidt (*Thronfahrt Jahvehs*, 1927) have denied the existence of these eschatological hymns. They object to this interpretation because an explicit reference to the understanding of the future is missing, whereas the prophets include an eschatological introduction, "on that day." They also object to the fact that the characteristic, demonic, mysterious tenor of the prophetic speech does not appear in them (cf. my "introduction" to Hans Schmidt, *Große Propheten*,[2] pp. xlviff; and S. Mowinckel, *Psalmenstudien*, vol. 2, pp. 15f; H. Schmidt, *Große Propheten*,[2] p. 5). Both scholars overlook the fact, however, that the prophetic counterparts which I have just discussed also do not generally possess the introduction which they find lacking. It is precisely by this means that the mystery is given to the poetry, as is particularly clearly illustrated in Ps 4 (cf. further ¶9).

It is, of course, not easy to recognize these eschatological hymns as such. They usually appear with perfect verbs to portray the mighty deeds of God as having already occurred (Isa 44:23; 61:10; Pss 46:7; 47:9; 48:4-7; 98:1-3; cf. Luke 1:51-54, 68f; etc.). As a result, it appears to be earlier than the natural element of relating these poems to historical events. However, the eschatological interpretation can be proven by a series of considerations: one cannot find the glorified components mentioned in these poems in the history of Israel, but they do completely *agree with prophetic predictions*. In addition, the psalms themselves occasionally reference the occurrence of the fulfillment of the promises (cf. Pss 48:9, 11; 68:23; 149:9; Luke 1:55, 70, 72f; Ps 93:5; Mic 7:20; Sir 36:20f). As we have just demonstrated (¶51), it is particularly impressive that the psalmists have only followed the prophets in penetrating the hymn with eschatological material. The dependence of the hymnic poets upon the prophets also becomes clear in the fact that they sometimes venture out to allow God to appear and speak (Pss 46:11; 68:23; 75:3f; cf. 84:7f). Such action is unheard of in the remainder of the transmitted hymns of Israel (cf. ¶24), but quite common in prophetic speech. Accordingly, the perfect verb of the eschatological psalms should be understood analogously to the prophetic perfect. When the great festival of the end time was celebrated and these songs were sung, the awesome act of God will already have occurred.

One may also explain that the eschatological songs sound like hymnic victory songs (¶¶41, 50) based on the nature of the eschatological songs (Pss 46:9; 48:13ff; Isa 33:20). They treat a mighty victory which YHWH would have attained. Ps 68:18f contains motifs of the worldly victory song, sung when the king entered, which are transferred to YHWH when he enters Zion. The conclusion of the eschatological victory songs periodically contains commands to the community to look at God's wonderful deed and to tell about it (48:13ff; 46:9; [76:1f]; cf. 66:5; Isa 37:13). Concerning the contents of the prediction in these poems, cf. the article "Endhoffnung der Psalmisten" in my *Reden und Aufsätzen*, pp. 123ff and ¶9. Concerning "Magnificat und Benedictus, compare *Festgabe an A. v. Harnack*, pp. 43ff.

53. Finally, we must briefly consider "YHWH's enthronement songs" (Pss 47; 93; 96:7-13; 97; 99 (¶3). They certainly stem from a different origin, but are closely related in content to the "eschatological psalms." They are also influenced by prophecy and have taken up threads of eschatology. Both genres are also very close to one another in form. The call to rejoice and to praise was also characteristic of the enthronement songs (§3, ¶¶3, 11). From that point the genres influenced one another, and created mixed forms. Ps 98, an eschatological hymn, contains motifs of the other genre, while the opposite is true of the enthronement song in Ps 97, which echoes a hymn-like conclusion (97:10-12). Also Ps 47, from the same genre, contains several hymnic forms (47:2f,7f). In Ps 96, a typically fashioned psalm (1-6) has been unnaturally attached to an enthronement psalm (cf. §3, ¶7). S. Mowinckel (*Psalmenstudien*, vol 2, 1922) and Hans Schmidt, *Thronfahrt Jahves*, 1927) treat the enthronement psalms differently (see §3, ¶¶8, 11).

IV. The Relationship of Hymns to Other Genres

54. Among other things, the great significance that the hymn apparently possessed can be noted in the fact that it *strongly influenced other genres*. We will present the dependencies in detail when we present the other genres, but here will provide a brief overview so that the reader may find all the hymn material together in one place.

The *thanksgiving song of the individual* comes particularly into view. It was originally sung during a thanksgiving offering in peaceful thanksgiving following deliverance from a great crisis (cf. §7). Both genres have influenced one another since the basic mood of these poems is related to the hymns. Thus, the *introduction* of the thanksgiving song frequently manifests the expressive hymnic form (cf. Pss 9:2f; 18:2f; 30:2; 34:2-4; 116:1; 138:1f; Sir 51:1), or the personal thanksgiving song is fashioned as a more common hymn (cf. Pss 66:1-12; 118:1-4; Dan 2:20-22;). Frequently, the celebratory conclusion is formed similarly to the hymn (cf. Pss 18:50f; 30:13; 32:11; 35:27; 66:20; 107:8f, 15f, 21f, 31f; Isa 38:18-20; Sir 51:12; cf. also Pss. Sol. 16:5). Elsewhere, a second part can follow the thanksgiving song in the form of a hymn (Pss 18:32-49; cf. 103:4ff), or an extensive hymnic conclusion can be attached later (Ps 107:33-42). At other times one finds a hymn in the middle of the thanksgiving song (Pss 30:5f; 40:5f; 138:4-6). Cf. §7, ¶8.

At the thanksgiving offering, the leader of the celebration tends to *invite the participants* to join with him. These invitations bear the form of a hymnic introduction (Pss 22:24f; 30:5f; 32:11; 34:4; 118:1-4, 24). Also, the song that the participants sing is a hymn in its form (Jer 33:11; Ps 106:1; 107:1; 118:1-4, 29; 136:1-3, 26; Sir 51:1ff; cf. also 1 Chr 16:34; 2 Chr 20:21. Thus, at this point, the thanksgiving song and the hymn flow together. See especially Ps 100, a song in hymnic form that was sung when entering the temple. Cf. §7, ¶7.

Only occasionally does the opposite happen where the thanksgiving song influences the hymn, such as when the personal life of the thanksgiving songs penetrates the hymn (cf. Pss 18:32-49; 92:5, 11f, 16; 103:2-5; 144:1f; 1 Sam 2:1; and the Song of the Three Men). In these cases, the act of God which the singers praise (¶28) is the act of deliverance which they have just experienced (cf. §7, ¶8).

One frequently finds prayers in the prose materials which are essentially thanksgiving to God according to their content, but whose form is hymnic. Cf. ¶14.

55. The "complaint songs" are far removed from the hymns in which the tone of the moaning and the entreaty is expressed loudly and, as a result, are differentiated from the sound of jubilation in the hymns as starkly as possible. Nevertheless, even these two opposites have sometimes been attracted, leading to several borrowings.

First, one notes those complaint songs in which the *people* express their pain and their desires at the great lamentation festival (cf. §4).

These poems begin regularly with a *call to YHWH* in which the divine name is enriched by several divine epithets. This seldom happens in Psalms, but more frequently outside the Psalter (¶¶19-21). Finally, it is fashioned into a type of hymn (cf. Ps 80:2; 1 Kgs 8:23; Isa 37:16; Jer 14:8; 32:17-22; Hab 1:12f; Neh 1:5; 9:6-15; Dan 9:4; Pr Azar 3-5; Add Esth 3:2-4; 1 Macc 4:30; 2 Macc 1:24f; 3 Macc 2:2; 6:2; Pss. Sol. 17:1-3; 4 Ezra 8:20-23; Apoc Bar 21:4-17; 48:2-10). Thus, a hymn can introduce a complaint song (Pss 44:2-4; 106:1-3; Isa 63:7), or a transmitted hymn can be supplemented by later material as an introduction to a complaint song (Ps 89:2, 3, 6-19; cf. §4 ¶12). Even the royal complaint, which is related to the communal complaint, can begin similarly (Ps 144:1f).

At times, these elements that recall the hymn stand in the middle of the complaint song (Lam 5:19), as with the hymnic narratives (Pss 74:12-17; 80:9-12). Cf. §4 ¶12.

As frequently happens in the individual complaint songs (cf. ¶56 [§6,24]), the vow concludes the communal complaint once. In response to his salvation, the psalmist vows to sing the thanksgiving song to the helpful God. This type of vow manifests hymnic form (Ps 79:13), which is typical for the thanksgiving song.

56. Those *complaint songs*, in which *the pious individual pours out his heart to God* and longs for help from God, are related to the communal complaint in their outline (cf. §6). The hymns are even incorporated here on occasion, essentially in the same way.

Thus, the "call" is sometimes constructed in the form of a hymn (¶¶19-21). Compare Jer 11:20; 17:12f; Tob 3:2, 11; Wis 9:1-3; cf. Pss. Sol. 5:1f (cf. §6 ¶¶10, 28).

All kinds of hymnic elements are very frequently found in the middle of the poem, even in the psalter. These hymnic elements express the singer's *trust*, and thus kindle the singer's hope in a way designed to make God intervene. Cf. Pss 11:4-7; 16:7, 9b, 10; 22:4-6; 25:8-10; 86:5, 8-10, 15; 102:13-23, 26-29; 119:12, 39, 54, 68, 72, 75, 89-91, 97,

98, 129, 137, 138, 140, 142, 156, 160; Lam 3:22f, 25; 5:19; Pss. Sol. 5:9-11. Cf. Also Pss 36:6-10 and 77:14-21 (cf. §6 ¶24; §7 ¶3).

Very seldom does the complaint song influence the hymn. A hymnic poet inserts the complaint song motif of a melancholy observation about human finitude in order to enhance the praise of the eternal nature of divine grace (Ps 103:14-16). In 90:1-12, tones of both genres are united in a moving blast (cf. also Sir 18:1-7, 8-14).

The petitions appear now and then in the conclusion of the hymns (cf. ¶36, p. 20). The petitions stem from the complaint song, as can be seen especially clearly when the hymn blends into a complaint song. This is the judgment of a researcher who works from the perspective of the Old Testament. In the Babylonian material, the combination of hymn and complaint is very common. Someone, like Fr. Stummer (*Journal of the Society of Oriental Research* 8 [1924]: 127), who observes this combination on the basis of the Babylonian material would presume that this blending was original. Only the future will decide which of these two observations is more correct. It will possess the Babylonian material more completely, and can recognize its internal history.

On the whole, the hymn contributed considerably more to the complaint than it received. The hymn proved to be the genre that was stronger and more capable of internal development.

57. Hymnic elements are frequently found in the prophetic books. One finds the prophetic and the hymnic elements combined especially in the salvific prophets, with Deutero-Isaiah foremost among them (cf. H. Greßmann, *ZAW* 34 [1914]: 283f). The same enthusiastic mood for the majestic God resides in both genres, and has enabled the confluence. The hymn penetrates the prophetic material in following places:

(a) *Eschatological hymns* are found especially at the conclusion of salvific pro-nouncements (cf. ¶51).

(b) The *introductions and conclusions* of the oracle, "thus says YHWH" and "I am YHWH," are frequently expanded by adding divine attributes that are similar to hymns (cf. ¶21).

(c) One also finds similar hymnic expansions in the *invocations of prayers*, especially in prophetic complaints (cf. ¶¶19-21).

(d) In addition, one finds *scattered hymnic elements*, of varying lengths, in *other passages*. Thus, Isaiah hears a hymn commence when standing before the seraphim. The hymn also penetrates the prophetic warning to fear only YHWH (Jer 10:6f, 10, 12-16; cf. further Isa 40:12-17, 22-24, 26, 28f; 63:7; Jer 2:6; 5:22, 24; 51:15f; Nah 1). Amos 4:13; 5:8; 9:5f are later insertions from a foreign hand.

(e) Corresponding to the characteristic forcefulness of the prophetic spirit, they love to turn folk expressions on their head. The jubilation songs typically begin with the words, "Rejoice, Israel." Hosea then begins cruelly and surprisingly by saying, "Do not rejoice, Israel" (Hos 9:1; cf. Isa 14:29). Cf. my introduction to Hans Schmidt's "Große Propheten,"[2] p. lxviii.

By contrast, the influence of the prophets on hymnic poetry was also very great. The eschatological hymns imitate the orientation of the prophets (cf. ¶51). Also, other hymns occasionally take up the most beautiful speeches of the salvific prophets (cf. especially Ps 103, ¶49, see the commentary). This influence of prophetic religion upon the hymns was certainly very significant. Thus, it is possible to explain that the divine perspective of the hymns so clearly agrees with that of the prophets (cf. ¶63). Cf. also ¶59.

58. It is easy to understand that the *victory song* has a close relationship with the hymn. Particular hymns were sung occasionally at the victory celebration (cf. ¶¶41, 50). Forms of the victory song permeated the hymn (Ps 66:5), especially the eschatological hymn (¶52, p. 57). Again, the influence also operates the other way around: a regular hymn, Judg 5:3-5 , forms the beginning of Deborah's victory song (v. 2 is a variant of v. 9).

59. The hymn plays a significant role in passages that contain *mixed elements* from several genres, even those performed by different voices that we call "liturgies (§11). These liturgies sometimes begin with a short hymn (Pss 24:1f; 106:1-3; Isa 63:7). Or, the hymn stands at the conclusion of a mixed genre poem, especially after an immediately preceding oracle (Pss 12:7-9; 68:33ff; 115:16-18; 118:28f; Mic 7:18ff; Deut 33:26-29; Pss. Sol. 8:34. At other times, hymnic elements frame an oracle or a prediction (cf. Ps 75:2, 5-11; Pss. Sol. 18:1-4, 10-12). Enthusiastic praises respond to the scornful words of the enemies (Pss 36:6-10; 115:3-8). A priestly blessing follows the priestly hymn of Ps 134:1, 2. The prophetic didactic poem of Deut 32 contains hymnic components among others, toward the beginning (3f) and at the end (43). The prophetic liturgies of Pss 81 and 95 are quite peculiar. They begin joyously with hymns (Pss 81:2-6a; 95:1-7), only to continue with warnings. In the *mixed poems* of Pss 90 and 139 that stem from a later period, the tenor of the hymn (90:1, 2, 4; 139:14-18) agrees with that of the complaint (¶¶36, 56). In the alphabetic poem of Ps 9, an eschatological hymn (9:6-13, 16, 17) mixes inorganically with the individual song of thanksgiving (¶54). Concerning Ps 89:2f, 6-19, see ¶55.

60. The spirit of the *wisdom poem*, with its peaceful observation, generally deviates from the hymn considerably. However, the tenor of the later hymns becomes more contemplative and more subdued, so that on occasion, the thoughts of wisdom teaching, especially teaching on retaliation (§10 ¶¶1, 2), could enter (Pss 97:10; 107:42; 111:10; cf. §10 ¶3). These speeches usually stand at the end of the poem. Once, the hymnic poet begins the wisdom poem with the celebratory form of the introduction (§10 ¶4) because he wants to recite his material, the sacral history, not only to honor God, but also to teach subsequent generations (Ps 78:1f). Further, the admonitions which are quite typical for the wisdom poetry (§10 ¶5) are occasionally inserted by the hymnic poets, and are perhaps influenced by these admonitions.

In the book of Job, the most exalted thoughts receive hymnic form. This holds true whether the book of Job must present the contemplated power of God about which human beings may not conjecture (9:4-12; 25:2f; 38f), or God's heavenly wisdom, which mortals cannot comprehend (11:10f; 12:13-25; 26:5-14),and even the admonition enters the hymn (5:9-16; 36:22–37:13). Elihu also makes use of hymnic motifs in order to present the irreproachable righteousness of the ruler of the world (34:18-30).

The book of Sirach (cf. W. Baumgartner, *ZAW* 34 [1914]: 169ff) contains a series of hymns (39:12-35; 42:15–43:33; 45:25; 50:22) and hymn motifs (10:14-17; 16:18f, 26ff; 17:29f; 18:1-7). These hymns in Sirach stand in stark contrast to the largely older book of Proverbs, which has none. By this point, however, the hymn already appears to be in complete deterioration. Portrayals of nature appear in the foreground, and push the exaltation of YHWH into the background (43). Above all, wisdom thought penetrates into the hymn (39:17a, 21-30; 42:22-24) and the prosaic meaning of "the wise" redirects the energy of the hymn considerably so that the details provide more of a cheerful than an elevated impression on the current reader. Compare the rather unenthusiastic word in

39:26: "The foundation of human life is water, fire, iron, and salt," etc. In addition, wisdom forms enter the hymn (39:12f, 28, 32). A hymnic portrayal (16:26ff) gradually dissolves into instruction. Smaller hymnic pieces are mixed with admonitions (10:14-17; 16:18f; 17:29-32). Compare further W. Baumgartner's explanations.

The hymn deteriorates even more in the *Psalms of Solomon*, where the doctrine of retribution that is characteristic of wisdom dominates (§10, ¶¶1, 2). Here, there is no longer an independent hymn. However, hymnic elements are generally lacking in reflection. Hymnic elements pierce the theodicy (2:33-37; 8:24, 34). Observations concerning the fate of the righteous (§10, ¶6) or a narrative concerning God's righteous judgment upon the wicked. Or a blessing upon the pious, as is customary in wisdom poetry (§10, ¶6), follows a shorter or longer hymnic piece (6:6; 10:5-8).

V. The Internal History of the Hymns

61. We have already provided several observations concerning the internal *history of the hymns* (cf. ¶¶7, 10, 14, 18, 23, 24, 28, 29, 34, 36, 38, 41, 44, 49, 50, 51, 52, 57, 60). We must still make several additional notes and attempt to develop a comprehensive picture.

The *beginnings of the hymn* lie in *the oldest period we can reach*, as is generally the case with the religious lyric of Israel (cf. §12). The situations of the hymns, i.e, mainly annual festivals and national festivals, appear alongside the very oldest narratives and are included in the earliest prophets (cf. ¶38-41). Hymnic poetry, as we have seen (cf. ¶38ff), grew out of the worship service, which must have taken place in the earliest time. The prophets already battled against the cult and the singing of hymns (cf. Amos 5:23). Even individual hymns or hymnic elements are know to us in this time. The song of Miriam, which apparently belonged to a saga (cf. "Märchen im AT," p. 108), but which must stem from a very early time, already bears the form which repeats so often in later times (¶2, 15, 18): "Sing to YHWH, for . . . , " or according to another transmission, "I will sing to YHWH, for . . . " (cf. ¶11). And the final form going back to the song of the individual singer is already found in the hymnic introduction (¶58) of the Deborah song: "I will sing, I will sing to YHWH, I will play for YHWH, the God of Israel." (Judg 5:3). Even the seraphim's song in Isaiah (6:3), completely exhibits the outline of a hymnic piece. Typically, YHWH is the subject of the first sentence, along with a praiseworthy divine attribute as predicate adjective: "YHWH Sebaoth is holy." The second sentence, "The whole earth is full of his honor," is a very common deviation of this type of speech (cf. ¶¶26, 29). The numerous contacts regarding form and content with Egyptian and Babylonian hymns argues for an early origin of the Israelite hymn (cf. ¶46). Precisely from these similarities, we may deduce that Israel learned the artistic expression of the hymn as it gradually developed in Canaan. We see confirmation of this supposition in the fact that the Amarna correspondence already occasionally contain hymnic allusions (cf. Fr. Böhl, *Theologisches Literaturblatt* 35 [1914]: 337ff; also cf. the commentary, to Ps 139:8, and J. A. Knudtzon, *El-Amarna-Tafeln*, 147:9ff, which even has hymnic attributes in relative sentences, and J.A. Knudtzon, ibid, 144:15f: "die Einführung des Hymnus des Einzelnen). There is no objection to this early placement of the hymn in Israel, so that the people manifest this type of poetry in developed form. On the spiritual level, it places Israel's religion in the line of the great cultural religions (cf. Fr. Heiler, *Gebet*,[2-5] p. 161). It follows, even more importantly, from this observation that Israel was by no means as

undeveloped in ancient times as the older Wellhausen school thought, and as S. Mowinckel, more recently, would have us believe.

62. The situation of the hymn, the annual festival, and the victory festival, were repeated innumerable times in the subsequent history of Israel. Therefore, Israel sang the
hymn throughout its entire history. The transmitted hymns also range over this vast time
period. One should thus expect this type of poetry to display an extraordinarily rich
history where clearly developing differences appear. That is, however, not the case. To
be sure, the contents of the hymn experience many changes, but most of the hymn
remained the same, as the classification in ¶46 showed. The forms, especially, demonstrate
a notable consistency throughout the centuries (cf. ¶36). Just as, according to the saga,
Miriam once sang, "Sing to YHWH, for he is highly exalted," so it was in the song of the
three men: "Praise the Lord, for he has taken us from the netherworld" (Pr Azar 65). Here
one can observe the almost unbelievable tenacity that literary forms and poems for the
worship service could possess. For the modern reader, this really creates an irritating problem, since it dramatically complicates the positioning of individual songs. Nevertheless,
we are able to say a little more about the details.

We may, with certainty, accept the preexilic origin in those places where Israelite
kings are mentioned. That happens in 89:19 and 1 Sam 2:10. The royal thanksgiving
psalm of Ps 18:32-49 contains hymnic forms (cf. ¶54; §5, ¶6). Ps 8:5 is used by the royal
lament of Ps 144:3, and even Ps 8 itself belongs to this earlier period. A prayer for the
ruling king (84:9, 10; cf. §5, ¶2) has been added to the "Zion song" of Ps 84 when it was
used for the public worship service. Thus, even this hymn stemmed from the monarchical
period. Several of the psalms belong to the Northern Kingdom (Pss 29; 81:2-6b; 89:2, 3,
6-19; cf. the commentary). One can see then that the hymn was obviously fostered in the
Northern Kingdom. One cannot, however, recognize rudimentary differences to the Judean
psalms. The adoption of these songs for Jerusalemite worship is only comprehensible in
the earlier period when both people groups still felt united by religion, or at least before
they did not yet hate each other completely (thus, before Ezra's reforms at the very latest).
It is notable that the mythological elements appear so prominently in Pss 29 and 89:2, 3,
6-19. This is also a sure sign of an older period. Ps 19:1-7, whose second portion could
originally derive from a sun-hymn, sounds just as old. Thus, one finds nine psalms which
can be ascribed to the preexilic period with great certainty. Among these, Pss 8 and 84
are uniquely preserved. Additionally, one can include several hymnic songs, or portions
of songs, outside the psalter, like the Song of Miriam, perhaps even in its expanded form.
One may also include the song of the seraphim (Isa 6), as well as Deut 33:26-29, etc.
Thus, the judgment appears to be correct that the formal expression of the Israelite hymn
maintained its shape during this time. Still, we can well imagine that a collection of
hymns which came strictly from this time period would have left a considerably different
impression than the hymns of our current psalter. In such a collection the mythological
elements and the relationships to the sanctuaries, and their worship services, would appear
more prominently. Currently, however, these older hymns appear in purified form, or at
least they have obtained another perspective by their association with newer poems.

63. *In the age of the writing prophets, the genre came under their influence.* The
eschatological hymns provide clear evidence of this influence (¶¶51, 52). The prophetic
spirit that lived in the future and the majestic images produced by that sprit provided such
a powerful impression that even the hymnic poets were determined by it. As with the

future, the hymnic poets also conceived YHWH's and Israel's past according to the model of the prophets. Even the presentations of sacral history in the hymns express prophetic thoughts and would be inconceivable without the prophets (¶50). Powerful liturgies with hymnic components (Pss 81; 95) are worthy imitations of prophetic entities (¶59). Ps 103 borrows its most beautiful sayings from prophetic speech (¶¶49, 57). The total impression is of particular significance, however, whereby the thoughts about God in the hymns agree on the whole with the prophets (¶57). So one may say that Israel's hymn reached its majestic height when it was filled with prophetic spirit. This flowering of the hymn should be sought in the *seventh and sixth centuries*. It is during this same time that prophecy also influenced the composition of the law and the historical narrative. One can thereby see that the beginning of prophetic influence does not coincide with the exile. Further, one can see that the exile created no division in hymnic poetry. It is therefore incorrect to raise the question for each individual hymn whether it was preexilic or postexilic.

64. In the following centuries, the hymn attained its greatest popularity among the people. One recognizes from the writings of the postexilic period how much that period enjoyed its festivals, especially from Ezra, Nehemiah, Chronicles, and the books of Maccabees (cf. ¶41). The community and the individual (¶44) allowed no opportunity to pass in which one could sing a hymn. And in the Jerusalem temple the praise songs to YHWH resounded day and night (1 Chr 9:33). One can understand how earlier research could conclude that these centuries that were so enamored with the *performance* of hymns could also have been the particular age of the *composition* of hymns. However, anyone knowledgeable with the history of literature and music knows that the times of origination of an art form is often far removed from its popularity among the people. In Goethe's and Beethoven's time, there were no Goethe clubs and no one had established any Beethoven monuments. The fact that the blossoming of the hymn did not occur in that late epoch, can be shown by the fact that the law, *on the whole, did not affect the hymn*. Glorification of the law occurs relatively seldom in hymns, and only in such cases where, for other reasons, we must also ascribe a late date within the whole developmental perspective (Pss 19:8-11; 119:39, 54, 72, 86, 90, 97f, 103, 127, 129f, 137f, 142-144, 151, 160, 164; cf. Pss 111:7f; 147:19; cf. ¶¶26, 48). We therefore conclude, with every confidence, that the hymn already possessed a completely ensconced form. At least in the case of the hymn, it is not possible to say that the origin of psalmody presupposed the existence of the post-exilic law, a belief frequently articulated today. Even the numerous allusions to the creation accounts (cf. ¶50) are not on the whole dependent upon the priestly code. Rather, these allusions presuppose older, more colorful, and in part mythological, transmission. Exceptions are rare (cf. Pss 33:9; 136:8f; 148:4). Ps 8:6f and especially Ps 104 are places where the content relates to Genesis 1. However, these places operate quite freely, and do not treat the story as an inviable revelation given once and for all. Perhaps these passages know the story in an older form rather than reflect the "priestly code."

65. *Characteristics of later hymnic poetry* include, above all, mixtures with other genres and the liturgies (cf. ¶59). In addition, there is a certain slackening of the forms (cf. ¶¶16, 23, 24, 29), as with the appearance of the "I" of the singer (cf. ¶¶50, 54) among others. The poem in Ps 139:1-18 is especially noteworthy in which the poet profoundly considers his relationship to YHWH that penetrates and masters him. This relationship per-meates everything so much that the old stringent forms of the hymn retreat into the back-

ground, providing a strong subjectivization of such an originally objectively directed genre.

66. The following are *characteristics of the latest poetry*. The independence and creative power of the singers has ceased. The songs which the later singers produce imitate the old models, and use current expressions that finally result in a "sacerdotal" poetry arising from common formulas. The energy of the ancient poets makes room for a tired, suppressed tone where expansiveness and accumulation replace powerful brevity. In addition, the latest poetry lacks a rigid order. One is increasingly satisfied with merely piling line upon line. The outward decoration of the alphabetic form appears particularly pleasing to this period, a decorative form which can only be appreciated by the eyes while offering nothing for the ear or the spirit. Also, the influx of "wisdom" that was favored in the latest period, demonstrates how much the freshness and enthusiasm diminished (cf. ¶60). The observation of scribal dependencies (especially of Deutero-Isaiah and the priestly code) and linguistic usage (cf ¶12) are of value for determining the date. Accordingly, the following belong to this repercussion of hymnic poetry: Pss 33; 68; 96; 98; 100; 105; 111; 113; 135; 136; 145; 147; 148; 150.

The large expansion and the notable connection of a hymn-like beginning followed by a complaint are characteristic of the prose prayers of that time (cf. ¶55). The latter is a sign of renewed Babylonian influence (¶36, cf. Fr. Stummer, *Journal of the Society of Oriental Research* 8 [1924]: 131).

The question is now raised, when was this latest period of biblical hymnody? Today, one would usually be inclined to suggest the Maccabean period. However, the Chronicler leads to a different conclusion. At that time, the most frequently performed verse was the hymnic thanksgiving song (§7, ¶7):

> Give thanks to YHWH, for he is good,
>   for his grace endures forever.

The Chronicler introduces the verse on multiple occasions and derives it from David (1 Chr 16:7, 34, 41; 2 Chr 5:13; 7:3; 20:21). The Chronicler seems to think about this verse in particular when he assures that the hymns were performed "according to the manner of David" (Ezra 3:10f) or "with the words of David and the seer Asaph (2 Chr 29:30). Still, he also introduces a larger hymn (1 Chr 16:8-36), an alleged hymn of David, consisting of Pss 105:1-15; 96:1b-13a; 106:1, 47f, and finally, it even contained a praise song that was incorporated onto the end of the fourth book of Psalms, transposed into the form of a narrative. Accordingly, around 300 such late hymns as Pss 96 and 105 were already considered immeasurably old. One may even say that the Psalter was already closed at that time and was believed to be a work of David (§12).

Additional indirect proofs for this dating include the following. The musical instruments mentioned in, *minnîm* and *'ūgāb*, Ps 150:4, are already missing in Chronicles. Above all, the most weighty such proof is that the decomposition of the forms in the later books, such as Sirach and the Psalms of Solomon, has already increased to a large degree (cf. ¶60).

67. The time period in which the book of Psalms was closed conceived the book as a whole to be *tehillîm* ("hymns"), as the book's superscription indicates. By no means, however, were all of the songs originally hymns. They were also sung in public worship to honor YHWH.

Hymnody did not, however, perish at that time. Rather, it continued for a long time without a recognizable pause, as the hymnic elements in Daniel, the apocrypha, and in the Psalms of Solomon demonstrate.

§3 Songs about YHWH's Enthronement

The following is an appendix to the hymns. It is a small genre in which the investigation of the matter must take a somewhat different course. However, it rests on the same principles, and at any rate could not be omitted from this position.

I. Form and Content

Ausgewählte Psalmen[4] 1917, p. 134ff. — H. Greßmann, *Ursprüng der israelitisch-jüdischen Eschatologie*, 1905, pp. 294ff.

1. Those psalms that begin with the words, "YHWH has become king" (Pss 93; 97; 99), are related to the "eschatological hymns" (§2, ¶¶51, 52). Pss 47 and 96:10ff are comparable in that they contain these characteristic words even though not as the first phrase (Ps 47:9; 96:10). Ps 10:16 also constitutes a recollection of these songs where the poet of a complaint song, who has reached the height of certainty, takes up this motif in addition to other eschatological motifs. The last echoes are in the New Testament (Rev 19:6f; 11:17f). It helps to understand this psalm if one recognizes that the words "He has become king" are also used for earthly rulers at significant places. When the new king is addressed, one finds the royal cry: "Absalom/Jehu has become king." (2 Sam 15:10; 2 Kgs 9:13). The fact that these words are so intended in the Psalms can be seen from Ps 96:10: "Say among the nations, 'YHWH has become king.' " This corresponds to 2 Sam 15:10 where Absalom sent secret messengers to all the tribes of Israel with the commission, "As soon as you hear the trumpet sound, say, 'Absalom has become king in Hebron." Accordingly, these Psalms celebrate *YHWH's enthronement*. The idea that a god would become king is already found in the Babylonian creation poem: ["When the gods, his fathers, saw the success of his utterance, they rejoiced and paid homage: 'Marduk is king.' They submitted to him the scepter, throne, and royal apparel (?)." From E. Ebeling in H. Greßmann, *Altorientalische Texte und Bilder,*[2] 1926, p. 117.] The same image has been carried over to YHWH by the prophets of Israel, who, so they say, once became king on Zion (Isa 24:23; cf 52:7; Mic 4:7; Ezek 20:33; Rev 11:15.17; 19:6).

The psalms already mentioned portray this idea of YHWH's enthronement. Since these poems lead with the words "YHWH has become king" in a prominent position and since they are also full of images of enthronement, one can accept that they not only use the royal "address" to YHWH, but that they *imitate the motifs from the royal poems and carry them over into the spiritual realm.* A similar example of such a process can be seen when during the reformation period, secular songs were transformed into spiritual ones. So, for example, during that time the love song "Innsbruck, I Must Leave You" became a song about death, "O world, I must leave you." (W. Baumgartner further references similar cases from the German folk song in J. W. Bruinier, *Deutsches Volkslied,*[5] 1914, pp. 47, 75, 78, 110; and in O. Boeckel, *Psychologie der Volksdichtung,*[2] 1913, pp. 151, 154, 168, 355 (fn 3). Cf. further A. Erman, *Hymnen an das Diadem der Pharaonen,* 1911. These are songs that celebrate the crown, but later were used for the cult of a god.)

2. The royal poems that were sung on the day of the anointing of the young ruler, and which display this outline, are no longer preserved. This deficiency is not unusual given the generally scanty amount of Israel's worldly poetry that has come to us. Pss 2; 101; and 110 presuppose the same celebration (cf. §5, ¶6) but are different in form. However, it is possible to gain a view from these royal songs in which one represents the situation of the enthronement from the reports of the historical books. Thereafter, although with all due caution, one can attempt to recognize the worldly model shining through in the spiritual poems we have before us.

The *process of the enthronement* is described in 1 Sam 10:24ff; 11:15; 2 Sam 15:10; 1 Kgs 1; 2 Kgs 9:13; 11:12ff; cf. 1 Chr 12:39ff; 29:22ff (cf. S. Mowinckel, *Psalmen-studien*, vol. 2, 1922, p. 6f.). In the most extensive reports two different actions can be differentiated: first, the new ruler is anointed on a holy site at the hand of a priest and adorned with the crown. Then, however, he "ascends" in a celebratory parade (*'ālāh*) and seats himself on the royal throne (1 Kgs 1:34, 38ff, 44ff; 2 Kgs 11:12ff; 1 Chr 29:23). The day begins with a festive tone. Flutes are blown (1 Kgs 1:40); trumpets (signal horns) bellow round about the king (1 Kgs 1:34, 39, 41; 2 Kgs 9:13; 11:14) with a sound that is then passed on from place to place so that it echoes throughout the entire land (2 Sam 15:10). As we hear over and over, it is a day of joy and rejoicing (1 Sam 10:24; 11:15; 1 Kgs 1:40; 2 Kgs 11:14, 20; 1 Chr 12:40; 29:22). The people rejoice (*hērîă'* in 1 Sam 10:24) so that the earth might burst with their cry (1 Kgs 1:40). This is called the king's rejoicing (*terū'at melek* in Num 23:21). The great personages of the kingdom are assembled around the king: the elders and the heads of the people (2 Sam 5:3; Deut 33:5), the ministers, and soldiers (1 Kgs 1:7ff, 19, 25, 38, 44; 2 Kgs 11:14; 1 Chr 29:24). Whoever appears before the king prostrates himself (1 Kgs 1:47, 53), brings gifts (1 Sam 10:27), and commences with blessings: May God make your name majestic and your throne exalted (1 Kgs 1:47, 37). A celebratory sacrifice and a sacrificial meal take place (1 Sam 11:15; 2 Sam 15:12; 1 Kgs 1:18f, 25; cf. perhaps Isa 25:6ff; Ezek 39:17ff). The herald carries the message throughout the land (Isa 52:7): "He has become king." And those who hear it, clap their hands (2 Kgs 11:12) and join in: "He has become king" (2 Sam 15:10); "The king lives" (1 Sam 10:24; 1 Kgs 1:25, 34; 2 Kgs 11:12). Thus, "the kingdom is summoned" (Isa 34:12). One may consider the words of Goethe in "Elepnor" (II, 2) in these portrayals: "An old king drives the hopes of human beings deep into their heart and imprisons them there. The sight of a new sovereign, however, liberates the long bound desires. In ecstasy, they press forward. They, the wise and the fool, greatly enjoy the breath that had been so sorely lacking." There were similar enthronements in Assyria whereby the new ruler, adorned with the signs of his authority, sits on his throne in the throne room. All present prostrate themselves before him and kiss his feet. His kingdom is summoned and the greatest desires expressed (cf. B. Meißner, *Babylon und Assur*, vol. 1, 1920, p. 63; and E. Klauber, *Assyrisches Beamtentum*, 1910, pp. 19f. The same holds true for Egypt. Cf. A. Wiedermann, *Das Alte Ägypten*, 1920, p. 59 [and A. Erman[2] = H. Ranke, *Ägypten und ägyptisches Leben im Altertum*, 1923, pp. 69ff; cf. also *A Thousand and One Nights*, Littmann, vol. 1, pp. 702f, 732f; vol. 2, p. 144]).

3. It is this type of day that is the right day for the *song of the court singer*. An enthronement poem of this kind would have begun with the *call to the king*. It would have taken it up and performed it poetically. He has become king! He has sat on the throne of the king of Israel (Pss 99:1; 47:9) and his throne is founded upon righteousness and jus-

tice (97:2). He has put on the royal garments (Ps 93:1). He has "ascended" in the fortress amid rejoicing (*terū'āh*) at the blaring of the horn (47:6). He has performed powerful deeds (Pss 47:4f; 93:1; 96:10). He created justice and righteousness in Israel (Ps 99:4). Now he takes the throne in his royal majesty (Pss 97:2ff). The great ones of Israel stand among his servants (96:6; cf. 97:2), and the princes of conquered peoples rushed here from great distances to be gathered before him (Ps 47:10). Heralds announce him in all the world (Ps 97:6). Reverently, the poet names the center of the kingdom (2 Sam 15:10; Ps 9:12) and the extent of the new empire. The conquered ones shudder before him (Ps 99:1). The subjects rejoice at the justice of the government (Ps 97:8ff) that now breaks forth (Ps 99:4). Standing alongside these descriptions of royal majesty, a large portion of the poem is filled with *commands* to rejoice and celebrate the majesty of the new king (Pss 47:2; 96:11f; 97:1, 12; 98:4; cf. 9:12) with trumpets and horns (Ps 98:6), with singing (Pss 47:7f; 98:5), and praising (Ps 99:5, 9), with the zither and with loud noise (Ps 98:5), by clapping hands (Ps 47:2; 98:8), by prostrating oneself (99:5, 9), and proclaiming to all the world, "He has become king" (Ps 96:10). The enthronement song would have proceeded in this manner. The details may remain uncertain, but they are relatively insignificant for understanding the whole.

4. In the above mentioned psalms, these worldly royal psalms are adapted *to YHWH as king and his future kingdom*. The earlier period had already named YHWH "king," a concept that was also prevalent among other Semitic peoples (cf. Robertson Smith-Stübe, *Religion der Semiten*, 1899, p. 27, 45ff, 66; Eduard Meyer, *Geschichte des Altertums,*[2] vol. 1/2, 1909, p. 372). In so doing, of course, they considered Israel as the empire of YHWH, and they believed in a present kingdom of God. Cf. 1 Kgs 22:19; Isa 6:5; Num 23:21; Deut 33:5; cf. also 1 Sam 8:7; 12:12; Jer 10:7, 10; Isa 41:21; Mal 1:14; etc. These thoughts also echo in the psalms: Pss 24:7; 29:10; 74:12; 103:19; 145:1,11; Exod 15:18; etc. However, during the suffering times of foreign rule, the contradiction between belief and appearance led them to believe in a future kingdom of YHWH because one could hardly deny that the present showed them very little of his gracious lordship over his people. They could also hardly deny that now other powers conducted their cruel dominion over Israel and the world (Isa 26:13). However, faith turned even more to the conviction that YHWH himself would one day take the reins of the government (Isa 24:23). The prophets had already preceded with this idea of a kingdom of YHWH in the final time. Ezekiel had prophesied it (20:33). Deutero-Isaiah heard the voice of the herald who proclaimed the royal call to Zion: "Your king has become king." (Isa 52:7). Cf. also, Isa 33:22; Mic 2:13; 4:7; Zech 14:9,16f; Zeph 3:15; Obad 21. The psalmists transferred the prophetic use of the royal call to YHWH himself, and rendered it into entire poems that imitated the worldly songs. Accordingly, *these psalms should be understood eschatologically* as can be seen in the description of the origin of the poems. It also proceeds clearly enough from their entire content. One need only compare passages like Ps 47:4 that speak of the subjection of the heathens to Israel; that is, of Israel's future worldly rule. Or, one should consider passages like Pss 96:13 and 98:9 that speak of YHWH's "coming" to judge the world. Following the prophetic proclamation, the singers poured out everything that they knew to say regarding the end time using the form of these enthronement poems, YHWH's "judgments" (Ps 97:8), and "miracles" (98:1). They spoke about the overthrow of the heathen (Ps 47:4) and YHWH's faithfulness and grace toward Israel (Ps 98:2f). *One understands*

*these psalms when one recognizes the form of the enthronement songs and their
eschatological content.*

5. According to the form, these psalms glorify YHWH as the new king of the world.
He is the king (Pss 47:3, 8; 98:6; 99:4), and has just now become king (Pss 93:1; 97:1;
99:1; 47:9; 96:10). He has now taken his holy throne (Ps 47:9) that is carried by cherubs
(Ps 99:1) or, according to another spiritualized concept, by justice and righteousness (Ps
97:2). He puts on majesty and power as royal garments (93:1). He also "ascends" amid
shouting (*terūāh*) and trumpet blast (Ps 47:6) after which he performs his deeds (Ps
98:1f), subjugates the nations to Israel (47:4), refortifies the earth (Pss 93:1; 96:10), and
creates the new just order in Israel (Ps 99:4). The singer delightfully portrays his royal
appearance (Ps 97:2ff). The nobles of the peoples of the entire world stand beside his
throne alongside the children of Abraham (Ps 47:10), or—again spiritualized—it means
that majesty and splendor (96:6) surround him. Another expression uses clouds and
darkness (Ps 97:2). Or, the singer recalls from the sacred history that Moses, Aaron, and
Samuel are among his priests (Ps 99:6). The heavens proclaim his justice as heralds (Ps
97:6). Fire precedes him as a forerunner (Ps 97:3). Zion is his residence (cf. also Ps 9:12).
All nations are subjects of his empire (Ps 99:2). The subjugated nations must tremble (Ps
99:1) while Zion will rejoice concerning its God (Ps 97:8). His kingdom is a kingdom of
justice (Ps 99:4) and of grace (Ps 98:2f) and lasts forever just as his throne has been
established from time immemorial (Ps 93:2). This government shall be welcomed with a
loud shout (*hērî'a*, Ps 98:4, 6; cf. Zeph 3:14), or hand clapping and trumpet blasting from
the entire world (cf. above, ¶3).

6. The material of this poetry is eschatology. All the psalms agree that YHWH's future
reign is a world empire encompassing all nations. All gods bow in the dust (Ps 97:7) before the one who has now proven himself as the highest (Ps 47:3) in the entire world (Ps
97:9). At the same time, it is an empire of complete justice (Ps 96:13; 97:2, 6; 98:9, especially Ps 99). Mythological material enters as well. The attack of the sea and a universal
earthquake precede the new order. Then YHWH appears in the majesty of the volcano god
(Ps 97:2ff).

7. The time of the poems is given in that they presuppose prophetic eschatology.
They often have no particular characteristics, although Ps 93 is characterized by its powerful brevity, and Ps 99 by its moral seriousness. Most frequently, the eschatological hymns
sound like Deutero-Isaiah. Nevertheless, they provide a good picture of the powerful faith
of Judaism in the coming kingdom of YHWH, a faith which, in the manner of the ancient
prophets, sees the future as having already occurred and thus can even now raise the royal
call. Nowhere do any particular causes appear that are tied to a particular time period.
According to the above-mentioned material, it is understandable that this genre possesses
a close relationship *to the hymns* and has been mixed with them (Pss 47; 97; 98; and
especially 96 [§2, ¶53]).

II. The Cultic Situation and History of the Enthronement Songs

8. I wrote the preceding section (I) of this chapter in 1913, and then reworked it in
1919/1920. I printed it at this point so the reader could see how I have wrestled with this
material for many years. I placed a few additions in square brackets. In the following section (II) I have avoided repetition where possible. In the meantime, the situation of the
discipline has shifted to the degree that S. Mowinckel has discovered a festival in his mas-

sive, original, and extremely fertile work from 1922, *Psalmenstudien II, Das Thronbesteig-ungsfest Jahwähs und der Ursprung der Eschatologie*. He claims this festival provides the reason, not just for the above-mentioned Psalms, but, to many other psalms as well. The recently published work of H. Schmidt (*Die Thronfahrt Jahvehs*, 1927), where he basically agrees, provides illustrations of this festival in his lively and insightful manner.

Both believe that the festival, which will be treated here, is one which celebrates the *entry of YHWH* into his sanctuary. He has become king, and he now enters Zion in order to be honored by his people as king. The voices of those singers accompanying him resound in order to rejoice about the one who is enthroned.

Mowinckel brings together those songs that clearly presuppose such an enthronement festival (those which we believe presuppose this festival will be demonstrated subsequent-ly). He combines these psalms with a whole host of other psalms which possess a certain affinity with them in some respect. In this category he also includes those psalms in par-ticular that were, in his opinion, sung at the "Fall Festival." Mowinckel also perceived that the festival of enthronement was celebrated at the new year, and adds the supposition (which P. Volz had already expressed in *Neujahrsfest Jahwes*, 1912) that the New Year's festival and the autumn Harvest Festival should be seen together. On the basis of these combinations, Mowinckel presents a worship service of celebration with an abundance of ideas. In this service, the old year concludes, with its troubles and its disappointments, and the new begins with its wishes and its hopes. In this service, one is grateful for the benefi-cence of the old time and expects the same for the coming year. In this service, YHWH again becomes king and thus takes possession of his holy place. And so many additional thoughts attach themselves that finally, for the researcher who is daring and interested in revitalization, this festival appears as the "most important operation" of all for Israelite religion (p. 316). Accordingly, one is not surprised that the Psalms as a whole are related to this celebration. For Mowinckel, it is the powerful magnet toward which a large portion of the psalmic poetry is attracted. As a result, he can finally present the surprising thesis that the lyric of the New Year Festival gave rise to Old Testament eschatology. The con-tent of the eschatology originated from this festival (p. 226). By contrast, H. Schmidt registers far more caution, and eliminates a whole series of texts that his predecessor re-lated to the festival. However, Schmidt does maintain another portion of these texts.

If one wishes to attain a firm foundation for this question, one must first ascertain *which psalms one may accept whose origin is related to an enthronement festival*. Every-thing depends upon the greatest caution and reservation in this investigation. If we allow fantasy to have full rein in this task, we enter an area in which everything is possible and nothing is certain any longer. So, the following would be characteristic of the enthrone-ment festival as S. Mowinckel and H. Schmidt conceive it: (1) that YHWH becomes king on this day; and (2) that to do so, he *enters his sanctuary* in order to mount his throne. However, when these two indicators do not come together in a psalm, we can only speak of an "enthronement festival" if other very reliable criteria yield this conclusion. Thus, we begin the investigation in this case with the "life setting" (§1, ¶¶4-6), and in so doing be-lieve we possess the right and the obligation to do so. However, the fundamental question is this: which *psalms belong to a very specific festival*? Now one can hardly deny, that according to this measuring device, the psalms mentioned by our very esteemed friends are insufficient to support their claims. It would go well beyond the scope of this book, if we attempted to demonstrate every detail. Several significant examples must suffice.

Ps 100 (S. Mowinckel, p. 3; H. Schmidt, p. 6) is a song that was sung when the community entered YHWH's courts (cf. §2, ¶40). However, we hear just as little of the fact that YHWH himself has already entered the temple and that YHWH is king or is recrowned in this festival. Rather, all that we learn from the superscription (also confirmed by the concluding verses in 100:4f), is that the song was sung with the celebration of the "thanksgiving sacrifice (tōdāh, cf. §7). We do not receive a more specific statement regarding the date of the festival calendar. The belief that the psalm belongs specifically to the enthronement festival thus hangs entirely in the air.

The same thing appears even more clearly in Ps 48 (S. Mowinckel, pp. 3f, 105f; H. Schmidt, p. 28). In this psalm, we hear that YHWH is "the great king" (48:3), but we hear nothing to the effect that he has just become king. To be sure, a procession is announced here, but not *a parade into the sanctuary*. Rather, the procession is more clearly *a march around the walls of the city* (48:13f; cf §2, ¶41). Our friends accept that this march could have belonged to the enthronement festival, where the march was held at the celebratory festival on a later day. But, who can prove that? Is it not more natural to presume that an entirely different festival is presupposed here, one that contained a very different perspective, namely YHWH's protection of the holy city during its great trouble?

Ps 65:12 also speaks of another march. I am also inclined to accept that it treats the path of YHWH over the fields in a divine chariot, whose tracks leave behind fertility according to the belief of that time (cf. the commentary). But why must this happen specifically on that day (S. Mowinckel, 137ff, 161; H. Schmidt, pp. 20f)? Nothing else in this psalm speaks about YHWH's enthronement, and the song manifestly belongs in a time of the year in which the grain already sprouts in the valleys (cf. 65:14). H. Schmidt (p. 20) is in error when he believes that the poem presupposes "the beginning of the rainy season," just as when S. Mowinckel thinks of a harvest thanksgiving song. Rather, the psalm is much more a *song of spring*, and it is not possible that it belongs to *New Year's day*, at the end of the dry season, where both researchers place the enthronement festival.

Ps 132 presupposes a festival that is related to the throne voyage of YHWH in a certain way. The basic thought occurs in both: YHWH comes on the current day to his sanctuary. But this thought is expressed quite differently both times, for in Ps 132 (§5, ¶¶3, 6) it is the God who has been without a home for a long time, who finally receives his own dependable home by the pious care of David. At the enthronement festival, however, the powerful ruler triumphantly takes the throne of the world in Zion. In addition, a major emphasis in Ps 132 is the promise for the dynasty, which receives the divine blessing at the same site because of the piety of the ancestor. By contrast, Ps 132 lacks the idea that YHWH becomes king in this festival. So here too, one can neither prove, nor show probability, that the same festival lies behind this psalm (contra S. Mowinckel, p. 112f; H. Schmidt, p. 36).

Ps 81 was related to the Fall Festival by rabbinic tradition. This reference, however, is not attested until such a late period that we may not deduce that much from it for the earlier time. The blowing of the ram's horn (81:4) is typical for the enthronement festival, but it is not an incontrovertible clue since this usage occurs with other festivals as well (compare the commentary, contra S. Mowinckel, pp. 86ff; H. Schmidt, p. 35). Additionally, the psalm does not speak of YHWH's kingship, much less of his coronation. There is also nothing said of his entry into Zion, and though the psalm may refer to wheat and oil that he would give to his obedient people (81:17), nothing demonstrates that this reference should be understood the goods of a "New Year" (S. Mowinckel, p. 218; H. Schmidt, p. 36).

Ps 15 most clearly presupposes a specific worship service. The priest communicates an answer for the laity to the question of their condition if they wish entry onto the holy mountain (cf. §11). However, the text does not offer a single word regarding which festival would have included this kind of question and answer (contra S. Mowinckel, p. 269). We will treat the related Ps 24 subsequently.

H. Schmidt (p. 41) believes that Ps 2 relates to the festival of the throne voyage of God, while we conceive it as the enthronement song of a human king (§5, ¶6). We now have rather specific information on the Babylonian New Year's festival from H. Zimmern, *Das babylonische Neujahrsfest*, 1926 = Alter Orient XXV/3 (cf. also H. Zimmern, *Berichte der philol.-hist Kl. der Sächs*. Geschichte der Wissenshaft zu Leipzig LVIII. 1903, p. 126ff; and LXX, 1918, vol. 5). During the Babylonian New Year's festival the king receives his kingdom *anew* from the hand of the high priest (H. Zimmern, *Babylonische Neujarsfest*, p. 12). This Babylonian practice does not prove, however, that the same thing occurred in Jerusalem, and nothing in the psalm mentions it since the kingship is not *returned* to the king but newly bestowed upon him. Finally, one finds nothing in this poem to indicate that YHWH has just become king in Zion or just made his entry.

Now I will cease. The following picture has satisfactorily developed from that which has been presented. There are a whole series of different celebratory events in the Israelite-Jewish worship service, and here and there some of them may have even been related to one another. How would such a group of priests have been maintained if they only infrequently had something to do during the year? Mowinckel, however, has combined this diversity and directed his attention rather one-sidedly to a New Year's festival. He has seen "Helen in every woman."

So what do I think is the ultimate reason for these apparent errors? *Mowinckel has not proceeded stringently enough in his assignation of those psalms belonging to this festival.* From the beginning he should have kept the presumed worship situation in mind, and he should have asked whether this psalm fit the enthronement festival. Also, he should not have combined the genres and their forms, whose differences he recognized. Instead, Mowinckel allowed himself to be led far too easily by the alleged similarity of *thoughts*. However, these thoughts are only part of the whole, that is generally capable of being transformed. As a result, taking the parts by themselves does not provide a solid foundation for a study of genres. Thus, Mowinckel jumps from one genre to another, combining many psalms that belong to very different festivals.

The situation is somewhat different with H. Schmidt, but he also shows disdain for the bit and the bridle, which a strict literary critical methodology provides for the researcher. Thus, his own fantasy carries him along without any restraints.

A few particularly clear examples will suffice to show how both researchers combine material that is entirely diverse. Ps 130, the famous song of confession so full of humility, is related by Mowinckel (pp. 131f, 166) and H. Schmidt (pp. 33f) to the night before the enthronement festival since one "waits" on the morning, as the latter explains it. However, this "waiting" is a very common term in the complaint songs generally (cf. §6, ¶19), and the image of the watcher who waits on the morning does not prove that the song was composed specifically for the night. And even if that was the case, the author could have sung many of the complaints at night (cf. §6, ¶4). So why should this beautiful song relate specifically to the New Year's festival? S. Mowinckel (pp. 4f) has ascribed all of the "pilgrimage songs" to this festival in spite of the fact that these psalms originally belong to very different genres and worship situations (cf. the commentary). At least here, H. Schmidt (*Theologische Literaturzeitung* 49 [1924], col. 78) objected in a more cautious manner.

Thus, the ground on which the whole structure was erected, has proven to be very unstable. Not much remains from the hypotheses so loftily built upon one another.

9. While it is easy enough to perform this unfortunately necessary task of destruction, it is much more difficult to say what we can *affirm confidently*. The author must confess that he wavered a long time over which path to take to find an exit from this labyrinth of difficult questions before, he believes, finally finding the trail. Ps 47 offers a relatively firm entry point where both researchers have begun (S. Mowinckel, p. 3f; H. Schmidt, p. 11). Certain traces in the text presume specific worship actions. I think even future research will evaluate Mowinckel's enduring contribution to be the discovery of these traces and the deduction of a festival from them. This contribution is even greater in that he has brought our attention to something new, namely, the connection between psalms and worship (something that was of course not entirely unknown to us earlier).

Ps 47 treats the cheering of the entire world (47:8) to the God who sits on his throne (47:9) after he has climbed onto it (47:6)—also amid great rejoicing (cf. ¶¶2, 3 and the commentary to 47:6). We presume *two festal events* afterward: (1) YHWH's march to the sanctuary; and (2) the glorification of the God enthroned there, both with the joyful shouting of the congregation.

One could raise the argument against this presumption that the Old Testament never expressly testifies to such a festival. However, this objection loses its force when one notes that a whole series of other worship events can only be deduced from the psalms, and are not known to us anywhere else (cf. e.g., §2, ¶¶40-42). Nevertheless, it remains a grievance, that anything we would like to say about this festival, can only be done by *supposition*. In addition, the allusions that are given in such festival poems tend to be rather inexact (§2, ¶45). In so doing, one opens the gate and the door to error, a difficulty which the two researchers have not made sufficiently clear.

First, it is clear that YHWH *is glorified as king in this festival*. This religious festival thus corresponds in details to the model of the enthronement of the earthly king who goes up (*'ālāh*, cf. ¶2) to his palace in order that he might receive homage. What we have said in section I concerning this imitation is thus essentially confirmed. Alongside this observation, I would not ascribe any particular value to the fact that there would also have been worldly royal songs of this type that echo in the psalms (¶¶3, 4). It is enough to note that thoughts and customs that were originally used of the earthly king have here been transferred to God. We observe similar things in the Babylonian festival of Marduk's entry into his temple (cf. ¶10). There, for example, god and goddess, as well as king and queen, are enthroned alongside one another (H. Zimmern, *Babyl. Neujahrsfest*, 1926, pp. 5f). The lesser gods gather themselves before the chief god as the vassals before their lord (p. 14), and they appear before him—so it goes in a related description—arranged precisely in rank and dignity, just like in the court (p. 17). Generally, the crowning of the divine "king" is fashioned according to the crowning of a human ruler, and the entry of a divine king is fashioned according to the entry of a human king.

Which psalms belong to this throne festival of YHWH? At this point, the *study of the form* fortunately comes to our aid, especially by observing *the first words* of the poem. Otherwise, the entry is the most reliable characteristic of the genre (cf. §1, ¶8, p. 17). So Pss 93; 97; and 99 clearly belong together as a group, according to the beginning clause "YHWH became king." Ps 47 should be included here as well where the saying is repeated twice (47:8,9) and where it dominates the subject matter. Ps 96:7ff is just as certain, where the sentence stands in a very important position. The *worship situation* is portrayed quite differently in these psalms. This is most clear in Pss 47 and 96:7ff, which speak of the march (entry) of God. By contrast, Pss 93; 97; and 99 do not speak of this entry. In Ps 98, the matter is reversed since it does not possess the characteristic introductory formula. Instead, the conclusion (98:9) agrees almost identically with the last sentences of 96:13, and is also closely related to the worship situation of this psalm. Here too, we find a joyfully expected entry (98:9) of the divine "king" (98:6) who comes to judge the earth. Thus, he will now take power. The first part of the psalm sounds more like an eschatological hymn §2, ¶53). In these cases, both characteristics of the little genre work together so that we need not doubt that all these psalms belong to the same festival.

It is quite different in Ps 10:16-18. This passage occurs at the end of a "communal complaint" (Ps 10) as a description of the "assurance of being heard" (§4, ¶11) where the fulfillment of the poor sufferer's desire is portrayed enthusiastically. It begins with a sentence which elsewhere tends to stand at the beginning of the enthronement songs (10:16). However, an entry cannot be intended here since Pss 9 and 10 constitute an acrostic poem that, from the outset, would only be conceivable as a written work. This passage is therefore to be considered an imitation of these poems.

Along with the passage just mentioned, one can also include verses 9:8f, 12, that come from the same psalm, although it is highly mixed. These verses belong to an eschatological hymn (9:6-13, 16, 17f), and whose leading formal movements contain the enthronement. They depend almost literally upon other easily recognizable enthronement songs (cf. especially 9:9 = 96:13; 98:9). This passage is also then an allusion.

Should other psalms be considered part of this group? What about the entry liturgy of Ps 24:7-10 (cf. §1, ¶6, p. 11 and §11)? This text also contains reference to the entry of the "king" YHWH into his temple. However, the main thoughts of the other psalms are completely missing from this text, namely the ideas that YHWH becomes king in this festival and takes the throne. One must therefore leave this text out of the equation. There could very well have been different advent festivals in the long history of Israelite worship (cf. Ps 132; §2, ¶52, p. 56). One can read more about Ps 24:7-10 in the commentary. It may be different for Ps 24 as a whole, which appears to be compiled by a later hand using various, older, small poems for the purpose of a performance. Since the first part of this entire composition (24:1,2) treats YHWH's creation of the world, and since creation of the world is one of the main ideas of the New Years festival in Babylon (cf. ¶10), one might suppose that the *entire liturgy* is determined by this festive day (cf. S. Mowinckel, p. 3f; H. Schmidt, p. 19f). However, the form of this liturgy deviates considerably from enthronement psalms. It would be more accurate to accept this liturgy as portrayals of the *songs of rejoicing* which Zion should sing when YHWH *returns*. The wonderful summons: "Your God is king" recalls Isa 52:7-10, where the prophet is thinking of the rejoicing of an enthronement song as one would have previously experienced it in the homeland. He conceptualizes the future rejoicing according to this model. One could also conceive the less significant passage in Zeph 3:14-17 in a similar light. The texts in Ps 68:18f, 25f remain uncertain on this issue. To be sure, they treat the entry of God into Jerusalem, but they could just as easily be drawing upon the model of a universal entry following a victory (§5, ¶6). Likewise, there are only a few places where the reference to an enthronement festival can come into play. The paucity of this event is not surprising since we possess very few psalms that we could relate with certainty to *specific* festivals.

10. Now we turn to the festival at which these psalms might have been sung.

Nowhere in the historical reports or in the legal material have we received a reference to this kind of enthronement festival. Some (S. Mowinckel, p. 43) have wanted to relate the saying from the Bileam speeches in Num 23:21 to this festival: "YHWH, his God, is with him, and a royal shout is in him." This word shout (*teru'āh*) can certainly be used in this context (¶¶2, 3, 5), but that does not mean that it must have the very specific connotation in every instance. Rather, Israel and the pious one rejoices over its God-king whenever they see his countenance (cf. Job 33:26). The people would naturally have shouted "hurrah" before its king, not just at his enthronement, but also at every other festal opportunity where the ruler appeared before the people. A "royal shout" is thus a shout like the nations tended to voice before their kings. This passage wants to say that Israel broke into such a shout before YHWH because they had every reason to do so. Even though they did not have an earthly ruler at that time, Israel did have a king in its midst.

By contrast, on Babylonian-Assyrian soil, there was an important festival held at every important cultic site. This festival displays more than a passing similarity to the presumed Hebrew festival. In this festival, one of the main elements is that the God-king enters his sanctuary anew during a powerful procession in which the entire people participate. In Babylon, the enthroned Marduk again sits in his temple *Esagil* from that time. The narrative that belongs to this festival is the famous creation myth whose climax comes when all of the other gods pay homage by calling out, "Marduk is king!" It would be conceivable that the Babylonian festival was taken over by Israel (as recently suggested by A. Freiherr von Gall, Βασιλεια του Θεου, 1926, p.21f). The faith of Israel would have contrasted the Babylonian call "Marduk is king" with their own call, "YHWH has become king." The conclusion of this chapter (¶11, p. 77) provides a comparison of the relevant poems of both parties. One cannot observe a literal dependence between the two. Only *one place* exhibits a certain similarity of form, if one compares Ps 47:6 with the Babylonian verses:

> The lord of Babylon set out. The lands kneel before him . . .
> Side by side with Ishtar of Babylon
> Their servants go up with the playing of flutes.
> All of Babylon goes up with jubilation.
> (H. Zimmern, *Das babylonische Neujahrsfest*, p. 18)

Several ceremonial practices of the "great day of reconciliation" appear to be borrowed from the same festival (H. Zimmern, ibid., p. 11).

From the outset, one may assume as probable that the Israelite festival began as an *annual* festival since festivals representing a divine event commonly began as annual festivals. Rabbinic tradition about Ps 47 suggests that this festival occurred at the *New Year*, as does the fact that the Babylonian festival took place at this time. However, there is no express mention of the new year in the "enthronement psalms" which we ascertained had a significant degree of probability.

We are also not poorly informed about the New Year. The beginning of the year must have been figured by the few who already were trained in astronomy (even though this would have been scanty enough) in order to date contracts and other documents (Isa 10:1). This would have been the case from the beginning of the Assyrian period. It is a very different question as to whether the day would have been celebrated by the people. In the accounts of the great pilgrimage festivals (Exod 23:14ff; 34:18, 22; Deut 16), there is no mention of a New Year's festival. This fact also leads with great certainty to the conclusion that this festival was at least not very widely known in ancient times, and could by no means have been the most significant of all the feasts.

P. Volz (*Neujahrsfest Jahwehs*, p. 12ff), and later S. Mowinckel (p. 83ff) and H. Schmidt (p. 25) have already associated the festival with the "feast of booths," the main festival of ancient Israel since both fall together at approximately the same time of the year. However, one should note that these two festivals are very different in their basic ideas. The festival of booths looks back on the gifts of the "gathering" received in the current year and expresses thanksgiving to the divinity for them. The New Year's festival, however, by its very nature looks to the future. This festival begins a new time while the festival of booth, which is consistently recounted as the last of the great pilgrimage festivals, represents the conclusion of the whole series of festivals. Even the origin and the type of the two events are very different. New Year's day would be set by the calendar, while the Fall Festival falls on different dates. As long as it was celebrated according to nature, each time depended upon the climate of the location and the year's weather. This situation later led to different opinions as to whether is should be placed before the New Year (as in Exod 23:16) or after it (as is presumed in the Gezer calendar; cf. H. Greßmann, *Altorientalische Texte zum AT*,[2] 1926, p. 444). We do have one reference that does appear to speak of both festivals together in Zech 14:16ff, which only means that the two days come so close together that one can occasionally mention them in the same breath. The types of the two festivals remain, however, quite different. Indubitably, Mowinckel and H. Schmidt thus combine more than a few psalms or psalm motifs with the New Year's festival that have, or appear to have, a relationship to the Fall Festival (cf. A. von Gall, Βασιλεια του Θεου, p. 21).

It is also possible to comment upon the time in which the New Year's festival came to Israel. It is doubtful that ancient Israel would have known about it (cf. above). As a whole, the prophetic references to the royal summons of YHWH that stems from the enthronement festival stem from a later time, at the earliest not long before the exile (cf. ¶4). The legal passages that speak about the New Year's festival (Lev 23:24f; Num 29:1-5; cf. Lev 25:9; Ezek 40:1; Ezra 3:6; Neh 8:2) also belong to this late period. The similarity that the presumed Israelite festival demonstrates with the Babylonian suggests that it is fashioned after the foreign festival (cf. above, p. 75). Now let us suppose with confidence that the Israelite festal calendar, which earlier had followed the relationships of the harvest as dictated by nature, later was fixed along astronomical lines under the influence of the dominant Babylonian culture. We may therefore seek the introduction of the New Year's festival in the worship of Jerusalem during this epoch, whose beginning we would have to place in the late monarchic period (cf. A. von Gall, Βασιλεια του Θεου, p. 21). However, since the enthronement of YHWH would not have begun at this place during the exile, we must imagine that this festival was celebrated in the time before and after the exile, although how long cannot be determined (cf. A. von Gall, Βασιλεια του

Θεου, p. 21). Later, as the reaction to the Babylonian religion dissipated, it would have lost its significance until it was finally forgotten. The latest allusions to this festival are still perhaps found in the prayers of the synagogal New Year's festival (cf. P. Fiebig, *Rosh ha-schana*, 1914, pp. 45ff).

After all is said, we have attained several more or less probable ideas with which we must expand and change the picture presented in part I.

(a) The enthronement psalms were performed in Jerusalem on New Year's day to celebrate the throne voyage of YHWH (as S. Mowinckel and H. Schmidt have seen).

(b) This celebration perhaps arose as an imitation and a reaction to the Babylonian New Year's festival during the latter monarchic period (as A. von Gall recently notes).

(c) At the same time, the celebration of the enthronement of the earthly king, as they would have often experienced it, would have been the model for the practices of this festival as well as the thoughts which they would have combined with it.

11. Now, let us address the *contents of the transmitted psalms* in this new light. They are so few in number, and so small, but so diverse in the material they combine, that their significance is difficult to determine.

First, we ask whether the Babylonian elements reverberate through them, and if so, to what extent. In the description of the festal procession, the Babylonian and Israelite poems are related to one another in *one* passage (¶10, p. 75). In the remainder, massive differences exist. The Babylonian poems generally use the typical connections of hymnic address to the divinity and petition for the sanctuary, the city, and the high priest. They are generally spoken by the high priest. By contrast, the Hebrew poets proceed with their own preferred form of the choral hymn (cf §2, ¶¶26, 46). We would thus further presume that the Hebrew poets generally exhibited considerable independence in relationship to the Babylonian elements. This is the same attitude which we have accepted also led to the distinctive substitution of their own YHWH for the foreign Marduk in an act of defiant faith. It is also this attitude which caused them to leave the date of the festival in the fall, remaining true to the ancient Israelite custom, rather than the Babylonian date which fell in the spring. However, one trace of Babylonian influence can be seen, even if it is not clear. Ps 93:3f is apparently related to YHWH's victory over the water, and is accordingly perhaps an allusion to the Babylonian myth of Marduk's battle. This narrative belongs to the creation myth, and we now know with certainty (cf. H. Zimmern, *Das babylonische Neujahrsfest*, p. 7) that the Babylonian festal story is specific for the New Year (New Year is the repetition and a celebration of the memory of the origin of the world). For these reasons, it can be suggested that this festal narrative was taken over from Babylon by Israel at the same time as the festival. Speaking for this assumption is the fact that the overthrow of the water is a motif that coincides very well with the end of the rainy season, which is when the Babylonian New Year occurs according to Babylonian reckoning. On the other hand, it is a genuine Hebrew train of thought when YHWH appears in clouds and darkness, with fire and lightning, in the shaking of the earth, and in the melting of the mountains (i.e., in the horror of the volcano, see Ps 97:2ff).

Next, we ask how much can be said about the *festival of YHWH's enthronement* based on the texts? We learn very little concerning the specific actions of the celebration: the "ascent" of God (47:6); the "entry" (into the holy site [96:13; 98:9]); and the homage itself paid by those gathered (96:7-9), who are dressed in festal clothing as they enter the courts of YHWH, where they fall down and present him with gifts (96:8, 9). We hear especially about the noise of rejoicing: the singing (47:7; etc.) and the trumpet blowing that accompanied this action (47:6). This description of the worship elements recedes behind the image of an earthly enthronement (cf. ¶5). God is conceived as the king sitting on the throne (47:9) with expensive clothes (93:1), with the subjects gathered before him from near and far (cf. ¶3). We cannot say in every instance whether, and if so how, these images correspond to the cultic reality. We have no way of knowing whether they used some type of divine symbol, or what it might have been if they did. The strong accentuation of the image of the enthroned king is a particularly Israelite touch. When the priests of Jerusalem adopted this festival from Babylon, they made this well-known image into the center of the celebration.

The fundamental mood of the *songs belonging to the festival* is one of joyful enchantment over the God whose imminence was experienced in the actions of this festal day. A simple people unaccustomed to thinking clarifies this kind of abstract thinking in that they do not conceive these things as continually present, but as having happened, and embodied in actions whereby they attain an unprecedented perceptual power. The *fundamental idea* of these poems is that YHWH becomes king *on that particular day* and enters. The fact that this happens on New Years day is appealing enough, for the soul gladly believes that with the New Year everything can become new, and that everything hoped for but never received will now come to pass. In our texts only Ps 93:3f (see above, p. 77) plays on this date, and then only somewhat vaguely.

We divide the entire material into *three parts*.

(a) There are many *commands to rejoice* that are identical in tone to the hymnic introduction (§2, ¶2), which explains why these two genres are sometimes combined (§2, ¶53).

(b) There are short allusions to YHWH's *deeds* which are thought to have *just happened* and which develop such great enthusiasm among the people. First, there are all kinds of deviations in the speech that he has now become king. Thus, sentences are expressed like 47:8, 9a, or "He sits upon his holy throne" (47:9b); or, expressed more loftily: "He clothed himself in majesty" (93:1). Very seldom does this form allude to the entities of the festival celebration: "He went up with a cry of jubilation" (47:6). And as the human king mounts the throne—like the founder of a new dynasty— after he has first performed military deeds, so it is here with God: "He has performed miracles. His right hand and his holy arm had helped him" (Ps 98:1-3, if the psalm is a unity [cf. §2, ¶53]). They could also have referred to mythological deed in these contexts, as with the conquering of the primal sea (Ps 93:3f, cf. above p. 77), a deed which primitive thought may have imagined as having just occurred. Or, there is another idea that God had created order in Israel.

(c) In addition, there are all kinds of *descriptions*, mostly timeless, that present the *condition of YHWH's enthronement* according to the context of the poem. Thus, YHWH is terrible (47:3), holy (99:4), and "majestic in the heights" (93:4). Here one should also include the great men who have stood in YHWH's service (99:6ff). Something of the energetic tone of the songs is lacking in the concluding section of Ps 97 with its rather thin presentation of YHWH's reign among humanity.

Also, the sentences listed under b) and c) are not all that far removed from sentences that are typical of the hymn (sometimes even the content as well). Cf. §2, ¶¶25, 28. However, this observation does not give the researcher the right to conclude that these hymnic motifs are part of the enthronement psalms in general (contra S. Mowinckel).

(d) A new idea occurs with all of this, one which is repeatedly proclaimed in various deviations and which provides a surprising turn to the whole. If Mowinckel had recognized the great significance of this idea (as I already noted, though perhaps not forcefully enough, regarding Ps 97 in "Ausgewählten Psalmen," 1st ed., 1904, p. 158ff), he would have arrived at a completely different conceptualization of the transmitted songs. The enthronement poems do not just speak about the experience of Israel, or praise that which YHWH had done in their context. Rather, their field of vision stretches much wider. They speak about the *coming of a new universal kingdom.* YHWH has become king *over all the earth* (Ps 47:8); and "*king over the nations*" (47:9). The great salvific act that he had performed occurs before the entire world: "The *ends of the earth* saw the salvation of our God" (98:1-3; Isa 52:10); he conquered "*peoples*" and "*nations*" (47:4). He is now called "a great king *over all the earth*" (47:3), the "*Lord of all the world*" (97:5), the "most exalted one *over all the world*" (97:9), "who is exalted *over all the nations*" (99:2), "whereby *all those serving images* doubt" and "*all gods* sink before him in the dust" (97:7), the "*highest of all gods*" (97:9). He is now come to judge "*the earth*" and "*the peoples*" (96:13; 98:9). The *honored ones of the nations* are gathered to pay homage before his throne (47:10). The "*princes of the world*" belong to him (47:11). All of these words are too numerous and too serious to be set aside as the exaggerations of increased intoxication of the festival (H. Schmidt, p. 12). Also, if one just considers these words as "the self-evident conclusion from the work of creation," the expression of a universalism that one should "not overestimate" (S. Mowinckel, p. 182), then one has misunderstood them greatly. By contrast these things appear so great and powerful to the psalmists themselves that they cannot do enough to call all peoples, indeed, every being of this world, to praise this huge God enthusiastically: heaven and earth, sea and meadow, the many islands, streams and mountains (Pss 47:2; 96:7-12; 97:1; 98:1, 4, 7f; 99:1). A conquest has now occurred, the likes of which are unprecedented, and an entirely new world order has been established. This is the reason that the fanfare is so loud. And how could Zion not raise its voice and rejoice (97:8)! He has "placed the nations under our feet" (47:4), and "done away with the rebellious ones" (Zeph 3:15)! Now, the "heathen have disappeared from YHWH's land" (Ps 10:16). "Zion need no longer fear evil" (Zeph 3:15). And he has bestowed upon us such an expansive country as would befit a world power (47:5). There, enthroned in heaven above, "on the *cherubim*," i.e., on the highest throne of the world (99:1), and here below on the earth there is a kingdom of righteousness (Pss 96:13; 98:9; 99:3f). That is truly a majestic message for Zion: its God has now become king of the world (Isa 52:7). What an abundance of salvation is enclosed within these words.

It should not be difficult to conceive the origin of these enthusiastic portrayals from Israel's soul. They describe how the most intense desire of Israel's heart could be fulfilled. Faith that the world would be overturned would create this certainty in a time when the people were greatly oppressed under the rule of a foreign power, when foreign gods triumphed, when YHWH's name was shamed, and when the wicked sat in power. There can be no suggestion that this faith already belonged to the oldest time of Israel and stemmed from the cult. Rather, this idea is the achievement of the *prophetic spirit,* and prophetic poets have produced it in transmitted form, including enthronement songs among other forms. In their hand, these songs were a means to express that YHWH is the one who enters and takes the throne as *king of the world.* It is YHWH who now takes up his kingdom *over all nations.* From now on, Zion is the center of the world (Isa 52:7; Ps 97:8;

99:2). So the people were transported into the future with unprecedented power, and must experience the coming day as the present.

From this starting point, several passages of this poetry become intelligible that would be quite difficult without the eschatological relationship. The arrival of YHWH in the horror of the volcano and thunder (Ps 97:2ff), a thought which seems rather out of place in this festival, is immediately explainable since it is an element of eschatology (cf. Isa 29:6; 30:27ff; Hab 3; etc). Further, the fact that the earth totters until YHWH steadies it (Pss 93:1; 96:10) was originally a mythological component that was related to the primal time and the end time. It also appears in Persia and Egypt as an image of disarray and reordering by the earthly king (cf. the commentary to 75:4). However, it cannot easily be understood as an experience of the worship service, and can hardly be understood as anything other than the future. So, the fantasy of the prophets, with the help of ancient motifs, clarifies the decisive paragraph. It brings the last appearance of YHWH. The prophetic poets use the old Babylonian motif of the New Year's festival for the same purpose by transferring the divinity's battle against the waters from the primal time to the end time (Ps 93:3ff., cf. the commentary to Ps 46).

We have additional evidence for this eschatological conceptualization of the enthronement songs. The same thing happens with the "eschatological hymns" or the other genres that have been adapted from the prophets by their relationship to the future (§1, ¶2; §2, ¶¶51, 52; §9). We can even name the great prophet who first accomplished this step with the enthronement poetry, and the prophet whom the poets of the enthronement psalms imitated. It was *Deutero-Isaiah* (52:7-10). It is then no wonder that the prophetic predictions and those psalms that were influenced by them agree closely with the contents of this poetry (cf. §9, and the commentary).

Mowinckel has gone an entirely different direction. He considers many psalms and psalm passages to be enthronement poetry if their content demonstrates any type of connection with the enthronement poems. He then wants to explain all of the material from the worship service. In places where the prophets touch upon this content, they deviate from this worship service. However, if that researcher is finally of the opinion that the entire eschatology of Israel derives from the enthronement festival, about which, in reality, we know precious little and whose significance could never have been very great, then he is really placing a heavy load on a very little piece of thread. Cf. also §9.

Schematic Summary of the Development of Enthronement Psalms

Babylonian New Year's Festival   Israelite Enthronement Festival
(and its festival poetry)   of the earthly king (royal summons)

YHWH's Enthronement Festival
and its festival songs in Jerusalem

Eschatological Reinterpretation by Deutero-Isaiah

Received Enthronement Psalms

§4 Communal Complaint Songs

Ausgewählte Psalmen,[4] pp. 106f — *RGG Art.* "Psalmen 4." — E. Balla, *Das Ich der Psalmen,* pp. 65ff — W. Staerk, *Lyrik in den "Schriften des AT,"* vol. 3/1,[2] pp. 118ff. — M. Jastrow, *Religion Babyloniens und Assyriens,* vol. 2, pp. 1ff — Hans Schmidt, "Hosea 6:1-6," *Sellin Festschrift,* 1927, pp. 111ff.

1. This genre includes the following psalms: 44; (58); 74; 79; 80; 83; (106); (125); Lam 5 (1 Macc 3:50-53); Sir 33:1-13a; 36:16b-22 (Pr Azar = Addition to Daniel 1:3-22; Pss. Sol. [4]; 7; [9]). In addition, one can include the following from liturgies, mixed genres, and reworkings: Ps 9:18-21; 10:1-18; 12:2-5; 33:20ff; 53:7; 60:3-7, 11-14; 68:29-32; 77:8-10; 82:8; 85:5-8; 89:39-52; 90:13-17; 94:1-7; 104:35; 108:13f; 115:1f; 123:2-4; 126:4-6; 129:5-8; Lam 1:9ef, 11e, 18ab, 20abcd, 21af, 22ab; 2:20a; 3:40-51; Pss. Sol. 11:8f; 17:21-25. It also includes the following prophetic texts, especially from prophetic liturgies: Isa 26:8-14a, 16-19a; 33:2, 7-9; 40:27cd; 49:14, 24; 51:9f; 58:3a; 59:9-15b; 63:11–64:11; Jer 3:4f, 22b-25; 4:10; 10:19-21, 23-25; 14:2-6, 7-9, 19-22; 31:18f; Hos 6:1-3; 14:3f; Joel 1:18-20; 2:17; Mic 7:7-10, 14-17. One should also include the mostly prose individual prayers, especially by the leaders of the people during times of public need: Josh 7:7-9; Exod 32:11-13; Deut 9:25-29; 32:17-25; Hab 1:2-4, 12-17; Ezra 9:6-15; Neh 1:5-11; 9:6-37; Dan 9:4-19; 1 Macc 2:7-13; 4:30-33; 2 Macc 1:24-29; 15:22-24; 3 Macc 2:2-20; 6:2-15; Jdt 9:2-14; Add Esth 3:1-10, 14-30; Pr Azar; Bar 1:15-3:8; Pss. Sol. 2; 5; 8; 4 Ezra 8:6-16, 20-36; Apoc Bar 21; 48. One should also include the prayers for the king (Pss 20:2-6, 10; 72; and 28:8f; 61:7f; 63:12a; 84:9f; 1 Sam 2:10de) and the prayers of the king (Isa 37:16-20; 2 Chr 14:10; 20:6-12) and the royal complaint (Ps 144:1-10). Finally, one should include the petitions in the royal prayer (132:1-10; 144:5-10) and the references to royal petitions (18:4, 7; 20:5).

2. The *setting of the genre* in the worship service is the "fast" (*sōm*), a great complaint festival which the community tended to hold now and then in response to general calamities (cf. W. Baumgartner, *Beiträge zur alttestamentlichen Wissenschaft,* K. Budde. ed., 1920, pp. 12ff.). The Wellhausen school is incorrect in its opinion that "the basic tenor of the ancient Hebrew cult was joy." (Cf. R. Smend, *Alttestamentliche Religionsgeschichte,*[1]1893, p. 125; [2]1899, p. 142). They did not recognize the great significance that the festival of mourning had for the religion. Also, the fact that these events could not be included among the regularly occurring annual festivals contributed to their being overlooked. Nevertheless, these events are presupposed and described in several passages: cf. Deut 9:13; Josh 7:6; Judg 20:23, 26ff; 21:2ff; 1 Sam 7:6; 1 Kgs 8:33-36, 44; 21:9, 12; Isa 15:2ff, 12; 16:7ff, 12; 29:4; 32:11f; 33:7ff; 58:3ff; Jer 2:27; 3:21, 25; 4:8; 6:26; 14:2; 36:6, 9; 49:3; Hos 7:14; Joel 1:1–2:17; Amos 5:16f; Jonah 3:5ff; Mic 1:8-12, 16; 4:14; Zech 7:3ff; Ezra 8:21; Neh 9:1; Petition of Baboas 15, 20f; Esth 4:3, 16; 2 Chr 20:3ff; 1 Macc 1:25-28; 3:47-54; 4:39f; 2 Macc 1:23; 3:15-21; 3 Macc 5:25, 50f; Jdt 4:8-15; etc.

The *cause* of these celebrations are generally all types of communal calamities: war, imprisonment (exile), pestilence, drought, famine (1 Kgs 8:33ff, 44ff; 2 Chr 20:9); aberration (Hos 7:14); locust plagues (Joel 1:2, etc.). These misfortunes may have already happened, they may be impending (Deut 9:25; Jonah 3:9), or may be feared to be imminent (Esth 4:3; Ezra 8:21ff). When the calamity lasted a long time, these complaints would be repeated (as in Elephantine, Petition of Baboas 15, 20f). There could even be specific days set aside for the complaint (Zech 7), or the festival could last for several days (Deut 9:25; Esth 4:16).

The lament festival was held at the sanctuary (Judg 20:23, 26; 21:2; 1 Sam 7:6; 1 Kgs 8:33, 35; Isa 15:2; 16:12; Jer 36:6, 9; cf 3:21; Hos 7:14; Joel 1:14; 2 Chr 20:9; 1 Macc 3:46; 4:37ff; Jdt 4:11; Bar 1:14. All the people gather together (1 Sam 7:5; Jer 36:6, 9). Everyone should take part, including the elderly, the women, and the children (Joel 2:16; Jonah 3:5; 2 Chr 20:13; Petition of Baboas 15; 2 Macc 3:18-21; Jdt 4:10. One hoped especially that the plight of the helpless would move God. Here and there we hear of general complaint and lament (Joel 1:5ff; Isa 24:11; 33:7; Jer 9:9, 17ff; 1 Macc 1:25-28): in the streets, in the market place, on the rooftops (Isa 15:3; Amos 5:16f), and in the gates (Jer 14:2). We hear of a communal lament (Isa 13:6f; 14:31; 23:1, 10; Jer 22:20; 25:34, 36; Zeph 1:10f, 14; Zech 11:2f), which culminates in a worship celebration (Joel 1:14). The celebration would first be "called" (1 Kgs 21:9, 12; Isa 22:12; Jer 36:9; Ezra 8:21; Jonah 3:5, 7; 2 Chr 20:3). The fasting and the gathered community (*qāhāl, 'ǎsārāh*) would be "consecrated" to YHWH (Joel 1:14; 2:15f) by ceremonies that are not conveyed to us. According to 1 Kgs 21:9, the celebration takes place *under the direction of a leader* who was chosen for the task.

The holy act of "fasting before YHWH" (Jer 36:9) characteristically arises *from the withholding* of food and drink (Deut 9:9, 18; Judg 20:26; 1 Sam 7:6; Isa 58:3ff; Neh 9:1; Jonah 3:7; Esth 4:16; 1 Macc 3:47; Jdt 4:13; Bar 1:5) in precise contrast to the joyous festivals in which the consumption of the sacrificial meat before YHWH plays such an important role. One should also abstain from marital relations and from anointing one's self with oil (Petition of Baboas 20) and from civil business (Isa 58:3; cf. Jer 29:5f). In addition, people tear their *clothes* or take them off (Josh 7:6; Isa 32:11; Mic 1:8; Joel 2:13; Jonah 3:6; 1 Macc 3:47; 4:39). They *beat themselves on the hip* (Jer 31:19). They cut themselves (Mic 4:14; Hos 7:14). They gird themselves with sackcloth (Isa 22:12; 58:5; Jer 4:8; 6:26; 49:3; Joel 1:8; Jonah 3:5, 6, 8; Neh 9:1; Petition of Baboas 15, 20; Esth 4:3; 1 Macc 3:47; 2 Macc 3:19; Jdt 4:10). They shave themselves bald (Isa 15:2; 22:12; Mic 1:16), and cover themselves with *dust or ashes* (Josh 7:6; Neh 9:1; 1 Macc 3:47; 4:39; Jdt 4:11, 15). They fall to the ground (Deut 9:18; Ps 44:26; Isa 29:4; Jer 3:25; 7:2; 14:2; 26:2; Jonah 3:6; 3 Macc 5:50; Jdt 4:11) on *sackcloth* (Isa 58:5; Esther 4:3). They roll around in the ashes and dust (Jer 6:26; Mic 1:10). They throw themselves on *their knees* (2 Macc 3:21), *on their face* (Josh 7:6; 1 Macc 4:40). Everyone raises *their hands toward the sky* (Lam 2:19; 3:41; 2 Macc 3:20; 15:21; 3 Macc 5:25). Even the priests clothe themselves with sackcloth (Joel 1:13; Jdt 4:14), and lament (Joel 1:9). They throw dirt and ashes on themselves (Neh 9:1; 1 Macc 4:39; Jdt 4:14). They even cover the altar with sackcloth (Jdt 4:12). They stand crying before the porch and the altar (Joel 2:17), and throw themselves down before the altar in their priestly garments (2 Macc 3:15) or spend the night in sackcloth in the sanctuary (Joel 1:13). Sacrifices are occasionally mentioned (Ps 4:6; 1 Sam 7:9; 2 Macc 1:23), including: *'ōlāh* and *minhāh* (Jer 14:12) or *'ōlôt* and *šelāmîm* (Judg 20:26; 21:4; cf. also Jdt 4:14). Alongside of these elements, one also finds the pouring of water before YHWH (1 Sam 7:6; Lam 2:19). All of this leads to the strongest possible impression of heart rending lamentation and tumultuous entreaty by a quite passionately moved people who are in great distress.

Therefore, the center of the festival is situated in a general "weeping before YHWH" (Judg 20:23, 26; 21:2; Mic 1:8; Zech 7:3), a loud lament (Jer 14:12, using *rinnāh*; 1 Kgs 8:33, 35, 38, 45; Jonah 3:8; Ezra 8:21ff; 10:1), howling and screaming (Isa 15:2ff; 16:7; Jer 4:8; Hos 7:14; Joel 1:5, 8; 2:1; Mic 1:8; 1 Macc 3:54; 3 Macc 5:7, 51; Jdt 4:12), raising a call to heaven (3 Macc 3:50; 4:40; 2 Macc 3:15), a light whimpering and whispering like a bird chirping (Isa 29:4). Fasting, weeping and lamenting (*spd*) belong together (Isa 22:12; Joel 2:12; Zech 7:3; Esth 4:3). The sound of the human voice was supported by the *sound of the trumpet* so that YHWH might hear it in heaven (2 Chr 13:14; 1 Macc 3:54; 4:40; cf. Joel 2:1, 15). Here and there, the prayer of *the priests* is mentioned expressly (2:17; cf. 1:9, 13; 2 Macc 3:15; Jdt 4:15). The various *groups of the people* were lamented chorally, and they prayed, which explains why individual groups were summoned (Joel 1; cf. also Zech 12:12-14).

In this situation, the common expression for the "prayer" was *hitpallēl* (1 Kgs 8:28-30, 44, 48, 54; Jer 7:16; 11:4; Dan 9:4, 20; Neh 1:4, 6) in times of public distress, particularly for the king, the one praying, and those for whom intercession was made. "Prayer" is called *tefillāh* (1 Kgs 8:28f, 45, 49, 54; 9:3; 2 Kgs 19:4; Isa 37:4; Jer 7:16; 11:14; Dan 9:3, 17, 21; Neh 1:6, 11; Ps 102:18). Other expressions include: *rinnāh* ("lament," cf. above), *tehinnāh* (supplication, 1 Kgs 8:28, 45, 49, 52, 54; 9:3; Dan 9:20; etc.).

The *thoughts of this "festival day"* need no clarification, and they are expressed often enough. In great distress, Israel turns to its God (*šûb* in 1 Kgs 8:47f; Hos 6:1; 14:3; Joel 2:12; Lam 3:40) who has sent this plague for the punishment of sins. Israel confesses its sin (1 Sam 7:6; 1 Kgs 8:47; Neh 9:2) and seeks his compassion (*drš*, 2 Chr 20:3). The fast and the remaining castigations (*'innāh nefeš* in Isa 58:3, 5; *hit'annāh* in Ezra 8:21; Jdt 4:9; nif '*al nzr* in Zech 7:3) serve the purpose of strengthening the prayer so that "the sound might be heard on high" (Isa 58:4). May YHWH "see" the fast and "hear" lamentation (Isa 58:3f; cf. Jdt 4:15). "Perhaps God will repent, and be sorry, and turn away from his fierce anger, so that we will not be destroyed" (Jonah 3:9; cf. Joel 2:14). At another time, the thoughts of sin retreat, and the fast only serves to lift up the prayer, e.g., with a dangerous trip (Ezra 8:21ff), or after the destruction of the temple from Elephantine. It is also conceivable that one asks for *the oracle* (¶14) in ancient times, as in Judg 20:23, 27f. This was an opportunity that the prophet used (Jer 36:4ff; cf. also Isa 37:21ff). Several times we expressly hear the words that would have been spoken during this complaint: "We have sinned before YHWH." (1 Sam 7:6; cf. 1 Kgs 8:47); "Why, YHWH, God of Israel, has this happened in Israel?" (Jdt 21:3ff; cf. Josh 7:7-9) "Get up and help us." (Jer 2:27; cf. 1 Macc 3:50-53). Joel 2:17 communicates a prayer of the priests on such an occasion:

> YHWH, have compassion on your people.
> Do not shame your inheritance,
> So that the heathen mock them;
> Why should it be said among the heathen:
> "Where is your God?"

In 2 Chr 20:6ff, we read an extensive prayer of the king in the name of his people on a day of fasting. We also hear, especially in sagas and legends, the prayers of individuals who intercede and who pray aloud for the people (cf. above, ¶1) in which the petitions of the leader reflect those of the people gathered for the fast. It could be that this is how the prayers would have sounded. On these occasions, those witnessing the suffering would be named, as elsewhere with the people (Deut 9:18; Josh 7:6; Dan 9:3; Ezra 9:3-5; Neh 1:4; 9:1; 1 Macc 2:14).

Several of the fasting customs mentioned in the preceding discussion would have originated late. Nevertheless, many of these are already found in the Babylonian examples (H. Zimmern, *KAT,*[3] pp. 603f; E. Behrens, *Assyrisch-Babylonische Briefe kultischen. Inhalts,* 1906, p. 19), and recur in Hebrew dirges (H. Jahnow, *Hebräisches Leichenlied,* see "Trauerbräuche" in the index, esp. pp. 164f). The antiquity of the entire practice, which is also attested in Moab and Ammon (Isa 15:2; 16:12; Jer 49:3) cannot be doubted. The oldest allusion to the practice is the Naboth narrative (1 Kgs 21:9, 12). Several older prophetic passages also demonstrate the antiquity (cf. especially Hos 7:14; Isa 22:12; 29:4; 32:11f; Jer 3:21, 25; etc.).

The public *funeral service* should not be confused with these days of complaint. The former tends to take place after a defeat in battle (1 Sam 31:13; 2 Sam 1:12; Jer 7:29). Both may have often taken place together since public catastrophe would also bring suffering to the individual families so that the general complaint was mixed with the mourning for the corpse. The main differences, however, are that the funeral service knows no hope and does not occur in the sanctuary, since according to the ancient belief of Israel, the dead have no relationship to YHWH (H. Jahnow, *Hebräisches Leichenlied,* p. 56). However, it is often difficult to ascertain which of the two events is intended with the prophetic allusions.

3. The *received communal "complaints"* were performed on these days of fasting. The evidence for this statement, insofar as any more evidence is even required, can be deduced from the agreement of these songs with the fasting prayers appearing in Joel 2:17 and 2 Chr 20:6ff. Also, one finds allusions to fasting customs of lying on the ground and throwing dirt upon oneself in the complaint songs (Ps 44:26; Jer 3:25). *One must therefore visualize the prominently portrayed practices of the lament festival if one wants to understand this poetry.*

4. In its pure form, the naming of YHWH in the vocative *within the first few words* is characteristic of this genre, as well as for prayers in general (cf. Pss 12:2; 44:2; 60:3; 74:1; 79:1; 80:2; 83:2; 94:1; 115:1; Isa 26:8, 16; 33:2; Lam 5:1; Sir 33:1; Pss. Sol. 7:1; etc.). The same is true *with new paragraphs* of the complaints, or with "mixed poems" (§11), where the complaint begins, or elsewhere at the beginning of the "petition" (Pss 10:1; 68:29; 74:10; 80:5; 85:5; 89:47; 90:13; 123:3; 125:4; 126:4; Lam 1:9e, 11e, 20a; 2:20a; Isa 33:2; 64:8; etc.), or with *new paragraphs of the petition* (Pss 83:14; 79:9; 94:3, 5; Jer 14:8). The same is also true of the beginning elements of the *conclusions* (Pss 74:22; 79:12; 80:4; 83:19; 85:8; 89:51f; Isa 64:11; etc.). Compare §1, ¶8, p. 17 concerning agreement between the beginning and end, especially in those places where the petition concludes the entire poem (Pss 44:24; 89:51; 123:3; 125:4; Lam 5:21; Pss. Sol. 9:8f; etc.). Sometimes, this vocative is scattered elsewhere (Pss 83:17; 89:50; Jer 31:18; Joel 1:19). This practice is explained from an early time when the ones praying recognized many gods, meaning that the prayer must first state the name of the god to whom it is directed so that god would hear the prayer and attend to it. The same practice occurs in the individual complaint song (cf. §6, ¶10, where there is even a more extensive presentation). It is therefore understandable that this calling upon the name of God in the most important

position would be repeated in the subsequent prayer. Those praying thus originally made certain that the god paid attention to their words. One thus recognizes that the primary emphasis for those praying comes with the *petition*, as is perhaps self-evident.

Usually, the name that is called is just YHWH. Occasionally, this name is circumscribed or expanded, as in the following formulas: "Lord" ('*ădōnay*, Ps 79:12; 89:51); "my God" (83:14); "God of our salvation" (79:9; 85:5); "YHWH Sebaoth" (80:8, 15); "Shepherd of Israel" (80:2); "YHWH, avenging God" (94:1); "Judge of the earth" (94:2); Almighty God" (Sir 33:1); "Lord, God of our fathers" (Pr Azar 3). Sometimes this call is expanded in a manner similar to the hymns (cf. e.g.): "Hear, Shepherd of Israel, who watches over 'Joseph's sheep, ' who appears enthroned on the cherubim" (80:2); "The hope of Israel, its healer in the time of need" (Jer 14:8). Cf. ¶12 for a discussion of the way that these hymnic expansions (§2, ¶¶9-12) can stretch into the entire first hymnic section of the poem in a later period. Those places which do not contain 'a call at the beginning of the poem represent exceptional cases. For example, Ps 58 and Pss. Sol. 4 begin with an indignant address to the godless and their gods. See also Ps 106; Hos 6:1-3; 14:3f; and Pss. Sol. 9.

Due to the nature of the prayer as such, the God is addressed as "you" (singular). This "you" appears regularly throughout the entire complaint, no matter whether the complaint is communal or individual (§6, ¶25). This happens because the prayer is not defined (as one tends to do today) as a conversation (or dialogue) with God. Rather, the prayer is a *speech to God*. Even this venture of the heart in child-like trust, when one speaks to God and "pours out one's heart" before him, is peculiar for the prayer of antiquity (Fr. Heiler, *Gebet*,[2-5] pp. 147f.). Here, the basic presupposition is that one can say something to God that could influence him. From this supposition comes the particular warmth of the Old Testament prayer that still moves and enthralls us.

Nevertheless, in certain passages in the complaint songs the perception of standing *before God* and speaking to God recedes somewhat while contemplation of speaking *about God* dominates for those praying. The same thing occurs in the individual complaints (§6, ¶25), as well as the communal complaints. In these cases one speaks of YHWH in the *third person*. This occurs when the more peaceful mood of *trust* enters the heart instead of fervent longing so that those praying actualize for the present what God will certainly accomplish (Pss 10:16; 125:1f; Mic 7:9-10; Lam 5:19; cf. ¶10). Or, this occurs when the last word contains the "affirmation of having been heard" after everything else that has been said in the poem (Pss. Sol. 9:11; 11:9; cf. ¶11). Also, instead of the "petition, "Help, YHWH," a less demanding form of address to God appears, namely, the "*wish*." The wish expresses that which one desires and hopes, and that which might be (¶8). This same kind of third person speech frequently appears in several other instances, including: when one portrays the *godless opponent* (Ps 10:4; Isa 26:10; Pss. Sol. 4:21); when one portrays the *enemy's speech* (Pss 83:13; 94:7; 115:2; ¶¶7, 9); when one recounts the doubting words of the innocent one (10:1); and, self-evidently, when one reports the divine *deeds of the past* (106:8; Pss Sol 9:1). Similar things happen in other cases. Sometimes, "he" stands in parallel with "you" (44:9; 125:5), or in the same context (10:4f; 68:32; 90:16f). All of this occurs in the individual complaint as well (§6, ¶25).

5. The song is sung by a plural "we," which is Israel. This "we" is characteristic of the communal complaint as compared to the individual complaint (§6). This use of "we" does not occur in Babylonian materials, as far as I am able to determine, even though many "complaint songs" occur there as well, also those addressing public crises. If this

observation holds true, it would be very important for conceptualizing a distinction between the Babylonian and Israelite religion. In Israel, a *community* exists as the *conveyer of the worship service*. There is no such phenomenon in Babylon, where the king also stands in the foreground of the religion. The same is true of the hymn (§2, ¶11). One finds this type of prayer spoken by a choir relatively infrequently among primitive peoples (Fr. Heiler, *Gebet*,[2-5] p. 56).

Following Joel 2:17, one may accept that in the Israelite form of performance these songs were performed originally by a *choir*, like the priests, in the name of the gathered community. Occasionally the poets chose a more lively form, in which they placed the prayer in the mouth of Zion (Mic 7:7-10), whereby reference to "your people" and "we" follows (cf. Pss 129:1-3; Pss. Sol. 1; Isa 40:27; 49:14; Jer 3:4f; 10:19-22; 31:18f; cf. E. Balla, *Ich der Psalmen*, 1912, pp. 114ff, and my essay, "Micha-Schluß," *Zeitschrift für Semitistik* 2 [1924]: 155f). This poetry, where the "I" = Zion, would have been voiced originally by an individual during the complaint festival. It would have been rather impressive when Zion appeared and spoke words of suffering and hope on the same day. It is also marvelously poetic when the tribal ancestress Rachel climbs out of her grave and is portrayed as lamenting (Jer 31:15). There must also have been a setting in which the *king* or the chief priest spoke such a prayer. Such was frequently the case in the Babylonian materials (cf. W. Schrank, *Babylonische Sühnrite*, 1908, see the index under "König also Büßer;" H. Zimmern, *Babylonische Hymnen und Gebete*, pp. 7f; H. Zimmern, *Babylonische Neujahrsfest*, 1926, pp. 4-6; A. Ungnad, *Religion der Babylonier und Assyrer*, 1921, pp. 207ff, 209ff, 212ff, 222; M. Jastrow, *Die Religion Babylon und Assur*, vol. 2, pp. 5ff, cites numerous examples.). Ps 20:5 also presupposes a prayer of this type. One of these royal complaints appears in 144:5-10 (cf. §5, ¶6). Prose prayers delivered by the king in times of public distress can be found in Isa 37:16-20; 2 Chr 14:10; 20:6-12. In earlier times, the leader of the people prayed in this manner (Josh 7:7-9). In later times, the high priest appeared in place of the ruler (3 Macc 2:1ff; cf. 2 Macc 1:23). Or, someone speaks for the community: a leader (Neh 9:6 [LXX?], 37; 1 Macc 4:30-33), the eldest (3 Macc 6:1), or a distinguished person (3 Macc 6:1ff; cf. Josh 7:6). Thus, already Naboth was placed at the head of the people on the day of festival, in order to express the celebratory petition (1 Kgs 21:9, 12). This form of prayer where the father of the family, the chief of the tribe, or the priest prays for his own, is already quite common among uncultured peoples (cf. Fr. Heiler, *Gebet*,[2-5] p. 54). The prophets took up this custom of public prayer at the complaint festival, and occasionally appeared as the one praying for the community (Isa 59:9-12; Jer 10:23-25; 14:2-9, 19-22; cf. Hab 1:2-4, 12-17). The "I" that appears alongside the "we" in the communal complaint is also explained in this setting: Israel's military leader prays (Ps 60:11); Ps 89:47-52 speaks of YHWH's anointed one (89:52) after the plural in 89:48, 51. According to the context, this speaker would be the one aspiring to the throne from the family of David, who must have taken a particular position in the worship of the Jewish community. The "I" that has created so many difficulties for commentators in several places is simply to be understood as the leader of the holy gathering: Pss 44:5, 7, 16; 68:25; 74:12; 83:14 (106:4). Cf. Ps 44:7 and §6, ¶3.

6. These complaint songs contain the cry of doubt and the cry for help of a tormented people whose own sacred perceptions have also been offended. It is a complaint so heart-rending and at the same time so lingering that it will perhaps never again be heard in the

world. The glowing breath of lamentation and supplication hit us in the face from these poems.

Thus, the *main categories* are provided into which these songs are divided (the same is true for the individual complaints): 1. a lamenting *complaint* over the misfortune; 2. a supplicational *petition* to YHWH to change the misfortune, whereby; 3. all types of thoughts appear in which one reproaches one's self for consolation or speaks before YHWH in order that he will hear and intervene. Sometimes the poet himself clearly distinguishes these parts. Thus, Pss 44:10-17 expresses the complaint, after which follows (in 44:18-23) the contemplations which YHWH should decide. The petition (44:24-27) closes the entire complaint. Similarly, Ps 89:39-46 contains the complaint, 89:47-50 contains the same contemplations provoking God; and 89:51f contains the petition. Ps 83:3-9 contains the complaint, and 83:10-19 contains the petition. Isa 33:2 contains the petition, 33:7-9 the complaint. Or, the entire poem is comprised almost exclusively of complaint (Lam 5) or petition (Sir 33:1-13; 36:16-22; cf. 2 Macc 1:24-29). Where the complaint begins the poem, an introductory petition tends to stand (a cry for help) at the beginning (Pss 12:2; 80:2f; 83:2; 94:1f; cf 74:2f), or conclude the poem (Jer 14:9). The latter also occurs in Babylonian royal prayers (H. Zimmern, *Babylonische Hymnen und Gebete*, p. 8; A. Ungnad, *Religion der Babylonier und Assyrer*, p. 209).

Sometimes, the complaints are not expressly spoken, but are implicitly included in the petition as in Sir 33:9, 11; 36:18; 2 Macc 1:24-29. The *reasons given for divine intervention* are almost always spoken at the point of the petition (cf. ¶10), or the complaint contains a form whose thoughts indirectly proceed to arouse God to come to the people's aid and to enflame God's anger against God's opponent (Pss 44:26; 74:1f, 10, 18; 79:1, 7; 89:39f; etc.; cf. ¶9).

7. The complaints contained in the communal complaint songs of the psalter are almost exclusively *political* in nature (44:10-17, 20, 23-25; 60:3-5, 12; 74:4-11; 79:1-4; 80:5-7, 13f; 83:3-9; 85:6; 89:39-46; 123:3f; cf. Isa 26:14a, 17f; 33:7-9; 40:27; 49:14; 63:17-19; 64:5f, 9f; Jer 10:25; 31:18; Hab 1:13-16; Lam 1:9f; 3:42-51; 5:2-18; Pr Azar 9f, 14f). Jer 14:2-6 complains about the lack of rain, and Joel 1:18-20 complains about a locust plague. Compare the Babylonian-Assyrian complaint songs with their extensive portrayals of general distress in P. Jensen *KB*, vol. 6/2, pp. 82ff. and in A. Ungnad, *Religion der Babylonier und Assyrer*, pp. 208f, 210f, 216, 222.

Canaan's soil was not very fertile and left many cases of misfortune. Plague was also not unknown. These psalms demonstrate that Israel was very politically involved, more so than it was concerned about these disasters. It perceived its unfortunate political fate from its longstanding lack of peace. Since the Assyrian period it had been ruled by one foreign power after another. Even Judaism in postexilic Jerusalem was only a small colony groaning under heavy pressure from the world empire, entangled in wars, and threatened on every side by ill-intentioned neighbors. The longer this lasted, the more splintered the people became. Scattered Jews lived throughout the entire Middle Eastern world. In addition, internal relationships were lamentable. These were not only addressed in communal complaints (Pss 10:2-11; 12:2f, 5; 94:3-7; cf. 125:5; Hab 1:2-4; Pss. Sol. 4), but understandably, even more in the individual complaint songs (cf. §6, ¶8). They are occasionally even addressed in the wisdom songs (cf. Ps 73:6-11) where the rich and the powerful are conceived has having fallen away from the religion and from the people. They are associated with the same status as the sojourners and the foreigners, and they profit ruthlessly from their power over the poor and the marginalized. And from there, the entire world of the time groaned under the mismanagement of the world empire (58:2-6).

From all of this harassment, the proud Jew obtained the distinct impression of having been delivered over to shame. They were accustomed to looking over the border to see what the neighboring countries were saying about them. Now, however, they were sickened by the thought that those neighboring countries were mocking them: "His name has become a shame and disgrace among the nations (cf. the commentary to Pss 44:14-17; see also 79:4, 10, 12; 80:7; 89:42, 51f; 115:2; 123:3f; Jer 31:19; Lam 1:9; 3:45f; Joel 2:17; 1 Macc 1:28; Pr Azar 10).

The pious ones perceived these distresses as both *moral and (especially) religious*. They were shocked to see the same play acted out everywhere: lies and falsehoods dominated the earth; the godless unashamedly killed widows and orphans; thieves and murderers lurked everywhere; blood was poured out like water (Ps 79:3); and no one received proper justice (58:2f; 94:5f). And YHWH allows all of this to happen. The communal complaint songs (as with the individual complaint songs, see §6, ¶8) love to present this whole terrible situation impressively, and to portray the actions of the wicked extensively (cf. also Ps 73). In so doing (see also §6, ¶8), they also place *speeches* in the mouths of the godless to explain their arrogant attitudes and their criminal plans (cf Pss 12:5; 14:1; 74:8; 83:5, 13; 94:7; cf. also 2:3). The fact that Israel's anger heavily colored these words against these people can be seen in the people's vehemence (cf. especially, 12:5). These speeches are portrayed as "sneering" and "slander" (Pss 74:10, 18; 75:5f; 79:4, 12; 123:4).

The political misfortune is particularly conceived as *religious distress*. It is YHWH's people whom the nations want to exterminate. They graze on YHWH's vine (83:4f). It is his name that the foolish people slander (74:18), his temple that is shamed (74:3ff; 79:1), his dwelling that is ruined (79:7), and his holy city that is destroyed (79:1).

In this situation, the people suffer under the belief that this misfortune reveals YHWH's wrath (60:3; 74:1; 79:5; 80:5; 85:6; 89:47; Isa 63:4; Jer 31:18; Lam 5:22). YHWH has "rejected" (74:1), "insulted" (44:10), "offended" (60:3), and "sold" Israel "like cattle" (44:12f). He forgets the "trouble and distress" of his people (44:25); "does not allow himself to see any longer" (89:47); "hides his face before his people" (44:25; Isa 64:6; cf. Ps 10:1); and "holds his right hand 'in the midst of' his breast" (74:11). He sleeps (44:24). Israel's path is hidden from him (Isa 40:27); and indeed it is slaughtered because of him (Ps 44:23). He has transferred control of the world to other divine beings who misuse that power (58:2f), and left the whole earth to godless power (Hab 1:13ff).

Thus, this belief increased the natural pain of the people. The terrible fate which they now experience contradicts that which they had confidently believed. For this reason, one constantly finds the apprehensive question "Why?" that characterizes the complaint songs (even the individual complaints, §6, ¶11): "*Why* should the heathen say, 'Now where is your god?'" (Pss 79:10; 115:2; Joel 2:17; Mic 7:10). "*Why* do you forget us forever?" (Lam 5:20); "*Why* do you cause us to stray from your ways?" (Isa 63:7; cf. also Pss 10:1, 13; 44:24f; 74:1, 11; 80:13; Exod 32:11; Josh 7:7; Judg 21:3; Isa 58:3; 63:17; Jer 14:8; Hab 1:13). In the Babylonian royal complaint songs, see A. Ungnad, *Religion der Babylonier und Assyrer*, p. 209.

Alongside this apprehensive "Why?" stands the impatient question, "How long?" "*How long* will the adversary slander?" (74:10); "*How long* will you continue to be angry?" (79:5); "*How long* will the wicked rejoice?" (94:3; cf. also 80:5; 89:47; 90:13; [also 85:6]). For the Babylonian royal complaints, cf. H. Zimmern, *Babylonische Hymnen und Gebete*, p. 8; M. Jastrow, *Religion Babyloniens und Assyriens*, vol. 2, pp. 16, 43, 109; A. Ungnad, *Religion der Babylonier und Assyrer*, pp. 210, 222. For those suffering so greatly, it seems as if the distress has been upon them for an eternity (cf. Pss 44:16, 23f; 74:1, 10, 19, 23; 77:8; 79:5; 85:6; 89:47; Lam 5:20; Jer 3:5; Hab 1:17). Occasionally one finds other questions of doubt (e.g., Isa 49:24).

8. The *petitions and wishes* to change the judgment correspond to the complaints, even in terms of the tenor of suffering. Also, YHWH is sometimes notably humanized, even for Israelite concepts: Pss 9:18-20; 10:12-15; 12:4; 44:24, 27; 58:7-12; 60:6f, 13; 74:2f, 18-23; 79:5-13; 80:2-4, 8, 15-20; 83:10-19; 85:5, 7f; 89:47-52; 90:13-15; 94:1f; 106:4f, 47; 115:1; 125:4f; 126:4; 129:5-8; Isa 26:11ff; 33:2; 37:17, 20; 51:9; 63:19ff; Jer 10:24f; 14:9, 21; Joel 2:17; Mic 7:14-17; Lam 5:21; Dan 9:16ff; Neh 1:6, 11; 9:32; 2 Chr 14:10; 1 Macc 4:31-33; 2 Macc 15:23f; 3 Macc 2:17ff; 6:9ff; Jdt 9:8ff; Add Esth 3:8-10; Pr Azar 11f, 19-21; Sir 33:1-13a; 36:16b-22; Pss Sol 4:6-8, 14-22; 7:1-8. In Babylonian royal complaints, cf. A. Ungnad, *Religion der Babylonier und Assyrer*, pp. 211f.

In Hebrew, the usual tense for what I call the petition is the *imperative*. The *jussive* is less common, and I call it the wish (cf. ¶4). Petitions (and one should include the negative forms using *'al* plus the jussive) include the following: "pay attention," "hear" (Ps 80:2; Isa 37:17); "look," "see" (Pss 74:20; 80:15; Isa 37:17; 63:15; 64:8; cf. Lam 1:9e, 11e, 20a; 2:20a; 5:1); "wake up" (Ps 44:24); "stand up," "raise yourself" (9:20; 10:12; 44:27; 74:22; 82:8; 94:2; Jer 2:27); "plead your case" (Ps 74:22); "appear" (80:2; 94:1); "don't forget" (10:12; 74:23); "think" (74:2, 18; 89:48, 51; 106:4; 137:7; Exod 32:13; Jer 14:21; Lam 5:1; Neh 1:8); "turn back" (Isa 63:17); "restore us" (Pss 80:4, 8, 15, 20; 85:5; Jer 31:18; Lam 5:21); "change our fate" (Ps 126:4); "visit" (106:4); "have compassion" (90:13; 123:3; Joel 2:17; Isa 33:2; Jer 2:27); "Let go of your wrath" (Exod 32:12; cf. Ps 85:5); "Do not reject forever" (Ps 44:24); "Do not be too angry" (Isa 64:8); "Do not remember our guilt forever" (Isa 64:8; cf Deut 9:27); "Forgive our sins" (Ps 79:9; cf. Jer 14:7); "Do not hold the iniquity of our ancestors against us" (Ps 79:8); "Let us see your grace" (85:8); "show your face" (80:4, 8, 20); "save" and "help us" (44:27; 79:9, 11; 106:47; cf. Jer 2:27). Apart from these petitions, one also finds terrible petitions against the heathens (68:31; 74:22f; 79:6, 12; 83:10-15, 17).

In addition to the petitions, one also finds the less common "*wish*" (or the curse) using the jussive. "Wishes" include: "May the wicked go to the underworld" (Ps 9:18a); "YHWH, cut off flattering lips" (12:4); "May sinners disappear from the earth" (104:35a). Other examples include: 68:30, 32a, 31c, 32b (compare the commentary); 74:21; 79:10cd, 11a; 83:16, 17b, 18f; 90:16f; 125:5; 129:5f; Mic 7:10, 14e; Lam 1:21f, 22a.

However, the petitions are far more prevalent. One usually finds wishes only as a continuation of the conclusion of the petition throughout (cf Pss 12:4; 74:21; 79:10cd, 11a; 83:18f; 90:16f; 104:34f; 125:5). Thus, the wish that the heathen will be shamed frequently stands at the conclusion of the poem (83:17f; 129:5; Mic 7:16; Pr Azar 21). "May they learn, YHWH, that you alone are God (1 Kgs 19:19; cf. also 59:14; 83:19; Sir 33:5; 36:22; Jdt 9:14; Pr Azar 22).

Sometimes, the prayer takes the more timid form of the interrogative sentence: "Will you revive us again? (Pss 85:7; cf. 60:11; Isa 63:11; 64:11; Jer 3:5; Hab 1:17; 2 Chr 20:12).

Even the piety of the individual is full of vehement desires. However, there were pious hearts who could renounce every great desire. The Jew can renounce for himself, but not for his people.

9. These laments and petitions seek to move YHWH's heart, and are thus spoken in a form that one hopes will accomplish this purpose. For this reason, the portrayals should stir YHWH with the entire community's *unceasing complaint* and *supplication* as well as the apprehension of the pious ones, even using images from nature: Pss 10:11; 44:26; 80:6; 123:2; Isa 26:8f; 33:7-9; 59:11; Jer 14:2-6; Joel 1:20; Lam 1:20f; 3:48-51; 5:14-17; 3 Macc 6:14. See 1 Macc 1:25-28 and the general whining in the Babylonian complaints in P. Jensen, *KB*, vol. 6/2, pp. 82f; A. Ungnad, *Religion der Babylonier und Assyrer*, pp. 208f. The same is true among primitive peoples (cf. Fr. Heiler, *Gebet*,[2-5] p. 89). Thus, YHWH is remonstrated over and over again that *this matter concerns* him, which is why the people constantly repeat: "your people," "your inheritance;" "your possession:" (Pss 74:2; 79:1; 83:4; 94:5; Deut 9:26; Isa 63:17; 64:8; Joel 2:17; Mic 7:14; Sir 36:17f; 3 Macc 6:3; Pss. Sol. 7:2); "your congregation" (74:2); the "sheep of your inheritance" (Mic 7:14); the "sheep of your meadow" (Ps 74:1); the "man of your right hand" (Ps 80:18); "your anointed" (89:39, 52); "your sanctuary" (Isa 63:18); "your holy throne (Jer 14:21). From the other side, they refer to "your enemy" (Pss 74:23; 83:3; etc.).

Thus, even in the complaint proper, that which concerns YHWH is not suppressed. To the contrary, it is intentionally accentuated *in order to irritate him* and to inflame his terrible wrath against his enemy. So Pss 74 and 79 begin with the destruction of the sanctuary and only thereafter speak of the suffering of the congregation (74:19-21; 79:2-4). For the same reason, the complaints also emphasize that the enemies do not just shame Israel, but that they also maliciously slander YHWH (cf. Pss 10:4, 13; 74:10, 23; 79:12; 83:3; 94:7; Isa 37:17). He could not listen contentedly to that! The complaint songs also tend to express the wicked words of the opponent (Pss 10:4, 6, 13; 12:5; 74:8; 83:5, 13; 94:7; 115:2; Exod 32:12; Deut 9:28f [¶4, 7]) with the expectation that their meaning would not be hidden from God!

10. The thoughts remaining in the background of these phrases are expressed explicitly relatively frequently. One then *reports all kinds of rationale for stirring divine intervention* (¶6), i.e., considerations which God will favorably ponder and then act (cf. ¶4). One thus presents the case to YHWH, that he must act *for the sake of his name*; that is, for his own honor (79:9; 115:1). "Why should the heathen say, 'Where is your God?' (79:10; 115:2)." See Jer 14:21; Pr Azar 11. "We are called by your name (Jer 14:9)." We are "clothed in your name (2 Chr 14:10)." "What will you do for your great name (Josh 7:9)." Give honor to your name (Ps 115:1; Pr Azar 20). "Because your name lives among us, we will find compassion (Ps 7:6)."

Or, one calls upon YHWH's grace (Pss 44:8; 115:1; Pr Azar 19; Pss. Sol. 7:5), or on the beautiful *past* when YHWH came to their aid, especially at the *exodus* and the conquest of Canaan (Pss 44:2-4; 74:2; 80:9-12; Isa 63:11-14; Mic 7:15; Exod 32:11; Deut 9:26; Neh 1:10; 9:7ff; 2 Chr 20:7; Sir 33:4). One calls on the *covenant and the promises* (Pss 89:50; 125:3; Jer 14:21; Mic 7:20; Exod 32:13; Neh 1:8f; Sir 36:20; Pr Azar 11-13; Pss. Sol. 7:10; 9:8-10). One also calls to YHWH with a statement about the close association with his people that YHWH created. "You are my king and my God (Pss 44:5; 74:12; cf. 2 Chr 14:10; Jer 31:18)." You are "Israel's hope" (Jer 14:8), "protector" (Pss Sol 7:7), and "father" (Isa 64:7). And they are "your servants" and "your people" (Deut 9:29; Neh 1:10;

cf. Pss. Sol. 9:8; and the performances of Isa 63:19; 26:13), the "sheep of your field" (Ps 79:13), the "work of your hands" (Isa 64:7). It is impossible that YHWH will forget this grace that he has demonstrated to his people. He cannot act differently than in the past. He cannot break the covenant or take back the promises!

They can also hope to rouse divine compassion by portraying their *own helplessness*. "We are so weak (Ps 79:8; Pr Azar 14)," "so transitory" as humans (Ps 89:48f), and so utterly dependent on your grace (Isa 64:7). Also, God would favorably welcome statements that *help* comes only *from him* who alone is God and apart from whom there is no aid (Ps 60:13; Isa 37:16; Jer 3:23; 14:22; 2 Chr 14:10; 20:6; Sir 33:5).

YHWH could not refuse the petition of his people when it assured him that they *relied entirely on him and his compassion*, not on sword and bow, nor on their own righteousness (Pss 10:14; 33:20-22; 44:7f; Dan 9:18; cf. Jer 14:8; Pss. Sol. 7:6-9; 9:10). YHWH could not refuse the petition of his people when they reported to him that he was the holy and pure God who could not look on the wrong that had now befallen Israel (Hab 1:12f). Though these words were spoken, sometimes in archaic style, with the parallel intention of affecting God; nevertheless, one cannot fail to recognize that genuine religious feeling resonates within them as well. Sometimes, only this feeling is expressed. The pious heart is aware of its own confidence, and is strengthened by the fact that it is powerfully expressed. We can label these confident outpourings "words of comfort," especially those that speak about YHWH in the third person (cf . ¶4). One example would be Ps 125:1-3; cf. 126:5f; Hos 6:1-3). The same holds true for the individual complaint song (§6, ¶19).

Occasionally, the affirmation becomes so prominent in the prayers that the complaint, which is normally the chief characteristic of the genre, is silenced completely, thereby expressing only the petition and the affirmation. We have labeled these poems "psalms of confidence" (Ps 125; Mic 7:7-10; Pss. Sol. 7; cf. 2 Chr 14:10). Similar things occur in the individual complaint song (§6, ¶27).

Frequently, all kinds of gruesome images of ruin (Ps 58:7-10) are added to the curse of the enemy, with *examples of horrifying divine judgment* from the past (Pss 83:10-12; 1 Macc 4:30; 2 Macc 15:22; 3 Macc 2:4-8; 6:4-8; Jdt 9:2-4). These renderings may have originally been conceived as an "analogy to magic." Naming the ancient name should arouse the ancient power. In the transmitted texts, however, they serve the higher goal of reminding God of his own power and strengthening the confidence of those praying.

The rationale for instigating divine intervention also includes the fact that the people penitently confess their own sin and implore YHWH's compassion. Mentioning one example is not very difficult among the Israelites, as with the ancient Middle East in general. Israel is convinced from the outset that its misfortune must be pronounced to the divinity when any type of injustice or oversight is experienced (cf. §6, ¶5). One may thus accept that this confession of sin was a typical component of the complaint song (Ps 79:8f; Lam 1:18, 20; 3:42). This confession clearly occurs (1 Sam 7:6) in the ceremonies of the genre (cf. ¶2). The prophets have taken up these "songs of confession," albeit from a much higher standpoint. They knew nothing of a stuffy and shy self-cringing attitude under the violent fate. Rather, they possessed the moral recognition that this people, whose sins the prophets knew all too well, had deserved the righteous punishment of God. The prophets composed this kind of confessional prayer both as the one praying and, because of their great privilege, as the intercessor for their people (Isa 59:12f; 64:4, 6, 8; Jer 14:7, 20; Mic 7:9). It is particularly moving when the prophets voice such a prayer *for the future*. With tears of longing in their eyes, the prophets think of the time when Israel's hard heart will become soft, and when the people will finally finally find their way back to their God. The prophets even sing the song that implores the compassion of YHWH (Hos 6:1-3; 14:3f; Jer 3:22-25; 31:19). They influence a portion of the prayers of Judaism. Compare the professions of guilt and the "general confessions" (Ps 106; 1 Kgs 8:47; Dan 9:5ff; Ezra 9:6ff; Neh 1:7; 9:16ff; Bar 1:15ff; Pr Azar 6f; 4 Ezra 3; 4ff). This prophetic influence must have first occurred during the exile and then later become the dominant mood (Lam 1:18, 20; 3:42; Mic 7:9; Ps 106; 1 Kgs 8:47). Beginning in this period, the prophets (especially Ezekiel) also influenced the idea of theodicy which became one of the main ideas of such "confessions." We alone bear the guilt for all the current misfortune, for YHWH, who has struck us so hard, has no guilt. He remains unpunishable (Lam 1:18; [Isa 59:1; Deut 32:4]; Ezra 9:15; Neh 9:33; Dan 9:7, 14; Pr Azar 4, 10; Bar 1:15; 2:6; Pss. Sol. 2:15ff; 8:7ff; 9:2).

It is even more apparent that the majority of the communal complaints transmitted in the psalter do not know the moods of remorse and repentance. Ps 44 even argues passionately against this idea (cf. 44:18-23). May we, from this fact, only see a sign of Jewish self-righteousness from the age of law, or should we infer that which is not intended, a firm characteristic of the people of that time? Can they judge themselves independently of their cruel fate, thereby rejecting the confession of guilt that was customary in this ancient context? The same parallel between psalms of repentance and innocence also exists in the "individual complaint songs" (§6, ¶26). The confession of innocence from the Babylonian king on the fifth of Nisan can be found in H. Zimmern, *Babylonische Neujahrsfest*, p. 12: "I have not sinned, o Lord of the Lands, I was not negligent toward your divinity." (etc.)

11. It is customary to express complete "certainty of having been heard" at the end of the complaint: Pss 10:16-18; 12:8f; 60:14; 79:13; 126:5f; Mic 7:19f; Pss. Sol. 7:8, 10; 9:11; 11:9. Not infrequently, the petition flows into these thoughts. From the hearing of the prayer, may all the world recognize YHWH's greatness. Then the enemies will be ashamed and YHWH's pious ones will rejoice over his power (Pss 9:21; 10:18; 58:11f; 106:47; Isa 37:20; 1 Macc 4:33; 2 Macc 1:27; 3 Macc 2:20; 6:15; Add Esth 3:10). Cf. Also ¶8 and the prayer of the Babylonian high priest: "for this reason, they proclaim your renown . . . ; praise your name" [in H. Zimmern, *Babylonische Neujahrsfest*, p. 6]). As this happens, then the poems occasionally conclude with an explicit *vow*. Someday the delivered will honor YHWH full of rejoicing because of his help (Pss 20:6; 21:14; 79:13; 80:19; 144:9f; cf. Hos 14:4). A similar movement occurs in the individual complaint songs (§6, ¶24).

Thus, the complaint song, which began so lamentingly, ends with the tone of rejoicing certainty. Those praying have run the gamut from deep anxiety, even despair, to the full height of certainty that YHWH lives and helps. This presents a beautiful image for every true prayer. Since one finds similar elements at the end of the individual complaint, and since it is probable that the "certainty of being heard" goes back to an oracle expressed at the end (cf §6, ¶23), then one should suppose that the same thing happens here. In support of this supposition, one can mention that the portraits of the future that appear in this position are sometimes related to prophetic predictions (Ps 10:16f; cf. §9).

12. From the preceding discussion, it is clear that the communal complaints are quite similar to the "*individual complaint songs*" in their outline and in many details, even

though there are also strong deviations that are explained by the nature of the material. In the communal complaints, the "we" takes the lead role, while the "I" does so in the individual songs. The one complains about national distress, while the other complains about individual distresses, especially illness. For the one, anger over the neighboring people's ridicule is characteristic, while for the other it is the image of the trip into the underworld (§6, ¶5). Cf. E. Balla, *Ich der Psalmen*, pp. 69f.). See ¶5 concerning Zion as "I," where communal poetry borrowed from poetry of the individual (cf. §6, ¶2).

On the other hand, at times the individual and communal poetry stand in relationship to one another. The prayer of 2 Macc 1:24-29 was, according to 1:23, spoken antiphonally by Jonathon and the priests, together with the people. Also, it was not just the king, the leader, or the man of God (¶1, 2, 5, 10) who turned to God in times of public distress. Rather, the common man felt so deeply about the fate of the homeland, that he naturally turned to his God (cf. Ezra 9; Neh 1:5-11; Jdt 9:2-14; Pr Azar; Add Esth 3:1ff, 14ff). It is only a small step from leading a prayer to an intercessory prayer like Moses and the prophets practiced. One also finds traces of such in the psalms. In Ps 137:7-9, a true adherent of Zion hurls a curse at the one who destroyed his homeland. In Ps 102, the psalmist complains about his own suffering and the curse of his days (102:2-12), and comforts himself with the certainty of Zion's glorious future (102:13-23). In Ps 77, the poet muses over the sad fact that God has left his people. In so doing, the poet takes up motifs from the communal complaints. Ps 94 connects complaints and petitions in common social (94:1-7) and personal torment (94:16-23). In reverse order, the poet of Ps 123 speaks first of himself and then concludes using "we" with other pious ones (123:2-4). Cf. also Pss. Sol. 2:22-25; 5. In the acrostic poem of Lam 3, the author placed a complaint about the suffering of his people (3:40-51) together with his own complaints and petitions. This association of components of public and private complaint songs also occurs frequently in the Babylonian material (cf. M. Jastrow, *Die Religion Babylon und Assur*, vol. 2, pp. 29f). Several songs of individual poets have been supplemented at the end with intercession for the ruler for the performance in the royal temple of Jerusalem (cf. Pss 28:8f; 61:7f; 63:12a; 84:9f; 1 Sam 2:10d, e; cf. §5, ¶2). The association of different genres, public and private, appears to be quite inorganic, including a communal complaint within the alphabetic poem of Ps 9 and 10 (cf. 9:18-10:18).

The hymns (§2) stand in stark contrast to the communal complaint songs. The latter contain apprehensive lamentation, while the former contain spellbinding rejoicing and happiness. The piety of the people contained in the psalms that is expressed simultaneously in these two genres must have resolved powerful internal contradictions. Both, however, demonstrate a passion that tends to go to the extremes, a characteristic of Israel and of Judaism generally.

It is characteristic of the emotional power of that time, however, that precisely these two genres have attracted each other (§2, ¶55). Such poetry sustains the starkest contrasts; indeed, it even seeks them out intentionally. The poets of Israel did not cautiously dilute the colliding of the enthusiastic faith expressed by the hymns, with the suffering reality which the communal complaint songs lament. Rather, the clash was strengthened in order to assail God more urgently. Thus, for example, the "summons" of the communal complaint (¶4) is expanded by all kinds of *honorific titles* for the divinity that bear a hymnic form, until it results in the entire first section of the poem that represents a hymn: Ps 80:2; 1 Kgs 8:23f; Isa 37:16; Jer 14:8; 32:17-22; Hab 1:12f; Neh 1:5; 9:6-15; Dan 9:4;

Pr Azar 3-5; Add Esther 3:2-4; 1 Macc 4:30; 2 Macc 1:24f; 3 Macc 2:2; 6:2; Pss Sol 17:1-3; 4 Ezra 8:20-23; Bar 21:4-17; 48:2-10. The same happens occasionally in the royal complaint songs (Ps 144:1f) and in the "individual complaint songs (Jer 17:12f; Pr Man 1-7; Tob 3:2, 11; Pss Sol 5:1). Even Babylonian complaint songs very frequently begin with a hymnic introduction (cf. M. Jastrow, *Die Religion Babylon und Assur*, vol. 2, pp. 3ff for numerous examples; cf. also Fr. Stummer, *Sumerischen-akkadischen Parallelen*, pp. 11ff). Sometimes, these honorific titles proceed with a particularly celebratory form of address from the mention of the divine name (Ps 80:2ff; cf. 94:1f), as also occurs in the Babylonian material (Fr. Stummer, pp. 16ff). For these mixtures, cf. W. Baumgartner, *Klagegedichte des Jeremia*, pp. 41, 82; *Genesis-Kommentar*,[3-5] p. 358. This practice would originally have intended to put the deity in a favorable mood toward the one praying, or indeed to flatter the deity. However, it corresponds to a higher stage of respect that one perceives before YHWH. Before one considers coming before him with petitions, one should praise him. This praise song simultaneously places divine power impressively in view. It thus includes a strong element of trust. The powerful and gracious God will even hear this prayer. So the royal complaint of Ps 144:1-10 begins with a hymn (144:1-2), which praises God's help in the past. Ps 44 starts with a hymn-like narrative, which justifies the complete trust in YHWH's help (44:5-9), which then stands in shocking contrast to the lamenting complaint that follows. In Pss 80 and 74, the hymn-like narratives paint such a different picture compared to the sad poem, and are placed in the middle of the poem (cf. 80:9-12; 74:12-17). In Ps 89, a later independent hymn (89:2, 3, 6-19) served as the foundation for a more comprehensive composition that culminates in complaint and petition. Ps 115 contrasts a word of slander from the heathen (115:2), a hymn to YHWH (115:3), and a related speech mocking idols (115:4-8). This combination of an entire hymn first became typical in the later period, especially in prose prayers (§2, ¶55). Earlier, it was common in Babylonian materials. This suggests that the literature of Israel was again influenced by the Babylonian in the later period (cf. Fr. Stummer, *Journal of the Society of Oriental Research* 8 [1924]: 131). Sometimes a hymnic speech stands at the end of the complaint song (Mic 7:18; Lam 5:19; cf. Pss. Sol. 8:34). While in all of these cases, the hymn stands in stark contrast to the lamentation and supplication of the complaint song, in Ps 106 (a general confession of Israel), the hymn serves the purpose of appropriately introducing the whole with a praise of YHWH (106:1-3). Isa 63:7 begins similarly, in hymnic form, only to continue with a communal complaint (63:11c-64:11).

13. In later times, *different productions conclude* relatively frequently with *petitions* that derive from communal complaints. Examples include: the "*communal song of thanksgiving*" (§2, ¶41) in Ps 129 (cf. 129:5-8); the "*psalm of confidence*" (¶10) in Ps 123 (cf. 123:3f); the *prophetic poetry* (§9) in Pss 53; 82; Pss. Sol. 11 (cf. 53:7; 82:8; Pss Sol 11:8f); the *historical summary* in Ps 106 (cf. 106:47), Pss. Sol. 9 (cf. 9:8-11). The same is true for *the hymns* of Ps 33 (cf. 33:20-22) and 104 (cf. 104:35). One poem, Ps 90, woven together by hymnic and general complaint attitudes has been expanded by a communal complaint (cf. 90:13-17). In Ps 115, a larger liturgical composition begins with these echoes (cf. 115:1f).

In a late period in the history of the Psalms (cf. §12), the transformation of the *dirge* is conducted with several motifs of the communal complaint, as transpires in Lam 1, 2, and 4 which H. Jahnow has exquisitely described (*Hebräisches Leichenlied*, 1923, [cf. the subject index under "Königspsalmen]). This type of melding is all the more noteworthy since the dirge and complaint are a world apart in terms of their type (cf. ¶2). On the other hand, both genres do have a certain, distant relationship that dominates the complaints. Moreover, the dirge normally concerns the *death of an individual*, but in Lamentations it is related to Zion's misfortune. Thus, it has been filled with political elements, thereby coming closer to the communal complaint. Thus, several elements, which were originally characteristic of the communal complaint, found their way into Lamentations. The element in which YHWH is occasionally the subject was normally not possible in the dirge (cf. 1:5c, 12e, 13-15, 17f; 2:1-9, 17-19, 21f; 4:11, 16). This reference to YHWH is clear in the "*summons*" using his name (1:9e, 11e, 20a; 2:20a); the *petition* to him to look upon Zion's suffering and to listen to its moaning (1:9e, 11e, 20e, 21a; 2:20a); the "curse" of the enemies (1:21f, 22a [¶8]) with the *petition* against them (1:22b); the *confession of sin* (1:18b, 20d; 4:6, 13) combined with the theodicy (1:18a [¶10]); and finally, several of the complaints proper follow the subject of the communal complaint more closely than the dirge (cf. especially 1:9f, 20a, b, c, 21a). In this manner, the originally *secular* genre of the dirge has been transformed into a *religious* poem (H. Jahnow).

14. The communal complaint has a close relationship to the *oracle*. Anyone unfamiliar with Hebrew thought patterns may not easily recognize the relationship with the oracle since it appears fairly infrequently. However, for anyone who is knowledgeable, it appears quite natural. The God who was addressed in the complaint song responds in the oracle to the lamentation of his people (cf., "Micha-Schluß," pp. 161f; "Jesaja 33," *ZAW* 42 [1924]: 194f). We have already noticed that it was customary to consult YHWH during the festival (Judg 20:23, 27; cf. ¶2). The saga tells about the oracle that ensued from the sanctuary (Judg 20:23, 28). We hear something similar in the saga of Joshua, who complains about the destitute condition of Israel. He prays and receives a response to his prayer (Josh 7:7f). Similarly, we also see this in the legend of the Chronicler. The king arranges a fast during a time of war, and expresses the complaint prayer himself. An Asaphite responds inspired by YHWH, and proclaims divine help (2 Chr 20:3ff). Likewise, YHWH's oracle responds to Hezekiah's prayer through Isaiah (2 Kgs 19:14ff, 20ff). During the communal fast arranged by Jehoiakim, Jeremiah had instructed Baruch to read YHWH's word aloud (Jer 36). Joel provides the communal complaint that the priests were to cry aloud on the festival day in response to the locust plague. Immediately thereafter, he narrates the gracious promises that YHWH had spoken in response (2:18ff). Habakkuk sings Israel's complaint song in a time of great distress, and then reports how he received an oracle of consolation afterward (1:12f; 2:1ff). According to the transmitted text in Daniel 9, the man of God prays a long confessional prayer for his people until an angel appeared to him and communicated the key to the future. Thus, we may visualize that, according to Israelite custom, when a communal complaint was finished, the voice of the priest or another representative of God would be raised in response to the humiliated people. It is thus all the more shocking, and a sure sign of God's wrath, when the oracle is omitted (Ps 74:9).

The Babylonian custom corresponds to the Israelite custom, in which an oracle promising salvation is affixed to the royal complaint song. For examples, see H. Zimmern, *Babylonische Hymnen und Gebete*, p. 8; vol. 2, pp. 20f; *Babylonisches Neujahrsfest*, p. 12; J. Pinckert, *Hymnen und Gebete an Nebo*, pp. 17ff. The same holds true for Egyptian custom, see A. Erman and H. Ranke, *Agypten*, p. 467. The evangelical liturgies offered in the name of the congregation on the day of confession are also quite similar. There the pronouncement of the forgiveness of sins by the clergy tends to follow the confession. The Israelite prophets took up this custom and formed "liturgies" (§11). In these liturgies, the complaint of the people is expressed first, then the deity's voice begins to promise salvation for the end time. This vision of the future sounds all the more majestic since it stands out dramatically against the dark background of the congregation's mourning and supplication. It thunders all the more powerfully in the ears of the people when the prophetic response does not speak of YHWH's grace, as expected, but of his wrath. We find this connection between communal complaint and oracle in Isa 26:8-14a, 14bf; 26:16-18, 19-21; 32:2, 3-6; 33:7-9, 10-12; 49:14, 15ff; 49:24, 25f; 59:9-15b, 15c-20; 63:7-64:11; 65; Jer 3:22b-25; 4:1f; 14:2-9, 10; 14:19-22; 15:1f; 31:18f, 20; 51:34f, 36ff; Hos 6:1-3, 4-6; 14:3f, 5-9; Mic 7:7-10, 11-13; 7:14-17, 18-20; Hab 1:2-4, 5ff; 1:12-17; 2:1ff; cf. also Joel 1:5-2:11 with the oracle in 2:12-14; and 2:15-17 with 2:18-27. See also Zions dirge and complaint in Bar 4:9-29 with the oracle in 4:30ff. A complicated connections of the two pieces is found in Isa 40:27-31, where Israel's cry of pain (40:27c, d) is cited in the prophet's consolation speech. It should be noted that this combination of complaint and oracle often repeats twice in succession (cf. "Micha-Schluß," pp. 171f; "Jesaia 33," pp. 199f). The same combination occurs in the individual complaints §6, ¶28).

These "liturgies" are also received in the *Psalms*. The royal song in Ps 20 first contains intercession for the ruler, followed by an oracle. Likewise, prayer and oracle stand alongside one another in Ps 132 as it would have been performed in the royal temple of Jerusalem. In Ps 60 an oracle is framed by a complaint, whose occasion is an unfortunate military campaign. Here, we have liturgies before us that flow from the life of Israel. By contrast, Pss 12; 85; and 126 *are imitations of prophetic liturgies*. In Ps 12, a soothing oracle follows an angry communal complaint (12:2-5). This oracle states that the time of salvation has now arrived (12:6), after which a hymn-like speech closes the entire psalm. Ps 85 begins powerfully with an oracle (85:2-4) after which the community responds with longing (85:5-8). This longing is then again resolved with an enthusiastic oracle (85:9-14). Ps 126 is simpler. It begins with an oracle (126:1-3) and continues in the tone of the communal complaint (126:4-6). Also in Pss. Sol. 17, the prayer of the people concerning the messiah (17:21-25) gradually gives way to the divine promise about him (in 17:26ff). The dependence of these liturgies on the prophetic liturgies is recognized by their prophetic content and by the fact that they speak about the end time (cf. §9; §11). The distinctive attractive beauty of the majority of these liturgies is recognized in the fact that both ends of the pendulum, between which the piety of that circle swings, are expressed in the same poem. They swing between the lamentation of the present and the enthusiastic hope for the future, feeling both with the same passion. The result is that the same poem truly and comprehensively discloses the entire spiritual life. In the future, may these liturgies receive their due since to this point they have seldom been recognized as such, nor understood.

15. As we have described them, communal complaint songs were performed by Israel *from the earliest period* (cf ¶2) *through the latest period*. The faith expressed in them is on the whole already the faith of ancient Israel. It is a faith which clings to God in every distress, and a piety which was particularly nurtured in the circles of the salvific prophets and which Judaism fulfilled. As a result, the same poems were updated and revised repeatedly, which explains the characteristic *imprecise tone* of almost all of these songs. To be precise about this characteristic, one should be clear that these compositions are not

so much those of an individual poet flowing from a unique situation as they are formulas that were repeatedly reused in new situations, with perhaps very little change. The same is true for Babylonian poetry (M. Jastrow, *Die Religion Babylon und Assur*, vol. 2, pp. 10f, 61f, 116; cf. §1, ¶4).

Of course, this formulaic repetition explains why *determining the chronology* of these psalms is so extraordinarily difficult. First, it is conceivable the material transmitted to us in the psalter perhaps belongs completely to the *postexilic* period. This transmitted material persisted as that which was most preferred and most usable at the time of the collection. Ps 80 stems from the area of the earlier Northern tribes. Lam 5 may have been sung during one of the festivals at the ruins of Jerusalem, like the ones mentioned in Zech 7. Ps 106 is its antithesis from the east. Ps 89 was performed in the name of the Jewish aspirant to the throne in the Jerusalem community. Ps 83 speaks of the attacks of all the neighboring nations. Ps 125 speaks ambiguously of the "scepter of wickedness," meaning the sinful dominion of the ruling empire. Pss 74 and 79 (cf. Ps 44) are related to specific events (perhaps the same or similar ones to which Isa 63:18; 64:9f; and Joel 4:3f refer). In these events the temple is desecrated and burned, Jerusalem is in great danger, and the people suffer "for the sake of YHWH." Recent commentators usually think of the Maccabean religious persecution for these and other poems. However, our knowledge of this late period of Judaism is so full of holes that this assignation must remain dubious. Several observations also speak against this date, and the possibility that Pss 44; 74; 79; and 83 belong within the time of Ezra to Alexander the Great must remain open (cf. the commentary to these psalms). How imprecisely we can really determine these psalms can also be seen in Ps 60 where an older oracle (stemming from the time of the downfall of the Assyrian empire, at the earliest) was later taken up on the occasion of a flight to Edom after a defeat. We are completely in the dark as to when these events might have occurred and why they were reworked in Ps 108.

§5 Royal Psalms

"Königspsalmen," *Preußischen Jahrbücher* 158 (1914), pp. 42ff — H. Greßmann, *Der Ursprung der israelitisch-jüdischen Eschatologie*, 1905, p. 250 — S. Mowinckel, *Psalmenstudien*, vol. 2, 1922, pp. 299ff.

1. We consider the following in this group: Pss 2; 18; 20; 21; 45; 72; 101; 110; 132; 144:1-11; cf. 89:47-52.

Confusion regarding the meaning of these psalms is extraordinarily great (cf. ¶26). We will attempt to bring clarity to the whole, not by observing them in isolation as has generally occurred until now, but by explaining them in the context they share. We will also compare them with similar material from the other psalms and the rest of the Old Testament, as well as the Babylonian-Assyrian and Egyptian writings.

2. The internal unity of the above mentioned psalms stems from the fact that they are *concerned entirely with kings*. Since kings ruled Israel for centuries, one can accept that these poems relate to those kings. First, we suggest that they relate to Judean rulers since the psalter stems from Jewish hands. We will depart from these presuppositions only in cases where significant ideas to the contrary emerge.

A preliminary glance at the *designations referring to the ruler in these psalms* confirms the appropriateness of our assumption. He is called: "the king" (Pss 20:10; 21:2, 8; 45:2, 6, 12; 72:1); the "son of the king" (72:1); "YHWH's king" (2:6; 18:51); "YHWH's anointed" ([2:2]; 18:51; 20:7; 89:52; 132:10); "YHWH's servant" (89:51). He resides in Zion ([2:6]; 20:3; 110:2; 132:13); "YHWH's city" (101:8). His ancestor is David ([18:51]; 89:50; 132:10, 17; 144:10). His God is YHWH in all of the psalms. His people are called: "Jacob" (20:2); YHWH's people (72:2). In several of the songs the king himself appears in order to speak (Pss 2; 18; 101; 132:1-10; 144:1-11; cf. also 89:47-52). At the conclusion of these passages, according to Hebrew custom (cf. the commentary to Ps 18:51), the "I" who is speaking designates himself as "YHWH's king" (18:51); his "servant" (89:51); and anointed (18:51; 89:52; 132:10); and counts himself among "the kings" (144:10). The duties which he is praised for fulfilling in Ps 101 are the duties of a ruler.

We reach the same conclusion from the *intercession for the ruler* which has been added to several poems of a pious individual (cf. ¶10), including: Pss 28:8f; 61:7f; 63:12a; 84:9f; 1 Sam 2:10d, e. In these psalms, the ruler is called the "king" (Pss 61:7; 63:12a), YHWH's king (1 Sam 2:10), and YHWH's anointed (Pss 28:8; 84:10; 1 Sam 2:10). He sits on the throne "before YHWH" (61:8). His people are YHWH's people and inheritance (28:8f). He is "our" (meaning Israel's) "shield" (84:10). Cf. the commentary to Ps 28:8f.

If we probe all of these psalms as a group, the above-mentioned references lead us to conceptualize *reigning native kings*. Their Davidic ancestry argues against relating them to the ruler of a foreign power and against interpreting them as Maccabean rulers. Their residence in Zion also argues against the explanation of a foreign ruler. Intercessions that are only understandable for the present ruler argue against an interpretation as the messiah. See further discussion in ¶26.

We can already determine at this point that Ps 45 apparently stems from the Northern Kingdom (cf. ¶20, 25), while Ps 89:47-52 is ascribed to the descendent to the throne from the house of David following the collapse of the state (cf. ¶20, 25).

3. Our task is now to seek the *life setting* of the royal psalms. First, we should look at the many celebrations that are organized by the Israelite kings. Every village in antiquity and in the present holds festivals designed to present the splendor and majesty of the kingdom (Esth 1:4). They do so in order to make the boredom of life more bearable for so many idle people who flock before the ruler. We hear relatively little about these festivals in the Old Testament historical books. We can deduce additional information about them from the royal psalms. The *enthronement* of the new ruler began quite festively, as we recognized from the references in the historical books as well as in the poems about YHWH's enthronement (§3, ¶2, 5). The sound of the trumpet rings far and wide across the country. "He has become king!" Songs that praise the ruler are sung at the festal *royal table* (1 Sam 25:36; 2 Sam 9:10ff; 19:36; 1 Kgs 5:2f). We even hear explicitly that the voice of the male and female singers would have been a delight at the royal meal (2 Sam 19:36). In addition, there may have been *special festivals*, like the birthday of the ruler or the anniversary of his taking power, that would have resounded with jubilation (Hos 7:5; Pss 21; 72). Another celebration is the marriage of the prince (Ps 45).

Other days have a *clearly religious* meaning. David's *transferring the ark* to Zion (2 Sam 6:5, 15) and Solomon's *temple dedication* (1 Kgs 8) initiated a great festival. Ps 132 allows one to deduce a festival that was dedicated to the *founding of the royal house and its sanctuary* (cf. Also Ps 78:68-72). The day *when the king went to war* was also begun in celebration (Pss 20; 144:1-10; cf. 1 Sam 13:9ff; 2 Chr 14:10; 20:4ff), as well as the day he returned crowned in victory, and safe from all danger (cf. Ps 18, especially 18:33-49; 20:6; 68:18f). He returned while young women beating drums in the midst of singers and musicians came to meet him (cf. Ps 68:25f; see the commentary for the text). The history of Saul talks about these *celebrations of victory*. It also provides a song that was sung on such occasions (1 Sam 18:6f; cf. also 1 Sam 15:15). They would undertake *acts of atonement* (§6, ¶4) during severe illness of the ruler or a member of his house (cf. occasions like those in 2 Sam 12:16; 2 Kgs 20), and the great *thanksgiving celebrations* when God had healed the illness (cf. ¶6). It is also self-evident that upon the death of the king, a prince or one of the dignitaries would conduct a *dirge* in his honor. These are portrayed for us in 1 Sam 31:13; 2 Sam 1:12; 3:31ff; 1 Kgs 14:18; Jer 34:5; 2 Chr 16:14; 21:19; 35:25. Dirges that have been preserved that would have been sung in this context include:1 Sam 1:17ff; 2 Sam 3:33f, as well as those imitated by the prophets Isa 14; Ezek 19; 27; 28:11f; 32.

The "house of David" had a particularly honored role in postexilic complaint festivals (Zech 12:12). The complaint of the descendant of David in Ps 89:47ff should be understood in this context.

4. We can find additional confirmation that we are developing the image properly from the fact that similar celebrations took place in the Assyrian court. As is natural, the Assyrian king, as well as the Egyptian Pharaoh (cf. §3, ¶2), experienced a festival at his *enthronement*. He enjoyed himself when sitting and drinking wine in his wine arbor with his court band. Cf. the well-known image of Ashurbanipal in H. Greßmann, *Altorientalische Texte und Bilder*, 1927, vol. 2, illustrations 148f. He experienced festivals at the *completion of palaces and canals*, and at the *dedication of a new residence or fort*. He

organized festivities in the *palace of defeated rulers*, and returned home after a *successfully completed military campaign*. He entered the capital city at the head of his troops in a triumphant parade to singing and playing. If, however, the ruler passes away, a great *mourning festival* takes place, which would have to include the song of mourning. Cf. E. Klauber, *Assyrisches Beamtum*, 1910, pp. 15ff; Br. Meißner, *Babylonien und Assyrien*, vol. 1, 1920, pp. 64f, 71, 79, 331. We also hear of a celebratory reception at the border following a victorious campaign (cf. A. Wiedmann, *Das Alte Ägypten*, p. 61).

Regarding *days of complaint* during national crisis, e.g., an enemy threat or illness of the ruler when he sings the complaint song himself, see M. Jastrow, *Die Religion Babylon und Assur*, vol. 1, p. 442; vol. 2, pp. 5ff; and W. Schrank, *Babylonische Sühnrite*, 1908, pp. 36n.1, 46, 48, 49, 51, etc. Ritual instructions for the king's atonement prayer can be found in P. Jensen, *KB*, vol. 6/2, pp. 56ff. For the king's thanksgiving songs from the *victory celebration*, or after *healing* occurred, see §7, ¶11. An illustration of Assyrian *royal sacrifice* accompanied by music can be seen in Br. Meißner, *Babylonien und Assyrien*, vol. 1, illustration 48.

We have other reports of the courtly festivities of foreign rulers preserved in the occasional references in the *Old Testament*. There we hear that the pharaoh tended to celebrate his *birthday* with a pardon (Gen 40:20). We learn that the Chaldean ruler had a mighty statue dedicated with the participation of the whole empire, in which the moment of celebration was marked with music (Dan 3). We learn that Belshazzar gave a *festive meal* where songs were sung (Dan 5), and that the Persian king celebrated his enthronement (Esth 1).

Repeatedly we learn that which also proceeds from the material composed for us; namely, that singing and music played a major role at all of these festivities. There were also professional singers at the ancient Indian courts (cf. J. Hertel, *Indische Märchen*, 1921, p. 221n.1). In a letter (printed in the "*Berliner Tageblatt*," 13 [1903], p. 5) king Menelik of Abysinnia had one of the court poets sing for himself and his guests at the court table during dessert. And even a nephew of the great Babylonian king *Narâm-Sin* did not think himself too refined to exercise the office of a harpist for the god *Sin* (cf. Br. Meißner, *Babylonien und Assyrien*, vol. 1, p. 332).

5. It is crucial to recognize that royal psalms *were performed at some type of court festivity*. We do not need to look much further for their poets and singers. They were members of the royal band about which we have already spoken (cf. Also Ps 45:9; Qoh 2:8). The court singers of Jerusalem were famous as demonstrated by the Assyrian report in which Senacherib included the temple choir among the fineries he demanded from Hezekiah (cf. E. Ebeling in H. Greßmann, *Altorientalische Texte und Bilder*,[2] 1926, p. 354). The extent to which the pleasant craft of making music was held in high esteem can also be seen in the fact that even the kings themselves were not ashamed to appear as singers. David was Israel's greatest poet, and Solomon himself delivered a dedicatory speech at the temple dedication (cf. 1 Kgs 8:12f). There are also a series of psalms in which the kings speak in the first person (cf. ¶2), either as the poets or as spectators while the real singers took over these mundane duties for them, just as the German princes usually drew upon reliable men for their speeches and summons. One may hold open this same question for the famous sun song of Amenophis IV.

The *general situation of the songs* has now become clear. They were performed in the presence of the king and his dignitaries in the palace or in the sanctuary. The majestic

wonder of the room is evident in its venerable splendor, in the expensive, colorful garments of all of the gathered nobles, including the first person of the state in all his ornate
dress, in the glittering weapons of his body guards, and in the whirling clouds of expensive incense. One should keep all of this in mind in order to understand this poetry. Then,
the singer enters this lordly arena, and he strums loudly on the strings and "his heart
overflows with inspired words" (cf. Ps 45:2). One thinks on the introduction of Schiller's
"Barons of Hapsburg" or Goethe's "Singer." Here, insufficiency and scanty resources have
no place. Rather, the song of the enraptured poets wafts into a more beautiful world that
might be more pleasing to the king. One cannot inquire too precisely from these euphoric
singers about the piece of reality hidden behind his effusive portrayals. The same contrast
between the elaborate words honoring the king and the relationships of the empire has
been noted in the court poetry of Egypt by A. Erman (*Ägypten*, 1885, p. 86; revised edition by H. Ranke, 1923, p. 57) and in later Indian court poetry by M. Winternitz
(*Geschichte der indischen Literatur*, 1908, vol. 1, p. 75). At the same time it is significant
to know that the court singer speaks, but *not the people*. The very king who is so highly
praised, is perhaps the same one for whom the conspirator sharpens the dagger in silence
or against whom the prophet's sermon thunders in the market place.

6. Nevertheless, the *particular occasions of the individual royal poems* are often clear.
If we are correct, the singer rejoices at the *enthronement festival* when he takes up the
herald's royal summons: "He has become king." These are perhaps the songs which were
later recast for YHWH's future kingdom so that they attained the form in which we now
have them (cf. §3, ¶3 [pp. 67f], and ¶9 [pp. 73f]). During these days, the poet may also
proclaim the divine selection of the ruler and the ruler's priesthood (Ps 110). Or, the poet
creates an entire drama in which the subjugated peoples try to rebel against him, but he
keeps them in bonds (Ps 2). Or, the poet proclaims the honorable foundation of the king's
government in his name (cf. Ps 101). On the *anniversary* of the ruler's taking power, the
poet sings about the ruler's majesty and righteousness, his victories over his enemies, and
about his reign over the whole world (Pss 21; 72). On their *wedding day*, the poet
glorifies the royal pair, closing with beautiful wishes for the royal bed (cf. Ps 45). On the
day celebrating the *founding of the sanctuary*, a liturgy was performed which dramatically
portrayed how the ancestor David brought the ark of YHWH to Zion. In this liturgy, the
poet provided an oracle in which God promises to bless David and David's house (Ps
132). Other emphases sounded in the Psalms include those days when the king *goes to
war* with his army and a celebratory worship service takes place in the temple. The ruler
himself prays and calls to his God for help against his enemies (cf. Ps 144:1-11). One
may also compare the royal prayers spoken in prose during threats of war (2 Kgs 19:15-
19; 2 Chr 14:10; 20:6-12; cf §4, ¶5). At the same time, however, the temple singers offer
intercession, and a divine oracle proclaims victory for him (Ps 20). The prophetic text in
Isa 45:1-7 imitates this type of royal oracle delivered at the time of departure for war. If
the prince then returns home triumphantly, a song is sung portraying the prince's *festive
entry*. One such song, transferred to YHWH, is found in Ps 68:18ff, with his procession
described in 68:25f (cf. §3, ¶9 [p. 73]). Ps 20:6 announces this kind of *victory song*. Then,
the king himself voices his majestic *thanksgiving song* (cf. Ps 18). We then read a portion
of this same poem taken up by an individual in a "thanksgiving liturgy" (§7, ¶9) in Ps
118:10-12. A whole series of victory songs are echoed in Ps 18:33-49 (cf. the commentary
to this passage). Another kind of thanksgiving song was performed for the king when they

celebrated his *healing from severe illness* with a festival. An example of this type of song is placed in the mouth of Hezekiah in Isa 38:9. During a communal complaint festival (§4, ¶2), the last heir of David's tribe sings his *complaint song* and implores YHWH to consider his distress (Ps 89:47ff). *Dirges* that were once held in the prince's court have not been transmitted to us in the psalter. These songs would not belong in a song book like the psalter because the psalter is concerned with YHWH and not the dead (§4, ¶2, p. 85). However, 2 Chr 35:25 mentions dirges for Josiah. One can add that the apocrypha ascribes a *complaint song* to Manasseh after he was taken prisoner.

Further, one can mention the relatively common *royal oracle* that is submitted following the inquiry of the king. They appear almost exclusively in *prose* or an account of them is merely narrated (cf. 1 Sam 14:41a, b; 14:42a, b; 23:2a, b; 23:12a, b; 2 Sam 2:1 [with question and answer appearing twice]; 5:19a, b; 5:23a, 23b-24; 24:10, 12ff; 24:17, 18; 1 Kgs 14:5, 12; 22:6, 7, 11f; 22:15; 22:16, 17; 2 Kgs 1:2, 6; 6:33; 7:1; 22:11-14, 15-20; Jer 38:14, 17f; 38:19, 20-22).

7. In addition, several related passages should be noted, even though they do not belong to the royal songs in a technical sense, because they possess *such a close relationship to a particular occasion*. The Bileam speeches (Num 24:7ff, 17f) that prophesy about the kingdom of David and Saul would have been performed by a singer at David's court. One can also relate the promise of a coming ruler in *Jacob's blessing* (Gen 49:10-12) to Solomon, whose name sounds like the currently corrupted form *šylh*. In both cases, older poems honoring the great princes were used and continued. Even David himself proclaimed the fortune of a righteous monarch in lively sentences in his "last words" (2 Sam 23:1-7). He declared that one from his house would stand at God's side while the godless enemies would have to go into the fire. There is no objection to the genuineness of the song (cf. *Preußisches Jahrbuch*, 158 [1914]: 66n.1).

It is also conceivable that they often celebrated the *memory of the founding ancestor* in the court of Jerusalem. We possess several passages in later psalms that echo this selection (cf. Pss; 89:20-38; 78:68-72), just as Nathan's oracle transmitted in 2 Sam 7:8ff would then also go back to a poem (cf. H. Greßmann, *Schriften des Alten Testaments*, vol. 2/1, 1921,² p. 138, and the commentary to 89:20-38; 78:68-72).

8. There are an extraordinary number of songs that would have been sung at the royal court according to this reconstruction, along with a correspondingly large number of court festivals. Royal psalms are thus not really a self-contained "genre" like the other categories we have seen in this "introduction." Rather, royal songs are comprised of a whole series of genres which can be immediately distinguished from one another by their different causes. Among these royal songs there are several which should be placed with the *songs of the people*. Thus, the royal song of thanksgiving belongs with the communal thanksgiving songs (§2, ¶41, 50). This is especially true for the royal complaint songs, which are followed by oracle, combined with the communal complaint to which God also responds (§4, ¶14). Further, one can note those royal poems that are related to genres that otherwise belong to the *private citizen*. For example, the outline of the prayer that the king speaks in response to the enemy threat belongs to the *complaint songs* (§6), while the thanksgiving song after the victory belongs, by form and content, to the "*individual thanksgiving song*" (§7). This is explained by the fact that the royal psalms have *borrowed* from the corresponding private genres. Such is especially true for the first part of Ps 18 (cf. the commentary) and 144:3, which adopts Ps 8:5.

9. It is far more common to find places in which individual poems contain sentences that are only understandable from the mouth of the king. These places must have been taken *from royal psalms into private poems.* We perceive that the Israelite ruler speaking a joyful prayer of thanksgiving feels surrounded by the nations of the entire world who then listen to his words: "I will thank you among the peoples." (Ps 18:50) However, sometimes the private citizen praises this way in his complaint: "I will thank you, YHWH, among the nations, and play for you before the nations." (Ps 57:10) When this happens, it should not be understood from the relationship of a typical Israelite. Rather, it is more understandable as a saying that originally came to the king but has now penetrated the speech of the individual. Similar cases from the songs of individuals include: "I will sing to you *before the gods.*" (Ps 138:1); "All the *kings of the earth* will acknowledge you, for they have heard the words of your mouth" (with which you have promised me life). (Ps 138:4). One may also compare Ps 119:46: "I speak of your testimonies before *kings.*" This transferral also helps to explain why the psalmist calls forth the universal judgment of YHWH over *all nations*: "Wake up, 'my God, ' 'bring forth' judgment; YHWH, judge the nations (Ps 7:7, 9a); "overthrow *the nations* in your wrath, 'YHWH.'" (Ps 56:8); "Awake, punish *all the heathen.*" (59:6); "But you, YHWH, laugh at them you mock *all the heathens.*" (Ps 59:9). It can also been seen in something less grandiose: "judge me, YHWH, plead my case against *an unholy people.*" (Ps 43:1). The same holds true for cases in which the individual poet portrays his victory over the nations by God's intervention using a thanksgiving song: "All the nations surrounded me. I will cut them off in the name of YHWH." (Ps 118:10-12); "You have pled my case and my controversy. *You sat on your throne*, a righteous judge." (Ps 9:5). It is no longer unusual when Ps 9 combines motifs of the individual thanksgiving song (9:2-5, 14f) with common eschatological motifs that have a national character. The king is even allowed, in the same breath, to speak of his own wanderings and of those of his people, since he feels the situation of his people is his own.

We also understand the *images of war* that are so common in the songs of the individuals in the same way. In these songs, the enemies campaign against him, but he does not care whether ten thousand camp against him (cf. Pss 3:7; 27:3; 55:22; 56:2f; 59:5; 62:4; 109:3; 120:7; 140:3, 8; Jer 1:19; Job 30:12ff; Pss. Sol. 12:3; cf. Odes Sol. 5:4ff; Compare the commentary to Ps 3:7; 118:10; 138:1). All of these words are appropriate for a king, but they would never have occurred to a private citizen if they were not already available to him. These words appeared in royal songs and the private citizen imitated them. We would also trace such all-encompassing words as the thanksgiving songs introduced in Ps 22:28ff back to events of these lively royal poems in which all the ends of the earth, even the dead and those not yet born, will praise God's deed to the psalmist. The same is true when the triumphant psalmist compares himself with a wild animal standing with raised horns (cf. Ps 92:11; 1 Sam 2:1; cf. Ps 75:5, 11; 148:14; 89:18). The horn is originally the symbol of divine power (cf. the Babylonian horned crown), before it became the symbol of the king's power (cf. the victory stela of Narâmsin in H. Greßmann, *Altorientalische Texte und Bilder*, 1927, vol. 2, illustration 43), of the people in the Old Testament, and finally of the individual. The triumphant feeling of the psalmist appears especially at the conclusion of the poem. "I will cut down all the horns of the wicked (Ps 75:11); "He makes my feet like the hinds' feet and lets me walk on my heights (Hab 3:19). This last verse is taken from the royal thanksgiving song in Ps 18:34.

Even the concept that God "takes up" the psalmist like a child (Ps 27:10) was first said of kings (Ps 2:7; see the commentary). Also, the influence of the royal poetry on the songs of the private citizen is confirmed by the Babylonian writings (M. Jastrow, *Die Religion Babylon und Assur*, vol. 2, pp. 29f; 65f; 79f; 84; 106; 117). We conclude from this evidence that the royal songs had a profound influence upon private poetry, especially in the thanksgiving and complaint songs. In older times royal psalms would have been numerous and impressive. Those that we now by chance possess are only proof of a type of poetry that was once far more abundant.

The same can be said for the portrayals in Ps 18:30, 33ff where one finds a whole range of victory songs (cf. ¶6 and the commentary at those locations). At the same time we may raise the question whether the royal poetry was in fact the older type from which private singing of psalms first developed in a more sophisticated era. It may seem remarkable or even impossible that this imparting of attitudes, indeed even entire literary genres, would have been possible from the rulers to common mortals. However, according to its counterpart, it is not impossible. M. Jastrow (see above) finds both genres have the same relationship in Babylonian materials. The Egyptian service to the dead provides a good counterpart for this type of internal history since it began with the king and only later took place with the subjects. First, the pharaoh built a pyramid as a burial site, then later the subjects followed him in this example. One need only consider the pyramid of Cestius in Rome. "Originally conceived for the deceased king, the idea of divine existence in heaven was adopted for favored persons when they died as well." (A. Erman, *Ägyptische Religion*,[2] 1909, p. 114). "At the end of the Old Kingdom, the texts that had been used for the health of the Pharaoh, are now used to the private citizen." (From G. Roeder, *Urkunden zur Religion des alten Ägypten*, [1]1915 and [2]1923, p. xxviii. See also A. Erman [*Ägypten*, 1885, p. 86; revised edition by H. Ranke, 1923, p. 347; A. Erman, *Ägyptische Religion*,[2] pp. 123, 129; Ed. Meyer, *Geschichte des Altertums*, vol. 1/2,[2] 1909, §205 n.117.) "So it finally happened that things which tended to be placed in the grave of the dead king, were found with the mummy of the common person, even the two crowns of the two lands." (H. Schäfer, *Zeitschrift für die ägyptische Sprache und Altertumskunde* 43 [1906]: 70.) K. Sethe originally made this observation. Even Egyptian names were adopted from kings into the private sector (cf. H. Grapow, *Bildliche Ausdrücke des Ägyptischen*, 1924, p. 20). See also §6, ¶5.

10. We have already seen that several private psalms contained *intercessions for the king*; specifically complaint songs, hymns, and "Zion Songs" (§2, ¶52). These intercessions are also found among primitive peoples for the chief, in ancient China for the emperor, and elsewhere (cf. Fr. Heiler, *Gebet*,[2-5] pp. 70, 460f. They are also found in Judaism for the ruler of the world empire (cf. J. Boehmer, ZAW 26 [1906]: 149) and in Egypt (A. Erman, *Die Literatur der Ägypten*, pp. 362f).

In several passages in the psalter one can readily recognize that this kind of intercession was first added by a later hand since the passages currently stand in the wrong position. Such is the case in Pss 61:7f; 63:12a; 84:9f. Compare the commentary to Ps 28:8 for a Babylonian/Assyrian counterpart where the subject of royal intercession is treated specifically. One wonders whether a particularly devoted subject was moved to add this intercession, or whether—as seems more likely—it came about when the psalm was adjusted for performance in the royal temple in Jerusalem. If the latter is true, it would follow that songs of the individual also had their place in worship at the royal sanctuary.

Perhaps this occurred in a later period. The individual hymn of Ps 89:2, 3, 6-19 provides evidence for this suggestion when it mentions the king of Israel, the shield of YHWH, at the end.

11. Before we attempt to assemble the thoughts of the royal psalms we must first discuss *the context* which such an explanation of the details and the total situation presupposes.

These poems sing of the king as the ruler of Israel, as the true servant of the national God. It is clear from the outset that the character of the people and its religion arises from these poems. However, one must ask whether it suffices to explain these songs solely on the basis of Israel and YHWH. Rather, we should investigate whether Israelite kingship is solely a native establishment, or whether foreign influences also appear. Perhaps this influence will even shed some light on the meaning of the royal psalms. We thus insert a section here that treats the *relationship of Israel's monarchy to foreign countries*.

It appears that Israelite monarchy was founded in a time of enthusiasm for YHWH by a seer of YHWH, or at least one working in YHWH's name. However, we can also find hints that one could also find great resistance among the ancient clans directed toward this innovation (cf. Judg 9:8ff). Even later one finds evidence that the monarchy was considered to be an imitation of the foreign governmental systems (1 Sam 8:20). The inauguration of Israelite monarchy itself demonstrates the accuracy of this belief, especially when it attains its prominence and can reveal its essential attributes. King Solomon built and decorated a *royal fortress* from foreign materials with the help of foreign construction workers, and of course, according to a foreign design. The *temple* of Solomon arose in the same manner. Solomon's *lion throne* (1 Kgs 10:18ff), *the sundial* (2 Kgs 20:11), and the *sacrificial altar* of Ahaz (2 Kgs 16:10ff) imitated foreign designs, as is even reported of the latter. Even the hallowed act of *anointing the king* was a Canaanite (Knudtzon, *El-Amarna-Briefe*, nr. 51, p. 319), Babylonian, and Egyptian practice (A. Bertholet, *Kulturgeschichte Israels*, 1920, p. 81; B. Meißner, *Babylon und Assur*, vol. 1, p. 63).

State life and its *procedures* were taken from foreign countries. One thinks of the royal "book of the day's transactions," i.e., a state journal comparable to the Alexander the Great's *Ephemerides* and the Hellenistic *hypomnematismoi* known from the Papyri. This convention was already known in Egypt and Assyria, and later, among Roman officials (cf. Ed. Meyer, *Die Geschichte des Altertums*, vol. 3/1, 1901, p. 47). It contained items that were quite non-Israelite, and about which the true Israelite moaned and muttered, including: *forts, chariots and wagons, census data*, and *taxes*.

In addition, other elements show how much the Israelite/Judean state was inclined toward foreign countries: the *covenants* that the kings made at times with foreign rulers against the inclination of the people; the *foreign worship practices* the kings introduced in Israel in order to make the capital city the center of a wider area or to seal a covenant with a neighbor; the *actions* which they pursue with foreign countries, sometimes ones that are very distant; and the trading centers they established in foreign capitals (1 Kgs 20:34).

Court life in Israel also imitated foreign models. Israel's king received the foreign ruler's *visit* or *emissaries* in the court (cf 1 Kgs 10:1ff; 2 Kgs 20:12ff). David already possessed a *harem* like the surrounding princes. Ps 45 glorifies the wedding of an Israelite king with the daughter of a foreign king, and Solomon even brought home an Egyptian princess. These *political marriages* were very common in the ancient Middle East. One can mention the marriage of Tutmoses IV with the daughter of the *Mittanni* king Artatama (Breasted/Ranke, *Die Geschichte Ägyptens*, 1911, p. 274), or the marriage of Amenophis III with a sister of Kadešman-Harbe of Babylon (Knudtzon, *El-Amarna-Tafel*, vol. 1, nr. 1, pp. 60f) and his marriage with Giluḥepa, daughter of Tušrattu from Mittanni (Knudtzon, *El-Amarna-Briefe*, vol. 1, nr. 16, p. 131), or the marriage of Ramses II with the daughter of the Hittite king Ḫattušil (Breasted/Ranke, *Die Geschichte Ägyptens*, p.340f), or the marriage of the Scythian king Bartatua with a daughter of Asarhaddon (Br. Meißner, *Könige von Babel und Assur*, 1926, p. 218). The marriage of Cambyses with an Egyptian or of Alexander with Roxane (Meißner, *Babylonien und Assyrien*, vol. 1, p. 61). There would have thus been a group of *foreigners* at the Israelite court, including the men and women that a foreign prince would wish to bring as their companions or servants. Also included would have been foreign body guards about whom we sometimes hear (2 Sam 8:18; 15:18ff; 20:23), the artists that the king had brought from afar, the merchants who formed their own trade centers at the time (1 Kgs 20:34), priests from foreign sanctuaries. Even the government ministers could be foreign, as perhaps with Shebna in Isa 22:15ff. In reality, even the king himself, the first man of the state, to whom Israel had so gladly looked up to as the representative of indigenous existence, could been born to a foreign mother. How could the king have understood his people? The prophets' battle against the kings can be explained to some degree because they embodied a significant portion of the Ancient Israelite manner of reacting against a monarchy that was constantly leaning toward foreign countries. However, no matter how much friends of the fatherland protected themselves against this development, or tried to keep it at bay (Deut 17:14ff), no one could change this because it was part of the nature of kingship. Kingship was only following the inner law of its existence.

12. Where were these foreign models found that the monarchy of Israel strived to follow? Understandably, the first was Canaanite, followed, as we could demonstrate with examples, by Phoenician and occasionally Aramaic (for the latter, see 2 Kgs 16:10ff). However, anyone who knows the history of the Ancient Near East knows that when foreign elements penetrated Israel, it generally came from Babylonian/Assyrian culture on the one side and Egyptian culture on the other. It has been known for a long time and recently confirmed by excavations in Palestine that all of Asia Minor was dependent upon these two cultures. It can also be accepted without qualification that this dependence would have been known at the court of the Israelite king. The Babylonian/Assyrian and the Egyptian rulers would have been the prominent models of the Israelite and Judean princes, whether directly or indirectly. They would have done so just like the the smaller despots of Germany looked to the sun kings of France for their exalted models. Just as Napoleon I demanded the hand of the Austrian princess as recognition of his house, Solomon would have looked with joy upon the relationship with the daughter of the Egyptian king as the recognition of his kingship by the much older and more distinguished Egyptian monarchy.

We can recognize how much the Israelite court imitated the Babylonian and Egyptian courts by a plethora of small threads. Several of these can be mentioned here. Among the women of the royal household, the *queen mother* occupied the highest rank in the Ancient Near East. This was well known in Assyria (Br. Meißner, *Babylonien und Assyrien*, vol.

1, p. 74), in Egypt (cf. A. Erman/Ranke, *Ägypten*, p. 86), and also in Israel (1 Kgs 15:13; 2 Kgs 10:13; Jer 13:18; 22:26; Ezek 19:1; etc.).

The Old Babylonian kings already placed a high value on marrying an *Egyptian princess* without being able to do so (Br. Meißner, *Babylonien und Assyrien*, vol. 1, p. 61). The honor which then befell Solomon should be all the more esteemed.

"One of the first acts of the Egyptian king tended to be *seizing the harem of his predecessor*" (A. Wiedmann, *Das alte Ägypten*, 1920, p. 60). The same practice is narrated about Absalom (cf. 2 Sam 16:21f).

It is well known that the sons of David held the office of priest (2 Sam 8:18). The same practice occurred in Babylon and Assyria (Br. Meißner, *Babylonien und Assyrien*, vol. 1, 55, 63, 77; cf. also Erman/Ranke, *Ägypten*, p. 89) among the princes and princesses.

The *visit of a monarch*, as when we are told that the queen of Sheba visited Solomon, took place from very early times. The Hittite king employed this royal visit following the establishment of peace with the Pharaoh (cf. Ed. Meyer, *Geschichte des Altertums*, vol. 1, 1884, p. 285.

The king received guests while standing at the "*royal window*." This greeting at the royal window was often portrayed in Egypt. Jezebel received Jehu at such a place (cf. H. Greßmann, *Altorientalische Texte und Bilder*,[2] 1927, illustrations 190, 80, p. 61; and *Schriften des Alten Testaments*, vol. 2/1,[2] p. 312.

Solomon's throne was guarded by lions like the Pharaoh's portable seat (cf. Erman/Ranke, *Ägypten*, p. 68).

Solomon's *trade* with distant countries imitated older princes. Babylonian/Assyrian and Egyptian rulers had already been significant controllers of trade (Br. Meißner, *Babylonien und Assyrien*, vol. 1, pp. 53f, 336f; and Erman/Ranke, *Ägypten*, pp. 607ff).

Israelite rulers employed famous artists from distant lands (1 Kgs 7:13f), which was no different than the Hittite kings (Br. Meißner, *Babylonien und Assyrien*, vol. 1, pp. 229f).

It is well known that the kings of Israel took the use of horses from Egypt. A common practice among the Assyrians and the Hittites was continued in Israel in which a "third man" rode on the royal chariot along with the warrior and the driver. The life of the ruler was entrusted to this man, and he enjoyed a particularly prominent position in the life of the court (2 Kgs 7:2; cf. Br. Meißner, *Babylonien und Assyrien*, vol. 1, p. 93). The *troops* were divided into a small standing army and the drafted populace, as with the Babylonians (Br. Meißner, *Babylonien und Assyrien*, vol. 1, p. 85) and the Hittites (cf. E. Forrer, *Mitteilungen der deutschen Or-Geschichte*, Dec. 1921, ¶61, p. 35).

The court title "friend of the king" (2 Sam 15:37; 16:16; 1 Kgs 4:5) that was already in use in Canaan prior to Israel (Gen 26:26) appears to stem from Egyptian practice (cf. A. Wiedemann, *Das alte Ägypten*, p. 63; and Erman/Ranke, *Ägypten*, p. 85). Any subject granted an audience with the king was said to "*look on the king's face*," a phrase repeated among the Israelites (2 Sam 14:24, 32) and among the Assyrians (Br. Meißner, *Babylonien und Assyrien*, vol. 1, p. 70). That subject had to *bow before the king* as before a god and *kiss his feet*. (For Israel, see 1 Kgs 1:16, 23; for Assyria, see E. Klauber, *Assyrisches Beamtum*, pp. 14f; Meißner, *Babylonien und Assyrien*, vol. 1, pp. 63, 70; for Egypt, Erman/Ranke, *Ägypten*, p. 82.) The subject speaks "before the king," not "to him" (cf. Esth 1:16; 7:9; E. Klauber, *Assyrisches Beamtum*, p. 15; Meißner, *Babylonien und Assyrien*, vol. 1, p. 70).

The custom of *swearing by the king* is found among the Egyptians (Gen 42:15f), Israelites (cf. the commentary to Ps 63:12), and the Assyrians (Meißner, *Babylonien und Assyrien*, vol. 1, p. 150). His loyal subjects call him "*breath of life*" (Lam 4:20), an expression also encountered in the El-Amarna texts (cf. J.A. Knudtzon, *El-Amarna-Tafeln*, Tablet 141 3:2, 7, 10, 13, 37; 143:15, 17; 144:2, 8). In Egypt, the ruler is called "the air for every nose through which one breathes" (cf. E. Roeder, *Urkunden zur Religion des alten Ägypten*, p. 74. See also H. Grapow, *Bildliche Ausdrücke des Ägyptischen*, 1924, p. 122. H. Greßmann first made this observation in *Protestantenblatt* 49 [1916]: col. 327).

Enough of the details. From what has been presented we can see again and again that Israel's court life was dependent upon the court life of older established cultures.

13. Now we also know that there were *royal songs* in Babylonian/Assyrian and in Egyptian courts as well. When we add the other monuments of Ancient Near Eastern court style, particularly the extremely instructional representations, we have enough remains of court life and speech to understand these poems completely. It is self-evident that we should compare the Israelite songs with these other elements to see whether they agree with them, and if so, how they agree. If we find a close connection, we may assume from the previous discussion that the poetry of Israel imitated the foreign model.

14. The *collective material* of the Israel's royal song naturally divides into several categories: *praises of the prince's majesty*, as well as portrayals of YHWH's *grace* that the prince experienced (these can be general in nature or for a victory which has just occurred); *prayers of the king* and *intercession for the king*; *royal oracles*; and, finally, presentations of his *righteousness and piety*. This material sometimes dominates an entire psalm. Ps 110 contains a royal oracle. Ps 18 portrays YHWH's grace and the king's victory. Ps 101 speaks of the king's obligations. Ps 144:1-11 contains a royal prayer. At other times, the material is combined. For example, Ps 18 also speaks of the king's piety, and in the intercession of Ps 72, we also hear of his righteous judgment (72:12-14). The diverse material can even be combined side by side as in a liturgy. Thus, in Ps 20:2-6, 7-9, 10 we find intercession, an oracle, and a concluding intercession respectively. In Ps 21:2-8, 9-13, 14, we read a portrayal of YHWH's grace, followed by an intercession, and then a concluding word. Naturally, in these last two examples, we can accept the change of speakers. Ps 132 presents a very dramatic performance.

15. Next, *glorification of the ruler* and his court. The song praises his wonderful beauty (Ps 45:3), and his charming speech (45:3). It also praises the splendor of the royal decorations (45:5), the pleasant aroma wafting from his clothes (45:9), and the harps of his singers (45:9, cf. text notes) on the wedding day. It also praises the gold-laced dress of the young queen (45:10) and the colorful costumes of her attendants (45:15). It praises the eternal throne (45:7) and the ruler's powerful military campaigns, as well as those that still await him (45:4f). Further, it praises the large number of chariots, prisoners, and tribute that comes back with him after a victory (Ps 68:18f). Note that the purely worldly descriptions appear almost exclusively in Ps 45. By contrast, they are quite typical for the "enthronement songs," whose existence is of course debated (§3, ¶3).

16. In other portrayals of this type, pious thoughts accentuate that it is YHWH's *grace* which has so richly blessed the prince. These are not absent in Ps 45. YHWH "chose" him (45:8), "anointed him with joyous oil" (45:8), "placed the golden crown on his head"

(21:4), and "made him 'rule' on Zion" (2:6). YHWH fulfilled the king's prayer (21:3, 5) and "met him with beautiful blessings" (21:4). YHWH's revelation was given to him (2:7-9; cf. 2 Sam 23; 1 Kgs 9:2ff; Prov 16:10). The king received "splendor and majesty" through YHWH's help (21:6). The king rejoices in YHWH's protection (21:2; cf. 28:8). YHWH heard the king's prayer during war and protected him from his enemies (18:18-20). YHWH prepared the king for battle (cf Ps 144:1) and gave him the empire in victory (18:33ff). For this reason, he presents his song of thanksgiving in Ps 18. YHWH remains the source of the king's blessing forever (21:7).

In grand style, the songs praise the grace with which YHWH has inundated the king's *ancestor David* (Pss 89:20-38; 132:11-18; cf. 2 Sam 7:8ff; Ps 78:68-72; Isa 55:3). Cf. also the portrayals of the call of Cyrus in Deutero-Isaiah that echo the poetic glorifications of the Israelite ruler (cf. ¶23).

17. Other places repeat this and similar material as *intercession* for the king or *his own prayer* (concerning the difference between the two, see §4, ¶8). Examples of these intercessions can be seen in Ps 72:15, and in the prayers mentioned in ¶2, 10, and in 1 Kgs 2:45. Examples of the king's own prayer can be found in 2 Kgs 19:15-19; 2 Chr 14:10; 20:4ff. "YHWH, look upon our shield; look upon his anointed countenance" (84:10). May YHWH fulfill his plans (20:5). "May YHWH give him power and exalt the horn" (1 Sam 2:10). "Let favor and grace protect him" (Ps 61:8b). "So may he rejoice in 'YHWH'" (63:12). In the distress of battle protect him from his enemies (20:2; cf. 89:23f) and "send him help from the sanctuary" (20:3). "The right hand" of the king 'manifests' "awesome deeds" (45:5). May "your sharp arrows 'scare' the nations, and the king's enemy lose courage" (45:6). May his hand proceed against all his enemies and devour them in flames like a god (21:9f). May they accomplish nothing against him, and may they disappear with his entire family (21:11ff). May YHWH grant him lordship over all the earth (72:8-11).

The king himself also prays. Hear the wicked word that the enemy has spoken, and "deliver us from his hand" (2 Kgs 19:16, 19). Help us, YHWH, our God" (2 Chr 14:10). "Bow your heavens and come down . . . "Save me from the evil sword, and free me from the hand of the foreigner" (Ps 144:5, 10c, 11a, b). And later, his last descendant implores, "consider 'what happens to me forever' . . . Think on the reproach of your servant, Lord" (Ps 89:48, 51). In ancient times, there is also the prayer for the proper dominion of the ruler: May YHWH give him righteous speech that he may rule Israel in righteousness (72:1f). "Righteousness sprouts in his days" (72:7). The hills and mountains will carry salvation and righteousness for the people (72:3). Especially, may he speak properly to the poor (72:2, 4). May the land yield rich harvest in its time (72:16), and may it do so forever. May the king rule properly "as long as the sun appears" (72:5). "May his days be 'like the days' from generation to generation" (61:7). "He is enthroned forever 'before YHWH's countenance" (61:8). "May David's throne last forever before YHWH (1 Kgs 2:45; 89:29f), or at least may the ruler's *name* endure into perpetuity" (72:17; 45:18). And "may your sons take the place of their father" (45:17).

In the *parallels*, one finds *petitions* for YHWH's people standing alongside these royal wishes (28:9). Less common are the commands to the king: "Gird your sword on your loins, o warrior" (45:4). "Lift yourself up in the protection of YHWH" (21:14). For the king's subjects, one desires that "the one who swears by him (i.e., by the king) be praised" (63:12).

18. The *oracle* promises the ruler what the prayer desired for him. YHWH 'lifts the ruler onto his lap' and calls him his son (2:7; cf. 89:27f; 2 Sam 7:14). From the time of his birth, the ruler is 'majestic' and 'holy' (110:3). YHWH makes him a priest (110:4). YHWH gives him the seat at his own right hand (110:1). The ruler's concern is God's concern (Ps 2). YHWH presents the nations to the ruler as an inheritance" (2:8) so that he can "shatter them with an iron rod" (2:9). YHWH makes "his enemies as a footstool" (110:1). The ruler receives eternal life (21:5). The dew of his youth 'flows from the dawn' (110:3). His priesthood lasts forever (110:4). His royal house exists forever (Pss 132:12, 17; cf. 89:37f; 2 Sam 7:16). "YHWH clothes his enemies in disgrace" (132:18).

Sometimes these oracles take on the form of YHWH's oath in order to remove all doubt, as particularly in the case of the promise to the ancestor David (cf. Ps 89:36; 110:4; 132:11). The ruler himself speaks several royal oracles (Ps 2:7-9; 2 Sam 23). YHWH's promise to Cyrus (Isa 45:1-7, especially 2f) should be understood in light of these royal oracles where God goes before his anointed onto the battle field to open fortresses for him and to open hidden treasures for him (cf. ¶23).

19. The poets lay great value on the *righteousness and piety* of the prince. The "scepter of the empire is a righteous scepter" (Ps 45:7). When he goes into battle, he fights "for the good cause" (45:5). On the other hand, as one learned well enough in the World War, one is convinced that the enemies are villains, an innate weakness of all states and peoples. One thinks the enemies are presumptuous emperors (Pss 2; 21:12; 144:7ff), thorns to be thrown into the fire (2 Sam 23:7). Thus, YHWH's grace blessed him rightly: "Because he loves righteousness and hates the wicked, YHWH chose him" (45:8). Because he obeyed all the commandments, YHWH did to him "according to his innocence" and delivered him from his enemies (18:21-25). The king deserved all the gracious gifts because he trusts in YHWH unerringly (21:8). World dominion is due him because he delivered the poor from the oppression of 'the rich' (72:12-14). YHWH swore on account of the ancestor's piety (Ps 132; cf. 78:72). Thus, David himself revealed the fate of a righteous ruler in celebratory words (2 Sam 23). Thus, the song can pray, "consider the king's sacrifice" (Ps 20:4) or "remember David's affliction" (132:1).

Warnings are not spoken to the ruler because that would be unseemly. By contrast, the poet risks warning the young queen on the wedding day (Ps 45:11f). It is, however, an immediate *type of threat*, as well as a sign of how important the righteous dominion of the prince is to the poet, when Ps 72 prays for the prince's righteous dominion (cf ¶17). The same thoughts lie behind the prophecy to David's house which sets a punishment for overstepping God's law, even though the punishment is relatively mild (89:31-34; cf. 132:12; 2 Sam 7:14f). The same is true when the poet praises the prince in a celebratory pronouncement because he has faithfully fulfilled all the royal duties: "'practice' grace and righteousness, walk in purity." Walk only in faithfulness, but all the wicked will perish, etc (Ps 101).

20. As a whole these details provide a relatively consistent *overview*. It presents the *picture* of a happy, righteous king, blessed by God. The king remains certain of divine help even in the midst of distress. Only the heart of a king could crave the prayer which his loyal subjects express for him and the oracle which his God proclaims. Our tested hypothesis is thus confirmed that these poems are to be conceived as a unit (¶2). Specific details are naturally subject to change. Thus, Ps 45 is differentiated from the remainder

on the basis of its worldly tone (cf. ¶15), while Ps 89:39ff differs from others by its painful complaint over the fall of the kingdom, etc.

Repeatedly, the characteristic *indefinite type of speech* stands out. No kings are named with the exception of the ancestor David and the archetype Melchizadek. No specific political situations are explicitly tied to real events. These poems do not portray a particular king as such. Rather, the singers carry the ideal ruler in their heart which they place upon the rulers of their time like a wonderful majestic coat. The songs can thus be readily transferred from one ruler to another, just as royal hymns of the present or the recent past can be transferred. The same characteristic formality appears in other genres (§1, ¶4; §4, ¶15). The same is true for the Assyrian/Babylonian examples of this type (cf. O. Weber, *Literatur der Babylonier und Assyrer*, 1907, p. 116).

Further, it is characteristic that the *royal psalms are also religious poetry*, which lies in the nature of the subject. Even for us, the national state is one of the highest moral entities of our people for which we pray. This attitude was true in a special way for Israel, whose religion was a national religion that stood in a close relationship to the state.

The first rule of this *state religion* in Israel, as in all nations of antiquity which lived under kings, was that the *prince stands in an especially close relationship to the God of the people*. The royal court attends to this relationship so that God himself will protect the ruler on his perilous height. We selected the following statements as illustrations: YHWH is "his God" (1 Sam 13:13; 25:29; 2 Sam 14:11; Isa 7:10); our king is "his (YHWH's) king" (89:19); his "anointed" (cf. ¶2); "his servant" (89:51; see also 89:21; 2 Sam 3:18); YHWH is "at his right hand" (Ps 110:5). YHWH has 'placed him on his lap' and chosen him as his son" (2:7; see also 89:27f; 2 Sam 7:14); and given him the priesthood (110:4). YHWH gives him his thoughts (72:1, see also the commentary to Ps 2:7-9). He devours his enemies in flames like a god (21:10). In Ps 18 mythological material is apparently even transferred to him (cf 18:17). One names him alongside YHWH (2:2f; cf 1 Kgs 21:10, 13; Isa 8:21; Zech 12:8; Prov 24:21; etc.). One swears by the king as one would swear by a god (cf. 1 Sam 17:55; 25:26; 2 Sam 11:11; 15:21). He towers above things human (Ps 45:3), and is even called "god," albeit seldom (45:7; cf. the commentary to 110:2).

The song of the court singer praises the prince quite highly, but do not forget that YHWH is above him. The victory song in Ps 20:6 does not praise the king himself, but praises the God who helped him. Similarly, the thanksgiving song in Ps 18 does not primarily praise the ruler, but the God who intervened on his behalf. Everything glorious which the king possesses and which the oracle promises for the future stems from above, as is proclaimed repeatedly. The king becomes cognizant of how much he depends on YHWH especially in times of distress (Pss 144; 89:39ff).

21. The majority of the material communicated in these poems readily attaches itself to that which we know elsewhere about Israelite kingship (cf. the previous discussion as well as the arguments in the commentary). One may add that the role of *priest* was also given to the king of Judah (Ps 110:4). We have many other traces that show the value the kings of Israel and Judah have placed on the priesthood (cf. the commentary to this passage). The effusiveness that appears so strong in these poems corresponds entirely to the situation in which they are sung (cf. ¶5).

Thus, one may also explain the fact that *immortality* is promised to the king (Pss 21:5; 45:3, 7; 61:7f; 72:5; 110:3f). This desire appears elsewhere in the Old Testament (1 Kgs 1:31; Neh 2:3; Dan 2:4; 3:9). Several passages demonstrate that this idea should not be taken too literally since the poet is satisfied that the king's name (Pss 45:18; 72:17) or the king's house lasts forever (89:29f, 37f; 132:12; 2 Sam 7:16; 1 Kgs 2:4, 45; 9:4f).

The *battle portrayals*, violent by any measure, are also explained in this way (Pss 18:38ff; 21:9ff; 45:5; 110:5-7; also those about Cyrus in Isa 41:2ff; 45:1ff; ¶23). Characteristically, these make no mention of the armies, without which no battle could be fought. Rather, the honor for the victory goes solely to the prince. Such is also the result of the stormy inspiration of these court poets.

They risk ascribing *world dominion* to their ruler (Pss 2:8; 18:44-46, 48; 45:13; 72:8-11; 110:5-7; 144:2). We are people of reality, and to us this idea appears completely impossible for the kings of Israel or even Judah, even though it could be said in the Israelite royal courts. The same is even expressed about David in later passages (Ps 89:26, 28; Isa 55:4; cf. also 2 Sam 7:9).

22. If we compare this royal image with the *Babylonian and Egyptian* royal songs, we find a great deal of similarity.

First, we grant that there are *similar forms*. Foreign rulers are also accustomed to receiving *oracles* from the divinity (cf. M. Jastrow, *Die Religion Babylon und Assur*, vol. 1, pp. 414, 416, 417, 418, 521, 523; vol. 2, pp. 145, 157ff; H. Zimmern, *Babylonische Hymnen und Gebete*, vol. 2, pp. 20f; O. Weber, *Literatur der Babylonier und Assyrer*, pp. 181ff, 189f; E. Klauber, *Assyrisches Beamtentum*, 1910, pp. 20f; A. Erman/Ranke, *Ägypten*, p. 646). The Old Testament also narrates accounts of these revelations to foreign rulers on occasion (Gen 20:3ff; 41; Isa 36:10; Dan 2; 4; 5; 2 Chr 35:21). An Assyrian oracle in poetic style can be found in M. Jastrow, *Die Religion Babylon und Assur*, vol. 1, pp. 443f, 521, and Old Sumerian examples can be found in H. Zimmern, *König Lipit-Ištars Vergöttlichung*, 1916, pp. 13, 15 (3:32ff); 17 (3:8ff, 18ff, 35ff). Egyptian examples are in Erman/Ranke, *Ägypten*, p. 468 and G. Roeder, *Urkunden zur Religion des alten Ägypten*, pp. 157, 158ff, 181f. Hittite examples appear in A. Goetze, *Hethitische Texte*, vol. 1, 1925, pp. 7, 11, 23, 31), and an Aramaic example appears in H. Greßmann, *Altorientalische Texte zum Alten Testament*,[2] p. 444n.12.

There are an extraordinary number of *royal prayers* in Babylonian and Assyrian texts, see M. Jastrow, *Die Religion Babylon und Assur*, vol. 1, pp. 394ff, 406ff, especially complaint songs, see ibid, pp. 431, 472f, 492, 507f, 511f, 523f, 525, 536f; vol. 2, pp. 10, 21, 31, 43f, 63, 75f, 97f, 106-117. Zimmern, *Babylonische Hymnen und Gebete*, vol. 1, pp. 8, 9; A. Ungnad, *Die Religion der Babylonier und Assyrer*, pp. 172ff, 180f, 182ff. As with the Hebrew examples, these prayers were normally spoken at times of enemy attack, or personal illness (cf. ¶3, above). Egyptian royal prayers are found in A. Erman/Ranke, *Ägypten*, pp. 467f; Roeder, *Urkunden zur Religion des alten Ägypten*, p. 83.

Intercessions for the king are also found in M. Jastrow, *Die Religion Babylon und Assur*, vol. 1, pp. 398f, 427, 521, and n. 2; Zimmern, *Babylonische Hymnen und Gebete*, vol. 1, p. 8; A. Ungnad, *Die Religion der Babylonier und Assyrer*, pp. 171f. These were perhaps spoken at the coronation (cf. Br. Meißner, *Babylonien und Assyrien*, vol. 1, pp. 63f) or during the daily practice of the priest (ibid, p. 75), or loyal subject (ibid, p. 136). These intercessions occasionally received additions by the scribes, as perhaps also happened in certain psalms (cf. ¶2; for examples, see the commentary to 28:8f; and the commentary to 72:1, 15). Egyptian intercessions for the king are found in G. Roeder, *Urkunden zur Religion des alten Ägypten*, pp. 65, 70f, 72, 76, 77, 80f, 81, 86, 87, 93.

The *connection between prayer and oracle* (¶14) is also found in Babylonian and Egyptian (cf. the commentary to 20:7; M. Jastrow, *Die Religion Babylon und Assur*, vol. 1, pp. 442ff = A. Ungnad, *Die Religion der Babylonier und Assyrer*, pp. 180ff = P. Jensen, *KB* 6/2, pp. 136ff; M. Jastrow, *Die Religion Babylon und Assur*, vol. 2, pp. 43f [where the oracle presupposes the complaint]; A. Erman/Ranke, *Ägypten*, pp. 467f. There are also Babylonian *royal thanksgiving songs* §7, ¶11). *Glorifications of the king* are particularly frequent in Egyptian materials (see A. Erman/Ranke, *Ägypten*, pp. 58f, 72f, 76, 83, 466; G. Roeder, *Urkunden zur Religion des alten Ägypten*, pp. 72, 74, 75, 78, 79; and H. Zimmern, *Babylonische Hymnen und Gebete*, vol. 1, pp. 8f).

Above all, we find the same *effusive* tone, or one which is even more effusive, especially in Egypt.

In addition, an abundance of specific contacts are also expressed on occasion. The Assyrian ruler also places great value on the fact that he holds a *righteous scepter* (cf. H. Zimmern, *König Lipit-Ištars Vergöttlichung*, p. 17 [3:23]; and the commentary to Ps 45:7). He also wants to shatter his enemies *"like clay pots"* (cf. the commentary to Ps 2:9). The subjects *swear by him* (cf. the commentary to 63:12). Conquered peoples must *kiss his feet* (cf. the commentary to Ps 2:11). Both of these appear elsewhere in the world empires (cf. ¶12). The prayer expresses the desire that the deity *give the king justice and righteousness*. The prayer of Israel is no different than the one of Assyria (cf. the commentary to Ps 72:1). Even the foreign poems gladly accent the *confidence* that sits by the deity (cf. M. Jastrow, *Die Religion Babylon und Assur*, vol. 1, 395, 444, and Ps 21;8). The Hittite Ḫattušiliš says about his goddess, Ištar of Šamḫaš, "I will take my refuge in god continually." (Cf. A. Goetze, *Hethitische Texte*, vol. 1, p. 47). One passage has its counterpart in an Egyptian royal song that appears to be as completely Israelite as Ps 20:8f. It expresses the *contempt of any worldly means of help* in contrast to divine help (cf. the commentary). It is particularly impressive that the conceptualization of Ps 18:35 reappears also in an Egyptian royal song. YHWH teaches the Judean king to *shoot the bow* like Seth of Tutmoses (see the commentary). When the prince wishes to take his place at the *right hand of God* while his enemies must serve him like a footstool, then both must have been educated in Egypt (cf. the commentary to Ps 110:1). Egyptian images also present ideas that the goddess takes the king up to her lap, which appears to reappear in the Hebrew. The same is true in Assyrian (cf. the commentary to Ps 2:7). One must look at these texts themselves in order to evaluate the specific connections.

These concepts are attested among the world empires, even though they have given such difficulties to commentators because of their tremendous overstatements or for other reasons (cf. ¶21). Recent research does not want to believe in the *priesthood* of the king of Zion (110:4). However, it is this office that most clearly presents the close association with the deity. Rulers of Babylon, Assyria, and Egypt have placed the greatest value upon this office (cf. the commentary to Ps 110:4).

To us, it is too much to wish the king *eternal life*, especially in the strong expressions used by the Israelite court singers to express these thoughts. Nevertheless, Babylonian and Assyrian rulers have quite similar prayers and promises. "I strengthen the foundation of my throne into perpetuity like the building of *Etemenanki*" (i.e., the temple tower of Babylon; M. Jastrow, *Die Religion Babylon und Assur*, vol. 1, p. 400). Or, may the goddess "determine a long life for me, and strengthen my government like heaven and earth." (M. Jastrow, *Die Religion Babylon und Assur*, vol. 1, 419; other examples can be found on 394, 395, 396, 397, 403, 521, 525; and in H. Zimmern, *König Lipit-Ištars Vergöttlichung*, 1916, pp. 15 [3:45]; 17 [3:21]).

The Egyptian court style is even more ostentatious. They write ideas like the scribe who ascribes "millions of years" to the gods which they present to the Pharaoh (cf. A. Erman/Ranke, *Ägypten*, p. 324). Or they record that the gods have written his name on the leaves of the holy tree (ibid, p. 396). They write about the way that the gods hold the *ankh* (the symbol of life) in front of him (cf. e.g., B.R. Lepsius, *Denkmaler aus Aegypten und Aethiopien*, 1849-1856, vol. 8, page 14). Or, they write about the way the gods pour water over him, water that comes straight from the *ankh*, thus making it the water of life, (B.R. Lepsius, *Denkmaler aus Aegypten und Aethiopien*, vol. 6, page 124; vol. 7, p. 238). The god repeatedly assures the pharaoh, "I will give you life into perpetuity . . .; your name will exist as long as the heavens exist." (A. Erman/Ranke, *Ägypten*, p. 325). Or, "my beloved bodily son, I will give you millions of festival times in life, longevity, and purity" (A. Erman/Ranke, *Ägypten*, p. 384). One can observe the partial, almost literal, agreement with Pss 72:5; 89:37f. Similar wishes are also found in Phoenician (cf. the inscription of Yehaw-melek from Byblos (H. Greßmann, *Altorientalische Texte zum Alten Testament*,[2] p. 446 [3:9f]).

Further, the immense *battle images*, which stood out in the biblical royal psalms, are favorites used to glorify the Babylonian-Assyrian and Egyptian ruler. Cf. the commentary to Pss 18:23; 21:13 and the so-called "poem of Pentauert" in (H. Greßmann, *Altorientalische Texte zum Alten Testament*,[2] p. 468), which states:

> Look, none of you wants to stand before me in battle. Your heart becomes weak in your body. You cannot shoot and you do not find the courage to hold your lance. I let them fall into the water as the crocodiles fall into it. They fall over one another, and I kill those whom I choose. None of them looks behind them, and none turns around. Anyone who falls does not get back up.

One should also note something else we found remarkable in the biblical royal songs (cf ¶21). Namely, the presentation and the poem celebrate the king so highly, that nothing is left for the soldiers to do. He is the primal powerful hero who conquers the enemy almost by himself. This situation is very different among the Hittites, who possessed a great value for the individual, and who never credited to the king what one of his generals had completed (cf. E. Forrer, *Mitteilungen der deutschen Orient-Gesellschaft* 61 [1921]: 35).

The belief that the king was the *son of the god* (Pss 2:7; 89:27f) is also relatively common in the Ancient Near Eastern empires (cf. the commentary to 2:7). His adoption as a child by being placed upon the lap, that is stated in 2:7a (according to the corrected text), was spoken in Assyrian materials and represented in Egyptian materials (cf. the commentary to 2:7a). Also the fact that the king is sometimes addressed as "god" is not surprising (Pss 45:7; cf. 110:2). It was common to honor kings as gods, especially in the Old Babylonian Kingdom (E. Klauber, *Assyrisches Beamtum*, 1910, p. 11). In Egypt (cf. A. Jirku, *Altorientalischer Kommentar zum Alten Testament*, 1923, p. 226; Chr. Jeremias, *Vergöttlichung der babylonisch-assyrischen Könige*, 1919), they were already accustomed to seeing the Pharaoh as "the good god" during his lifetime (A. Erman, *Ägyptische Religion*,[2] p. 48).

The *ideal of world domination*, which seemed so unusual to us for the kings of Israel and Judah, appears natural for the much larger empires of the Babylonians, Assyrians, and Egyptians. Their kings ruled for long periods of time over many peoples. It is no wonder that they would have desired and claimed that the whole world should fall at their feet. In Babylon and Assyria, they named the ruler "king of the world," "king of the four parts of the world," and "king of all the world." Ashurbanipal says that the earth was given to him from sunrise to sunset. Sargon takes possession of the four parts of the world from the sunrise to the sunset (A. Jeremias, *Handbuch der altorientalischen Geisteskultur*, 1913, pp. 178f). "Hammurabi received lordship over all humanity after the introduction of his famous lawbook" (A. Ungnad, in H. Greßmann, *Altorientalische Texte und Bilder*, vol. 1, p. 141 = E. Ebeling, in H. Greßmann, *Altorientalische Texte und Bilder*,[2] vol. 1, pp. 380f; cf. H. Zimmern, *König Lipit-Ištars Vergöttlichung*, p. 15 [3:40ff]). The priests sing to the pharaoh, "Your axe encounters the heart of every foreign land, and their princes fall before your sword" (A. Erman/Ranke, *Ägypten*, p. 640). Or, the pharaoh himself says, "I defy all peoples, even if I am utterly alone" (A. Erman/Ranke, *Ägypten*, p. 636). He is praised as "the one who sets his boundaries in any country he wants" (A. Erman/Ranke, *Ägypten*, p. 640). Additional examples can be found in (Breasted/Ranke, *Die Geschichte Ägyptens*, 1911, pp. 199, 268). Even in Israel, the Assyrian, Chaldean, and Persian empires were conceived as determined to possess the whole world (Isa 14:26; Jer 27:6; Dan 2:38; 3:31; 5:18f, 26).

23. In previous observations, we confirmed that the Israelite royal court perceived its lofty image in the great world rulers (cf. ¶12). Accordingly there is no question as to how one should explain the close relationship of the biblical royal psalms to the Ancient Near Eastern statements. The *poetry of Israel imitated the foreign pattern*. The Israelite court singers attempted to keep up by using the enthusiastic or pretentious manner of speech that was common in the foreign courts. This pattern sheds light upon the mention of the name "Melchizadek" (Ps 110:4). In so doing, a non-Israelite image of a Judean king is specifically named. We can imagine that the Egyptian and Babylonian pattern came to Israel via Canaanite influence, whether by entire songs or by individual concepts. Accepting this premise is made easier by the fact that several passages are found in the El-Amarna correspondence from the Canaanite city-kings to the pharaoh which may be conceived as the works or imitations of royal poetry (cf. Fr. Böhl, *Theologisches Literaturblatt* 35 [1914]: 337ff). Here are several examples: "My lord is the sun-god who daily rises over the countries, . . . through whose friendly word I have life, but I lament when it is oppressed. (My lord is) the one power who resides in peace in the entire land, who causes his thunder to roar in the skies like Adad, so that the whole country rises before his thunder" (J.A. Knudtzon, *El-Amarna-Briefe*, nr. 147, 3:5-15; translated by Fr. Böhl, *Theologisches Literaturblatt* 35 [1914]: 339). "You give me life and you give me death. I look to your face" (J. A. Knudtzon, *El-Amarna-Briefe*, nr. 169, 3:7-9). The Canaanite prince calls himself, "the dust of your feet, the ground on which you walk, the seat where you sit, the stool for your feet" (J. A. Knudtzon, *El-Amarna-Briefe*, nr. 195, 3:5-10). The deification of the king is also accented here. Other remnants of these royal poems are cited in the commentary to Ps 27:8; 123:2; and 139:8.

In addition, there are *internal reasons* arguing for the dependency of Israelite poetry on Babylonian-Egyptian poetry. The ideal of a world empire is just as understandable in a big state as in a small one, making powerless Israel arrogantly presumptive (cf. ¶22). A world situation, as presumed in Ps 2 where the nations of the world rebel at the enthronement of the new ruler, never occurs in Israel. It is much more common in the world empires. Here we have a concrete example of an imitation of a foreign pattern by

Israelite court poetry. H. Greßmann first noted this imitation (*Der Ursprung der israelitisch-jüdischen Eschatologie*, 1905, pp. 253f; see the commentary to Ps 2). One may thus accept without qualification that designating the ruler as "God" or "the son of God" did not arise in Israel but in the polytheistic thought of the nations.

In this context, we can solve a small, but significant problem which R. Kittel has posed (*ZAW* 18 [1898]: 149ff). Deutero-Isaiah's prediction about Cyrus (Isa 44:28; 45:1ff; cf. 41:2ff) agrees with the official inscription in which the Babylonian priest exalted his entry into the temple in Babylon (*KB* 3/2, pp. 120ff), where the portrayal of his divine calling is noteworthy. R. Kittel asks whether the Israelite prophet is dependent upon the Babylonian text or vice versa. He denies both, and proposes that this kind of speech was typical Babylonian court style (which can be supported with examples), and that Deutero-Isaiah imitated this style. However, it is much better to presume that Deutero-Isaiah spoke in this style because for a long time one tended to speak about the kings of Israel and Judah in this way. The similarity of his words with the Cyrus cylinder can then be explained by the fact that the Israelite court style drew upon the Babylonian court as its model (cf ¶12, 22). It is thus no wonder that the portrayal of Cyrus' victorious campaign and world empire have their counterpart in Israelite royal psalms (cf. ¶18, 21).

24. If we now wish to ascertain the *character of Israelite royal poetry* after everything we have learned, then we must investigate whether it can be differentiated from foreign royal poetry, and if so, to what extent. First, one notes the *poetic greatness* of the biblical royal psalms. They have an impressive power, liveliness, and diversity that far surpasses the Babylonian-Assyrian, and especially the Egyptian royal poetry with its monotonous torrent of phrases (A. Erman, *Ägypten*,[1] p. 91). Even in this section, Israel shows itself to be the most poetically gifted people, by far, among all peoples of the Ancient Near East.

At the same time, however, the *majesty of its religion* stands out. Israel, who was monotheistically determined from the beginning, completely rejected the deification of the kings as occurred in the world empires. Calling the king "god" is found quite seldom (cf. ¶20). Divine sonship of the king developed from "natural sonship" into an "adopted sonship." The idea that YHWH would have sons of his own body would have been an abomination to Israel (cf. the commentary to Ps 2). The singer even affirms that YHWH is above the kings. God is owed honor above the ruler (cf. ¶20). The singer prefers to praise YHWH's grace that rules over him rather than the merit of YHWH's person (¶15f). Prayers to the king, like those known in Egypt (A. Erman/Ranke, *Ägypten*, p. 72), would have been impossible in Israel. Thus, when compared with other Ancient Near Eastern royal poetry, Israelite court poetry receives decidedly higher marks. The Christian song "God Save the Queen" could have arisen from Ps 20, but not from Babylonian or Egyptian poetry. At the same time, it is to Israel's credit that the ideal of *righteousness* is accentuated so strongly, even though it does appear in foreign (especially Babylonian) poetry as well (cf. the commentary to Ps 72:1; cf. ¶19). Israel's innate sense of righteousness which lived with terrifying power in the great prophets is not foreign to these royal singers.

S. Mowinckel (*Psalmenstudien*, vol. 2, 1922, pp. 299ff) presented the Israelite concept of kingship quite differently than we have presented it. He laid the foundation for a "primitive" concept which is not attested in the Old Testament itself. According to him, one would have seen that the "great 'I' of the community, the particular bearer of human existence, was simultaneously embodied in 'mythic' manner by a representative" (p. 300). "God communicated with the people" through kings. Accordingly, deification of the kings in ancient Israel was a "living religion" (p. 302). From this point, all traces of the Israelite image of the king are explained entirely. Mowinckel, however, completely overlooked the strong influence of the concepts of the world states. How could an idea like the world domination of the prince have arisen from "primitive" soil?

25. *Dating.* We have to place the origin of Israelite royal poetry in that time when foreign concepts and court customs would have flowed into Israel. This could have happened already in the time of the first kings, especially Solomon. We know that the poets already exalted Saul, David, and perhaps even Solomon (¶7). Because of the impre-cise manner of speech, it makes no sense to try to place individual songs in the time of a specific king. Since the psalter originated from Jerusalem, it is only natural that Judean psalms would predominate the royal psalms (cf.¶2). Further, we can presume that the psalter contains those royal psalms that would have been especially popular in the late period of the monarchy. Therefore, the transmitted works would generally stem from this time. We would relate Ps 20 to a later Judean king because of its specific spiritual tenor. The same would be especially true for Ps 18 because of its magnitude, verbosity, and repetitions. In addition, one can mention its use of older songs, its legal spirit, and finally its late vocabulary (cf. the commentary to the psalm). Ps 144:1-10 imitates Ps 18, and should be dated even later. Ps 132, with its values placed on God's "covenant" and "witness" (132:12), and with its mention of the sons of the sons of David (132:12), also belongs to this time. We can recognize a characteristic prophetic touch in Ps 101 which is silent about sacrifices, gifts, buildings, and endowments, speaking instead only about the king's just verdicts. Similar observations could be made for Ps 72. A song like Ps 89 forms the close of the entire development, where the last Davidide raises his lamenting voice after the fall of the state. Several songs stand out for their particularly powerful tone: Pss 2; 45; 72; 110. Among these, Ps 45 plays a special role. It emphasizes worldly praise of the ruler (¶15). He is addressed as "god" (45:7). It is characteristic that this song says nothing about David or Zion, perhaps because it derives from the Northern Kingdom. Since the glorified prince possesses a long series of royal ancestors, one might think of Jeroboam II.

26. *Current research* into the dating of the royal psalms shows an amazing state of complete confusion. The reasons can be stated as follows:

(a) As with Psalm research in general (cf. §1, ¶2, p. 5), concentrating on the individual songs limits one to attempting to understand and explain each psalm in isolation. Even a man like Wellhausen simultaneously presented *four* different explana-tions for eight royal psalms (cf. *Preußisches Jahrbuch* 158 [1914]: 42f).

(b) No one took seriously, or at least not seriously enough, the Babylonian-Assyrian and the Egyptian counterparts, even those that have been available for a long time. In so doing, they gave up one of the chief means of understanding.

(c) The general assumptions of Wellhausen and his school have proven to be particularly unhelpful. They believe that *the psalms* as a whole are *postexilic* (cf. §12). Because this prejudice existed, there could be no preexilic royal psalms, or at least very few. As a result, one creates some of the most unusual gyrations in order to escape the most self-evident explanation.

The most frequently presented opinion argues that the kings in these psalms were the *Maccabean priestly rulers* who accepted the title "king" after 105 B.C.E. One tends to explain Pss 2 and 110 in this way (most recently, K. Budde, *Die schönsten Psalmen*, 1915, p. 117 for Ps 110 and E. Kautzsch/A. Bertholet, *Heilige Schrift des ATs³*, vol. 2, 1923, pp. 121f, 243f). But both poems contain royal oracles and yet we hear expressly that the divine oracle had ceased in that late period, which was painfully missing at the time when the Maccabeans were raised to princes (cf. 1 Macc 4:46; 9:27; 14:41). Would this "monster" (K. Budde, *Die Geschichte der althebräischen Literatur*, 1906, p. 265) against whom the pious ones of that time fought so bitterly, really have been praised so highly and these songs adopted into the psalm collection? And we even have enough songs from the "postcanonical" period to be able to measure the royal songs against them. However, these late poems are powerless, reflecting corroded imitations of ancient patterns. They are far removed from the outstanding flourish of the songs in Pss 2 and 110. See the discussion of this late date in §12. We will refrain from addressing the question here as to whether there are, or even could be, any Maccabean poems in the psalter at all.

For many, the *priesthood* about which Ps 110:4 speaks would seem to be a more solid foundation for Maccabean dating. However, the psalm does not promise that a priest would become king, rather, it promises a king will become a priest. This idea was common in the Ancient Near East. The acrostic to Simeon which one wishes to read from the first sentences of the poem, derives from the "time of uncertainty" of meter (cf. the commentary to Ps 110 for a discussion of both). The mention of Melchizedek (Ps 110:4) appears at first glance to indicate a late date since this form otherwise appears only in late legends. But why could one not argue the reverse, that this figure was very old since it already occurs in the royal poetry? See my commentary. Why does one date Ps 2 in this late period just because it expresses the world domination by the king of Zion? Should one really believe that this idea could not already belong to the monarchic period? It is impossible to ascribe Maccabean origins to these royal songs which speak of David and his family (cf. ¶2). The Maccabeans were not Davidides, and for this reason were held as unworthy in pious circles (cf. Pss. Sol. 17:4-6).

The idea that David composed several of the psalms (or at least that they were dedicated to him) derives from the time before the Maccabeans. The collector of the Samuel book already preserved this opinion for Ps 18. However, in the psalm *texts* there is not one clear reference to him as the author, not even in Ps 18. Its character stands out dramatically from the ancient poet heroes (cf. ¶25), and it also contains no concrete reference to David (contra Wellhausen. See the commentary).

It is quite common to relate the majority of these poems to the messiah. That was the explanation of the synagogues which no longer possessed kingship. Because of this explanation these poems were incorporated into the Psalms (e.g., Pss 2; 72:8-11; 110). Even today, they are sometimes represented in this manner. However, we have shown in the preceding discussion that this group of psalms does not relate to a future king, but to the ruling king. Such is particularly clear in those passages which pray for the ruler (¶17, 2), or which proclaim an oracle for him (cf. ¶18). The messiah appears in full possession of his majesty (cf. the commentary to Ps 72). Ps 2 deserves similar consideration. There, the ruler does not yet possess the world empire. Rather, it has only been promised to him (cf. the commentary). To be sure, the picture of the ideal king painted by the royal psalms is quite similar to the portrait of the messiah which the prophet has in mind. Some want to explain the commonalities with the idea that the characteristics of the future king have been transferred to the current king (Ewald, Keßler, Kittel, Staerk[2]). However, it is much simpler to accept that both conceptualizations derive from common stock. The ideal image which the court poets equate with their kings is the same one which the prophets see in the future (cf. the commentary to Ps 72). Of course, it makes a great deal of difference whether the court singer sees this ideal in the present, or if the much more exalted prophet, who disavows the present, seeks the ideal with a glowing heart in the future (cf. §9).

Some have contemplated heathen rulers because they did not credit Israelite-Judean princes (e.g., Wellhausen, for Pss 45; 72; and Budde for Ps 45). However, the king who worships YHWH as his God (45:8) and who is anointed by YHWH would be difficult to explain outside Israel. Even less explainable, are those passages like Ps 72:2 where the king rules YHWH's people and turns his righteousness to YHWH's suffering ones, the marginalized in Israel. This latter situation of course applies to the entire group (cf ¶2).

It is hardly worth the time to refute the belief that several of the royal songs should be interpreted for the *personified community*, even though someone like Wellhausen has expressed this position for Pss 2, 20, 21, and 101. This interpretation proceeds from Isa 55:3f, where the eternal grace once promised to David is now transferred to Israel. The people, as before with David, now obtain an eternal covenant with YHWH and become king of the nations. Because of this prophetic message, some now believe they possess the right to interpret the "king" of the psalms as Israel. But how can YHWH call Israel the son who was begotten "today" (Ps 2:7) when God had long ago chosen his people? And how can Israel be called "YHWH's king" (Ps 2:6)? It is far more appropriate to call YHWH Israel's king, while only the ruler of Israel would be called YHWH's king. And even Ps 101, concerning the message that the ruler will only allow the upright to serve him (101:6), some have not been shy in a really outrageous confusion of the times by interpreting it as the "service of the community" (Baethgen). These interpretations, however, have created utter despair because they *did not want* the simple and self-evident explanation to be true in which the royal psalms should be interpreted as references to Israelite-Judean princes.

We mention the presupposition only in passing that the royal wedding song (Ps 45) glorifies a typical wedding couple because it was the common practice of the day to celebrate the bride groom as king. However, nothing in the psalm points to this transferred meaning (cf. the commentary to Ps 45).

Nevertheless, our interpretation that these songs are related to Israelite-Judean kings has never been completely silenced (cf. K. Budde, *Die Geschichte der althebräischen Literatur*, 1896, p. 265, regarding Pss 20 and 21; C. Steuernagel, *Einleitung in das Alte Testament*, 1912, p. 753, regarding Pss 45 and 72).

Additional literature for dating the individual royal psalms appears in the commentary.

§6 Individual Complaint Songs

Ausgewählte Psalmen,[4] Index heading "Klagelieder des Einzelnen" — *RGG Art.* "Psalmen 7, 15." — E. Balla, *Das Ich der Psalmen*, pp. 13ff, 47ff, 76ff — W. Staerk, *Lyrik in den "Schriften des AT,"* vol. 3/1,[2] 1920, pp. 118ff, 140ff. — W. Baumgartner, *Klagegedichte des Jeremia*, 1917. — S. Mowinckel, *Psalmenstudien*, vol. 1, Åwän, 1921.

1. The following poems representing this genre have been preserved in the psalter: Pss 3; 5; 6; 7; 13; 17; 22; 25; 26; 27:7-14; 28; 31; 35; 38; 39; 42; 43; 51; 54; 55; 56; 57; 59; 61; 63; 64; 69; 70; 71; 86; 88; 102; 109; 120; 130; 140; 141; 142; 143. Lam 3 belongs to the same genre, as do the "psalms of confidence" which have developed from the complaint psalms (¶27): Pss 4; 11; 16; 23; 27:1-6; 62; 131. Several passages from the "liturgies and mixed genres" (¶28; §11) belong here: Pss 19:13f; 36:2-5, 11-13; 77:2-7; 94:16-23; 118:25; 119:5f, 8, 10f, 12b, 15-53, 55-63, 65-67, 69-71, 73f, 75c-85, 86b-88, 92-95, 97, 98b, 99b, 100b, 101, 102a, 104bc, 106-125, 127, 129b, 131-136, 139, 140b, 141, 143, 144b, 145-151, 153-155, 156b-159, 161-163, 165, 169f, 173-176; 121:1, 3; 123:1; 139:19-24. In addition, see the "freer style of poetry" (¶28; §11; Ps 52), and "individual thanksgiving songs" (¶28; §7, ¶8; 30:10f; 31:23b; 32:5c,d; 41:5-11; 66:18b; 116:4bc, 5f, 11b, 16b; Isa 38:10-14; Jonah 2:5; Sir 51:10, 11ab). Individual complaints appear at the *conclusion of thanksgiving songs in smaller passages* (Pss 40:12; 118:25; 138:8c) and *larger passages* (Ps 40:14-18; Pss. Sol. 16:6-15). They also appear at the *conclusion of hymns* (¶28; §2, ¶36; Pss 19:13f; 104:31-35; 139:19, 23f; [29:11; 33:22; 1 Sam 2:10d, e]), as well as *communal complaints* (¶28; §4, ¶12; 77:2-7; 94:16-23; 123:1; [Ezra 9:6a]). Individual complaint songs are imitated in *Jeremiah's complaint songs* (Jer 11:18-20; 15:15-21; 17:12-18; 18:18-23; 20:10-13). Compare also the related passages in Jer 12:1-6; 15:10-12; 20:7-9, 14-18. One hears the echo of complaint songs in several of the speeches of *Job*, especially those where he complains about his pain and the cruelty of his friends, when he assails God, and when he protests his innocence (Job 6:2-7:21; 9:25-10:22; 13:23-14:22; 16:6-17:9; 19:7-20; 23:2-17; 29:1-31:37; cf. also 3:3-26). In the *apocrypha*, the following passages belong to the complaint songs: Sir 51:10, 11ab; cf. 17:25; 21:1; 28:2f; 31:31; 38:9-11; 39:5; also 14:17-19; 17:27f; 18:8-10; 22:27-23:6 (cf. W. Baumgartner, *ZAW* 34 [1914]: 181-186); Pr Man; and Pss. Sol. 5:2-8; 12:1-3; 16:6-15. One should also compare the similarly structured *communal complaint songs* (§4, ¶12), the royal complaints from the royal psalms (Pss 144:1-11; 89:39-52; §5, ¶6; §4, ¶5;), and the *individual thanksgiving songs* that form the counterpart to the complaint songs (§7, ¶10). Finally, compare the *prose prayers* in the narrative books to the degree that they are similar to the material in the complaint songs, as in: Gen 4:13f; 32:10-13; 43:14; Deut 3:23-25; 1 Sam 1:10f; 2 Sam 12:16; 24:10, 17; 1 Kgs 8:37ff; 19:4; 2 Kgs 20:2f; Jonah 1:14; 1 Chr 29:10-19; Tob 3:1-6, 11-15; 4:19; 8:5-7; Jdt 9:2-14; 13:4f, 7; Sus 35. Cf. ¶7 and §4, ¶12 for the prayer of the individual during public distress. The Babylonian-Assyrian counterparts are of particular significance for understanding this genre (cf. especially M. Jastrow, *Die Religion Babylon und Assur*, vol. 2, pp. 1ff; and the account in E. Balla, *Das Ich der Psalmen*, pp. 76ff.). Additional literature will be mentioned in

the following discussion. Only a few examples can be cited in our discussion from the extraordinarily extensive Babylonian genre (J. Begrich counts more than 100 examples).

2. The individual complaint songs form the *basic material* of the psalter. They stand out from other genres by their number alone. It would thus appear that a number of these poems found their way into the worship service of the royal temple in Jerusalem (Pss 28; 61; 63; cf. §5, ¶2, 10). These poems were so popular and so moving to every heart, that one could not dispense with them in the royal worship encounter. This also explains why the motifs of this genre and the poetry in general are sometimes placed in the mouth of Zion (Mic 7:7-10; cf. Ps 129:1-3; Pss. Sol. 1; Isa 40:27; 49:14; Jer 3:4f; 10:19-22, 23; 31:18f. Cf. §4, ¶5). This individual poetry pulls Israel's heart strings more than communal poetry. The individual poetry is therefore far more richly developed, and the communal piety borrowed much from it.

3. It was thus the gravest mistake that psalm research in general could have made, when they completely misunderstood such lively individual poetry and universally related the "I" of the complaint songs to the "community." This allegorical interpretation, which already appeared in the Targum and Midrash, has recently come to light in Smend, *ZAW* 8 (1888): 49ff, though not without opposition, especially by B. Duhm. It has greatly influenced the Wellhausen school with many deviations until E. Balla, *Das Ich der Psalmen* (1912), provided a blow that will be hard to overcome (literature in E. Balla, *Das Ich der Psalmen*, pp. 1ff). The main objections against this interpretation are cited here briefly. Personification of that type would require complete pathos in the *first person* (e.g., Lam 1:9, 11-16; etc.). This interpretation should only be accepted where the poet makes it explicit (Ps 129:1; Isa 40:27; 49:21), or where the meaning demands such an interpretation (Mic 7:7; Isa 61:10; Pss. Sol. 1) in order to avoid being arbitrary. However, wherever these rather uncommon cases do not appear (cf. §4, ¶5), the explanation of the "I" as the poet is so natural, even self-evident, that any deviation from it should be perceived as a tasteless error and should be resisted with all one's strength. In fact, in every other worldly and religious poetry, the "I" is always the poet with very few exceptions. Accordingly, it is unnecessary to bring evidence that such was also the case for psalmody, but evidence can be brought in abundance. In Jeremiah's complaint songs (cf. ¶1), which are quite similar to the complaint songs of the psalter, the "I" is Jeremiah, i.e., an individual. The book of Job contains Job's complaints (cf. ¶1), again used for an individual. Later, even those persons who added the superscriptions understood the "I" songs as songs based on the experience of individual persons. For this reason, they could easily presume David was the author of so many psalms. In many cases they even sought the particular events when the songs would have been composed. Occasionally we even find the statement, "complaint song of one suffering, when he is despised, and pours out his concerns to YHWH" (Ps 102:1). Also, one can mention the complaint song of Manasseh, the thanksgiving song of Jonah and Hezekiah, and the hymn of Hannah, all of which are ascribed to individuals, and must therefore be understood individually. It is quite clear that Jesus ben Sirach intended his "I" songs to be understood as himself (e.g., the allegorical love story in 51:13ff and the thanksgiving psalms in 51:1ff). The New Testament even preserves a song in which a person from sacred history appears in the hymn of Mary (Luke 1:46ff). It is particularly convincing to note that the Babylonian material undoubtedly relates to individuals. Here one frequently cites the passage in which the one praying can insert their own name (cf. E. Balla, *Das Ich der Psalmen*, p. 80; Fr. Stummer,

Sumerischen-akkadischen Parallelen, 1922, pp. 68ff). And finally, one can note the abundance of personal expressions in these songs in the psalter where the "I" is clearly differentiated from other Israelites: "You have removed my friends from me (88:9)." "I have become a stranger to my own brothers (69:9)." "Father and mother leave me (27:10)." "I was young and became old (37:25)." YHWH, when you save me, "I will tell your praise to my brothers (22:23)." In these and many other passages, an allegorical understanding of the "I" would lead to a very unnatural reading.

Finally, we are in a position with the individual psalm genres to state the class to which the poet belongs, though not the specific person. In several of the royal psalms, like Ps 18, the ruling king speaks (§5, ¶2, 5). In other royal psalms, like Ps 45, it is the king's loyal singers (§5, ¶5). The sages speak in the wisdom poems, like Ps 37 (§10, ¶4). In the thanksgiving songs, the one who has been delivered from great distress speaks at his sacrifice (§7, ¶2), and in the complaint songs, it is the one who is imploring YHWH for help. The explanation of the "I" to the community is nothing more than the left-over of an earlier, commonly used allegorical interpretation of the holy scripture. It is not a fitting tribute to the Old Testament discipline of recent time that this thoroughly antiquated concept has once again received acclaim.

One can see from Ps 30 how old this reinterpretation is. Originally an "individual thanksgiving psalm" (§7, ¶9), Ps 30 was reinterpreted in the Maccabean time to refer to Zion according to the superscription and was used for the temple festival. By contrast, this reinterpretation should not be accepted in places where components of communal poetry have been added to the song of an individual, either by the poet himself (Pss 69:36f; 130:7f) or by a later hand (Pss 25:22; 51:20f; 131:3). These communal components include predictions, petitions, and warnings for Zion. The same holds true for other passages that join the individual and communal elements (cf. Pss 77; 94; 102; 123). In these instances, one should not under any circumstance grasp at the psychologically impossible statement that "the I of the poet merges into the I of the community." Nor should one proceed from the presupposition that the community reinterpreted what were originally individual complaint songs for themselves. Rather, it is quite natural that the pious poet would also consider his own people when he has finished with himself, or that he first speaks of Israel and then of himself, or even that he mixes the two together (cf. ¶28; with E. Balla, *Das Ich der Psalmen,* pp. 128ff, contra S. Mowinckel, *Psalmenstudien,* vol. 1, pp. 163ff).

4. The *life-setting of the genre* is not so easy to recognize, since the poetry often proceeds with general expressions. However, it is precisely from this point that the explanation is provided. One should seek its setting in the worship service and accept the fact that the poetry derives from cultic formulas (§1, ¶4).

It has been clear from the beginning of this study, in other words for decades, that the genre of individual complaint songs belongs originally to certain *worship activities* ("Israelitische Literatur" in "Kultur der Gegenwart," vol. 1/7, 1906, pp. 64f, 89). The counterpart of the communal complaint songs adds to the evidence because the same is true for it (§4, ¶2). Also the Babylonian parallels often explicitly mention the rites behind the texts that were to be performed during the singing (H. Zimmern, *Babylonische Hymnen und Gebete,* vol. 1, p. 6). One may also mention a passage like Ps 51:9, where just such an action is mentioned ("Purify me with hyssop, that I might be pure."). The following have agreed with me: E. Balla, *Das Ich der Psalmen,* p. 14; W. Baumgartner,

Klagegedichte des Jeremia, p. 26; W. Staerk, *Lyrik in den "Schriften des AT,"* vol. 3/1,[2] p. 118; R. Kittel, *Psalmen*,[3,4] pp. xxxii, xxxiv, and xxxvi; S. Mowinckel, *Psalmenstudien*, vol. 1, p. 137. Admittedly, I did not initially find many indications of worship performance in the transmitted poems of this type, so that I even doubted whether *these songs* were even intended for performance. I thought it more likely that one should treat these songs as *imitations* of the older worship songs (*RGG*,[1] "Psalmen," ¶7, 15). In the meantime, Mowinckel has compiled a whole series of additional "traces of the cultic mood of the complaint song" (*Psalmenstudien*, vol. 1, pp. 140ff). While I certainly do not agree with everything, much of what he says withstands scrutiny, so that the question should be considered again. As a result, a new series of observations follows. At the same time, we will examine Mowinckel's contrasting belief that every individual complaint song should be understood cultically (S. Mowinckel, *Psalmenstudien*, vol. 1, p. 137).

We begin this investigation with several psalm passages in which the *place* of prayer is mentioned explicitly in Pss 5:8 ("But I, by your great grace, may enter your house, and bow down in worship before you before your holy temple.") and 28:2 ("'Look' when I raise my hands to your holy sanctuary."). In these instances, we have a self-portrayal from the one praying while drawing near to the *holy setting of the deity* in complete cognizance of the tremendous grace allotted to him. He prostrates himself in the forecourt, facing the temple and raising his hands to implore protection.

The sanctuary and God are named together in the celebratory and very ancient "summons" (¶10) of the complaint song in Jer 17:12-18. This combination is only conceivable, if it was customary to speak this kind of prayer in sight of the temple.

The *time* of the prayer is sometimes also mentioned explicitly. Generally, these places mention the *dawn* as the time when the sacrifice is incinerated,[1] or when one expects an oracle[2] or intercession.[3] This kind of praying early is also attested explicitly.[4] One also finds the prayer is spoken in the evening in the hour of the evening dough offering.[5] This hour would have been seen as a "time of grace."[6] It is doubtful whether one can determine from the texts themselves if the nightly complaint songs[7] have anything to do with the worship times.

It is particularly clear that the complaint psalm belongs to the worship service in which it is sung in those places where the sacrifice is named. Ps 5 presupposes that the psalmist stands beside his sacrifice.[8] The fact that this custom continued into the late period can be seen from Sir 38:9-11 where the one praying is admonished to consider a *minḥāh*, an *'azkārāh*, and a fat offering, that is a meat offering, in addition to the prayer

---

[1] 2 Kgs 3:29; 16:15; Amos 4:4; Ezek 46:13ff; also Exod 29:39; Lev 6:5; Num 28:4; cf. Gen 28:18.

[2] Ps 5:4.

[3] Pss 30:6; 46:6; 90:14; 143:8.

[4] Pss 5:4; 57:9; 59:17; 88:14; 119:147.

[5] Exod 29:41; Lev 6:13; Num 28:4f; 1 Kgs 18:29, 36; 2 Kgs 16:15; Ezra 9:4; Dan 9:21.

[6] For this expression, cf. the commentary to Ps 69:14. Ps 141 is a complaint song for the evening time. See also Pss 4:9; 30:6; (55:18); Dan 6:11.

[7] Pss 6; (57; 59); 63; 77; as well as 102:8; and Isa 38:13.

[8] Ps 5:4: "In the morning, I called to you."

for healing and the purification of the hands.[9] Ps 141:2 also attests to the fact that in ancient times *minḥāh* and incense offerings were already associated with the complaint songs, even though this passage contains the poem itself in place of the sacrifice.[10] From these and similar examples, one sees that the genre once belonged to certain types of sacrifices. This conclusion is confirmed by corresponding observations in the communal complaint songs.[11]

Another trail that leads to the same conclusion manifests itself in the relationship of the complaint song to the *oracle*.[12] Ps 5:4 shows this relationship quite clearly: "In the morning I called to you and watched for you." The appearance of YHWH, which the psalmist foresees here, was expected in the context of sacrifice according to the text. Perhaps, it arises in a sacrificial sign.[13] These kinds of revelations while sacrificing are also mentioned elsewhere on occasion.[14] One would have thought similarly[15] when one prayed, "Show me a sign."[16] In the frequent expression, "I wait for your word,"[17] one perhaps finds the "word of YHWH" to be the divine revelation which the poet hopes to hear, and which will give the poet back his life and health.[18] Finally, it is not overly clever to suggest that the expression which Hab 2:1 uses for the prophet's watch for revelation,[19] "I look to you", is primarily encountered literally with variations in the complaint songs.[20] It would have originally related to the singer's watching for revelation at the sacrifice. These ideas become more probable with the observation that one frequently finds an oracle in the communal complaint songs,[21] as well as the poems Jeremiah composed in the tone of this genre.[22] All of this evidence provides solid rationale that the conspicuous mood swing that one notices in the "certainty of having been heard" following the final complaint and petition was originally precipitated by a divine message. This message

---

[9]Perhaps the superscription *lehazkîr* among the complaint songs in Pss 38 and 70 is related to this *'azkārāh* sacrifice. (Baethgen)

[10]Similar things can be said for Ps 40:7f and 51:18f, which presume the custom of bringing the *'ôlāh* and *ḥăṭā'āh* (whole and sin offering) or *zebaḥ* and *'ôlāh* (partial and whole offering). See details in the commentary.

[11]Cf. §4, ¶2.

[12]Cf. ¶23.

[13]See the commentary for a Babylonian counterpart.

[14]See the narratives of Cain and Abel (Gen 4); Balaam (Num 23:3); and Zechariah (Luke 1:11). Cf. also Gen 15:11. Cf. Fr. Küchler, *Abhandlungen W.W. Grafen, v. Baudissin überreicht*, 1918, 295f.

[15]See the commentary for a Babylonian counterpart.

[16]Ps 86:17.

[17]Pss 130:5; 138:4. See also footnote 20, p. 125.

[18]Cf. the commentary to Ps 130:5.

[19]See also Isa 21:6.

[20]Ps 5:4; Mic 7:7; Pss 38:16; 119:74, 81, 114, 147; 130:7.

[21]§4, ¶14.

[22]Cf. ¶23. In our texts the oracle is almost always lacking. Only Ps 62:12ff concludes a similar poem with a revelation which the poet had just received (cf. also Ps 91:14-16). In the Assyrian liturgy for Ashurbannipal (§5, ¶22) the comforting response from the mouth of the priest follows the king's prayer. Ps 121 perhaps contains a similar conversation. See the commentary to that text.

assured God had heard and thereby created the psychological presupposition for that motif.[23] Finally, one should consider whether the admonitions to wait and trust, which sometimes conclude the complaints, should be conceived as echoes of a priestly admonition and comfort.[24]

Further, the occasional mention of *washings and purifications* (which are frequent in Babylonian materials) point to the association of the genre with the cult.[25] These references include "wipe off" and "wash" in Ps 51:4, 9b, the purification of the hands as an act of absolution (Sir 38:10) and the expiation by waving Hysop (Ps 51:9a).[26]

Several other actions indicate an origin in worship for these songs, in which several descriptions provide an idea of the association with the cult. The one praying tears clothes and coat, shaves the hair of his head and beard, casts himself onto the ground in the dust, and raises his hands to God while on his knees, etc.[27] The complaint songs contain no consistent portrayal of this type, although they do portray an abundance of individual threads that belong in this suggested context. The one praying fasts a long time in order to attract God's grace.[28] He wears the "sackcloth" of the sinner,[29] and calls himself "black" in this respect.[30] He compares himself with the wineskin covered with soot hanging in the oven.[31] He is also covered with dirt.[32] Stretched out on the ground in sackcloth and ashes, he complains and implores.[33] When praying, he stretches out his hands toward the sanctuary.[34] These actions are approximately those which the Babylonian confessor undertakes,[35] and which were performed during the communal complaint in Israel.[36] One should also note, that the singers of the complaint songs were only men. Women do not sing these songs.[37] This also leads one to conclude that in the ancient Israelite view, the complaint song belonged in the worship service where women had no place.

---

[23]*'attāh yāda'tî*. Cf. Ps 20:7 (royal liturgy); 56:10c; 140:13.

[24]Pss 27:14; 42:6f; 55:23; cf. ¶28.

[25]Cf. W. Schrank, *Babylonische Sühnriten*, 1908, see the index under "*Waschung*."

[26]Job 9:30 also contains an allusion. By contrast, "washing the hands in innocence" (Ps 26:6) describes the beginning of the worship act in general and does not belong in this context.

[27]Cf. 2 Sam 12:16; Job 1:20; 2:8; 42:6; and Ezra 9:3-5; 10:1.

[28]Pss 35:13; 69:11; 102:5; 109:24; Isa 58:5; Sir 31:31; §17.

[29]Pss 30:12; 35:13; 69:12; Isa 58:5; Job 16:15. In Babylonian materials, sackcloth (woven from black goat's hair) is the clothing of the sinner. Cf. Br. Meißner, *Babylonien und Assyrien*, vol. 1, 1920, p. 409.

[30]*Qôdēr* in Pss 35:14; 38:7; 42:10; 43:2; Job 30:28.

[31]Ps 119:83.

[32]Also in Babylonian materials, the delinquent seeks "to create a mood by means of a dirty garment." See Meißner, *Babylonien und Assyrien*, vol. 1, 1920, p. 409.

[33]Ps 5:8; Lam 3:16; Isa 58:5. He kneels (1 Kgs 8:34), bows deeply (Pss 35:14; 38:7; 119:107; Isa 60:14), bows his head (Isa 58:5) in the dust (Ps 119:25; Job 16:18; Lam 3:16).

[34]Pss 28:2; 141:2; contrast Ezra 9:6.

[35]W. Schrank, *Babylonische Sühnrite*, pp. 58ff.

[36]Cf. §4, ¶2. The customs for the funeral lament are quite similar, which Israel itself noted (cf. Ps 35:14).

[37]By contrast, women play an important role in funeral celebrations (cf. H. Jahnow, *Hebräisches Leichenlied*, 1923, see the index under "*Frauen*").

If all of this evidence leads to the conclusion that the genre originally belonged to the cult, this does not mean (which must be stressed against Mowinckel) that the psalms *as we have them* which are from this genre show this connection as a whole, or even to any great degree.

As evidence, there are more than a few complaint songs that were composed *a considerable distance from the sanctuary.*[38] Every possible objection to locating psalms in the diaspora is silenced by the apocryphal complaint song of Manasseh, which the author placed in the mouth of the king who was held in prison in Babylon. It is self-evident that such poems must be understood as a strictly private outpouring of their psalmists, and that they were not specified for worship performance.

Occasionally the complaint songs express desire for YHWH and Zion. The singer painfully misses the marvelous surroundings of the holy temple. He would like to walk there and "see YHWH's face,"[39] "go to the altar,"[40] and "be YHWH's guest forever."[41] He buries himself in the majestic reminiscence of earlier pilgrimage journeys,[42] etc. These and similar psalms could only be spoken at a site removed from the sanctuary, and thus it would be impossible that they accompanied a worship act. The same is true for those complaint songs which speak in shorter, partially pictorial suggestions, and for those in which the singer believes himself to be cut off from YHWH's sight,[43] so that he states his desire "to see YHWH's face," to "be satisfied with the sight of your form,"[44] "to find refuge in the shadow of your wings,"[45] etc. One can readily see that these desires are not conceivable in the sanctuary from Ps 27:4, where the singer demands only one thing from YHWH: "to see YHWH's friendliness and to observe his temple." This kind of passionate desire could only arise in a heart of one who is painfully lacking what he most desires at the present time.

One may deduce a similar situation for the poet in places which portray the poet's adversary. We hear that opponents surround him,[46] seek him out, lie in wait for him,[47] gloat over his misfortune,[48] taunt him, and laugh at him.[49] When we hear these things, we are not led to a worship service setting but to a situation of life outside where the one praying suffers, separated from YHWH's help,[50] where he cannot hide in YHWH's protection, and where he feels "god has left him."[51] All of these scenes transfer us to a place in the midst of life, but not in a worship service, where the psalmist quarrels with his

---

[38]For details, see the commentary to Pss 16; 42/43; 55; 61; 120.

[39]Ps 42:3.

[40]Ps 43:4.

[41]Ps 61:5.

[42]Pss 42:5; (55:15). See also the complaint song inserted into the thanksgiving song of Jonah 2:5.

[43]Ps 31:23.

[44]Ps 17:15.

[45]Pss 57:2; cf. 17:8; (52:10; 23:6).

[46]Pss 22:13, 17; cf. 17:9, 11.

[47]Ps 59:4, etc.

[48]Ps 22:18.

[49]Pss 22:7-9; 42:11; 102:9. Cf. the account of this material and the previous references in ¶8.

[50]Ps 22:2.

[51]Ps 22:2.

opponents,[52] but desperate friends must comfort.[53] In addition, "Jeremiah's complaint songs" as well as those in Job borrow from the complaint psalms but contain no actions performed in a worship setting.[54]

The two alphabetic complaint songs, Pss 25 and Lam 3, show how far the genre has been removed from its "life setting." These two could only have been composed for a written form, to please the eyes, as would be true for all psalms so arranged. One can no longer think about a performance for these songs.

The same would also be true for those passages that speak of an *aversion to sacrifice.* These passages include the famous sentence in Ps 51:18 which speaks unambiguously.[55] Of course, these utterances do not completely exclude participation in the cult which could of course include other endeavors.[56] However, there is notably little talk of atonements, and the clearest speech about *ritual cleansing* can only be pictorial since the sins it treats are of such an internal nature that it could hardly concern the priests.[57] Other passages also attest to places whereby the psalmic poet has deviated from the practice of the worship service and strives to spiritualize it. It is not necessary to seek out the temple in order to pray. Even from a distance, one can stretch out one's hands toward the temple.[58] Or, one can demonstrate this attitude to YHWH without thought to Zion.[59] But even this action is lacking. One could also simply raise one's eyes[60] or bear one's soul to God.[61] These words show how little it appeared necessary to performs specific customs while speaking the complaint. The prayer times also demonstrate the same deviation. References such as "all day," "the whole day," and "day and night" show that the entreaty occurred un-relentingly.[62]

In certain psalms we can provide more than the negative evidence and specify the place they occupied in life more clearly. In a number of instances, one should think of the bed,[63] especially the sick-bed.[64] The latter is particularly clear in the inserted complaint psalm 41:5-11 which speaks of the visit of a hypocritical friend. It is also evident that this type of prayer takes place *at night.* If the sleep that is craved does not occur, then one feels the pain even more, thus reawakening internal suffering, concerns, and questions. This time is recognizable in the expression that the pious had suffered and prayed "until morning."[65] The situation of the sick person is far worse when he finds himself on the

---

[52]Pss 4:3ff; 22:8ff; 62:4ff; etc.

[53]Pss 4:7ff; 11:1ff; 62:9ff; etc.

[54]Jer 17:12ff is an exception insofar as it alludes to a prayer offered earlier in the sanctuary.

[55]Cf. also 40:7c, 8. This thought appears more frequently in the thanksgiving songs (§7, ¶8).

[56]Cf. Mowinckel, *Psalmenstudien,* vol. 1, pp. 140ff.

[57]Ps 51:4ff.

[58]1 Kgs 8:38; Dan 6:11; cf. Tob 3:11.

[59]Pss 88:10; 143:6.

[60]Pss 121:1; 123:1; cf. Isa 38:14.

[61]Pss 25:1; 86:4; 143:8.

[62]Pss 22:3; 32:3; 42:4; 55:18; 88:2; cf. 38:7. The one complaining also goes around in sackcloth "constantly," even during regular daily activities (Pss 35:14; 38:7; 42:10; 43:3; see also Job 30:28).

[63]Pss 63:7; 77:3, 5.

[64]Ps 6:7; cf. Isa 38:3.

[65]Isa 38:13; cf. Pss 6:7; 63:7; 77:7; 102:8. Job also speaks of his "painful nights" (7:3ff; 30:17).

dungheap, having to sit in ashes and excrement, as is told of Job.[66] These settings are referenced in phrases like: "YHWH has thrown me into the dust, I became like dust and ash;" "I eat ash like bread."[67] Mowinckel doubted whether one would have tended to write poems in painful situations as frequently as would appear in these poems.[68] But who knows whether or not it is natural for the soul to seek eternal compassion in painful nights and when fearing death. And who knows whether or not these verses flooded forth from the poetically gifted in these difficult hours. Consider Rückert's "At Midnight." And if the one praying cannot write, he can have a friend write the poem the next morning.[69]

Other examples of the genre presuppose that one speaks them *on the bed before going to sleep*.[70] In addition, we hear that *prisoners* cry their refrain to YHWH from the darkness.[71] Even the sailor in danger of running aground calls to God.[72] Thus, one can speak a complaint song to YHWH in several settings outside of the worship service.

Also the received psalm texts thoroughly contradict Mowinckel's acceptance of the fact that they were only composed as worship service formulas by "professional poets among the temple personnel" for use by the laity.[73] That would hold true for the Babylonian poetry whose monotony bears the stamp of this origin. It would be a great injustice, however, to accept this argument for the biblical songs. Of course they manifest traces of this formulaic origin. On the other hand, because of their wonderfully dynamic nature and their abundant diversity,[74] one cannot deny that many of the complaint psalms clearly demonstrate that they were "not typical of the normal mood of religiosity of the time."[75]

The question is also not as simple as Mowinckel indicates by dividing the poems into worship service poetry and nonworship service poetry. Rather, one has to consider all kinds of transitional forms which are very briefly indicated below.[76] Mowinckel is correct that one cannot derive convincing rationale from the relatively few allusions to the

---

[66]Job 2:8.

[67]Job 30:19; Ps 102:10; cf. Lam 3:16.

[68]Cf. Mowinckel, *Psalmenstudien*, vol. 6, p. 13.

[69]Contra Mowinckel, *Psalmenstudien*, vol. 6, p. 14.

[70]Ps 4. Cf. also Ps 55:18 and Dan 6:11.

[71]Ps 107:10ff. The prayer of Manasseh is a prisoner's complaint song. Cf. ¶26.

[72]Ps 107:23ff; Jonah 1:14.

[73]Cf. Mowinckel, *Psalmenstudien*, vol. 1, p. 138; vol. 6, p. 68.

[74]See especially, ¶28.

[75]Contra Mowinckel, *Psalmenstudien*, vol. 1, p. 157; vol. 6, pp. 24f. See also §1, ¶8, p. 20; §2, ¶44, p. 46.

[76]At one end of the spectrum, we note the case where the prayer was sung at a worship service. A second case occurs in passages which do not involve the worship service. These conclusions can be deduced because involvement in the worship service is specifically rejected (Ps 51:18f) or because it is momentarily impossible (Ps 51:20; Pr Azar 15; Neh 1:4). In other cases, the prayer is at least spoken outside the house of God or in a holy hour (Pss 28:2; 141:2; Ezra 9:5ff; 10:1). In this case, the prayer may serve as the substitute for the sacrifice (Ps 141:2; Pr Azar 16). Or, one prays in the direction of the sanctuary (1 Kgs 8:38) or prays during the time for the sacrifice when at a distance (Dan 6:11). Finally, the place and time of the prayer have completely disappeared, as with the prose prayer of Neh 1:4. Generally, no one can decide to which class the individual transmitted psalms belong.

worship service.[77] Generally, however, Mowinckel's opinions appear to us to be built upon too narrow a foundation relying upon observations that are too one-sided.[78]

5. It is awkward to speak about the *personal situation of the one praying*. The signals of the psalmist are notably drab and prefer general allusions along with images that are not easy to explain.[79] One reason is certain. This style of the genre originates from cultic formulas.[80] In addition, one must consider whether the poetry has been reworked later for use by the community, thereby freeing it from overly individual tendencies. The training for this type of speech would have also contributed in that the poet would often place less value on the external negative experience than upon the spiritual impressions excited them. For the singer of Ps 41, the illness affects him less emotionally than the provocative taunting words of his enemies. The consciousness of his own sin torments the singer of Ps 51 more than his bodily suffering. One should also understand that the view of researchers concerning how to understand these allusions varies considerably even into the present. Our obligation in the following is therefore to be more cautious. Proceeding from what is clear and certain, we will attempt small steps in approaching those things that are more difficult to conceive.

Every poem presumes a *smaller or larger* circle without which even a partial understanding of the poem would not be possible. This circle should also be presumed for the complaint songs from the outset. The fact that it is nowhere mentioned outside the psalter does not detract from its existence. What passage from the received writings should speak about it? This circle is above all recognizable from the thanksgiving songs, the counterpart to the complaint songs?[81] In this context, only the poet's understanding to those people can be more closely observed. We can imagine that their eyes look at his fate quite sympathetically. We can imagine that they suffer with him just as they celebrate with him after his deliverance.[82] On the other side, the position of the psalmist should also not be conceived too prominently, and should not be equated without qualification to the position enjoyed by famous poets today. Perhaps nothing shows how much less ancient poets were valued, compared to the modern poet, as the fact that the names of the psalmists have not been transmitted, meaning they apparently did not care about their own fame. In addition, the experience of the singer was not so much seen as something unique, but as a particularly clear example of a common event.

It is characteristic of almost all complaint songs that the psalmist has composed them in *apparently life-threatening situations*,[83] such as the "distress," "danger," and "fear" which they mention so often in these songs.[84]

---

[77]Mowinckel, *Psalmenstudien*, vol. 6, p. 20.

[78]Concerning the internal history of the genre, see ¶30.

[79]They speak of their "opponents," "sins," "distress," and "fears," without making clear how these should be conceived.

[80]Cf. ¶4 and §1, ¶4.

[81]§7, ¶10; cf. Also the thanksgiving songs at the conclusion of the complaint songs (§7, ¶2). The circle will be more carefully described in §7, ¶8.

[82]Cf. the commentary to Ps 22:23-27.

[83]Pss 77 and 120 are exceptions.

[84]Pss 25:17; 31:10, 22, 23; 42:10; 71:20; 86:7; 102:3.

These prayers do not treat everyday occurrences. Rather, they treat the *terrible decision between life and death*. The relationship between the enemies and the one praying also concerns who will live and who will die. They strive to kill him, and he wants to gloat over their destruction.[85] For this reason, one finds the extreme anger that blows from these poems, or the cruel, passionate tone which the psalmist takes. Here is the place where *the religion of the psalms confronts death*.[86]

Several times the poet speaks about this mortal threat:[87] "my days 'stretch out' like a shadow, and I wither like grass. Shortness of days is my lot.[88] The threat to life proceeds further from the words he cites from his enemies that wait on his death in order to bury him.[89] They are recognizable in the vocabulary of his petition.[90] Not infrequently, the poet speaks as though his life approaches the *underworld*: "My soul is full of pain. My life draws near to the underworld.[91] *Now is the last chance for YHWH to intervene* if he wants to help. More frequently, the poet's fear of death has amplified this presentation. He is displaced *into the underworld* and attests to all its horrors. One should also note that in this context, the sinister word "sheol" is avoided.[92] The complaint songs prefer to use suggestive images for sheol: the grave, the pit, the cistern.[93] Even these references are infrequent. They are encountered more frequently in the materially related genre of the individual thanksgiving song.[94] Occasionally, the complaint songs speak more clearly when they mention the "waters of the underworld,"[95] their "torrents and breakers,"[96] or their terrible "streams."[97] One should also observe that the more tormented and dubious the mood is, the clearer the references to the underworld appear: "Help me YHWH, for the water is already up to my neck. I am sinking in the mud of the deep and there is no solid ground. I am sinking into the depths, and the stream sweeps me away."[98]

More painful than anything else for the one praying is the fact that in the underworld, he will be *lost to YHWH's help*. The power of YHWH's help does not reach down into the gruesome deep. He performs no miracles there. No prayer is raised there, and no worship of God. No one remembers him in the land of forgottenness.[99] Hence, the complaint of Hezekiah states: "I will no longer see YHWH in the land of the living."[100]

---

[85]Ps 54:5, 9.

[86]Cf. ¶12.

[87]To this point by Gunkel; from here on by Begrich.

[88]Ps 102:12, 24, 25a; cf. further 109:23.

[89]Pss 22:19; 41:6, 9.

[90]Pss 13:4; 51:16; 143:7.

[91]Pss 88:4:cf. also 51:16.

[92]With the exceptions of Ps 88:4; Isa 38:10; Syr. Apoc. Ps 4:3 (M. Noth, "Die fünf syrisch überlieferten apokryphen Psalmen," *ZAW* n.F. 7 [1930]: pp. 1ff.).

[93]*šahat* (Ps 30:10); *be'ēr* (Ps 69:16); *bôr* (Pss 28:1; 88:5; 143:7).

[94]*šahat* (Pss 103:4; 107:20; Isa 38:17; Jonah 2:7; Sir 51:2; cf. also Job 33:24, 28); *bôr* (30:4; 40:3; Lam 3:53, 55).

[95]Ps 69:2ff, 15; Lam 3:54.

[96]Ps 42:8, or the thanksgiving song of Jonah 2:4.

[97]Ps 69:3, 16; or the thanksgiving song of Jonah 2:4.

[98]Ps 69:2f; cf. further 69:15f.

[99]Cf. Pss 6:6; 28:1; 30:10; 88:11-13; 115:16f.

[100]Isa 38:11; cf. further Pss 42:8; 130:1; (141:7); 143:7.

Presentations of the underworld as presented in the Israelite complaint songs are also known in *Egyptian and Babylonian* and are borrowed from there by Israel.[101] It is all the more amazing that the Babylonian counterparts to the Israelite genre scarcely use these references when portraying the distress.[102]

How should one understand the emotional petitions for liberation from the underworld? The interpretation of a hope and a desire for a *life beyond death and the grave* that is often attempted[103] would be a foreign concept introduced into the complaint songs. Whoever wishes to come close to the proper understanding cannot observe these passages in isolation. Rather, these passages must be taken together with the corresponding references in the materially related individual thanksgiving song,[104] and they must be conceptualized in this context.

The soul's journey into the underworld appears far more clearly in the thanksgiving song than in the complaint. It is encountered in the narrative of the situation and deliverance,[105] and describes the condition from which the deliverance of the recovered one proceeded: "Constantly I cried to YHWH, and he inclined toward me. . . H pulled me out of the 'corrupt' grave, the muddy excrement, and placed my feet upon the rocks, and gave me sure footing."[106] "YHWH, my God, I implored you, and you helped me. You brought my soul out of the underworld, from which you called me to life from those sinking into the grave."[107] The context of the thanksgiving song's material with the corresponding references from the complaint song becomes even clearer when one considers that the formerly sung complaint song can appear in the position of the portrayal of the distress in the thanksgiving song.[108] In this case, the journey of the soul into the underworld is stated exactly as in the independent complaint song." "What use is my blood to you if I sink to the grave? Can dust thank you or proclaim your faithfulness?[109] Given this material relationship, the soul's journey cannot be understood differently than in the thanksgiving song. The petition for liberation from sheol does not mean life after death, but a return to earthly life upon which the psalmist hangs every fibre of his being.[110] The presentation of the complaint song whereby the one praying believes himself already to be in the underworld, can accordingly only be understood as a particularly strong, fantastic expression for the most extreme mortal danger, and the most bitter divine abandonment.

---

[101]See the commentary to Ps 18, p. 62.

[102]They only appear in the prayers of the priests for the sick: "Thrown in the water of mud, grab him by the hand (H. Zimmern, *Babylonische Hymnen und Gebete*, vol. 1, p. 24, 3:55)." "The faces of darkness have taken him, and they bring him to the place of ju(dgment) (ibid., p. 27, 3:30)." "Your servant lies in the opening of the morass. Let him arise from your anger, and tear him from the swamp (ibid., p. 27, 3:41f)."

[103]Cf. the commentary to Pss 16:10; 17:15; 49:16; 73:23f.

[104]Cf. E. Balla, *Ich der Psalmen*, p. 137; and §7, ¶4 and ¶10.

[105]§7, ¶4 and ¶10.

[106]Ps 40:2-3.

[107]Ps 30:3f. Further, cf. Pss 9:14; 30:10; 41:5-10; 71:20; 103:4; 107:18; 116:3; Isa 38:10f, 14; Jonah 2:3-7; Job 33:28; Sir 51:2, 5, 6, 9; Pr Azar 65; Odes Sol. 29:4.

[108]§7, ¶8.

[109]Ps 30:10; cf. footnote 132.

[110]Jonah 2:5; Isa 38:11.

How did the poetry choose specifically this image of the hades journey? A mythological meaning, as has often been suggested, is hardly appropriate.[111] It appears more likely that concepts continue to live that were developed in primitive relationships. One can observe in different parts of the world that *fainting and unconsciousness* are perceived as death. The soul then wanders to the banks of the river of death,[112] or flies far away to the ruler of the kingdom of the dead.[113] The soul returns from there if the person believed dead opens their eyes again. Since we encounter the same concept among Israel's neighbors, the Greeks,[114] and the Babylonians,[115] the corresponding references cannot be interpreted any other way.[116] This becomes even clearer when one recognizes that belief in life after death is only conceivable with full clarity with the latest stage in the history of Israelite-Jewish religion.[117]

The complaint song and the thanksgiving song speak with a different mood about the soul's journey into the underworld. This different mood yields a particular mode of expression for the complaint song. The thanksgiving song speaks clearly and unambiguously about this journey and does not avoid the word "sheol."[118] In so doing, the individual complaint song is more reserved and avoids this word.[119] If one looks more closely one can see that this designation for the underworld only appears where the one praying *believes he is close to entering* the underworld or where he petitions not to be *abandoned* to the underworld. As soon as the pious one says that he has fallen into sheol, with all its horrors, the clarity disappears. Suggestive images like grave, cistern, well, or individual references like the dust of death or torrents of water appear in place of clearer statements. Why does this difference happen? Apparently, the background lies in trepida-

---

[111]Sellin, *Zwölfprophetenbuch*,[2,3] p. 295; A. Jeremias, *Altes Testament im Lichte des Alten Orients*,[4] p. 723; W.W. v. Baudissin, *Adonis und Esmun*, 1911, p. 409.

[112]So it is with the Algonquin Indians. Tylor, *Anfänge der Kultur*, vol. 1, pp. 429f.

[113]So it was in ancient India, see Oldenberg, *Religion des Veda*, p. 526. Further, cf. Albert Schweitzer, *Zwischen Wasser und Urwald*, 1923, p. 65, in which someone with a stroke and narcosis was considered dead by the natives of Congo. The doctor "first killed the sick person, and then healed them. Afterward, he woke them up again." Similar things are found in Chinese fairy tales, where the soul of one who has fainted, or who is inebriated, left its bodily shell to enter the underworld. Cf. R. Wilhelm, *Chinesische Volkmärchen*, 1919, pp. 117, 125, 186, 284f, 366.

[114]It is said of the powerless Andromache by Ilias (5:467): ἀπὸ δὲ ψυχὴν ἐκάπυσσεν ("She exhaled her soul."). Similarly, one finds the words of Sarpedon (5:696): τὸν δ' ἔλιπε ψυξή ("But his soul left him.").

[115]"Because the critically ill person is already deemed dead, the physician is viewed as one who raises the dead. The Babylonian goddess Gula, the patron saint of the physicians, carries the nickname "lady raising the dead." Fr. Delitzsch, *Zweiter Vortrag über Babel und Bibel*, p. 18. Cf. also the prayer to Nimurta, "who must go down to the underworld, whose body you may carry back." Ungnad, *Religion der Babylonier und Assyrer*, 1921, p. 177.

[116]For the entirety, cf. E. Samter, *Volkskunde im altsprachlichen Unterricht*, vol. 1, 1923, pp. 102f, who first related these concepts to an explanation of the Psalms.

[117]Isa 26:19; Dan 12:2. The thought first appears as an unprecedented innovation in Isa 53:10ff. For those places (Pss 17:15; 49:16; 73:23ff) where R. Kittel (*Die hellenistische Mysterienreligion und das Alte Testament*, pp. 88ff) finds the hope of resurrection expressed, see the commentary.

[118]Pss 9:14; 18:5f; 30:4; (71:20); 86:13; 116:3; Jonah 2:3; Isa 38:10; Sir 51:2, 6, 9; Pr Azar 88.

[119]Pss 6:6; 88:4; 141:7; Syriac Apocryphal Psalms 4:3; cf. ZAW (1930): pp. 1ff.

tion before the underworld and belief in the sinister power of the name when expressed.[120] Thus, it becomes characteristic that the moment the poet wants to express the deepest distress of the throbbing pain, he is confronted in horror by the specific expression which he has to use. The situation is very different with the poet of the thanksgiving song. For him, the underworld has lost all of its horror in the context of the joyous thanksgiving festival. He can speak unhampered about his past mortal distress and does not need to shy away from the word "sheol."[121]

No *specific situation* for the one praying is clear from the portrayals of mortal distress. They are too generally maintained. Seldom is it clearly expressed whether sickness, misfortune, or persecution from enemies have created the problem. More commonly, the images of the complaint contradict one another and do not allow themselves to be coordinated into one self-contained situation. For example, *within a single context*, the singer of Ps 22 asks for liberation from wild animals and deliverance from the sword that persecutes him. He believes himself to be already in the underworld, then he sees that wild animals have been turned loose on him that want to rob him of his life. Then he speaks of himself as one who is deathly ill whose belongings are divided by those who survive him.[122]

These observations should serve as a warning to us against taking the individual images and concepts which occur in the complaint literally in every case. Three observations should warn us against conceiving these images as the realistic reflection of the situation of the one praying. It is often impossible to coordinate the individual references of the complaint in the graphic depictions created by the images. From this recognition, one can see how unbelievably difficult it often is to communicate the specific distress standing behind the complaint. One can see how little tangible material the psalmist provides about the external situation.

Conversely, these observations about the discontinuity of the images make it completely clear that whatever unites these images has to be sought outside the images themselves. This unity may lie in the spiritual condition of the poet. The poet does not place as much weight on a completely faithful reflection of the external circumstances as he does on communicating the internal circumstances, by expressing the impressions which the external events release in him. He wants to "pour out his sorrow before YHWH."[123] He reaches for images that powerfully and poignantly reflect his pain and distress, his abandonment, and his betrayal. He appropriates an image as an expression of his feeling to the extent that it appropriately suggests the mood of his spiritual condition. If one image does not suffice, then he multiplies images unconcerned about whether their appearances agree as long as they shock and provoke with their burning colors. In other words, they provide a dynamic impression of what is occurring in his soul.

6. Though it is often impossible to determine the particular distress of an individual psalm, the individual images do allow satisfying results for the genre as a whole.

---

[120]See the previous note.

[121]For the same reason, the complaint song inserted into the thanksgiving song in Isa 38:10ff speaks very openly of sheol.

[122]See also Pss: 42:7-11; 69:2f, 5f, 9.

[123]Ps 102:1. Cf. also Ps 42:5.

Sickness represents one easily recognizable cause of the complaint song. We find many vivid assertions at this point. For example, when it says every part of his flesh is injured,[124] or that his wounds fester and stink,[125] one thinks of *external wounds*. References point toward *internal illness* far more frequently. Flesh disappears from disease.[126] Skin and flesh cling to the leg.[127] The hips are full of burning.[128] The bones become brittle.[129] The heart is singed like grass.[130] The palate is as dry as a clay pot, and the tongue clings to the jaw.[131] Many of these places are spoken by someone suffering from a very high fever.[132] The Syrian Apocryphal Psalm 3:19 speaks of leprosy.

Other places speak clearly of illness, but *nothing more definitive* can be deduced. In these passages, for example, it is said that the legs of the one complaining are broken,[133] or that they break apart,[134] or that nothing is well any longer.[135] The one praying feels withered,[136] poured out like water.[137] His heart melts like wax inside his body,[138] his skin oozes,[139] the light of his eyes goes out,[140] and his days go faster than a weaver's loom.[141]

Metaphorical expressions speak *quite generally*. They mention YHWH's terrible *arrows* that pierce the one who is sick,[142] or they speak of YHWH's heavily laden hand.[143] Sometimes the sickness is only recognizable in the petition for healing.[144]

A number of passages reveal no concern for the *origin of the illness*. The one praying simply states what torments and pains him to YHWH. It does not matter to the psalmist whether the illness stems from himself or has no connection to him. The psalmist is concerned with what affects him internally. He is only concerned with making sure YHWH hears him and heals him.[145]

---

[124]Ps 38:4, 8.

[125]Ps 38:6, cf. also 38:9.

[126]Ps 109:24.

[127]Ps 102:6.

[128]Ps 38:8.

[129]Ps 32:3.

[130]Ps 102:5.

[131]Ps 22:16; cf. further Pss 6:3; 102:4; Lam 3:4; Job 30:30; 33:21.

[132]See also the emaciation from fever (Ps 102:5; Job 16:8). The counting of bones also belongs here (22:18). Ps 102:5 speaks of scorning food as a result of illness.

[133]Pss 51:10; cf. 69:27; Lam 3:4.

[134]Ps 22:15.

[135]Ps 38:4; cf. 42:11.

[136]Ps 6:3.

[137]Ps 22:15.

[138]Ps 22:15; cf. 38:11.

[139]Job 7:5.

[140]Ps 38:11.

[141]Job 7:6; cf. also Pss 31:11; 38:11, 18; 40:13; 102:6; Job 7:5; 16:7, 13; 30:27.

[142]Ps 38:3; Job 6:4.

[143]Pss 38; 39.

[144]Ps 13:4 is relatively clear: "Illumine my eyes (that have become dull with sickness and sorrow) so that I do not pass away into death." By contrast, some are quite general: "Heal me." (Jer 17:14); see also Sir 28:3.

[145]Pss 13:4; 22:15f, 18f; 28:1; 30:10f; 42:11; (41:5ff); Isa 38:10ff; Jer 15:18(?); 17:14; Job 7:5.

A profound manner of thought stands alongside this immediate and apparently primitive manner of thought. It seeks the *connection between* YHWH *and the illness*, which is very different from the Babylonian prayer where illness and distress are generally traced back to evil demons and magicians.[146] Even at this point one can see how Israelite religion sought to trace everything that happens in the world back to YHWH, and to understand everything in relationship to YHWH.

The context between YHWH and illness is usually one in which YHWH operates directly, with his own hand so to speak.[147] In order to understand this concept, one must recognize that the natural causes of much suffering were virtually unknown at the time. Only much later do we find any reference to the physician's art used against illness.[148] It is noteworthy, however, that even in the later period, the counsel given to the sick person is first to pray to YHWH for healing, and to think about expiation. Only then should one turn to the physician whom the Lord has also created.[149]

The idea of doubting whether God has anything to do with illness stands in more or less clear opposition, and is equally terrifying, to the thought that God sends the suffering. YHWH forgets the one praying,[150] leaves him,[151] disowns him,[152] and rejects him.[153] Expressions like these continue.[154]

Even more oppressive is the idea that YHWH is indifferent. Instead, the one praying thinks that YHWH acts *in wrath*.[155] YHWH sends the suffering while in this disposition.[156] Such suffering can include a plague sent by YHWH,[157] or a curse which derives from YHWH.[158] YHWH intends to use these elements to punish[159] and to chasten.[160] The one praying is under the impression that his God has become his "enemy."[161]

Divine wrath is not without cause. *Sin and guilt* instigate it. It is significant that the Israelite does not present his God as an arbitrary God. YHWH does not act without reason. If the one praying has taken ill, he must recognize in complete contrition that *his offense* has caused YHWH's wrath to spew. The first thing he can do to rid himself of the illness is to set aside its cause, meaning to seek YHWH's forgiveness humbly. For this reason, many of the complaint songs that ask for healing from illness begin with a complaint or a petition related to sin and YHWH's wrath: "Do not punish me in wrath."[162] "My sins

---

[146]Ungnad, *Religion der Babylonier und Assyrer*, pp. 179, 205, 219, 246, 247, etc.

[147]Pss 38:3, 4; 39:11; 51:10; 69:27; Job 4:7; 6:4; 7:12, 14ff; 9:3, 4; 10:2ff, 14ff; 13:23ff; 16:13.

[148]Sir 38:1ff.

[149]Sir 38:9ff.

[150]Pss 13:2; 42:10.

[151]Pss 22:2; 71:9, 11, 18.

[152]Jonah 2:5; cf. Ps 31:23.

[153]Pss 43:2; 71:9; 88:15.

[154]Pss 13:2; 22:2, 12, 20; 28:1; 35:22; 88:15.

[155]Pss 6:2; 38:2; 88:8, 17; 102:11; Job 16:9, 12-14; 19:11.

[156]See previous note.

[157]Ps 39:11.

[158]Pss 38:4; 102:11.

[159]Pss 6:2; 38:4; 39:12.

[160]Pss 6:2; 39:12.

[161]Job 13:24.

[162]Pss 6:2; 38:2.

have overtaken me, and I cannot bear them."[163] One occasionally finds an explicit confession of sin full of pain and horror at the events.[164]

Protestant Christians are used to seeing these passages with peaceful acceptance, finding a piece of their own experience therein. This is not without reason! But one should also be critical of the doctrine of retribution that stands behind this conceptualization of illness. In many cases, this conceptualization threatens the veracity of the person. Someone of a weak disposition could be in danger of accusing one's self of unconscious sin just to be healed.[165] By contrast, it is a sign of a strong spirit and a truthful conscience when the singer of Ps 26, like Job, rebels against the idea of guilt and protests his innocence vehemently.[166] However, where the appearance of illness really serves to encounter the conscience, it could be that the confession of sin, with its internal emphasis, no longer merely served the goal of healing. In this case, the thoughts of illness retreat before the deeper thoughts about deserving YHWH's wrath. The highest desire of the one praying then becomes to seek and to find YHWH. This mode of thinking dominates Ps 51.

Mowinckel attempts to demonstrate *other causes of illness*. See ¶8 concerning their type and appropriateness.

Statements about the illness of the one praying do not take up all that much space. However, in the history of the genre sickness would have originally been the *characteristic* distress. For support of this statement, note that in the parallels of the Babylonian genre, the petition for healing still occupies a large amount of space.[167] In addition, the complaint elements of Job frequently speak of his illness.[168] The most convincing passages of all occur when Jeremiah imitates the genre. He describes the condition from which he wants to be delivered as a wound when it really has to do with vindication of his prophecy and the ridicule which he must endure for the sake of YHWH.[169] He petitions for healing.[170] The use of this expression by the prophet can only be understood if complaint about bodily pain and a petition for healing were common elements of the genre which he adopts.

7. *Internal distresses* are also common reasons why the psalmist creates the complaint song. These distresses include: being removed from Zion, the holy site which he seeks with all his soul. Songs like Pss 42 and 120 make it easy to recognize what the pious Judean misses and lacks from the foreign land. They also show the great longing for the holy mountain of God and his longing for its shaded environs.[171]

---

[163]Ps 40:13; cf. also 27:9; 38:4.

[164]Pss 38:5, 19; 40:13; 51:5-7; 69:6.

[165]Compare the commentary to Ps 32.

[166]Job 9:21; 13:3ff; 27:2ff.

[167]Cf. Ungnad, *Religion der Babylonier und Assyrer*, pp. 179, 198, 204ff, 217ff. E. Ebeling, *Quellen zur Kenntnis der babylonischen Religion*, vol. 1, pp. 21, 32, 37, 42; vol. 2, pp. 14, 27, 30, 38, etc.

[168]Job 6:4, 12; 7:3ff; 9:25ff; 10:18ff; 16:6ff; etc.

[169]Jer 15:18.

[170]Jer 17:14.

[171]Cf. Pss 42:2f, 5, 7; 43:3; 63:2; also Pss 55; 61.

In addition, *all kinds of heavy thoughts* drive the pious Israelite to complain and pray. Often, these thoughts are only indirectly acquired. We hear of "concern," "sorrow,"[172] "distress of the heart" and "discomfort."[173] His heart turns within himself while fear and horror come over him.[174] He finds no rest,[175] and he is scared to sleep at night.[176] He is overwhelmed with suffering,[177] and he sees his past in a gloomy light.[178]

Where these heavy thoughts are most comprehensible, one encounters things like the *transitory nature of one's own life* which climaxes in a wistful consideration of the *shortness of life and human suffering* in general: "Every person stands only 'as' nothing. Man walks along just like an apparition. He piles up 'riches' for nothing and does not know to whom they will be left."[179]

In other places the poet's own experience retreats completely into the background. The *distress and fate* of his people concerns him instead. These include the offense of Israel and the absence of YHWH's grace.[180]

Even the doctrine of retribution, with the difficult questions it presents, can cause a complaint song. Even though in many cases sickness and distress can be interpreted as YHWH's punishment for sin and guilt,[181] this doctrine does not encompass the fulness of human life. Sometimes it appears in stark tension with the conscience and its self-assessment. It becomes a subject of the complaint. One of the first moderate objections to the doctrine can be heard in the declarations of innocence found in the genre itself.[182] The poet of Job is one of the first to break with the doctrine. He seeks an answer to the tormenting question why YHWH afflicts the pious while allowing the wicked to live and gain strength.[183] "I am innocent. My soul does not bother me. I curse my life. It is immaterial. Therefore I say: He kills the pious as well as the wicked. If his 'whip' kills suddenly, he mocks the doubt of the innocent. The earth is given into the hand of the wicked."[184]

It is far more common that the Israelite is driven to prayer when he feels *mocked* and *defamed*. His easily wounded sense of honor is deeply offended, and he impetuously demands satisfaction and revenge from God. He speaks with provocative words about this desire. He is a "worm" who has been miserably crushed,[185] scorned by the people,[186] and

---

[172]Pss 13:3; 55:3.
[173]Ps 25:17f.
[174]Ps 55:5.
[175]Pss 22:3; 77:5.
[176]Ps 56:9.
[177]Ps 88:4.
[178]Ps 88:16; cf. also utterances in Pss 31:10, 11; 69:30; 86:1.
[179]Ps 39:6f; cf. further the extensive complaints in Job 7:7-18; 14:1-12.
[180]Pss 77; 94.
[181]Cf. ¶6.
[182]Cf. ¶26.
[183]Job 21:7ff.
[184]Job 9:21-24. See also 13:23ff; 16:15-18; 23:1ff; 29:1-31:3.
[185]Ps 22:7.
[186]Ps 22:7.

disputed by his friends.[187] His disgrace lasts all day long,[188] and it is so deadly that it breaks his heart, etc.[189]

All of these distresses are *internal distresses, spiritual torments*. They are sufficiently clear to us because the singers bring them up in the first line and express their thoughts and their perceptions.[190] When one attempts to portray the external processes which brought the one praying into distress, then once again, this search yields only partial clarification, and only in genuinely imprecise lines. Two elements can be ascertained.

Sometimes one can recognize that a *trial* and its proceedings can cause the complaint. However, specific, vivid references are seldom perceptible. He has to return what he did not steal.[191] He points out the burden of his own property offense.[192] False witnesses threaten to destroy him by their assertions.[193] Several places indicate the one praying is in prison.[194] He implores YHWH to be released from jail.[195] He demands righteousness. "Make it right."[196] "Pronounce judgment."[197] These few references allow an approximate presentation of the situation of the one praying. All of the details remain in the dark, however, as to the type of trial that will decide the matter. Will it be a judge's verdict or God's judgment? Is the accused free or in custody? Is he is threatened in the temple or in the courthouse? In addition, several expressions are apparently not meant to be taken literally. Rather, they are to be understood metaphorically.[198] Therefore, it would seem rather presumptuous for us to deduce a particular situation for a specific prayer of the accused based on this evidence.[199]

Do the dark *powers of magic* also cause a complaint? Mowinckel has recently accepted this cause. He generally wants to see these powers as the distress of the one praying.[200] N. Nicolsky has taken up this thesis more cautiously.[201] We will delay treatment until the next section which deals with the question of whether magic is involved with the individual complaint song.

8. The distress that takes up the most space by far in the complaint and petition is the contempt of the enemy. The question of its meaning has become a hot topic once again

---

[187]Ps 31:12.

[188]Ps 102:9.

[189]Pss 69:21; cf. further 27:11; 31:19, 21; 35:16, 19, 21; 38:17; 39:9; 40:16; 42:10, 11; 43:2; 54:7; 55:13; 69:10, 20; 109:25; 142:5; Job 17:2; 19:14-19.

[190]Cf. ¶5, p. 134.

[191]Ps 69:5.

[192]Ps 7:5ff.

[193]Pss 27:12; 35:11.

[194]Ps 88:9; 107:10ff; Lam 3:7; and perhaps Ps 118:5 (cf. H. Schmidt, *Das Gebet des Angeklagten im AT*, 1928, p. 8). Ps 31:9 is less clear since imprisonment can only be confirmed through dubious conclusions. Ps 142:8 is difficult to understand in a literal sense (cf. 142:4, c, d, 5).

[195]Ps 142:8.

[196]Ps 26:1.

[197]Pss 7:7; cf. further 7:8; 17:2; 35:1; 43:1.

[198]Compare the commentary to the passages mentioned in footnote 191 (p. 139) to footnote 197 (p. 139).

[199]Contra H. Schmidt, *Das Gebet des Angeklagten im AT*, 1928. For specifics, see ¶26.

[200]S. Mowinckel, *Psalmenstudien*, vol. 1, 1921.

[201]N. Nicolsky, *Spuren magischer Formeln in den Psalmen*, BZAW 46, Gießen: 1929.

by Mowinckel's investigation. Since the last study of this subject[202] did not pursue Mowinckel's statements closely enough, and since that study regrettably covered only the first book of the psalter, it is recommended that we carefully pursue the question step by step. The importance of the subject and the necessity of a precise examination of its modern meaning, forces one to consider the framework of this section in a rather wider relationship to the remainder.

The *enemies of the pious* are mentioned everywhere.[203] From the abundance of designations, one can see that material was available which the complaint singers put to use. We will explain these designations while including the corresponding statements from the thanksgiving songs.[204]

The one praying calls his opponents "his enemies" most frequently. In addition, one finds designations like persecutor, adversary, slanderer, hater, opponent, etc."[205] These expressions characteristically relate to the person of the one praying by using the suffix. Alongside these expressions one finds others characterizing the enemies according to their essence. One encounters the expression *rāšā'*, an expression that originally belonged to the legal realm that was used to designate the guilty party, but later received the meaning "wicked, godless" In more general contexts.[206] The enemies are characterized as "arrogant," "violent," "Impudent," "lying witnesses," "evil persons," "impious people," and so

---

[202]G. Marschall, *Die "Gottlosen" des ersten Psalmbuches*, 1929.

[203]3:2f, 8; 5:9; 6:9; 7:2f, 6, 7, 13-17; 13:3, 5; 17:9-12, 13f; 22:8f, 13f, 17-19; 23:5; 25:2, 19; 27:2f, 6, 11f; 31:5, 12, 14; 35:1-8, 11-21, 24-26; 38:20; 39:9; 40:15f; 41:6-9, 12; 42:4, 10f, 43:1f; 54:5, 7, 9; 55:4, 13, 19-22, 24; 56:2-8, 10; 57:5-7; 59:2-6, 7-9, 11-14; 61:4; 62:4f; 63:10f; 64:2-7, 8f, 69:5, 10-12, 15-29; 71:4, 10f, 13; 86:14, 17; 102:9; 109:2-5, 6-20, 25, 28f, 31; 119:21, 42, 51, 53, 61, 69f, 78, 84-87, 95, 110, 115, 118f, 121f, 134, 136, 139, 150, 155, 157f, 161; 120:2-4, 6, 7; 140:2-4, 5f, 9, 10-12; 141:9f, 142:4, 5, 7; 143:3, 9, 12; (144:10); Job 16:9f; 30:1f, 9-15; Jer 11:18-20; 15:15; 17:15, 18; 18:18, 20-23; 20:10-13; Lam 3:34-36, 52f, 58-66; Pss. Sol. 12:1-6.

[204]They treat the same material: see §7, ¶7.

[205]These designations include: "my enemies," *'ôyebay* (Pss 3:8; 6:11; [9:4]; 17:19; [18:4]; 25:2, 19; 27:2, 6; [30:2]; 31:16; 35:19a; 38:20; (41:3); 41:6; 54:9; 55:13; 56:10a; 59:2; 69:5, 19; 71:10; 102:9; 143:12), *'ôyebî* (Pss 13:3, 5; [18:18; 41:12]), *'ôyēb* (Pss 7:6; 31:9; 42:10; 43:2; 55:4; 61:4; 64:2; 143:3), *sāray* (Pss 3:2; 13:5; 27:2, 12; Job 16:9), *sôreray* (Pss 7:7; 31:12; 42:11; 69:20; 143:12); "my persecutors," *rôdepay* (Pss 7:2; 142:7; Jer 15:15; 17:18; 20:11), *meraddepay* (Ps 31:16); "my adversaries," *mitqômemay* (Ps 59:2; Job 27:7; 17:7 [without suffix]), *qāmay* (Ps 18:49); "my slanderers," *sôreray* (Pss 5:9; 27:11; 54:7; 56:3; 59:11); "those hating me," *sône'ay* (Pss 35:19b; 38:20; 41:8; 69:5; 86:17), *mesan'ay* (Pss 55:13; [18:41]); "my opponents," *yerîbay* (Ps 35:1), *lôhămay* (Pss 35:1; 56:2, 3); "those seeking my life," *mebaqšê napšî* (Pss 35:4; 40:15); "those keeping my life" (Ps 71:10); "those suing my soul," *sôtenê napšî* (Pss 71:13; 109:31; and also Ps 109:29). This expression is ambiguous and could mean "sue" as well as "confront". Cf. 1 Sam 29:4; 1 Kgs 5:18; 11:14, 23, 25); "those planning disaster against me," *hôšebê rā'ātî* (35:4); "those seeking my disaster," *mebaqšê rā'ātî* (Ps 71:13); "those finding pleasure in my disaster," *hăpsê rā'ātî* (Ps 40:15); "the one robbing me," *gôzelî* (Ps 35:10); "the one mocking me," *mehôlelî* (Ps 102:9).

[206]Pss 55:4; 71:4; and 140:5 use the singular while 3:8; 11:2; and 17:9 use the plural.

forth.[207] Among these expressions, one finds the term that Mowinckel used as his starting point only five times, *pô'ălê 'āwen*,[208] and only once for the expression *bôgedê 'awen*.[209]

Alongside these short expressions stand a whole series of *statements* portraying the *motives* of the enemies. These statements preserve a certain image of the enemies, but as a whole they present very general references with little concrete details. By contrast, the impression of the enemies' conduct upon the pious, and the response to that conduct, is quite clear.

These portrayals prefer to speak pictorially of the opponents. They gladly portray the enemy as an attacking *enemy troop*.[210] The one complaining sees himself surrounded by an enemy army,[211] while arrows are shot at him,[212] the enemies run against him as they would a sinking wall and an overthrown wall.[213] Correspondingly, the *sword* in the enemies hand is often mentioned,[214] or their *bows and arrows*.[215]

Another element that is characteristic for the psalmist's enemy is taken from the *hunt*. The opponents lay secret *nets* before the pious like those one tends to lay in the animal's pathway.[216] They dig graves in his path so that the unsuspecting will fall into them.[217] Or, they chase him like one would chase a wild animal on a hunt.[218]

Another series of images portray the enemy as *robbers*.[219] The previous series had already suggested the enemies' deceit and cunning, but they appear here openly: "the 'murderer' waits in ambush, 'to kill' the innocent in hiding. His eyes scout for the weak. . . . He lies in wait for someone in distress. He captures someone in distress, pulling that person into his net. 'The innocents are thrown down, ' and overpowered."[220]

Other passages speak of the enemies as they would about wild beasts, which allows the psalmists' fear of them to be recognized. They bear their teeth,[221] tear open their

---

[207]"evil doer," *merê'îm* (Pss 22:17; 27:2; 64:3); "impudent" *'azzîm* (Ps 59:4); "arrogant," *zêdîm* (Pss 54:5; 86:14); "haughty," *gê'îm* (Ps 59:6; 140:6a); "violent," *'arîsîm* (Pss 54:5; 86:14); "crooked," *me'awêl* (Ps 71:4; cf. Job 16:11), *hômēs* (Ps 71:4); "strong," *hāzāk* (Ps 35:10); "lying witnesses," *'ēdê šeqer* (Ps 27:12); "evil persons," *'adām rā'* (Ps 140:2); "men of violence," *'îš hămāsîm* (140:2, 5), *'îš hāmās* (Ps 18:49); "deceitful and shifty men," *'îš mîrmāh we'aūlāh* (Pss 43:1; 55:24; 59:3); "impious people," *gôy hāsîd* (Ps 43:1).

[208]Pss 5:6; 6:9; 59:3; 64:3; 141:9.

[209]Pss 59:6. In Pss 28:3 and 141:4, *pô'ălê 'āwen* also appear, but these do not designate the enemies of the one praying, rather a class of people with whom the pious ones do not wish to be damned.

[210]Pss 3:7; 27:3; 55:19b; 56:2; 59:5; 62:4; 109:3; 120:7; 140:3, 8; Jer 20:17; Pss. Sol. 12:3.

[211]Pss 27:3; cf. 3:7; 17:9.

[212]Ps 55:19.

[213]Ps 62:4.

[214]Pss 7:13; 37:14; (55:22); 57:5; 59:8; 64:4.

[215]Pss 7:13f; 11:2; 37:14; cf. 57:5; 64:4; 120:4.

[216]Pss 9:16; 31:5; 35:8; 57:7; 140:6

[217]Pss 7:16; 35:7; 57:7; 141:6f; Jer 18:22.

[218]Ps 22:17.

[219]Pss 10:3, 8ff; 35:10ff; 37:12; 56:7; 59:4; Lam 3:52.

[220]Ps 10:8ff.

[221]Pss 35:16; cf. 37:12.

mouth,[222] and yearn to feed on his flesh.[223] There are lions that threaten the one praying,[224] as well as enraged bulls,[225] or biting dogs.[226] May God crush their bite,[227] and shatter their teeth.[228]

These images could make one think about openly violent actions. Alongside these images stand *nonpictorial portrayals* of the enemies' activities. They allow one to recognize that the one praying really complains about *their crooked ways, their secret opinions, and their irritating, disdainful words.*[229] They threaten him without any cause,[230] and they plan murderous attacks against his life.[231] Or, at the very least they wait for his death so they can bury him.[232] Most of the time, the psalmist fears the *thoughts and tongue* of the enemy: "There is no truth in 'their' mouth. Their insides are corrupt. Their throat is an open grave, but their tongue flatters."[233] They taunt and slander the suffering,[234] and rejoice over his plight.[235] They do not speak of peace for those who are quiet in the land. On the contrary, they point to words of betrayal[236] and slander.[237] They convey hateful speeches. They come apparently to comfort the sufferer,[238] but they only make him ill.[239] They accuse him falsely of a crime.[240] In short, they attribute everything wicked to the loyal YHWH follower.[241] They rob him of all dignity and honor.[242]

Several places demonstrate clearly the enemies' words and thoughts which deeply wound the one praying. The one praying *communicates the enemies' words* to God in his prayer.[243] Their *mocking and their feeling of triumph* are the things that wound him. That which they expected finally comes to pass: "Ha, we have seen it with our own eyes."[244] "We have devoured him, and we have consumed him."[245] "He will no longer get up from

---

[222]Pss 35:21; cf. 22:14.

[223]Ps 27:2.

[224]Pss 7:3; 22:14; cf. 10:9; 17:12; 35:17.

[225]Ps 22:13.

[226]Ps 22:17.

[227]Ps 58:7; cf. Job 29:17.

[228]Ps 3:8.

[229]Pss 25:19; 27:12; 31:12; 35:15ff; 38:12f; 41:10; 55:4f; 69:8; 88:9, 19; Job 11:13-19; Jer 12:6; 20:18.

[230]Ps 38:20.

[231]Pss 31:5, 14; cf. 35:4; 40:15.

[232]Ps 22:19.

[233]Pss 5:10; cf. 55:22.

[234]Pss 31:12ff; 35:15; 42:11; 55:13; 102:9; 109:25.

[235]Pss 13:5; 35:15, 19, 26; 38:17.

[236]Pss 35:20; 36:4.

[237]Pss 4:3ff; 5:10; 27:11.

[238]Pss 3:3; 4:3ff; 5:10; 17:10; 41:6ff.

[239]Pss 69:22; cf. 5:10; 28:3; Jer 9:7.

[240]Pss 27:12; 35:11; 69:5.

[241]Ps 5:9f.

[242]Pss 3:3ff; 4:3; 69:20ff.

[243]Pss 3:3; 22:9; 35:21, 25b; 40:16; 41:6, 9; 42:4, 11; 64:6f; 71:11; Jer 11:19; 17:5; 18:18; 20:10.

[244]Ps 35:21.

[245]Pss 35:24; cf. 40:16.

the place where he lies."[246] "He will get no help from his God."[247] These words hit and wound, particularly when the one praying has become uncertain whether his God will help him. It is certainly no accident that on occasion the mocking question is repeated twice: "Where is your God now?"[248] Would that not make an impression upon him?

One of these words allows one to recognize more clearly than the others the thoughts that the enemies harbor: "Who regards 'us, ' or can see through our secrets? The fraud has succeeded. The bosom has been tricked. The heart is deep."[249] Accordingly, they do not just stand in *opposition to the pious*, but also to YHWH. The psalmist often accentuates this fact in order to cause God to intervene. The enemies defy YHWH,[250] and they pay no attention to his action.[251] They speak against him disparagingly and arrogantly: "He surmises nothing. He is no god."[252] They consider themselves secure before him, but they are far from his statutes.[253]

A confusing array of individual references expand the complaint songs when portraying the enemies. One can deduce without difficulty that the one praying fears their persecution will kill him or their mocking will cause him great pain. However, it is understandable that the discipline is not satisfied with this type of general and trite statements. If one wants to make progress, one should not employ the vivid imagery even though it appears to suggest itself.[254] These images are penetrated and combined with various nonmetaphorical portrayals, thereby losing sharpness and clarity. More often, one should recognize that the images of war, of the hunt, of thievery, etc., do not reflect the facts of the case but are comparisons for something else. However, that raises the difficult question which of these references are *intended literally* as characteristics of the enemy, thereby allowing one to find *something more definitive*.

Mowinckel correctly sees the *starting point* for the meaning of the enemies in the word *'awen* that occasionally appears in the designation of the enemies and their motives.[255] He understands it as "spell." The term *pô'alê 'awen* are thus magicians and he finds these almost everywhere in the enemies of the complaint songs.

The evidence for this belief proceeds from the incontrovertible fact that the same thing is said about the enemies in general as about the *pô'alê 'awen* in particular. If this concept really describes magicians, then according to Mowinckel, the parallel words that

---

[246]Ps 41:9.

[247]Ps 3:3.

[248]Ps 42:4, 11.

[249]Ps 64:6f.

[250]Ps 5:11.

[251]Ps 28:5.

[252]Pss 10:4; cf. 17:10; 10:13.

[253]Ps 10:5.

[254]This would be especially true for the statements about war. Taking them literally forbids one to interchange them with references of another type (cf. 7:13 with 7:3, 10, 15f; 55:19bf with 55:22, 24; 56:2 with 56:6f; and 57:5a with 57:5b-7; etc.). The fact is that those praying are not the great politicians, but are common private citizens. The model used for these utterances should be sought in the *royal complaint songs* that are imitated by the individual complaint songs (cf. §5, ¶9). In the process, the individual complaint songs lose their literal meaning and become images and symbols. For a parallel process in Egypt, see A. Erman, *Ägyptische Religion*, 1909, p. 114.

[255]He constantly transcribes the original form as *'aūn*.

are interchanged with it must also mean magic. However, if these portrayals of the enemies should be understood in the sense of magic, where they are found in parallel with *pô'alê 'awen*, then other portrayals of the enemies that do not use the term cannot be taken any other way. By this conclusion, Mowinckel finds numerous traces of magicians in the individual complaint songs. He concludes, on the basis of the unity, that the portrayals of the unity should generally be interpreted as magicians.[256]

Should his view be accepted?

One should certainly concede to Mowinckel that *'awen* means something dark, scared of the light, and secret, which does not coincide with rational concepts. One should even concede that sometimes it means magic.[257] However, that does not prove that *'awen* should be universally understood in this sense. Whoever would interpret in this way would have to argue that this word consistently had such a meaning over the course of the history of the language and that it was not subjected to any historical changes.

In addition to this general objection, a whole series of specific objections appear. First, one should object to the manner of argument that the significance of the parallel word is overstated. Words that appear together as parallel elements do not have to mean the same thing. It is entirely sufficient if they come together for a specific effect. "How" they come together is not yet determined. However, in an unbiased examination, the parallel words of our context rest in the condition of the hostility toward the pious.

It is thus conceivable that Mowinckel pushes a designation of the enemy *into the foreground* which demonstrably stands *clearly in the background*.[258] One does *violence to the material* if designations for the enemy that are readily comprehensible in one arena of images are interpreted magically just because they stand in parallel with an expression in which *'awen* appears.[259]

In addition, Mowinckel himself has to concede that the generally accepted meaning of "wicked" fits very well in many Old Testament passages.[260] He thereby admits that in many cases a nonmagic meaning is better than the one he suggests.

These considerations argue convincingly against Mowinckel's thesis. This impression gains even more stature to the point of complete refutation when one contemplates the relationship in which they stand to the distresses of the one praying.

---

[256]See various locations in *Psalmenstudien*, vol. 1.

[257]He may have proven that for Isa 58:9 (cf. *Psalmenstudien*, p. 8) where reference to holding out the finger stands alongside the *'awen* speech, which is a well-known action of magic (cf. examples in J. Hempel, "Die israelitischen Anschauungen von Segen und Fluch," *ZDMG* 79 [1925]: p. 25n.2).

[258]Only the following passages in the complaint songs speak of *'awen* speeches or actions: Pss 5:6; 6:9; 7:15; 10:7; (28:3); 41:7; 55:4; 56:8 (?); 59:3, 6; 64:3; 141:(4), 9.

[259]Mowinckel's treatment of Ps 59 is illuminating in this respect (see *Psalmenstudien*, vol. 1., pp. 67, 69, 132). The introductory words contain the expression *pô'alê 'awen* in parallel with *'ôyebay, mitqômemay, 'anšê dāmîm* and *'azzîm*. The fact that *'azzîm* ("strong") could fit well with the designation of demons in this context cannot be proven. By choosing this explanation, the exegete is deciding for *one possibility* of understanding. Methodologically, one has to work in exactly the opposite direction by moving from the indisputable statements to the unknown *pô'alê 'awen*.

[260]Mowinckel, *Psalmenstudien*, vol. 1., p. 57.

According to Mowinckel, the magical enemies inflict *illnesses* upon the pious.[261] The lying words and the whispering speeches, that flow forth from their tongue, as well as the placing of the trap and the laying of the net should all be related to magic words[262] and magic actions.[263] According to Mowinckel, the enemies are the "primary" evil, and they were perceived as such by those suffering. They were perceived as such to the degree that frequently the one suffering *completely ignores* the "secondary" evil, the sickness caused by the enemies. With painful emanations he implores only for *deliverance from his enemies*. If this happens, so we should believe, then the illness caused by the enemies will disappear by itself.[264]

These explications proceed from the fact, accurate by itself, that one often finds complaints about *enemies and illness* side by side.[265] However, one encounters *complaints about the enemies alone* even more frequently.[266] One must ask whether his interpretation of the condition is correct. Here, *one must strongly object to Mowinckel.*

Mowinckel's interpretation of the relationship between enemies and illness mentioned in the first group rests on his understanding of considerably fewer psalms which must be further checked below against his theory. However, even if one grants he is correct, should one object immediately to this understanding based on the large number of complaint songs in which it is not possible to recognize a connection between enemies and illness? If one must recognize the possibility of another context, then by no means can one ascribe the illness of the one praying to those psalms which only speak of enemies. Mowinckel's conclusions thereby appear to be rash and hasty.

One can add the following individual items to this general consideration.

Several things do not point toward magic: the fact that the enemies' chief weapon is the tongue, that they speak *šāū* and *kāzāb*, that they act in secret, and that they whisper. These things do not indicate magic unless one has already convinced oneself to interpret everything from the peripheral expression *pô'alê 'awen*. That which the psalmist understands by the words of his enemies proceeds from his citation of their vocabulary.[267] If it were magical incantations, we would certainly expect clear mention of that which had touched him and wounded him so deeply, here where the singer speaks aloud. Instead, *these passages, of which there are more than a few, are completely silent about magic.* According to them, the problem for the one praying is the bitter slander and the caustic mocking, nothing more. Mowinckel naturally wants us to know that the mock is only "another form of the curse which intends to make the weak weaker."[268] However, this conceptualization does not justify the central position of those words in the complaint. Those words really do not treat a secondary matter for the one praying.[269] The remaining texts

---

[261]Mowinckel, *Psalmenstudien*, vol. 1, pp. 5ff, 9ff, 17f, 19f, etc.

[262]Mowinckel, *Psalmenstudien*, vol. 1, pp. 15ff, 22, 23, 39, etc.

[263]Mowinckel, *Psalmenstudien*, vol. 1, pp. 20, 28, 42.

[264]Mowinckel, *Psalmenstudien*, vol. 1, pp. 101ff.

[265]Pss 3; 6; 13; 17; 22; 27:7ff; 28; 31; 40:14-16; 41:5-11; 42; etc.

[266]Pss 4; 5; 7; 11; 25(?); 52; 55; 57; 59; 62; 63; 64; 120; 123; 140; 142; etc.

[267]Cf. p. 142, note 242.

[268]Mowinckel, *Psalmenstudien*, vol. 1, p. 104.

[269]Compare the treatment of Ps 42 on p. 143.

can readily be understood without magical background when the psalmist refers to slander and mocking.

The individual thanksgiving songs offer a further counter-argument because they treat the same material as the complaint songs.[270] These songs think far less about deliverance from enemies than about deliverance from sickness and other distresses.[271] If the enemies were really the cause of all distress, or if the sick person really attributed everything to their removal, or if the sick person believed that the illness would disappear by itself with them, then the one offering thanksgiving would have mentioned them in the first position. The one offering thanksgiving would not bypass them in silence.

The complaint songs stemming from the *diaspora* and seeking the enemies in specific nationalities also argue against Mowinckel.[272]

The most serious objection, however, comes from comparing the statements of the complaint songs with the utterances which Job, when he is ill, makes against his friends who torment him with the speeches. To claim that these friends are magicians who caused Job's illness will not suffice. These men try comfort and to help him. When Job describes these men with expressions used by the complaint poets concerning their enemies, it is then impossible to ascribe magical meaning to these words.[273] Above all, the Job passages are convincing because, for Job as for the complaint singers, the pious one finds himself confronting persons whom he perceives as enemies. Also, a relationship between the illness and the enemies occasionally exists, but in Job it clearly does not exist in a magical cause.

For all of these reasons, Mowinckel's belief that the enemies of the psalmist are magicians does not withstand scrutiny to the extent that he claims. Do they at least hold up for the small group of passages from which he took his far-reaching conclusions?[274] One must also object to these passages. At no point, do these passages clearly say that the enemies called forth the illnesses. One has to contrast this with the fact that the one praying uses *unambiguous words* to trace his suffering back to YHWH.[275] Rather, closer

---

[270]Cf. ¶5.

[271]Pss 22:23ff; 28:6f; 30; 31:22ff; 34; 40; 103:1-5; 138; Jonah 2; Isa 38:15; Pr Azar 65.

[272]Pss 55:20; 120:5. Mowinckel does believe about the last passage that, "v. 5 should be understood metaphorically. It does not provide a reason for romantic considerations over a Jew living in exile or the pain of the diaspora" (Mowinckel, *Psalmenstudien*, vol. 1, p. 45). However, this is a decree, not evidence.

[273]Job describes his friends as "those spreading lies," *ṭōfelê šeqer*, (13:4; cf. Pss 5:7; 69:5). The friends speak '*awlāh* and *remîyāh* (Pss 13:7; cf. Pss 5:7; 7:15; 34:14; 35:20; 38:13; 43:1). Job calls his friends *menaḥămê 'āmāl* (16:2; cf. Pss 7:15; 10:7). Job is angry about his friend's "windy speech" (*dibrê rûaḥ*) in 16:3. According to *Psalmentstudien*, vol. 1, p. 39, however, *rûaḥ* should be a synonym for magician. Job knows that his friends harbor thoughts of *mezimmôt* and *maḥăšābôt* with which they wish to exercise "violence" (*ḥāmās*) against him (21:27; cf. Pss 10:7-11; 56:6). In secret the friends defend god's position (13:10; cf. the secretive action of the enemies of the psalmist). One also finds the images of the hunt (19:22). One hears the tenor of the psalmists enemies when Job's friends think: "We will pursue him and find the cause 'in him'" (19:28). These are just a few examples. Comparing the psalm passages cited, which Mowinckel interprets magically, shows how risky it is.

[274]Pss 6:3-8; 28:3-4; 41:6, 12; 69:21. See *Psalmenstudien*, vol. 1, pp. 9f, 17ff, 100.

[275]Cf. ¶6. See also H. Schmidt, *Gebet des Angeklagten im AT*, p. 31.

examination of the vocabulary demonstrates that Mowinckel introduced the decisive elements himself.[276]

Do the complaint songs recognize demonic powers in ways other than the cause of illness? Only Ps 91 clearly mentions these powers, but it is a psalm that does not belong in this context.[277] Nicolsky wants to find them in other passages, including complaint songs.[278] However, his presentation is unconvincing, in part because it is presented using Mowinckel's rationale which we have already treated. Or, can words such as these about Ps 18:5-6 be taken as serious proof? "The . . . quotes already mentioned remove any doubt that the waves of 'death,' the streams of Belial, Sheol's gang, and the net of "death" describe demonic powers which have attacked the author of the psalm."

If Mowinckel's starting point for interpreting the enemies is impossible, then the only remaining possibility is to approach them *as in the Job passages*. Immediately, of course, *two difficulties* are apparent. First, it can be shown that the images used for the relationship of the friends to Job do not correspond to one another materially. Do they want to chase him like a wild beast? Do they really go around lying about him? Are they really trying to do violence to him?[279] To ask these questions is to refute them. Rather, it is clear that the images want to express the impression which the friends' words and deeds have on Job. Further, it shows how passionately the words are expressed. Job is not trying to provide an objective portrayal. He wants to express his internal desire and to liberate himself from the unbearable tension of his soul. It cannot be overstated that one has to keep both aspects in mind if one wishes to interpret the singer's enemies. They protect against

---

[276]In Ps 28, the relationship of the one praying to the *rešā'îm* and the *pô'ălê 'āwen* does not function as the central point. Rather, he prays for preservation from them. The destiny of the wicked must be included, as well as vengeance for their action because they have not bothered with YHWH. The portrayal of the expected deliverance at the conclusion of the psalm only thinks about healing, not about the liberation from enemies which one would expect according to Mowinckel.

The sentence in Ps 6:8 ("My eye is dull from concern and fainter than all my enemies" [according to Mowinckel]) follows the portrayal of the illness and the pain. This sentence does not lead the impartial reader to conclude that the illness was caused by the enemies. Sorrow and sadness from their torments are completely understandable without relying upon magic.

In 41:5-11, Mowinckel introduced the decisive element: the one praying "presupposes that they (the enemies) are not satisfied with having put him in a sickbed" (*Psalmenstudien*, vol. 1, p. 17). Nothing can be discovered about this idea in the text. This interpretation also runs aground in 41:7. If this passage really intended a magician, it would be expected that the *'āwen* had spoken directly to the one praying, who is already sick. However, one would not expect him to go inside, drag him out, and address him outside (Hempel, "Die israelitischen Anschauungen von Segen und Fluch," 24ff).

In Ps 69, only one sentence supports Mowinckel's view: "I am sick because of my friends" (*Psalmenstudien*, vol. 1, p. 100). Otherwise nothing supports his interpretation. Rather, the psalmist clearly attributes his illness to YHWH. This sentence rests upon a very dubious conjecture. Mowinckel relocates *kol ṣôrrāy* from 69:20 to a place behind *wā'ānúšāh* in v. 21 and inserts *min* in front of it.

[277]See the commentary to Ps 91.

[278]See discussion of Pss 7; 18; 35; 58; 69; 109; 141 in N. Nicolsky, *Spuren magischer Formeln in den Psalmen*, BZAW 46, Gießen, 1929.

[279]Cf. above, p. 146, footnote 273.

falsely deducing what the material denies, namely clarity and certainty concerning all details.[280]

The first thing one should realize is that the one praying characteristically sees himself surrounded by a world of enemies. This world cannot be explained solely on the basis of the passionate exaggeration of the one suffering. One comes closer to understanding when one proceeds from the original cause of the complaint song, extreme illness and terrifying mortal danger.[281] The way in which it is possible that someone wrestling with death has the whole world as an enemy can be understood by starting with the observations Lévy/Bruhl has collected from the world of primitive tribes.[282]

If someone is beset by extreme illness, whose causes are not readily discernible (and very few were for primitive peoples), then that person's relationship to the surroundings are fundamentally changed. That person suspects demonic powers at work behind the invisible and unfathomable suffering, from which one must protect one's self in all circumstances. The poor ones to be pitied have wasted away because of the "wicked death." How should one relate to these people? "If one rushes to help them, one attempts the impossible: tearing them away from death when they are already more than halfway dead. It appears that it is trying to evoke an irresistible feeling of human sympathy. However, an irresistible feeling of fear and horror almost always leads the primitive people to do exactly the opposite."[283] One seeks to resolve the coherency with an unfortunate person, so that the circle in which he lives does not also encounter misfortune. Thus, "in a single second . . . the person who was a companion, a friend, or a relative, now becomes a stranger, an enemy, a subject of horror and hate.[284] From this standpoint, it becomes clear how sometimes the *outcast* is left by everyone, and if he appears again in their midst he is banished for the second time.

"For the same reason they never help someone who is drowning, or a person in any other kind of mortal danger. But when he cries in doubt, they flee from there as quickly as they can, or they even stone him in order to end it. Even women who have emergencies while bearing children cannot cry out because all the world would then run away and leave them without remaining to help.[285]

An instinctive egotistical feeling of sin, as can be observed among primitive peoples, may have originally been what made the Israelite who was praying see himself surrounded by enemies. One can easily see that occur when one remembers the inhuman treatment of the unfortunate ones in Israel who were cast out, or if one compares the shocking portrayal of Job 19:13-19, where everyone, including his wife, turns away from him in disgust. The fact that the gruesome treatment of those cast out was still typical in Jesus' time shows how long these primitive feelings lasted into more advanced times of human development which no longer explained the terrible impression of sickness magically.[286]

---

[280]This statement also contradicts Marshall who believes he is able to deduce specific groups of enemies for specific psalms, such as oppressors of the poor, personal enemies, and accusers.

[281]Cf. ¶6.

[282]L. Lévy-Bruhl, *Die geistige Welt der Primitiven*, 1927.

[283]Lévy-Bruhl, *Die geistige Welt der Primitiven*, p. 261.

[284]Lévy-Bruhl, *Die geistige Welt der Primitiven*, p. 263.

[285]Lévy-Bruhl, *Die geistige Welt der Primitiven*, p. 264.

[286]Luke 17:11-19.

A further example can be seen in the flight of the people of Wittenberg when the plague broke out in 1527.

Now, we would err if we believed had found *the* explanation of all the animosity toward the one suffering in the outbreak of the primitive feelings. This explanation would not explain the fact that enemies are very frequently castigated without even mentioning illness.[287] This reason is not known to Lamentations as we have received it. Therein one can see that Lamentations is not an example of a very primitive thought, and that one may not overemphasize primitive sounding references in them. These poems do not show of a dull-witted belief in incomprehensible demonic powers that exclude anyone asking "why" this happened. Here, a rational theory is offered, incorporating a specific, comprehensible reason for the illness of the one suffering. Thus, one finds the widely proliferated *doctrine of retribution* in Israel. Further, it is characteristic of Hebrew thought, in distinction to the primitive rationale of the feeling of horror, that the doctrine of retribution was not limited to the area of extreme illness or another mortal danger. Rather, the doctrine of retribution sought to explain every adversity which humans encountered. From that point, enemies arose for anyone who was afflicted, perhaps even in places where the primitives were not afraid.

Whoever has to suffer has been stricken by YHWH because of sin. One retreats from someone like this, especially if he has been stricken with a bad illness.[288] The declaration that YHWH has stricken the one suffering may be the only thing that one says about him.[289] The one who is sick, however, has perhaps become uncertain whether or not YHWH really afflicts him because of sin. In his spiritual irritation, he perceives the uncompassionate nature of such declarations and thereby feels himself wounded in his innermost being. Job's friends become enemies by these words, just as the men who visit the singer of Pss 41 and 69 become enemies, even though their intention is to comfort. That which the visitors say is only perceived by the one suffering as "poison" and "vinegar."[290] In his mistrust, when they only sought to gather by him, he even attributes to them what they could be saying about him outside.[291] When the neighbors appear in this respect, how else would the judgment and the conduct of the surroundings seem? To the one suffering *everyone* would appear *as enemies*, before whom *he alone* is left, destitute of all help.

A whole series of statements about the enemies could be understood in this way. Of course, the problem is not yet surmounted. Several instances demand yet another meaning, including the large number of enemies, their desire to harm, their taunting and their pleasure at someone else's pain, and finally their animosity to YHWH himself.[292]

Here contexts come into play which can perhaps best be explained by the *relationship of the one praying to his enemies*. The singers prefer to designate themselves as "poor."[293] In contrast, one can see that their enemies must be seen as rich and prosperous. Ps 119:78,

---

[287]Compare p. 145, footnote 266.

[288]Lévy-Bruhl, *Die geistige Welt der Primitiven*, p.17ff, 44ff, 242ff.

[289]As with Job's friends, so Pss 3:3; 41:9.

[290]Ps 69:22.

[291]Ps 41:7.

[292]Pss 13:3, 5; 18:18, 49; 41:12; and 55:13 speak only of an enemy. See also perhaps 7:6; 31:9; 42:10; 43:3; 61:4; 64:2 if they do not intend *'ōyēb* collectively.

[293]Pss 10:2; 12:6; 22:25; 35:10; 40:18; 86:1; 109:22; 140:13; 4:8 (cf. the commentary).

121, 134 speak explicitly of persecution by the godless rich. These persons practice the wickedness that the prophets have so often rebuked: false accusations, procuring false witnesses for the tribunal in order to corrupt the poor.[294] However, the rich do not stand in opposition to the poor as individuals but as *a type*. Thus, the psalmist often speaks of himself in the third person: "the enemy lies in wait to capture the one suffering."[295] YHWH will not forget the suffering before his enemies.[296] Indeed, enemies and pious are specifically contrasted as groups: "YHWH, let them 'confess.' Let their plots fail. Push them out 'according to' their many sins, for they offer defiance. But all whom you have rescued will rejoice. Those who love your name will always exult and be happy about you 'all the time.' "[297]

These sentences allow one to recognize that the hostility can extend beyond the relationship from person to person. It concerns *groups* who oppose one another. They are separated from one another by *social contrast*. The pious belong to the lower classes. The rich and the powerful stand over against them. They are the ruling powers which pre-supposes that they are often named in connection with the other nations, that is with the heathen, with whom they apparently have relationships.[298]

Religious contrast appears alongside the social contrast. The poor one believed him-self pious and is convinced the *rich are wicked*. The poor one believes the rich persecute him because of his religion. To identify the contrast more specifically, it is important to note that the enemies are never castigated for the worship of idols. The primary sin of the preexilic people no longer plays a role in the psalms. They are accused of not having YHWH before them and having no fear of God.[299] They are accused of openly acting wickedly. Even when they are warned, they only respond with impudent speech. "YHWH does not see. Jacob's God has no understanding."[300] "How would God know of this? Is there knowledge with the Most High?"[301] It could be that through these statements the psalmists perceive the influence of the "heathen."[302]

According to these words, and similar ones, the enemies do not believe the sentence that means everything to the pious, namely, that God judges rightly, that he distinguishes between right and wrong, that the righteous remains but the godless pass away. It apparently concerns the enlightened rich who are mistaken about the doctrine of retribution, and now must suffer the consequences.[303] From their standpoint, they have only ridicule for the pious who finds misfortune and whose trust in God is now really put to the test. They now try to make him fall. The pious one, however, retaliates with all his heart. He hates them with all his being, not just because they are *his* enemies, but in *the*

---

[294]Pss 7:4ff; 27:12; 35:11.
[295]Ps 10:9.
[296]Pss 9:13; 10:12; cf. 35:20; 69:7.
[297]Ps 5:11-12.
[298]Pss 7:7ff; 9:16ff; 56:8; 59:6.
[299]Ps 36:2.
[300]Ps 94:7.
[301]Pss 73:11, cf. further 10:3ff, 11.
[302]Cf. footnote 295, p. 150.
[303]Compare Qoh 2:16; 4:1-3; 7:15; Sir 16:17-23.

name of religion: "YHWH, shall I not hate those that hate you; should I not abhor those who abhor you? Indeed, I hate them completely. They are enemies to me."[304]

Seen in this context, one can understand that the individual praying really can have a large number of enemies. From this point, one understands the passionate and very irritated tone which the psalmists strike against their enemies. They are battling for their holiest ideal, their trust in God, which every worldly person is trying to drag into the dust. For this reason, one also understands why the enemies are so frequently mentioned, not just in connection with illness. Every case of misfortune must have been a cause for their hostility.

The question is whether one can draw out anything more from these statements concerning the psalmists' enemies. The fact that there were factions, along with their general characteristics, scarcely offers a valid basis for further statements. From the beginning, postexilic Judaism knew a polarity between the pious and children of the world. The material contents are only very briefly suggested. Those returning home after 520 found a group of inhabitants who had remained in the land and who knew nothing of the religious development of Babylonian Judaism. The returnees had to come to grips with those who had remained. Later returnees attached themselves closely with the population of the land and its neighbors, so that Ezra and Nehemiah had to purify the community with force. In this way, difficulties arose within Judaism itself, about which the books of Ezra and Nehemiah occasionally provide information. After the dark period of the fourth and third centuries the influence of Greek culture on Judaism began to be noticeable. It reached its climax in the ruthless Hellenization of Antiochus Epiphanes. The Maccabean revolt was directed against this Hellenization and against the Hellenistic collaborators, and it found support in the circles of the 'Ασιδαῖοι. However, the Maccabeans and their adherents soon became secularized and appear in opposition to the pious. A new split appears. In the time of Jesus, the Pharisees and the Sadducees stood in opposition to one another. It appears risky to identify the psalmists' enemies with a specific group of secularized Jews. Pss. Sol. 12:1-3 certainly thinks of the children of the world from the Maccabean time when it petitions for deliverance from the evil and lawless man or from the lawless and slanderous tongue. However, the ancient psalms of the canon speak in a similar manner about the singer's enemies.[305] The fixed style of the complaint song constantly portrays the opponents from differing times using the same images and expressions. This style prohibits closer inspection. One must be satisfied with this conclusion.

9. There are fewer complaints about *relatives, friends, and acquaintances* than complaints about enemies if one looks at the amount of material. That is understandable since this subject treats very personal experience that would not be of the more general significance as the resistance of a hostile group. However, if one looks at the subject, the action of close persons strikes the one praying much deeper: "'If' only 'my' enemy had burdened me, 'then I could seek refuge.' 'If' only the one who hates me had done something great against me, I could hide from him. But you are a person like me, me friend and confidant. We attended to sweet fellowship in YHWH's temple."[306] This bitter mood is perhaps under-

---

[304]Ps 139:21f.

[305]Pss 5:10; 10:7; 27:12; 41:6ff. See also Jer 20:13 with its contrast of "poor" and evil. See the discussion in Baumgartner, *Klagegedichte des Jeremia*, p. 51.

[306]Ps 55:15.

standable. Instead of standing by him and comforting him, the people closest to him retreat from the one praying because he is deemed marked by YHWH to his brothers, relatives, acquaintances, guests, servants, maidservants, even his own wife.[307] He has become a horror to everyone.[308] One can understand if the terrible stress of the one praying makes known the oppressiveness of being left in a cruel manner, causing the one praying to utter wild curses concerning those who have so painfully disappointed him: "May they go 'quaking.' 'Let death fall' over them. May they go to hell trembling, traveling there in their horror."[309] One can also understand if the friends that visit him become hated enemies to him because he attributes to them an intention that corresponds to the harmful effect of their words to him.[310]

10. Now, concerning the *arrangement of the complaint songs*.

The individual complaint song begins just like the communal complaint song,[311] with the *summons in the name of YHWH*. The summons regularly stands *among the first words of the first sentence.*[312] It appears far less frequently in other positions.[313] Passages where the psalm does not begin with the summons deviate so strongly from the normal style that the song should not be designated as an individual complaint song in the strict sense, even if it otherwise uses the motifs of the genre.[314]

The summons is repeated with *new sections* in the psalm, sometimes with the complaint or with the petition.[315] The summons appears particularly frequently in poems where the petition begins after the complaint.[316] It is also repeated at the beginning of the petition in general,[317] at its conclusion,[318] or in other locations.[319]

Observations concerning this address are important because one can see from whence the psalmist begins. In those places where he summons the name of YHWH, he renews his concern that YHWH really does hear him.

---

[307]Job 19:13-19; cf. Pss 27:10; 31:12; 38:12; 41:10; 55:13f; 88:9, 19; Jer 12:6; 20:10.

[308]Ps 31:12.

[309]Ps 55:15f.

[310]Pss 41:7; 55:22; cf. p. 149, footnotes 290 and 291.

[311]Cf §4, ¶4.

[312]Pss 3:2; 5:2; 6:2; 7:2; 13:2; 16:1; 17:1; 22:2; 25:1; 26:1; 27:7; 28:1; 31:2; 35:1; 38:2; etc.

[313]Pss 42:2; 120:2; Isa 38:14. The observations of this footnote and the previous footnote also hold true for the communal complaint, as well as the prayer in general. Cf. B. Stade, *Biblische Theologie des Alten Testaments*, vol. 1, p. 150, and Fr. Heiler, *Das Gebet*, 4th edition, pp. 58f.

[314]Pss 4; 11; 23; 39; 52; 119; Lam 3.

[315]Pss 3:4; 5:9; 6:5; 7:4, 7; 17:6; 31:10, 18, 20, 22; 38:10; 39:8; 69:6f, 17; 71:17; 77:12; 86:8, 12, 14; 88:14f; 119:33, 41; 130:3; 140:5; Lam 3:58; Jer 12:3; 17:14; 18:23.

[316]Pss 3:8; 5:11; 6:5; 13:4; 17:13; 22:20; 35:17, 22; 38:22f; 41:11; 43:1; 55:24; 56:8; 58:7; 69:14; 71:12; 88:14; 102:13; 142:6; (40:18; 41:11); Jer 18:19.

[317]Pss 5:9; 7:7; 17:13; 25:4, 11; 30:11; 31:4; 35:22f, 24; 39:13; 51:12, 16, 17; 86:4; 88:14; 109:21; 120:2; 139:19, 23; 140:9; 143:7. The same thing occurs in Babylonian material. Cf. Ungnad, *Religion der Babylonier und Assyrer*, pp. 198, 205, 206, 219, 220, 221, 223.

[318]Pss 3:8; 19:15; 38:22f; 43:4.

[319]Pss 4:9; 5:13; 6:3, 4; 7:9; 17:14; 25:6, 7; 26:11; 27:11; 31:6; 35:24; 38:10, 16; 54:7; 59:13; 69:30; 71:4f, 18f; 86:4, 5, 6; 140:8f; 143:9; Lam 3:58, 61, 64; Ps 119:12, 31, 52, 55, 64, 75, 108; Jer 15:16. The same thing happens in communal complaints, see §4, ¶4.

The most frequent name which one encounters in this context is "YHWH."[320] Other names alternate with YHWH, in part, in the form of appositionally expanded[321] address: "YHWH of hosts,"[322] "God of Israel,"[323] "God,"[324] "my God,"[325] "YHWH, my God,"[326] and "Lord."[327] These terms often express *what YHWH means for the one praying.* For this reason, one frequently finds that the first person suffix and comparative words are selected that express protection and help. At this point it will suffice to reference[328] these briefly since the subject of the occasion of the statements of confidence will be more extensively treated in ¶19.

One should observe that these names to not appear to be heaped upon one another in the Psalms. Israelites relate very differently at this point than the one praying in the Babylonian material. The Babylonian incorporates an abundance of honorific names for the divinity, to which a portrayal of the majesty of the summoned God is attached.[329] The Babylonian thereby desires to put his gods in a favorable mood, or to flatter them and seek to convince them to do what he implores. The Israelite acts differently to YHWH. From the outset, he trusts that YHWH will hear him and refuses to depend upon the external means of convincing by flattery.[330]

This difference coincides with the fact that the Israelite address, in contrast to the Babylonian, does not use the hymn-like expansion[331] using the relative sentence or the participle. This expansion helps explain what the heaping of addresses has expressed, and serves the flattering of the gods. However, the Israelite genre scorns this expansion.[332]

Outside of the canonical psalms one can find traces of arrangements of the summons corresponding to the Babylonian material in content and form. The two texts which will be mentioned here are Jer 17:12-18 and the Prayer of Manasseh. The Jeremiah text begins with a heaping of summonses, of which the first three (remarkably similar to Babylonian and Israelite) references relate to the sanctuary while the last two are directed to YHWH.[333]

---

[320]Pss 3:2, 4, 8; 4:7, 9; 5:2, 9, 11; 6:2, 3, 4, 5; 7:2, 4, 7; 13:1; 17:13, 14; 22:20; 25:1, 4, 6, 11; etc.

[321]See §2, ¶19.

[322]Ps 69:7.

[323]Ps 69:7.

[324]'ēl; see 16:1; 17:6.

[325]Pss 3:8; 22:2; 30:11; 35:23; 38:16, 22; 40:18.

[326]Pss 7:2, 4; 13:4; 43:4; 88:2; 109:26.

[327]Pss 35:17; 38:10; 39:8; 51:17; 59:12; 86:4f, 8, 15; Lam 3:58.

[328]Ps 19:15; 22:20; 27:9; 28:1; 31:6; 38:23; 59:10; 140:8. Similarly, the same thing happens in communal complaints. See §4, ¶4.

[329]Cf. Fr. Stummer *Sumerisch-akkadische Parallelen zum Aufbau alttestamentlicher Psalmen,* 1922, pp. 11ff; J. Begrich, "Die Vertrauensäußerungen im israeltischen Klageliede des Einzelnen und in seinem babylonischen Gegenstück," *ZAW,* new series 5 (1928): 230. Recently also W. G. Kunstmann, *Die babylonische Gebetsbeschwörung,* Leipziger Semitische Studien, new series 2, 1932.

[330]Cf. Begrich, *ZAW* new series 5 (1928): 250-251, 254.

[331]Cf. ¶2, §20.

[332]Cf. Begrich, *ZAW* new series 5 (1928): 251.

[333]Perhaps there is a textual error. Is something missing from the beginning of *yōšēb*? (Supposition of Gunkel.)

As more commonly occurs in Babylonian material, the name of God does not stand in the first position. Rather, it comes later for the sake of the climax. It is attached to the "portrayal of majesty" using an independent clause.[334] It is general and widely preserved: "All who leave you will come to nought; those who deviate from you are ascribed to the underworld." A personal relationship to the God who is addressed is not clear. The emotion of trust, the characteristic element of the Israelite complaint song, is subsumed under the homage of God, as in the Babylonian material.[335]

The *Prayer of Manasseh* agrees even more closely with the Babylonian forms. The confession of sin begins with v. 9. In v. 13 the petition for forgiveness follows. An eight verse summons and portrayal of majesty precedes: "Lord, all powerful, heavenly God of our fathers Abraham, Isaac, and Jacob and their righteous seed." These names are expanded in participial style as in the Babylonian forms.[336] Their content really belongs to hymnic themes, the praise of the creator: "The one who created the heavens and the earth, together with all its adornment, who bound the host by the word of his command, you are the one who enclosed and sealed the deep with your fearful, majestic name."[337] The participle is continued by the relative sentence. In place of the direct praise in which YHWH is the subject, there appears an indirect praise in which he is the object of the sentence. The continuation states: "Before whose power everything shudders and trembles." The portrayal of majesty then follows. It is limited, as in several Babylonian prayers, to the fertility of YHWH against the sins and the immeasurable nature of his grace. The praise of grace holds the last word, to which the hope that the prayer will be heard is attached: "For the majesty of your splendor cannot be endured. Your anger cannot be endured. Your anger threatens the sinners. The grace you promise is immeasurable and incomprehensible. For you, Lord, are the highest, most compassionate, long-suffering and very gracious. You repent of human sufferings." Here we clearly find the Babylonian form. The content also shows Babylonian influence, observable in the connection of the emotion of trust and the homage of God. Of course, Israelite material comes to the forefront with regard to content.[338]

11. Next to the summons we find one of the most important components of the genre, the complaint.[339] It is not always expressed as an independent motif, but in those psalms lacking a complaint, it stands very much in the background.[340]

---

[334]Terms according to Stummer, *Sumerisch-akkadische Parallelen*, p. 9.

[335]See the details in Begrich, *ZAW* new series 5 (1928): 249.

[336]*ZAW* new series 5 (1928): 231.

[337]Cf. §2, ¶48, 50.

[338]This form of summons appears much more regularly in the communal complaint. Cf. the examples in §4, ¶12.

[339]Pss 3:2-5; 5:10; 6:3, 4, 7-8; 10:1-11; 13:1-3; 22:2-3, 7-9, 13-19; 27:10; 31:10-14; 35:7, 11-16, 20-21; 38:3-21; 40:13; 41:6-9; 42:2-4, 7-12; 43:3; 54:5; 55:4-6, 10c-12, 13-15b, 19b-22; 56:3; 57:5; 59:4, 7-8; 64:4-7; 69:1b-5, 8-13, 20-22; 86:14; 88:4-10, 15-19; 102:4-12, 24-25; 109:2-5, 22-25; 120:5-7; 140:3-4, 5-6; 142:4c-5; 143:3-4; Jer 11:18-19; 15:18; 17:15; 18:18; 20:10; (15:10; 20:7-9, 14-18); Job 6:4-7, 11-12, 21-23; 7:2-6, 12-21; 10:1, 18-22; 13:23-26; 16:6, 20-17:2, 4-9; 19:7-20; 23:2; 29:1-30:3; Pr. Man. 9-10; Pss. Sol. 12:2; Isa 38:10-14; Jonah 2; (Ps 66:18).

[340]Pss 7; 17; 28; 39; 51; 61; 63; 71; 130; 141; Pss. Sol. 5:2-8; 16:5-16.

That which oppresses and torments the heart of the one praying flows unrestrictedly in the complaint. "He pours out his soul before YHWH."[341] It unfolds a picture of his suffering and despondence. The complaints are often expressed generally. The one praying "is afraid,"[342] and his soul is bewildered.[343] He is filled with worries and concerns.[344] He has lost his courage.[345] Occasionally the psalmist speaks more clearly. He is ill. He hangs suspended in mortal danger. Mostly, his enemies are coping with him.[346] In all of this trouble, he suffers from the awareness that God has left him.

That which torments and oppresses him will not let him go. His suffering follows him deep into the night and into his sleep, granting him no peace. His sorrow continues day and night.[347] The night pierces his bones.[348] His tears are his food day and night.[349]

One approaches the characteristic life of this motif when one asks about the *form of the complaint*. Two elements are found in the main part, the *narrative* and the *portrayal*. The narrative differentiates itself from the thanksgiving song's narrative in that what is communicated never appears entirely in the past. Rather, it is still operative in the present. One could describe the tense specifically as *perfectum praesens*. Ps 22:15 is an example of this: "I have been poured out like water. All of my limbs have dissolved. My heart has become like wax, melted within me." Or, Ps 69:21f says: "I waited for 'a comforter, ' but there was none. I waited for sympathizers, but did not find them. They gave me poison as bread for comfort, and made me drink vinegar for my thirst."[350]

The *portrayal* highlights references to the immediate present. Here, one generally finds the imperfect as the tense. The nominal sentence alternates with it: "Every night I wet my bed. My couch flows with tears."[351] My palate is as dry as a pot, and my tongue cleaves to my jaw."[352] The portrayals far outnumber the narrative references with which they alternate, which betrays the inner turmoil of the psalmists. Everything about which they complain is very close to them and the emotional fantasy, including death and the underworld.

From here, we can delve more deeply into the motif. Israelite prayer is not naive. The complaint is not formed without intention. The *goal* of *moving* YHWH dominates the motif.[353] The complaint should challenge YHWH's honor (as with the complaint about enemies) and excite his anger, or the complaint should move him. Therefore, one should present the points of complaint as heatedly as possible. One prefers to choose the moment when everything stands under the blade of the knife. YHWH must now decide whether he will help. Otherwise, it will be too late: "Powerful steers surround me, Bashan's strong

---

[341]Pss 42:5; cf. 102:1.

[342]Ps 31:10.

[343]Ps 6:4.

[344]Pss 13:3; 31:10.

[345]Pss 40:13; cf. further 6:8; 25:16; 38:9; 40:18; 42:6, 12; 43:5; 119:141, 143, 153.

[346]Cf. ¶6-9.

[347]Ps 13:3.

[348]Job 30:17.

[349]Pss 42:4; cf. also 22:3; 32:4; 55:11; Jer 8:23.

[350]Cf. Pss 6:3, 4, 8; 22:13f; 27:10; 31:10, 12; 35:7; 38:3; etc.

[351]Ps 6:7.

[352]Pss 22:16; cf. also 3:3; 5:10; 6:7; 10:2ff; 22:7f, 16-19; 31:10b; 35:11f, 20; 38:4f; etc.

[353]The same is true for the communal complaint. See §4, ¶9.

ones surround me. 'His' vengeance cuts me off like a marauding, roaring lion.[354] "They divide my garments among themselves and cast lots for my clothing."[355] "I hear many whispering all around me. Too often, they counsel against me, plotting revenge to take my life."[356]

Or, one cites the *words of the enemies* directly, so YHWH will be inflamed. One also seeks that which would irritate him most. "He 'turned' to YHWH as the one who would deliver and save him, because he loved him."[357] "Ha, we have seen it with our own eyes."[358] If the one praying wishes to move YHWH, he presents himself in the foreground in contrast to the enemies. He portrays himself so pitifully and sympathetically that he hopes God can do nothing more than listen to him. He is so battered that he can no longer endure God's wrath.[359] He can count all of his bones.[360] The dust of death is already on his lips.[361] He sinks in the mire of the deep, and the river of the underworld threatens to take him away.[362] On occasion, the portrayal escalates when the one praying describes himself as having been left by God: "I have been cast out from before your eyes;"[363] "The Lord will not hear me."[364] He gladly strengthens the effectiveness of the complaint so that one contrasts the impudent instigation of the enemies with the pitiful nature of his own situation.[365] Or, the one praying accentuates the way he acted in their position over against the actions of his opponents.[366] The agitation in these contrasts betrays the painful torrents for the one praying. It becomes most visible in the characteristic reformulation of the portrayal in the *form of the question*.[367] In place of the simple portrayal, "my enemies are many," one finds, "how many are my enemies?"[368] Indeed, the one praying hurls the impatient question in YHWH's face: "Why, YHWH, do you stand in the distance? Why do you hide in times 'of distress?'"[369] "My God, my God, why have you forsaken me?" These questions which one finds here and there mostly begin with "why." One seeks an explanation for that which has happened. Less frequently, these questions begin with "what."[370] Petitions posed with an interrogative pronoun offer a counterpart.[371]

One perceives that the agitated complaints of the inwardly shaken person sometimes forget the distance between God and humans. Sometimes the complaint brings an accusa-

---

[354]Ps 22:13-14.
[355]Ps 22:19.
[356]Pss 31:14; cf. 35:12; 38:11; 54:5.
[357]Ps 22:9.
[358]Ps 35:21. See also the references in ¶8, p. 142, footnote 243.
[359]Ps 6:3-4.
[360]Ps 22:18.
[361]Ps 22:16.
[362]Ps 69:3.
[363]Ps 31:23.
[364]Pss 66:18; 116:10; Jonah 2:5; Isa 38:10-14.
[365]Pss 22:7-9, 13-16, 17-19; 31:10-12, 13-14; 42:7-11; etc.
[366]Ps 35:13f.
[367]This also happens in the communal complaint. See §4, ¶7.
[368]Ps 3:2.
[369]Ps 10:1.
[370]Pss 42:6, 12; 43:3.
[371]Cf. ¶16.

tion against God. It appears that the feeling of several psalmists took offence at these complaints.[372] The more polite piety of these poets instinctively perceived that the loud, noisy, wild complaints went too far. They felt that the stormy intimidation of YHWH, or the murmuring and rumbling against him could easily lead to presumptuousness. That may be the reason why the complaint recedes in several psalms. The psalmist of Ps 39 certainly had this perception. "He does not want to prepare the spectacle for the godless one who gladly observes his pain in which the pious one quarrels with his God."[373]

The Babylonian counterpart does not remove the remarkable life of the Israelite complaint. It certainly contains the same or similar material: illness and suffering, fear, distress and complaint, offence by the king and princes, divine wrath, mortal danger, etc.[374] However, the Babylonian counterpart generally expresses these elements in a genuinely passionless manner: "According to your weighty command, according to the heat of your powerful divinity, I became . . . sick and tormented with pain. Your servant siezed and pursued the hand of the spirit of the dead, magic, and suffering. He has become healthy and well."[375] Portrayals of the moving complaint, or the miserable condition of the one praying, are not found all that often: "I look around, but no one takes me by the hand. I cry, but no one comes to my side. I let loose with laments but no one hears me. I am full of suffering. I am defeated, and no longer look up."[376] Occasionally the complaint is raised to the vividness of metaphorical speech: "I totter like a flood blown about by an evil wind. My heart soars and flutters like a bird in the sky. I complain like a dove day and night. I am oppressed and I cry pitifully. My mind is tormented from woe and sorrow.[377] We hear about "daily misery,"[378] about "calling without being heard,"[379] and about "moaning and groaning."[380] One cannot fail to see the similar elements in these references to those in the Israelite complaint. However, they are quite uncommon, and they do not determine the essence of the motif to be remotely like the Hebrew complaints.

12. The most significant part of the complaint song is the *petition*.[381] It is the heart

---

[372]Pss 7; 17; 28; 39; 51; 61; 63; 71; 130; 141; Pss. Sol. 5:2-8; 16:5-16.

[373]See the commentary to this passage.

[374]Schollmeyer, *Sumerisch-babylonische Hymnen und Gebete an Šamaš*, pp. 98:14ff, 18f; 106:25; 114:15; Ebeling, *Quellen zur Kenntnis der babylonischen Religion*, vol. 1, pp. 37:35ff; 45:30; vol. 2, 38:17; Ungnad, *Religion der Babylonier und Assyrer*, pp. 206:40; 220:75ff; 223:13; see also Kunstmann, *Die babylonische Gebetsbeschwörung*, pp. 16ff.

[375]Ungnad, *Religion der Babylonier und Assyrer*, pp. 179:10-14; cf. 223:11-14.

[376]Ungnad, *Religion der Babylonier und Assyrer*, pp. 225:35-38.

[377]Ungnad, *Religion der Babylonier und Assyrer*, 220:62-66. Cf. Zimmern, *Babylonische Hymnen und Gebete*, vol. 1, p. 26.

[378]Ungnad, *Religion der Babylonier und Assyrer*, 206:39.

[379]Ungnad, *Religion der Babylonier und Assyrer*, 223:14.

[380]Zimmern, *Babylonische Hymnen und Gebete*, vol. 1, pp. 25, 26.

[381]Pss 3:8; 5:2f, 9, 11; 6:2, 3, 5; 7:2, 7, 9; 13:4; 16:1; 17:1ff, 6-9, 13, 14; 19:13-15; 22:12, 20-22; 25:4, 6, 7, 16-20; 26:1f, 9; 27:7-12; 28:1-4; 30:11; 31:2, 3, 10, 16, 17; 35:1-3, 22-24; 36:11; 38:2, 22, 23; 39:9, 11, 13, 14; 40:14, 18; 41:5, 11; 43:1, 3; 51:3, 4, 9-14, 16; 54:3, 4, 7; 55:2, 3; 56:2, 4, 8, 9; 57:2; 59:2, 3, 5, 6, 12, 13; 61:2, 3; 64:2, 3; 69:2, 14, 15, 17-19, 24, 25-28; 71:2-4, 9, 12, 18; 86:1-4, 6, 11, 16; 88:3; 102:2-4, 25; 109:1, 6, 21, 26; 116:4; 118:25; 119:8, 10, 12, 17-19, 22, 25-29, 31, 33-40, 43, 49, 58, 64, 66, 68, 73, 86, 88, 94, 107, 108, 116, 117, 121, 122, 124, 125, 132-135, 144, 149; 120:2; 130:2; 138:8; 139:23f; 140:2, 7, 9; 141:1, 3, 4, 8; 142:7, 8; 143:1, 2, 7-

of the genre, which is understandable since the efforts of the praying are designed to obtain something from God.

The given form of the petition is the *imperative*. The imperative attaches to an *abundance of contents*.

We should begin with *petitions of a general nature*, the primary one being those which seek to inspire YHWH to *hear the prayer* various statements. "Hear me."[382] "Hear my voice."[383] "Hear my speech,"[384] or "examine my words."[385] "Examine my tears."[386] "Listen to my loud crying,"[387] and "incline your ear to me."[388] One encounters an abundance of different types of formulations as the passages cited in the footnotes allow one to see more clearly.

The parallel Babylonian genre also indicates corresponding petitions. "Hear my entreaty. Accept my fervent petitions and prayers."[389] "Hear my speech, accept my entreaty, and hear my prayer."[390]

The *general prayer* that YHWH might favorably notice the matter of the one praying stands close to the petitions mentioned above. Here, one finds short sayings. "Look."[391] "See,"[392] or "observe."[393] The deviation in Job 14:6 and 39:14 is quite original. They request that YHWH look away, exactly the opposite of what is typical. These Job texts presume that God looks at the singer with anger. It is better for this person that God not look at him. Maybe then he will forget the punishment and pain.

The Babylonian genre also manifests points of contact to the Israelite genre at this point: "come here,"[394] "arise,"[395] "look at me,"[396] "turn to me."[397] The relationship to an object, such as to the one praying, places this last petition simultaneously into the arena we will treat next. All of these texts characteristically begin with a petition to "hear."

12; Isa 38:14; Jer 12:3; 15:15; 17:14, 17f; 18:19, 23; Lam 3:19, 63; Sir 51:10; Pr Man 13; Syriac Apocryphal Psalms 3:1, 3-21; 4:2, 6, 13.

[382]Ps 119:145.

[383]Pss 27:7; 64:2; 119:149; 130:2.

[384]Ps 17:6.

[385]Pss 5:2; see also 17:2; 54:4; 55:2; 86:6; 140:7; 141:1; 143:1.

[386]Ps 39:13.

[387]Pss 5:3; see also 86:6.

[388]Pss 17:6; 31:3; 86:1; 88:3; 102:2; Syriac Apocryphal Psalms 3:3; see also 5:2; 17:1; 27:8; 28:1, 2; 30:11; 39:13; 54:4; 55:3; 61:2; 102:3; 119:169, 170; 142:7; 143:1; Jer 18:19.

[389]Ungnad, *Religion der Babylonier und Assyrer*, 175:56.

[390]Ungnad, *Religion der Babylonier und Assyrer*, 205:25-30; see also 177:22-23; 219:43-44; 221:91-92; 222:99-100; 223:19; 226:46; Ebeling, *Quellen zur Kenntnis der babylonischen Religion*, vol. 22:9; 37:36; vol. 2, 12:22; 44:17; etc.

[391]Pss 25:19; 59:5; 119:159; Lam 1:9, 11, 20; 2:20; 5:1.

[392]Pss 13:4; 74:20; 80:15; Isa 64:8; Lam 2:20; 3:63.

[393]Ps 74:20.

[394]Ungnad, *Religion der Babylonier und Assyrer*, 205:29.

[395]Schollmeyer, *Sumerisch-babylonische Hymnen und Gebete an Šamaš*, 99:24; 108:7.

[396]Ungnad, *Religion der Babylonier und Assyrer*, pp. 177:4, 22; 219:43; 221:92; 223:19; Ebeling, *Quellen zur Kenntnis der babylonischen Religion*, vol. 1, pp. 22:9; 37:36.

[397]Ungnad, *Religion der Babylonier und Assyrer*, 177:25.

Occasionally the brief petition is *expanded* by *that which* YHWH *should see*. "Look at my suffering and my distress."[398] Some petitions are even more urgent, e.g., "Do not hide your face,"[399] and the petition to think and not reject YHWH's servant.[400]

The petition for *gracious intervention* can be added to these petitions. It is so generally preserved that it expresses the excitement of the one complaining and his urgent demand for immediate help. If it appears when the affirmation of being heard is omitted, as though YHWH is sleeping, then the petition attempts to pull him away from his sleep: "wake up."[401] The summons seeks to disturb him from the contemplative rest in which God does not pay attention to the one suffering. "Arise."[402] "Stand up."[403] The innocent one wishes to speed divine intervention. "Hurry to me."[404] "Hurry to help."[405] "Do not tarry."[406] The pious one moans to YHWH. "Do not retreat."[407] "Do not leave me."[408] "Do not stay far from me."[409] He demands: "Visit me."[410] "Intervene for me."[411] "Come close to my soul,"[412] etc.

After these calls to pay attention and to come to help, the petition transitions to the *main point*. One also finds an abundance of common expressions here which do not allow one to recognize the specific item which is bothering the one praying. They only express the demand in general terms. "Have compassion on me."[413] "Help me."[414] "Support me."[415] "Save my soul,"[416] etc.

The Babylonian counterpart also knows this petition. "Help me."[417] "Do not be antagonistic."[418] "Be gracious to me,"[419] etc.

---

[398]Pss 25:18; cf. 119:153.

[399]Pss 27:9; 69:18; 102:3; 143:7.

[400]Pss 25:7; 27:9; Jer 15:15. For similar petitions, see Pss 25:6, 16; 31:17; 69:17; 86:12; 119:132, 135; Lam 3:19.

[401]Pss 7:7; 59:6; cf. further 35:23; 59:5.

[402]Pss 3:8; 17:13.

[403]Pss 3:8; 7:7; 17:13; 35:2.

[404]Ps 40:18.

[405]Pss 22:20; 38:23; 40:14; 71:12.

[406]Ps 40:18.

[407]Ps 55:2.

[408]Pss 27:9; 71:9; 119:8.

[409]Pss 22:12, 20; 35:22; 38:22; 71:12. Cf. also 28:1; 35:22; 39:13; 83:2; 109:1.

[410]Jer 15:15; cf. 119:176.

[411]Isa 38:14; cf. Ps 119:122.

[412]Pss 69:19; cf. 35:3; 119:124.

[413]Pss 6:3; 25:16; 26:11; 27:8; 30:11; 31:10; 41:5, 11; 51:3; 56:2; 57:2; 86:3, 16; 119:58, 132.

[414]Pss 3:8; 6:5; 7:2; 22:22; 31:17; 54:3; 59:3; 69:2; 86:2; 109:26; 118:25; 119:86, 94, 146; Jer 17:14.

[415]Ps 119:116.

[416]Pss 35:17; cf. further, 6:5; 7:2; 18:8, 13; 25:20; 26:11; 30:11; 39:9; 43:1; 51:16; 59:2f; 61:3; 64:2; 69:15, 17; 71:2; 86:2; 109:21, 26; 116:4; 119:17, 38, 49, 117, 122, 134, 153, 154, 170, 173; 140:2, 5; 141:9; 142:7; 143:9.

[417]Ebeling, *Quellen zur Kenntnis der babylonischen Religion*, vol. 2, 43:14; 44:18.

[418]Ebeling, *Quellen zur Kenntnis der babylonischen Religion*, vol. 2, 38:20.

[419]Ungnad, *Religion der Babylonier und Assyrer*, 177:3; 219:45.

The distress is of course reflected in the petitions since it forms the cause of the complaint. The material presented in ¶¶5-9 appears here. However, even here the petition remains relatively generalized. The petitions, for example, that entreat the departure of illness do not allow one to recognize what causes the one praying to suffer. One finds words like: "Heal me."[420] "Heal my soul,"[421] or "support me that I might live."[422] The parallel Babylonian petitions are likewise general.[423]

Sometimes, however, the *specific, observable references* are clear. The psalmist thus asks that God might illumine the psalmist's eyes,[424] raise him up,[425] or pay attention to his sleepless nights.[426] The *feeling of the nearness of death* and the *abandonment to the underworld* are expressed on occasion. "Do not gather me up in half of my days."[427] "Save me from the 'land of silence.'"[428]

Next to illness, the *enemies* appear in the petition, "Look how numerous my enemies are."[429] "Save me from the hand of my enemies and my persecutors."[430] "Do not leave me to my oppressors.[431] These petitions do not confront the enemies directly. Rather, they only seek deliverance or protection from them. Petitions that attack the enemies will be treated in ¶15.

In other petitions, the one complaining appears as one imploring help as he seeks justice before the judge's bench. "Judge me."[432] "Vindicate me."[433] "Take my case."[434] Correspondingly, the Babylonian prays to Šamaš or Ištar: "Judge me rightly, decide my case.[435] The psalmist further petitions YHWH to *recognize the psalmist's honor*. He petitions for the restoration of his standing before the opponents,[436] or for *protection when approaching God*.[437] The complaint about being removed from YHWH's sanctuary and his blessed nearness corresponds to the petition for a pilgrimage.[438]

---

[420]Ps 6:3; Jer 17:14.

[421]Ps 41:5

[422]Pss 119:116; cf. further 119:25, 40, 88, 107, 149, 154, 156, 159.

[423]Ungnad, *Religion der Babylonier und Assyrer*, pp. 175:62; 178:19-20; 180:22; 198:10; 199:20; 206:51-52; Zimmern, *Babylonische Hymnen und Gebete*, vol. 1, pp. 18:25; 27:45; Ebeling, *Quellen zur Kenntnis der babylonischen Religion*, vol. 1, p. 11:9.

[424]Ps 13:4.

[425]Ps 119:28.

[426]Ps 56:9; especially 56:9b.

[427]Ps 102:25.

[428]Ps 51:16.

[429]Ps 25:19.

[430]Ps 31:6.

[431]Pss 119:21; cf. 17:13, 14; 27:12; 28:3; 35:17; 39:9; 64:3; Syriac Apocryphal Psalm 3:7.

[432]Pss 7:9; 35:23, 24; 43:1; 54:3.

[433]Ps 26:1.

[434]Pss 119:154; 43:1.

[435]Ebeling, *Quellen zur Kenntnis der babylonischen Religion*, vol. 1, p. 27; Revers, vol. 1, pp. 31:25; 42:16; 45:31; vol. 2, pp. 30:24; 38:18; Schollmeyer, *Sumerisch-babylonische Hymnen und Gebete an Šamaš*, pp. 49:26; 70:5; 119:11; 121:7.

[436]Pss 39:9; 69:7; 119:22, 31b, 37, 116; Jer 15:15; 17:17; Syriac Apocryphal Psalm 3:9.

[437]Pss 17:8; 86:16.

[438]Pss 27:4; 61:5; cf. also 43:4.

In complaint songs, typically brief petitions such as those described at the beginning of the section generally appear alongside the first address. They do not yet contain the specific petition for help which comes when the complaint has portrayed the distress. Here, one only wishes to direct YHWH's attention to one's self. This petition should be designated as an "introductory cry for help." The Babylonian counterparts have a similar function.[439] The introductory cry for help can be very brief: "YHWH, hear my voice 'on the day' that I call."[440] If the one praying is very anxious, or if he no longer expects help, the short petitions can be piled on top of one another. In Ps 102:2-3, the same thought is heavily accented by a six-fold deviation: "YHWH, hear my prayer. May my crying come before you. Do not hide your face from me. 'Pay attention' on the day that I am afraid. Incline your ear to me. On the day I cry, hear me quickly."[441]

Multiple *portrayals of praying* stand in *close connection to the petition*.[442] Their position is mostly at the *beginning of the songs* where they appear in connection with the introductory cry for help. Occasionally, they show traces which help one imagine how the complaint was spoken. Since this was treated more exactly in ¶4, only a few examples of the form are required at this point. "In the early morning I called to you and stretched out 'to you;'"[443] "'I sing' a prayer by myself to the God of my life.[444] The portrayal of praying above all expresses the *urgency* of the prayer. It is not uncommon to find "I call," or "I cry."[445] However, frequently it is not sufficient for the psalmist to say, "I pray," or "I entreat."[446] The expressions are generally more daring. The pious one aims at YHWH's heart because he knows no help otherwise. "I flee to you, YHWH."[447] In so doing, the one praying gladly places his internal condition in the foreground in order to make an impression upon YHWH. If he is convinced of his innocence, he makes YHWH aware of that. "I pray with lips separated from deceit."[448] More frequently, the despondent voice states, "My eyes cry from above."[449] "My soul melts unceasingly."[450] "My soul pants like a hind,"[451] or "my cry is louder than a lion's roar."[452] Even the doubter's disappointment finds expression here. "I call by day, but you do not answer me, and by night, but I find no rest."[453] This element attains the following form for the repentant sinner: "I will

---

[439]See the examples given on p. 158.

[440]Ps 27:7.

[441]Cf. to other cries for help: Pss 5:2f; 17:1; 28:1; 31:3; 41:5; 55:2-3; 61:2; 64:2; 86:1; 88:3; 109:1; 130:1-2; 140:1-2; 143:1; Syriac Apocryphal Psalm 3:1, 3ff.

[442]One encounters these in detail in Pss 88:2, 10, 14; 102:2-6; 142:2, 3, 6.

[443]Ps 5:4.

[444]Ps 42:9.

[445]Pss 17:1; 28:2; 31:18; 38:9; 57:3; 61:3; 69:4; 77:2; 88:2, 10; 102:6; 119:146; 130:1; 141:1.

[446]Cf. Pss 5:4; 27:8; 63:2; 77:2; 119:58.

[447]Pss 7:2; 31:2; 71:1; cf. 141:8.

[448]Ps 17:1.

[449]Isa 38:14.

[450]Ps 77:3.

[451]Ps 42:2.

[452]Pss 38:9; see also 42:3; 63:2.

[453]Pss 22:3; see also 25:5; 38:16.

confess my misdeeds to YHWH."[454] Whoever wishes to remain constant on account of YHWH will say, "My heart 'entreats me' to fear your name."[455]

The Babylonian complaint also knows this portrayal of prayer in the "self-introduction of the one praying."[456] As in the Hebrew one enters the rite of prayer. "I have made no preparations for sacrifice to you."[457] "I have cast myself down."[458] "I kneel down,"[459] etc. The distress and urgency of the one praying also finds expression here, although less frequently and less dynamically than in the Hebrew. The one praying adds a brief reference to himself to the portrayal of the prayer: "I call to you, suffering and wretchedly, tormented by pain, your servant.[460] "Faint and oppressed, I look to your face."[461] The desire and demand of the one praying is recognizable less frequently: "I trust confidently, my Lady, in you. My mind is directed to you. I entreat you."[462] One can hardly fail to notice that at this point the Babylonian genre comes close to the Hebrew, materially as well as the expression.

13. Several petitions stand out for their peculiar nature from the large number of petitions. First, there are the *confessional petitions*.[463] His first desire is forgiveness of sins by YHWH. "Forgive all my sins."[464] "Blot out my wickedness."[465] "Forgive me, o YHWH, forgive me. Do not snatch me up with my sins. Do not be angry with me forever. Do not preserve my wicked deeds."[466] The one praying in Ps 130 is reserved and shy. He does not risk leading off with his own desire. He only petitions for notice and reminds YHWH of his right to pardon. Occasionally, the one confessing asks forgiveness for actions lying in the distant past.[467] These petitions occasionally allude to the atonement rites of the cult, from which the genre proceeded.[468] "Take away my sin with hyssop."[469] "Wash me pure of my guilt."[470] These petitions are also well known from the Babylonian material.[471]

---

[454]Ps 32:5.

[455]Ps 86:11.

[456]Terminology from Stummer *Sumerisch-akkadische Parallelen zum Aufbau alttestamentlicher Psalmen*, p. 9.

[457]Ungnad, *Religion der Babylonier und Assyrer*, 177:17; Ebeling, *Quellen zur Kenntnis der babylonischen Religion*, vol. 2, 12:20.

[458]Ebeling, *Quellen zur Kenntnis der babylonischen Religion*, vol. 1, pp. 5:33; 24:11ff.

[459]Ebeling, *Quellen zur Kenntnis der babylonischen Religion*, vol. 1, p. 45:31; vol. 2, 38:17; see also Ungnad, *Religion der Babylonier und Assyrer*, 205:27; 206:42ff; 221:79; 247:12ff; Schollmeyer, *Sumerisch-babylonische Hymnen und Gebete an Šamaš*, pp. 58:11; 65:10ff; 70:5; Ebeling, *Quellen zur Kenntnis der babylonischen Religion*, vol. 2, pp. 14:31; 17:27.

[460]Ungnad, *Religion der Babylonier und Assyrer*, p. 219:42.

[461]Ebeling, *Quellen zur Kenntnis der babylonischen Religion*, vol. 2, pp. 13:20; 38:17.

[462]Ungnad, *Religion der Babylonier und Assyrer*, 221:79; cf. 217:1.

[463]Cf. ¶21 and ¶26.

[464]Ps 25:18.

[465]Ps 51:3.

[466]Pr Man 13; Ps 25:11; 51:11.

[467]Ps 25:7.

[468]Cf. ¶4.

[469]Ps 51:9.

[470]Ps 51:4, cf. 51:9.

[471]See Zimmern, *Babylonische Hymnen und Gebete*, vol. 1, pp. 25-27.

In addition to the desire for wiping out guilt, the explicit *petition for the removal or lessening of punishment* recedes. Significantly, this petition appears in the forefront only in those places which downplay the consciousness of personal sinfulness. "Do not punish me in wrath."[472] This petition stands in conjunction with the petition for forgiveness only in the Prayer of Manasseh. However, even there it appears in the second position, in contrast to the passages already cited.[473] In the Prayer of Manasseh, it is not the petition for the removal of the punishment, but only the desire that he not die. It is noteworthy that those praying the confessional complaint songs have peace with God in the first position, and that the question of their own punishment is not addressed until the second position, which offers a very remarkable deepening of the petition.

Petitions of the *innocent* present the exact opposite to the petition of the one confessing. Conscious of his blamelessness he demands the strictest investigation from YHWH. "Test me."[474] Examine my kidneys and heart."[475] He urges the divine judge, "vindicate me."[476] The one praying beseeches YHWH to recognize his innocence, and not to leave him to fall to the fate of sinners.[477]

If the petitions treated thus far stand in direct connection with the distress of the one praying, others develop forcefully beyond this limitation. These cases concern *conversion and restitution* through YHWH. The pious one begins to see that he is not capable of avoiding future sins, and he petitions that YHWH himself should give him teaching and instruction. "Teach me your statutes."[478] "Let my heart not incline to wicked words."[479] "Put a guard on my mouth,"[480] etc.

It is characteristic of these petitions that they petition for *protection from sin*. Other petitions lead even deeper. They do not remain stationary at this point. Rather, they seek YHWH's *assistance* for a *new life*. "Let me walk in your truth."[481] "Teach me to do your will."[482] "Assist me with the spirit of obedience."[483] Finally, the ultimate and deepest petition comes very close to the New Testament: "YHWH, create in me a clean heart. Give me a new, steadfast spirit in my breast." "Do not take your holy spirit from me."[484]

One also encounters these petitions for higher good in the Babylonian complaints. "Put truth in my mouth. Let good be in my heart."[485]

Petitions of this type do not appear frequently in Hebrew, even though they are more numerous than in Babylonian. Until this desire, the piety of the complaint singers does not

---

[472]Pss 6:2; 38:2; cf. 143:2; Syriac Apocryphal Psalms 3:9.

[473]Pr Man 13.

[474]Ps 26:2; Jer 12:3.

[475]Pss 26:2, cf. 139:23f.

[476]Pss 7:9; 26:1; 35:24; 43:1.

[477]Ps 26:9; (28:3); Pss. Sol. 13:5; 16:5.

[478]Ps 119:12, 26, 64, 124, 135.

[479]Ps 141:4.

[480]Ps 141:3; similar petitions are found in 5:9; 25:4; 27:10, 11; 86:11; 90:12; 119:10, 18, 19, 29, 36, 43, 66, 68, 108, 125, 133; 143:8.

[481]Ps 25:5; cf. 86:11.

[482]Ps 143:10.

[483]Ps 51:14.

[484]Ps 51:12-13.

[485]Ungnad, *Religion der Babylonier und Assyrer*, 179:14-15 = 199:12-13.

ascend as a rule. The highest element which most of them reached was the petition for the protection from sin. There is no doubt that the spiritualization of the prayer inside psalmody represents a higher developmental stage.

14. In addition to the petitions the genre knows *wishes*. Here, YHWH is addressed and commanded to do something. Normally, the form of the *jussive* dominates, *especially in the third person*.[486] The first or second person is seldom used in this context. The same kinds of material appears also in these wishes as were contained in the petitions: the wish for YHWH's attention,[487] for YHWH's help and compassion,[488] for deliverance from enemies,[489] the desire for salvation and healing,[490] the desire for proper justice,[491] and the desire to be near the sanctuary.[492] Higher good is not missing from these desires. They wish to avoid sitting with those committing misdeeds,[493] to cling to YHWH's statutes,[494] or to continue to follow YHWH.[495]

Several examples will illustrate the form of these wishes. "Let your hand come to help me."[496] "May he reach from heaven and help me."[497] "Let not the foot of pride trample on me."[498] Examples of the use of the first and second person include the following sentences. "May your light and your faithfulness lead me, and conduct me to your holy mountain."[499] "I want to be saved."[500] "I would like to be a guest in your tent forever."[501]

The *Babylonian genre* knows similar wishes. Several examples can demonstrate. "May my prayer and my entreaty reach you."[502] "May your fierce heart find rest, and your angry mind be soothed."[503] Examples of the first person include: "May I live by your breath."[504] May I succeed in what I desire;[505] and "may I walk before your face, and be full of life."[506]

---

[486]Sometimes, the final sentence in place of the wish, perhaps introduced with *"pen,"* "lest" (Ps 13:5; 28:1).

[487]Pss 69:14; 102:2; 119:169f; 141:2.

[488]Pss 57:4; 119:41, 76, 173.

[489]Pss 36:12; 119:122.

[490]Pss 69:16; 119:17, 77, 116, 117, 175.

[491]Pss 7:8; 17:2; 119:175.

[492]Ps 17:8; 43:3, 4; 61:5.

[493]Ps 141:4.

[494]Ps 119:80.

[495]Pss 31:4; see also 25:21; 63:6; 119:5, 18, 27, 34, 73, 125, 133; 143:10.

[496]Ps 119:173.

[497]Ps 57:4.

[498]Ps 36:12.

[499]Ps 43:3.

[500]Ps 119:117.

[501]Ps 61:5.

[502]Ungnad, *Religion der Babylonier und Assyrer*, pp. 222:99.

[503]Ungnad, *Religion der Babylonier und Assyrer*, pp. 176:64; 222:11.

[504]Ungnad, *Religion der Babylonier und Assyrer*, p. 176:65.

[505]Ungnad, *Religion der Babylonier und Assyrer*, p. 178:21.

[506]Ebeling, *Quellen zur Kenntnis der babylonischen Religion*, vol. 1, p. 6:33.

Two elements distinguish the wish from the petition. The first is praising YHWH's *favor and grace* and *singing the thanksgiving song* for him. These wishes always stand at *the conclusion* of the complaint song or one of its components in case one loses one's way in several similar paths. "May I rejoice and shout over your grace."[507] "May I always rejoice and multiply all your praise."[508] "May I proclaim the great deeds of YHWH."[509] It is characteristic for these wishes that they use only the first person. Only a few deviations alternate with this characteristic: "my lips,"[510] "my tongue,"[511] and "my bones."[512]

Wishes for friends constitute the second special element.[513] At the end of the complaint song, when the complaint and petition have been completed, the thoughts of the one praying turn to the friends and include them in the wishes. These wishes seek to create trust and hope for other poor and suffering people from the same happy deliverance of the one bringing the complaint. "May your pious ones turn to me."[514] "Let those rejoice who want my victory, and let them always say, 'Great is YHWH who desires the salvation of his servant.'"[515]

15. The petitions and wishes which take up a lot of space in the complaint songs are those directed *against the enemies of the one praying*. In the petitions, all the pain of the one complaining surges forth in an inexorable desire for vengeance. The mildest form which one encounters is that YHWH intervene on behalf of his pious one: "Strive against those who strive against me. Draw forth spear and hatchet against my persecutors."[516] The following even appears relatively reserved: "Let their plots fail."[517] It is typical that these petitions are relatively difficult to find, for the psalmist shows no compassion in desiring the downfall of his opponents. "Pour out your curse on them."[518] "Destroy my enemies."[519] "Exterminate all those who are feuding with my soul."[520] However, simply expressing his thoughts of rage do not calm the rage of the one complaining. In gory detail, he paints a picture of how YHWH will kill them. "Appoint over him a wicked judge."[521] "Break the arm of the wicked."[522] "Let their loins ever stagger."[523] "Gather them up like sheep for the slaughter."[524] His desire for vengeance even follows the descendants of his opponent:

---

[507]Ps 31:8.

[508]Ps 71:14.

[509]Pss 71:16; cf. also 35:9, 28; 43:4; 51:10, 16; 63:6; 71:15; 109:30; 119:171, 172.

[510]Ps 119:171.

[511]Pss 35:28; 51:16; 119:172.

[512]Pss 35:10; 51:10.

[513]See ¶5 and ¶8.

[514]Ps 119:79.

[515]Ps 35:27. Cf. also 5:12; 40:17; 52:8; 69:7; 119:74; 142:8.

[516]Pss 35:1, 3; cf. 17:13.

[517]Pss 5:11; cf. also 7:7, 9a.

[518]Ps 69:25.

[519]Ps 143:12.

[520]Ps 143:12; cf. also 17:14; 54:7; Jer 15:15.

[521]Ps 109:6.

[522]Ps 10:15.

[523]Ps 69:24.

[524]Jer 12:5.

"Give their sons over to hunger."[525] One can take that to mean there should be no escalation, but the Israelite does know of one. He petitions YHWH not to forgive his opponent's guilt. "Reckon their wickedness."[526] "Strike them 'according to' the quantity of their sins."[527] "Do not forgive their sins."[528] It is even more terrible when the one praying does not stop there, but petitions YHWH to deliver their guilt even deeper into guilt: "pile guilt on top of guilt."[529]

It should be noted that the *wishes against the enemies* just about double the *petitions* against the enemies. The wishes deliberately provide more possibilities for the psalmist's pain and seeking vengeance. The manner of destruction is portrayed here in blazing colors, by far more blazing than in the petitions. It is thus all the more remarkable that the wishes against the enemies *almost never mention YHWH*. The enemy and that which belongs to the enemy are the subject of the sentence and the jussive is the predicate that relates to the enemies' judgment and downfall. It is frequently wished that the enemies and their plans will experience bitter disappointment. "May those who wish my misfortune retreat and be ashamed."[530] "Let them be dressed in disgrace and shame."[531] "May those despising me not raise their head."[532] Wishes that only want to avert the opponents enjoyment of their pain sound somewhat milder. "They should not rejoice on my account."[533] "'Stop them from' cursing and lying."[534] "May the evil of the wicked come to an end."[535] Typically, these milder sentences are relatively few. Reserved response toward the enemies does not come easily for the Israelite. On the contrary, the Israelite wishes them death and destruction. "May their days not be complete."[536] "May they go shaking down to hell."[537] "Let them be blotted out of the book of life."[538] "May the godless come to disgrace, may they be silenced in the underworld."[539]

One can perceive the full effect of the cruelty of these wishes when one considers the anxiety and fear with which the one praying thought of the underworld.[540] Even here the search for vengeance has a preference for specific details. The wicked should be destroyed in the manner in which he tried to bring down the pious one. "May 'your' net which you

---

[525]Jer 18:21.

[526]Ps 28:4.

[527]Ps 5:11.

[528]Jer 18:23; cf. also Pss 10:15; 59:6; Jer 15:15.

[529]Ps 69:28. For a Babylonian petition against an enemy, see Ungnad, *Religion der Babylonier und Assyrer*, 221.

[530]Ps 40:15.

[531]Ps 35:26.

[532]Ps 140:10; cf. also Pss 6:11; 31:18; 35:4; 40:16; 56:10; 71:13; 86:17; 109:29; 119:78; Jer 17:18.

[533]Pss 35:24; 38:17.

[534]Ps 59:13.

[535]Pss 7:10; cf. further 25:2; 35:19, 24, 25.

[536]Ps 55:24.

[537]Ps 55:16.

[538]Pss 69:29; cf. 9:18.

[539]Ps 31:18; cf. also 63:10.

[540]Cf. ¶5.

laid catch you, and force you into the grave."[541] "May the wicked fall upon the one defaming me."[542] They should become ill.[543] They should stumble over that which is next to them.[544] One wishes they were eaten by scavengers.[545] The bitterness does not stop with the relatives and the descendants of the opponent. "May their wives lose their children."[546] "'The body of their sons will be filled' with their inheritance (sins and curse). 'May they be full' of that and still leave the rest to their own children."[547]

There are only a few wishes in which YHWH is the subject. "May God tear you down."[548] "May the abundance of your anger take hold of them."[549] "May the guilt of his father be remembered, and the sins of his mother not be erased; let them be before YHWH for all time so that he removed his memory from the earth."[550] The one praying these psalms is a world apart from the singer of the 51st psalm. The latter is conscious of his great unworthiness before YHWH, and is unable to think in anger about the wicked. He therefore wishes: "May the wicked learn your ways so that the sinners return to you."[551]

The difference in the form of the wishes is not without importance. Those wishes which contain no trace of the mention of YHWH betray their origin in *primitive-magic thought*. This is the form of the *curse*, which the above mentioned quotes offer.[552] Such curses work by themselves and require no other power.[553] One may now observe how rigidly the curse formula preserved its form into the latest times. Compare Pss. Sol. 12:5: "May the slanderous tongue go to destruction in flames of fire."[554] Rarely is the power of the wish derived from the name of YHWH introduced into the formula. It would be wrong if one believed the singers of the complaint songs were fully cognizant of a belief in the magical power of the words of these wishes, or that they presumed they could tap into the power of YHWH by uttering them. Rather, they stand under the influence of the fixed form. This form betrays the type of self-actualizing magical curse operative in Israel from time immemorial. The fact that these formulas were not thought to be more than self-actualizing is seen first in their locations within prayers, which turn to YHWH, and further in the fact that the petition and wish stand so close together and can be interchanged.[555]

The *wishes for the pious ones from the one praying* form the counterpart to these curses. They belong with the just mentioned wishes in terms of content and are more frequently placed alongside the curses. The form of the wish is the ancient pattern of the

---

[541]Ps 35:8.

[542]Ps 54:7.

[543]Ps 69:24.

[544]Ps 69:23, 26.

[545]Ps 63:11.

[546]Jer 18:21f.

[547]Pss 17:14; cf. further 31:19; 35:5, 6; 55:16; 56:8; 57:5; 63:10-11; 64:9; 86:17; 109:9ff; etc.

[548]Ps 52:7.

[549]Ps 69:25.

[550]Pss 109:15; cf. 139:19.

[551]Ps 51:15.

[552]Cf. §8, ¶18, 19. Cf. Hempel, "Die israelitischen Anschauungen von Segen und Fluch," pp. 55f.

[553]Cf. §8, ¶14. Cf. Hempel, "Die israelitischen Anschauungen von Segen und Fluch," p. 55.

[554]Cf. Hempel, "Die israelitischen Anschauungen von Segen und Fluch," p. 66.

[555]E.g. Pss 9:18-21; 56:8-10a; 59:12-14; 69:23-26, 28-29; 109:6-15, 28-29; Pss. Sol. 12:5f.

blessing formula, as the connection with the curses makes clear.[556] This formula also concerns originally self-actualizing words that carry their operative power in themselves.[557]

Wishes against the enemies and *wishes for one's self* are often placed together at the conclusion of the complaint song. They meet in this order[558] or in reverse order.[559] Wishes for the enemies and for friends and pious ones generally prefer to stand at the conclusion.[560] In so doing, the blessing takes the last word, which is understandable. One desires the destruction of the enemy or at least that the enemy be shamed. One seeks to insure YHWH's blessing for one's self and one's closest associates.

How did the curse and blessing formulas find their way into the prayer when they originally had nothing to do with that genre? Two factors are perhaps important, one related to content and the other a formal element. Petitions and wishes have the *same goal*, repelling the enemy and making him harmless on the one hand and the healing and good fortune of the one praying on the other. The petitions, curse formulas, and blessing formulas also have a *common form*. Hebrew knows a wish form that is materially different from the blessing and curse. It is found specifically in places where a person of lesser standing petitions someone of higher standing and that person wishes to avoid direct address and imperative forms. "May your maid speak before your ears, and may you hear the words of your maid."[561] "May Abishag of Sunem be given as wife to your brother."[562] It is important that these last words, as well as those from Solomon, be designated as "petition." This kind of wish petition also alternates with the imperative petition.[563]

It should perhaps not be doubted that in the religious petition, as in the worldly petition, that the wish form arose alongside the imperative form. The wishes point in that direction. They have nothing to do with the content of the blessing or the curse. Compare, for instance, "May my prayer come before you, and my cry approach you."[564] It is not extraordinary, given the close relationship of the petitions to the words of blessing and curse, that the two types of speech have been connected. It is significant from a history of religion standpoint that the prayer has taken the leading role rather than the magical formula. The latter is subordinated to the former, causing the formula to lose its magical characteristic, even where YHWH's name was not incorporated or where it does not display any other relationship to YHWH. It has become a petition. The ancient formula has experienced an internal change. It is expected that whatever happens comes from YHWH.

16. We should now briefly consider a particular form of the petition, the reproachful question. It has a close relationship to the complaint. This question only appears in places where the one praying wrestles with liberation from his arduous distress. It never appears with the petitions for higher goods. The *reproachful question in the complaint* is related

---

[556]Cf. §8, ¶9.

[557]Cf. Hempel, "Die israelitischen Anschauungen von Segen und Fluch," pp. 31f.

[558]Pss 17:14f; 35:4-10; 55:15-19; etc.

[559]Ps 57:4f.

[560]Pss 5:11f; 35:26f; 40:15-17; 64:8-11; etc.

[561]1 Sam 25:24.

[562]1 Kgs 2:21. See also Gen 13:3; 41:33-34; 1 Sam 17:32; 19:4; 25:25-27; 26:19; 2 Sam 13:24; 14:4; etc.

[563]Cf. 1 Sam 25:24ff; 2 Sam 14:4, 11; 2 Kgs 5:15, 17ff.

[564]Cf. the beginning of ¶14 where one can find additional examples.

to this form of petition. The complaint, as with the petition preserved in this interrogative form, appear together so that they betray an accusing, excited mood. However, while the complaint seeks the solution to the tormenting question "why?," the petition impatiently looks for the end of the suffering condition. The question "when?" is characteristic for it. "When will I come and see YHWH's face?"[565] "When will you act rightly toward my persecutors?"[566] "When will you comfort me?"[567] It is instructive to observe how complaint and petition mix together in precisely these ardent questions. The material belongs to the former while the form belongs to the latter: "How long, YHWH, will you continually forget me? How long will you hide your face from me? How long shall I bear the cares of my soul, or the grief of my heart day and night? How long will my enemy triumph over me?"[568] Understandably, these petitions are relatively rare. Their vehemence and impatience stand in almost unbearable tension to the position of the one praying to YHWH as a servant to his master. One may ascribe it perhaps to the sensitivity of the psalmists that they almost never draw upon this form which is so understandably human.[569]

If one overviews the abundance of petitions and wishes that flow like a violent stream through the complaint songs, one looks deep into the heart of the one praying in the psalter. This flood of demands so strongly expressed in the complaint songs appears all the more noticeable since a fine and delicate practice in Israel in ancient time had already appeared. In this custom, a petition was not expressed to someone in a higher position. Rather, one was satisfied with portraying the situation while leaving the wish to others. These petitions and wishes, so numerous and so clearly expressed, would have sounded far too coarse to one with more delicate ears.[570] This is also evidence that the development of the complaint songs belongs to a very ancient period.

The noise of these petitions, which goes to such great lengths to suggest one's own will to God, stands in stark contrast to the silent petition given in the New Testament: "Not what I will, but what you will." While these components of the complaint song evidence human ego more than faith in God, the opposite is true in those passages whose purpose is to justify the petitions. These will be treated in the following.

17. The goal of the complaint song is to *obtain something from YHWH*. In order to avoid missing this goal, the one praying strives *to move* the heart of God with everything he says.[571] Several points were already touched upon in the portrayal of the complaint.[572] It is the last moment for YHWH if he wants to help.[573] Or, the one praying casts such a pitiful image of himself that no compassionate being could look at him without deep sym-

---

[565]Ps 42:3.

[566]Ps 119:84.

[567]Ps 119:82.

[568]Pss 13:1-3; see also 6:4; 35:17.

[569]Similar impatient petitions beginning with "how long?" can be found occasionally in Babylonian material. Cf. Ungnad, *Religion der Babylonier und Assyrer*, 218, 219, 220, 221.

[570]Cf. Gunkel, *Meisterwerke Hebräischer Erzählungskunst*, vol. 1: *Geschichten von Elisa*, pp. 20, 25.

[571]The same is true for the communal complaint. See §4, ¶9.

[572]Cf. p. 155.

[573]See the examples in ¶11, p. 155.

pathy. Should not the same image have an effect on YHWH?[574] The portrayals of petitions, cries, and complaints also serves the purpose of stirring YHWH.[575] The introduction of the burdensome speeches of the enemies also serves the same purpose. These speeches call into doubt YHWH's inclination and power to help.[576] In addition, one can note the numerous portrayals of the *bodily condition*.[577] In contrast to the communal complaint, one should observe that the thought recedes that the deity must accept its own concern.[578] The request of the one praying is only seldom equated with the concern of YHWH, and then only hesitantly.[579] This fact corresponds with the fact that the one praying only rarely designates himself as God's servant (and therefore his possession). He could not reveal this light-heartedly.[580]

18. The psalmist also knows a number of "rationale for divine intervention."[581] They should make an impression on YHWH, but at the same time they should *comfort the heart of the one complaining* at the moment he speaks them and they should insure the help of God. They are a warning for YHWH to help. For the pious, they are a beam or a board with which the ravages of a shipwreck can be clamped together.

Corresponding to the nature of the matter, these rationale relate closely to the petition.[582] The shortest form in which they appear is the *prepositional phrase*.[583] Generally, the grace, steadfastness, righteousness, name, or speech of YHWH emerges, which is understandable since one would hope for help based upon these qualities. "Lead me according to your righteousness."[584] "Help me on account of your grace."[585] "Do away with my wickedness according to your abundant compassion,[586] etc. Occasionally, the *enemies and slanderers* also appear with the preposition. Here the psalmist places the events before YHWH in order to cause him to intervene. "Lead me . . . on account of my enemies."[587] "Lead me on a level path on account of those slandering me."[588] Ps 13:5 states what the one praying hopes to say in this way using a final negative sentence. This final sentence constitutes another attachment of the rationale to the petition: "For my enemy does not say, 'I have overcome him.' My opponents do not rejoice that I have wavered." This last example moves to another form.

19. Confidence in YHWH is the preferred and the most frequently stated reason why the poets of the complaint songs offer their petition. One finds an abundance of expres-

---

[574]See, for example, Pss 6:3ff; 22:7, 15-16, 18-19; 88:4-10.

[575]See the end of ¶12, p. 161.

[576]See ¶8, p. 141.

[577]See ¶4, p. 126

[578]Cf §4, ¶9.

[579]Pss 5:11; 69:8, 10.

[580]Pss 19:12f; 27:9; 31:17; 69:18; 86:2, 4, 16.

[581]The same is true for the communal complaint. See §4, ¶6.

[582]The same is true for the communal complaint. See §4, ¶6, 10.

[583]It is formed with *le*, *be*, or *lema'an*.

[584]Ps 5:9.

[585]Ps 6:5.

[586]Pss 51:3; see also 25:7, 11; 31:2f; 35:24; 69:14, 17; 71:2; 109:21; 119:25, 28, 40, 58, 107, 116, 169, 170.

[587]Ps 5:9.

[588]Ps 27:11.

sions here. One can recognize that confidence is the particular foundation of the petition.[589] A number of expressions simply express the *fact of confidence in YHWH* without further delineating its content or reason. One can designate these as *assurances or protestations* of confidence. These are frequently attached by *kî* (for) because of the causal relationship in which they stand to the petitions. Very frequently the psalmist speaks in simple and therefore very moving words: "I trust in you."[590] Or, the psalmist accentuates how incessantly he depends upon YHWH. "I keep YHWH before me always."[591] "My eyes always look to YHWH."[592] The following assurance sounds even more certain: "My soul still belongs to YHWH."[593] Indeed, the confidence escalates in tone to the point of a happy and secure certainty which requires nothing more than to petition for what he hopes will happen. Therefore, he foregoes the form of the prayer, that is the address to the deity.[594] "Before whom shall I be afraid?" "Before whom shall I be uneasy?"[595] "And must I also enter the dark ravine? I fear no judgment."[596] "I trust in YHWH. I am not afraid. What can mortals do to me?"[597]

These expressions of firm, unconfused trust, however, are only the highpoint. It is understandably human when the one praying becomes disconcerted with the long delay of help and has to wrestle internally with his trust. He then casts his heart to God in stormy desire. The utterance of trust and the portrayal of the prayer melt together into a single expression. "I hide myself in you YHWH."[598] "My soul hides in you.[599] "I hide myself in the shadow of your wing."[600] "I fly to you."[601] Or, the expression of peaceful trust becomes imbalanced toward the side of longing and hope. "I long for you the whole day."[602] "I hope on YHWH with the soul and long for his word."[603] "I hope for your salvation."[604] The greater the temptation, the more pictorial and urgent the sentences become: "My soul longs for your salvation."[605] Impressive comparisons heighten the effect. "My soul yearns for you like a withering countryside."[606] "My body pines for you like dry land pines for water.[607] "My soul longs for you, YHWH, like a hind longs for streams of water."[608] If the

---

[589]See also the communal complaints in §4, ¶10, page 91.

[590]Pss 13:6; 25:2; 26:1; 31:7, 15; 55:24; 56:4; 119:42, 66; 143:8; see also 16:1; 57:2.

[591]Ps 16:8.

[592]Pss 25:15; see also 119:82; 141:8.

[593]Ps 62:2.

[594]Cf. ¶25.

[595]Ps 27:1.

[596]Ps 23:4.

[597]Pss 56:5bc, 12; see also 5:5; 23:4; 25:3; 27:2; 54:7; 59:9, 11; 119:21, 118ff, 155; Syriac Apocryphal Psalm 3:24-27.

[598]Pss 71:2; cf. 31:2.

[599]Pss 57:2; see also 11:1; and 141:8.

[600]Ps 61:5.

[601]Pss 7:2; 11:1; 16:1; 31:2; 71:1.

[602]Ps 25:5.

[603]Ps 130:6.

[604]Pss 119:166; see also 38:16; 39:8; 59:10; 119:81, 144, 147, 166; Mic 7:7; Lam 3:24.

[605]Pss 119:81; cf. 119:82, 123; cf. 63:2.

[606]Ps 143:6.

[607]Ps 63:2.

expectations of the one praying are not fulfilled, if his resistance will no longer hold up, then he warns himself not to lose confidence. "Why do you melt, my soul? Why do you groan? Long for YHWH. One day I will thank him, the one helping my countenance and my God."[609] It is instructive to observe how in those places where the pious one seeks to rouse himself to trust, the connection to YHWH in the form of the prayer is lost. Then the psalmist speaks of God in the third person.[610]

Alongside the protestations of confidence, a series of other expressions appear that speak of the *reason and content of the confidence*. *Mixed forms* produce the transitions. "I speak to YHWH; you are my God,"[611] "but I trust in you, YHWH; I say, 'you are my God.'"[612] The form of these words is provided as the introduction unfolds.[613] They are closely associated with the form of the Babylonian portrayal of majesty. One encounters the accented "you" here as well. This accented you can stand at the beginning or the end of the sentence. A predicate follows it which expresses a property of the deity. "You are strong, my lady. Your name is exalted. You light the heaven and earth, strong daughter of Sin."[614] "Creator of everything in heaven and earth, you are Šamaš."[615] "YHWH, you are a shield around me, the honor that raises my head."[616] "For you are my refuge and my fortress." Despite the formal relationship, however, the *content, purpose, and position* of these sentences are different in the Israelite complaint songs than in the Babylonian. In the Babylonian complaints, these sentences stand in conjunction with the introductory address. By contrast, they never do in the Israelite. The Babylonian examples pile honorary predicates of far-reaching breadth to flatter the god in order to incline him to grant the petition of the one praying. In the Hebrew complaint song, however, the content of the predicate is an expression of what YHWH means *for the one praying*. Therefore, the first person suffix frequently appears, as in "my God," "my rock," etc. Its intention is to express the confidence of the pious in order to show how he clings to god."[617]

The Israelite genre consciously found an amazing abundance of expressions for that which YHWH signified for his pious ones. Their content largely rests upon the words of the address,[618] and often corresponds with the contents of the petition.[619] Therefore, we should here present the entire material. YHWH is designated as "my God" extremely frequently.[620] For the one praying, different expressions declare that God is the confidence,[621] the hope,[622] the God of his life[623] and his salvation,[624] his light,[625] his savior

---

[608]Ps 42:2.

[609]Pss 42:6, 7, 12; 43:5; cf. 55:23.

[610]Cf. ¶25.

[611]Ps 140:7.

[612]Ps 31:15.

[613]Ps 3:4; 22:10, 11; 25:5; 31:4, 5, 15; 40:18; 43:2; 71:3, 5; 86:2; 140:7; 142:6; 143:10.

[614]Ungnad, *Religion der Babylonier und Assyrer*, 217.

[615]Schollmeyer, *Sumerisch-babylonische Hymnen und Gebete an Šamaš*, 98.

[616]Ps 3:4.

[617]For details, see J. Begrich ZAW, 1928, pp. 221ff.

[618]Cf. ¶10.

[619]Pss 30:11; 31:3; 35:3; 57:2; 61:3; 71:3.

[620]Pss 3:8; 7:2, 4, 7; 13:4; 22:1, 11; 25:2; 31:15; 35:23; 38:16, 22; 40:18; 42:7, 12; 43:4, 5; 59:2; 63:2; 69:4; 71:4; 109:26; 140:7; 143:10.

[621]Pss 22:10; 71:5.

and redeemer.[626] The innocent one turns to his just God,[627] the one who is shamed calls God his honor.[628] Different expressions describe YHWH as the psalmist's help.[629] Indeed the expressions also select very clever comparisons. YHWH is a "place of refuge,"[630] a "steep mountain,"[631] a "cliff,"[632] a "fort,"[633] a "strong tower,"[634] or even a wonderful, all-encompassing shield.[635] In addition, one finds an image that was originally at home in the communal complaint, the picture of the true shepherd.[636] The singer of Ps 23 very cleverly transferred the image to an individual person. The predicates mentioned in Ps 23 are combined with one another in various ways, and are occasionally piled upon one another if the one praying is really full of unrest.[637]

Standing alongside the statements expressing what YHWH is to the pious, one finds other statements which state *what he does for the pious*. He will listen to the pious, as is often accented. "If I cry aloud to YHWH, he will hear me."[638] "You will answer me."[639] In addition, all kinds of sentences appear which say that the one praying is supplied by God with his help, grace, and intercession. "YHWH keeps me."[640] "He will help me."[641] "He will hide me in 'his' hut on the day of judgment. He provides me with shade in the shadow of his tent, and raises me high upon the cliffs."[642]

The *shade* which appears in the protestations of confidence also returns in the other statements about the reason and content of the confidence. The one praying does not always soar to a happy confidence without qualification. He first has to rouse himself to that pitch. If he can find nothing that will stimulate his confidence, he turns his eyes to his surroundings and seeks comfort in the common experience of the pious. A reflective piece enters the genre at this point. These utterances which we now address can thus be designated as "comforting thought."[643]

---

[622]Ps 71:5.

[623]Ps 42:3, 9.

[624]Pss 25:5; 27:9; Mic 7:7; cf. also 27:1.

[625]Ps 27:1.

[626]Pss 19:15; 40:18; 70:6.

[627]Ps 17:1.

[628]Pss 3:4; also 16:1, 5, 6; 31:6; 43:2; 54:6; 142:6.

[629]Pss 22:20; 27:1, 9; 35:3; 38:23; 40:18; 42:6, 12; 43:5; 70:6.

[630]Pss 61:4; 142:6; Jer 17:17; cf. 31:5; 43:2; 22:20; 59:10; 140:8.

[631]Pss 31:4; 71:3.

[632]Pss 19:5; 28:1; 31:3.

[633]Pss 31:3, 4; 71:3; cf. 59:10.

[634]Ps 61:4.

[635]Pss 3:4 cf. 7:11.

[636]Cf. §4, ¶4, p. 86.

[637]Pss 3:4; 31:5, 6.

[638]Ps 3:5.

[639]Pss 38:16; 17:6; cf. 4:4; 55:19; Mic 7:7.

[640]Ps 3:6.

[641]Ps 55:17.

[642]Pss 27:5; see also 16:11; 23:3, 4, 5, 6; 25:15; 27:4; 31:6; 55:11; 59:9; 119:6, 50; 140:6.

[643]For comforting thoughts in the communal complaint, see §4, ¶10.

The *experience of the one remaining true to* YHWH stands in the foreground. "None who wait on you will come to shame."[644] "The honest ones will see your face."[645] Mostly, however, YHWH appears in these sentences powerfully in the foreground. That is not accidental, for the one who is beaten down hopes only in him alone for salvation. Therefore, he can only establish himself on YHWH's deeds, and can only comfort himself by reflecting upon YHWH's being. Thus he looks at everything from above, not from the perspective of the pious one's experience. He then comes into contact with hymnic spheres.[646] It is hymnic material which proceeds from the comforting thought, and this is how the form of the hymnic sentence enters the complaint song. "YHWH is good to those who hope in him."[647] "YHWH is good and true."[648] "YHWH is the one helping the honest heart."[649] In these sentences which speak of YHWH in the third person, the relationship to him is already lost. The form of prayer is abandoned. The reference to the general teaching shows how the personal relationship to YHWH begins to loosen. There is still something more solid in those sentences which have the same content of the previous ones but which still used the second person. "You are good and reconciling.[650] "None compare to you among the gods."[651] "You are good and you act with goodness."[652]

20. The battle and wrestling for the psalmists' confidence makes it apparent from the outset that the complaint song knows *other motifs* which effectively support the petition. One presents the *brevity of human life* to YHWH, so that YHWH can do something and the one praying will not be taken away before his time. "'I make' known to you my end."[653] "I incline myself toward you like a shadow. I go forth, but am blown away like locusts 'and am no more.'"[654] "Consider 'how I go forth forever.' Have you created all human children for nothing?"[655] At the same time, one reminds YHWH of what YHWH loses if he delivers his worshipers to the underworld. "In death, one does not think of you."[656] "What good is my blood to you so that I should go to the grave? Can dust thank you or proclaim your faithfulness?"[657] Or, the poet turns his glance to the happy future of his people where YHWH will appear in the newly constructed Zion with his majesty, and the prayer of the departed one will be heard.[658]

The consideration of YHWH's *sovereignty and eternity* is not very far from these ideas. This material is then also bound with the eschatological material of Ps 102:12ff. The poet

---

[644]Pss 25:3; 71:6, 17.

[645]Pss 11:7; cf. 119:165.

[646]Cf. §2, ¶56 and §6, ¶28.

[647]Lam 3:25.

[648]Ps 25:8.

[649]Pss 7:11; see also 7:12; 25:6, 8, 9, 10, 14; Jer 11:20; Lam 3:23; Syriac Apocryphal Psalms 3:23f.

[650]Ps 86:5.

[651]Ps 86:8.

[652]Pss 119:68; cf. 22:4; 31:7; 86:10; Lam 3:22f. See ¶25 concerning the alternation of persons.

[653]Ps 39:5.

[654]Ps 109:23.

[655]Ps 89:48; see also 39:6; 119:8f, 83.

[656]Ps 6:6.

[657]Ps 30:10; see also 88:11-13.

[658]Ps 102:13-23; cf. §9, ¶24, 25.

finally conquers the pain of his fleeting life by thinking about that which continues eternally, the essence of YHWH that remains the same when everything changes. His lordship over Jacob and his recognition by his enemies are the thoughts with which Ps 59 impresses upon YHWH.[659] YHWH's sovereignty is the last thing mentioned in the petition of Ps 130: "Forgiveness is with him so that he might be feared."

The one praying occasionally recounts a call to the wonderful knowledge of YHWH, which is related to the idea of sovereignty. "YHWH, you know all their deadly plans against me."[660] Or, one reminds YHWH of the praise songs that he has sung to him (and therein the complaint song comes close to its Babylonian counterpart), and he sings: "My praise will always go to you."[661]

Another reason for comfort is that the *godless will find no place with YHWH*. "You have no pleasure in wickedness. No evil one may be a guest of yours. Fools may not appear before your eyes. You hate all those doing wrong, those speaking lies, the man of deceit. And 'you shy away from' murder, YHWH."[662]

Or, one challenges YHWH that his honor is endangered by the appeal of the one complaining: "Know that I am suffering disgrace on your account."[663]

In this paragraph, one should especially observe the psalmists' ideas about their *personal experience*. These ideas form the rationale previously mentioned over against a larger group by themselves. The recollection is essentially dominated by the past tense according to its own nature: "I have been cast to you from my mother's womb. You have been my God since I was on my mother's lap."[664] "You have been a help to me. 'I found my nest' in the shadow of your wings. My soul clung to you. Your justice kept me upright."[665] "YHWH, you have taught me since I was a youth."[666] Though these recollections essentially preserve the form of the prayer, other examples lose the connection with the form: "I will think of this and my soul shudders within me, so that I might one day go to the 'tent of majesty, ' to YHWH's house, with the sound of rejoicing and thanksgiving, 'the noise' of the pilgrims."[667] Or, one remembers how the lot almost would have been different if YHWH had not helped. "They had almost abandoned me to the earth."[668] "Had YHWH not been my help, my soul would already lay in the land of silence."[669] Sometimes these recollections are combined with a word about the *blessing and purpose* of the suffering. It should purify and lead to YHWH. One might suggest that the recollections of one's own life take the place of these observations. However, it is no accident that this idea does not appear in the complaint songs themselves. The complaint songs are too immediate, too little controlled by reflection. This idea first appears in Ps 119, a poem

---

[659]Pss 59:14; see also 109:27.

[660]Jer 18:23; cf. 12:3.

[661]Ps 71:6; similarly, 109:1; Jer 17:14; cf. *ZAW* (1928): 250.

[662]Pss 5:5-7; cf. 31:7.

[663]Jer 15:15; Ps 68:8, 10.

[664]Ps 22:11.

[665]Ps 63:8-9.

[666]Pss 71:17; cf. 3:5; 4:2; 119:50, 65, 71, 73.

[667]Ps 42:5.

[668]Ps 119:87.

[669]Pss 94:17; see also 94:18; 119:92.

that for various reasons belongs to the latest period of psalmody. "Before I had to suffer, I must have erred, but now I accept your judgment."[670] "It was healthy for me that I was humbled so that I might learn your statutes."[671] The specific place of this thought is the individual thanksgiving song.[672]

21. Finally, one should mention the rationale of the *innocent and the penitent*. The innocent one places his pious conviction before YHWH: "I am pious."[673] He knows nothing of wicked deeds: "'I did not overstep' your command regarding bloody' deeds. . . My step does not tread on the path of the robber. I did not deviate from your tracks."[674] Conscious of his innocence the one praying laments. "They hate me without reason."[675] "Though I am not guilty and have not erred, they run at me and make me an example."[676] It is quite sufficient for him that he may enter YHWH's house. That is also proof of his innocence: "But I may enter your house by your great grace, and cast myself down in fear before you in front of your holy temple."[677]

By fending off any reasons of guilt, however, these rationale disappear. The one praying calls upon his *deserved conduct*. One should thereby observe the complete lack of worship activities. The psalmist portrays his *humility*: "I am mute. I do not open my mouth, for you have done it."[678] Or, he is zealous for YHWH and his honor. "Zeal for your house consumed me."[679] "My zeal kills me because my enemies forget your words."[680] He calls himself to strive for good: "They feud with me because I search out good."[681] This thought includes a large part of the innocence motif since the law had decisively begun to determine Jewish piety. *Love of YHWH's law* is expressed repeatedly. "I love your ordinances."[682] "I crave your law."[683] "The path of your commands pleases me."[684]

The *rationale of the penitent one* is completely different. It contains no reference to innocence and lawfulness, no self-conscious citation of good deeds. The one confessing stands under the convicting conscience of *God's righteous anger over his sins*. This can be expressed in the petition itself. "Forgive me my guilt even though it is great."[685] Generally, the confession of sin is expressed in a particular sentence. "I confess my

---

[670]Ps 119:67.

[671]Ps 119:71.

[672]See §7, ¶4.

[673]Ps 86:2.

[674]Pss 17:3-5; see also 26:4-5.

[675]Ps 35:7, 19.

[676]Ps 59:4.

[677]Ps 5:8; see also 26:6-8.

[678]Ps 39:10, similarly 39:2-4.

[679]Ps 69:10.

[680]Ps 119:139.

[681]Ps 38:21.

[682]Ps 119:159.

[683]Ps 119:30.

[684]Ps 119:35; see also 119:11, 13, 14, 22, 23, 24, 25, 30, 32, 47, 51, 55, 56, 58, 59, 60, 61, 67, 69, 70, 77, 78, 83, 87, 94, 99, 100, 101, 102, 104, 105, 109, 110, 111, 119, 121, 128, 129, 141, 157, 158, 159, 161, 162, 163, 166, 167, 168, 173, 176. See also 17:4; 19:12; 26:3.

[685]Ps 25:11.

wickedness."[686] "My faults go over my head."[687] "My sins have hemmed me in, and I cannot bear them. They are more than the hairs on my head. My courage has left me."[688] For the inwardly pious person praying, confession of sins does not include concession to his environment that he is wicked. He protests explicitly against the supposition that blood clings to his hands, or that he has oppressed the widow and the orphan, etc. He gives his confession a form which avoids any misunderstanding. "I have sinned against you alone."[689] "You alone know my faults."[690] It is a comfort for the one praying that he does not stand alone before YHWH in his convictional guilt. It is the fate of humanity generally to sin. The singer of Ps 51 therefore adds to his personal confession, "I am surrounded by sin."[691] The psalmist hopes that just as YHWH is forgiving toward humanity in general, he will also forgive the individual. The prayer of Manasseh states: "Your grace that you promise is immeasurable, incomprehensible . . . Humans suffering repent to you. You promise forgiveness of sins according to your compassionate goodness to the one who errs. According to the abundance of your compassion you decree confession for sinners so they might be saved."[692] Ps 130 expresses the same thoughts less verbosely, and more deeply and finely: "Forgiveness belongs to you, so that one might fear you."[693]

22. How are the aforementioned individual components arranged with respect to the complaint song as a whole? The flow of the genre is presented here in its simplest form. For the freer form, see ¶28.

Normally, the complaint song begins with the summons to YHWH.[694] If he is going to help he must be made aware that everything which the one praying says is directed *to him*.[695] Those psalms which do not begin with the summons are either not complaint songs in the narrower sense,[696] or the situation of the one praying is quite special. Ps 39 and Isa 38:10ff both begin without address: Ps 39 because the poet wants to bear his suffering in silent devotion, and Isa 38 because the one praying is full of doubt and has lost faith that YHWH will hear him.

The summons often does not stand by itself. Rather, it is placed within the "introductory cry for help." In these cases the summons is not the first but the third or fourth word.[697]

A *brief portrayal of the praying* occasionally precedes the introductory cry of help, separated by the summons. Examples include: "I bow myself to you, YHWH. Do not let

---

[686]Ps 51:5.

[687]Ps 38:5.

[688]Pss 40:13; cf. 32:5; 38:19; 88:17.

[689]Ps 51:6.

[690]Ps 69:6.

[691]Pss 51:7; cf. 130:3; Syriac Apocryphal Psalms 3:10.

[692]Pr Man 6-7.

[693]Ps 130:4.

[694]Cf. ¶10.

[695]The following begin with addresses: Pss 3; 5; 6; 7; 17; 22; 26; 27:7ff; 28; 31; 42; 51; 54; 55; 56; 57; 59; 61; 63; 64; 69; 70; 71; 86; 88; 102; 109; 130; 140; 141; 143; Sir 51:10; Pr Man; Ps 41:5.

[696]See ¶27.

[697]Pss 5:2-3; 17:1; 27:7; 28:1; 31:2; 55:2-3; 61:2; 64:2; 86:1; 88:3.

me be ashamed any more. Incline your ear to me. Hurry to save me."[698] At times, the summons *stands by itself with the portrayal of praying* at the beginning of the poem: "YHWH, my God, I flee to you."[699] The summons is not, however, limited to the beginning of the poem. It returns again at the important places of the poem (cf. the details in the numerous examples given in ¶10).

The summons and the cry for help can follow the *complaint*.[700] If a cry for help is lacking, the complaint is attached directly to the summons.[701] Such is the case where the complaint begins with the impassioned question: "My God, my God, why have you forsaken me?"[702]

The petition follows the complaint.[703] However, the passion and the tempestuous tension which lives in the genre means that the order is not always fixed. The *movement of the form* more closely corresponds to the movement of the mood. The complaint song can begin with the petition rather than with the complaint if the desire for liberation overwhelms the impulse to speak the complaint.[704] Or, *the petition can be attached to the portrayal of praying* which accompanies the address.[705] However, in most cases the petition follows the introductory cry for help.[706] The complaint is then attached to the petition.[707]

The petition and complaint can be repeated. Excitement causes the psalmists to wander, until it is expressed and finds peace. Those cases move from complaint to petition, from petition back to complaint and back again to petition.[708] The Babylonian material also knows this alternation.[709] With this variation the complaint can hold the final position.[710] Far more frequently, however, the petition stands at the end where the expression of hope appears.[711]

The various rationale specifying why YHWH should intervene stand in connection with the complaint and petition. They are found behind the complaint and before the petition,[712] between petitions,[713] between complaints,[714] between petition and complaint,[715] after the

---

[698]Pss 31:2f; see also 28:1; 71:1-2; 88:2-3; 120:1-2; 130:1-2; 142:1-4.

[699]Pss 7:2; see also 42:2-3; 63:2-3.

[700]Pss 42:4; 54:3-5; 55:4-6; 88:2ff; 102:2ff; 109:1-5; 142:2-5; 143:1-4.

[701]Pss 3:2-3; 13:2-3; 22:2-3.

[702]Pss 22:2.

[703]Pss 13:4-5; 56:4; 69:6ff; 109:6ff.

[704]Pss 6:2; 35:2; 38:2; 40:14ff; 41:5ff; 51:3-4; 57:2; 59:2-3; 140:2ff.

[705]Pss 7:2; 71:1-2.

[706]Pss 17:1-3; 27:7ff; 28:2-3; 31:3ff; 61:3; 64:3; 86:2ff; 141:3ff; 143:2ff.

[707]Pss 6:7ff; 27:10; 35:7; 38:3ff; 40:18; 41:6-10; 54:5; 57:5; 59:4; 64:4ff; 69:2ff; 140:6; 143:3-4.

[708]Pss 5:9, 10, 11; 17:6-14; 22:2-3, 7-12, 13-22; 27:7ff; 31:10ff; 35:1-10, 11ff; 38:1ff; 40:14ff; etc.

[709]Ungnad, *Religion der Babylonier und Assyrer*, pp. 205:27ff; 218:27ff.

[710]Pss 6:8; 88:10, 19; 120:5-7.

[711]5:11-12; 13:4-5; 17:13ff; 22:12, 22; 31:19; 35:9-10, 26-27; 38:22-23; 39:14; 40:18; 41:11; 43:1-4; 51:17; 55:19; 56:9; 59:12-14; etc.

[712]Pss 13:4-7; 22:10-11; 31:15-16; 38:16, 19-20; 54:6; 59:10-11; 69:6; 71:5-6; 86:15; 140:7-9; 142:6-7; 143:5-6.

[713]Pss 5:5-8; 7:4-6; 17:3-5; 26:3-8; 31:4-6; 51:5-8; 61:4-5; 71:3; 86:3; 141:8.

[714]Pss 22:4-6; 42:5; 88:10-13.

[715]Pss 43:2; 56:4.

petition by itself,[716] after the complaint by itself,[717] and finally, between the address and the petition.[718]

The individual components of the genre are often clearly broken off and therefore the transitions are not difficult to recognize. For example, the appearance of "but you" (we'attāh) marks the place where the complaint song turns away from the distress of the one praying and the hostilities of his opponents to the expression of confidence or the reason for trust.[719] Or the word marks the place where the complaint song changes to the petition of YHWH.[720] Similarly, "but I" (weānōkî, wă'anî) accents the transition to a new component. It leads from the portrayal of the hostile proceedings to the expression of confidence.[721] It separates the innocence motif from the complaint about the opponents,[722] or it leads from the petition and the confidence motif back to the bitter complaint.[723]

The complaint song can conclude in this fashion and with its components in this order. It can thereby preserve the complaint as the last word.[724] More frequently, the petition stands at the end,[725] and less often in imperative form.[726] It is more common for a wish to stand at the end. The wish relatively seldom relates directly to the one praying.[727] Generally, the poet looks away from himself and either thinks of his enemies, his friends, or the pious in general.[728] However, the wish does not stop with the narrow circle of the pious. It grows from there and stretches over all humanity. Even if humanity cannot create trust from the event because they are not YHWH's pious, they should still be impressed with his action: "May all humanity be afraid, interpret his action, and recognize his work. May the righteous rejoice in YHWH, and may all pious hearts triumph."[729] The conclusion sometimes has a full-toned sound. May the pious "always" have cause to celebrate.[730]

Several less common conclusions appear in conjunction with the petition. With the direct relationship, it is not strange for the last petition to conclude with the motif in which the various "rationale" stand close to it. This motif appears in direct relationship with the petition: "Come quickly to help me, Lord, my salvation."[731] It appears more frequently as an independent element: "May innocence and honesty protect me. For I wait for you, YHWH."[732] The stages also appear here that were observed with the expressions

---

[716]Pss 63:7-9; 86:5-7, 8-10; 130:3-4.

[717]Ps 102:13-23, 25-29.

[718]Pr Man 4-8.

[719]Pss 22:4, 10; 86:15; 102:13.

[720]Pss 41:11; 59:6; 109:21.

[721]Ps 13:6.

[722]Ps 5:8.

[723]Pss 22:7; 40:18; 69:30; 88:14.

[724]Ps 120:5-7, perhaps also Ps 88:11 if the text is transmitted without abbreviation.

[725]Pss 17:13-15; 35:24-27; 38:22-23; 39:14; 40:18; 41:11; 43:1-4; 63:10-12; 64:8-11; 86:14-17; 141:8-10; 142:6-8; 143:12.

[726]Pss 39:11-14; 40:18; 41:11; 143:12.

[727]Pss 17:12; 141:10; similarly 43:3-4.

[728]Pss 63:10f; 86:14ff; 35:27; 142:8.

[729]Ps 64:10-11.

[730]Pss 35:27; cf. 19:15.

[731]Ps 38:23.

[732]Pss 25:21; cf. 143:12.

of confidence. Sometimes one finds self-admonition in the conclusion: hold fast to YHWH.[733]

The multistaged ordering of the individual components sometimes receives a *tighter structuring*. The complaint song is thereby arranged into two parts with the same flow.[734] Then it twice moves from the complaint to the petition.[735] Or, the complaint song moves from the summons to the certainty of being heard, to the vow,[736] in order to sink back into the depth of the complaint, before returning to the path of certainty once again.[737] Ps 71 even strives toward this goal three times. One can observe the same arrangement in Babylonian materials.[738] This arrangement allows one to divide the various moods more clearly and to isolate them more sharply. They would otherwise flow into and through one another. Thus, in Ps 22:2-12 the complaint, confidence, and reasons for comfort dominate while in Ps 22:13-22 the deep, doubting complaint has control. The relationship in Ps 35 is similar. One should particularly mention the conclusions. Part one concludes with the wish for healing and the wish to be able to praise YHWH. Part two no longer thinks about the one praying, but on the pious and their comfort. Therefore it wishes that they might express the praise for the salvation of the one praying. Similar observations could be made for the other references cited.

23. A number of complaint songs have a *special form for the conclusion* beyond the parts already described to this point.[739] This form was mentioned in passing at the end of the previous section. It concerns the certainty of being heard and the vow. First, let us turn to the *certainty of being heard*.

At the conclusion of the complaint songs, it is not uncommon to be able to observe a very noteworthy, abrupt change in the mood of the one praying. He still complains in a heart rending manner, and petitions importunely that he be heard and liberated. In the next instant he speaks with a comforting and happy soul like a person who no longer needs to petition, like one who is sure and certain he has been heard. This certainty knows various stages. It is certainly no accident that it is materially associated with the expression of confidence found in connection with the petition. It is the same confidence expressed in both places. The expressions of certainty are differentiated, however, with regard to their location to the petition. The motif of confidence carries the petition which is built upon it. The certainty no longer serves this purpose. The expressions of confidence stand free of any reference back to the intentions of the one praying. One can readily understand that the expressions of certainty do not recognize the vacillations and nuances of the statements of confidence. There is no longer any wrestling. The degree of certainty is a different type.

---

[733]Pss 27:14; 55:23; see also the refrain in 42:6, 12; 46:5.

[734]The same thing happens in the hymn (§2, ¶6), in the communal complaint (§4, ¶14), and in the individual thanksgiving song (§7, ¶9).

[735]Pss 22:2-12, 13-22; 59:2-6, 7-15; 69:1-7, 8-13; 88:2-10, 11-13, 14-19; 102:2-23, 24-29; 109:1-20, 21-31; 140:2-6, 7-12.

[736]Cf. ¶23, ¶24.

[737]Pss 31:2-9, 10-25; 35:1-10, 11-27; 86:1-13, 14-17.

[738]Ebeling, *Quellen zur Kenntnis der babylonischen Religion*, vol. 1, 6:39-50; 6:1-7:18.

[739]They also appear in the communal complaint. See §4, ¶11.

The simplest expression of certainty is closely associated with the expression of unshakeable confidence as encountered in conjunction with the petition: "I trust your grace, 'YHWH.' "[740] "I am like a green olive tree in the house 'of YHWH.' I trust 'YHWH's' grace for ever and always."[741] The material of the thoughts of comfort also appears. "You bless the righteous, YHWH, 'with salvation' and 'protect him' like a shield. You crown him with favor."[742] "'YHWH' is my shield 'that protects me, ' the helper of the honest heart." "'YHWH' judges the righteous and 'repays the one who' curses every day."[743] In contrast to the confidence motif and the reasons for comfort, one can no longer ascertain any wrestling with confidence. Rather, the certainty escalates into a broader realm from the narrow circle of personal relationships. Ps 61:6 makes that unmistakable with the words, "You guarantee 'the supplication' of those who fear your name." These words precede the following: "for you, YHWH, examine my vow." One should also consider it an escalation when those thoughts dealing with the reasons for comfort abandon the form of the prayer and speak of YHWH in the third person.[744] The one praying is so certain that he no longer needs the support that he sought in expressions of confidence and reasons of comfort.[745]

From this point, one can understand how the one praying brings himself to see that which he petitions as certain. Examples from Jeremiah will illustrate: "But YHWH the Lord judges rightly. He examines heart and soul. I will see my vengeance on them, for I have cast my matter to you."[746] "But YHWH is with me like a mighty hero, therefore my opponents must stumble."[747] The material of the petition appears here, but it is no longer conceived in the form of the imperative or the wish. Rather, it appears in the form of certain expectation. It is no accident that the first person, the one praying, can be the subject of the assertion.[748]

Expressions of certainty like those just mentioned are found relatively commonly in the complaint songs. Soon they speak of YHWH in the third person, but also in the second person as the example from Ps 61:6 mentioned above: "You do not give my life over to the underworld. You do not let the pious see the grave. You make known to me the path of life. There is an abundance of joy before your countenance, and delight in your laws always."[749] "YHWH is my fortress, my God the protecting rock. He repays them for their wickedness, and destroys them because of their evil.[750] The certainty is so great that one deals with the entry of that which was petitioned without ever thinking that YHWH has done it: "And now my head is raised above my enemies roundabout."[751] The assertion which follows relies upon the statements of confidence: "Indeed, he whets his sword for

---

[740]Ps 13:6.

[741]Ps 52:10; cf. 55:24.

[742]Ps 5:13.

[743]Ps 7:11f.

[744]One can observe the difference in the reasons for comfort which have a corresponding form. See ¶19, pp. 171 and 174.

[745]Jer 11:20; 20:11.

[746]Jer 11:20.

[747]Jer 20:11.

[748]Jer 11:20.

[749]Pss 16:10-11; see also 55:24.

[750]Pss 94:22-23; cf. 130:7-8.

[751]Ps 27:6.

himself. He holds the bow in tension and aims. He prepares the murder weapons for himself. He polishes his own spear."[752] On occasion, the one praying accentuates his certainty very strongly at the beginning of the motif: "This I know. 'YHWH' is for me. With 'YHWH' 'I conduct my affairs.' I trust in 'YHWH.' I am not afraid. What can mortals do to me?[753]

In all of these sentences the psalmist sees the fulfillment of his petition very close at hand. The tense in which he speaks is therefore *imperfect*. However, sentences containing the highest degree of certainty that can be attained stand in the *perfect* tense. In these cases, the one praying sees a time fast approaching which is triumphantly already fulfilled and completed. He sees why he prayed so longingly: "You have struck all my enemies on the cheek. The teeth of the wicked are broken.[754] "The evil-doers shuddered. They have fallen and will not get back up."[755] These sentences usually follow the petition,[756] but at times the expression of certainty is attached directly to the complaint. In this case a very peculiar effect arises with the polarity that is created. Ps 6 is perhaps the most illustrative example. The psalmist still complains: "I swim in my bed every night. My couch flows with tears. My eyes are heavy with grief, and become feeble in all 'my distress.'" The mood then changes suddenly: "Get away from me, all you evil-doers, for YHWH has heard the sound of my crying. YHWH has accepted my prayer. They shall be ashamed and terribly afraid. All my enemies must cease immediately."[757]

How does one explain the sudden change of mood which is so noticeable in this motif? Does it concern an internal process of the one praying? After all of the turmoil of the internal struggle, after the despondency or the doubt, does the heart of the one praying finally find stillness and confidence? Or, is this change dependent upon an external event? Fr. Küchler believes that a priestly oracle would have originally appeared within the genre before the affirmation of being heard.[758] He believes the oracle would have been confirmed that the one praying had been heard on the basis of some type of sacrifice or the like. One cannot support this argument based upon the narrative passages mentioned by Küchler because they concern places where the oracle is incorporated in cases where it is unclear which of the various possibilities someone will choose.[759] The reference to Ps 5:4 is more convincing, where the one praying prepares his sacrifice in the morning and stretches himself out before YHWH. In this instance it actually appears to lead to the expectation of a decision by YHWH in conjunction with the sacrifice.[760] However, this reference stands completely isolated within the individual complaint songs. The parallel communal complaint also offers no oracle. Only in liturgies can one deduce that an oracle

---

[752]Ps 7:13-14.

[753]Pss 56:10-12; cf. 140:13ff; and 20:7.

[754]Ps 3:8.

[755]Pss 36:13; see also 26:12; 57:7; Jer 20:11c.

[756]Pss 3:8; 26:12; 36:13.

[757]Pss 6:8-11; see also 57:7; Jer 20:11.

[758]Fr. Küchler, *Das Priesterliche Orakel in Israel und Juda*, Abhandlungen zur semitischen Religionskunde und Sprachwissenschaft, published by W.W. Grafen von Baudissin, p. 285.

[759]Gen 25:22ff; 2 Sam 5:19, 23ff; 21:1.

[760]Compare the commentary at this passage.

follows the Israelite complaint song.[761] The most important evidence is perhaps the fact that a divine oracle follows as the response in the complaint poetry of Jeremiah and in texts which are similar to the complaint songs.[762] But could this oracle not constitute a deviation, evidenced by the fact that Jeremiah is simultaneously *the one praying and a prophet*? One could of course say that passages like Pss 56:10 and 140:13, with the phrases "now I know" are best understandable if a divine oracle immediately preceded. But one could also conceivably make the observation that in Jer 11:18-20 and 20:10-12 the complaint and the petition follow the certainty of having been heard. The uncertainty which the above mentioned passages leave is overcome, in our opinion, when one incorporates the texts of Deutero-Isaiah mentioned in the footnote below.[763] In our opinion, they certainly lead to the conclusion that a priestly salvation oracle originally preceded the certainty of being heard and that even Deutero-Isaiah knew this salvation oracle with the individual complaint song. He shows elsewhere in his prophecy that he is heavily dependent upon religious lyric. He took up this form in order to express the message of salvation contained in it. The fact that these oracles are not transmitted in conjunction with the text of the complaint songs is apparently explained by the fact that the poet would not have access to their vocabulary, and therefore could not make them a component of his poetry.

It is illuminating that the change of mood could be completed on the basis of the divine decision addressed above which assures the one praying of the fulfillment of his petition. A fixed association existed between oracle and petition in the cult even as late as the end of the preexilic period, as can be deduced from Deutero-Isaiah. This association formed a fixed style that continued to operate more widely. One should be clear that the priestly oracle does not constitute the entire explanation for the certainty of being heard. There are numerous complaint songs which have never presupposed such an oracle, those without cultic ties. One has to consider these as the consequences of a fixed style.[764] This consequence would only be possible because bringing one's self to the point of fixed certainty is elsewhere characteristic of the prayer itself. "In the prayer itself, a wonderful metamorphosis is completed unconsciously and unintentionally, often quite suddenly. The feeling of uncertainty and reservation is dissolved by the happy awareness of protection and being hidden in the hand of a protective higher power. Certainty breaks through doubt and questioning. From the fear comes confidence, and from the anxiety and timidity comes the courage of rejoicing in the future. Desires and wishes become internal assets and possessions."[765] From this experience, Luther writes to Melancthon, "I have prayed for you. . . . I have felt the amen in my heart.[766] From this experience, Calvin formulated the rule of prayer: "In the midst of misgivings, fear, and wavering, we should force

---

[761]Cf. §4, ¶14 and §11, ¶15.

[762]Jer 15:15-21.

[763]Isa 41:8ff, 14ff; 43:1-2, 5a; 49:15; 54:4ff; cf. 51:7f. The proof should be reserved for a special investigation which exceeds the framework of this work. Since one does not encounter a priestly salvation oracle within Psalms, the introduction to the psalms can be ignored for this topic at this point with no harm to the comprehensiveness.

[764]So Küchler himself (*Das Priesterliche Orakel in Israel und Juda*, p. 300).

[765]Fr. Heiler, *Gebet*,[4] 1921, p. 380.

[766]L. Enders, *M. Luthers Briefwechsel*, vol. 8, p. 52; vol. 3, pp. 85ff.

ourselves to pray until we find illumination which calms us. If our hearts waver, and are disturbed, we may not give up until faith proceeds victoriously from the battle."[767]

24. The complaint song can now conclude with the certainty of having been heard.[768] Not infrequently, however, another specific component can follow, the *vow*. This component is usually at the end of the Babylonian complaint song, where it follows immediately upon the complaint and petition, and where it appears as a concluding, particularly effective means of convincing God. In the Hebrew complaint song, the vow is separated from the petition, thereby casting this element in another light. It is no longer the means of convincing, it is the *expression of a feeling of thankfulness which has welled up*.

The cultic situation of the complaint song and the thanksgiving song[769] suggests that originally the one praying pledged a *thanksgiving sacrifice*. This custom is only preserved in traces in the complaint songs of the psalter. "I will freely bring you offerings."[770] "Your vows are incumbent upon me, YHWH. I will pay you with a thanksgiving offering."[771]

The thanksgiving song[772] is closely associated with the thanksgiving offering by the situation, so it is only natural when they appear together. "I will sing and play to YHWH."[773] "I will thank your name."[774] Finally, the vow of the thanksgiving song gradually replaced the vow of the thanksgiving offering. Traces of this process can be seen in Pss 40:7f; 51:18; and 69:31ff, places that speak of YHWH not wanting the sacrifice. In Pss 40 and 69 the thanksgiving song returns to its place. The complaint song or its analogous components quite frequently conclude with this vow of the thanksgiving song.[775]

The *form of the vow* is of course a sentence whose verb stands in the first person, since the one praying is himself the one considering how to act. The mode is either the *imperfect*[776] or the cohortative.[777] As an example, we can cite: "I will thank YHWH for he is righteous, and I will sing the name of the most high."[778] The Babylonian vow corresponds to the Hebrew materially as well as formally: "I will praise your greatness, I will exalt you."[779]

The complaint song cannot just use the simple vow of the thanksgiving song. The certainty of being heard drives the singer further. In his enthusiasm, he already voices the

---

[767]Heiler, *Das Gebet*,[4] p. 383.

[768]Pss 3:8; 5:13; 6:9-11; 36:13; 51:18-19; 55:24; 63:10-11; 140:13-14.

[769]§7, ¶2.

[770]Ps 54:8.

[771]Pss 56:13; cf. 61:9. In Ps 27:6 the offering of jubilation appears in place of the thanksgiving offering, though it does not belong to the complaint songs in the strictest sense.

[772]Cf. §7, ¶2.

[773]Ps 27:6.

[774]Pss 54:8; cf. 61:9.

[775]Pss 7:18; 13:6; 22:23ff; 26:12; 27:6; (28:6f); 31:8f; 35:9f, 27f; 42:6; 43:4f; 51:15-17; 54:8; 56:13f; 57:8f; 59:17; 61:9; 63:5, 6; 69:31ff; 71:8, 14-16, 18ff; 86:12ff; 109:30; 119:7; 140:14; 142:8; Jer 20:13; Sir 51:11; see also Ps 21:14.

[776]Pss 7:18; 26:12; 42:6, 12; 43:5; 54:8; 57:10; 59:17; 63:5; 69:31b; 71:14, 16, 22; 86:12; 109:30; 119:7; Sir 51:11b.

[777]Pss 7:18; 13:6; 22:23; 27:6; 43:4; 51:15; 54:8; 57:8, 9; 61:9; 69:31; 71:22; 86:12; Sir 51:11.

[778]Ps 7:18.

[779]Ebeling, *Quellen zur Kenntnis der babylonischen Religion*, vol. 1, p. 18:19; cf. 6:49; 20:24; vol. 2, p. 14:26; etc.

thanksgiving song that he will sing after deliverance occurs. That is how the thanksgiving song enters the genre.[780] The simplest form appears: "I will sing to YHWH who has acted kindly toward me."[781] One also finds the revised form of the thanksgiving song with an address to those participating in the celebration, warnings, etc.[782] Because of the enthusiasm to which the psalmist raises himself, the thanksgiving song occasionally adopts *hymnic forms*.[783] Indeed, the thanksgiving song grows beyond the contemplation of the salvific act. It turns to YHWH's help for the pious in general, thereby joining in the *hymn*.[784] Or, the one praying is not satisfied that he should offer thanks by himself. He includes ever larger circles in his thanksgiving, and escalates from there into the *high tones of the hymn*.[785]

Similarly, the Babylonian genre can conclude with hymnic words: "May the heavens rejoice in you, Apsu, and be happy about you. May the great gods rejoice over you. May the gods, the Igigi, speak well of you."[786] "I will praise your divine power and strength before the blackheaded people. Ištar is exalted. Ištar is queen. The lady is exalted. The lady is queen. Irnini, the daughter of Sin, has no one like you."[787]

It is understandable that this full-toned conclusion also prefers grand terms. The praise shall resound "day by day,"[788] "all morning,"[789] "the whole day,"[790] even "the entire life."[791] Even the unborn generation shall join in singing with heaven and earth, the living, and those who have passed away.[792] This also has Babylonian parallels.[793]

Alongside these strong and powerful tones of the vow stand those which are *quieter and more subdued*. The *wish* appears in place of the psalmist's self-confident conclusion: may YHWH grant that the one praying can sing a thanksgiving song or even a hymn.[794] Even the tone of the hymn seems subdued.[795] The vow in 142:8 appears very cautious and specifically designed as a means of convincing: "Free my from prison so that I might praise your name."

---

[780]Pss 13:6; 22:24ff; 28:6-7; 31:22ff; 54; 56:14; 59:17; 69:33ff; 71:14-16, 20ff; 86:12-13; 144:9-10.

[781]Ps 13:6.

[782]Pss 22:24ff; 31:22ff; et.

[783]Pss 28:6; 31:22.

[784]Ps 31:20ff.

[785]Pss 22:28ff; 69:35-37. Hymns appearing without the mediation of the thanksgiving song appear in Jer 20:13; Ps 57:8ff; cf. §2, ¶54, 56; §7, ¶3, 5, 7, 8.

[786]Ebeling, *Quellen zur Kenntnis der babylonischen Religion*, vol. 1, p. 11:20-23.

[787]Ungnad, *Religion der Babylonier und Assyrer*, 222:102-105; see also Ebeling, *Quellen zur Kenntnis der babylonischen Religion*, vol. 45:35; and Ungnad, pp. 178:22-25.

[788]Ps 61:9.

[789]Ps 59:17.

[790]Pss 35:28; 71:8, 15, 24.

[791]Ps 63:5.

[792]Ps 22:28ff.

[793]Stummer *Sumerisch-akkadische Parallelen zum Aufbau alttestamentlicher Psalmen*, pp. 105f. Ps 22:24ff comes especially close to an Egyptian thanksgiving song. Cf. §7, ¶12.

[794]Pss 35:9, 10, 28; 43:4; 63:6; 71:8, 14.

[795]Pss 69:35; 142:8.

With the genre's greater distance from its original life-setting, other contents appear in place of the thanksgiving song. One finds perhaps *vows of piety* in general. It is no accident that this vow is found in a mixed poem of the later period, Ps 119. The old forms speak of the fact that the one praying will preserve the speech of YHWH,[796] meditate on his statutes, and observe his path.[797] There are more vows of this type.[798]

25. It has already been mentioned that sometimes YHWH is *addressed*, and then is spoken about in the *third person*. Now we will investigate the change more closely to discover the *reasons* for the change.

Inside the complaint song, naming YHWH in the *third person* appears more often in the *confidence motif* than in the related *certainty of being heard*.[799] In the latter, the task of the prayer form lies in the fact that the one praying no longer requires the dependence on YHWH (cf. ¶23). With the expression of confidence one occasionally encounters an escalation to the point of certainty. Then, the one praying no longer finds dependence necessary: "'YHWH' is my helper. The lord is the support of my soul."[800] I laid down and fell asleep, now I am awake, for YHWH supports me.[801] By contrast when an immediate confidence is lacking, this can be explained if the reason for comfort, recalling one's own experience, speaks of YHWH in the third person: "I will think about and pour out my soul within me as I once went to the 'majestic tent, ' to YHWH house, with the sound of rejoicing and of thanksgiving, the 'noise' of the pilgrim.[802] For the same reason, the *self-admonitions* speak the same thing.[803] The lack of immediate confidence is also identified with avoiding the address of YHWH when *portraying someone praying*.[804] Naturally, one can also not address YHWH when admonishing others.[805]

The "wishes"[806] introduce YHWH in the third person, especially the curses.[807] The avoidance of the direct address is explained by the fact that blessing and curse words originally followed the wishes, and these carried their own power. They did not derive from YHWH (cf. ¶15). Naturally, the words of the opponents who slander those suffering also speak about YHWH in the third person. The enemies have no living relationship to YHWH.[808] Finally, the fact that the *thanksgiving song and the hymn* at the end of the poem usually do not address God can be explained by the essence of these two genres.[809] Alternation between second and third person occurs in the same context without any detectable reason (see Pss 43:3f; 54:8f; 56:14; 62:12-13; 71:16; Jer 11:20).

---

[796]Ps 119:8.

[797]Ps 119:15.

[798]Ps 119:17, 27, 44, 46, 47, 48, 93, 106, 115, 117, 145.

[799]3:5-7; 6:10; 7:12; 25:15; 27:13; 42:5, 6, 12; 43:5; 54:6; 55:17; 56:10, 12; 59:11; 102:17-23; 130:5, 7; 140:8, 13; Lam 3:22, 24; Ps 94:17, 22; Jer 11, 20.

[800]Ps 54:6.

[801]Pss 3:6; cf. 59:11.

[802]Ps 42:5. Cf. ¶19 and ZAW 1928, pp. 256f.

[803]Pss 42:6f, 12; 43:5; 55:23; cf. 27:14.

[804]Pss 42:5f; 55:17; 57:3; 69:4; 77:2-4; 120:1; 142:2f.

[805]Pss 31:24; 130:7.

[806]Pss 27:10; 35:9; 42:3; 43:4; 71:16; etc.

[807]Pss 52:7; 64:8; 109:15; 140:11.

[808]Pss 3:3; 22:9; 42:4, 11; 71:11; etc.

[809]See §2, ¶24; §7, ¶4.

26. With the completion of the previous discussion the form and contents of the complaint songs have been paraphrased generally. From this discussion, the nuances of several subcategories stand out. These subcategories attain their particular characteristics by the recession of other components thus accentuating one component. This accented component takes up the largest portion of the space in the poem, at least greater than the other components.

The heavily accentuated assurance of innocence[810] is characteristic for the *song of innocence*.[811] In addition to the forms described in ¶21 the song of innocence sometimes follows the extraordinarily impressive form of the *qualified self-curse*: "If I practice haughtiness, if dishonesty is on my hands, if I have done evil to the one who has retaliated against me, or if I have robbed the one who contends against me, then may the enemy pursue my soul and capture me. May he stomp my soul into the ground and lay my liver in the dust."[812] The one praying thus separates himself from the activities of the sinners.[813] The petition in the songs of innocence makes the same sharp distinction. One implores YHWH's punishment and revenge upon the godless,[814] while, in contrast, petitioning and wishing help and salvation for one's self.[815]

Songs of confession represent another group which can be clearly distinguished as a subcategory from the mass of complaint songs.[816] Pss 6, 38, and 69 stand between the songs of confession and the typical complaint songs because they have the *confession of sin* which is characteristic of the songs of confession. The characteristic element for the songs of confession is the painful awareness of having sinned against YHWH and deserving the punishment. Within the song of confession, this awareness appears in the confession of sins appearing dominantly in the foreground.[817] Likewise, songs of confession have grown from the Babylonian genre by the heavy accentuation of the consciousness of sin and the confession of sin.[818]

It is understandable that complaints about external distress and indeed complaints in general are generally lacking in these psalms. It is also understandable that the petition desires nothing more than "atonement,"[819] "forgiveness,"[820] "remission of punishment,"[821] or "renewal of the inner person to a God-pleasing life."[822] Even the rationale of the prayer achieves its own character from the basic mood of these psalms. The petition is bound solely to YHWH's grace and fidelity,[823] and his own willingness to forgive sin.[824]

---

[810]Pss 6:5-8; 7:4-6; 17:3-5; 26:1-8; cf. 119:101, 104, 128.

[811]Pss 5; 7; 17; 26. Similarly, see Job 23:10-12.

[812]Ps 7:4-6; Job 31:5-40 is similarly constructed.

[813]Pss 5:5-7; 17:10-11; 26:4-5.

[814]Pss 5:11; 7:10; 17:13-14.

[815]Pss 5:12; 17:8f, 15; 26:11.

[816]Pss 51; 130; Prayer of Manasseh.

[817]Ps 51:5-8; Pr Man 9, 12; Pss 38:19; 69:6. A confession of sin is preserved indirectly in Ps 130:3f.

[818]Zimmern, *Babylonische Hymnen und Gebete*, vol. 1, pp. 17f, 22f, 25.

[819]Ps 51:3b-4a; Pr Man 13.

[820]Ps 51:3, 11; Pr Man 13.

[821]Pss 6:2; 38:2; 51:10.

[822]Ps 51:12-14.

[823]Ps 51:3ab.

Finally, one needs to mention the so-called *curse and revenge psalms* in this context. The striving for retaliation against the enemies is that which distinguishes these psalms from the usual genre. This retaliation appears in other complaint songs alongside other contents of the petition,[825] but here seems to be the *only goal* of the prayer.[826] Here, the ancient curse formulas that entered the complaint song[827] are multiplied and appear painfully cruel. As gruesome as these curses sound to us today, it is nevertheless clear that the psalmist expresses them with a clear conscience and expects that God will fulfill his curses.

H. Schmidt has endeavored to demonstrate the "prayer of the accused" as another subcategory.[828] He distinguishes more precisely between prayers of the accused[829] and prayers of the ill who are also accused.[830] According to him they share a situation unique to themselves.[831] those praying find themselves *under investigation in prison*. Since they have not yet proven their innocence, they will be cast before *divine judgment* at the holy place. Before this judgment, according to Schmidt, the accused petitions YHWH that he might speak a righteous judgment for him, and cleanse him from all suspicion. He hopes for God's decision during the night in which he has prostrated himself in silence in the temple.[832] The validating divine speech is completed after the one praying awakens with happy confidence. The confidence allows him to speak the words of certainty, of triumph, and of thanksgiving that we read at the conclusion of these poems. This is the situation from which the individual references of each psalm are to be understood according to H. Schmidt.

As strong an impression as the vividly described situation may conjure up for the origin of the prayer, there are nevertheless a number of *thoughts* which make the presence of the aforementioned subcategory dubious. The fundamental passages to which H. Schmidt refers speak only of divine judgment.[833] The fact that the accused has been released from detention is not mentioned, a fact which deserves more inspection since nothing is known elsewhere about such a detention in Israel. It is not clear why the context of 1 Kgs 8:30ff, which is silent about a prayer of the accused in conjunction with divine judgment, should allow one to deduce this detention. To be sure, prayers (of the people) are mentioned immediately (1 Kgs 8:32) to which YHWH might listen. But can one deduce from that reference that one should envision a prayer about the divine judgment from this section which *would have its fixed position inside the ritual*? The text, which requires that YHWH hear the oath which the accused must take to YHWH, is understandable by itself and requires no expansion. YHWH must hear him because he is still in the

---

[824]Ps 130:3f, 7; Pr Man 7-8, 13.

[825]Pss 17:13-14; 28:4; 31:18f; 35:26; 40:15f; 52:7; etc.

[826]Ps 109; Jer 18:18-23.

[827]Cf. ¶15, p. 167.

[828]H. Schmidt, *Das Gebet der Angeklagten im AT*, 1928.

[829]Pss 3; 4; 5; 7; 11; 13; 17; 26; 27; 31; 54; 55; 56; 57; 59; 94; 140; 142.

[830]Pss 25; 28; 31; 35; 38; 41; 69; 86; 102; 109.

[831]This situation is deduced from 1 Kgs 8; Deut 17; Exod 22; Num 5; Elephantine Papyri, number 27.

[832]H. Schmidt, *Das Gebet der Angeklagten im AT*, 1928, p. 28.

[833]H. Schmidt, *Das Gebet der Angeklagten im AT*, p. 252, footnote 16.

position of deciding the legal case. YHWH is just as necessary here as in the distress of the people related in that which follows.

The allusions of the psalms themselves are not clear, not explicit enough. If the ones praying are petitioning for liberation from detention and imprisonment,[834] one could more readily think the consciousness rebels against the propriety of *a prison term*.[835] However, the reference to imprisonment could also be meant purely metaphorically. The graphic account in Job 13:27 can be cited here as particularly impressive. Job, whose situation is well known, speaks like a prisoner and protests to YHWH that his feet have been placed in stocks. One can also think about *mēṣar* in Ps 118:5?[836] Is "tribulation" not also possible?[837] Ps 31:9 says: "You have let my feet step into freedom."[838] Does this statement force one to conclude that the one praying was previously in prison? Would not "narrowness" or "distress" be better antonymns to "breadth," which is what *merḥāb* primarily signifies?[839] In addition, other references do not point with certainty to a situation like the one H. Schmidt presumes. The petition that YHWH speak justly need not go with a divine judgment. It can be intended completely metaphorically.[840] One may also recall the metaphorically intended petition for security.[841]

The fact that the extreme change of mood between the beginning and end of the aforementioned prayers could be understood from two different situations of the one praying, before and after the divine judgment, would at first glance seem to argue strongly for H. Schmidt's thesis. However, upon closer inspection misgivings are also registered. The same difference in mood is also found in psalms which cannot be designated as prayers of the accused.[842] These psalms cannot be separated from the others. The fact that a priestly oracle within the cult could cause the change within the same situation argues against placing the texts in two situations, and against the total picture of H. Schmidt.[843] The fact that the change of mood characterizes the prayer beyond the borders of Israel also argues against his thesis (cf. the end of ¶23). In view of these various difficulties, it is questionable whether the relationship of the passages (Pss 3:5, 6; 4:5; 17:15; 57:4; 139:18b) is correctly preserved in the idea of oracular sleep in the temple even though it might otherwise be very illuminating. The thanksgiving song of Syriac Apocryphal Psalm 3:30 speaks about revelatory sleep during illness, but not about imprisonment.[844]

If, after everything has been investigated, one must be very careful about accepting a prayer of the accused which stands out from the other complaint songs as a subcategory, then one may make more confident statements for another subcategory. The next section will treat this other subcategory.

---

[834]Pss 118:5; 142:8; 107:10.
[835]Concerning the prison term in the postexilic period, see Ezra 7:26.
[836]So H. Schmidt, *Das Gebet der Angeklagten im AT*, p. 8.
[837]Cf. Ps 116:3; Lam 1:3.
[838]Following H. Schmidt, *Das Gebet der Angeklagten im AT*, p. 11.
[839]Cf. Pss 4:2; 18:7.
[840]Cf. Pss 43:1; 119:154.
[841]Cf. Isa 38:17; Job 17:3.
[842]Pss 6; 22; 36; 61; Jer 11:18ff; 20:10ff.
[843]See §6, ¶23, p. 182.
[844]Contra M. Noth, "Die fünf syrisch überlieferten apokryphen Psalmen," p. 15.

27. The genre experiences its most effective reformulation in the *song of confidence*.[845] Its central part is the *expression of confidence*, especially in the form where the confidence escalates to the point that the prayer no longer requires dependence on YHWH. It should not be astonishing therefore that the song of confidence overwhelmingly speaks of YHWH *in the third person*. It is very instructive to observe how much the independent excitation of confidence increasingly pushes back the other motifs of the genre.[846]

Ps 16 stands closest to the complaint songs. It has the address along with the description in 16:1. The prayer form is maintained throughout almost the entire psalm. However, it is noteworthy that after the opening expression of confidence using "you" (16:5), the expression in 16:5 escalates to "he" at the point which clearly heralds the discontinuation of the dependence. Only at the end does the psalm return to prayer. The confidence motif takes a large amount of space in 16:2-10. The one praying knows that YHWH controls his fate, that YHWH stands ever at his side, and that his body may rest in surety. Thus, anxiety and distress are conquered internally, and it is conceivable that complaint, petition, and vow are lacking. In addition to Ps 16, the beautiful Ps 131 stands closest to the original genre. It knows the address, and almost the entire psalm preserves the prayer form. At the end, there stands an admonition to Israel to long for YHWH. The psalm displaces important components of the genre, the complaint, petition, and certainty. As the psalmist himself expresses, he has a peaceful, still heart with no great wishes and requests.

The remaining songs of confidence abandon the prayer form (the characteristic element of the complaint) in the certainty of confidence. However, the origin of the genre is even more clearly recognizable in the reformulation of the individual impulses. So Ps 11 begins with a portrayal of praying. The material of the complaint appears, but it is not introduced as the words of the one praying. Rather, it is introduced as the objection of another who the pious is protecting: "How could you say to me?" The pious one depicts his confidence in God loftily. He speaks in hymnic tones about how YHWH is enthroned in the heavens, examines humans, hates doers of violence, chooses the righteous. That which would normally be the petition is incorporated into the expression of confidence and reformulated in the form of a statement: "He reigns fiery 'coals' and brimstone on the wicked. Burning wind is released into their cup of fate." The song of confidence concludes with thoughts about the righteous, just like the complaint song closes with wishes for the righteous. However, these ideas about the righteous also appear in characteristic fashion in the form of statements: "'The honest ones' may look on your face." (11:7).

In Ps 27:1-6, the situation of the complaint song also shines through clearly. YHWH stands at the beginning as the first word, naturally as the subject of an assertion, to which the expression of confidence is attached. The material of the complaint, which would otherwise tend to come here, appears throughout: "Villains attack me to eat my flesh. My opponents, and those opposing me, must stumble. When they build camps against me, my heart is without fear. When they make war against me, I remain comforted." In place of the petition only the wish of the one praying appears, but it is not introduced as a petition, rather as a narrative: "I asked one thing from YHWH, after which he demanded of me that

---

[845] Pss 4; 11; 16; 23; 27:1-6; 62; 131.

[846] Marschall, pp. 40 and 45, disputes the idea that the song of confidence proceeded from the individual complaint song.

I look upon YHWH's friendliness and observe his temple." In 27:5 the expression of confidence is attached, the certainty of having been heard and the vow of a thanksgiving song.

Ps 62 begins with the material of the complaint which is formed at the beginning as a question from the innocent directed to enemies: "How long will you storm a man?" The expression of certain confidence follows in 62:2-8. As in Ps 131, a warning to the pious ones that they place their hope in YHWH is attached. In conclusion the singer calls upon a revelation given him by YHWH. God protects in his grace.

Ps 23 deviates considerably more from the genre. It incorporates a confidence motif from the beginning. It lacks a complaint and petition. The occasional address to YHWH and the appearance of the enemies in 23:5 are what remains of the origins. At the end the expression escalates to full tones, thereby recalling the complaint songs. However, that which would otherwise be a wish, is here expressed with peaceful surety as being completely certain: "Only goodness and love will follow me all the days of my life, and 'I remain' in the house of YHWH for a long time."

The separation of genres is strongest in Ps 4. It begins like a thanksgiving song with the narrative of deliverance. It has no complaint and no petition, not even a reformulated one. The elements which do relate to the complaint song include the remembrance of past deliverance, citing the words of others, and the admonition to confidence addressed to others.[847] Otherwise the song has completely grown beyond the genre from which it originated. Among all the components of the complaint song, only the expression of confidence leads to a significant reformulation of the genre (or one might even say to a genre which has branched off of it). This fact proves the characteristic life of this specific motif better than any portrayal might.

28. The songs of confidence and their loosening of the genre lead to the observation of *freer forms of the complaint song*. The freer style is formed by the psalmists striving to speak more dynamically and more vividly. They adopt forms in their poetry which do not belong to that poetry from the beginning. They have been observed scattered periodically throughout the preceding discussion, but are now gathered specifically.

In impatient questions the complaint is encountered at the beginning of the poem in a freer style rather than in simple assertions.[848] In order to present the image of the opponent to YHWH as dramatically as possible, the singer is not satisfied with a simple portrayal of their motivation. He presents to YHWH *their own words* as an unimpeachable witness of their wicked intention. The psalmist thereby incorporates into the genre other persons' *words of ridicule*, an element that was originally foreign to the genre.[849] The *words of the pious* form the counterpart. Occasionally at the end the complaint song wishes that the pious might praise YHWH. In the freer style these words of praise are introduced.[850] The liveliness of the complaint song occasionally escalates to the point that the one praying no longer complains to YHWH about the action of the enemies. Instead, the one praying addresses the enemies himself with an angry question.[851] The *address to*

---

[847]See this location in the commentary.

[848]Pss 13:1-3; 22:2; 52:2; 62:4; 58:2; Pss. Sol. 4:1.

[849]Pss 3:3; 4:7; 10:6; 11:1ff; 22:9; 35:21, 25; 40:16; 41:6, 9; 42:4, 11; 71:11; etc. Cf. ¶8, p. 142.

[850]Pss 35:27; 40:17; 58:12.

[851]Pss 52:2; 58:2; 62:4. Addresses to the opponents outside the introductory question is found also in 6:9; 119:115.

the friends is the counterpart to the address to the enemies. It seeks to create comfort and confidence in YHWH from the psalmist's own experience.[852] The warnings thus enter the genre. The warning then appears to deviate further in the form of the self-admonition not to lose confidence.[853] The petition, like the complaint, is occasionally expressed in the form of a question in the freer style. The fervent desire for liberation from torment creates a particularly urgent expression in the question.

A *lyrical outpouring* even appears once between complaints where one would normally find the petition. In this lyric outpouring, the one praying expresses how gladly he would like to be displaced from the desolate activities which he has revealed.[854]

The complaint song concludes with the *vow of the thanksgiving song*. The psalmist is sure of being heard so he pronounces the thanksgiving song in advance (cf. ¶24). In so doing, the materially related genre appears in relationship to the complaint song.[855] If the singer's enthusiasm grows, the thanksgiving song attaches the *hymn* to the genre.[856] Hymnic tones also penetrate at other points, specifically in the expression of confidence.[857] If the confidence sinks, the observation of one's own experience is no longer operative, then one recalls YHWH's deeds to the fathers and his gracious being in general. He thereby enters the material of the hymn.[858] Hymnic tones *in the address* of the complaint songs are found in Jer 17:12-18 and Pr Man 1-7.[859] The intention is to remind YHWH of his deeds and his essence in order to make known that one expects help from him.[860] In Ps 123 the genre is mixed with the complaint song of the people. The singer's personal distress is the distress of his nation. The mixture of the two genres is accomplished by similar means in Ps 77. *Individual motifs* from the complaint song enter into the individual complaint songs. The complaint of the people enters Lam 3:42-48. Ps 23 takes the expression of confidence from the communal complaint song. The image of YHWH as the shepherd of the pious ones is originally at home in the communal complaint (cf. Ps 80, etc.). Intercessory *wishes for the king and people* occasionally appear at the end and may also derive from communal complaints.[861] Sometimes, *eschatology* appears in trace amounts in the complaint song. The singer in Ps 102 comforts himself in the hope which is already granted to Israel in the present. If the one praying proceeds into all kinds of ideas of comfort, then even *speeches of pious wisdom* are occasionally blended into the individual complaint.[862] Indeed the complaint song even enters into the mixed form *of the liturgy*. In Ps 121, it even alternates with the answer of the priest.[863] One can hardly fail

---

[852]Pss 4:4-6; 31:24; 62:9; 131:3; cf. 130:7.

[853]Pss 27:14; 42:6, 7, 12; 43:5; 55:23.

[854]Ps 55:7-10b. See the commentary.

[855]Cf. 13:6; 22:24; 28:6-7; 31:22ff; 54:9; 56:14; 69:33; 71:14-16, 20ff; 86:12-13; 144:9-10. The opposite also occurs when the complaint song enters the thanksgiving song. See §7, ¶8.

[856]Cf. ¶24; Pss 22:28ff; 31:20ff; 57:8ff; 69:35-37; Jer 20:13.

[857]Cf. ¶19 and §2, ¶56.

[858]Pss 22:5-6; 25:8-10; 36:8-10; 86:5, 15; 130:4, 7; 143:5.

[859]See ¶10; §2, ¶56.

[860]Cf. ¶19, §2, ¶56.

[861]Pss 28:8; 61:7; 63:12; 1 Sam 2:10d, e.

[862]Pss 25:12; 119:1, 2, 9; Lam 3:26-29; cf. §10, ¶3.

[863]See the commentary and §11, ¶15.

to see that the complaint song attained significant vibrance and capacities for expression by the enrichment of the free style.

29. Did the Hebrews have an *expression* which summarized the songs of the genre as has been described in the previous discussion which allowed them to be consciously grouped together? One can answer affirmatively. The Hebrew technical term for the individual complaint song is *tefillāh*. This can be confirmed from the psalms belonging here. A large number begin by petitioning that YHWH might hear their *tefillāh*, and notice it.[864] The singer of Ps 6 rejoices in the certainty that YHWH has accepted his *tefillāh* (Ps 6:10). The one praying in Jonah 2 narrates: "as my soul despaired, I thought of YHWH. My *tefillāh* came to you, to your temple" (Jonah 2:8). The thanksgiving songs introducing these words of prayer teach us the kind of prayer he spoke in this distress.[865] It is the complaint song of the individual which appears in these places. Because of these various passages it is not debatable that the expression relates to the complaint song. One can only ask whether *tefillāh* is really a technical term designating a genre. Several terms alternate with this word as synonyms: *teḥinnāh*,[866] *taḥănunîm*,[867] *taḥănūnōt*,[868] *rinnāh*,[869] *šaw'āh*.[870] However, if one compares the appearance of the parallel words with the appearance of *tefillāh* one can scarcely doubt that *tefillāh* is the specific designation of the genre. This conclusion is then confirmed with the superscriptions of Pss 17:1; 86:1; 102:1; 142:1. They name the subsequent psalm as a *tefillāh*. The fact that the expression should be understood as a technical term is beyond doubt. It is only questionable whether the superscription intends the original use of the complaint song or whether it characterizes the psalm according to its usage in later worship services where the more original life setting and the later performance type need not be hidden.[871] This anxiety is superfluous. The mass of psalms described in the superscription as *tefillāh* belong to the genre of "individual complaint songs." Ps 102 is of particular importance where not only does the self-designation of the psalm agree with the superscription, but the word *tefillāh* in the superscription contains an explanation which reflects the situation of the complaint song quite clearly. "This is a *tefillāh* of one who suffers, when he is disheartened and pours out his sorrows before YHWH." It can be stated as all but certain that the Hebrew designated the complaint of the individual as *tefillāh*.

Because of the lack of sharp conceptual thought among the Israelite people of the time, the term *tefillāh* is of course not limited to the complaint songs. The term also designates the situation and the goal of similar genres. Thus, the communal complaint song is designated with the same expression.[872] In addition, one should also mention the

---

[864]Pss 17:2; 39:13; 54:4; 55:2; 61:2; 69:14; 86:6; 88:3, 14; 102:2; 141:2.

[865]§7, ¶8.

[866]Pss 6:10; 55:2.

[867]Ps 143:1.

[868]Ps 86:2.

[869]Pss 17:1; 61:2; 88:3.

[870]Pss 39:13; 102:2.

[871]One need only consider Ps 30, which is an individual thanksgiving song, was used according to the superscription as a song at the temple dedication.

[872]Cf. §4, ¶2, p. 84.

prose prayer of the individual in this context.[873] It is distinguished from the complaint song of the individual only through the external form. This lack of sharp conceptual differentiation is not noticeable in that uncertainty never dominated the individual cases as to which genre was intended.

30. In conclusion we attempt to write the internal history of the genre. The individual complaint song proceeds from the cult and its purposes. Several allusions preserved in the various psalms point in this direction.[874] In its oldest form, the complaint song should be conceived as *formulaic*, to be utilized by the one praying in different situations. This situation resulted in a specific *formulaic quality, a general nature, and a tediousness* in the forms of expression.[875] This formulaic character is encountered in a large number of the Babylonian counterparts. They are specified for use by any adherent, and therefore they leave blank the name of the one praying and his father.[876]

The oldest form of the Israelite individual complaint song may have been simple enough. Since no examples of these have been preserved, they can only be reached by deduction. We have conceptualized their size and structure similarly to those of the short complaint songs of Pss 28; 54; 61, etc. A complaint song of this type would have encompassed address, complaint, petition, perhaps the certainty of having been heard, and the vow of a thanksgiving offering. The latter may perhaps have signified one last means of convincing, as in the Babylonian examples originally. One could perhaps see Ps 142:8 as the last vestige of the original genre. All of these components were expressed as simply as possible, and would have been very similar to the Babylonian counterpart in their formulaic nature.

The similarity of the Israelite and Babylonian genres that also appears elsewhere once again raises the question of the relationship between the two.[877] On historical grounds the Israelite genre must be dependent upon the Babylonian. But how can one conceptualize this dependency more closely? If there was not originally an individual complaint song in Palestine, one could accept that the Babylonian genre found entry and adoption in the time of the Babylonian cultural influence. One would then note the numerous points of contact between the Israelite complaint song and its Babylonian counterpart as traces of the borrowing which had been preserved by the independent reformulation and expansion of the genre, first among the Canaanites and then among the Israelites.

However, perhaps the dependency should be conceived completely differently. It is perhaps more likely that the Babylonian and Israelite genres had nothing to do with one another from the beginning. Or, should one not believe that one could have prayed to the divinity in the various distresses of existence before the Babylonian cultural influence. Everywhere that a person raises hands to pray, one finds the same components of the prayer and the same order of these components. Even the contents correspond to a large

---

[873]2 Sam 7:27; 1 Kgs 9:3; 2 Kgs 20:5.

[874]Cf. ¶4.

[875]§1, ¶4.

[876]Ungnad, *Religion der Babylonier und Assyrer*, 205 (see also pp. 177, 179, 223, etc): "I, _____, son of _____, whose god is _____, whose goddess is _____, I call you in the middle of the night.

[877]Cf. ¶10, 11, 12, 13, 14, 19, 22, 24.

degree.[878] Seen in this light, the relationship between the Babylonian and Israelite genres rests to a large degree not upon borrowing, but upon the character of prayer in general. From this parallelism of genres it is now understandable that later connecting threads could have been spun from the Israelite to the Babylonian material, and that the Israelite complaint song had been enriched from the Babylonian. The history of Palestine from the Amarna time to the times when Assyrian gods had to be honored in the temple in Jerusalem shows the ways in which Babylonian cult lyric could have attained influence upon the Israelite genre. One would have taken details from the Babylonian poetry, exactly as one would have adopted particular images and concepts from Egyptian poetry while leaving others behind.[879]

In the course of history the individual complaint song was gradually released internally from the cultic acts related to it. One can see this in the fact that references to the cult and its situation are much more sparse in the thanksgiving songs, where one can observe, that the number of complaint songs preserved for us significantly exceeds the number of thanksgiving songs.[880] The one praying no longer requires the cult activity in order to walk in relationship with his God. It would be too hasty, however, to deduce from this fact that complaint songs demonstrating no trace of a relationship to the cult were no longer prayed at sacrifice activities.[881] The Babylonian parallels caution us against too hastily making that decision. The Babylonian songs also show an internal separation from the cult. However, so many accompanying rituals attest to the fact that they were simultaneously prayed in the cult.[882] Prophetic polemic then appeared, arguing for the separation of the Hebrew complaint song from worship (which did not yet include opposition to the complaint song).[883] The separation of sacrifice and cult would have been strengthened by this influence.

External separation runs parallel to the *internal* separation. Mowinckel has attempted to prove the contrary, that almost all of the psalms were composed for the cult.[884] A number of complaint songs, however, argue to the contrary. There are psalms that are clearly sung *far from the sanctuary*.[885] There are psalms where the one praying finds himself in the diaspora,[886] and those which clearly make known the desire for YHWH and his holy mountain.[887]

The external separation of the prayer from the holy sites very probably begins *already in the preexilic period*. That is particularly clear with Ps 61, a poem from the diaspora.

---

[878]Cf. Fr. Heiler, *Gebet,*[4] 1921, pp. 58ff.

[879]In this context one can point to the concept of the protective movement of YHWH (Pss 17:8; 36:8; 57:2; 61:5; 63:8) that certainly goes back to the widely disseminate Egyptian view of gods who protected with wings. See the commentary to Ps 17:8 for examples.

[880]Cf. §7, ¶10.

[881]Cf. ¶4.

[882]Cf. J. Begrich, *ZAW*, 1928, p. 230; E. Ebeling, in Ebert, *Reallexikon der Vorgeschichte*, vol. 4, p. 184.

[883]Cf. Pss 51 and 69 and the commentary for them.

[884]S. Mowinckel, *Psalmenstudien*, vol. 1, pp. 137ff.

[885]So Pss 27; 42; 61; 120; 55.

[886]Pss 42:7; 55:20; 61:3; 120:5.

[887]Pss 27:4; 42:5; 43:3, 4; 61:5. See also ¶4 for details and further examples can be found of the internal separation of the genre from the cult.

It has had an ending added expressing wishes for the king and the people. They have very likely been added when the song was published for use in the royal temple in Jerusalem. Since these wishes continually relate to the ruling king, the current form of Ps 61 must have already belonged to the preexilic period. One may deduce a similar relationship for Ps 63.[888] In addition, one can point to the complaint songs of Jeremiah, which with the exception of 17:12-18, do not show any trace of external or internal relationship to the cult. The fact that the law had no significance at this stage of the genre's history offers an additional observation pointing in the same direction. Only with the beginning of the dissolution of the style did the law achieve influence over the genre.[889] Accordingly, there can be no doubt that the development of the complaint songs into spiritual songs first commenced in the legalistic (postexilic) period.

This development, which starts in the preexilic period can be traced into the late period. The following individual points can be made: In Ps 42, the one praying in northern Canaan feels removed from YHWH and longs for the holy mountain. This psalm belongs in the time after Deuteronomy.[890] According to the framing narrative, Job should be placed somewhere in the land of Uz. Job sits in sackcloth and ashes, and constantly proceeds in the style of the complaint song. The late Prayer of Manasseh finally presupposes the imprisonment of the one praying (v. 9). It is not overly clever if one deduces that the complaint song became acclimated to the Israelite household,[891] similar to the thanksgiving song.[892] Cultically bound poetry was also preserved alongside this poetry that was becoming free of the cult.[893]

The *personal life* enters the genre to the degree that the complaint song grows away from the cult and becomes a spiritual song. Of course, this development could not entirely eliminate the impression of the original formulaic quality. Rather, the style formed by long usage never completely lost its prominence. Thus, it is constantly difficult to perceive the difficulty under which the poets suffer. Nevertheless, that which grew to be incorporated into the complaint song as it began to be freed from the cult (and the cult's generalized forms and contents) includes the following: clever images, peculiar formulations, passionate outpouring of the complaint, imploring petition, and inner personal piety.

Here, one can see the starting point for the *later development*. The old, constricting forms are expanded. The size grows, and the contents become more fruitful.[894] Material and forms from other genres enter, as was attempted to be shown in ¶28. Clearly recognizable subgroups are formed, including the *song of innocence, the song of confession, the curse psalm, the revenge psalm*, and finally, though not least, the *song of confidence*.[895] In the latter, one can even follow developmental stages precisely.[896] Here, the original

---

[888]Cf. the commentary to this passage.

[889]See Ps 119 above all.

[890]See the commentary.

[891]One should understand Pss. Sol. 5:2-8; 12:1-3, and 16:6-15 in this way. The following also point in this direction: Tob 3:1-6, 11-15; 8:5-7; Jdt 9:2-4; 13:4, 7; Suzanna 35.

[892]§7, ¶8.

[893]Cf. Sir 38:11.

[894]See especially ¶13.

[895]Cf. ¶26 and ¶27.

[896]Cf. ¶27.

genre begins to change. A new shoot grows from the old root. The complaint songs of Jeremiah show how early the change from the rigid to the freer style begins, for there one encounters the characteristic form of that style, the introduction of the words of others.[897]

The constraints separating the material and forms in the genres from one another were lost to the degree that the genres of religious lyric were removed from their original life setting. The material and forms drew closer to one another, and mixtures occurred. The thanksgiving song could fall back into petition.[898] A complaint song motif can appear in a late hymn praising the law (Ps 19:8-15).[899] The connections become inorganic as each psalmist imagines specific material which then leads him to other materials.[900] These mixtures are found above all in the late alphabetic psalms that were composed for the enjoyment of the one reading, especially Ps 119:5.[901]

The *dissolution of forms* can be clearly seen in the *collection of the Psalms of Solomon*. There is no longer a pure genre of the individual complaint song. Pss. Sol. 16 appears as a mixture of a thanksgiving song (16:1-5) and a complaint song (16:6ff). Communal and individual complaint songs are combined in Pss. Sol. 12 (cf. 12:1-5 and 6). Pss. Sol. 12:5 is woven from hymn and complaint song (cf. 12:1-2 and 12:5ff). In these examples, the complaint has all but disappeared. It is lacking in 5 and 16. The vow is also gone. *Reflection* is that which is new to the genre and it also accelerated the process of dissolution. The original dynamism and immediacy which provided lyrical power to the complaint song has completely vanished. For example, one could compare the following sentences in the expanded expression of confidence (5:4ff): "Who could take something from that which you have made if you did not give it? Both humanity and its portion are weighed out. It cannot do anything more than that which you have determined."[902]

The Psalms of Solomon arose in the Maccabean period, more specifically in the first century B.C.[903] The dissolution of the genre can thereby be understood chronologically. If one compares the form that the complaint song has taken in this collection with the canonical psalms, the chronological distance is undeniable. The canonical collection must be older than the Maccabean period. Even Ps 119, which belongs to a relatively late period, arose before this epoch.[904]

The Maccabean period signifies the end of the old genre. If one looks from there back to the beginning of the genre, the following major lines of the history stand out. The complaint song of the individual begins in the confines of the cult, and lives from the material and the mood which the cult suggested. It attains size and depth when it is dissolved from the cult. However, this dissolution also becomes the core of its fall. The boundaries between it and the other genres are lost, and mixtures occur. Finally, reflection nests in

---

[897] Jer 11:19; 17:15; 18:18; 20:10.

[898] Ps 40:12 (§7, ¶8).

[899] §2, ¶56.

[900] Cf., e.g., Pss 9; 10.

[901] For details, see ¶28.

[902] Pss. Sol. 5:5f.

[903] See the Psalms of Solomon article in *RGG*,[2] vol. 5, col. 91.

[904] See the commentary, p. 516.

the genre in place of dynamic perception and immediate contemplation, corroding the genre completely.

§7 Individual Thanksgiving Songs[1]

Ausgewählte Psalmen, vol. 4, 1917, pp. 36ff, 210ff. — *RGG*,[2] "Psalmen," 6, 14. — E. Balla, *Das Ich der Psalmen*, 1912, pp. 29ff, 48, 57ff, 88ff. — *Zeitschrift für Missionskunde und Religionswissenschaft* 34, 1919, pp. 177ff, 211ff. — W. Staerk, *Lyrik in den "Schriften des AT,"* vol. 3/1,[2] 1920, pp. 88ff, 111ff. — W. Baumgartner, *ZAW* 34, 1914, pp. 178ff. — Hans Schmidt, *Religiöse Lyrik im Alten Testament*, 1912, pp. 28ff. — *ZAW* 40, 1922, pp. 1ff — J. Begrich, *Der Psalm des Hiskia*, 1926. — S. Mowinckel, *Psalmenstudien*, vol. 1, 1921, pp. 125ff; vol. 4, 1924, pp. 25, 28ff, 51ff, 65ff. — E. Reitzenstein, *Iranisches Erlösungsmysterium*, 1921, pp. 251ff.

1. We have twenty complete thanksgiving songs preserved.[2] In addition, we have several verses from alphabetic poems,[3] Job 33:19ff, which tells a small story about how one comes to a thanksgiving song,[4] and the thanksgiving songs that are extolled or cited at the end of complaint songs.[5] One should also mention the thanksgiving saying at the beginning of the royal complaint song in Ps 144:1ff, and finally those motifs of the thanksgiving songs which have entered the hymns.[6] One should also compare the thanksgiving songs of Israel,[7] especially Isa 12:1ff and the prose thanksgiving prayers.[8]

2. For this genre we are in the position of providing the original setting in the worship service with complete certainty. The thanksgiving psalm belongs originally to the thanksgiving offering. Both bear the name *tôdāh*. Several of the songs allow us to recognize clearly the cultic acts, such as the sacrifice.[9] The psalm may also mention the celebratory *act of raising the cup* before the drink offering, an act that was accompanied by calling to the name of YHWH. This act must have played a significant role in the thanksgiving sacrifice,[10] or it presupposes the celebratory *meal*,[11] the festive procession, or the

---

[1]By Gunkel.

[2]Pss 18; 30; 32; 34; 40:2-12; 41; 66; 92; (100); (107); 116; 118; 138; Isa 38:10-20; Job 33:26-28; Jonah 2:3-10; Sir 51; Pss. Sol. 15; 16; Odes Sol. 25; 29.

[3]Pss 9:2-5, 14f; 119:7, 26a, 65, 67, 71, 75, 92.

[4]Cf. B. Duhm, *Buch Hiob*, 1897, 162.

[5]Pss 7:18; 13:6; 22:23ff; 26:12b; 27:6; 28:6f; 31:8f, 20-25; 35:9, 18, 27; 40:17; 42:6f, 12; 43:4; 51:17; 52:11; 54:8f; 56:13; 57:9-12; 59:17; 61:9; 63:4-6; 69:31ff; 71:8, 14-16, 18cff; 86:12f; 109:30f; 140:14; 144:9f; Jer 20:13.

[6]Pss 92:5, 11f, 16; 103:2-5; 1 Sam 2:1; Pr Azar 65; (88); ¶8.

[7]§2, ¶41, 50; §8, ¶28.

[8]§2, ¶14, 54.

[9]Pss 66:13ff; 107:22; 116:17; 27:6 (*zibḥê terū'āh*, "offering of rejoicing"); 56:13; Jonah 2:10. They are frequently considered as *sacrifices of vows* (Pss 22:26; 56:13; 61:9; 66:14; 116:18; Jonah 2:10). Partial offering and meal offerings are especially mentioned (Ps 40:7). Occasionally *free will offerings* are spoken (Ps 54:8). Cf. the offering types in Lev 7:11ff; 22:17ff. Ps 66:15 also speaks of the grand *'ōlōt* (whole offering). The thanksgiving song takes place before the sacrifice (116:17ff; Jonah 2:10; cf. Ps 66:13ff).

[10]Ps 116:13.

[11]Ps 22:27.

"ring dance."[12] This procession begins outside the sanctuary,[13] in order to stop before the temple gates,[14] before marching through the "gates of righteousness"[15] in a line so the gathered community can encircle the altar.[16] Also, when there are several people gathered who wish to bring a thanksgiving offering, a festival procession occurs in the sanctuary for those bringing thanks.[17] For example, this happened from ancient times where the custom was to pay the vows for the year.[18] Sometimes we hear about a general situation in which the thanksgiving psalm is sung in the temple.[19]

In most thanksgiving songs the *one bringing the thanksgiving sings alone*. It is often presumed that a *group* of persons stands around this person who go by honorable names like the "pious," the "righteous," the "holy ones," "YHWH fearers," the "oppressed," etc.[20] These people gladly share his good fortune.[21] From Ps 22:27 one can deduce that these others are *the guests at the festive meal following the thanksgiving offering*, and from Ps 118 we can deduce that they are also *participants in the festival procession*. All the relatives, friends, acquaintances, and anyone else (as we picture it) encircle the one offering thanksgiving while rejoicing and shouting, and they eat the holy meal with him. Even the poor may be invited as with the other festival offerings.[22] The meat of the thanksgiving offering must of course be devoured on the same day according to the law.[23] All the people who are gathered in the sanctuary take part happily,[24] and join in the rejoicing. The fact that one has invited guests to the sacrifice, and especially guests for the "vow of sacrifice," is attested elsewhere.[25] When the festival meal was finished, at least in later times, the practice was to voice the thanksgiving song one more time in the worldly "community of the people," and in the "meet of the elders."[26]

The *basic mood* of these celebrations are characterized by all of these events. It provides the most beautiful hours in the life of the pious.

The center of the festival is the thanksgiving song. The fact that there are *words* that enter at this point corresponds to the spiritually advanced condition of Israel. The fact that these words preserve a *poetic form* is explained by the poetic giftedness of the people. Singing this type of song is usually called *hōdāh*. These songs are generally composed in the same circles which have responsibility for the worship and its order, namely the

---

[12]Ps 30:12.

[13]Ps 100:2, 4.

[14]Ps 66:13f.

[15]Ps 118:19. See the commentary for this passage.

[16]Ps 118:27. See the commentary to 26:6f.

[17]Cf. Jer 33:11 and ¶7.

[18]1 Sam 1:21.

[19]Jonah 2:5, 8; Pss 43:4; 138:2; Isa 38:20; cf. Pss 9:15; 41:13.

[20]Pss 22:24; 30:5; 32:11; 34:10; 66:16; 69:33; 118:15; cf. 34:7, 11; "a great community" in: 40:10f; 22:23, 26; 35:18; 107:32.

[21]Ps 34:4.

[22]Deut 14:27; 16:11, 14; 26:11.

[23]Lev 7:15; 22:29f.

[24]Pss 116:18; 118:1-4.

[25]Cf. Deut 33:19; 1 Sam 9:13, 22, 24; 2 Sam 13:23ff; 15:11; 1 Kgs 1:9, 19, 25, 41, 49; Amos 4:5; Zeph 1:7; Ezek 39:17; Prov 7:14.

[26]Ps 107:32.

priests or the appointed *singers* for the musical portion.[27] The harp and zither are the instruments used for the thanksgiving song.[28] The mood of these poems also flows from the type of celebration. They are full of inner thanks, and joyful happiness.

3. Many of the thanksgiving songs of the Israelite variety begin with a more or less "expanded introduction"[29] that communicates the intention and the content of the song. "I will thank you." "I will praise you."[30] "Give thanks." "Praise."[31] These thanksgiving songs may also close with words like these.[32] In addition, one encounters the conclusion in the *third person* plural jussive: "Let them thank."[33] The forms of these introductions are the same as those of the hymns.[34] In the hymnic thanksgiving prayers preserved in prose the typical introduction is, "Praise be. . . . "[35]

YHWH is an indispensable word for the "introduction." From the outset, the one offering thanks must express to which god his song is dedicated, just as the "summons" of the divine name is the main element at the sacrifice.[36] Syntactically, the word "YHWH" stands after the introduction's verbal form in the *vocative* or as the *object* of the thanksgiving and the praise. Also, where the thanksgiving song contains no introduction, it is almost unavoidable that the word YHWH falls within the first sentences. "YHWH" is *to the poem as though it were written in capital letters.* Only Ps 32:2 forms an exception where a more general sentence begins.

4. One of the most important elements never lacking from the thanksgiving song is the *narrative* of the fate of the one offering thanks. It is therefore a certain identifying marker for the genre. It is usually directed to the guests of the celebration: "Come [plural] and hear. I will tell you pious ones everything YHWH has done for my soul."[37] One can therefore explain why YHWH is spoken about in these contexts using the *third person.*[38] Only in a later style does the poem take the form of a "prayer"[39] in which YHWH is addressed directly.[40] This kind of report about his condition functions as the *holiest obligation* of the pious one. He should not hide what he has experienced by YHWH's gracious

---

[27]Cf. §1, ¶6.

[28]Pss 43:4; 71:22.

[29]§2, ¶8.

[30]Pss 9:2f; 18:2f; 30:2; 34:2f; 57:8f; 119:7; 138:1f; Isa 12:1; Sir 51:1.

[31]Pss 22:4; 107:1; etc. Compare especially the short thanksgiving songs at the conclusion of the complaint songs which usually consists of just an introduction of this type. Cf. §1, ¶8.

[32]Pss 18:50; 30:13; 32:11; 118:21, 28f; Sir 51:12; cf. Pss. Sol. 16:5; Syriac Apocryphal Psalm 5:11f.

[33]Ps 107:8, 15, 21, 31.

[34]§2, ¶11; §2, ¶3; cf. ¶8.

[35]§2, ¶14.

[36]Cf. Gen 12:8; Ps 116:13. As is self-evident the same is true for the hymn (§2, ¶ 15).

[37]Ps 66:16.

[38]Cf. Pss 18:4, 7, 9-15, 17ff, 42; 34:5, 7; 40:2-4; 66:16-20; 107:4-7, 10-14, 17-20, 23-30; 116:1-8; 118:5, 10-18; Isa 12:1bc, 2bc; 38:11; Jonah 2:8; Job 33:28; Sir 51:8,11f; Syr Apocryphal Psalms 5:3ff.

[39]§4, ¶4; §6, ¶10.

[40]Pss 18:16, 36f, 40, 44; 30:3f, 8ff; 32:4f; 41:13; 92:5, 11b; 116:16d; 118:21; 119:7, 26a, 65; 138:2ff; Isa 38:17; Jonah 2:3-7,8d; Sir 51:2f. The same change occurs in the hymns (§2, ¶24) and in the thanksgiving songs standing at the end of complaint songs (§6, ¶24).

help in the inner thoughts of his heart. Rather, it should be proclaimed before all the people in the great gathering, proclaimed with a loud voice to the honor of his God.[41] Given the great significance of this narrative it is understandable that it frequently stands *in the first position* in the poem, either right at the beginning itself,[42] or immediately after the "introduction."[43] It can stand right after a hymn (¶8) at the beginning of a particular thanksgiving song,[44] or after a "confession."[45] Sometimes the importance of the motif is seen by the fact that it is repeated one or more times,[46] or by the fact that it comprises almost all of the poem.[47]

By the preferential position of these reports, one recognizes especially clearly that the joyful telling of the gracious deeds of YHWH is the most important thing that the poet has to say.[48] The particular content of the thanksgiving song is the great change which has now occurred for the one offering thanks. Just as he had been in deadly distress and anxiety, already close to the portals of the underworld, now he again sees the golden light. Just as he had been repudiated and slandered, he is now the center of the beautiful festival. The narrative of the thanksgiving song presents this change.

One thereby observes that these poems do *not* treat *minor details*. The Israelite did not celebrate a festival or sing a song of this type for every kind of divine help. Rather, this celebration only occurred in matters of life and death, which corresponds to the utter seriousness of the Israelite religion—the same seriousness expressed by the complaint songs.[49]

Additionally, it is characteristic of these songs that the psalmists report about themselves but very seldom use specific references. This trait appears in other psalms as well and is explained by the fact that these poems go back to worship formulas.[50]

The narrative usually contains *three parts*: the report of the poet's distress, his summons to YHWH, and his deliverance. Jonah 2:3 presents a classic formulation: "I called in my distress to YHWH and he heard me."

In many instances, the psalmists' distress arises from an extreme illness which brought him close to death.[51] Other examples are communicated in Ps 107, where one finds *wanderers* who have lost their way in the wilderness, *prisoners* who were pining away in jail, sailors on the stormy sea that nearly breaks the ship.[52] We also have examples preserved from life if we ask in which cases the frequently mentioned vow is

---

[41]Pss 30:13; 40:10f; 71:18; 107:21f.

[42]Ps 40:2-4; Job 33:27b-28; Jonah 2:3-8; Pss. Sol. 15:1; 16:1-4.

[43]Pss 18:4ff; 30:2-4; 34:5; 107:4ff; 116:1-6; 138:2b-3; Sir 51:2ff; Syriac Apocryphal Psalms 5:3ff.

[44]Pss 66:13ff; 118:5; cf. 92:11f.

[45](¶5). Pss 32:3-5; 41:5ff.

[46]Pss 18:4-20, 33-46, 48f; 30:2-4, 7-12; 118:5, 10-18, 21-24.

[47]Cf. Pss 18; 107:1-32; Jonah 2:3ff; Sir 51.

[48]Cf. Pss 107:22.

[49]§6, ¶5.

[50]Cf. §1, ¶4; §6, ¶4.

[51]Cf. Pss 30:3f,10; 107:17-22; 116:8-10; 118:17f; Syriac Apocryphal Psalms 3:19-23, 29; cf. 103:3; Odes Sol. 25:9. See also the narratives in Job 33:19ff; Isa 38; and the superscription of Isa 38:9.

[52]"From many distresses" (Sir 51:3ff).

offered in the thanksgiving song.[53] The one who is banished or had to leave the homeland speaks the vow in the event of a happy return;[54] those who are shipwrecked speak during a storm.[55] The leader and the people speak it during the threat of war.[56] If divine help and deliverance from distress occurs, then the person must "pay" his vow while singing a thanksgiving song. These vows are already found among primitive peoples.[57]

It frequently happens that those suffering have experienced *opposition from enemies*, unjust accusations and wicked slander.[58] Ps 41:6-9 portrays how the critically ill person is tormented by the poisonous speech of those who will not believe in his innocence and expect him to die soon. Or we hear how the person who is ill suffered[59] from *being held in low esteem*,[60] even by his closest friends.[61] S. Mowinckel wishes to interpret the "enemies" of those singing the psalms in the individual complaint songs as evil magicians who have vexed the singers with illness. Mowinckel also expresses this explanation for the enemies in the thanksgiving songs.[62] However, his explanation does not seem satisfactory in any passage in this genre. Nowhere is it clearly expressed, or even made probable by the context, that the evil enemies have *caused* the psalmists' illness. Rather, they have only used the illness to slander and to accuse him.[63]

The royal poem of Ps 18:18ff, 33ff speaks about political opponents and hostile peoples. Pss. Sol. 16 is the first to speak of assistance in the battle *against sin*.

Very frequently the mortal danger to the one offering thanks is presented as a trip into the underworld, which is also a frequently occurring image in the complaint songs.[64] The following descriptions are also explained by this image: sinking into the great water, or into muck and mire, or into a deep cistern and the grave. The same images appear in the individual complaint songs, where the entire material has been treated extensively, including that which appears in the thanksgiving songs.[65]

Sometimes the psalmist includes a humiliating and sorrowful word with this narrative about the distress in which he states that he is at least partially to blame for the threat confronting him. He transgressed against God, perhaps by too much certainty.[66] In Ps 32,

---

[53]Pss 50:14; 56:13; 61:9; 66:13; 116:14-18; Jonah 2:10; cf. Pss 22:26; 61:6.

[54]2 Sam 15:8; Gen 28:20; 31:13.

[55]Jonah 1:16.

[56]Num 21:2; Judg 11:30ff; Isa 19:21; Nah 2:1.

[57]Fr. Heiler, *Gebet*,[4] 1921, p. 97.

[58]Cf. Pss 9:4; 30:2; 71:24; 92:12; 118:10-12, 22; 138:7; Sir 51:2ff; Odes Sol. 25:3, 10; 29:5, 10.

[59]See §6, ¶8, 9.

[60]Pss 116:11; 118:22; Ode Sol. 25:5.

[61]Ps 41:10.

[62]Cf. S. Mowinckel, *Psalmenstudien*, vol. 1, p. 124.

[63]Cf. the commentary to the appropriate passages.

[64]Cf. Pss 9:14; 30:4, 10; 40:3; 71:20; 103:4; 107:18; 116:3; Isa 38:10f, 14; Jonah 2:3-7; Job 33:28; Sir 51:2, 5, 6, 9; Pr Azar 65; Syriac Apocryphal Pss 5:3ff; Odes Sol. 29:4. The same occurs in the Babylonian (See the so-called Psalm of Job [¶11] in: E. Ebeling, with H. Greßmann, *Altorientalische Texte*,[2] 1926, p. 279) and Egyptian (see under ¶12) materials. See §6, ¶5.

[65]§6, ¶5.

[66]Ps 30:7. See also Pss 107:11, 17; Isa 38:17; Job 33:14; Pss. Sol. 16:3; cf. Ps 103:3; Isa 12:1; Syriac Apocryphal Psalms 3:9. See also the commentary to Ps 40:7.

the poet, calmly and contritely, offers thanks specifically for the forgiveness of sin.[67] He also tells specifically about his own unwillingness to confesses,[68] until his stubborn attitude was broken by suffering. He decided to confess his sin. He then experienced forgiveness by the grace of God. Divine training through suffering has its special place in the thanksgiving song.[69] If the deliverance is seen as something undeserved, then the thanksgiving song is somewhat different.[70] By contrast, the royal song in Ps 18 presents an extensive portrayal of how God rewards the singer's blameless disposition and recognized the singer's righteousness.[71] According to Ps 118:19f, the confirmation of the righteousness of the one offering thanks follows from the fact that he may walk through the "gate of righteousness" in the temple. For a similar ceremony in Babylonian materials, see ¶11.

However, the greater the distress has been, the more joyous the thanksgiving resounds from the whole heart. In the moment of the most extreme threat, when everything appeared to be at an end, the singer considered YHWH[72] at the last moment, and he called to YHWH for help.[73]

YHWH heard him in compassion,[74] and helped him. This help is also described in images of the trip to hades, especially in Ps 18. The gracious God forgave his sins[75] and healed him.[76]

The narrative is either preserved very briefly,[77] or it is more or less *conducted in broad strokes*. Frequently the report is first given quite briefly so that it can then be thoroughly expanded.[78]

The *order* in which the individual parts of the narrative are offered is left entirely to the poet. Usually, the poet begins with the summons,[79] or with the distress,[80] and not quite

---

[67]Cf. also Ps 103:3.

[68]See also Ps 119:71.

[69]See also Pss 119:67, 71, 75.

[70]Job 33:27; Pss. Sol. 16.

[71]Cf. Ps 18:21f. The same thing happens more smoothly in Pss 41:12f; 116:15f; see also 9:5; 92:8ff; 118:19f; Odes Sol. 25:12; 29:5.

[72]Ps 107:5, 18; Jonah 2:8; Sir 51:7f.

[73]Pss 18:7; 30:3; 107:6, 13, 19, 28.

[74]Pss 18:7; 22:5; 34:5, 7; 40:2; 66:19; 116:1; 118:5, 21; 138:3; Jonah 2:3,8; Sir 51:11; Syriac Apocryphal Psalms 3:28.

[75]Pss 32:5; 103:3; 107:17ff.

[76]Pss 30:3; 107:20; Syriac Apocryphal Psalm 3:28. The last passage portrays how healing was given in a dream to the one who was sick (Syriac Apocryphal Psalm 3:30). The same thing happens in the Babylonian "Job Psalm." Cf. ¶11.

[77]Pss 9:4f, 14; 22:25; 34:5; 71:20; 119:26a, 65a, 92; 138:3; Isa 12:1.

[78]Pss 18:4, 5-20; 30:2, 3f, 7-12; 66:17, 18f; 116:1f, 3f; 118:5, 10f; Jonah 2:3, 4-8; cf. Sir 51:1-6a, 6ff.

[79]Pss 18:4; 30:3; 34:5; (40:2); 66:17; 118:5; Jonah 2:3; Pss. Sol. 15:1; Syriac Apocryphal Psalms 3:1ff.

[80]Pss 18:5ff; 41:5; 107:4f, 10, 17f, 23ff; 116:3; Isa 12:1; 38:10ff; Jonah 2:4ff.

so often with the deliverance,[81] or the affirmation of having been heard.[82] Rarely, does he begin with the sin.[83]

5. A second main part of the thanksgiving song is the *confession* to YHWH as the one who delivered from distress. *Hōdāh* ("thank") also means "confess." Singing a thanksgiving song means to proclaim YHWH's grace before all people.[84] It should ring out loudly and joyously. No one else helped, either gods or humans. Only YHWH is faithful and helps his pious ones. I trust only him. The one offering thanks experienced that help for himself, and the other pious ones shall learn that from him. They shall find confirmation for the general statement from his example.[85] Thus, the confession expresses the *spiritual contents* of the thanksgiving song in relatively abstract form. "YHWH listens to his holy ones when they cry to him." Such is the fundamental thought of the simple, dogma-poor religion of these poems. It is easy enough to perceive in words, and relatively easy to understand, but difficult to believe and maintain every the distress of this life. The one offering thanks is expressing the same conviction that the one complaining expressed for comfort in his time of trouble.[86] It is thus no wonder that the contents of the "confession" of the thanksgiving song and the "expressions of confidence" in the complaint songs correspond to one another.

By its very nature, such proclamation is directed toward *others*,[87] and therefore normally speaks of YHWH in the *third person*.[88] Naturally, it stands at one of the most important places of the poem, so that it resounds powerfully in one's ears. It thus normally stands at the *conclusion of the narrative* as the result of the poet's experiences. The confession is seldom placed at the beginning as a *superscription* of the whole.[89]

Sometimes a small hymn appears in its place in a developed style (cf. ¶8), expressing a pious person's newly confirmed experience in the form of a hymnic component.[90] Or, knowledge is presented, which others should learn. It is presented in the form of a *blessing* over those who YHWH has delivered.[91] Or, instead of a *challenge to the pious*, one should observe the fate of the psalmist and should recognize YHWH's dominion.[92]

One can also see a "confession" of YHWH's help in Israel's "thanksgiving psalm" at the conclusion of the poem.[93] This kind of "confession" is also found in Egyptian monuments (see below, ¶12).

---

[81]Pss 30:2; 92:11; 138:3; Sir 51:2ff, 6b.

[82]Ps 116:1.

[83]Pss 30:7f; Job 33:27; Pss. Sol. 16:1ff.

[84]Job 33:26f; Pss 9:15; 22:26; 35:18; 40:10f; 51:17; 107:32; 109:30; cf. 116:17ff.

[85]Cf. Pss 18:26-28; 30:6; 31:24; 32:1f, 6ff; 34:6ff; 40:5; 41:2-4; 69:34; 92:13ff; 116:15; 118:6-9; 138:4-6, 7f; Isa 12:2ab.

[86]§6, ¶19.

[87]See especially Ps 34:6ff; Job 33:26f.

[88]Exceptions are Pss 18:26-28; 32:7; and 138:7 which speak of him in the second person.

[89]Pss 32:1f; 41:2-4.

[90]Cf. Pss 30:5f; 69:33f; 138:4-6; cf. also 1 Sam 2:3bff; §2, ¶18.

[91]Cf. Pss 32:1f; 40:5; 41:2-4. This kind of blessing can also be a hymnic type, as is particularly clear in 40:4f.

[92]Cf. Pss 31:24; 32:6f; 34:6-11.

[93]Ps 124:8; cf. Isa 12:2; §2, ¶41.

6. The third, admittedly less common, part of the thanksgiving psalm is the *announcement of the thanksgiving sacrifice*, most clearly expressed in Ps 66:13-15: "I enter your house with the whole offering. I pay my vow to you."[94] In the same words the psalmist responds to the question, "How shall I now thank YHWH?"[95] A sacrifice speech tends to accompany the sacrifice among less cultured peoples, especially with the thanksgiving sacrifice.[96] This announcement is directed with surging sentiments to YHWH himself, or it speaks of him in the *third person* like the remaining parts of the genre. At the same time, we can recognize from this type of material that the thanksgiving songs preceded the sacrifice. The sacrifice tends to follow immediately after the "announcement." This part, according to its nature, forms the last part of the thanksgiving song. At a later stage when the sacrificial animal was rejected (¶8), the thanksgiving saying takes the place of the announcement of the sacrifice.[97] An announcement of the thanksgiving saying is also found at the conclusion of the inscription of an Egyptian monument (see ¶12 below).

7. Another form sung by the rejoicing *choir of festival participants* stands alongside this individual form of the thanksgiving song. The thoughts of the festival guests also play a large role in the thanksgiving song of the individual as we have already seen.[98] The thanksgiving song was sung before them.[99] The thanksgiving offering was presented before them,[100] and the meal was shared with them.[101] However, they experience similar distress to the psalmist. They create new trust, fear,[102] and joy[103] from that which they now hear and see. In the background one sometimes finds the presupposition that the pious, like the poet himself, are poor and humiliated,[104] while the wealthy possessors of power turn their back on religion. This presupposition is also valid for many complaint songs and it is confirmed in the communal complaint songs.[105] We suggest that the psalmist commands this group to express their shared joy and to raise their happy voice with him.[106] This kind of song is then voiced during the festival meal (cf. Ps 22:27). Usually the choir of friends would have accompanied the one offering thanksgiving to the sanctuary with joyful singing.[107] According to Jer 33:11, the customary song in such parades that was also typical when several persons offering thanksgiving appeared together was the verse,[108] "Thank YHWH, for he is good, for he keeps his grace forever." One should thus consider

---

[94]Ps 116:13, 17-19; Jonah 2:10; cf. Pss 27:6; 118:19ff.

[95]Ps 116:12; Isa 38:15.

[96]Cf. Fr. Heiler, *Gebet*,⁴ 1920, pp. 76ff, 97. See also Ps 66:13f.

[97]Cf. Pss 18:50; 28:7d; 118:28; Isa 38:20.

[98]Cf. ¶2, 4, 5.

[99]Job 33:27; Pss 22:23; 52:11; 107:32; 109:30; cf. 9:15.

[100]Ps 116:18.

[101]Ps 22:27.

[102]Pss 22:24; 40:4.

[103]Pss 34:6; 69:33; 118:15f.

[104]Pss 22:25, 27; 34:3, 7, 11; 41:2; 69:33f; 109:21; 116:6; 138:6. See also Ps 18:28.

[105]§6, ¶8; §4, ¶7.

[106]Cf. Pss 22:24f; 30:5; 32:11; 34:4; 35:27; 69:33; 118:1-4,24; see also Syriac Apocryphal Psalms 5:1.

[107]Cf. Ps 118:22-25.

[108]This verse forms the first line of Pss 106; 107; 118:1-4, cf. 118:29; 136:1-3,26; Sir 51:1ff (cf. also 1 Chr 16:34; 2 Chr 20:21; 5:13; 7:3; Ezra 3:11; 1 Macc 4:24).

that this subcategory of the thanksgiving songs was originally sung with the thanksgiving sacrifice by the thanksgiving choir. The form of these songs belongs to the hymns.[109] Ps 100 communicates a hymn. According to the superscription, this psalm is "for the thanksgiving offering" since it is a choral hymn that was sung by the choir of festival participants. In a later period, the line "Thank YHWH for he is good" was then also still used as a hymn on other occasions.[110]

We suggest that a unified poetry was created from this kind of choral hymnic thanksgiving song and from the individual thanksgiving song. In Ps 66 the thanksgiving song of the festival giver in 66:13-20 follows the choral hymn in 66:1-12. The same is true for Ps 118:1-4,5ff. In Ps 118, we possess a grand thanksgiving festival liturgy where the voices of all the participants (the individual and his friends) ring out, along with the the blessing of the priest. Something similar is presupposed in Ps 26:6f.[111]

In Ps 107 we read another form of the choral thanksgiving song where those offering thanksgiving are arranged in four groups, and commanded by the priest to sing their thanksgiving song. The outline of every strophe follows the outline of the individual thanksgiving song. The psalm is apparently a mass thanksgiving song, perhaps conducted at the autumn festival.[112]

8. The simple form of the thanksgiving song as described above was later perceived to be too threadbare for the exuberant mood and was expanded by numerous means. First, other genres influenced the thanksgiving song.

The previous practice had been to introduce the words which the poet had spoken when in mortal fear. These words were placed at the point of the narrative, where the summons to YHWH was spoken. The same thing happened in an Egyptian monument (see ¶12). They bear the form of the *complaint song*,[113] and they are usually introduced with the words *'anî 'āmartî* ("I once said").[114] The poet recalls the previous time of complaint in order to bring the powerful change into view clearly and impressively. Once he was in deep pain, but now he is in joyous happiness.

Further, thanksgiving songs conclude with a short petition if something else remains for the one offering thanksgiving to wish.[115] This petition is again a motif of the complaint song. The thanksgiving song in Pss. Sol. 16:1-5 turns into an entire complaint song. A complaint song is added by a later hand to the thanksgiving song of Ps 40:1-12, just as a hymn in Ps 107:33-43 is added to the thanksgiving song of Ps 107:1-32. See the Syriac Apocryphal Psalms 3:37f for a petition for Israel at the conclusion of the thanksgiving song. The fact that the thanksgiving saying also has wishes attached is normal among primitive peoples.[116]

---

[109]§2, ¶5.

[110]2 Chr 5:13; 7:3; 20:21; Ezra 3:11; 1 Macc 4:24.

[111]See the commentary to this passage.

[112]See the commentary. A later hand added a hymn in 107:33-43.

[113]Pss 30:10f; 31:23b; 32:5ab; 41:5-11; 66:18; 116:4bc, 5f, 11b, 16a; Isa 38:10-14; Jonah 2:5; Sir 51:10, 11ab; Syriac Apocryphal Psalms 3:3-27.

[114]Pss 41:5; 66:18; 116:11; Isa 38:10f; Jonah 2:5; cf. 30:7; 31:23.

[115]Pss 40:12; 118:25; 138:8c.

[116]Cf. Fr. Heiler, *Gebet,* p. 97.

From the opposite side, the thanksgiving song also influences the complaint song when the complaint poet raises his affirmation of being heard to the level of "certainty" at the conclusion of his complaint and petition. The thanksgiving song also influences the complaint song when the complaint poet offers the thanksgiving song in advance, or even voices the thanksgiving psalm he will offer to God's honor.[117] This happens frequently.[118] Ps 57:8ff is especially noteworthy. It is a thanksgiving song clothed entirely in hymnic form. It appears to be taken from elsewhere and attached to a complaint song. Thus, the poem wonderfully and naturally presents the movement from an impugned heart to a conclusion where the heart still trusts.

The royal song in Ps 144:1f begins with a brief thanksgiving song.[119] Before the ruler delivers his petition for protection from his enemies to YHWH, he expresses his thanksgiving for the fact that YHWH has delivered him from his enemies to this point.

The fact that hymnic elements have penetrated the thanksgiving song has already been shown above in several examples.[120] This mixing of styles was even easier given the fact that both genres share the basic mood of jubilation over YHWH. The difference is that the thanksgiving songs rejoice about the *specific act* which God has just done for the one offering thanksgiving, while the hymns sing of the great deeds and majestic characteristics in general.[121] However, it was natural that the two genres influenced one another. The thanksgiving songs borrowed from the hymns. Sometimes the "introduction" of the thanksgiving songs bears a hymn-like form,[122] or the songs close with similar words.[123] The hymn can stand *in the middle* of the poem,[124] or the narrative can take this position.[125] A larger hymnic piece can precede the thanksgiving song,[126] or follow it.[127] Sometimes, towards the end of the poem, a "confession" is clothed in hymnic form.[128] The basic mood of the thanksgiving song, rejoicing and happiness, is powerfully accented by these hymnic pieces. Israel's thanksgiving song in Isa 12:1f also has a hymnic form, that is eschatologically changed by the prophet.[129]

The opposite is also true. The *thanksgiving songs have also colored the hymns* at times so that the thoughts of the thanksgiving song have penetrated those of the hymn. The poet sometimes included an expression of his thanksgiving for the divine kindness to himself in particularly impressive form when rejoicing over the wonderful rule of God

---

[117]§6, ¶24.

[118]See the examples mentioned in ¶1.

[119]§6, ¶28.

[120]¶¶3, 5, 7.

[121]§2, ¶54.

[122]Pss 9:2; 18:2f; 22:23f; 30:2; 34:2-4; 57:8f; 69:31; 71:15f, 18b, 22ff; 138:1f; Sir 51:1; cf. §3, ¶7.

[123]Pss 18:50f; 22:28f; 30:13; 32:11; 35:27; 69:35ff; 107:8f, 15f, 21f, 31f; Isa 38:18ff; Sir 51:12; (Pss 31:20-22); cf. 107:33-42; Pss. Sol. 16:5; and ¶3.

[124]Pss 30:5f; 40:5f; 138:4-6.

[125]Ps 92:11.

[126]Pss 66:1-12; 118:1-4; cf. Dan 2:20-22.

[127]Ps 18:32-49.

[128]¶5; cf. Pss 30:5f; 69:33; 138:4-6; cf. 40:5.

[129]Cf. §2, ¶41.

that stretches over all the world.[130] The *thanksgiving prayers* which are preserved in prose very commonly have a hymnic form.[131]

The *prophets* heavily influenced the overall mood of thanksgiving poetry,[132] but this influence appears infrequently in details. Thus, we sometimes find references to eschatology preserved at the end of the *hymnic pieces* when thanksgiving songs conclude individual complaint songs.[133]

The opposite is also true. One occasionally notices that the genre of the thanksgiving song has influenced prophetic material. Isa 12:1f is the small individual thanksgiving song related to Israel and reinterpreted eschatologically: "On that day, you (Israel) shall say, 'I thank you YHWH that you were angry with me. Your anger turned away and you comforted me.' "

Sometimes we find a blessing speech in place of the confession. So the one offering thanksgiving says, salvation comes to the man who keeps me close to YHWH. Like me, he will be delivered. The penetration of this form is grounded in the fact that the poet looks away from himself momentarily. He thinks of the other pious ones for whom he wishes the same heart-warming experiences.[134]

For the same reason one sometimes also finds a didactic element which belongs to the wisdom teaching by form and content.[135] When this occurs, the "confession" of the one offering thanks takes the form of wise doctrine and the festival guests become students to whom the instructor now proclaims his wisdom.[136] He also communicates "admonitions" which proceed from his fate, warnings that were common to wisdom poetry.[137]

An important change from a religiohistorical perspective occurs in the genre when it begins to *free itself from the thanksgiving sacrifice*. In many of these poems the sacrifice is not even mentioned.[138] Thus this stage of the psalm's development expresses the intellectual content and the spiritual mood of the singer more clearly than the sacrifice. Sometimes, consciously or unconsciously, the singer himself would be esteemed more highly than the sacrifice. This same attitude also appears in the Babylonian material where the vows concluding the complaint songs very frequently treat the praise and worship of the deity who has delivered, but these songs do not specifically treat sacrifices and ceremonies.[139] Even certain Egyptian monuments show a high esteem for thanksgiving songs that is similar to the Hebrew psalm passages already mentioned.[140] Of course this does not

[130]Cf. Ps 103:2-5 as well as Pss 18:32-49; 92:5, 11f, 16; 1 Sam 2:1; and Pr Azar 65 (88). Cf. §2, ¶54.

[131]Cf. §2, ¶¶14, 54; §7, ¶3.

[132]P. 206.

[133]Pss 22:28f; 69:36f. See the commentary.

[134]See ¶5.

[135]§10, ¶3.

[136]Cf. Pss 31:24; 32:6ff; 34:12ff; 51:15; Pss. Sol. 15:2ff, 7ff.

[137](§10, ¶5), cf. Pss 31:24a, 25; 32:8f; 34:12-15. Cf. also Sir 39:6 where wisdom speech and thanksgiving prayer stand together.

[138]Cf. Pss 9:15; 18:50; 30; 34; 41; Isa 38:20; Sir 51:11; Pss. Sol. 15:2ff; and the majority of the thanksgiving songs that are offered and sometimes cited at the end of the complaint songs (with the exception of Pss 22:26f; 27:6; 54:8; 56:13; 61:9).

[139]Cf. §6, ¶24.

[140]§10, ¶3.

mean that one should immediately accept that these songs wish to exclude the sacrifice.[141] However, neither can one necessarily accept the opposite position in every case, that the completion of the thanksgiving sacrifice was self-evidently presupposed. It is different in other passages, whose effect Mowinckel (*Psalmenstudien*, vol. 6, pp. 53ff) incorrectly seeks to downplay when he only finds "occasional hyperbolic formulations." These occasional passages explicitly, and with all clarity, reject sacrifice. They designate the psalm as all that God desires and all that God values.[142] When we ask why such a strong and far-reaching deviation from previous practice occurs, the consistently independent, and in large measure attractive, arguments of our friend appear to us to lack spiritual depth and poetic understanding. These arguments fail to recognize the religious pathos which stands out so markedly in these passages. He thinks this pathos represents an all too "human" self consciousness on the part of "professional psalmic poets" who wished to use these words to provide rank and prestige when comparing their own office with the sacrificial priest.[143] Also, the "anti-cultic polemic of the prophets" with which the position of these psalmists certainly coincides, has far deeper roots than the "natural reflex feelings of the simple, somewhat rationalistic man." These feelings turn against the extravagance of the "greed and avarice" of the priests."[144] It thus appears to us to be incorrect when Mowinckel (p. 56) asserts that these psalmic poets "stand in very positive relationship to the temple cult," and have generally undertaken only a *displacement of evaluation* for the individual events of the cult.[145] In other words they have preferred the cultic song of the singer to the sacrifice of the priest. Thus, Mowinckel was not able to see the great significance for world history which took place in the minds of these persons. By studying from the prophets, they learned to free themselves from the sacrificial worship in which their poetry had developed. *The soul steps before God, liberated from the bonds of the cult.* This change was also significant for the history of literature. The "spiritual thanksgiving song" arose from the *thanksgiving offering song.* One can also observe a corresponding phenomenon in other genres.[146] Now one can certainly not say that the old songs of worship must be separated *in details* from the later psalms liberated from the cult. Rather, the style is constrained so that the pious language generally remains the same. However, there is a big difference for piety whether this poem accompanies a holy action or whether it appears without any such support.

Nevertheless, not all of the poems liberated from sacrifice are that far removed from the worship service. It remained the practice to *sing the thanksgiving song in the sanctuary.*[147] The impression of the holy site would have been too much even for these minds who no longer valued the coarse sacrifice. The holy site with its expensive decorations, its many enthusiastic people, and its ancient memories left the indestructible feeling that the person is close to God and may even "see God's countenance" while there. It

---

[141]S. Mowinckel, *Psalmenstudien*, vol. 6, 1924, pp. 20f.

[142]Pss 40:7; 50:14; 51:17f; 69:31f. Cf. also Ps 63:6 where the singing is set in place of the sacrifice.

[143]Mowinckel, *Psalmenstudien*, vol. 6, pp. 57f.

[144]S. Mowinckel, *Psalmenstudien*, vol. 6, p. 55.

[145]S. Mowinckel, *Psalmenstudien*, vol. 6, p. 51.

[146]§1, ¶8; §2, ¶44; §6, ¶4, 28.

[147]Cf. Pss 9:15; 41:13; 43:4; 138:2; Isa 38:20.

would have remained a given to these persons if they wanted to voice a thanksgiving song, they would choose the sanctuary as the place to do so.

A further development was reached when one abandoned the sanctuary and sang the song for himself and his friends in his own house or somewhere else. The person who inserted the "Jonah psalm" into the prophetic booklet, greatly misunderstood it, thinking that such a thanksgiving song could be spoken in any situation and at any place, even in the belly of a fish. The "hymn of the three men" which concludes (65 [68]) with a thanksgiving song motif was even sung in a red-hot fiery oven. Even thanksgiving songs like Sir 51, and especially those in the Psalms of Solomon (15; 16) have as little to do with the sanctuary as with the holy meal. An alphabetic thanksgiving song, Ps 34, was never intended to be read aloud at any point. Rather, it was conceived for reading and with the eyes. Accordingly, nothing would stand in the way of locating the poems of this genre, which are silent about the sanctuary, within the house of the pious ones. However, we cannot be certain in this respect, since just a few of these songs exist.[148] One can more frequently observe the absence of the sanctuary and performance elements in the small thanksgiving songs at the conclusion of the complaint songs.[149] It apparently belongs to the style of these songs that they speak in very unspecific terms.

Another line runs alongside this line of development, one in which the thanksgiving psalm was originally composed by the *officials of the sanctuary* for use there (¶2). It is comparable to the songs that tend to stand at the end of our hymnbook and are designated "for specific cases," such as sickness, thunderstorms, and mortal danger on the sea. Later, however, this genre itself came into the hands of *the laity*, who put down their own experiential feelings in this form. Even when tracing this line, it appears to me that Mowinckel has not quite found the right path. He wants to accept that all of these poems stem from temple personnel, with very few exceptions. These exceptions as works of the laity betray a "more inferior language" and a style which is less regulated. He thinks their origin stems from the especially scrupulous pious ones who composed their own thanksgiving psalm in order to fulfill all righteousness.[150] But how, in a poem such as Ps 103, does one find a spirit which provides the scrupulous precision of the offering, but which thereby only leads to a weak "poem." It seems more proper that one use a very different measuring rod for these songs if one wishes to differentiate between worship formulas and those psalms composed by the ones offering thanksgiving. This measuring rod should ask whether or not examples are found in this genre which contain the inimitable touch of personal bubbling and the passion of a soul who has "been made fortunate by his God." Mowinckel (*Psalmenstudien*, vol. 6, p. 65) recognized this measuring rod, but it is questionable whether he was able to use it. We thus come to the point of determining the internal differences between these poems.

9. The *individually preserved thanksgiving songs* are the most readily differentiated from one another. To be sure, the basic mood remains the same, even if it appears in varying power and clarity. The mood is one of the joyful thanksgiving to the gracious

---

[148]Pss 32; 34; Sir 51; Pss. Sol. 15.

[149]Pss 7:18; 13:6; 28:6f; 31:8f, 20-25; 35:9; 57:8-12; 59:17; 63:4-6; 71:8, 14-16, 18c; 86:12f; 109:30f; Jer 20:13.

[150]So Pss 30; 103; 116; Sir 51. See S. Mowinckel, *Psalmenstudien*, vol. 6, pp. 65f. The psalms he mentions in that context (23; 73; 145; 146) are not thanksgiving songs.

helper on high from a deeply moved heart which has endured the fear of death. Several of the above mentioned pieces are indispensable. The individual poet, however, has the freedom to select first one piece and then another from the genre's storehouse and then to bring it into the light. We have songs in which the painful *complaint* which the singer once expressed in his distress (¶8) forms the center section[151] or the first section.[152] Sometimes the feeling of pain is so strong, even after the poet's change of heart that he cannot free himself from it very quickly. In addition, there are other poems in which the *hymnic* or *didactic* elements are particularly accented, according to the way the one offering thanks feels. There are poems in which the *narrative* is particularly extensive (Ps 18). There are also several in which the poet cannot just pour out his heavy heart just once, so he divides the entirety into *two parallel main parts which follow upon one another*.[153] In addition, there is another poem (Ps 34) in which the author has selected the alphabetic form, which is admittedly just an external decoration as with the thanksgiving liturgy in Ps 118 (¶7) or the mass thanksgiving song in Ps 107 (¶7), etc. Isa 12:1f is a very special poem in which Israel of the future should sing an individual thanksgiving song of this type, and where an eschatological hymn (12:3-6) has been attached. Here, one can perceive this allegorical transposition as particularly deep and spiritually perceptive. One other individual thanksgiving song (Ps 30), as shown by the superscription, has been reinterpreted to Israel's condition and sung at the temple consecration.[154] The alphabetic poem in Pss 9/10 has a special place in which pieces of different genres are completely mixed in an unnatural manner. Even motifs of the individual thanksgiving song (9:2-5,14f) are combined with those of the eschatological hymn (§2, ¶51). The baroque, all too pompous, thanksgiving song in Ps 18 is of great significance since it is placed in the mouth of a king of Judah.[155] It is apparent from the outset that these royal thanksgiving songs are by their nature older than those from private persons. They contain certain expressions that appear in the individual thanksgiving songs and stand out for their grandeur.[156]

If we summarize these observations, and return to the question with which we concluded ¶8, we have achieved a characteristic image which incorporates great differences within it, even when viewed from the perspective of the history of literature. On the one hand, one certainly reads much that is remarkably consistent, uniform, and impersonal and we accept without reservation that this phenomenon can be explained by the worship origins of the genre. The *sanctuary officials must have been the creators of this type of poetry* (¶2). We may find the oldest form of the genre in the *royal thanksgiving songs,*

---

[151]Ps 41:5-11.

[152]Isa 38:1-14; Syriac Apocryphal Psalms 3:3-27.

[153]Pss 18; 30; 116. See also ¶4. The same phenomenon happens in the hymn (§2, ¶36) and elsewhere (§4, ¶14; §6, ¶22).

[154]See also the superscription of Syriac Apocryphal Psalms 3, which relates this type of thanksgiving song to the return from the Babylonian exile.

[155]See also Ps 144:1f.

[156]Pss 9:5; 22:28ff; 57:10 (I will thank you, YHWH, *among the nations*, see also Ps 18:50); 108:4; 118:10-12 ("All the heathen surrounded me, I drove them off by YHWH's name."); 138:1 and especially 138:4 ("All the kings of the earth shall confess your, YHWH, for they have heard the words of your mouth" [through which the poet again attained life]). See also Syriac Apocryphal Psalms 3:13f; 5:1f; Odes Sol. 29:7. Concerning this transition from royal song to the song of the individual, see §5, ¶9 as well as in the individual complaint songs in §6, ¶8.

which would have been sung by the royal singers in the temple.[157] We possess examples of poems from this group of temple officials in the mass thanksgiving song of Ps 107 and the great thanksgiving liturgy of Ps 118. The "communal thanksgiving songs" would also be considered here. Mowinckel was right about these songs.

One the other hand, we also find much that is diverse, genuinely personal, and experiential, which does not coincide with such an interpretation. In these examples, the speaker is not a cultic official seeking to empathize from afar with the voices of the one offering thanksgiving. Rather, the one offering thanks is the one speaking. That person's heart is full from that which he has just experienced. In more than a few of these poems, the impression which those of us born later can still perceive is so strong that we do not for a moment doubt that those speaking so powerfully are speaking from their own experience. One can mention the personal demeanor of several psalms: the artistic arrangement of Ps 30 and Isa 38:10-20, the stark sense of a contrite feeling of confession in Ps 32, the shocking complaint beginning Ps 41, the rejoicing and triumph of Pss 92 and 138, the steadfast rejection of sacrifice in Ps 40, the depth of Ps 103 with its majestic conclusion, and Pss. Sol. 16.[158] The result is that *there were poets, and among them some very great poets*, who have formed these majestic creations, yet who did not, would not, or could not completely refashion *the traditional style*.

10. In explaining the thanksgiving songs, it is necessary to observe their relationship to the complaint songs of the individual (§6, ¶30). Both genres are similar in many respects, and correspond to one another like the two shells of a mussel. Both contain the portrayal of the distress. In the complaint songs, it is current while in the thanksgiving songs it belongs to the past. Both genres speak of deliverance, with the complaint songs anticipating it through the affirmation of having been heard while it has already occurred in the thanksgiving songs. The complaint song poets are comforted by the thoughts of God's faithfulness ("assurance of trust"[159]), which then appears as a "confession" in the thanksgiving songs. Both genres contain similar images and expressions. The same relationships are presupposed everywhere. Many complaint poets demand healing and restoration from God as vindication which God owes them because they are his pious ones (¶4; §6, ¶21), while many thanksgiving song poets see divine recognition of their innocence in the change that has occurred (¶4). In addition, both genres tend to borrow from one another.[160] These two kinds of songs sometimes come so close to one another, that only a very precise investigation of the linguistic form can differentiate them.[161]

Precisely because of this interrelationship, however, these two genres can be distinguished from one another. As an example of both the difference and the similarity let us take the possible deviations of the images of the hades journey in these types of songs.[162] The *complaint song complains*: I have been swallowed by the deep. Therefore the *petition* comes: YHWH, save my life from the grave. The *vow* concludes: I will thank you when you have raised my from the deep. The *thanksgiving song narrates* about the distress: I

---

[157]§5, ¶3, 5.
[158]See the commentary to the individual psalms.
[159]§6, ¶19.
[160]Cf. §6, ¶28; §7, ¶8.
[161]Cf. J. Begrich, *Der Psalm des Hiskia Jes 38*, and the commentary to Ps 41 and 116.
[162]§6, ¶5; §7, ¶4.

was once swallowed by the deep. Then it narrates about the *deliverance*: then you saved my life from the grave. It concludes with the *announcement of thanksgiving*: I will thank you because you have raised me from the deep. This type of comparison also teaches other things, including: the certainty that YHWH will not concede that his pious one should see the grave,[163] or that YHWH will redeem the soul of the pious by snatching him from the power of the underworld.[164] It does *not* teach general liberation from death (i.e., eternal life or immortality). Rather, it only *affirms the deliverance from the current mortal danger*. One sees this clearly from the thanksgiving songs, which offer thanks for salvation from death and the underworld in very similar words.[165] Similarly, when the complaint psalm expresses hope one should interpret it to mean that the singer wishes to see God's countenance in righteousness.[166] Even here, the counterparts in the thanksgiving songs show how this wish is to be understood. That for which the one complaining hoped and wished, the one offering thanks has experienced. After they have experienced God's help and even his declaration of vindication with it,[167] they have appeared before him (originally in the sanctuary) and have experienced blessed awareness of his nearness.[168] All difficulties disappear here, as soon as one finds the counterpart corresponding to the meaning.[169]

The thanksgiving songs are also differentiated from the complaint songs in their history by the fact that the sacrifice and ceremonies recede in the one, while the relationship to the sanctuary was preserved a long time in the other. Thus, we can well imagine that in the period in which the complaint song found its place in the home of the pious that the thanksgiving song still resounded from the temple. Mowinckel,[170] who holds this type of parallel development to be impossible, asks how in the world it would be possible to explain this phenomenon. We would respond that it would have been quite natural for the poor suffering persons to pour out their personal pain before their God in the stillness of their own little room. By contrast, the thanksgiving songs by their very nature belong to a public setting so that the one who was delivered should give honor to God before all the world.[171] Therefore, the thanksgiving songs did not lose its relationship to the sanctuary until much later.[172]

The entire life of the pious one takes its course in the change between the complaint song and the thanksgiving song. He thinks of his God at all the high points. In misfortune, he cries to God. When he has good fortune, he thanks God. The powerful feeling, indeed the fervor about which we must speak so often in this book,[173] makes the piety moving

---

[163]As in the psalm of confidence in Ps 16:10.

[164]Ps 49:16 is an insertion of this motif into a wisdom song.

[165]Cf. Pss 9:14; 18:17; 30:4; 118:18; Isa 38:17; Job 33:28; etc.

[166]Ps 17:15.

[167]¶4, p. 204 and ¶10, p. 213.

[168]Cf. Pss 41:13; 18:25.

[169]§6, ¶19, 23.

[170]S. Mowinckel, *Psalmenstudien*, vol. 6, p. 21.

[171]Cf. ¶2, 5, 7.

[172]Cf. ¶8.

[173]§2, ¶¶7, 8, 10, 13, 25, 33, 38, 39, 43, 46; 57; §3, ¶11; §4, ¶¶2, 6, 7, 9, 11, 14; §5, ¶¶5, 6, 9, 15, 20, 21, 22, 24, 25, 26; §6, ¶¶5, 11, 15, 16, 24, 28.

even in these contrasts. The same is true for the religion of the people.[174] Nevertheless, as one can see from the Psalms of Solomon in particular, as time passed the fervor became milder. The contrasts were leveled out and elements of both genres appeared together.[175]

There are noticeably fewer thanksgiving songs than complaint songs. Human beings are far less likely to think of God when things are going well than in times of distress, and poor blessed creatures that we are, we more often believe that we have cause to lament and implore than that we have cause to rejoice and be thankful. It was already that way among primitive peoples, and even now at the height of the history of praying, the petition far outweighs the thanksgiving.[176] However, in order to judge the relationship in the psalter fairly, one should compare the Babylonian religious poetry, where extraordinarily few thanksgiving sayings were transmitted in comparison to the abundance of complaints and petitions. Thus, even this case demonstrates the depth of Israelite piety in which they were far more capable than the Babylonians of not forgetting their God in the good times. The beautiful thought, "Do not forget, o my heart," first appeared on Israelite soil, but even here the admonition was not in great abundance.

11. We thus come to thanksgiving songs in the remainder of the Ancient Near East. The thanksgiving song has its counterparts in Phoenician, Aramaic, Babylonian, and especially in Egyptian religion. In Phoenician, the inscriptions of the votive stela recall thanksgiving. The inscription of Yahaw-melech of Gebal (Byblos) states: "I call to my Lady, the *Ba'alat* of Gebal for she hears my voice." "Then as soon as I called to my Lady, the *Ba'alat* of Gebal, she heard my voice and did well by me."[177] This stela tells of *a prayer which was heard*, and thus contains the main element of a Hebrew thanksgiving song. One should also compare the inscriptions from Idalion, Tamasos, and Malta,[178] and especially those from Pauli Gerrei.[179] The Aramaic inscription from Zakir of Hamath also narrates about an event of a prayer being heard.[180]

One sees that the Babylonians also knew these thanksgiving songs, since the vow of a thanksgiving saying also typically concluded the complaint song in Babylonian materials.[181] Just as in the Hebrew examples, the complaint song tended to resemble the introduction of a thanksgiving song.[182] The Babylonian thanksgiving songs which have been referenced are also similar in form to the hymns, and must have had their original setting in the cult (which is also comparable to the Hebrew examples). The Babylonian thanksgiving songs include others in their praise: "The people of my city wish to honor your

---

[174]§4, ¶12.

[175]Cf. Pss. Sol. 16 and ¶8, p. 207.

[176]Fr. Heiler, *Gebet*, pp. 349, 444, 463f.

[177]Lidzbarski, *Altsemitische Texte*, vol. 1, 1907, pp. 12ff; H. Greßmann, *Altorientalische Texte*,[2] 1926, p. 446.

[178]Lidzbarski, *Altsemitische Texte*, vol. 1, pp. 31, 33, 43 ("Because he heard the voices voice.").

[179]Lidzbarski, *Altsemitische Texte*, vol. 1, p.46 ("Because he heard his voice and healed him.").

[180]Lidzbarski, *Ephemeris III*, 1915, pp. 1ff; H. Greßmann, *Altorientalische Texte*,[2] 1926, pp. 443f.

[181]Cf. §6, ¶24.

[182]W. Schrank, *Babylonische Sühnriten*, pp. 55ff.

power." Two thanksgiving songs have come to us from kings, albeit in very corrupt form:[183]

> I will glorify (?) your deity, proclaim your power . . .
>   (Of Marduk), the compassionate one whose gift is near . . .
> Whose heart (was appeased), who shows mercy,
>   (Accepted) my supplication, turned his neck,
> Whose heart was appeased, and showed compassion,

Then a *narrative* of the destruction of the Elamites follows:

> The Elamite, who did not fear his great deity,
>   Spoke inappropriately (against) his noble deity.
> Your weapons (went forth) against the impudent Elamites,
>   You cast his army down, and broke his power.
> You destroyed (his numerous places), set them aflame (?)
>   (His) great . . . you conquered just like the storm-flood.

The second song is also a king's thanksgiving song. It tells of the terrible *enemy threat*, the constant supplication of the king, and then the *redemption* and *deliverance*. It concludes with the presentation of the magnificent sacrifice which is rendered in thankfulness to Marduk for his help. Both royal songs form counterparts to Ps 18.

One text contains an extensive thanksgiving song from a Babylonian *private citizen*, the first part of which has been known for a long time under the name of the "Job Psalm."[184] It was published in more complete form some time ago, although it is still somewhat fragmentary.[185]

The poem begins with a hymnic introduction: "I will praise the Lord of wisdom." A large gap in the text follows. At the end of the first tablet one finds an expansive portrayal of the earlier distress from the one praying along with the many melancholy thoughts which tormented him at the time. Once he was a zealously pious person and loyal subject, and then evil spirits and severe illness befell him. There was no incantation against them, so he had to spend the night in his own filth. His grave was already dug for him, and the dirge was already completed. "My entire country called out: he has been so mistreated. His enemy heard it and his face glazed over." Nevertheless, in all his suffering he remained strong in his faith. This takes us through the second tablet. The third tablet then relates three dream stories which he envisioned which promised him redemption. Marduk drove the evil demons from him and delivered him from the corruption. Marduk raised him from the river of brimstone, the stream of the underworld.[186] Ceremonies are now undertaken for him with which the priests of Esagil tended to promise health to those who were ill. He was led through twelve gates in each of which he was loaned a particular good. Then follows the hymn from the Babylonians who observed his astonishing healing.

---

[183]J. Hehn, *Hymnen und Gebete an Marduk*, Beiträge zur Assyriologie 5, 1905, pp. 326ff; 339ff; H. Zimmern, *Babylonische Hymnen und Gebete*, vol. 1, p. 7; A. Ungnad, *Religion der Babylonier und Assyrer*, 1921, pp. 199f.

[184]H. Zimmern, *Babylonische Hymnen und Gebete*, vol. 1, p. 28.

[185]Cf. B. Landsberger in Ed. Lehmann and H. Haas, *Textbuch zur Religionsgeschichte*,[2] 1926, pp. 273ff, including bibliography.

[186]Cf. the hades journey (¶4) to this image.

Then the Babylonians saw	that he had been made alive,
All their mouths	praised (his greatness);
Who but Marduk	could have brought him from death to life?
Which goddess but Ṣarpanit	could have presented him with life?
Marduk made it possible	to awake while in the grave;
Ṣarpanit understands	how to deliver from corruption.

Therefore, all people were commanded to praise Marduk "wherever the sun shines, the fire glows, the water flows, or the wind blows."

The poem coincides to a large degree with the genre of the Hebrew thanksgiving song. The narrative of distress and redemption is the main part here as well. Its introduction has a hymnic form, and concludes with a hymn which is placed in the mouth of the spectators. The distress arises from severe illness. Healing is described as awaking from the dead which by no means (as with the Hebrew version) should be considered to refer to immortality of the soul.[187] Accordingly the genre of the song can be affirmed with certainty. We conclude that the Babylonians also knew the genre of the thanksgiving song, and that this genre contained essentially the same elements as the Hebrew version. In this instance we have an example of how the explanation can fertilize both Babylonian and Hebrew disciplines simultaneously.

12. Perhaps even more significant are the *thanksgiving songs from Egypt* which have been preserved in monuments from the Thebian cemetery plot erected in the twelfth and thirteenth centuries by craftsmen and workers.[188]

The following is one of the more valuable texts:

1. Hymn of Amon Re,
     The lord of Karnak, the first one of Thebes,
   And honor before Amon of the city,
     The great god,
   The lord of this sanctuary,
     So great of beauty.
2. I write hymns to him in his name;
     I praise him who is as high as the heavens and as wide as the earth.
   I proclaim his power to anyone who comes,
     and to anyone who goes.
3. Protect yourselves before him;
   Let son and daughter proclaim it,
     Great and small alike.
   Say it from generation to generation,
     and to those not yet born.
   Say it to the fish in the water,
     and to the birds in the sky.
   Proclaim it to the one who knows it,
     and to the one who does not know it.
   Protect yourselves from him.
4. You, Amon, are the lord protector of the silent one,
     the one who comes when the poor call.
   I call to you in my grief,

---

[187] Cf. H. Zimmern, *ZDMG* 76 (1922): 49.

[188] A. Erman, *Sitzungsberichte der Berl. Ak. D. Wissenschaften* 49 (1911): pp. 1086ff; cf. *Reden und Ausätze*, 1913, pp. 141f.

and you come to deliver me.
>   You give breath to those who suffer,
>   And you deliver me, the one who is sitting (?).

5. You, Amon Re of Thebes, are the one
>   who delivers the one in the underworld . . .
>   If one calls to you, you will come from afar.

6. Neb-re, painter of Amon in the city of the dead, son of Pai, painter of Amon in the city of the dead, composed this song in the name of his lord, Amon, the lord of Thebes, who comes when the poor call.

7. He wrote hymns to his name,
>   because his power is so great,
>   And he wrote complaint songs before the whole country
>   On behalf of Night-Amon, the painter,
>   who was sick and close to death,
>   And had fallen by the power of Amon, for the sake (?) of his cow.

8. Then I noticed that the lord of the gods came as the north wind,
>   and how sweet air came before him,
>   So that he might deliver Night-Amon, the painter of Amon,
>   who was born by the house-wife Pasched.

9. He speaks: "The servant was used to sinning,
>   But the lord is used (?) to being gracious.
>   The Lord of Thebes is not angry all day long.
>   When he is angry, it is just for a moment, and nothing can withstand it.
>   The wind turned to us with favor,
>   Amon turned with (?) his air.
>   As surely as you live, you will be gracious,
>   and what has changed (?) for the better will not turn back."
>   Written by Neb-re, painter of Amon in the city of the dead.

10. He speaks: "I will make this monument in your name.
>   I will place this song on it as an inscription,
>   If you deliver for the writer Night-Amon."
>   Thus have I said, and you heard me.
>   Now, I do that which I promised.
>   You are the lord protector of the one who calls upon him,
>   who rejoices over right. You are lord of Thebes.
>   Composed by the painter Neb-re (and his) son Chai[189]

Neb-re erected this monument to the name of his God Amon in thankful recollection of the gracious deliverance of his son Night-Amon from severe illness. He also took the opportunity to write his own poem for this occasion. This song corresponds in every way to the biblical thanksgiving song. First, it has the same cause, the delivery *from illness* which is portrayed as a *redemption from the underworld*, just as in the Hebrew and Babylonian examples. The poem is designated as a hymn (praise song) and an "honor" in the superscription. It has a short petition included: "May he allow me to live in the vicinity of his temple.[190] It is a petition which sometimes concludes the Hebrew thanksgiving song (cf. ¶8 above). The song begins with a *hymn* to the compassionate god: heaven and earth shall be full of praise, even the unborn generations should hear of his grace,[191] and learn

---

[189]See also Erman, *Die Literatur der Ägypter*, 1923, pp. 383f; G. Roeder, *Urkunden zur Religion des Alten Ägypten*, 1915, pp. 52ff.
[190]Cf. Pss 27:4; 61:5.
[191]Cf. Ps 22:32.

fear before God.[192] The "confession"[193] to Amon follows in ¶5, who approaches at the cry of the poor (note the expression). He even redeems the one who languishes in the underworld, and the poet unwaveringly believes on his help the entire time. Following a superscription (6) a second poem begins gradually that contains the *narrative* of the events.[194] The poet reports about the *illness* of his son which is traced to sin.[195] He reports his *call* in hymns and complaint songs (Egyptian *Šnmh*, self-humiliation, prayer) to the god to whose grace he had testified (7). He then reports his being heard by god. All of this is precisely like the Hebrew examples. The subsequent passages (9, 10) once again return to the complaint song, which the poet had composed during his son's illness.[196] Even this song corresponds in structure and in thought precisely to a biblical complaint song. He comforts himself with all kinds of observations about the grace of God,[197] which he then elevates to the complete *certainty of having been heard*.[198] Soon anger will turn to grace, and the one who is then happily healed will no longer be sick. Finally, he spoke the *vow*[199] that he would engrave this song on a stone to the eternal memory of Amon, if he has compassion on the one who is ill (10). Then, the *announcement of thanksgiving* concludes the whole:[200] thus I spoke, and you heard me. Now, he fulfills his vow with joyful thanksgiving. He erects a stone and concludes with another "confession" of thankful belief. Whoever calls on god in belief, Amon will preserve him as lord protector. This song is so similar to the biblical thanksgiving song, that we would scarcely need to do more than change the names in order to change the Egyptian poem into a Hebrew poem. Even the piety which appears here is very close to the Israelite piety. Even this piety could have named a cultic proceeding if it had portrayed the sin he had committed. Of course an offence against the holy cow in Israel would be completely impossible.

One should also compare the thanksgiving song to the "highlights."[201] The thanksgiving song also contains a hymnic introduction with a short petition, as well as the *narrative about the sin, illness, summons, and the certainty of having been heard*. The summons cites the *complaint song* that had been spoken. The *conclusion* contains the confession directed to all the ears of the earth.[202]

It is not possible here to discuss why psalms that are so full of personal piety are otherwise lacking in Egypt. It is enough to note that the thanksgiving song was not just known to the Hebrews, but also existed among the Babylonians and Egyptians (and perhaps the Phoenicians and Aramaeans) in essentially the same form. It is difficult to

---

[192]See above, ¶7.

[193]See above, ¶5.

[194]Cf. ¶4 above.

[195]Cf. ¶4 above.

[196]Cf. ¶8.

[197]Assurance of confidence (§6, ¶19).

[198]Cf. §6, ¶23.

[199]§6, ¶24.

[200]See ¶6 above.

[201]A. Erman, *Sitzungsberichte der Berl. Ak. D. Wissenschaften* 49 (1911): 1098ff; G. Roeder, *Urkunden*, 57ff.

[202]Other Egyptian thanksgiving songs of the same type can be found in Erman, *Sitzungsberichte der Berl. Ak. D. Wissenschaften* 49 (1911): 1101f, 1105f, 1107f. Concerning the religion of these songs, see pp. 1108f.

circumvent the acceptance of historical context because of the surprising similarity of the Babylonian and Egyptian thanksgiving song with the biblical one. From a distance, we are thus able to see a precursor to Israelite religious poetry in this case as with other psalm genres.[203] Before the appearance of Israel in history, the great cultured peoples of Asia Minor already shared a literary possession which can be recognized precisely in the similarity of forms. Israel appropriated this treasure available to it. One can observe especially that both the poem of Neb-re as well as the "Job psalm" are lay poems, even though the cult existed in a completely unbroken line at that time, and even though the cult is presupposed in these poems. It is nevertheless remarkable that there are also similar inscriptions to the ones treated here on Hellenistic soil. The basic Hellenistic cult practice also corresponds to that presupposed in the biblical thanksgiving song.[204]

13. In conclusion, the individual observations should be arranged into a picture of the history of the thanksgiving song in Israel, even though only in broad strokes. The *thanksgiving offering song* is an element of the Israelite worship service and is traced back to the oldest period of Israel even with regard to its outline.[205] The foreign counterparts also argue for an early date for the origin of the genre.[206] Originally, these poems would also have been *formulas* composed by cult officials like other worship songs.[207] First, these songs would have been sung at the king's thanksgiving sacrifice, either by him or for him.[208] Royal thanksgiving songs are also preserved in Babylonian materials.[209] These songs then came to the subjects from the kings.[210] During the royal period in Israel poems dedicated to the ruler would have arisen alongside those which served the subjects until finally, with the fall of the kingdom, even the royal songs disappeared from life. Little wonder that so few of them were preserved.[211]

Another developmental line occurs when a newer, freer type of poetry arose from the older, strict type in which the thanksgiving song was enriched especially by borrowing from other genres, especially the hymn and the complaint song.[212] One cannot doubt that this reformulation occurred through significant poets who expressed their own fresh experience in these songs.[213] One can see how old this reformulation is from Ps 18, which already shows the newer style in full bloom.[214] Babylonian and Egyptian poems already led the way into this freer form.[215] By contrast, the frequently cited verse, "Thank YHWH for he is good, for his grace endures forever," is the older form because of its simplicity. It is first mentioned as a song of those offering thanks in Jer 33:11, but could stem from a much earlier time. At the same time a spirit *free of the cult* that penetrated the thanks-

---

[203]See §2, ¶¶46, 61; §3, ¶¶10, 11; §5, ¶23; §6, ¶30.

[204]Cf. R. Reitzenstein, *Iranisches Erlösungsmysterium*, 1921, p. 252n.1.

[205]§2, ¶61; §4, ¶15; §6, ¶30.

[206]¶¶11, 12.

[207]§1, ¶6, p. 13.

[208]¶9.

[209]¶11.

[210]¶9; cf. §5, ¶9; §6, ¶8.

[211]¶9.

[212]¶8.

[213]¶9.

[214]See the commentary.

[215]¶¶11, 12.

giving songs appears which must certainly derive from the influence of the great *prophets*[216] and their passionate battle against sacrifice.[217] This spirit even continued to be transmitted in the legal period.[218] For a long time, these poems would have been sung in the sanctuary, until they entered the house of the pious ones altogether.[219] In all of this, there would have been room for the individual poet who wished to express his own thanksgiving. There was no lack of these poems in Israel.[220] It is much easier to recognize for the complaint song than the thanksgiving song, but this developed poetry would have been nursed in a group of poor and oppressed people. The religious poetry of these "poor" is presumed by Jeremiah.[221] Finally, wisdom poetry, with its rational reflection, undermined the thanksgiving songs as well as the other lyric genres. In the canon, one can see only a few weak traces of this wisdom poetry.[222] By contrast, in the Psalms of Solomon there are two thanksgiving songs in which the outline can still be recognized, but it is overrun with reflection and other kinds of material.[223] Even in the well-phrased thanksgiving song of Sir 51:1ff, one can recognize all the signs of an ebbing of the spirit.[224] Odes of Solomon 25 and 29 then offer the final picture in which many threads of the old thanksgiving song continue to live. However, other images have also entered,[225] and mystical experiences have completely colored the whole and placed the older inherited traditions in a whole new light. The *overview* thus shows that the genre which stemmed from an early period, was maintained through the centuries with great tenacity. It was influenced by the prophets, but the legalistic period left only a trace behind.[226] One cannot recognize any influence from the exile on this type of poetry. However, a psalm like 103, which Deutero-Isaiah cites, shows that this type of poetry still blossomed after the exile.[227] From the examination of Sir 51 and Pss. Sol. 15 and 16, one would not be wrong in speaking of a particularly powerful blooming of the genre in the Maccabean period. Most of the poems of this type that were transmitted to us come from the later period of the genre's history, that is between the seventh and the fifth centuries.

---

[216]§9, part VII.

[217]¶8.

[218]See the commentary to Ps 40:7f.

[219]¶8.

[220]¶9.

[221]Cf. Jer 20:13. It does not matter if this passage is declared nongenuine (contra C.H. Cornhill, *Buch Jeremia*, 1905, p. 238; and P. Volz, *Jeremia*, 1922, p. 209).

[222]¶8.

[223]Pss. Sol. 15; 16.

[224]The same is true for the Syriac Apocryphal Psalm 5, where the usual form of thanksgiving song is transferred to David while chapter 3 appears more original and older.

[225]Ps 25:7, 8.

[226]Ps 40:7f.

[227]Cf. Isa 57:16; Isa 40:6ff.

§8 Smaller Genres

I. Sayings of Blessing and Curse; II. The Pilgrimage Song; III. The Victory Song; IV. The Thanksgiving Song of Israel; V. Legends; VI. The Torah

I. Sayings of Blessing and Curse

S. Mowinckel, *Psalmenstudien*, vol. 5: *Segen und Fluch in Israels Kult und Psalmendichtung*, Oslo, 1923 (Videnskapsselskapets Skrifter II, Hist.-filos. Kl. no. 3.) — J. Hempel, "Die israelitischen Anschauungen von Segen und Fluch im Lichte altorientalischer Parallelen," (*ZDMG* new series 4 [1925]: 20-110.) — *RGG* article, "Segen und Fluch." — N. Nikolsky, *Spuren magischer Formeln in den Psalmen*, BZAW 46, Gießen, 1927. — H. Schmidt, "Grüße und Glückwünsche im Psalter," *Theologische Studien und Kritiken*, vol. 103 (1931): 141ff.

1. Among the genres we will treat in this chapter, we begin with the "blessing saying"[1] and the "blessing wish."[2] We begin here because of attention to their significance and their frequency. The latter category also includes the wishes from the individual complaint song which relate to the pious ones in addition to the examples which are cited.[3]

2. The blessing, like its counterpart the curse, has its roots in the *conceptual world* of *magic* even though the magical character recedes further and further into the background in the course of the history of religion.[4] Nevertheless, the origin is clearly recognizable by its linguistic form even into the latest periods.

From the outset, the blessing is a *magical saying*. As such, it works from *its own power* and originally knows no connection to the power of YHWH. Examples include Gen 1:22, 28 ("Be fruitful and multiply.") and Gen 24:60 ("You are our sister. May you become a thousand ten thousands. And may your seed possess the gate of his enemy."). Once the blessing has been spoken, the one saying the blessing no longer has any power over it. It has become an *autonomous, independent* entity. Isaac cannot take back the blessing which Jacob surreptitiously obtained.[5] The goal of the blessing is to create an advantage for the one who is blessed, to increase his dynamic power, to provide wealth

---

[1]Pss 1:1-3; 2:12; 32:1-2; 33:12; 34:9; 40:5; 41:2-4; 65:5; 84:5, 6, 13; 89:16; 91:1-13; 94:12; 106:3; 112:1; 115:15; 118:26; 119:1-2; 127:5; 128:1; 137:8f; 144:15; 146:5. See also Gen 14:19; 27:29; Num 24:9; Deut 28:3-6; 33:24,29; Judg 17:2; 1 Sam 15:13; 23:21; 25:33; 26:25; 2 Sam 2:5; 1 Kgs 10:8; Isa 3:10; 19:25; 30:18; 56:2; Jer 17:7; Prov 3:13; 8:32,34; 14:21; 16:20; 28:14; 29:18; Job 5:17; Ruth 2:20; 3:10; Dan 12:12; Qoh 10:17; Tob 11:17 (א); 13:12, 14; Jdt 13:18; Sir 14:1, 2, 20; 25:8, 9; 26:1; 28:19; 31:8; 48:11; 50:28; 4 Macc 18:9; Pss. Sol. 4:26; 5:18; 6:1; 10:1; 18:7.
[2]Pss 115:12-14; 118:27a; 121:7-8; 122:6b, 7; 128:5-6; 129:8; 134:3; also 15:5; 24:5-6.
[3]See §6, ¶15, p. 167.
[4]See J. Hempel, *ZDMG*, new series 4 (1925): 60ff.
[5]Gen 27:35.

to his descendants, to furnish *šālôm*, "rest and security in an undamaged and unthreatened condition, or good fortune and health in the widest sense."[6]

3. *Anyone* can pronounce blessings as well as curses. The blessing thus does not appear to be bound originally with any fixed cultic situation. The occasions on which a blessing would have been spoken are extremely diverse. One blesses another in a greeting,[7] in a departure,[8] and upon returning home.[9] The traveler who passes a field at harvest time calls out a blessing upon the harvester.[10] The recipient of a good deed blesses the person who performed it.[11] The king thanks his loyal subjects by conveying a word of blessing through a messenger.[12] The subjects bless the ruler when he takes the throne.[13]

The effectiveness of the blessing does depend upon the one who expresses it. There are persons whose word was ascribed with special power to bless. In magical thought, these persons carry a special power.[14] These persons include someone who is dying,[15] the king,[16] and last but not least the *priests*.[17] Indeed, over the course of Israel's history, imparting the blessing became the *special privilege of the priest*.[18] He blessed the people[19] as well as the pious individual.[20] He blessed the sacrifice,[21] the pilgrims who came to YHWH's festival,[22] and the festal community who entered the gates of the sanctuary.[23] He even blessed those in the celebratory worship service.[24]

The words of blessing were often accompanied by *specific activities* suitable to their original magic character. However, since nothing appears within the blessings themselves indicating proof of these actions they are only mentioned in general terms here.[25]

4. The *forms* of the blessing are understood from the presuppositions described. The *imperative and the indicative* forms are the most original since they express the magical character most strongly. Both clearly express the conviction that the effectiveness stems from its own power. Examples of the imperative form are found in the wording of the

---

[6]See J. Hempel, *ZDMG*, new series 4 (1925): 51. One should also compare the finer details of this category which he presents.

[7]1 Kgs 1:31; 2 Kgs 4:29; Ruth 3:10.

[8]Gen 24:60.

[9]Tob 11:17 (א).

[10]Ps 129:8.

[11]Judg 17:2; 1 Sam 23:21; 25:33; Ruth 2:20.

[12]2 Sam 2:5.

[13]1 Kgs 1:47; see Mowinckel, *Psalmenstudien*, vol. 5, p. 10.

[14]Cf. G. Hölscher, *Die Propheten*, p. 90; Hempel, *ZDMG* new series 4 [1925]: 47; 49; 59f; 78; Mowinckel, *Psalmenstudien*, pp. 10f.

[15]Hempel, *ZDMG* new series 4 [1925]: 49.

[16]2 Sam 6:18; 1 Kgs 8:14, 55.

[17]Gen 14:19-20; Num 6:24-26; 1 Sam 2:20; 9:13.

[18]Num 6; Deut 10:8; 1 Chr 23:13; see Hempel, *ZDMG* new series 4 [1925]: 79.

[19]Num 6:24-26.

[20]Gen 14:19-20; 1 Sam 2:20.

[21]1 Sam 9:13.

[22]1 Sam 2:20.

[23]Ps 118:26; cf. 24:5-6.

[24]Pss 115:12-15; 134:3.

[25]S. Mowinckel, *Psalmenstudien*, vol. 5, p. 9; Hempel, *ZDMG* new series 4 [1925]: 26.

passages (Gen 1:28; 24:60) mentioned above (p. 222). Examples of the indicative forms include Gen 27:29 ("Blessed is the one who blesses you.") or 1 Sam 25:33 ("Blessed is your will, and blessed be you, that you have prevented me today from bloodshed.").

In addition to these two forms, a third can be added, the wish form: "May your seed take possession of the gate of your enemy" (Gen 24:60); and "Peoples shall serve you; Nations shall bow down before you" (Gen 27:29).

Of these three forms, the second and third became significant for psalmic poetry. We call them the "blessing speech" and the "blessing wish." The imperative form of the blessing is greatly decreased in comparison to these two because its nature makes it difficult to connect the effectiveness of the blessing to YHWH.

5. The *blessing saying* originally began with the passive participle *bārūk*, "blessed is." The *one receiving* the blessing follows the participle as the *subject*.[26] The subject appears in the *third person*,[27] but also the *second person*.[28] This form, where the self-efficacy of the magic saying is recognized by its indicative form, was reformulated based on the conviction that the blessing could only have its power from YHWH. The first step of this process provides a corresponding *expansion of the predicate*. Instead of the simple *bārūk* ("blessed is . . . "), it becomes *bārūk leyahwēh* ("blessed to YHWH is . . . "),[29] or *bārūk bešēm yahwēh* ("blessed in the name of YHWH is . . . ").[30]

Also, this reformulated formula expresses the belief that humans can be effectively blessed if only they would use the *miraculously powerful name of their God*. The name of YHWH is placed at the disposal of humans so they can use the power for their blessing, a power they do not possess on their own. In this respect, a *further reformulation of the blessing saying* takes the idea seriously that humans have no power over the blessing. The blessing saying is changed to the *blessing wish*: *yehî bārūk* ("may he be blessed").[31] Or, the word *bārūk* disappears completely from the blessing formula, giving way to the call for prosperity *'ašrê*,[32] after which follows the designation of the one who is blessed in a genitive construction.[33] In the same sense, though considerably less frequently, one finds *ṭôb le* ("fortunate is the one who . . . ")[34] and *ṭôb* ("fortunate is . . . ").[35]

This change of the ancient blessing formula may coincide with the belief which grew steadily over the course of history, that a real blessing was impossible for the laity. It could only come from priests. Therefore, one can maintain that the blessing saying which

---

[26]Gen 14:19; 27:29; Num 24:9; Deut 28:3-6; 33:24; 1 Sam 25:33; Isa 19:25; Jer 17:7.

[27]Gen 27:29; Num 24:9; Deut 33:24; Isa 19:25; Jer 17:7.

[28]Deut 28:3-6; 1 Sam 25:33; 26:25.

[29]Gen 14:19; Judg 17:2; 1 Sam 15:13; 23:21; 2 Sam 2:5; Ps 115:15; Ruth 2:20; 3:10; Jdt 13:18 (almost all of these examples are in the second person).

[30]Ps 118:26; see the commentary.

[31]Ruth 2:19.

[32]See S. Mowinckel, *Psalmenstudien*, vol. 5, p. 2; Hempel, ZDMG new series 4 [1925]: 23n.3.

[33]Deut 33:29; 1 Kgs 10:8; Isa 3:10; 30:18; 56:2; Pss 1:1; 2:12; 32:1, 2; 33:12; 34:9; 40:5; 41:1; 65:5; 84:5, 6, 13; 89:16; (91:1); 94:12; 106:3; 112:1; 119:1, 2; 127:5; 128:1; 137:8, 9; 144:15; 146:5; Prov 3:13; 8:34; 14:21; 16:20; 28:14; 29:18; Job 5:17-18; Dan 12:12; Qoh 10:17; Tob 13:14; Sir 14:1, 2, 20; 25:8, 9; 26:1; 28:19; 31:8; 48:11; 50:23; 4 Macc 18:9; Pss. Sol. 4:26; 5:18; 6:1; 10:1; 18:7.

[34]Ps 128:2.

[35]Ps 112:5.

is introduced with *'ašrê* was the characteristic blessing form for the laity. As H. Schmidt (*Theologische Studien und Kritiken*, 103 [1931]: 141ff) conveniently presumes, the blessing saying could well have been used in poems of greeting, as is still typical on Palestinian soil today. Its use, however, would not have been limited to those settings (see the various occasions upon which the laity speaks a blessing in ¶3). This presumption finds welcome additional evidence in the observation that the blessing saying beginning with *'ašrê* appears nowhere as the blessing of the priest, while the ancient form introduced with *bārūk* is demonstrable in examples of priestly blessings stemming precisely from the period in which only the priesthood had the privilege of carrying out a blessing.[36] The priestly formula contains the name of YHWH, as one would expect.

6. All of the blessing forms described originally existed as a predicate and subject or (with *'ašrê*) as the call to prosperity with the dependent genitive of the one being blessed. The blessing form designates the receiver of the blessing to the degree that the blessing treats *specific persons*. It suffices to have the *name*,[37] if the one receiving the blessing is addressed, or the *second person pronoun*,[38] or the *third person pronoun* if the person is not present, but is known.[39]

If no specific person is to receive the blessing, then a *more specific characteristic* is necessary using a *relative sentence*,[40] or a participle.[41] A substantive which designates the group more closely can precede these elements: *'enōš*,[42] *'ādām*,[43] *'îš*,[44] *geber*,[45] πλούσιος,[46] *gēr*,[47] and *'am*.[48] The following serve as examples: "Blessed is the man who trusts in YHWH."[49] "Salvation to all who flee to him."[50] The relative clauses and the participles are often paired together, and occasionally amassed in groups.[51] If these forms do not

---

[36]Pss 115:15; 118:26; see the commentary.

[37]Gen 14:19; Isa 19:25; Deut 33:24; cf. Deut 28:4,5.

[38]Deut 28:3,6; Judg 17:2; 1 Sam 15:13; 23:21; 25:33; 26:25; 2 Sam 2:5; Ps 115:15; Ruth 3:10; Jdt 13:18.

[39]Ruth 2:20. The same is true for *'ašrê*: Deut 33:29; 1 Kgs 10:8; Ps 128:2; Isa 32:20.

[40]1 Sam 25:33; 2 Sam 2:5; Isa 56:2; Jer 17:7; Pss 1:1; 32:2; 33:12; 34:9; 40:5; 65:5; 84:6; 94:12; 112:1; 137:8, 9; 144:15; 146:5; Prov 3:13; Job 5:17; Qoh 10:17; Tob 13:14; Sir 14:1, 2, 20; 25:8, 9 (LXX); 31:8; 50:28; Pss. Sol. 5:18; 6:1; 10:1.

[41]Gen 27:29; Num 24:9; 1 Kgs 10:8; Isa 30:18; 32:20; 56:2; Pss 2:12; 32:1; 41:2; 84:5,13; 89:16; 91:1-2; 106:3; 112:1,5; 118:26; 119:1, 2; 127:5; 128:1; Prov 8:32, 34; 28:14; Dan 12:12; Tob 13:14; Sir 28:19 (LXX); 48:11; 50:28; Pss. Sol. 4:26; 18:7.

[42]Job 5:17; Isa 56:2; Sir 14:1, 20.

[43]Ps 84:6,13; Prov 3:13; 8:34; 28:14.

[44]Pss 1:1; 112:1, 5; Sir 14:2; 50:28.

[45]Jer 17:7; Pss 34:9; 40:5; 94:12; 127:5.

[46]Sir 31:8.

[47]Ps 33:12.

[48]Pss 89:16; 144:15.

[49]Jer 17:7.

[50]Ps 2:12.

[51]1 Kgs 10:8; Isa 32:20; 56:2; Pss 1:1; 32:1-2; 33:12; 40:5; 65:5; 84:6; 89:16; 91:1-2; 94:12; 106:3; 112:1; 119:1-2; 128:1; 146:5; Prov 3:13.

yet characterize the one receiving the blessing, then extended *main clauses*[52] or an *infinitive with le* can be attached.[53]

7. The relative clause and participles frequently express the *reason why* one should receive the blessing. See 1 Sam 25:33 ("Blessed are you, who have hindered me today from bringing blood guilt upon myself, and who have helped me by your own hand."), 2 Sam 2:5 ("Blessed are you by YHWH, for you have done this kindness to Saul your lord, and buried him."), or 1 Kgs 10:8 ("Salvation to your 'wives,' and to your servants who stand continually before you that they may hear your wisdom.").

The ever increasing association of the blessing with YHWH apparently explains why the blessing, as it appears in the examples preserved for us, is used almost exclusively for the *challenges which YHWH religion holds for humans*. The relative sentences and the participles portray the *ideal image of Israelite piety*. Whoever receives YHWH's blessing, does not turn to foreign gods.[54] Rather, that person fears and worships only YHWH,[55] while trusting[56] YHWH without deviating.[57] That person willingly and gratefully sings as a warning to teach about his God.[58] He also rejoices when YHWH forgives his transgression.[59] He really seeks to remain innocent by word and deed,[60] and he avoids the company of sinners.[61] He joyfully immerses himself in God's law and God's command as the measuring rods for the way he conducts his life.[62] The details of a pious way of life are named as examples, including: faithfully keeping the sabbath, caring for justice, meekness toward the poor, and last but not least, the dynamic participation in the well-being and the woes of his people.[63] Finally, wisdom poetry recognizably influences the blessing saying.[64] The wisdom and insight which the pious attain through YHWH's instruction characterize him.[65]

The people of YHWH also appear in these formulas as the receivers of the blessing. They received the blessing not so much because they met the challenges of YHWH religion, but because of the special distinction which they experienced by YHWH's *election*.[66] They are praised as fortunate because YHWH is the God who helps them,[67] who allowed them

---

[52] Pss 1:2; 89:16b, 17.
[53] Prov 8:34.
[54] Ps 40:5.
[55] Pss 112:1; 128:1; Prov 28:14; Pss. Sol. 6:1.
[56] Pss 2:12; 34:9; 40:5; 84:6,13; 91:2; 146:5; Isa 30:18; Jer 17:7.
[57] Sir 14:2.
[58] Ps 94:12; Job 5:17; Pss. Sol. 10:1.
[59] Ps 32:1-2.
[60] Ps 32:2; Isa 56:2; Sir 25:8; 31:8.
[61] Ps 1:1.
[62] Pss 1:2; 112:1; 119:1-2; 128:1; see Prov 8:32.
[63] Isa 56:2; Pss 41:2; 106:3; 112:5; Tob 13:14.
[64] §10, ¶6.
[65] Prov 3:13; Sir 14:20; 25:8; 50:28; see Prov 8:34.
[66] Pss 33:12; 65:5; 144:15.
[67] Pss 146:5; see 91:1.

entry,[68] in whose house they may spend time,[69] and about whom they rejoice and celebrate.[70]

8. The form of the blessing saying described in ¶¶4-7 was occasionally somewhat *expanded.*[71] These expansions wish to explain *the extent to which* the one receiving the blessing should be praised as fortunate. Accordingly, they allow one to recognize the *content of the blessing.* They can be introduced with *kî* ("for"),[72] but they can also be attached without any introductory causal conjunction.[73] Since these sentences usually speak of the future, they generally appear in the future tense with either the imperfect[74] or the *perfectum consecutivum.*[75] Characteristically, this final form of the blessing saying preserves the words of the blessing in the character of a promise. The pious laity of the postexilic period are not able to do more than point to the promise which pious conduct should praise. There is no longer any trace of the idea that the pious one can create the blessing by speaking a magically effectual word. Even the more decisive form of the blessing wish is abandoned: "Salvation belongs to the man who fears, who really loves his commandments. His see will be famous in the land. The pious generation will be blessed. Wealth and riches are in his house and his righteousness exists forever."[76] "Happy is the one who dwells in the shade of the highest, who hides in the shadow of the almighty, (who speaks) to YHWH: 'my refuge and fortress, my God, whom I trust.' For he will deliver you from the net of the bird-catcher, (or the grave of) corruption, etc."[77] If Nicolsky had used the genre contexts somewhat more carefully with his "magical" interpretation of Ps 91, he would have avoided the danger of generalizing his observations about the magical character of individual ideas and expressions, and conceiving the entire psalm as an oath formula.

The promise of blessing may have proceeded from the *blessing wish,*[78] which is often attached to the blessing saying.[79] Evidence for this conclusion may also be found in the fact that the "promise of blessing," just like the "blessing wish," often used second person address.[80] The development which can be observed in the context of the blessing saying, perhaps also affected the blessing wish. Pss 15:5 and 24:5 are promises of blessing.[81]

9. The *blessing wish* was mentioned at the conclusion of the previous section. This form characteristically betrays a *level of uncertainty in the speaker's confidence in his own capacity for blessing.* Originally, the wish formula may have been valued the same as the

---

[68]Ps 118:26.

[69]Ps 84:5.

[70]Ps 89:16.

[71]Pss 1:3; 41:2-4; 89:18; 91:3ff; 112:2-3, 6-8; 127:5; 128:2-4; Isa 3:10; Jer 17:7; Prov 3:14; 8:35; Sir 28:20; Tob 13:14; Pss. Sol. 6:2ff; 10:2.

[72]Pss 89:18; 91:3; 112:6; 128:2; Prov 3:14; 8:35; Isa 3:10; Tob 13:14; Sir 50:28; Pss. Sol. 10:2.

[73]Jer 17:7; Pss 1:3; 41:2-4; 112:2-3.

[74]Pss 41:2-4; 112:2-3; 127:5; 128:2.

[75]Ps 1:1; Jer 17:7.

[76]Ps 112:1-3.

[77]Ps 91:1ff. (The text is somewhat different in the commentary.)

[78]Cf. ¶9.

[79]Deut 33:24; 1 Sam 26:25 (?); 2 Sam 2:5-6; etc.

[80]Pss 91:3-13; 128:2.

[81]See ¶9.

imperative form of the blessing, or at least have stood very close to it.[82] One should then translate it as, "It should be." However, the jussive increasingly attains the significance of a wish to the degree that one becomes aware that humans are unable to bless effectively by their own power. Accordingly, it should be rendered, "May it be."

The effectiveness of the blessing wish also did not originally require a connection to YHWH. The following examples illustration how close the blessing wish originally stood to the imperative blessing: "Blessed is Jael before women; before the women in the tent she is blessed (Judg 5:24). "Blessed is the house of your servant forever (2 Sam 7:29)."[83] The *structure of the blessing wish* contains the third or second person *passive jussive in the first position*. The *one receiving the blessing* follows as the *subject*. This form appears in reverse order *in the active*, where the one receiving the blessing appears as the object (cf. Gen 27:29: "The nations shall serve you; nations will bow down before you.").

The blessing wish, with the human uncertainty, accommodated to the association of the blessing to YHWH. His *name, powerful enough for miracles*, enters the formula. Only the name guarantees the blessing's effectiveness. The form of the blessing wish is rephrased in characteristic fashion so that YHWH *appears everywhere* as the *subject*, while the one receiving the blessing is consistently referenced as the object.[84] Usually, as in the original form, the jussive stands at the beginning, followed by the name of YHWH. The object of the blessing follows again: "May YHWH bless you and protect you (Num 6:24)." "May YHWH bless you from Zion (Pss 128:5; 134:3)." The verb appearing in the blessing wish is *bērek* ("bless").[85] It is occasionally expanded with a prepositional clause which clarifies the content of the blessing.[86] Other verbs also appear which *describe the content of the blessing*.[87] This form of the blessing wish, reformulated under the influence of YHWH religion, did not supplant the older forms of the blessing. As such, it witnesses to the tenacity with which the more primitive concepts were maintained as undercurrents. They often appear in connection with the form of the blessing wish just described. These more primitive concepts, however, are subordinated, bringing their originally disconnected intention into line with the belief that only YHWH is effective. See Gen 27:28ff: "May God give to you from the dew of heaven and from the fat of the earth and an abundance of grain and wine. May peoples serve you and nations fall down before you."[88] Even the imperative form of the blessing was preserved in this context (cf. Gen 27:28ff), where the citation continues: "be a hero for your brother." The same is true for Ps 128:5, 6. ¶8 already noted that the blessing wish occasionally becomes a simple promise of blessing, perhaps influenced by the blessing saying.

10. At least in the later period, the blessing wish appears to be the characteristic *priestly form* for communicating a blessing.[89] As far as one can observe, primitive blessing

---

[82]So S. Mowinckel, *Psalmenstudien*, vol. 5, p. 30.

[83]See also Gen 24:60; 27:29.

[84]Hempel, *ZDMG* new series 4 [1925]: 60ff.

[85]Gen 28:3; 48:16; Num 6:24; Deut 1:11; Pss 29:11; 115:12-14; 128:5; 134:3.

[86]Cf. Ps 29:11.

[87]Gen 28:3b-4; Num 6:25-26; Deut 1:11; Pss 29:11; 118:27; 121:7-8.

[88]Gen 48:16c provides a further example.

[89]Num 6:24-26; 1 Sam 2:20; Pss 115:12-14; 118:27; 121:7-8; 134:3; see the commentary to the Psalm passages.

formulas do not occur without the name YHWH in the blessing wishes which the priest expresses at the holy site. That is no accident. The core of Israelite religion manifests a sharp sense for that which is inwardly inconsistent with faith in YHWH. The *suppression* of other blessing forms can be explained by this attribute. The blessing saying, with the introduction *bārūk leyahwēh*, which originally belonged to the priest,[90] recedes noticeably behind the blessing wish, not to mention the imperative form of the blessing. The recognition that YHWH alone has the power to effect blessing becomes increasingly stronger. As a result, only the blessing wish appears in connection with the service of YHWH.

11. The *content* of the blessing, in the various formulas, encompasses everything which can make life stronger and richer. The blessing should bestow *life and success,*[91] peaceful, undisturbed *sleep,*[92] *numerous descendants,*[93] *success for all plans,*[94] *health and wealth,*[95] and *fame and prestige.*[96] The blessing should provide *protection and victory,*[97] *protection from harm,*[98] *healing from sickness,*[99] *deliverance on the day of judgment,*[100] and deliverance and prestige before enemies.[101] In short, the blessing can be expressed in one word: *šālôm.*[102]

The same content which was already characteristic of the blessing in its primitive stage comes to expression in the blessing forms described above.[103] The conceptual changes have not eliminated the content concerning the origin of the operative power of the blessing. That which the blessing sought to create in its original form was also the concern later. In the course of the history of the Israelite religion, however, other concerns entered which attest to the infiltration of a *richer and deeper piety*. The content of the blessing for these other concerns includes YHWH's pleasure,[104] and the application of his *grace and faithfulness.*[105] Or, the one who is blessed may see his desire by rejoicing over Jerusalem's good fortune[106] and over the majesty of the city of God.[107] The idea that the one who is blessed is protected from committing a sin leads even deeper. The one who is blessed will find *purification* if he does fall into sin.[108]

---

[90]See ¶5 above.

[91]Ps 1:3; Jer 17:8; 41:3; Prov 8:34; Sir 48:11.

[92]Ps 6:3.

[93]Pss 112:2; 128:3, 6.

[94]Pss 1:3; 41:3; 128:1; Isa 3:10; Deut 33:24; 1 Sam 26:5; Sir 50:28; Pss. Sol. 6:2.

[95]Ps 112:3.

[96]Pss 112:2; 127:5; Deut 33:24.

[97]Pss 89:18; 91:4.

[98]Pss 41:3; 91:5; 121:7-8; Pss. Sol. 6:2.

[99]Ps 41:3.

[100]Pss 41:2; 91:3; Pss. Sol. 6:1.

[101]Pss 41:4; 91:7ff; 127:5.

[102]Ps 29:11.

[103]Cf. S. Mowinckel, *Psalmenstudien*, vol. 5, pp. 5ff; Hempel, *ZDMG* new series 4 [1925]: 47ff.

[104]Prov 8:34; Pss. Sol. 6:9; 10:3.

[105]2 Sam 2:6.

[106]Ps 128:5.

[107]Tob 13:14.

[108]Pss. Sol. 10:1.

12. Various human desires are expressed in the words of blessing. These desires include the immediate necessities of everyday life as well as the concern for a deeper spirituality. This variation shows that we are dealing with a genre which was *widely known in Israel* and which enjoyed *great popularity*. Another observation leads to the same conclusion. The words of blessing appear nowhere as independent psalms. This fact is understandable because this genre is not a lyric genre. However, in spite of the fact that the words of blessing did not originate in psalmic poetry, they have acquired a home in psalmic poetry to an astonishing degree. They found their way into the various psalm genres. They always appear in the developed forms, never in the simple ones.

The blessing saying is found in the *hymn*,[109] in the *communal thanksgiving song*,[110] in the *communal complaint song* with a hymnic entry,[111] in the individual thanksgiving song,[112] in the *royal enthronement song*,[113] in *poetic curses*,[114] in *mixed poetry*,[115] in *liturgies*,[116] and especially in the wisdom poetry.[117] The blessing wish appears in the *pilgrimage song*,[118] in the *wisdom song*,[119] and in mixed poetry.[120] More frequently, after it lost its original character, the blessing wish entered the *petition* of the *individual complaint song* (§6, ¶15). However, it had a special place in the liturgies.[121]

13. Various causes have led to the intrusion of the words of blessing into the psalm genres mentioned. For the *hymn*, the *indirect praise of* YHWH comes into view. It pulls the *blessing saying* into the genre, which praises the pious and the people who have a powerful and helpful God like YHWH (§2, ¶32). Starting from the hymn, the blessing saying penetrates other genres in which the hymn had achieved influence. By this mediation, the blessing saying entered the *hymnically* fashioned *summons of the communal complaint* (§4, ¶12), thus entering the *hymnically* expanded conclusion of the communal thanksgiving song (§8, ¶37).

The cause for the *individual thanksgiving song* is somewhat different. Here, the blessing saying appears in place of the *confession* which is closely related to the hymn by form and content. It also attained its position under the influence of the hymn (§7, ¶8). However, for inclusion in the genre, the intention of the thanksgiving song itself is essentially decisive. The one offering thanks wishes to *strengthen and comfort* those suffering with him by telling of his deliverance. His experience is only one example for how YHWH helps his pious ones in general (§7, ¶5). Thus, "salvation belongs to the one

---

[109]Pss 33:12; 65:5; 84:5, 6, 13; 89:16; 146:5; (§2, ¶32).
[110]Ps 144:12-15; cf. Ps 65; see the commentary (§8, ¶37).
[111]Ps 106:3.
[112]Pss 32:1-3; 34:9; 40:5; 41:2-4 (§7, ¶8).
[113]Ps 2:12.
[114]Ps 137:8-9.
[115]Pss 94:12; 119:1-2; (§11, ¶11).
[116]Pss 115:15; 118:26; (§11, ¶24).
[117]Pss 1:1-3; 91:1-13; 112:1; 127:3-5; 128:1; Pss. Sol. 6:1; 10:1; (§10, ¶6).
[118]Ps 122:6-7; (§8, ¶22).
[119]Ps 128:5-6.
[120]Ps 129:8.
[121]Pss 15:5; 24:5-6; 115:12-15; 118:27a; 121:7-8; 134:3; (§11, ¶20, 21, 22, 24).

who flees to him." The *blessed fate of the pious* pulls the blessing saying into the thanksgiving song. The experiences of thanksgiving song's singer confirms this fate.

The same element operated even more strongly in the connection between the *blessing saying and wisdom poetry*. Wisdom poetry likes to concern itself with the pious. It *describes* his essence, and speaks of the *reward* that awaits him (§10, ¶6). However, this mood corresponds to the blessing saying by content and form. The relative sentences and participles contain nothing more than a *description of the pious righteous person*. Also, the significance of the sentences which express the *content* of the blessing is nothing more than *promises of reward* that will come to the righteous one (cf. ¶8). The fact that both genres prefer to speak in the second person connects them even more closely. Therefore, the blessing saying becomes the specific form for which *wisdom poetry* shows a certain preference.[122]

The appearance of the blessing saying is completely understandable in *liturgies*, which stem from the cult.[123] The priestly blessing has a fixed place in these liturgies. The fact that the blessing saying is found in *mixed poetry* is not astounding given its popularity.

By contrast, the *blessing wish* has exhibited a considerably *narrower influence* on psalmody, as the overview in ¶12 demonstrated. The frequent connection of the blessing saying and the blessing wish helps to explain the fact that the blessing wish appears in the wisdom song of Ps 128 which adopted the form of the blessing saying (cf. ¶8). The dominant dissolution of fixed genres explains the appearance of the blessing wish in *mixed poetry* (Ps 129). The pilgrimage song adopts the blessing wish in places where the pilgrim expresses *pious wishes* for the place of his desire (Ps 122). The influence of the blessing wish was strongest in the *individual complaint song* because it accommodates to the petition by content, intention, and form. Of course, by consolidating with the individual complaint song, the blessing wish lost its original essence. It became a *wishful petition* (§6, ¶15). By contrast, the blessing wish appears in *liturgies* in the actual sense of the word. The reason was treated with that of the blessing saying (see above).

14. The counterpart to the blessing, the curse, exercised far *less influence* on psalmody as illustrated in the breadth of its effect. It is found as an independent entity in Ps 119:21 and Ps 137 (see also Pss 1:4ff; 112:10). Elsewhere, by losing its original essence it enters the petition of the *individual and communal complaint song*.[124] The curse shares all the characteristics of the blessing. Like the blessing, it worked originally by its own power as a *magical word*. It knew no connection to YHWH and was an *independent power* over which the one cursing no longer had any control once he spoke the curse. The goal of the curse is to cause pain, and to hamper and destroy life.[125]

Originally, anyone could curse and bless. The curse is the weapon of one who was robbed against an unknown thief,[126] of the slave against his master,[127] of the hungry

---

[122]Cf. §10, ¶6.

[123]§11, ¶20, 21, 22, 24.

[124]See §6, ¶15 and §4, ¶8.

[125]Cf. S. Mowinckel, *Psalmenstudien*, vol. 5, pp. 61ff; Hempel, *ZDMG* new series 4 [1925]: 47ff.

[126]Judg 17:2.

[127]Prov 30:10.

against the king,[128] and the fugitive against his persecutor.[129] The curse also had its place in the cult as one can see by comparing Num 5 and Deut 27.

15. With regard to the relatively minor influence of the curse upon psalmody, these suggestions will suffice. Now, we turn to the *forms of the curse* and differentiate between the curse saying and the curse wish.

The curse saying corresponds completely to the blessing saying in its structure. Like the latter, the curse saying has an indicative form. It is introduced by the predicate *'ārūr* ("cursed is . . . ").[130] A *softening* of the curse into a woe saying beginning with *'ôy* ("woe") does not occur frequently.[131] The curse was preserved in its essence with more tenacity than the blessing, as demonstrated by the fact that the *name of* YHWH *did not enter* the curse saying, much in contrast to the blessing saying.[132] Only one form ("cursed before [*lifnê*] YHWH is") shows a very reserved connection between the name of YHWH and the curse saying.[133] As in the blessing saying, the subject follows the entry formula. Here the subject is the one who is cursed addressed in the second person.[134] If the subject is not self-evident, it is marked by relative sentences[135] or participles,[136] as in the blessing saying. Similarly, substantives can be used which state the cursed one more precisely: *hā'îš*,[137] *haggeber*.[138] As with the blessing saying, main clauses can be attached which more closely describe the *content* of the curse.[139] These clauses generally have the form of the curse wish. With its indicative character, this form may be the original continuation of the curse saying. However, these clauses confirm what has become[140] or will become[141] of the bewildered one by means of the curse. They address the one who is cursed, preferring the second person, like the sentences of the blessing saying.[142] By contrast, connections using *kî* are infrequent (Isa 3:11).

16. The curse saying itself was not made dependent upon the power of YHWH. However, since the curse saying is frequently directed against that which breaks the legal ordinances protected by YHWH,[143] there is a relationship between the curse saying and YHWH. This starting point led to a further development, in which the curse was also

---

[128]Isa 8:21.

[129]Judg 9:20, 29. See details in Hempel, *ZDMG* new series 4 [1925]: 39ff.

[130]Gen 3:14,17; 4:11; 9:25; 27:29; Num 24:9; Deut 27:15-26; 28:16-19; Josh 6:26; 9:23; Judg 21:18; 1 Sam 14:24, 28; 26:19; Jer 11:3; 17:5; 20:14, 15; 48:10; Mal 1:14; Tob 13:12.

[131]Num 21:29; Isa 3:11; Jer 13:27; 48:46; Ezek 24:6, 9; Sir 2:12, 13, 14; 41:8; see S. Mowinckel, Psalmenstudien, vol. 5, p. 2.

[132]Hempel, *ZDMG* new series 4 [1925]: 66.

[133]1 Sam 26:19; Josh 6:26.

[134]Gen 3:14; 4:11; Deut 28:16,19; Josh 9:23; Num 24:9; Jer 13:27; 48:46; Sir 2:14; 41:8.

[135]Deut 27:15,26; Josh 6:26; 1 Sam 14:14, 28; Jer 11:3; 17:5; 20:14, 15.

[136]Deut 27:16-25; Judg 21:18; Jer 48:10; Mal 1:14; Tob 13:12; Ps 119:21.

[137]Deut 27:15; Josh 6:26; 1 Sam 14:14, 28; Jer 11:3; 20:14.

[138]Jer 17:5; *hayyôm* in Jer 20:14.

[139]Gen 3:14, 17; 4:12; 9:25; Num 21:29; Josh 6:26; 9:23; Jer 13:27; 17:6; 20:14; 48:46; Sir 2:13; 41:8.

[140]Num 21:29; Jer 48:46.

[141]Jer 13:27; 17:6; Sir 2:13; 41:9.

[142]Gen 3:14,17; 4:12; Num 21:29; Josh 9:23; Jer 13:27; 48:46; Sir 41:9.

[143]Deut 27:15ff.

directed against those who do not meet the moral and *religious commands* which the worship of YHWH requires. The relative clauses and participles thereby *portray the godless* and provide a counterpart to the *description of the pious* in the blessing saying. This element includes the one who humbles the widow and the orphan, destroys boundary lines, or other things which Deut 27 considers legal faults. In addition, it includes anyone who worships idols,[144] who trusts in his own power and deviates from YHWH,[145] who loses trust in YHWH,[146] who abandons hope and patience,[147] who acts treacherously in YHWH's service,[148] or who acts suggestively.[149] In short, this element includes anyone who leaves the law of the almighty[150] for a word of the wicked.[151]

The curse saying is often coordinated with the blessing saying.[152] Originally, this connection would have sought to keep the word from causing pain to himself and his own.[153]

17. In contrast to the blessing saying, the curse saying scarcely penetrated psalmody. The majority of psalm genres offer no presuppositions for its acceptance. The communal and individual complaint songs come the closest to doing so, because the repulsion and the destruction of the enemy is one goal which they would share with the curse. The reason the complaint songs do not take up the curse lies in the fact that the curse saying, in contrast to the blessing saying, continually resisted being subjugated to YHWH.

The curse saying did gain a foothold in *mixed poetry* and in the *wisdom song*. Its appearance in mixed poetry was enabled by the blending of the boundaries of the old genres which were characteristic of this stage of psalmody. Nevertheless, the curse saying is rare in these places as well. The psalms preserved for us contain only one example (Ps 119:21).

The influence of the curse saying upon *wisdom poetry* is greater, but even there it remains considerably in the background. The curse saying coincides with the wisdom poetry in that it offers a practical *description of the godless* and his destiny. Specifically, the combination of blessing and curse, with its contrast of the pious and the godless, paved the way for the curse in wisdom poetry.[154]

However, one should also note that even in wisdom poetry, the curse saying, in the final analysis, was still perceived as something *foreign*. Especially in the psalms, the curse saying appears to be altered at the decisive point. Instead of *'ārūr* or *'ôy*, one finds "It is nothing for you" (*šāwū lākēm*),[155] or a statement stylizing the essence and fate of the

---

[144]Deut 27:15.

[145]Jer 17:6.

[146]Sir 2:13.

[147]Sir 2:14.

[148]Jer 48:10; cf. Mal 1:14.

[149]Sir 2:13.

[150]Sir 41:8; Deut 27:26; Jer 11:3; Ps 119:21.

[151]Isa 3:11; Sir 2:13; cf. Ps 119:21.

[152]Gen 9:25-26; 27:29; Num 24:9; Deut 28:3ff; Jer 17:5-8; Tob 13:12; Isa 3:10-11; cf. S. Mowinckel, *Psalmenstudien*, vol. 5, pp. 2, 97ff.

[153]Hempel, *ZDMG* new series 4 [1925]: 37ff.

[154]Isa 3:10-11; Jer 17:5-8.

[155]Ps 127:2; see the commentary.

godless. Cf. Ps 1:4ff: "The wicked are not like this, no they are not. They are like the chaff which the wind scatters. Therefore, the wicked will not remain in judgment, nor sinners in the righteous community, for YHWH knows the state of the righteous, but 'the hope' of the wicked is lost." Ps 112:10 describes the end of the godless quite similarly.

18. The structure of the *curse wish* corresponds to its counterpart, the blessing wish. It begins with the third person jussive. The designation of the cursed one follows as the subject: "Thus may your enemies perish, YHWH."[156] "Let him be the lowest servant to his brothers."[157] The usual order can be changed to accent the subject or the predicate noun (cf. Gen 9:26). The one being cursed also appears as the object: "Let fire go forth from Abimelek and devour the lords of Shechem . . . and let fire go forth from the lords of Shechem and devour Abimelek (Judg 9:25)."[158] The second person address appears less often in the various forms of the curse wish.[159] However, this sparsity could be due to the random nature of the material preserved. The self-curse of the oath naturally uses the first person: "If my steps depart from the path, or my heart goes after my eyes . . . let me sow and another reap."[160]

Both curses and blessings possess *power to infect another*. Anyone coming in contact with one who is cursed will himself share in the curse.[161] This belief is validated by the formula of the curse wish. It happens in a way which wishes for the opponent the same fate as one mentioned specifically by name who had been particularly visibly affected by the curse. The power of the curse wish to infect was communicated by inserting the curse-laden name. This power to infect proceeds from the one who is cursed. Jer 29:22 provides an example: "May YHWH make you like Zedekiah and Ahab who the king of Babylon roasted in fire."[162]

While the curse saying tenaciously preserved the ancient self-possessed power of the curse, YHWH religion influenced the curse wish. This influence is recognizable in the fact that the name of YHWH entered the formula. The effectiveness of the curse was derived from its power (cf. Jer 29:22). This change becomes understandable when one considers that the form of the wish allows one to recognize doubt in the effectiveness of the self-possessed power to curse (cf. ¶9).

19. In psalmody, the curse wish appears in its original manner only in Ps 137, a relatively late poem that arises from the time of the loosening and the mixing of fixed genres. The psalm begins like a communal complaint song. The poem then turns to hymnic tones so that it may finally speak of wild vengeance for Jerusalem's enemies. Curses are expressed (137:4-6) in the form of the self-curse mentioned above: "If I forget you, Jerusalem, may my right hand 'fail' and my tongue cleave to the roof of my mouth if I do not think of you." At the end one finds a blessing saying in a terrible reversal of the original meaning. The blessing saying concerns those who exercise cruel vengeance

---

[156]Judg 5:31.
[157]Gen 9:26.
[158]See also Num 5:22; 1 Kgs 2:32, 33.
[159]Num 5:21; Josh 7:25.
[160]Job 31:8. See also Job 31:10, 22, 40a.
[161]See 1 Sam 14:33; and the treatment by Hempel, *ZDMG* new series 4 [1925]: 30.
[162]See Hempel, *ZDMG* new series 4 [1925]: 67.

upon Jerusalem's enemy Babylon: "Blessed is the one who recompenses you; blessed is the one who seizes and smashes your children on the rocks" (137:8, 9).

However, the intervening piece (137:7) which comes between the curse wish and the blessing saying is no longer a curse. The material and intention may agree with the curse, but one has abandoned the magical underpinnings. The words have the form of a *petition* for YHWH to recompense: "Remember the sons of Edom for the day of Jerusalem. They said, 'Tear it down. Tear it down to the ground.' "

Thus, we noted the entry of the curse wish into the *individual and communal complaint song*. Often, the content and intention of the curse appear in the form of *a petition directed to YHWH* (as in Ps 137).[163] In so doing, it sometimes introduces someone who is particularly well known as being cursed (see above). "May it be for them as for Sisera, as for Jabin on the streams of Kishon, 'as at Midian,' which was recompensed by 'Encharod,' and became dung for the field." 'Make' the nobles like Orebe and all their princes like Zeeb."[164] However, this form is part of the last stage of the reformulation of the curse wish which resulted in its adoption into the genres already mentioned. The *entry of the curse wish in its original form* precedes this form. Its entry was made possible by the fact that the curse wish was closely associated in form and content with a particular type of petition, the wishful petition. When it became associated with the petition of the complaint song, the curse wish lost its ancient characteristic essence and turned into the petition itself.[165]

II. The Pilgrimage Song

W. Staerk, "Lyrik,"[2] in *Schriften des A.T. in Auswahl*, vol 3/1, 1920, pp. 245-47.

20. From antiquity, pilgrimages to the holy site were among the worship obligations for the Israelite.[166] Every male Israelite was commanded to go three times a year to the great festival to look upon YHWH's countenance. This command proved to be impossible relatively early, perhaps because of the distance. As a result, in Shilo *one pilgrimage* a year sufficed.[167] After Jerusalem became the only sanctuary of YHWH, it was completely impossible for many to make the long trip to the dwelling of YHWH on a regular basis during the year. The less frequently a pious individual was able to go to Jerusalem, the more his *desire* burned for the holy site.[168] He would have felt fortunate when his desire to see YHWH's sanctuary was fulfilled.[169] It is self-evident that the pilgrim acted with those of like mind. One traveled to Jerusalem with others at the same time, to the same festival so as to minimize the danger to a lone traveler.[170]

---

[163]Cf. §6, ¶15 and §4, ¶8.

[164]Ps 83:10; see Hempel, *ZDMG* new series 4 [1925]: 67.

[165]See details in §6, ¶15. For the content of the curse, consult §6, ¶15 and Hempel, *ZDMG* new series 4 [1925]: 47ff.

[166]Exod 23:17; 34:23; Deut 16:16.

[167]1 Sam 1:3, 21; 2:19.

[168]Jonah 2:5; Pss 42:5; 43:3; 63:3; 84:3, 5-6, 11; 87.

[169]Pss 122 and 84.

[170]See Luke 2:41 and the commentary to Ps 122 on p. 542.

This situation led to an independent minor genre, the pilgrimage song. Only one complete example, Ps 122, is preserved in Psalms, albeit in a later form. Ps 84 is closely related to it by content. Traces of pilgrimage songs are still found in Isa 2:3 (=Mic 4:2); Jer 31:6; and perhaps also Isa 30:29b (unless the latter simply speaks of a procession).[171] The very narrow condition of preserved examples makes it impossible to draw a precise picture of the genre. Nevertheless, the following can be recognized:

21. One sang these pilgrimage songs at the *beginning* of the pilgrimage when fellow travelers had gathered,[172] and at journey's destination after they entered the city of their common desire.[173] No examples show that these songs were sung along the way, but that is nevertheless probable.

The *content* provides all the *feelings and ideas* which the pilgrims fulfill. The first thing mentioned here is the *desire to go to Zion*,[174] the desire to see YHWH.[175] The content continually expresses the blessings and gifts of YHWH that one expects.[176] One voices the *praise of Jerusalem* as the center for the people of YHWH.[177] Envy is aroused for those who are able to linger continually in the holy site.[178] In the song voiced by the pilgrims when they reach their goal, one also finds the *recollection* of the completed journey which YHWH has graciously allowed to succeed.[179] The successful journey validates the *overwhelming impression of the city, its reliable fortifications, and its inspiring history.*[180]

The lack of older pilgrimage songs in complete form scarcely allows one to say anything regarding how the contents were formed. This much is clear. Originally a *group* spoke, which corresponds to the situation of the pilgrimage.[181] *Introductions* lead to the *main part* of the pilgrimage song. These introductions proceed from the concrete situation as with the hymn and the communal and individual thanksgiving songs. Introductions to pilgrimage songs from the beginning of the pilgrimage have been preserved. They use the first person plural cohortative form: "Let us go up" (na'ălleh);[182] "Let us go" (nelek).[183] A brief imperative with the meaning of an interjection of joy can begin: "go" (lekū,[184] qūmū[185]). The *destination* of the pilgrimage immediately follows the cohortative with *'el*: YHWH's house,[186] Zion,[187] YHWH's mountain,[188] or YHWH himself.[189]

---

[171]However, see the commentary to Ps 122.
[172]Isa 2:3; Mic 4:2; Jer 31:6; Ps 122:1b.
[173]Pss 122:2; see 84:3.
[174]Isa 2:3; Mic 4:2; Jer 31:6; Ps 84:2-3.
[175]Ps 84:8.
[176]Isa 2:3; Mic 4:2.
[177]Ps 122:3.
[178]Ps 84:5-6, 11.
[179]Ps 84:6-8.
[180]Ps 122:5, 6, 7.
[181]Isa 2:3; Mic 4:2; Jer 31:6; see also Pss 84:6-8; 122:2, 6.
[182]Isa 2:3; Mic 4:2; Jer 31:6.
[183]Ps 122:1.
[184]Isa 2:3; Mic 4:3.
[185]Jer 31:6.
[186]Ps 122:1; Isa 2:3; Mic 4:2.
[187]Jer 31:6.
[188]Isa 2:3; Mic 4:2.

22. The pilgrimage song increasingly expresses the feelings of an *individual*.[190] Perhaps this tendency should be associated with the desire to go to Zion which is so powerfully stated precisely in individual poems.[191] At this stage, forms originally foreign to the pilgrimage song entered, including: the *blessing saying* introduced with *'ašrê*,[192] the *blessing wish*,[193] the *portrayal of desire* which stemmed from the *individual complaint song*,[194] and consideration of the pious that operated in *wisdom poetry* (§10, ¶6).[195] One cannot deny the location of the situation of the contents and forms of expression which the genre experienced. On the other hand the mixing does lead to the dissolution of the original fixed forms and to the blurring of boundaries with other genres. As a result, the material and forms of the pilgrimage song wandered into another genre where the *enthusiasm for YHWH's sanctuary* also stood at the center, namely the Zion song. The Zion song also no longer knew the stringent forms of the hymn (§2, ¶52). Ps 84 preserves an example of this development.

Like other psalm genres, the pilgrimage song finally experienced a *change into an eschatological song*. Prophecy took control of it in order to lend its proclamations more vivid expression. YHWH comforts his people. In the future, one will again sing on Ephraim's mountain: "Go! Let us go up to Zion, to YHWH our God."[196] The prophets' keen expectation finds expression in the pilgrimage song that the peoples will turn to YHWH at the end of the days. Then they will come together and sing: "Go. Let us go up to YHWH's mountain, to the house of the God of Jacob. Let him teach us his ways, so that we may walk in his paths, for instruction goes forth from Zion and YHWH's word from Jerusalem."[197]

III. The Victory Song

23. Among Israel's experiences which found echoes in song, the *victory* was by no means least. The military sense of the people and the people's poetic gift demonstrate that victories became the subject of a particular genre, the *victory song*.[198] The goal of the victory song was to *laud the famous deeds of war* and to *praise the heroes* (see the examples given below). However, the purely secular mood of the victory song in the end did not agree with Israel's religion. No matter how powerfully the heroes may have performed, Israel knew that YHWH was the ultimate reason for victory. Trusting in YHWH's powerful state, the king and the people entered into battle.[199] As a result, it is consistent with the inner essence of Israel's religion that a form of the victory song arose in Israel which gives honor for the victory only to YHWH. We have no complete examples preserved of

---

[189]Jer 31:6.
[190]Pss 122:1, 8, 9; 84:3, 11.
[191]Jonah 2:5; Pss 42:5; 43:3f; 63:3; etc.
[192]Ps 84:5, 6.
[193]Pss 122:6f; cf. ¶12.
[194]Ps 84:3.
[195]Ps 84:11.
[196]Jer 31:6.
[197]Isa 2:3; Mic 4:2.
[198]Preserved examples include: Gen 4:23ff; 1 Sam 18:7; Judg 5.
[199]Cf. §4, ¶10; §5, ¶6.

this religious victory song. We have only bridge pieces, and most of these appear in later poetry.[200] Because of these circumstances it is not possible to provide a clear and penetrating description of the genre. We can, however, attain a certain image of the genre.

24. The situation in which the victory song belongs is the victory celebration. The victory celebration does not appear to be bound to a specific site based on the preserved reports. The simplest explanation, and also the most natural based upon the situation, is that the celebration took place before those of those who witnessed the victory: on the *battlefield*,[201] on the *field under the walls of the city* before which the opponent was defeated,[202] or in the tent camp of the victorious army.[203] In addition, victory celebrations are attested which were celebrated for the entire people to participate when the *victorious army returned to their homeland*.[204] The army appears at this festival in full combat attire with their victorious weapons,[205] crowned with olive branches. This victory celebration in the homeland may have often occurred at YHWH's holy place. However, the examples teach us that originally the victory celebration was not associated with the cult.

25. The *victory song* stands at the center of the victory celebration. Its mood is self-evident. Jubilation and cries of victory ring out in the tents.[206] The material is also self-evidently provided in the event, details, and presuppositions of the victory. They primarily express that YHWH gave the victory.[207] Various images expressed the manner in which YHWH accomplished the victory. He worked through weak humans who could do nothing under their own power.[208] He attacks with his own *powerful hand*.[209] He gets to his feet and casts horse and rider into the sea (Exod 15:21). Indeed, it suffices that YHWH *simply threatens* so that horse and rider become stupefied. The defiant combatant sinks into sleep.[210] Then the victory song feeds on the event accomplished. It looks to the battlefield where the enemies' weapons, the witnesses to their defeat, lie broken and burned according to war customs,[211] and the place where the enemy corpses lie.[212] The song rejoices over the spoils taken from the opponent.[213] The pitiful defeat of the conquered then turns very naturally to the enemy's *previous power*, which portrays the enemy as terribly threatening (in stark contrast to the current situation). The enemy was "violent," a "defiant combatant," a "roaring lion."[214] The horde of his warriors clogged the valleys,

---

[200]Pss 46:9f; 48:13f; 66:5-7; 76:4-7; 118:15; Isa 33:18; Jdt 16:4-6, 13; see also Exod 15:21; Ps 149.

[201]Exod 15:21; Pss 46:9; 66:5.

[202]Ps 48:13 (see the commentary).

[203]Ps 118:15.

[204]Jdt 15:13; Ps 149 (see the commentary, p. 620). Cf. 1 Sam 18:7.

[205]Jdt 15:13; Ps 149:5-7.

[206]Ps 118:15; cf. Jdt 15:12ff.

[207]Exod 15:21; Pss 46:9ff; 66:5ff; 76:4ff; 118:15; Jdt 16:5,13.

[208]Ps 149:4; Jdt 16:5, 12.

[209]Ps 118:15.

[210]Pss 76:6-7; cf. 46:7b.

[211]Pss 46:10; 76:4.

[212]Ps 76:6.

[213]Ps 76:5.

[214]Ps 76:5, 6.

and his horses covered the hills.[215] He thought he would wipe out Israel's population and plunder its possessions. YHWH destroyed all of these plans.

26. The *narrative* represents the usual form for expressing these thoughts and moods.[216] It speaks of YHWH in the third person because it intends to proclaim the message of YHWH's victory. The *hymn* and the closely related *communal thanksgiving song* represent forms of the actual narrative. YHWH, YHWH's arm, or YHWH's army are also the subject of the statement.[217] Similarly to the indirect praise of YHWH in the hymn (§2, ¶29, 30), one finds a form where the enemies constitute the subject while the form portrays their behavior when they attacked YHWH.[218] In the narrative of YHWH's victory, the enemy's earlier prowess appears in descriptive adjectives or pictorial expressions that are added to statements about the enemy.[219] This earlier prowess can also be the subject of an introductory narrative component.[220]

As with the hymn and the communal thanksgiving song,[221] *introductions* point to the main part of the victory song. These introductions grow out of the dynamic situation of the victory festival. They summon the people to the battlefield as witnesses to the victory. Originally, they may have called the people from the besieged city that was liberated by the victory. "Come and see YHWH's work."[222] A similar formula perhaps served as an introduction, but could also have been formed as a conclusion to the victory song. It commanded people to circle the city which had successfully resisted, to count the towers, and examine its ramparts and bastions.[223] The main part could be attached to these introductions by a relative sentence or participial construction, as in the hymn.[224]

27. It is easy to recognize that the victory song comes very close to the mood and style of the *hymn*. This relationship should be credited with the hymn enriching the victory song, a development which could only have been stimulated if the victory festival was celebrated at the holy place where the hymn had prominence. In this setting the hymnic introduction entered,[225] as did the hymnic main section.[226] In fact, not only did the hymn adopt the victory song by itself and combined its forms with those of the victory song,[227] it also essentially dislodged the victory song from its ancient setting (cf. §2, ¶41). Examples from the Maccabean period are characteristic. The victors voice a *hymn* at the temple, no longer a victory song when they return from victory, enter the conquered city, of successfully defend and attack.[228]

---

[215]Jdt 16:3.
[216]Exod 15:21; Pss 46:10; 66:6; 76:4; 118:15; Jdt 16:3-5,12.
[217]Exod 15:21; Pss 46:10; 66:5ff; 76:4; 118:15; 149:4; Jdt 16:5.
[218]Ps 76:5-7; Jdt 16:10, 11a; see also Isa 33:18.
[219]Ps 76:5, 6.
[220]Jdt 16:3-4.
[221]Cf. §2, ¶2-10; §8, ¶33.
[222]Expressions include: *lekū ḥăzū* (Ps 46:9); *lekū ū re'ū* (Ps 66:5). Both formulas say the same thing.
[223]Ps 48:13-14a.
[224]Ps 46:9, 10; cf. §2, ¶20, 12.
[225]Exod 15:21; Jdt 16:2.
[226]Pss 66:5-6; 118:15.
[227]Pss 66:1-7; 76:1-13; Exod 15:21; Ps 149 (§2, ¶58).
[228]1 Macc 13:47, 51; 2 Macc 3:30.

It is quite understandable that the victory song increasingly receded in favor of the hymn because there really were no real victories in Israel after the days of Jeroboam II. Without victories, the genre could not flourish. Under these historical relationships, the victory song might have completely disappeared from Israel's poetry, if it had not been perceived from the world of *eschatological* images. The subject of the genre became the victories which YHWH would accomplish at the *end time* over the nations which threaten his city.[229] However, the victory song was not able to add anything more to this arena by its own dynamic power. It could only be preserved in connection with the *eschatological hymnic poetry* (§, ¶41) or with the *prophetic liturgy* (Isa 33). However, it was only preserved within the specific boundaries encountered in the eschatological poems just cited as the individual forms and contents of the genre attest.

IV. The Thanksgiving Song of Israel

E. Balla, *Das Ich der Psalmen*. Forschungen zur Religion und Literatur des AT und NT, vol. 16, 1912, pp. 65f, 73f. — W. Staerk, "Lyrik,"[2] in *Schriften des A.T. in Auswahl*, vol 3/1, 1920, pp. 88f., 96, 110, 235. — W. Baumgartner, "Die literarischen Gattungen in der Weisheit des Jesus Sirach," *ZAW* (1914): 180.

28. Only a few complete examples of Israel's thanksgiving song have been preserved.[230] Perhaps it is accidental that we have no more exemplars of this genre, but more probably, the small number is explained by the fact that only a few communal thanksgiving songs existed in Israel. The human heart frequently and gladly turns to God with complaint and petition. However, after deliverance one forgets to give thanks to the helper.[231]

29. It is not easy to describe the genre's *original shape*, nor to provide the *places in life* from which the genre arose. The few examples accessible for our consideration indicate a *later style. Descriptions of the situation* are sparse overwhelmingly stem *from the late period* of psalmody.[232] For this reason, the gaps of our knowledge could only be closed by presumptions. We are thus forced to deductions from the parallel genres of the individual thanksgiving song and the communal complaint song, which treat the same material as the communal thanksgiving songs.

30. The "life setting" for Israel's thanksgiving song is a *cultic celebration at the sanctuary*. One may presume this statement based on the communal complaint song. If one besieged YHWH with petitions for liberation from trouble at the holy place,[233] then it would be quite probable that one would also thank YHWH at this place for changing the calamity. The *individual thanksgiving song* also suggests this conclusion since it proceeds from a cultic thanksgiving celebration.[234] This presumption also corresponds to the isolated notes about the communal thanksgiving song we do have from a later period. 1 Macc 4:54;

[229]Pss 46:9f; 48:13f; 76:4-7; Isa 33:18; see Ps 149.

[230]Pss 66:8-12; 67; 124; 129; Isa 12:3-6; Pss. Sol. 13:1-3. See also the transitional pieces in Isa 25:9; 2 Macc 15:34; Jdt 13:14, 17.

[231]§7, ¶10, p. 215.

[232]Jer 33:11; Neh 12:43; 1 Macc 4:24; 5:54; 13:51; 2 Macc 8:27; 10:7, 38; 15:34; Jdt 13:14, 17.

[233]§4, ¶2.

[234]§7, ¶2.

13:51; and 2 Macc 10:7,30ff allow one to recognize that the thanksgiving song was still celebrated on Zion in the Maccabean period whenever possible. Neh 12:43 and 1 Macc 5:54 mention the *sacrificial offering* which was brought for this occasion. We have almost no information concerning the *customs* followed in this festival. We only know of one rite, the creation of water from "holy sources," which appears to proceed from the singing of thanksgiving in a festival situation.[235]

31. Although the traces of the original character of the thanksgiving festival are quite limited, the *cause and mood* of this celebration are clearly recognizable. The community of YHWH held these celebrations when God graciously brought his produce into the land.[236] From the counterpart of the communal complaint festival, we may deduce that we are not treating a regularly occurring thanksgiving celebration that was coordinated with the communal complaint. Rather, it was something out of the ordinary. Israel called to YHWH when the harvest was endangered by a *lack of rain*,[237] by *misshapen plants*,[238] and *locust plague*.[239] Relatedly, one would have thanked YHWH when the *danger to the harvest* was happily *conquered*. The most frequent causes for Israel's thanksgiving celebrations were *political in nature*. They held such a thanksgiving festival in times when YHWH *helped* his people, *liberated them from enemy threat*, granted them *victory*,[240] or when YHWH delivered his holy temple from heathen defacers, and purified it.[241] One can compare the corresponding lines from the communal complaint song to these last passages.[242]

The *mood* of these celebrations is explained by their cause. Powerfully loud rejoicing and enthusiastic jubilation for God's help characterizes the festival. So it is hardly astonishing that one encounters a relatively large number of expressions for joy and shouting in the sparse number of attestations.[243] The human voice was accompanied by instruments.[244] In particular, *zithers*, *harps*, and *cymbals* are mentioned (1 Macc 13:51). The similarity of this festival with the celebrations when the hymn was sung is noteworthy (cf. §2, ¶38, 39, 40).

32. As with the individual thanksgiving celebration, the *communal thanksgiving song* expresses the thoughts and moods of the festival (§7, ¶2). Next, we observe its form.

As far as we can tell from the preserved traces, the genre knows three parts: an *introduction*, a *narrative main part*, and a *conclusion*. The first and the third can be omitted, but the third is unavoidable. The elements are correspondingly related to the individual thanksgiving song (§7, ¶3, 4).

---

[235]Isa 12:3.

[236]Ps 67.

[237]1 Kgs 8:33f, 44ff; 2 Chr 20:9.

[238]Hos 7:14.

[239]Joel 1-2 (§4, ¶2, 7).

[240]Isa 25:9; Pss 124; 129; 1 Macc 4:23-24; 5:50ff; 13:49ff; 2 Macc 8:27; 10:35ff; 15:34; Jdt 13:14, 17.

[241]2 Macc 10:1ff; 15:34.

[242]Pss 74:2, 3, 7; 79:1; Isa 63:18 (§4, ¶9).

[243]These include: *śāśōn* (Isa 12:3); *śāmaḥ* (Isa 25:9; Ps 67:5; and perhaps 1 Macc 5:54); *gîl* (Isa 25:9; and perhaps 1 Macc 5:54; 2 Macc 10:6); *rinnen* (Isa 12:6); *ṣāhal* (Isa 12:6).

[244]*Zimmer* (Isa 12:5).

The *introduction* usually speaks in second person imperatives.[245] It develops from the situation of the festival. Its goal is, first, to call the festival participants to praise the God who helps.[246] In this behavior the introduction corresponds to one of the more frequently occurring introductions of the individual thanksgiving song (§7, ¶3). Above all, it corresponds formally and materially with the entry form of the *hymn* (§2, ¶2). One may thus deduce that those moods related to the hymn enriched the opening of the communal thanksgiving song. One finds undeniably hymnic expressions alongside the introduction characteristic of the thanksgiving song (*hôdû*, "give thanks"). This introcution is transferred from here to the hymn (§2, ¶2).[247]

A further goal of the introduction is to summon the participants to *proclaim the saving act of* YHWH: *hôdî'û*, "make known" (Isa 12:4); *hazkîrû*, "call out" (Isa 12:4); *môda'at zôt*, "let this be known" (Isa 12:4). Here, Israel's thanksgiving song comes closer to the individual thanksgiving song (cf. §7, ¶4). At this point one finds the element characteristic of the genre. The thanksgiving song desires *to announce* the experience of YHWH's help (§7, ¶4).

The communal thanksgiving song probably originally addressed the *festival participants* as in the individual thanksgiving song (§7, ¶2 and 3). Traces of this custom appear in Isa 12:4-6 and Jdt 13:14. In the course of history the original circle expanded, perhaps under the influence of the hymn (§2, ¶7). One should tell YHWH's deeds among the nations.[248] In fact, the nations themselves are commanded to praise YHWH.[249]

One also encounters a passive introductory formula alongside the *active* one: *bārûk yhwh* (blessed be YHWH).[250] The passive formula appears in the *individual thanksgiving song* as well as the hymn (cf. §7, ¶3 and §2, ¶4). One can hardly determine whether this expression originally characterized the genres of the thanksgiving song or entered from the hymn (see the passages cited in §2, ¶14).

"YHWH" is the second word of the introduction as in the individual thanksgiving song.[251] The one who should be thanked is expressed right at the beginning (§7, ¶3). *Participles* can be attached to the name. These participles can briefly anticipate the content of the thanksgiving song narrative, as with the hymn (§2, ¶21): "Thanks to the one who created everything. Thanks to the one who saved Israel. Thanks to the one who gathered those who are scattered. Thanks to the one who built his city and his sanctuary. Thanks to the one who let a horn spring from the house of David."[252]

If the introduction is lacking, the name YHWH stands among the first words of the thanksgiving song narrative. The same thing happens in the individual thanksgiving song (§7, ¶3). The name YHWH does not normally appear in the vocative, but forms the object

---

[245]Ps 66:8; Isa 12:3-6; Jdt 13:14.

[246]Ps 66:8; Isa 12:3, 6; Jdt 13:14.

[247]These expressions include: *bārekû*, "praise" (Ps 66:8); *zammerû*, "play" (Isa 12:6); *rōnnî*, "rejoice" (Isa 12:6); *sahălî*, "cry aloud" (Isa 12:6); "praise" (apparently *hallelû*, Jdt 13:14); *qir'û bišmô*, "call his name" (Isa 12:3).

[248]Isa 12:4.

[249]Ps 67:4, 5, 6.

[250]Ps 124:6; 2 Macc 15:34; Jdt 13:17.

[251]Pss 66:8; 67:4, 6; Isa 12:4; Sir 51:12.

[252]Sir 51:12.

of the statement. Israel's thanksgiving song, like the individual thanksgiving song, was originally a report of God's help, not a prayer of thanksgiving (§7, ¶4).

33. The main element of the genre is the *narrative* (cf. ¶32).[253] If the narrative follows an introduction, the narrative is attached by means of *kî* ("for").[254] The same thing occurs with the individual thanksgiving song[255] and the hymn (§2, ¶18). The *relative sentence* serves as another form of transition.[256] In addition, the *participle* also makes the connection.[257] The same transitional forms appear in the hymn (§2, ¶20, 21) and the individual thanksgiving song.[258] Employment of the narrative without the introduction is also common.[259]

The narrative itself can contain *two parts*. It first treats the distress, specifically YHWH's *deliverance* from the distress.[260] The second part constitutes the essential element of the narrative. This part cannot be omitted from the genre, while a portrayal of the earlier distress can be omitted since it is often lacking.[261] YHWH is the subject of the important narrative element. It speaks about YHWH in the third person, as in the narrative of the individual thanksgiving song (§7, ¶4).[262] This is the original style (cf. ¶32). Only at a later stage does Israel's thanksgiving song, and especially the main element, adopt the form of the *prayer* and speak to YHWH in the second person.[263] This tendency also agrees with the parallel genre (§7, ¶4).

34. Directions similar to the introduction can stand at the conclusion of the narrative, as with the hymn (§2, ¶36) and the individual thanksgiving song (§7, ¶3). It could be accidental that no form using the second person imperative appears among the few examples preserved. Directions do appear in the jussive form in Ps 67:8: "Let the ends of the earth honor him." Another jussive forms a refrain (Ps 67:4, 6, 8): "Therefore, the nations should thank you, YHWH. All the nations should thank you." (See the commentary to this passage). In Isa 25:9 we find the first person plural: "Therefore, let us rejoice and shout with joy for his help."

These directions originally lead from the narrative back to the situation of the thanksgiving festival, as the last example shows. Because YHWH has helped, one should now praise him. At this point, as with the individual thanksgiving song (§7, ¶6), Israel's thanksgiving song also refers once to the *thanksgiving sacrifice*. The sparse nature of available examples prohibit one from more precise confirmation.

35. An *act of YHWH* toward *his people* forms the *content of the narrative*. The genre thus shows a close affinity with the hymn in this respect (§2, ¶28, 41, 50). However, upon

---

[253]Isa 12:4, 5, 6; 25:9; Pss 66:10; 67:2-3, 7; 124:6-7; 129:1-4; Sir 51:12; Pss. Sol. 13:1-3; 2 Macc 15:34; Jdt 13:14, 17; cf. also Neh 12:43; 1 Macc 5:54; 13:51; 2 Macc 8:27; 10:7, 38.

[254]Isa 12:4, 5, 6; Ps 66:10; Sir 51:12; see also Neh 12:43; 1 Macc 5:34; 13:51.

[255]Pss 13:6; 28:6; 30:2; 31:22; etc.

[256]Isa 12:6; Jdt 13:14.

[257]Ps 66:9; 2 Macc 15:34; Jdt 13:14.

[258]Ps 31:8 uses a relative sentence.

[259]Pss 67; 124; 129; Isa 25:9; Pss. Sol. 13:1ff.

[260]Pss 66:9-12; 124:1-7; 129:1-3; Pss. Sol. 13:1-3.

[261]Ps 67; Isa 12:3-6; 25:9; 2 Macc 15:34; Jdt 13:14; Sir 51:12.

[262]See Isa 12:4, 5, 6; 25:9; Pss 66:8; 124:6-7; 129:4; Pss. Sol. 13:1-3; 2 Macc 15:34; Jdt 13:14; Sir 51:12.

[263]Ps 67; Jdt 13:17.

closer inspection one can see a decisive difference between the narrative portions of the two genres. The hymn narrates praise to YHWH for what he did for Israel in antiquity (§2, ¶50). It pursues no other goal than to *honor* YHWH, speaking in a *disinterested piety* (§2, ¶46). In the communal thanksgiving song a *specific* act of YHWH stands at the center. The community shows *particular interest* in it. The thanksgiving song does not communicate some act of the distant past, but one from the *most recent history* whose effect still reaches into the present. It has thus introduced a sudden change in the relationships which were unbearable and caused them to pray to YHWH with a burning desire to change them.[264]

According to the available examples, the material of the narratives is overwhelmingly *political* in nature, as in the contrasting genre, the communal complaint song (§4, ¶7). It usually speaks rather nonconcretely using general and formal expressions about YHWH's help and its result.[265] Specific details related to the thanksgiving song are less frequently perceivable. However, 1 Macc 5:54 mentions the complete return of all the warriors, and 1 Macc 14:51 speaks about the expulsion of a great enemy from Israel. In this context, one should also note the way that the thanksgiving narrative speaks of YHWH's *deliverance of the temple.* Here, in a relatively late period for the genre, the particular historical character of the event being celebrated comes into play rather specifically. YHWH succeeded in cleansing his temple of heathens or he graciously preserved his place from being profaned.[266]

Other contents recede behind the contents of this type. Only Ps 67 speaks about the harvest. Other, less common, material can only be inferred since it does not appear in the few examples available to us. They can be deduced from the petitions and complaints of the communal complaint song (§4, ¶7) whose content is apparently related to the communal thanksgiving song so that it reflects the subject of the thanksgiving song narrative.

The formal and indeterminate nature of the statements typically do not allow one to determine the event more precisely. Apparently, this results from the same reason as the individual complaint song and thanksgiving song. The oldest form of the genres were cultic formulas, which must uniformly take account of the various cases which do appear (cf. §1, ¶4; §4, ¶15; §6, ¶4; §7, ¶4).

36. In spite of the small number of examples of Israel's thanksgiving song, one can nevertheless recognize that this genre had a relative abundant development.

First, one must confirm that the communal thanksgiving song, as with other genres, developed in *the spheres of the cult and the sanctuary* (§2, ¶44; §7, ¶8). Amazingly, no internal reason can be noted for separating the genre from the arena of the worship service. One has to seek the cause externally. One may sense the cause in the *suppression* of the *rural sanctuaries* associated with the centralization of the Jerusalem cult, as well as in the complete breakdown of the Jerusalem temple service during the exilic and early postexilic period. Under the influence of these historical relationships, YHWH's thankful community learned to abandon the holy site as the irreplaceable location of the thanksgiving festival. Also, the thanksgiving song was separated from sacrifice and temple. So

---

[264]Cf. "Today" in 2 Macc 8:27; Jdt 13:17; and "this night" in Jdt 13:14.

[265]Isa 25:9; Pss 66:12; 124:6; 129:4; Sir 51:12; 2 Macc 8:27; 10:38; Jdt 13:14, 17.

[266]2 Macc 10:7; 15:34; see Sir 51:12.

the people of the Maccabean period, after their temple was pillaged, unhesitantly sing their thanksgiving song at undedicated locations. The same is true for the population of Bethulah, which sang the thanksgiving song in their city.[267]

The simple, original form of the genre, which we have attempted to describe in the previous pages, was preserved into the latest period. It also participated in the dissolution of temple and sacrifice. However, many factors influenced the development of a more recent form. Describing this development and explaining the stipulations of its development is the final task which remains to be accomplished.

37. The genre was enriched when the hymn and the individual thanksgiving song influenced the communal thanksgiving song. It is not remarkable that the *hymn* found the path to the communal thanksgiving song (§2, ¶41). Both genres are closely related by their own *mood, material,* and *linguistic form.* The description of the introduction already touched upon the details.[268] Additional influence from the hymn should be observed in the excessive feeling of thanksgiving in which not only the festival participants but also *all* nations are commanded to thank YHWH.[269] The hymn also enters the narrative. The helpful action of YHWH takes its place among his *powerful deeds* in general.[270] The narrative of YHWH's deliverance praises YHWH's greatness,[271] or it praises his *rule over the nations.*[272]

In addition, the individual thanksgiving song attained influence over the related genre. The causes of this influence are diverse. One cause can be found in the great simplicity of the form of the communal thanksgiving song and in the poverty of its contents. Israel would have increasingly perceived something lacking in this respect. The more lively and abundant other forms became, the more the feeling would have grown that Israel's thanksgiving song was too monotonous, and that it was not an appropriate lyric expression of the mood that a thanksgiving festival community embodied. An enrichment of this type could not come from the presuppositions of the communal thanksgiving song for collective experiences and collective perceptions necessarily move in relatively small arenas. Thus, Israel's thanksgiving song had to borrow from the individual genre which had a greater deviation of material and a richer store of possibilities due to the greater diversity of experiences for the individual.

This change was also caused by something else. With the termination of an independent state, the particularly political nature of the contents in the thanksgiving narrative receded. The *desires of the religious community* come to the foreground. As a result, the individual thanksgiving song and the communal thanksgiving song became materially closer. Deliverance from hostility, from pursuit, from abuse and disgrace take a wider role (cf. §7, ¶4).[273] This concern becomes stronger since those who were faithful to YHWH could speak about YHWH's help against the hostility of their own populace. From this point, it is suggested that the material and the images from the individual thanksgiv-

---

[267]1 Macc 4:25; 2 Macc 8:27; Jdt 13:14, 17.
[268]See above, ¶32 and ¶35.
[269]Pss 66:8; 67:4, 5, 6, 8.
[270]Isa 12:4; Sir 51:12.
[271]Isa 12:6.
[272]Ps 67:5.
[273]Pss 124; 129; Pss. Sol. 13:1-3.

ing song extended into the narrative of the communal thanksgiving song. The group thanksgiving song may have accomplished the mediation, as described in §7, ¶7.

One encounters lines of thought from the individual thanksgiving song chiefly in rather late psalms.[274] Israel speaks very unpolitically about people attacking it. The activities of the opponent are characterized by lines of thought describing the enemy of the pious individual. The comparison of the latter with wild bloodthirsty animals recurs here, as does the comparison of entrapment using the example of the bird catcher. The individual genre (cf. §7, ¶4; §6, ¶5, 7, 8) borrows from the well-known image of the waters of death and the overflowing stream.[275] Occasionally, it even adopts the external form of the individual thanksgiving song so that Israel speaks as an individual person (Ps 129:1-3).

Among other genres, the blessing saying occasionally entered Israel's thanksgiving song, if one may ascribe Ps 144:12-15 to this genre.[276]

38. The genre develops further when it is removed from its original soil. It represents only a small step when the genre loses the connection to a specific event which has just happened. Instead of a specific helping act when YHWH helps the entire people, now the *whole series of YHWH's acts to Israel* enters the frame of the genre. Simultaneously, reflective consideration of the various saving deeds of YHWH in Israel's history replaces the immediate feeling that was so powerfully aroused by the experience of YHWH's help. It is easy to see that this change in the history of the genre could only proceed from those poems containing no introduction. These songs lacked connections to the situation. They also lacked the lyric forms of expression which were so well suited for introducing the thanksgiving song but which would not have united easily with a contemplative consideration of history.

Pss 124 and 129 offer examples of these reflective poems. The latter sees Israel's history, from its youth forward, as a chain of increasingly bitter hostility at the hands of the people's enemy. YHWH, however, broke the string of the wicked. The reflective element appears even stronger in Ps 124. This poem does not stop by observing actual history. Rather, it considers how the course of history would have gone if YHWH had not been with his people.

39. Poems of this type allow one to recognize how far the elements recede which constituted the genre of the communal thanksgiving song. The development which has been traced here necessarily leads to the *dissolution of the genre*. Among the preserved examples, Ps 129 and Pss. Sol. 13 even allow one to see this last stage of the history clearly. The first example connects the thanksgiving song narrative with wishful petitions filled with vengeance against all the enemies of Zion. The latter example provides a reason for a broad didactic treatment of the fates of those fearing God and the godless.

Thus, the history of Israel's thanksgiving song finally converges with the history of other genres, with the *communal complaint* (cf. §4, ¶13) and with *wisdom poetry*. The genre did not exercise decisive influence upon other types of poetry like it had itself experienced in abundance. See ¶32 above for a possible enrichment of the hymn by the thanksgiving song. The significance which Israel's thanksgiving song exerted upon

---

[274]See previous note.

[275]For these lines of thought, see Pss 124:2-5; 129:1-2, 4; Pss. Sol. 13:1-3.

[276]See the commentary for this passage.

prophecy is more tangible. Prophecy seized the thanksgiving song in order to express its future hopes more dynamically. Isa 12 preserves a thanksgiving song which Israel should sing when YHWH has completed his great saving act in the future. The form and the material of the genre remain untouched, as with the hymn (§2, ¶51). However, because of the context in which it placed Israel's thanksgiving song, prophecy incorporated new content into the old material and forms. Specifically prophecy incorporated enthusiastic *eschatological hope*.

V. Legends

W. Staerk, "Lyrik,"[2] in *Schriften des A.T. in Auswahl*, vol 3/1, 1920, pp. 276-84. — *RGG*[2] Article, 'Sagen und Legenden," II, ¶6.

40. The *legend* appears to be related to Israel's thanksgiving songs by the material. It does not appear independently in the preserved examples. Rather, it only occurs as a component of a very few psalms.[277] The psalms into which the legend entered, and to which the breadth of its material provided a particular impression, belong to various genres. Ps 78, like Deut 32, is a wisdom poem which presents the material of the legend from the vantage point of the admonition and indoctrination of Israel (§10, ¶3). Ps 105 is a hymn by form, although the appearance of warnings indicates it was a later pattern (105:4, 45). See §10, ¶6. Ps 106 is a communal complaint with a hymnic entry (cf. §4, ¶12). See also Isa 63:7–64:11. The very developed form that was moving toward the dissolution of the fixed form of the genres already mentioned shows that this passage belonged to a very late period of psalmody.

41. If one looks at the main elements of the various poems, one easily recognizes that no matter how they were used in the genre in which they were placed, they nevertheless depend upon a specific *literary type*, which was quite comprehensible materially as well as stylistically.

They have a common form, the *narrative*,[278] which is also perhaps recognizable behind Isa 63:7ff. The narrative is confined to a limited circle of material. The narrative is limited to YHWH's *deeds toward Israel* during the wandering from Egypt to the entry into Canaan.

In each context where one encounters the narratives. Either the *deeds of YHWH* are accented by themselves,[279] or the *sins of Israel* which YHWH had to punish during this period are pushed to the foreground. However, YHWH did not allow these sins to dissuade him from bringing about his ultimate goal, leading his people into the promised land.[280] A certain liberty dominates the handling of the material and its arrangement (see the commentary to Ps 106), but the shared material also shows itself in the specific nature of content. The natural stature and naivety of the old sagas has disappeared as well as their formal and substantive independence. Rather, the material is *summarized in unified fashion* and placed under a *dominant religious viewpoint*. It must be shown how YHWH has given

---

[277]Pss 78; 105; 106. Outside the psalter, see Deut 32 and Isa 63:7ff.

[278]Pss 78:12-72; 105:12-44; 106:7-46; Deut 32:10-25.

[279]As in Ps 105; Isa 63:11-14.

[280]Pss 78; 106.

the land to his people as a possession.[281] The good fortune of the chosen ones must be portrayed, so that the cowardly generation of the present time could set itself right.[282] The narrative of YHWH's deeds should strengthen trust in him, and fortify the obedience to his command.[283] At the same time, one detects a preference for the *miraculous* in these narratives. The miracles of antiquity are reported. Those which are especially noteworthy recur over and over: the Egyptian plagues up to the striking of the firstborn,[284] the march through the Red Sea,[285] the leading by columns of cloud and fire,[286] drinking from the rock,[287] feeding by manna and quail,[288] and similar lines of thought. The markers of the material which have been mentioned show that the old saga had changed into the legend.

42. One cannot accept that the legend ever formed an *independent psalm genre*. Rather, it is subsumed under known genres everywhere it appears in the psalms. First, observing that the legend never appears independently points in the direction of this conclusion. A second observation teaches us that this condition is not the result of a lengthy development within psalmody. In the psalms, the legend is thoroughly dependent upon the history of the material in the prose composition. Its development is completely understandable in this realm.[289] One should thus conclude that the legend developed elsewhere and only entered psalmody rather late.

The paranesis is the *place* where the legendary material was solidified into the shape characteristically appearing in the psalms. It is especially well known in Deuteronomy.[290] The narratives from the wilderness period were compiled to *admonish* Israel to trust YHWH, and to *warn* Israel against falling into sin and falling away from its God. They reported the various miracles and told about the wilderness generation's sins which YHWH had to punish severely. In this respect, two directions finally arose. One encounters these elements in the legends within the psalms already mentioned. This origin accounts for the *didactic tendency* of the final goal. The legend left traces of this origin in the psalms.[291] The legend type, created from Deuteronomic paranesis, developed considerably more broadly in the later period.[292] This later shape of the type is characterized by larger size and a closer connection to the final working of the Pentateuchal tradition. In broad strokes, this is the history of the legend in the realm outside lyrical poetry.

43. In its late form, dependent upon the written Pentateuch, the legend entered into psalmody via the *hymn*, the *communal complaint*, and the *instructional poem*. All of these genres accommodated the legend materially. The deeds of YHWH for his people in

---

[281]Ps 105:11.

[282]Ps 106:5.

[283]Ps 78:6ff.

[284]Pss 78:43-51; 105:27-36; 106:21-22.

[285]Pss 78:13; 106:7-12, 22; Isa 63:11-13.

[286]Pss 78:14; 105:39.

[287]Pss 78:15, 16; 105:41; 106:32.

[288]Pss 78:17-29; 105:40; 106:14-15.

[289]Cf. *RGG*,[2] "Sagen und Legenden," II, ¶6.

[290]Deut 4:1ff, 9ff, 23, 32; 7:17ff; 8:2ff; 9:7ff; 11:1ff; 29:1ff; see also Staerk, *RGG*,[2] "Sagen und Legenden," II, ¶6.

[291]Pss 78:1-4,6ff; 105:4ff, 45; Deut 32:1ff.

[292]Ezek 20:5ff; Neh 9:6ff; Dan 9:6ff; Acts 7:1ff; 13:16ff.

antiquity had already been a *theme of the hymn* for a long time (cf. §2, ¶50). The communal complaint referred to them as an effective *rationale for its petition* to YHWH (cf. §4, ¶10, p. 91). However, one saw evidence from an early period that YHWH chose Israel and could not abandon him because of the exodus from Egypt and entry into Canaan.[293] The *wisdom poem*, with its *instructional intention*, finally accommodated the ultimate goal of the legend type. Of course, as long as the genre's strict style was still in effect, the expanded form of the legend could not enter psalmody because the strict style allowed only brief allusions to the tradition of the time of election. That was only possible when the genres began to be completely reformulated. The earliest example of the legend penetrating may be Isa 63:7ff. In this passage, the expansiveness of the legend contrasts with the brevity demanded by the communal complaint song. However, in Pss 78, 105, and 106 the legends have conquered the resistance of the genres.

Consideration of the time of Israel's election, as practiced by the prophets, was connected relatively early with the consideration of Israel's history in general. It will suffice to reference the Deuteronomistic reworking of the Israelite history. It is thus not amazing that the consideration of the rest of the history of the people appears alongside the consideration of the time of election in the psalms.[294] The reason that this expansion of the legend entered may lie in the disintegration of the genres in general, but, positively, it may also be demanded by the development of the communal thanksgiving song. The latter started with the reference to the specific deed of YHWH for his people. Finally, at the end of its history it accomplished the consideration of Israel's history in general.

VI. The Torah

H. Gunkel, *Die israelitische Literatur*, pp. 76f (*Kultur der Gegenwart*, vol. VII); H. Greß-mann, "Die älteste Geschichtsschreibung und Prophetie,"[2] in *Schriften des AT in Auswahl*, vol. II/1, 1921, pp. 229ff; M. Haller, "Das Judentum,"[2] in *Schriften des AT in Auswahl*, vol. II/3, 1925, pp. 198ff; *RGG*[2] article, "Tora," ¶2. Details belonging here are treated by S. Mowinckel, *le décalogue*, Etudes d'histoire et de philosophie réligieuses 16, Paris, 1927; and by L. Köhler, "Der Dekalog, Nr. 9," *Theologische Rundschau*, new series 1, 1929.

44. The torah appears nowhere in the psalms as an independent genre. These only influence psalmody in *individual references*, and even these are relatively rare. If we leave aside the *torah liturgies*, which will be treated in §11, then it is found only in Ps 50:8,14f,22f . With deference to its rare occurrence, it is recommended that we portray the Torah only in broad strokes. We will consider more precisely only those details which are important for psalmody.

Communicating the torah is the particular task of the priests.[295] Its contents become clear from its purpose. It should make known to the laity the ordinances of the worship service. In addition, but only in a secondary role, it should make known the sentences of the law and morality. Apart from the torah liturgies, it is preserved in prose.

Other forms do not come into consideration in our context, but the form of the worship service torah is often the *imperative*, usually *singular*. This is explained by the

---

[293]See K. Galling, *Die Erwählungstraditionen Israels*, BZAW 48, 1928, pp. 5-26.
[294]Pss 78:56-72; 106:34-46; Deut 32.
[295]Deut 33:10; Jer 2:8; 18:18; Ezek 7:26; 22:26; Hos 4:6; Zeph 3:4; Hag 2:11; Mal 2:6.

fact that the priest had to turn to an individual when communicating torah. The following passages offer examples of this form of torah with its "you should" or "your should not." These include: Exod 12:46; Lev 11:4, 8, 11, 13, 24, 33, 43; etc.

Another form of the torah which overwhelmingly concerns the proclamation of the forbidden portrays that which repulses YHWH. It prefers to be connected to a negative imperative with an explanatory *kî*: "for this is an abomination before YHWH your God."[296] however, this form of the torah is also found as an independent entity, an example of which appears in Lev 20:13: "A man who lies with a man as one would lie with a woman. Both have committed an abomination." This form was once much more common than the postexilic priestly legal ruling still allows one to recognize as is shown by the imitations which are found precisely in this form of priestly torah among the prophets.[297]

Characteristically, the torah is communicated under *commission of YHWH* by the priest acting in his place.[298] The form itself shows that since YHWH himself frequently speaks, and YHWH is the "I" which frequently appears in the instructional sentences. Cf. Lev 19:4: "Do not turn to idols, nor make images. I am YHWH your God."[299] In these contexts, YHWH often even accentuates that he is the one speaking to those listening, and introduces himself. See the example just cited and Lev 19:10, 18, 25, etc.

The prophets gladly made use of both forms in opposition to the dominant cultic religion when speaking what they believed to be God's will for his people. The portrayal contains that which repulses YHWH, and Israel's *worship service* with all of its ordinances. The imperative commands that they turn away from external activities and fulfill the great *religious and moral challenges*: "I hate, I despise your festivals. I cannot accept your celebrations. . . . I take no pleasure in your cereal offerings. I do not regard the sacrifice of your fatted calves. Get away from me with the noise of your songs. I don't want to hear the playing of your harps. Let justice pour down like water, and righteousness like an ever-flowing stream." (Amos 5:21-24; see also the above-mentioned prophetic passages). When the prophets adopted the torah, it overwhelmingly served the speech to which it was bound. The torah may have preserved the rhythmic form which helped it enter psalmody.

Individual elements of the priestly torah entered psalmody in connection with the prophetic torah which developed from the priestly torah. These elements include the self-presentation ("I am YHWH your God." Ps 50:7c) and cultic instructions ("Sacrifice a thanksgiving song to YHWH, then you will pay your vow to the highest. Call to me on the day of distress, and I will deliver you and bring honor to you." Ps 50:14; see also 50:22, 23). If Ps 50 were the only time that the torah appeared in psalmody, the reason would be that no real internal relationship existed between torah and the lyric genres. These genres also excluded the torah as long as the strict style existed. Only at the point when the genres began to disintegrate and the boundaries between them started to be blurred, did the torah succeed in penetrating psalmody. However, because its nature was foreign to the lyric poetry, the torah was never able to exert much influence upon lyric poetry.

---

[296]Deut 7:25; see also Deut 17:1; 18:12; Lev 18:22.

[297]See Amos 5:21-22; Isa 1:11-15; Jer 6:20; 7:22; Isa 58:5; 66:3; Zech 7:5-6.

[298]See H. Greßmann, "Die älteste Geschichtsschreibung und Prophetie."

[299]See also Lev 19:1, 2, 4, 10, 18, 25; Amos 5:21-22; Isa 1:11ff; Jer 6:20; 7:22; Isa 58:5; 66:4; Zech 7:5.

§9 Prophetic Elements in the Psalms

H. Gunkel, *Reden und Aufsätze*, 1913, pp. 123ff. — H. Gunkel, *Ausgewählte Psalmen*,[4] 1917, see the index under "Propheten." — *RGG*[2] articles, "Psalmen," ¶¶11, 16, and "Propheten," ¶II B, 3. — E. Balla, *Das Ich der Psalmen*, 1912, pp. 103ff. — W. Staerk, "Lyrik," in *Schriften des AT*, vol. 3/1,[2] 1920, pp. 123, 150ff, 263, etc. — W. Baumgartner, *ZAW* 24 (1914): 186ff. — S. Mowinckel, *Psalmenstudien*, vol. 3, 1923.

Preceding sections have traced the influence of psalmody on the prophets.[1] Here, we will look at the reverse. How much have prophetic elements entered the psalms? Those psalms or psalm parts are called "prophetic" which relate to or depend upon prophetic form and content.

I. The Eschatological Material of the Psalms

1. Prophetic elements appear in the psalms in "eschatological hymns,"[2] "eschatological Zion songs,"[3] and "eschatological enthronement songs."[4] In addition, prophetic elements appear in "liturgies,"[5] in prophetic portions of "mixed liturgies,"[6] in prophetic "judgment speeches,"[7] "torah,"[8] and in rebuke, threat, and warning speeches.[9] In addition, certain passages show the influence of prophetic speech forms on other psalm genres, including the "hymn,"[10] the "individual complaint song,"[11] the "communal complaint song,"[12] and "mixed poetry."[13]

---

[1]§1, ¶2; §2, ¶¶19-21, 28, 51-57; §4, ¶¶1, 10, 14; §6, ¶¶1, 6, 10, 23, 28, 30; §10, ¶3.

[2]Pss 9:6-13, 16ff; 68; 98; 149; Pss. Sol. 11:1-6; Tob 13 (at the end); Luke 1:46f, 49-55, 68-75; see also Rev 4:11; 5:9f, 12, 13; 11:17f; 19:1f, 7f; (§2, ¶¶51, 52).

[3]Pss 46; 48; 76 (§2, ¶52).

[4]Pss 47; 93; 96:10ff (= 1 Chr 16:30b-33); 97; 99 (§2, ¶53; §3).

[5]Pss 75; 85; 126; Pss. Sol. 11; Bar 4:5–5:9 (§11, ¶¶19, 20).

[6]Pss 12:6; 81:6c-11; 95:7d-11; cf. Ps 60:8-10 (§2, ¶59; §4, ¶14; §11, ¶15).

[7]Ps 82.

[8]Ps 50.

[9]Pss 14 (=53); 81:6c-11; 95:7d-11. Concerning nn. 6-8, see H. Schmidt, *Große Propheten* 1923, pp. lxiff.

[10]Pss 103:9-12, 15-17; 147:2; Jer 16:19; Jdt 16:15,17. One could also make a case in Pss 34:19; 36:6-10; 108:5. Cf. §2, ¶¶49, 50, 57, 61.

[11]Pss 52:3ff (§6, ¶28); see also the "hymn in the individual complaint song" in Pss 69:36f; 86:9; 102:14-23, 27 (§6, ¶¶20, 28; §2, ¶51).

[12]Pss 10:16-18; 124:3; Pr Azar; Sir 33:1-13a; 36:12b-22 (§4, ¶11).

[13]Pss 94:13-15; 119:26; Deut 32.

The "dirge"[14] and "wisdom poetry"[15] scarcely show any prophetic influence. More often, the prophetic impact can only be noted in the conceptual material.[16]

2. The most extensive area of the whole is the *eschatology* of the psalms. Investigations of Old Testament eschatology frequently ignore, or only briefly mention it, because they do not recognize its lines of thought. However, if one arranges the material of the psalms by *genre*, the eschatological content stands out with great clarity in the poems and poem parts which are related to prophetic predictions. At the same time, however, one also sees that the eschatology of the psalms carries no "messianic" lines of thought as previous generations have erroneously sought to find. Proper understanding of the eschatology of psalms has essentially been demanded by the works of B. Stade, H. Greßmann, and most recently by S. Mowinckel.[17]

First, one should prove that the future hope of the psalms generally coincides with that portrayed in the prophetic books, even if both deviate in details. We will prove the matter by attaching the most significant lines of thought in the psalms to their counterparts in the prophets. We will coordinate the result in section III.

3. The following summarizes briefly the *content of the ultimate hope of the psalmist*: A "time" will come when great miracles will happen. The "time" (*mô'ēd*, *'ēt*) is the expression used,[18] which is simultaneously a prophetic expression.[19] Like the prophets, the psalmists are also convinced that the "time" is "near."[20] Even more forcefully, one finds the following: The hour has already "come."[21] YHWH himself "comes,"[22] and YHWH says, "Now I will rise."[23]

The fact that it will happen soon, in the briefest span of time, adds spice to the portrayal of the majestic and the marvelous. A mighty, religious power expressed this idea, and it has resounded repeatedly throughout the centuries. This idea does not concern an innocuous theoretical doctrine for the pious. Rather, it attests to a burning faith which will not be eliminated by any number of disappointments. If one expunges this faith in the nearness of events from biblical eschatology, one would tear out its heart.

4. To understand the *fundamental lines of thought* for this hope, we must first ask about the *words or short sentences* in which the entirety is summarized by the poets themselves. The most common expression is perhaps that YHWH will "act:" "It is time for

---

[14]Lam 1:5, 12-15, 17f; 2:1-8; 4:11, 16 (YHWH's wrath against Zion); 1:5, 8, 14, 18, 20, 22; 2:14; 4:6, 13 (Zion's weighty sin); 1:21d; 2:17 (references to prophetic prediction); 4:21f (expression of hope); see H. Jahnow, *Das Hebräische Leichenlied*, 1923, p. 170.

[15]Pss 34:19 (=Isa 57:15); 94:13-15; Sir 2:13f; 24:33; 32:22-25; 35:20f; 39:1; 44:3; 46:13–49:10.

[16]Cf. Pss 15:3-5b; 24:4; 40:7-9; 50:14; 51:17f; 63:6; 69:31f; 94:6; 106; 115:4-8 (§1, ¶8; §6, ¶¶4, 24, 28; §7, ¶¶8, 13; and §2, ¶¶57-63).

[17]B. Stade, "Die messianische Hoffnung im Psalter," in *Akademische Reden und Aufsätze*, 2nd ed., 1907, pp. 37ff. He still uses the expression "messianic," but it is understood in the general eschatological sense. H. Greßmann, *Ursprung der israelitisch-jüdischen Eschatologie*, 1905; *Der Messias*, 1929. S. Mowinckel, *Psalmenstudien*, vol. III, 1923.

[18]Pss 75:3; 102:14; 119:126.

[19]Hab 2:3; Dan 8:19; 11:27, 29, 35; cf. Sir 33:10; also Isa 10:12; 33:10.

[20]Pss 85:10; cf. Isa 5:19; 10:25; Hab 2:3.

[21]Pss 75:3; 102:14.

[22]Pss 96:13; 98:9; Isa 35:4; "He is there" in Isa 25:9; 35:4.

[23]Pss 12:6 (= Isa 57:15, literally); 43:19.

YHWH to act," or in English "to intervene."[24] Other expressions mean essentially the same thing, such as "make himself known,"[25] "show himself,"[26] or the expressions already mentioned ("He will rise,"[27] and "He will come." See above). Included in these statements, but as a silent counterpart, is the fact that YHWH has *not acted* for some time until now. Rather, he remains inactive or in hiding. This idea is expressed in the complaints of the communal complaints (§4, ¶7), whose relationship to the eschatological hope will be treated below under section III.

Several brief statements answer the question of the *content of YHWH's action*. He does "deeds,"[28] which means the same thing as, "He does a *great thing*,"[29] a "miracle,"[30] or more specifically, "deeds of judgment."[31] He has "become king" (§3, ¶1). He is "the highest one in all the world."[32] He is "raised higher than all the gods."[33] "He enters to establish the earth."[34] The fact that YHWH brings *grace* and *salvation for Israel* appears alongside this hope for YHWH's self-illumination[35] via world judgment and dominion.[36] He radiates "new light" for the just.[37] Throughout, *YHWH is the only one who acts*. People do not create this hope. The Old Testament consistently contradicts the idea of helping to build God's kingdom. People can resist it, but they will be defeated (Ps 68:2).

5. Immediately, we have to place sentences about *Israel's subjective mood* in these events alongside objective sentences about YHWH's action. The former continually expresses one idea. Specifically, YHWH's people will be filled with *joy* and *jubilation* in that time. Eschatological psalms and psalm parts echo this idea repeatedly. "Then our mouth is full of laughter and our tongue full of jubilation . . . YHWH has done a great thing for us. For that we are happy."[38] "Your right hand is full of grace, the mountain of Zion *rejoices*. Judah's daughters are happy because of your judgment."[39] The same is true among the prophets. Then there will be "*eternal joy* about your head. Bliss and *joy* reach them. Concern and sorrow flee."[40] "Then, the lame will jump like a deer, and the tongue of the mute will rejoice."[41] The festivals of *rejoicing* in the future are sketched in detail.[42]

---

[24]Ps 119:126; cf. Isa 44:23.

[25]Pss 9:17; 48:4; 76:2; cf. Isa 19:21; Ezek 35:11; 38:23.

[26]Ps 102:17; cf. Isa 60:2; Zech 9:14.

[27]Pss 12:6; 68:2; 102:14; and Isa 28:21; 33:10 for examples in the prophets.

[28]Pss 9:12; 46:9.

[29]Ps 126:2f (Joel 2:21).

[30]Pss 75:2; 96:3; 98:1; 105:2; Sir 33:6 (Isa 25:1).

[31]Pss 48:12; 97:8; cf. 91:7.

[32]Ps 97:9.

[33]Ps 97:9.

[34]Pss 96:13; 98:9.

[35]Isa 44:28.

[36]Pss 69:36; 85:10; 102:14; 130:8; 149:4; Sir 33:17; (Isa 30:18; 41:13, 14; 43:1; 44:23; 49:13; etc.).

[37]Ps 97:11 (Isa 9:1; 58:10).

[38]Ps 126:2f.

[39]Pss 48:11f; cf. also 97:8.

[40]Isa 35:10.

[41]Isa 35:6, see 12:3.

[42]Ps 68:27f and in the enthronement songs.

In the psalms and the prophets alike, people who experience these things are called to cry out with joy.[43] It is often made clear that the exuberant joy is a joy over YHWH who has done such a great miracle.[44] This rejoicing will echo in *religious* festivals. "They will 'praise' YHWH in choirs."[45] The prophets also speak about these YHWH festivals.[46] The psalmist's enthusiasm presents this rejoicing over the majesty of his God so powerfully that it seems all *peoples, heaven, and earth* are full of it. The prophets also agree.[47] However, YHWH himself will join in this jubilation.[48] The singers will not be quiet with this happiness: "I will be happy ever more, and will play to Jacob's God."[49]

From all of these elements, the *basic mood* of the eschatological psalms and psalm pieces arises. It is a joyful delight, an enthusiastic excitement for the singers. This observation should continually cause the present day commentator on the poem to pause over for each point. One could make no greater mistake than to depict and combine the details of hope as dry and empty. Rather one should always be conscious of that which is new, that all of this material arises from enthusiasm. As the prophet says, YHWH directs salvation over Jerusalem like a stream. Accordingly humans will rejoice marvelously: "You will see, and your heart will be happy. Your bones will sprout like grass."[50] People will sample preliminary joy in the present as a foretaste of the blessedness which they will perceive in the future.[51]

6. After gaining a sense of the *basic mood* of the eschatology, we return to the objective sentences of this hope about which we have already mentioned several things in ¶4.

Sometimes these sentences in the psalms appear isolated from their internal context.[52] At other times, they are partially melded with smaller or larger images, or combined superficially.[53] One example will clarify the situation: "YHWH, look down from your holy high place. Look to the earth from heaven to hear the prisoners who are moaning, to redeem the sons of death so that one might proclaim YHWH's name in Zion, and his praise in Jerusalem when nations and kingdoms are gathered together to serve YHWH."[54] Not until the later period do even more expansive presentations of the end appear. Thus, they are found in the communal complaint song where one prays for YHWH's deeds in the end time,[55] or in the description of the messiah's troops.[56] We can go a step further in this direction. In our modern way, we attempt to compile a *comprehensive picture of the hope*

---

[43]Pss 53:7; 97:12; 149:5; Isa 54:1; 66:10f; Jer 31:7; Zech 2:14.

[44]Pss 97:8, 12; 98:5; 149:1; Isa 12:6; 24:14; Zeph 3:14; Joel 2:21, 23.

[45]Ps 68:27.

[46]Isa 9:2; 12:3; 30:29.

[47]Pss 47:2; 69:35; 96:11ff; 97:1; 98:4, 7, 8; Isa 42:10-12; 44:23; see also Isa 52:8f; 55:12; Jer 31:7.

[48]Isa 65:18f.

[49]Ps 75:10. Hab 3:18 is very similar at the same point in the poem. Isa 25:1 has this idea at the beginning of the poem.

[50]Isa 66:12, 14.

[51]Ps 75:2 (cf. §2, ¶51).

[52]Pss 12:6; 86:9; 147:2; etc.

[53]See n. 254.

[54]Ps 102:20-23.

[55]Sir 33:1-13a; 36:16b-22.

[56]Pss. Sol. 17:26-43.

from these references, yet the spirit of ancient Israel was more bound to details and would not have been capable of this comprehensive picture. Even the prophetic books seldom contain multifaceted eschatological images, as in Isa 33.[57] We arrange the whole in "seven joys," according to the pattern of 4 Ezra 7:91.

7. The *first joy is the restoration of the city of Jerusalem and the people of Israel.* A time will come when God will liberate the prisoners,[58] and "gather" "Israel's scattered ones" from all the world.[59] Then YHWH leads those languishing in foreign prisons[60] back to the homeland,[61] and grants them a "dwelling and property" in Zion and the cities of Judah.[62] He "rebuilds Zion,"[63] and appears 'there' in his majesty.[64] The great change (*šûb, šebût*) thus occurs for Jacob in this manner since the old has been restored and the end has become the beginning. This expression comes from the prophets but also appears in the psalms and psalm parts.[65] Following consideration of this type, the prophets liked to depict how the wilderness period, with its majestic miracles, will be repeated at the end.[66] Ps 68 echoes this idea, alluding with secretive words to the people's miraculous nourishment from quail and manna in the wilderness.[67] Thus, one will not sow tears forever, and someday one will harvest with joy.[68]

Joy increases since the external change of fate for Israel will reveal an internal divine conversion. YHWH's *wrath will then cease, wrath* which burdened the unfortunate people for a long time. "You have forgiven the people their guilt, atoned for all 'their' sins, taken back all your anger, and stilled the 'heat' of your wrath."[69] The generation of the end time experiences the joyful return and salvation of Israel as the greatest proof of the grace and compassion of its God.[70]

And this train of thought cannot be forgotten: the land into which one will enter will bring forth *fertile harvest* again. "Our land saves its produce." This hope, so common among the prophets,[71] only appears in Ps 85:13 in the psalter.

8. The *second joy* is that the *rule of the nations* is then broken. "The heathen sink into the grave which they prepared."[72] In other words, they receive the same fate which they gave to others. This idea, however, is *morally rationalized*, since it presupposes that

---

[57]See also S. Mowinckel, *Psalmenstudien*, vol. 2, p. 312.

[58]Ps 102:21 (Zech 9:11f).

[59]Ps 147:2 (Isa 56:8; cf. 11:11f; 27:12f; 60:4, 9; 66:20; Jer 16:14f; Mic 4:6f; Zech 8:7; Tob 13:5).

[60]Ps 102:21 (Isa 42:7, 22; 49:9).

[61]Ps 68:7 (= Zech 8:8).

[62]Ps 69:36 (Amos 9:14).

[63]Pss 147:2; cf. 69:36 (Isa 44:26; 61:4; Mic 7:11; cf. Ezek 36:10).

[64]Ps 102:17; 85:10 (Isa 24:23; 60:1ff; Zech 2:9, 14).

[65]Ps 53:7 (=14:7); 85:2; 126:1, 4.

[66]Isa 11:15; 40:3; 41:17ff; 42:16; 43:19; 44:3, 27; 48:20f; 52:12; 35:6cd; Mic 7:14f.

[67]Ps 68:10-12.

[68]Ps 126:5.

[69]Ps 85:3f; cf. Lam 4:22; Deut 32:42. The same thing occurs in the prophets in Isa 33:24; 40:2; 43:25; 44:22; Mic 7:18f.

[70]Ps 102:14 (Isa 14:1; 49:13; 54:7f; Jer 30:18).

[71]Amos 9:13; Hos 2:23f; Isa 4:2; 30:23f; Jer 31:12, 14.

[72]Ps 9:16; see also 9:6, 9.

the dominion of the nations over the whole world is connected to an immense amount of injustice and violence.[73] Like the great prophets, the psalmist confidently expected a later time when YHWH would punish the tyrannical foreign rulers. "And the Lord will not delay and will not keep violence to himself until he has shattered the loins of the cruel ones and repaid the 'proud ones' with justice, until he has 'shattered' the scepter of pride, and has completely broken the rod of the wicked, until he conducts the case of his people and makes them rejoice with his help."[74]

The psalms, like the prophets, relatively frequently portray the desired overthrow of the world kingdoms as YHWH's *universal judgment*.[75] Various passages demonstrate how this type of judgment scene was presented. "YHWH has 'taken his seat' forever, and set up his throne for judgment." "Wake up, 'my God,' 'summon' a judgment. May YHWH judge the nations. The counsel of the gods surrounds you. Take your seat over them in the highest."[76] The sense is that YHWH will take his place on the throne elevated above all the gods, thereby sitting in judgment.[77] One should note, first, that the passages accentuate that YHWH's judgment will be issued *in complete righteousness*,[78] marking the moral motivation of this expectation. Second, one should observe that YHWH's judgment is issued over the (whole) world, over "the heathen," and over (all) nations.[79] This universal judgment differentiates the second joy from the first which only concerned Israel and Jerusalem. Third, one should not overlook the fact that the image of divine judgment was not only considered a one-time event, as in late Judaism and Christianity, but at the same time was also considered a lasting condition. In English, one could substitute the term "rule" for "judgment:" "YHWH has 'taken his seat' forever, and set up his throne for judgment."[80] Fourth, this image of universal judgment appears relatively frequently, but it is not the all-encompassing image of eschatology, either in the psalms or the prophets. For this reason, the linguistic usage of modern theologians, which uses the term for the entirety of future expectations, is not justified and should be abandoned.

Sometimes, other terms express the overthrow of the nations. For example, the nations will fade away or turn to dust. They will be trapped in their own net. The pride of their princes will be humiliated.[81] Another peculiar, particularly noteworthy image is that of the *dreadful cup*,[82] filled with the "wine of reeling" (Ps 60:5) which YHWH had served the nations. Whoever must drink from this cup eats, rests, reels, falls, and sleeps forever.[83] More common than all of these descriptions, however, is the image of *war* when the

---

[73]Cf. §4, ¶7, p. 88.

[74]Sir 35:22, 23, 25.

[75]Pss 9:9, 17; 76:9; 96:13.

[76]Pss 9:8; 7:7c, 9a, 8. See the commentary.

[77]Ps 47:9; cf. Isa 24:23; Dan 4:14; 7:10; Rev 4:4.

[78]Cf. Pss 9:9; 96:13; 98:9; 99:3f; also 75:3; cf. also 9:5; 75:8 (Jer 11:20).

[79]Pss 7:9; 9:6, 20; 76:9; 82:8; 94:2; 96:13; 97:6; 98:9 (cf. Isa 8:9; 13:11; 24:1; 28:22; 66:16; Jer 25:15ff; Joel 4:2f, 9ff; etc.).

[80]Ps 9:8.

[81]Pss 9:7, 16; 68:2f; 76:13.

[82]Ps 75:9 (Jer 25:15ff, 27; 49:12; 51:39; Isa 51:17ff; Ezek 23:31ff; cf. Greßmann, *Ursprung der israelitisch-jüdischen Eschatologie*, pp. 129ff.

[83]Ps 75:9 (Jer 25:15ff, 27; 49:12; Isa 51:17ff; Ezek 23:31ff; cf. Greßmann, *Ursprung der israelitisch-jüdischen Eschatologie*, pp. 129ff.

heathen attack YHWH and his sanctuary. The heathen are defeated (see the sixth joy in ¶12). If the researcher was not connecting these images through the New Testament, they would at least speak about the "last battle of the nations" in addition to "universal judgment."

Finally, one should note that the eschatology of the psalms generally does not speak about judgment *against Israel*. Israel has to this point experienced oppression and mistreatment, and at this point will receive salvation and grace, as can be seen among the salvation prophets, especially Deutero-Isaiah. The complaint songs wish shame and destruction upon the godless opponents, even if they are Israelites (§6, ¶15). Unlike the judgment prophets, the eschatology of the psalms does not really mention these wicked compatriots.[84] Thus, it is "wisdom," not the eschatology of the psalms, which speaks about dividing Israel into the wheat and tares through wrathful judgment of the wicked.[85] The psalmists' future hope also does not expect *Israel's repentant return* to YHWH, although the psalmists do occasionally summon the people to confess according to the pattern of the prophetic warning speech. Ps 99 serves as an exception that speaks of the "great and terrible" God who "established a just order 'in Jacob' and who created justice and righteousness." Already in antiquity, God demonstrated that, contrary to his preference for being a forgiving God, he could also be an "avenger for 'all' their wickedness."[86] The influence of the judgment prophets is clear from these words.[87]

This overthrow of the rule of violence fills Israel with a dynamic satisfaction. YHWH's people see with their own eyes that their God does not act arbitrarily.[88] Their confidence in him gains new power because there is a deity who judges the earth.[89] From these ideas, the singer's glance occasionally looks beyond Israel's borders and turns to the many oppressed peoples of the world. They should also receive justice in the great divine judgment.[90]

9. The overthrow of the great natural calamities of the end time is the subject of the *third joy*. These terrible events form the material of the Zion songs. Sometimes they form an entire *universal drama*, but they are usually portrayed only in brief allusions. Their controlling line of thought is a gruesome *universal earthquake*, in which the whole earth shakes and the mountains sink into the sea.[91] One encounters the same image in the prophets.[92] It also appears in the Psalms as a sign of the horrid moral confusion that will follow the end. The gods judging unjustly are the ones causing the shaking of the foundations of the earth.[93] However, at the end YHWH will intervene and affix the earth's

---

[84]For example, see Zeph 3:11.

[85]Ps 1:5 (§10, ¶6).

[86]Ps 99:1-4, 8bc.

[87]See also 94:13ff; Pss. Sol. 17:27, 36 (Ps 125:5).

[88]Pss 9:9, 10, 11, 13; 68:23; Deut 32:43 (Ps 69:34).

[89]Pss 9:10f; 58:11f.

[90]Pss 10:18; 58:11f; 76:10.

[91]Pss 46:3; 75:4; (Jdt 16:16).

[92]Isa 24:19; Hag 2:6.

[93]Pss 75:4; 82:5.

columns.[94] At the same time, the earthquake symbolizes the *new, certain world order* which YHWH will found.[95]

Another image of the destruction of the world speaks of the *roaring waters* that are flooding toward the earth, but which YHWH repels.[96] Fantasy ties this image with the concept of the universal earthquake so that the waters cause the world to shake.[97] YHWH's battle against the waters ultimately stems from Babylonian material, and also appears in the prophets.[98]

10. God's battle against the roaring ocean is combined with YHWH's *victory* over the attacking nations in the psalms as well as the prophets.[99] The *fourth joy* contains their overthrow. It is the preferred subject of the Zion songs.[100] The particular significance of the piece of the hopeful imagery is shown by the fact that we possess several extensive poems and several more allusions to it.

Many passages, including passages among the prophets, predict that one day the nations will attack while roaring.[101] The expression "roaring" (root *hmh*) is at times selected with specific reference to the comparison with the eschatological flood of waters.[102] We hear of kings and nations[103] which have bound themselves to this line.[104] The psalms do not say against whom they march, just as the prophets are sometimes silent on this issue.[105] However, the internal context of the texts make it clear that the last strike occurs outside the gates of Jerusalem.[106] This event is sometimes stated explicitly.[107] The prophets, but not the psalms, frequently say that the nations come from the north.[108] The prophets often explain that powerful groups of riders are the ones who storm over the world.[109] The psalms, by contrast, only specify these riders occasionally: "At your rebuke, God of Jacob, horse and 'rider are' made mute."[110] A crippling horror proceeds from these gruesome hordes.[111] In unconquerable trusting faith, the psalmist affirms that all of these terri-

---

[94]Pss 75:4; 93:1; cf. 96:10.

[95]The Egyptians and Persians also use the same image for the rep-ordering of the world, but not in an eschatological manner. Cf. §3, ¶11, pp. 79, 80, and the commentary to Ps 75.

[96]Ps 46:4. The same expression (*hāmāh*) used of "roaring" waters also appears in Ps 65:8; Isa 17:12; 51:15; etc.

[97]Pss 46:4; 93:3f; see the commentary.

[98]Isa 17:12ff; see also 8:7f.

[99]Pss 46 (65:8); Isa 17:12ff; 59:19; Jer 47:2.

[100]Pss 46; 48; 76. Also see Pss 9:6f; 68:13-15, 22, 24, 29, 31; 97:2, 5; 149:5ff.

[101]Isa 8:9f; 17:12-14; 29:5-7; 31:4-9; Jer 47:2f; Ezek 38; Joel 4:9f; Mic 4:11-13; Zeph 3:8; Zech 12:2ff; 14:12ff. etc.

[102]Ps 46:7 (Isa 17:12; Jer 6:23; 50:42).

[103]Pss 48:5; 68:13; 76:13; 149:8 (Jer 50:41; Ezek 38:2f).

[104]Ps 48:5 (Joel 4:9; Isa 8:9f). See the commentary, p. 206.

[105]Isa 8:9f; 17:17; Zeph 3:8.

[106]Pss 46:5ff; 48:4, 7; 76:3f; Isa 10:32; 29:7; 30:33; 31:4; 37:22ff; Joel 4:1f, 16; Mic 4:13; Zech 12:2ff.

[107]Isa 29:1f, 7; Jer 6:23; Ezek 38:8, 11f, 16, 18; 39:2.

[108]Jer 1:13ff; 6:22; 10:22; 13:20; 47:2; 50:3, 41; 51:48; Ezek 38:6, 15; 39:2.

[109]Jer 4:13, 29; 6:23; 8:16; 47:3; 50:42; Ezek 38:4, 15; 39:20; Hab 1:8; Zech 10:5; 12:4f.

[110]Ps 76:7.

[111]Jer 47:3; Hab 3:16.

ble deeds will not horrify Zion.[112] YHWH has selected this city in which to dwell, and he protects it with marvelous streams so that no enemy can set foot in it.[113] So, the holy city endures the time of distress. YHWH Sebaot is with you. Jacob's God is your fortress.[114]

The main element of the whole is *YHWH's intervention* in the world events, the greatest miracle that happens on earth. No one will see it. Only when it is over will one marvel at the "vastness" which will then be completely visible to all.[115] God's work tolerates no spectators. This great event is more or less briefly suggested in manifold variations. Sometimes it is mentioned in general terms that the nations will be destroyed, are destroyed forever, or that their cities lay in ruins, etc.[116] More frequently, we hear of the sudden flight and scattering of the mighty army using very powerful words: "scatter," "chase," "disperse," and "fade away."[117] The cause of the flight is a panicky horror, a genuine "YHWH-fright."[118] How does it happen? "As soon as they looked, the nations were horrified, bewildered, and banished."[119] It does not say what they saw, but the texts imply that they caught sight of YHWH in all his majesty bringing destruction.[120] Using another expression, the nations are "stunned" by the appearance of YHWH and fall into a trance from which there is no awakening.[121] In these contexts, the idea often appears that the deity "threatened" his enemies.[122] This expression (root *g'r*) was originally used for the battle cry of the opponent.[123] The expression was then used of the deity when his arrival forces back the arrogant waters. On the other hand, this expression is mentioned with fire,[124] and is understood as *thunder, the* powerful voice of YHWH.[125] Afterward, the "threat" of the heathens or of the earth in the end time should be conceived as a terrible thundering. YHWH roars from Zion so that the world quakes.[126] This thunder when YHWH appears to destroy the nations is occasionally connected to the *idea of judgment*. The content of the message of thunder is judgment: "You let judgment ring out from heaven. The earth is afraid and becomes silent."[127]

The prophets often present the appearance of YHWH in dazzling images. He comes with the earthquake and with a loud noise, in the thunderstorm and in flaming fire. His breath devours like a consuming blaze, and so forth.[128] Ps 97 utilizes this material eschatologically. "Fire goes before him, and burns all around his enemies." "Mountains

---

[112]Pss 46:3; see also 75:2, 10ff; Hab 3:15.
[113]Ps 46:5, which is understandable from Isa 33:21, 23ab, 22; Ezek 47.
[114]Ps 46:6, 8, 12.
[115]Pss 46:9; 48:13; Isa 33:13.
[116]Ps 9:6f; Isa 8:10.
[117]Pss 48:6, 7; 68:2, 31; Isa 17:13; 29:5; 31:8f; 33:3.
[118]Zech 14:13; cf. Ps 48:7; Isa 8:9; 31:9; 33:3.
[119]Ps 48:6.
[120]Ps 77:17; Isa 66:18f.
[121]Ps 76:6, 7.
[122]Pss 9:6; 68:31; 80:17; Isa 17:13; 66:15.
[123]Isa 30:17.
[124]Isa 66:15; Ps 80:17.
[125]Pss 104:7; see also 77:17f.
[126]Joel 4:16; see also Isa 33:3; Ps 46:7.
[127]Ps 76:9.
[128]Isa 29:6; 30:27, 30, 33; 33:12; Ezek 38:22; 39:6.

melt like wax."[129] One should thus consider the poem as an echo of the fantastic portrayal of the theophany. Significantly, in contrast to the prophetic material, God is considered to be seated on the throne (v. 2). Without raising his hand, he lets the fire that goes before him consume the enemies. By contrast, in a deeper layer YHWH elsewhere appears as a powerful warrior, who marches forth with many chariots, smashes the head of his opponent with his own hand, and returns with the captured prisoners.[130] No matter how diverse the ideas of this material may be, it is clear that an awesome, *terrifying wrath* of YHWH dominates all of them.[131] We have one hint about the *time* of the great overthrow. YHWH helps his city when the morning approaches. Destruction rules the earth in darkness. The divine deed succeeds when the light breaks through.[132]

While all of these passages treat God as the one acting, in several passages in the psalter *Israel* itself performs the great deed and takes its vengeance upon the heathen. The poor oppressed ones go forth into battle. YHWH gives them the victory over their enemies, whose blood flows in streams, etc.[133] The reward for this victory, however, is the world domination of YHWH's people. "YHWH forces peoples under us, and nations under our feet."[134]

11. With this great strike, the world received an entirely different outlook, and that is the *fifth joy* of the redeemed. When the text speaks of the fall of the "nations," it really means the *fall of the great world empires* in which the nations were entangled. It thus follows that the time in which all of this happens is "the end of the days," a prophetic expression avoided by the psalms even though the idea is intended. After the world empires are overthrown, no person on earth will be able to exercise violence.[135] Rather, eternal peace is now assured, so that all weapons are destroyed, and the warriors forever scattered or destroyed.[136] YHWH controls wars to the ends of the world.[137]

Along with this gift to all oppressed and exiled persons, one also finds that YHWH himself assumes the *kingship* and the *rule of the world*. This idea is often expressed.[138] After all of the confusion, the God who rules the world establishes *a kingdom of righteousness*. He speaks justice among the nations.[139]

The prophets and the psalmists frequently depict how the world rule arises. The whole world will willingly subject itself to YHWH because the nations have recognized his greatness in his mighty victory.[140] At the same time, however, YHWH announced his salvation before the eyes of the nations in the salvation and transfiguration of Zion so that

---

[129]Ps 97:3,5. The latter is almost literally like Mic 1:4.

[130]Ps 68:18, 19, 22 (Isa 42:13; 51:9f; Hab 3:8, 15).

[131]Ps 76:8, 13 (Ezek 38:18; Zeph 3:8; Hab 3:12).

[132]Ps 46:8 (see the commentary); Isa 17:14.

[133]Pss 58:11; 68:13, 24; 149:6, 8 (Mic 4:13; Zech 10:3ff; 12:5ff). The following speak of the booty: Pss 68:14; 76:5f (Isa 33:4; Mic 4:13; Ezek 39:9f; Zech 14:14).

[134]Ps 47:4.

[135]Ps 10:18.

[136]Pss 46:10; 68:31; 76:4, 6 (Hos 2:20; Isa 9:4; Ezek 39:9f).

[137]Ps 46:10; cf. Hos 2:20; Isa 11:6ff.

[138]Pss 9:9; 46:11; 47:3,11; 48:3; 95:3; 97:5; 99:2 (Isa 24:23; 52:7; Mic 4:7; Obad 21; Mal 1:14; Zech 14:9.

[139]Pss 96:13; 97:2, 6; 98:9; 99; and n. 140.

[140]Pss 46:11; 47:2l; Isa 66:19; Ezek 38:16, 23; 39:7.

all could see it.[141] It thus happens that the entire world raises a *hurricane of jubilant voices*. Zion rejoices and "the daughters of Judah exult over your judgment, YHWH.[142] The heathen say, "YHWH has done a great thing to you."[143] It then describes how the nations, those from great distances and the world powers, bring their tribute to YHWH.[144] This process is generally described in terms of a pilgrimage,[145] an image also preferred by prophetic predictions.[146]

The hope for the association of heathens with YHWH unites the political (the subjugation under his world rule) with the religious (conversion to his deity). If the political elements appear in the forefront, a glorification of *Israel as the people ruling the world* can be attached. It then emphasizes that YHWH has subjected the nations to Israel and placed the nations under its feet.[147] The Jewish community, a very small people, could wish nothing more than that YHWH might expand their inheritance.[148]

12. We generally find the hope for Israel's world rule and expansion in the late and latest prophets. It is very uncommon in the psalms, where instead, the expectation of the sanctuary on Zion stands out more clearly. This transfiguration of the holy place is the *sixth joy*. With this idea, a peculiarly *provincial* idea penetrates the universally oriented image of the future expectation. YHWH "chose" only this place from among all the sanctuaries of the world. Though the many shapes of the mountains of Bashan may tower above tiny Zion, YHWH nevertheless desired only Zion for his dwelling place. Thus, universalism and particularism are melded together into a unit with powerful force in this eschatology so that the great world events climax in this place. The horde of nations break forth to Zion as the final place of asylum.[149] The hostile armies are destroyed there.[150] There, YHWH reveals himself as refuge.[151] There, YHWH marches from the battlefield in triumphal parade as victor.[152] There, he sits on the world's throne,[153] where he receives homage from the nobles of the nations.[154] The celebratory return of YHWH takes place at this location,[155] along with the triumphal weapon dance of the men of Israel.[156] Finally, the praise of those who are saved accompanies all these events with songs of rejoicing.[157] Accordingly, one understands that redeemed Jerusalem receives the most majestic predicates as "the most beautiful of the hills," "the charm of the entire world," and "the

---

[141]Ps 98:2, 3 (Isa 52:10; 59:16; 63:5).
[142]Ps 97:8.
[143]Pss 126:2; cf. 76:11; Joel 2:21.
[144]Pss 68:30, 32a, 31c, 32b; 76:12; 86:9; 102:23.
[145]Pss 22:28; 86:9; 102:23.
[146]Isa 2:2f; 18:7; 60:3ff; 66:18, 23; Jer 16:19; Mic 7:12; Zeph 3:10; Zech 14:16.
[147]Ps 47:4 (Isa 14:2; 49:23; 54:3; 60:10f; Obad 18ff).
[148]Ps 47:5; see also Isa 26:15; 27:6; 30:23; 54:3; Mic 7:14; Zech 9:7; 10:10; 12:6; etc.
[149]Ps 46:5, 6, 8; cf. Isa 7:14; 31:5; Zech 12:8.
[150]Pss 48:7; 76:4.
[151]Pss 48:4; 76:2; Isa 45:17.
[152]Pss 68:18ff; 76:12; 149:8.
[153]See §3, ¶3; Ezek 43:1ff.
[154]Ps 47:10.
[155]Ps 68:25-28.
[156]Ps 149.
[157]Pss 48; 68:20, 21, 23; 102:19, 22f; cf. Isa 12:4ff (§3).

fortress of the great king."[158] In the concluding image of the unit YHWH remains on Zion forever,[159] where he receives the honor of the entire world. Thus, Zion becomes the "end of the north," the "highest mountain of the earth,"[160] or, expressed nonmythologically, the *center* or *apex of the world.* "This is the plan for the earth, and this is the hand which is stretched over the nations."[161]

13. While all of this occurs on earth, even *greater things* happen *in heaven,* which is the *seventh joy.* Once YHWH has subdued humanity on earth, then in heaven "all gods sink in the dust before him."[162] One portrayal indicates how this occurs. YHWH appears in the council of the gods, meaning the national gods of the heathens, the heavenly lords of the world empires. He then snaps at them fearlessly: "You have wickedly misused my confidence. I thought you would rule the world in righteousness, in a manner worthy of your high rank as sons of the highest. But now you have shown that you possess neither understanding nor insight. You validate the wicked and destroy the rights of the poor. Therefore, all the earth's strongholds will totter. You will die like normal humans."[163] One should imagine that now YHWH executes the gods, the last echo of an original divine battle.[164] Afterward, God himself takes the scepter to rule the world. One encounters similar judgment speeches from YHWH against the gods in Deutero-Isaiah.[165] These passages express the conviction that the gods of the heathen must fall because they do not fulfill the commands of righteousness, and that victory belongs to YHWH's religion because it is the *religion of morality.*

Other ideas of the heavenly procedures speak about YHWH sitting upon the cherubim, the highest throne of the world.[166] The assembly of the subservient gods surround YHWH.[167] In these imaginative images the psalms present the victory of monotheism over polytheism. In its purest form, the victory is expressed: "On that day YHWH will be one and his name will be one."[168] When the gods fall, their servants must also doubt and recognize the futility of idol worship.[169] Such thoughts are prominent in Deutero-Isaiah.[170]

14. Anyone who feels the effects of the abundance of eschatological hopes, will perceive how these portrayals awaken the enthusiasm, and will understand that Ps 85

---

[158]Ps 48:2f (Isa 60:14; 62:4, 12; Jer 3:17; Zech 8:3).

[159]Ps 68:17 (Ezek 43:7).

[160]Ps 48:3; Isa 2:2. For predictions about Zion and the future among the later prophets, cf. Isa 4:2ff; 49:14ff; 52:1-12; 54; 60; 61; 62; Zeph 3:14; Zech 2:5ff; 8:1ff; etc. Tob 13:16 is an echo of Isa 54:11ff.

[161]Isa 14:26.

[162]Ps 97:7.

[163]Ps 82. See the commentary.

[164]See the commentary, p. 361.

[165]Isa 41:21ff; 44:7ff; 45:20ff; according to Isa 24:21ff, sent the gods to prison before the final "return." Behind Ps 58 stands the expectation that YHWH will set aside the unrighteous rule of the gods.

[166]Pss 99:1; cf. 97:9; Isa 33:5.

[167]Pss 7:8; 97:7.

[168]Zech 14:9.

[169]Ps 97:7; Jer 16:19f.

[170]Isa 42:17; 45:16; Jer 10:14.

concludes with the most complete exuberance. Words cannot express how majestic everything shall be. "Then we will be as though we are dreaming."[171]

So, is the comprehensive picture *internally unified* or not? Several different viewpoints can be noted with *very different conclusions*. If one looks at the impression of the whole, one can hardly fail to note that the individual parts converge to form a unity. The tone of rejoicing and jubilation summarizes everything. We must decide otherwise, however, if we look at the *origin* of the parts. One can separate the mythological portrayals (which we already addressed, pp. 257ff) from many others. One occasionally hears echoes of originally Babylonian material (pp. 257ff), but also Egyptian and Persian (pp. 257ff). The same judgment holds true when we look at the *value* of the individual. We appraise the particularly religious elements more highly than the hope for the people, even if we do not overlook its immeasurably great significance for the continuation of Israel. The *estimations of time* also lead to various conclusions. Thus, faith in the indestructibility of the holy city and hope for its restoration (which presumes the present destruction) belong to different times. Even more obvious differences appear in the following sections when we consider the psychological origin of the images of the future (section III) and their relationship to those of the prophets (section IV).

II. The Forms of the Eschatological Contents

15. Now we turn to the forms which express the eschatology of the psalms. First, we should mention the *songs of jubilation for the future*. These should be voiced when everything has happened. They also appear rather frequently among the prophets.[172] These poems have similar forms to the *hymns*.[173] The recognizable hymnic style appears throughout using the *imperative introduction* (with the subsequent *kî*)[174] the hymnic *participle*,[175] the narrative main part (with the *perfect* or historical *imperfect*),[176] etc. One encounters the same form among the prophets fairly regularly.[177]

The content makes these hymns *eschatological hymns*. While the typical hymns rejoice over divine deeds which have happened, the eschatological hymns praise the great deeds of God which belong to the future. In this context, the historical tenor of the typical hymn takes on the significance of the anticipatory *prophetic perfect*.[178] "He has performed miracles. His own right hand and his holy arm have helped him."[179] "YHWH has dealt graciously with his people."[180] The same thing happens in prophetic texts: "YHWH had compassion upon his people."[181] Sometimes *wishes* conclude the eschatological hymns, using the form of the *jussive*. "May the wicked go to the underworld." "May the man not be ob-

---

[171]Pss 126:1; cf. 85:10ff.

[172]Isa 12; 25:1-5; 26:1-6; 42:10-12; 49:13; 52:9f. For other examples, see §2, ¶51.

[173]Pss 98; 149; and 68. Ps 9:6-13, 16 can also be mentioned from among the mixed poems.

[174]Pss 98:1; 149:1, 4; §2, ¶18, 51.

[175]Pss 9:12f; 68:5, 33f, 36; 98:4ff; §2, ¶21.

[176]Pss 9:13; 98:1-3; 149:4; §2, ¶28.

[177]Isa 42:10; 44:23; 49:13; 52:9; 54:1; cf. 12:4-6.

[178]Gesenius-Kautzsch, *Hebräische Grammatik*, 28th ed., 1909, §106n.

[179]Ps 98:1.

[180]Pss 149:4; see also 9:13; 98:2-3; 149:4 uses the imperfect.

[181]Isa 49:13; 52:9; 44:23.

stinate, and may you judge the heathen."[182] One also finds *imperative petitions* to YHWH fulfilling the eschatological hope. "Arise, YHWH." "Rebuke the wild animals of the reeds."[183]

16. The "eschatological Zion songs" and the "eschatological enthronement songs" are related to the hymns. The similarity of the content in the eschatological song of Zion also appears in the form at times. It also has the anticipatory *prophetic perfect*. "He thundered so that the earth 'heaved'" "'YHWH' revealed his palaces as refuge."[184] These perfects not only portray YHWH's action, in the Zion song they also overwhelmingly portray the *opponents' actions* or the *effect upon the spectator*. "Nations roared. Kingdoms 'surged.' Truly, kings have come home 'bound.' As soon as they looked, they were horrified, bewildered, and scared away."[185] In addition, one finds *timeless sentences with a general content*. Most of these are nominal sentences in Hebrew which contain truths taken from past events. "YHWH is shelter and refuge for us." "The high one is in their midst so they do not falter."[186] Occasionally, the eschatological Zion songs conclude with the command to look upon YHWH's deeds and say: "Now come and look upon YHWH's works." "Traverse Zion, encircle it. . . . "[187]

The *songs of YHWH's enthronement* should be placed in this context to the degree that they are filled with eschatological content. The deeds of YHWH belonging to the future are also described in the form of the *perfect* and its variations. "For 'YHWH' has become king over the nations." He forced subjected nations to us. . . . " "He strengthened the earth so that it does not falter."[188] The events and the devices associated with YHWH's appearance to rule form the material. In addition, one finds *portrayals of the majestic future in nominal sentences* as well as descriptive *imperfects and perfects*. "'The princes' of the world belong to YHWH. YHWH is majestic on high."[189] The accompanying circumstances of the great eschatological deeds provide the content for these forms.

In addition to the relationship to the dominating mood, the great similarity of the genres mentioned in terms of form and content is explained especially by common dependence upon prophetic eschatology.[190]

17. Certain *hymnic passages* relate to the eschatological hymns, although they are milder in tone. These passages treat YHWH's future works as future events and therefore use the *predictive imperfect* to depict these works. "YHWH builds (participle) Jerusalem. He will gather (imperfect) the scattered ones of Israel." "The nations must come to you."[191] These passages are often found in the *individual complaint songs* in connection

---

[182]Ps 9:18, 20.

[183]Pss 9:20; 68:31; see also 9:21; 68:29, 30, 32; 53:7 = 14:7; 58:11f; 82:8; Pss. Sol. 11:8f; cf. §2, ¶36. Ps 68 belongs here as a whole even though other material and forms have been incorporated.

[184]Pss 46:7; 48:4; see also 76:4, 5.

[185]Pss 46:7; 48:5f; see also 76:3, 6, 9 (98:3).

[186]Ps 46:1, 6; see also 46:8, 12; 48:2f; 76:2, 8, 13 (Isa 12:4; Luke 1:68).

[187]Pss 46:9; 48:13f; see also 66:5; 76:12; Isa 33:13; §2, ¶52.

[188]Pss 47:4, 9; 93:1; see also 47:10; 93:3, 5; 96:13; 97:7; 99:4.

[189]Pss 47:11; 93:4; see also 47:10; 93:3, 5; 96:13; 97:7; 99:4.

[190]§2, ¶¶51, 52, 53.

[191]Ps 147:2; Jer 16:19.

with the reasons for confidence or with the certainty of being heard. These motifs have also been influenced by the hymn.[192]

18. Several *eschatological statements* are found in the "prophetic liturgies" (§11, ¶20).[193] One of these statements appears as the word of YHWH himself without any introduction. Others appear as human speech,[194] including one with a specific introduction: "I will listen carefully to what YHWH will say. . . . "[195] The tense of the statements either appears in the *imperfect* or *perfect*, though the latter is preferred. An example can be cited for each form. "Now, I will arise, says YHWH."[196] "YHWH, you have shown favor to your land. You have changed Jacob's fate and forgiven the guilt of your people."[197] The forms also appear in mixed style in which the statement begins with the perfect and continues with the imperfect.[198,199]

19. Further, one encounters the eschatological thought world in the communal complaint song, especially in the *certainty of being heard,*[200] the motif of confidence,[201] and the *petition.*[202] Their characteristic forms encompass the material. The *perfect* appears in the certainty of having been heard which takes up the request as though it had already occurred. "YHWH 'became' king forever and ever. The heathen have disappeared from the land."[203] By chance, the imperfect does not appear, though it would have been used if the highest degree of certainty had not been reached. Instead, the *future infinitive* appears: (You have heard the desire of the oppressed), "so that a person will no longer exercise violence upon the earth."[204]

The imperfect is the tense of the confidence motif. "The godless scepter will not remain upon the possession of the righteous ones."[205] While the form of both motifs remains close to the form of prophetic prediction, the *petition* departs from it more clearly. The form of the petition is the *imperative* or the *jussive* expressing a wish. "May you raise your hand against the foreign nations." "The one who thinks himself saved will be consumed in the wrath of fire. May the oppressor of your people reach an end.[206]

20. Finally, one should consider the eschatological passages in wisdom poetry.[207] One consistently finds the *predictive imperfect*. Wisdom poetry facilitates the preservation of

---

[192]Pss 68:9; 69:36f; 102:14, 15 (§6, ¶¶20, 28). A hymnic command precedes the words of Ps 69:35 and Deut 32:43 which should be related to a current rejoicing. The same happens in Tob 13:15f, while Lam 4:21 is intended ironically.

[193]Pss 75:3f, 7-9; 85:2-4, 9-14; 126:1-3.

[194]Pss 85:2-4, 9-14; 126:1-3.

[195]Ps 85:9.

[196]Ps 12:6.

[197]Ps 85:2ff.

[198]Ps 126:1, 2; cf. 85:11-14.

[199]To this point, Gunkel; from here, Begrich.

[200]Ps 10:16-18.

[201]Ps 125:3.

[202]Sir 33:1ff.

[203]Ps 10:16; see also 10:17.

[204]Ps 10:18.

[205]Ps 125:3.

[206]Sir 33:3, 11; see also Sir 33:2, 5, 8, 9, 10, 12, 13; 36:18, 19, 20, 21.

[207]Ps 94:14-15; Sir 32:22-26; and 47:22.

the original form of the eschatological statements in its own way. It tends to speak of the future destiny of the pious and the godless using the *imperfect* in the blessing saying and curse saying.[208]

III. Eschatology's Penetration of the Psalms

21. How did the eschatological hopes of the prophets find their way into the poetry of the psalms? We choose the *communal complaint song* as the *starting point* for the answer because it points out the decisive rationale for lyric's turning to the hope of the end time. Also, it makes clear where various considerations and accents of the eschatological concepts originate throughout the individual psalm genres.

Prophetic proclamation promises a healthy, enthusiastic future for Israel.[209] The current time filled with suffering, then, stands as a pitiful and deplorable contrast for the Israelite in the exilic and postexilic period. Nothing in that period corresponds in even the slightest way to the happy condition of the blessed end time. In almost every respect the current time is only a tragically distorted contrasting image. Present and future appear together in tension, a tension under which the pious suffer and moan. The measure of the hard and unbearable nature increases so that their days grow darker. Against this dark background, the light image of the future appears that much brighter and more majestic. From this spiritual condition of the pious, it is conceivable that the urgent and impatient petition of their complaint song is inadequate in its wish to be relieved of external suffering and distress. Rather, its demands turn with burning desire from the mournful present to the coming of the promised future. The spiritual torment caused by the contrast of the two times can really only be solved in this way. "Turn to the promises made in your name." "Let your prophets be confirmed."[210]

22. This condition of the communal complaint to the world of eschatology results in the fact that only *one part* of the ideas about the end time find an echo, specifically those ideas which form the contrast to the distress of the present. This section will specify these ideas more precisely. Simultaneously, it will look at the commonly preserved sentences of the previous section and clarify the details with which the petitions embrace the eschatological ideas.

The distress of the present time expressed by the complaints and petitions of the complaint songs has the following lines of thought. Israel *lies on the ground*, trampled underfoot and mistreated.[211] Its citizens are scattered among the nations. Foreign nations and their princes exercise *oppressive rule*.[212] The holy city is disgraced.[213] The *pride of Israel* is wounded unbelievably deeply. It can only think of the foreign army in the harshest expressions. Its rule consists only of *tyrannical oppression* and continual breaking of the law.[214] Its regents are nothing more than wicked persons and criminals, slayers of

---

[208]Cf. §8, ¶¶8, 15; §10, ¶6.
[209]See the portrayal in section I.
[210]Sir 36:20, 21.
[211]Pss 94:5; 106:47; Sir 33:13a; Pss. Sol. 8:28; 17:16ff.
[212]Ps 94:2; Sir 33:8, 9, 11, 12; Pss. Sol. 8:30.
[213]Sir 33:18-19.
[214]Pss 58; 94:2, 5; Sir 33:11.

widows and orphans.[215] In addition, they openly treat the defeated ones with the self-conscious lordly *pride of the victor*. Israel can only hear their presumptuous word in anger. "There is no one besides us."[216] How pitiful Israel appeared next to them. *All* joy was taken from them. Only mourning and moaning remained.[217] An elderly man who has become weak and powerless[218] is the same as a dead man.[219] The torment is sharpened when the worshipper of YHWH must see how those who defeated Israel *despise* YHWH who was not able to help his people. The torment is sharpened when the worshiper of YHWH must listen to the boastful words, "YHWH does not see. Jacob's God has no understanding."[220] They hear the *arrogance of those blaspheming God* in the prideful call, "There is no one except us."[221] And YHWH endures it all. Is it any wonder that Jews transgress against him and say, "There is no God."[222] The most stinging jab amidst all this suffering, however, is that the pious ones must say that all the distress and the impudent arrogance of the foreign rulers are ultimately caused by *YHWH's wrath* toward his own people.[223] He has taken away his grace and his compassion.[224]

The complaining community of YHWH turns its longing glance from this threatening situation to promises of the end time, with their radiant contrasts: Israel's *liberation* and *restoration*,[225] gathering its *citizens from where they have been scattered*,[226] the *overthrowing of foreign rule and unjust governments of violence*,[227] the *redemption of the holy city, and the glorification of the temple on Zion*.[228] From the sadness of the present time, one longs for the great *joy of the final days*.[229] From the distress of the time one longs for the *good fortune of the chosen ones*.[230] From the weakness of the moment one longs for the *eagle-like power of youth* in the end time.[231] From death one longs for *life*.[232] The taunting and mockery which they experience turns their desire to the promised *punishment of the oppressor*.[233] The arbitrary nature and lawlessness which they experience causes them to look to the future establishment of a *just government over all the world*.[234] Above all, however, the religious contrasts to the distress are important to the pious person. The pious

---

[215]Ps 94:3-5.
[216]Sir 33:12.
[217]Ps 106:5.
[218]Lam 5:21.
[219]Ps 85:7.
[220]Ps 94:7.
[221]Sir 33:12.
[222]Ps 53:2.
[223]Ps 85:5, 6.
[224]Pss 85:8; 106:4, 5, 47; Sir 36:17, 18; Pss. Sol. 8:27.
[225]Ps 85:8; Sir 33:13a; Pss. Sol. 11:7; 17:21.
[226]Ps 106:5, 47; Sir 33:13a; Pss. Sol. 8:28; 17:44.
[227]Pss 7:9; 94:2ff; Sir 33:9, 11, 12; Ps 56:6c; Pss. Sol. 8:30; 17:22.
[228]Ps 53:7; Sir 36:18, 19; Pss. Sol. 11:7; 17:22.
[229]Pss 85:7; 106:5.
[230]Ps 106:5.
[231]Lam 5:21.
[232]Ps 85:7.
[233]Ps 94:2; Sir 36:20.
[234]Ps 94:2; Sir 33:11.

person ultimately longs for the moment in which God shows himself in *all power and holiness* over against taunt of the heathen.[235] The pious one longs for the time when God will put *to flight and destroy* the opponent with his powerful right hand,[236] the time when God strikes all pride to the ground, and when he *forces* the marvelous recognition of his *uniqueness and his divine dignity*.[237] The pious one longs for the promised *turning of divine wrath*,[238] for the *kindling of his grace*,[239] and for the appearance of his *powerful help*.[240]

At various points, this portrayal betrays something of the mood with which the genre perceives the eschatological thoughts and ideas. Their *characteristic richness*, however, is only revealed with a closer inspection of the vocabulary of the petitions. The burning excess of the forms of expression in the petitions allows one to imagine how unbearable the one praying perceived the tension between now and then, and how powerfully the desires of the petitions exerted themselves. The manifold *shadings of the basic tenor* will not escape the careful reader. Various bitter perceptions of the time of distress call forth these shadings. Those tormented by the abundance of suffering confront YHWH with questions that are full of vehement impatience. "How long, YHWH, will the wicked; how long will the wicked rejoice?"[241] "Will you be angry with us forever?" "Will you not revive us again?"[242] They can no longer wait until the time YHWH considers right for coming. They push him forward impetuously: "Hasten the time."[243] They disrespectfully venture to make him remember the assurance he swore, as though he could forget his word. They mean the words of promise to his prophets. "Consider your oath."[244] The petition indulges in expressions of superlative power as it presents a painfully strong desire, allowing free reign for the *feeling of vengeance* to the one suffering. "YHWH, avenging God, avenging God 'appear.' Rise. Judge the earth. Repay the proud ones for what they have done."[245] "Execute your vengeance. Pour out your wrath. Annihilate the adversary. Destroy the enemy." "The one trying to escape will be consumed in the wrath of fire. Those corrupting your people will find destruction."[246] Elsewhere, a *religious demand for vengeance* replaces the *naive national demand for vengeance* which breaks forth here. This religious demand longs for the revenge for the suffering of YHWH. YHWH should take revenge on the wicked who speak boastfully and presumptuously.[247] "Shatter the heads of the princes, your enemies who say there is no one except us."[248] However, punishment alone will not suffice. "Raise your hand against the foreign nations. Show

---

[235]Sir 33:4.

[236]Sir 33:8, 9.

[237]Sir 33:1, 3, 5, 12; 36:22; Ps 94:4, 7; Pss. Sol. 17:28ff.

[238]Ps 85:5, 6.

[239]Pss 85:8; 106:4; Sir 33:17, 18.

[240]Pss 85:8; 106:4, 47; Sir 36:19; Pss. Sol. 8:27, 28; 17:45.

[241]Ps 94:3.

[242]Ps 85:6, 7.

[243]Sir 33:10.

[244]Sir 33:10.

[245]Ps 94:1-2.

[246]Sir 33:8, 11; cf. Also Ps 7:9.

[247]Ps 94:1ff.

[248]Sir 33:12.

them your power." "They should recognize what we have known, that there is no God except you, Lord."[249]

Petitions like these show that the prophetic predictions have found a dynamic echo in the hearts of the pious. They also show, of course, how far removed the mood is which encompasses the eschatological content here from the joyful mood of the prophetic words. However, the strength of the perceptions encountered in the communal complaint lets one suspect that the petitions could escalate to an enthusiasm which comes close to the prophetic trance.

23. The presupposition of this escalation is the rock solid conviction that the promises of majestic salvation in the future was no pleasing illusion to buoy them. Rather, they were absolutely certain and reliable because YHWH stood behind them. They were given in his name. He strengthened them with a *celebratory oath*, providing them with the highest degree of certainty that one could conceive.[250] Therefore, the pious ones, without succumbing to doubt, could hold fast to the belief that all the blessings of the end time would come. Uncertainty only ruled concerning the *time of fulfillment*. This faith in YHWH's promises is expressed in clear words in psalms of different genres. The careful observer, however, recognizes in these expressions that he has found in them a very significant *essential line of folk piety* extending beyond the boundaries of the individual genres.[251]

While this belief scarcely appears in days of tolerable fortune, in times of distress it breaks forth with strong dynamic power. It penetrates the communal complaint song in the *confidence motif* and in the *assurance of having been heard*. It sustains YHWH worshippers and prevents them from sinking into doubt. They base their petitions for the change of the distress upon it. The more irritating the external suffering, the more burning the spiritual torment, and the closer the temptation to doubt, the stronger they cling to YHWH's promise and the greater the power to resist the distress they possess. The eschatological hopes are expressed with a *confidence* which approaches the tone of prophetic predictions. "The godless scepter will not remain over the possession of the righteous."[252] "The heathen will not conquer us." "You will have compassion upon the family of Israel forever and you will not repel it." "You will set us upright at the time of your help, and will be gracious to the house of Jacob on the day which you promise."[253] Occasionally, an urgent prayer for salvation from the current distress rings with the joyful tone of *certainty* that speaks in the past tense.[254] "YHWH became king forever and ever. The heathen disappeared from his land."[255]

24. The power and the dynamic nature of the unwavering confidence in YHWH's promise also shows itself in the way that the *individual complaint song* conceives it. From the outset, the individual complaint song stands far removed from hopes about the end

---

[249]Sir 33:3, 5.

[250]Sir 33:10; Mic 7:20; Luke 1:73.

[251]It appears in the *communal complaint* (Sir 33:10; 36:19, 20; Pss. Sol. 7:9; 9:18f; 11:9 [Mic 7:20]), in the hymn (Pss 68:23; 149:9; Luke 1:55, 70, 73), and in the Zion song (Ps 48:9).

[252]Ps 125:5.

[253]Pss. Sol. 7:6, 8, 9. For similar expressions of this confidence which the prophets speak in the imperfect, see Ps 94:14; Pss. Sol. 12:8; 17:3.

[254]Cf. §4, ¶11; §6, ¶23.

[255]Ps 9:16.

time. In times of distress and the entreaties for his personal life, the one praying can become uncertain whether his God will help him. All the reasons for comfort do not enable him to restore his shattered trust to which he had clung previously by recalling his own and his ancestors' experience, or being aware of YHWH's gracious rule. If this happens, then he flees to the majestic final expectation for his people to see whether he may find comfort and assurance from that vantage point. The final expectation removes the cares and questions by YHWH's *sworn reaffirmation* to which all reasons for comfort are otherwise exposed without exception. The sinner who does not dare believe in the forgiveness of his own sins may feel quite comforted when he considers that YHWH will forgive all guilt in the blessed future for YHWH's people of which he is a member.[256] It must be internally liberating for the one praying who is suffering from utter hopelessness, or the one who feels burdened by YHWH's curse and also is mockingly slandered by enemies. How liberating it must be when that person turns his eyes to the promise for the future in whose glowing image he encounters the idea that YHWH will turn to the prayer of the one who is forsaken.[257]

If the penetration of eschatological faith into the genre shows its dynamic power, then above all it is shown by the tone in which it is expressed. Its prominence above all other motifs conveying the petition makes it understandable why it is only encountered in the optimistic confidence motif and in the assurance of being heard. This belief is not exposed to a wrestling with certainty. "He will redeem Israel from all its sins."[258] Under its influence, the certainty of having been heard,[259] which is itself frequently exaggerated, escalates to the point of the *certainty of the prophetic proclamation*. It even takes the form, content, and claim of prophetic proclamation. "You will rise, and have compassion on Zion. . . . Then the nations will 'see your' name, and all the kings of earth (will see) your majesty, for YHWH rebuilds Zion and appears 'there' in his majesty. He attends to the prayer of the forsaken one and does not despise 'their entreaty.' That will be written for the future generation so that the newly created people might praise YHWH," etc.[260]

However, even when the individual complaint song does not require attachment to the final expectation for Israel, it cannot resist the power of eschatological faith. We thus learn how strongly that belief must have dominated the life of Israel at times. The one praying may wrestle with himself to the point of the happy premonition of his own deliverance. He then turns his attention to the many who are suffering who look for comfort in their distress and for the security of being heard. If so, then his own experience which imparts trust and hope meets the promise of YHWH which proclaims the salvation of the people and with it the liberation from fear and suffering.[261]

25. We would greatly underestimate the significance of eschatological faith for the genre, however, if we understood it in the sense of the one praying gaining comfort and certainty for the present by a *deduction* based upon YHWH's assurance for his people in the distant future. In other words, we would underestimate the significance if we thought

---

[256]Ps 130:8.
[257]Ps 102:13ff.
[258]Ps 130:8.
[259]Cf. §6, ¶23.
[260]Ps 102:14, 16-19.
[261]Ps 69:33ff.

it worked in the following manner: if YHWH promises a hearing and deliverance for the future, then despite all the bitter experience of the present, YHWH is ultimately gracious and compassionate, and he will ultimately help me in my current troubles. In this context, the eschatological thought could only appear as a *leading motif* in the petition while its appearance in the *certainty of having been heard* and its victorious tone would be virtually incomprehensible. In addition, one should note that the vocabulary of the pertinent texts knows nothing of a mediated deliberation. Rather, the context is *spontaneous and immediate*. The pious ones live with the rock solid conviction that the change of times which has been promised stands just outside the door. This change will bring an end to all distress and anxiety for the one fearing God. Therefore, the individual who is praying can be certain about deliverance from his personal troubles. "You will rise to be compassionate to Zion . . . for 'the hour has come' to the gracious to him."[262]

Expressions of this type will cause the perceptive person to recognize the *escalation* of the eschatological belief into a burning, intoxicating, thrilling *enthusiastic* piety.

How does blessed certainty arise in the hearts of the pious ones of Israel that "the hour has come" for YHWH "to be gracious" to Zion,[263] or that it is "time for YHWH to act?" Words like these show the way. From prophetic prediction, Israel knows that a time of extreme distress and hostility precedes the great change bringing salvation at the end of the days.[264] The present time grows increasingly gloomy as its particular references approach the gruesome image that the prophets have presented for the days before YHWH's intervention. When this happens, then far from letting itself be discouraged and oppressed, eschatological faith sees a majestic confirmation of that which it believes. Specifically, it sees an undeniable sign that the last days have begun. Now, the hour has come for YHWH to be gracious to Zion. Only a few more days and the suffering of this time will be conquered and YHWH's eternal kingdom will break forth with all of the goods and gifts which are so longingly desired.

An unbelievable *frenzy of joy* overwhelms the pious ones with this confirmation of their faith. Only this kind of frenzy could solve the problem of the most terrible inner tension. It is a particular contrast to the bitter distress, fear, and pain in which they still find themselves. With an incomparable *impatience* that is only comprehensible in this situation, they wait for the complete confirmation that YHWH will act. It is indeed time. With unparalleled boldness and with a flood of demands which only the highest degree of earthly torment could produce, their powerful imagination transcends the time that still divides them from YHWH's coming. Their imagination hurries to his entry with rejoicing. It indulges in the alluring images of prophetic promises. It comforts itself with the burning hunger of promised triumphs that allow one to forget all the illnesses of this time. The more passionately the enthusiastic piety throws itself into this world so majestically close, the deeper the world of suffering and distress surrounding them sinks away. With their ecstatic eye they see the present as a blessed time though its fulfillment is still quite far away.

26. One can easily understand how the contents of the final hope at this stage could only find corresponding lyrical expression in the *hymn*, and in those genres closely

---

[262]Ps 102:14.

[263]Pss 102:14; 119:126.

[264]See the details provided in the portrayal in section I.

associated with the *content* and the *leading mood* of the hymn. Only in the hymn do joy and enthusiasm come alive in a manner which is closely enough related to eschatological material that its expressions could simultaneously encompass the entire world. Both the content and the leading mood contain an act of YHWH as the center point. This act glorifies him and shows his greatness surpassing all nations and gods, but it simultaneously bestows deliverance and honor to his people. Hymnic and eschatological piety also concur in that they praise the deeds of YHWH which have happened and belong to the past. An essential challenge of the penetration of the eschatological thought world into the above mentioned genres is thereby signified. The prophets illustratively preceded folk piety and also expressed their joyful certainty of the end time in lyrical form.[265]

The *character* of the individual genres determines the *selection* and *accentuation* of the eschatological ideas. Turning to the hymn, if we ask which ideas regarding the end time find an echo here, it immediately becomes clear that the hymn in general was not used in eschatology. Rather, one of its forms adopted the material and forms of the victory song for its own.[266] Only the victory hymn provides the possibility for the poet to speak of an event in the recent past whose dynamic after-effects still affect the present. Only the victory hymn also provides a place to express the eschatological hope appropriately, a hope whose dominant train of thought is YHWH's victory over the nations.

Thus, one can understand that the hymn contains the ideas which step to the foreground that are associated with the *conquest of the nations by YHWH*: YHWH's powerful *arousal* against his opponents,[267] his glowing victory,[268] the destruction of the hostile assembly and their cities,[269] capturing their king and their princes,[270] the liberation of their own prisoners,[271] and the *division of an abundant booty*.[272] Those are the deeds of deliverance which the victory hymn praises as having just happened.[273] The *victor's triumphal entry* follows, providing the penetration of further eschatological ideas: the celebratory entry of the victorious YHWH,[274] and the beginning of a *just government encompassing the world*.[275] However, the city YHWH enters is the holy city of Zion, which he has chosen as the center of his dominion.[276]

The eschatologically flourishing thoughts about Zion can only be mentioned briefly in the victory song when the entry of the victor into his city is addressed. These thoughts push their way to center stage in the Zion songs. This genre specifically praises the sanctuary (cf. §2, ¶52). Here, the distresses of the end time are portrayed which *threaten*

---

[265]Cf. §2, ¶51 for the hymn; §2, ¶52 for the Zion song; §3, ¶11 for the enthronement song; §8, ¶39 for the communal thanksgiving song; and §8, ¶22 for the pilgrimage song.

[266]Cf. §2, ¶¶41, 50, 51; §8, ¶27.

[267]Ps 68:2-3.

[268]Pss 9:6, 13; 68:13; 98:1.

[269]Pss 9:7; 68:22.

[270]Pss 68:19; 149:8.

[271]Ps 68:6-7.

[272]Ps 68:13ff.

[273]Cf. 9:10; 98:2, 3; 149:4.

[274]Pss 68:16-18; 98:9.

[275]Pss 68:19; 98:9.

[276]Pss 68:30ff; 98:9.

the holy city: the shaking of the world and the danger of flood,[277] the nations' attack against God's city,[278] and their lamentable destruction before its walls.[279] This genre speaks about the *marvelous protection* by God's torrents.[280] With particular pride, this genre states that this city is YHWH's city and residence.[281]

Other eschatological ideas find expression in the *enthronement songs*. Since this genre is dominated by the entry of the king, his proclamation, and enthronement, here the light shines upon YHWH's coming kingship. It shines on YHWH's proclamation as king,[282] on his march to the throne,[283] the homage of the nations,[284] and the appearance of his universal, just government.[285] The battle with the nations is considered here *in advance*. YHWH marches from the battlefield.[286] The eschatological shuddering of the earth also leads the way.[287]

27. It is characteristic of the *enthusiastic mood* which encompasses the eschatological ideas that it is insufficient to express the original possibilities, joys, and excitement. It is not satisfactory to summon the entire breadth of the nations of the world to praise the majestic God[288] (which the hymn also does at its climax).[289] Instead, it demands a whole "new song."[290] Only such a new song could be suitable for the unparalleled events of the end time. The same joy-filled words are repeated tirelessly ("Sing to 'our God,' sing! Sing to our king, sing! . . . Sing an artistic song!"[291]), which is overpowering to the Israelite with a mildly escalated feeling. The liveliness and the arousing nature of the leading mood then becomes recognizable as the above mentioned genres are transported into the midst of the eschatological elements. This liveliness is also recognizable when moments like these *are sought out* that abound in the various feelings and filled with the utmost tension. They are pushed into the center of focus. YHWH defeats the nations, and is called out as king. Now his entry is prepared, his majestic entrance and thus the *beginning* of a just kingdom. YHWH has graced his people with victory. Now the victors, holding the blood-drenched sword, *stand* and *sing* the victory song to their God. The manacled kings and princes of the nations are before them, those against whom the judgment shall be completed.[292] *Mythological ideas* are revitalized and stand out clearly in the assertions of the poetry: the *shaking of the world* at the end time,[293] the nations' attack and YHWH's

---

[277]Ps 46:2-4.
[278]Pss 46:7-8; 48:5-6.
[279]Pss 46:9ff; 48:7-8; 76:4, 5-6.
[280]Pss 46:5; see 48:2-4.
[281]Pss 46:5; 76:3; 48:2-4.
[282]Pss 10:16; 47:8; 93:1; 96:10; 97:1; 99:1.
[283]Ps 47:6.
[284]Pss 47:9-11; 96:7-9.
[285]Pss 96:13; 97:8; 99:4.
[286]Ps 47:4-5.
[287]Pss 93:1, 3; 96:10; 97:2ff.
[288]Pss 47:2; 96:1, 3, 7; 97:1; 98:4; 99:1.
[289]Cf. §2, ¶7.
[290]Pss 96:1; 98:1; 149:1; cf. Isa 42:10.
[291]Ps 47:7; see also 96:1f, 7f, 13; 98:9.
[292]Pss 96; 149; see also 9:6ff; 46; 47; 48; 68; 76; 97; 98.
[293]Ps 46; 93.

intervention,[294] the miraculous stream around the city of God,[295] YHWH's terrible appearance,[296] and the raising of Zion to the mountain of the north.[297] It is also decisive that the events of the last time appear to be almost completely associated with the *interests of the people*. He expanded "our" inheritance, the "pride of Jacob" whom he loved.[298] He was a God of help in "our" suffering.[299] With the victory over the nations he "considered" "his love and faithfulness for the house of Israel."[300] To take vengeance upon the nations is the majesty loaned to his pious ones.[301] Finally, it is also characteristic of the mood that the present distress in which the pious now stand, is somehow affected. Thus, this enthusiastic piety gladly tarries over those ideas which stand in illuminating contrast to the present situation by painting them *more broadly*. It indulges in the images of *revenge*.[302] It is revived by the *triumph* which has been granted to YHWH's despised people.[303] It rejoices over the *peace* which will now follow the anguish of a time of war.[304]

28. If prophetic prediction finds an echo in psalmody that closely approximates prophetic joy and certainty, then it is not strange that the last step would be taken so that a prophetic form, the oracle, would itself enter psalmody. The place within psalmody which comes into question is the *liturgy*. For a long time the oracle had a role in the liturgy.[305] Just as the divine promise tended to follow the typical communal complaint song which expresses that the song has been heard,[306] so the *prediction of salvation* follows the petition for the change of destiny and the introduction of the time of salvation. "I will listen to what YHWH says. 'Truly,' he speaks of salvation for his people and to his faithful ones 'and to those who turn to him, full of hope.' Indeed, his help is near for the pious so that 'his' majesty might dwell in our land," etc.[307] Or, the community sings a hymn in eschatological jubilation that is followed by God's own voice confirms the certainty. "When I perceive the time, I will hold a just court myself. When the earth totters along with its inhabitants, I will secure its columns myself."[308] Again, the combination is different in that the petitioning community places the great saving deed of God before them, in prophetic style with rejoicing and jubilation, as though it has already happened. The community zealously longs for the completion of that about which the prophets were so certain.[309]

---

[294]Pss 46; 48; 76.

[295]Pss 46:5; 48:2-4.

[296]Pss 68; 97.

[297]Pss 48:3; 68:16; 76:3.

[298]Ps 47:4-5.

[299]Ps 68:20.

[300]Ps 98:3.

[301]Pss 149:9; etc. See also 47:10; 48; 76; 99.

[302]Pss 68:24; 76:13; 97:8; 149:5f; Deut 32:43; Jdt 16:18.

[303]Pss 47:10; 68:4ff.

[304]Ps 46:9ff.

[305]Cf. §11.

[306]Cf. §4, ¶14.

[307]Ps 85:9ff.

[308]Ps 75:3-4.

[309]Ps 126.

IV. Eschatological Psalms in Relation
to the Eschatology of the Prophetic Books

29. The character of the *eschatology of the psalms* can be more clearly determined by a comparison with the *eschatology of the prophetic books*. In so doing, it becomes clear immediately how much psalmody presupposes prophetic predictions and appropriates its material. We begin with the most superficial example as the clearest. A number of *expressions* that are characteristic of prophetic proclamation about the future reappear in psalmody in the same sense. Prophecy speaks of a specific time (*mô'ēd*, or *'ēt*) when YHWH will bring salvation.[310] The same is true for the psalms.[311] The prophets know that his coming is near (*qārôb*).[312] One psalm uses the same word in a corresponding context.[313] Prophetic expressions for the eschatological deed of YHWH reappear in the psalms: "act" (*'āśāh*), "make known" (*nôda'*), "show" (*nir'āh*), "arise" (*qūm*).[314] The decision in the battle against the nations in both cases leads to YHWH's rebuke in which the word *g' r* is used.[315] A particular line of thought for prophetic eschatology is the *radiating of divine light*.[316] It is found again in prophetic formulation[317] where Zion is the *object of rejoicing* (*māśôś*).[318] Ps 48:3 speaks of its future destiny using the same word.

30. Individual expressions and entire sentences of prophetic prediction are also taken up, an indication of the esteem in which piety held these formulations. The expression, "Now I will arise, says YHWH," is encountered again in the response to the promissory oracle.[319] Ps 102:14 clearly alludes to this expression at the beginning of the certainty of having been heard: "You will arise and show compassion to Zion." One finds the message of prophetic certainty: "YHWH has done a great thing."[320] The message that YHWH will gather the *scattered ones* of his people is expressed in words in one psalm which undeniably echo words of the prophets.[321] Ps 68:7 stands in a similar relationship to prophetic texts when it speaks of the YHWH's return of the most isolated and the liberation of those captured.[322] The prediction that *the nations will see YHWH's majesty* is reiterated in the Psalms with the same expressions.[323] The prophetic expression of the "breaking of

---

[310]Hab 2:3; Dan 8:19; 11:27, 29, 35; 12:1, 4.

[311]Pss 75:3; 102:14; 119:126.

[312]Isa 5:19; 13:6; Joel 1:15; 4:14.

[313]Ps 85:10.

[314]Pss 119:126 (Isa 44:23); 9:17; 48:4; 76:2 (Isa 19:21; Ezek 35:11; 38:21); 102:17 (Isa 60:2; Zech 9:14); 12:6; 68:2; 102:14 (Isa 28:23; 33:10).

[315]Isa 17:13; 66:15; Pss 68:31; 76:7.

[316]*'ôr nāgāh* (Isa 9:1), *wezārah 'ôrekāh* (Isa 58:10); see also Isa 60:2 (*yizrah yhwh*).

[317]Ps 97:11 (*'ôr zārah*).

[318]Isa 60:15; 65:18; see also 62:5.

[319]Ps 12:6; Isa 33:10; and 28:21.

[320]Ps 126:2, 3 (*higdîl yhwh la'sôt*); Joel 2:21.

[321]Ps 147:2; cf. Isa 27:13; 56:8; Jer 30:17; Mic 4:6; Zeph 3:19.

[322]Isa 42:7, 22; 49:9.

[323]Cf. Isa 60:2 (*ūkebôdô 'ālayik yērā'eh*) with Ps 102:17 (*nir'āh bikbôdô*) and Isa 66:19 (pronouncement of YHWH's majesty on those who do not *rā'ū kebôdô*) with Ps 97:6 (*rā'ū kōl hā'ammîm kebôdô*).

the bow, sword, and club" is almost literally congruent with a psalm passage.[324] The sentence "YHWH helped with his right hand and his holy arm" corresponds to the vocabulary of eschatological passages.[325] Ps 98:3 agrees literally with all of Isa 52:10b. Examples like those provided could be multiplied, but we stop in order to keep another point in view which is important for the relationship of prophecy to psalmody.

31. There are places in the eschatological psalms which can only be understood from prophetic eschatology. The words "the mountain of Zion is the end of the north"[326] is only made accessible to understanding when one recognizes that it presumes the prophetic expectation that, in the final times, Zion will occupy the place of the high mountain of God in the north. Originally, Zaphon appeared in place of the mountain of Baal.[327] Or, one can think of the idea that the city of God will be encircled by a stream full of water, which does not correspond to the reality of Jerusalem.[328] Even here the words presuppose an expectation that rests upon the predictions of the prophets. When Zion becomes the mountain of the world, transfigured to the site of paradise, then the wonderful stream of paradise full of tributaries will go forth from it.[329] Passages like the ones cited make it quite clear that the eschatological ideas they contain are presumed to be known. Psalmody here lives undeniably in the hopes which prophetic prediction first ignited.

If one accepts that the eschatological psalmic poetry often makes direct reference to prophetic prediction,[330] then one can see that no matter where one begins, the eschatology of the psalms presumes the prophetic proclamation about the future and shows itself to be dependent upon that proclamation. Psalmic poetry should thus not be seen as the place in which eschatology developed and which then influenced the prophets.[331] That relationship should instead be seen from the reverse perspective, a result that was already anticipated through the discourse concerning the enthronement songs, which Mowinckel considered the source of eschatology.[332]

32. The full range of prophetic eschatology was not adopted by psalmody. This fact is also important for understanding the relationship between psalmody and prophecy. Beginning again with the superficial elements, then certain expressions of prophetic expectation about the end do not appear. We can search in vain for expressions like "the end of the days" or the "day of YHWH" in psalms influenced by eschatology. Significant contents of prophecy are also lacking. The psalms mentioned know of *no final judgment against Israel*. They know nothing of the *wicked citizens of their own people*. They do not expect a *repentance of the people* to their God at the end of the days (see ¶8). In other words, only the eschatology of the *salvific prophets* with its light, Israel-friendly message

---

[324]Hos 2:20 and Ps 76:4.

[325](*hôšî'āh lô yemînô ūzerôa kōdšô*) cf. Isa 59:16 (*wattôša' lô zerô'ô*) and 63:5 (*wattôša' lî zerô'î*). It echoes Isa 52:10.

[326]Ps 48:3.

[327]Cf. O. Eißfeldt, *Baal Saphon, Zeus Kasios und der Durchzug der Israeliten durchs Meer*, Halle, 1932. See also the commentary to this passage.

[328]Ps 46:5.

[329]See the commentary to Ps 46:5.

[330]See above, p. 269.

[331]Contra Mowinckel, *Psalmenstudien*, vol. 2.

[332]Cf. §3, ¶¶8ff.

found an echo in psalmody, not the eschatology of the *great prophets of judgment*. In addition, the hope for a messiah is unknown. The psalms know of no human king of salvation. Their final expectation only knows of an act of YHWH, of a coming kingdom of the God of Israel. This condition of the eschatological psalms is perhaps associated with its origin in the postexilic period when the messianic hope receded among the prophets (see section VIII). Only after the completion of the canonical psalter, when the messianic hope was revived in Judaism, did psalmic poetry also utilize it.[333]

Now, we should consider the fact that *YHWH's universal rule* and *the place of Israel* as the ruling people in his kingdom essentially recede in the psalms while the later prophets give special attention to them.[334] This difference can perhaps be explained by the fact that the poets of the psalms are primarily interested in the promised removal of the present distress.

The selection made by psalmody from the prophetic final expectations once again confirms that the psalms are not the point of origin for eschatology. Rather, they presuppose the prophets. In comparison to the prophets, psalmody consistently stands at a second stage which imitates that which was original to the prophets.

V. Other Prophetic Genres in the Psalms

33. The influence of other prophetic genres on psalmody cannot remotely be compared to the relatively broad incorporation of eschatological material and forms. However, it is present and can be demonstrated clearly enough from the available traces.

34. From these prophetic genres, we encounter the *word of rebuke* three times.[335] The *threat* is found only once.[336] See Ps 95 for an unexpressed threat like those which can appear in the prophets. Examples of prophetic *judgment speeches* do not appear in pure form in the psalter. Rather, they are mixed with other genres.[337] Finally, one encounters the prophetic *torah*,[338] and the admonition.[339] The genres most characteristic of the prophets of judgment, the rebuke and the threat, exercised the least influence on psalmody if one surveys the evidence. We will discuss the reason for this later. First, the fact of the influence should be demonstrated.

The evidence can be presented which shows that the forms and content characteristic of the rebuke and threat recur in the above mentioned passages. First, the forms: among the introductory formulas of the rebuke one finds the *command to hear*. "Hear the word of YHWH you scoffers."[340] "Hear YHWH's word, Israelites."[341] Relatedly, the rebuking section of Ps 50:7ff begins, by form, with a speech of accusation (cf. ¶36). "Hear, my people. Thus will I speak." the rebuke itself begins with an *indignant question*. "Why is it that

---

[333]Cf. Pss. Sol. 17:23ff; 18:6ff.

[334]See the end of ¶11 and the beginning of ¶12.

[335]Pss 50:16-20; 53:1-4, 5-6; and perhaps 81:9-12. Perhaps Ps 52:3ff is formed in imitation of a prophetic rebuke speech.

[336]Ps 53:6.

[337]Pss 50; 82.

[338]Ps 50:14-15, 22-23.

[339]Pss 81:14; 82:3-4; 95:8-11.

[340]Isa 28:14.

[341]Hos 4:1. See also Hos 5:1; Jer 2:4; Mic 3:1,9.

you climb on the roofs?"[342] "What have you done, and who are you that you have here hewn out a grave?"[343] The beginning of the rebuke in 50:16 corresponds to that: "What are you thinking, reciting my statutes and taking my commands in your mouth?" The same is true for the beginning of Ps 52:3: "Why do you commend evil, 'o man,' 'against the pious' all the time?" Occasionally the indignant question is raised because those being rebuked know better than they are acting: "Hear, heads of Jacob, judges in the house of Israel. Is it not for you to know right? But you hate good and love evil. . . . "[344] The rebuke in Ps 53:5f is formed the same way: "Do the evil-doers who are 'leading' my people 'astray' have no insight? They eat 'YHWH's' bread, but do not call on his name."

The rebuke likes to introduce the *words used by those being rebuked* with a form of *'āmār*: "Woe to those bearing sins . . . who say, Let him hurry. Let him hasten his deed so that we see it."[345] Ps 53:2 agrees with this practice: "The fool says in his heart, there is no God." In the context of prophetic rebukes we often find *historical overviews* which allow the guilt of those being rebuked to appear vividly in contrast to the deeds of YHWH.[346] A corresponding overview is found in a rebuking context in Ps 81:9ff.

The rebuke frequently turns *directly to those being rebuked* in the second person.[347] The state of Pss 50:16ff and 81:9ff corresponds to this pattern. Even the angry address in Ps 52:3 can be understood from this perspective. However, no less frequently those being rebuked are addressed in the third person.[348] Ps 53:2 follows this form of rebuke. The agreements coincide even in the details. One can compare how the *all encompassing nature of the guilt* is accentuated.[349]

The contents agree with the forms. The one being rebuked is designated as *nābāl*.[350] Another designation is "pô'ālê 'āwen."[351] The objection of the disgusting wickedness is expressed similarly.[352] The expression that there is no one who does good has its prophetic counterpart.[353] The sentence, "Everyone turns away," has its formal and material prophetic correspondence.[354] The accusation that they did not ask YHWH is found in both places.[355] In addition, one can mention: *inattention to discipline*,[356] *not listening to YHWH's voice*,[357]

---

[342]Isa 22:1.

[343]Isa 22:16; see also Jer 4:30; Ezek 18:2.

[344]Mic 3:1-2.

[345]Isa 5:19; see also Amos 6:13; 8:5; Isa 5:20; 10:9ff, 13ff; 28:15; 29:15; Hos 2:7; 10:3; 12:9; Jer 2:20, 25, 35; 8:8.

[346]Amos 2:9ff; Hos 11:1ff; Jer 2:1ff; 3:6ff; 7:29ff; Mic 6:3ff; Ezek 16; 20; 23.

[347]Isa 5:8ff; 22:1ff, 16ff; 28:14ff; 30:1ff; Amos 4:1-3; 5:18ff; 6:13; 8:4ff; etc.

[348]Isa 1:23; 5:11-12, 18-19, 20, 22-23; 8:6; 10:5ff; 28:1ff; 31:1ff; Amos 6:3-7; Hos 4:7-8, 10ff; Mic 2:1ff; 3:2, 5, 11; etc.

[349]The expression in Ps 53:4, *kullô sāg*, has its prophetic parallel in Isa 1:23, *kullô 'ôhēb šōhad werôdēf šalmônîm*, or in Isa 9:16, *kî kullô hānēf ūmēra'*. See also Jer 6:13; 8:6,10; cf. Also Isa 56:10; Jer 6:28; 9:1; Hos 7:4. Cf. *yahdāw ne'elāhū* in Ps 53:4 with *yahdāw šābērū 'ôl* in Jer 5:5.

[350]Ps 53:2; Isa 32:6; cf. Jer 3:22

[351]Ps 53:5; Hos 6:8; Isa 31:2; see also Isa 32:6; 59:6.

[352]Ps 53:2; Isa 1:4; Jer 6:28; Ezek 16:52; Zeph 3:7.

[353]Ps 53:2,4; Isa 59:4; 64:6; Jer 8:6.

[354]Ps 53:4; Jer 6:28; 8:6.

[355]Ps 53:3; Isa 9:12; 31:1; Jer 10:21; Zeph 1:6.

[356]Ps 50:17; Jer 2:30; 5:3; 32:33; 35:13; Zeph 3:2; cf. Jer. 7:28; 17:23.

friendship with thieves,[358] *adultery,*[359] and *deceptive* and *lying speech.*[360] The rebuke against the priests in Ps 53:5f has its prophetic counterpart.[361] Individual ideas which recur in psalmody include the *neglect of priestly knowledge,*[362] and *leading the people astray.*[363]

In prophecy, the rebuke is most closely associated with the threat. This connection is found in the psalms only once.[364] One cannot make a comparison with the prophetic threat because of the brevity and because of the corruption of the text.[365] In this context it should be noted that, like the prophets, psalmody does know the veiled, unexpressed threat.[366]

35. The careful observer cannot miss the fact that the rebuke and the threat which are imitated in the psalms show remarkably little contact with the 8th and 7th century prophets. The passionately driving manner is lacking, as is the raging cry of *hôy* used to prod those being rebuked, the terrifying *lākēn* of the threat, and the specific concrete objections. Instead, a greater stillness generally dominates the imitating words of the psalms. The contents are more general. The colors are more pale. The distance from the preexilic judgment prophets can be clearly traced. The contact of the psalm elements with the postexilic prophets stands out more clearly. The psalm elements speak with the forms of the postexilic prophets and treat their contents. One can compare the passages cited above. With this recognition, we come close to answering the question why the rebuke and the threat appear so infrequently in psalmody. It is easy to understand that the lyric material suppressed the gloomier words of the prophets rather than the reserved ones which avoid mention of the people. The fact that the rebuke and threat appear so seldom in psalmody is grounded in postexilic prophecy. In postexilic prophecy the rebuke and threat recede dramatically in comparison to preexilic prophecy. For this reason, it is understandable that it would hardly come into play more frequently in psalmody.

36. *Prophetic judgment speeches* utilize several performance forms, but the preserved examples in psalmody only imitate the *speech of the accuser at the trial*[367] and the *speech of the judge.*[368] Since the judge speaks about his own case in the latter example, it comes close to the first form in the element of the accusation.

As with the rebuke and threat, we will examine the agreement of *form and content* with the prophets. The judgment speech elicits a *portrayal of the judgment scene.*[369] In the accuser's speech *heaven and earth* are brought to judgment.[370] It begins with the *summons*

---

[357]Ps 81:12; Isa 66:4; Jer 7:13, 24, 26, 27; 9:12; 11:8; 35:14; Zeph 3:2.

[358]Ps 50:18; cf. Isa 1:23.

[359]Ps 50:18; perhaps Jer 23:10; Mal 3:5.

[360]Ps 50:19; Isa 32:7; 59:3, 4, 7; Jer 8:10; 9:7; Mal 3:5.

[361]Hos 4:4ff; 5:1ff; 6:9; Isa 28:7; Jer 2:8; 4:9; 5:31; 6:13; 8:10; 14:18; Ezek 22:26; Mic 3:11; Zeph 3:4; Mal 1:6; 2:1ff.

[362]Cf. Ps 50:5b, 6a with Hos 4:6; Jer 2:8; Mal 1:6; 2:2, 7f.

[363]Cf. Ps 53:5a with Hos 4:5; Mal 2:8.

[364]Ps 53:6b.

[365]See the details in the commentary.

[366]Cf. Ps 95:7ff; with Isa 5:7; 29:14; Jer 5:29; 9:8; Amos 5:19-20; 8:7.

[367]Ps 50:7-13.

[368]Ps 82:3-7; see Isa 41:21ff.

[369]Ps 82:1; Isa 3:13.

[370]Ps 50:6, as with Isa 1:2. Also in the defense speeches of Jer 2:12 and Mic 6:1ff.

to the accused.[371] It proceeds to the other parties using the *second person.*[372] It begins with a placating *question directed to the opponents.*[373] Next, it undermines the opponents' excuses in order to move forward to the particular point of contention.[374]

The judges speech begins by *addressing the accused.*[375] He lays forth the point of contention in an accusatory tone. He confirms[376] that the opponent has *no response* and is silent. This confirmation happens in a way in which the judge, perhaps turning to the spectators, speaks about the silent ones in the third person.[377] Then, the *proven guilt* is expressed[378] with the final word pronouncing the *judgment.*[379] The situation then turns again to the parties over whom the judgment was issued.[380]

37. *Agreements in content* appear alongside the agreements in form. It is YHWH who appears in the heavens as judge.[381] YHWH appears as the accuser of his people.[382] YHWH is the judge who speaks the verdict.[383] The accused are YHWH's *own people*[384] or the *gods of the nations.*[385] YHWH speaks the judgment to them.[386] The reason for YHWH's reprimand to his people is the *over evaluation of the cult* and the neglect of other *obligations.*[387] YHWH accuses the gods that they *judge unjustly* and favor the wicked.[388] The battle against breaking the law and favoritism can be illustrated in prophecy from Amos onward.[389] The idea that the gods have *neither understanding nor insight* was a prophetic idea since Deutero-Isaiah.[390] The corresponding speech in Isa 41:24, 29 has a similar affirmation to the judgment speech in Ps 82:5. Additional agreements of content can scarcely be cited. However, those already cited, when taken with the formal agreements, suffice to confirm that psalmody also used the prophetic judgment speech as a model.

---

[371]Ps 50:7, as with Jer 2:4. One should also compare Isa 1:2, Mic 6:3 summons to take note proceeds against the judges, not the other parties.

[372]Pss 50:8, 9, 12; 82:2, 3, 4, 6, 7; like Isa 3:14b-15; Jer 2:5ff, 29ff; Mic 6:3ff.

[373]Ps 82:2; like Isa 3:14; see also Jer 2:5; Mic 6:3.

[374]Ps 50:8ff; like Isa 43:22ff.

[375]Ps 82:2; like Isa 43:22ff.

[376]Ps 82:5; like Isa 41:24, 26, 28.

[377]Ps 82:5; like Isa 41:26, 28; see also Isa 43:9.

[378]Ps 82:5; like Isa 41:24, 26, 28.

[379]Ps 82:6-7; and Isa 41:29.

[380]Isa 41:29, by contrast, speaks in the third person, a deviation which can be explained by the fact that the unfriendly parties stole away early without waiting for the verdict.

[381]Ps 50:6; like Isa 1:2; Jer 2:12; Mic 6:2.

[382]Ps 50:7ff; like Isa 1:2-3; 3:14; see also the accusatory sections of the defense speech in Jer 2:8, 11.

[383]Ps 82:2ff; like Isa 41:29.

[384]Ps 50:7ff; like Isa 1:2-3, 18-20; 3:14b-15; 43:22-28; Jer 2:4ff, 29ff; Mic 6:3ff.

[385]Ps 82:2ff; like Isa 41:21ff; 44:6ff.

[386]Ps 82:6-7; like Isa 41:29.

[387]Ps 50:8ff. This genuine prophetic idea is expressed in a judgment speech in Isa 43:22ff.

[388]Ps 82:2ff.

[389]Usually the rebuke and threat speak about it. One encounters it in YHWH's accusatory speech in Isa 3:13ff.

[390]Cf. Ps 82:5; Isa 44:9, 18.

38. The influence of the *prophetic torah* upon psalmody is slight. This lone genre imitating a priestly form of speech (cf. §8, ¶44, p. 250) echoes only in isolated tones.[391] It does not appear as an independent unit. By comparing the above-mentioned passages with the prophetic *tôrôt*,[392] one can recognize the lines of thought which arose from the torah of the prophets. First, one can point to the *commanding imperative*,[393] then the *angry address*.[394] The *refusal of the sacrifice* and the placing of other commands constitute the prophetic elements.[395]

So much for the agreements. If one looks closer, one can ascertain characteristic differences. In imitating prophetic speech, the polemic against sacrifice is *abundantly more rationalistic*.[396] Above all the prophetic *tôrôt* and their imitations differ from one another with regard to what they demand in place of the commonly refused sacrifice. The prophets demand fulfillment of the commands of the law,[397] turning to the ways of YHWH,[398] grace, and the confession of God.[399] The imitation of the prophetic torah also knows about impeccable conduct. However, the imitation does not place this command in such stark contrast to the cult as the prophets do. Rather, the imitation places it above a command which though it stands in contrast to sacrifice it does not leave the realm of the cult itself. Specifically, it demands the *thanksgiving song* instead of the thanksgiving offering. The border of the prophetic influence can thus be recognized in this attitude. The prophets certainly succeeded in breaking the overvaluation of the sacrifice in cultic religion. However, they were unable to get the entire content of their torah accepted. Relatedly, the poetry of the psalms certainly imitated the prophetic torah which had become so significant, but it was not able to appropriate the ultimate ideas of the prophetic torah. This imitation remained in the middle between the original priestly teaching and the radical prophetic command.

39. More so than the torah, the *admonition* influenced psalmody.[400] The imitated pattern is easy to recognize in the psalms by form and content. In the prophets, the admonition is addressed to the *people* and its contents are the well-known prophetic commands. "Judge the 'oppressed,' the orphans. Give the suffering and the poor his right. Save the humble and those thirsting. Take them from the hand of the wicked."[401] One of the ancient prophets could just as easily have spoken these words.[402] The general

---

[391]Ps 50:14-15, 22-23.

[392]Amos 5:21-24; Hos 6:6; Isa 1:10-17; 58:6-7; 66:3ff; Jer 6:20; 7:21.

[393]Ps 50:14, 15, 22; Isa 1:16, 17; see also Jer 7:21.

[394]"You who forget God" (Ps 50:22). Compare Isa 1:10: "Hear the word of YHWH, you judges of Sodom. Pay attention to the torah of our God, people of Gomorrah."

[395]Cf. Ps 50:14-15, 22-23 with the comprehensive *tôrôt* of the prophets.

[396]See the commentary, pp. 216f.

[397]Amos 5:24; Isa 1:16-17; 58:6f.

[398]Jer 7:23.

[399]Hos 6:6.

[400]See the examples under ¶33.

[401]Ps 82:3-4.

[402]See, e.g., Amos 5:15: "Hate evil and love good. Judge rightly in the gate." Or Jer 21:11: "Judge rightly in the morning, and save those who have been robbed from the hand of the oppressor." Additional prophetic counterparts are found in Jer 22:3f; Isa 56:6f; 56:1; Zech 7:9; 8:16; Jer 7:3; see also Isa 1:16-17.

admonition not to harden the heart and to listen to YHWH has prophetic parallels,[403] as does the command to listen and walk in the ways of YHWH.[404]

The prophetic admonition is supported by a *threat*,[405] a promise,[406] or both.[407] Relatedly, a promise[408] or a threat[409] follows the admonition in the psalm. Both the promise and the threat are qualified.[410]

The prophetic admonition is occasionally attached to a *historical example* in order to convince.[411] The imitation in psalmody does the same.[412]

VI. The Situation of the Prophetic Psalms

40. The investigation of the prophetic influence upon psalmody points beyond the results attained. It also raises the question how one should conceive the details of the "life setting" of the prophetic psalms. One can easily see that one should distinguish the individual and the communal complaint song from the prophetic psalms, as well as the mixed poem.[413] All of these types may be influenced by prophetic speech. Their external situation is not affected by the prophets. The question for the remainder of the prophetic psalms, however, is all the more pressing. If one wishes to find a satisfactory explanation, it would seem necessary to divide the question into two subsidiary questions. First, one should ask how to conceptualize the external situation for the *eschatological hymn*, the *eschatological song of Zion*, and the *eschatological enthronement song*. Then one should ask how to conceptualize the life setting for the prophetically influenced *mixed liturgy*, the *judgment speech*, *torah*, the *rebuke*, *threat*, and *admonition*. This distinction does justice to the undeniable differences between the two groups. The first group concerns songs from a group which are thoroughly lyrical, not prophetic, even though prophetic forms are occasionally adopted. The prophetic influence essentially affects the content of the psalms. Nevertheless, the prophetic influence provides a certain character and makes them into a special group within their genre. In the second group, the prophetic form appears alongside prophetic contents. The prophetic form even dominates, thereby raising the question how one should conceptualize *the appearance of a prophetic speaker* in the context of a poem which has been influenced.

41. We begin with the first group whose particular genres either derive from the hymn or are influenced by it.[414] The fact that these psalms derive from a *cultic event* can scarcely be doubted for various reasons. The *particular manner* of the worship celebration can be deduced by an inquiring glance for a simple reason. It can be deduced because the

---

[403]Cf. Ps 95:7bff with Amos 5:4b-6; Jer 4:3; 7:3, 4; 13:15; Isa 55:6f.

[404]Ps 81:14; see also Jer 2:19; 7:2, 3; 14:15; Isa 55:6f.

[405]Amos 5:4-6; Jer 4:3ff; 7:1-15; 13:15ff; 21:11ff.

[406]Amos 5:15; Jer 3:12, 14ff; 4:1f.

[407]Jer 18; Ezek 18.

[408]Ps 81:15-17.

[409]Ps 95:11.

[410]Like Amos 5:15; Jer 4:1ff; 21:12; 23:16-20.

[411]Jer 7:23f; Ezek 20:18ff; Zech 1:3ff.

[412]Ps 95:7ff.

[413]¶¶21, 22, 23, 24, 25.

[414]Cf. §2, ¶¶51, 52, 53.

world in which the psalms live, to which their allusions refer, and from which they derive their material is a *world of hopes* and wishes. It is not the world of the present time in which the songs were sung.

The following reasons make cultic performance probable. First, one may point out that the hymn sung by a group almost always relates to a worship service. Eschatological hymns cannot be evaluated differently.[415] Then, the texts allow one to recognize numerous passages which belong to a *worship celebration* of the anticipated end time. Thus the hymn of Ps 149 would have been sung on Zion to music and dancing when Israel humiliated its enemies and to the leaders of the captive nations. Or, the framework where Ps 68 belongs is a festival on Zion in which YHWH the victor makes a triumphal entry with the booty, and the tribes of Israel, arranged in choirs, praise their God.[416] The conclusion which appears to be suggested is that poems which are so closely bound internally to the cult in their portrayals of the future, were also really sung in the worship service of the present. The especially high evaluation of the holy place also leads in this direction, especially as encountered in the Zion songs.[417] In addition, it is important that when the prophets speak of singing hymns in the future, they conceive nothing more than this singing in the *festal worship services*.[418] From this deduction one must conclude that the eschatological songs were used in the cult of the current time. In connection with these observations the fact gains significance that several of the eschatological songs mentioned were transmitted in collections which were undoubtedly compiled for the purpose of the worship service.[419] Using the example of Ps 30 with many psalms, one can correctly ask whether the cultic use attested later was intended for the particular poem from the beginning. However, no doubt can arise in the case of the songs mentioned in association with the observations noted above. Rather, as can be confirmed, everything points to the fact that the eschatological psalms must have had their place in the worship service of the community looking into the future.

We are lacking the necessary indicators for designating the *worship celebration* itself. The researcher can only rely upon *cautious suppositions* at this point. One may perhaps say the following with judicious reservation. At a certain point, eschatological expectation also entered the cult as it gripped the piety of the people with increasing strength. The enthusiastic mood, whose appearance section III attempted to clarify, brought about worship services which revolved around the future. The enthusiastic, dynamic, imaginative power presented them as already part of the blessed present. In celebrations of this type, the choral singers of the temple would have sung the eschatological psalms. They would have thereby expressed that which so powerfully moved the hearts of the pious community. The commentary to Ps 149 (p. 620) supposes that the great vividness of the scenic references created a situation where the eschatological psalms were perhaps

---

[415]Pss 68:5, 25; 98:1; 149:1, 2, 5; 48:2, 10, 13, 14, 15; 76:12; 47:4, 5, 7; 97:12; 99:5, 9.

[416]For other allusions to a worship setting, see Pss 9:12; 48:1-4, 9, 10, 12, 13, 14; 96:8, 9; 99:2, 9.

[417]Cf. Pss 46:5, 6; 48:2, 3, 4, 9, 10, 12, 13, 14; 76:3, 4; cf. Also 68:16-18, 25, 30, 36; 99:2.

[418]See the allusions in Isa 30:29; Jer 31:4; 33:11; Nah 2:1.

[419]Cf. §13, ¶¶11, 12. The enthronement song in Ps 47 and the Zion songs of 46 and 48 stand in the songbook of the Korahite singers' guild. The Zion song of Ps 76 in the stands in the songbook of the Asaph guild.

performed as "spiritual plays." However, acceptance of this idea is perhaps unnecessary. We know nothing with certainty regarding the reality of spiritual plays in the Israelite/Judean cult. On the other hand, the dynamic vividness may be explained with complete satisfaction by the enthusiastic liveliness with which the fantasy of the pious escalated in the events of the last days.

42. One also has to think of cultic performance in the psalms of the *second group*. Such is clear for the liturgies without further comment.[420] Things are less simple with Pss 50; 53; 82. In the last two psalms mentioned, the change between the prophetic and the petitioning voice could most readily be traced back to *liturgical use*. The simple imitation of cultic forms in a cult-free orientation appears less likely. These conclusions gain convincing power from the observation that Ps 82 (like the liturgies in Pss 75, 81, and 85) was transmitted in the song books of the temple singers. Like Pss 75 and 81, Ps 82 belongs to the Asaph collection. If Ps 82 is determined to have been performed in the worship service, then one may accept the same for Ps 53, whose structure is similar. By contrast, it is difficult to accept that Ps 50 was composed for cultic usage.[421] Perhaps Ps 50 was adopted later into the cult and in that context should be considered with the songbook of the Asaph guild.

43. But how should one consider the *prophetic word* in the psalms that were *recited* in the cult? S. Mowinckel[422] considers these words as a fixed, original component of cultic poetry, and believes they were spoken by *prophets who were counted among the personnel of the sanctuary*. He sees their origin in the ancient seers who existed in connection with the temple and the cult. Originally, the *nebî'îm* were not temple servants,[423] but over time replaced them, shaping the essence of temple prophecy. This process was thus made possible by the fact "that the *nebî'îm* were originally representatives of the community seized by the ecstasy of the orgiastic rapture of the cult festival. They were incited to ecstasy by divine power as it really should have happened, ideally and theoretically, for the whole community."[424]

According to Mowinckel, we should thus accept that the prophetic psalms should be conceived by the presuppositions of the cult, and that one cannot speak of an imitation of prophetic modes of speech by later worship services. Mowinckel's thesis stands and falls with the evidence for *cultic prophecy*. Closer inspection of this evidence hardly appears convincing.

First, the starting point of his line of thinking appears vulnerable. He is certainly correct in the sentence that in the cultic psalms the words of YHWH express a "cultic reality."[425] However, when he considers *every divine communication in the worship service* as a *prophetic* utterance, one must object. In addition, and more dubiously, he understands the word prophet in a sense that is far removed from its original usage, as he himself probably knows.[426] He gives the expression such breadth that the priest and the *nābî'* can

---

[420]Pss 75; 81; 85; 95; cf. §11, ¶20.
[421]Despite W. Caspari, "Kultpsalm 50," in *ZAW* 4, new series, pp. 254ff.
[422]Mowinckel *Psalmenstudien*, vol. 3.
[423]Mowinckel, *Psalmenstudien*, vol. 3, p. 16.
[424]Mowinckel, *Psalmenstudien*, vol. 3, p. 17.
[425]Mowinckel, *Psalmenstudien*, vol. 3, p. 2.
[426]Mowinckel, *Psalmenstudien*, vol. 3, p. 5.

be considered together. A purely formal concept is thereby certainly created which is distinguished from the "theological language" in that is not infused with any kind of specific content. This idea is lacking. It only perceives the formal, external agreements between priest and *nābî'*, while ignoring the characteristic differences between the two. However, these differences cannot be confused without damaging consequences. The manner in which the priest and the *nābî'* communicate their divine speeches is just as different as the origin of their oracles. The priest obtains his revelation by *technical means*,[427] while the prophet obtains his revelation in the condition of ecstasy peculiar to him. This difference explains the form of the two oracles. The priestly oracle is *clear* and *still*, while the prophetic oracle is *agitated, erratic*, and *dark*. Without doubt the priest gains the capacity for communicating the oracle by the particular character of his office. However, one should not believe that he also acquires *prophetic inspiration* from this character. The relatively numerous passages concerning the priesthood in the Old Testament do not provide any indication which leads to this idea. Mowinckel (*Psalmenstudien*, vol. 3, p. 4) thus finds it necessary to reference John 11:5, a passage which can hardly serve as a simple reference for late Jewish belief.[428] The language itself conceptually distinguishes priest and prophet as the words *kōhēn* and *nābî'* attest, apparently because of the impression of essential differences overriding that which they have in common.

These considerations raise doubt about the availability of cult prophets. This doubt increases when one more closely observes the *references* which attest to cult prophets according to Mowinckel.

One must eliminate 1 Kgs 18:16ff from those passages which Mowinckel has compiled (*Psalmenstudien*, vol. 3, pp. 17ff)[429] in which the *nebî'îm* were supposed to have conducted festivals and cultic actions. Here, the expression *nebî'îm* serves as the term used for *Phoenician priests*. One must ask whether or not the term was chosen because of the characteristic ecstatic activity that was foreign to Israelite priests but which corresponded to the prophets they knew. If so, this passage proves nothing. One should not forget that one encounters the "Ba'al priests" as *sacrificial priests not as communicators of oracles*. None of the remaining passages show the prophets in connection with a cultic activity. The fact that they speak at holy places cannot be used naively to connect them with cultic activity, since such activity is nowhere recognizable in the context of the text. In every case, the appearance of the prophets can be understood by the fact that they would find the greatest audience for their message at these holy places.[430]

Also, the fact that we encounter *nebî'îm* in places where there are sanctuaries[431] does not prove the cultic character of the *nebî'îm*. If it is correct that the *nebî'îm* were fanatical worshipers of YHWH (which they were), what could be more understandable than that they also have a respect for his sanctuary, and that they would seek to locate their organization in the vicinity of the holy places?

---

[427]So Mowinckel himself, *Psalmenstudien*, vol. 3, p. 4.

[428]Cf. W. Bauer on this passage, in Lietzmann's *Handbuch zum Neuen Testament*.

[429]1 Sam 10:5ff; 19:19ff; 1 Kgs 18:16ff; Jer 26; 28; 36; cf. also 1 Kgs 22; 2 Kgs 3:15; 4:38; Ezek 8:1-3; 11:1ff, 24f.

[430]Cf. Amos in Bethel.

[431]1 Sam 10:5; 2 Kgs 2:35; 4:38.

The combination of priests and prophets[432] has absolutely no convincing power. It depends very much upon the viewpoint under which they are combined. Mic 3:11 and Jer 18:18 clearly demonstrate this viewpoint is not cultic. In these passages, counselors and judges stand alongside priests and prophets, but no one attempts to maintain the first two are cultic officials. Decisive for the Jeremiah passages that combine priest and prophet is the fact that both are *religious authorities* of the people, and that in a similar way both stand in a hostile relationship to Jeremiah.

Finally, one should emphatically contest the idea that Jer 29:26 "without doubt" attests to the institution of temple prophets.[433] The sentence only speaks of the priest who was made overseer in the house of YHWH "for every crazy person and anyone behaving like a prophet" so that he can place that person in stocks and neck irons. Mowinckel asserts that the cult prophets should be understood among those prophets over whom the high priest has jurisdiction. One should instead think of prophets like Jeremiah and Amos against whom the high priest had to *intervene as the one responsible for the order of the worship service and the sanctuary*.

Despite Mowinckel, 1 Chr 15:22, 27 cannot be considered as undamaged. Moreover, it seems rather unlikely that once can deduce a "director of oracle concerns" from this context treating the carrying of the ark of YHWH.

In contrast to this situation, one cannot deduce that Jeremiah and Ezekiel were of priestly origin. Even 2 Chr 20:14ff cannot be used in this context. Mowinckel sees this late passage as evidence that the *cult prophets* in the postexilic period were adopted into a series of Levitical singers (Mowinckel, *Psalmenstudien*, vol. 3, p. 521). Anyone who contests Mowinckel's opening sentence will discover nothing more than prophetic influence upon the postexilic cult.

Anyone critically evaluating these ideas will see that cult prophets are really a very *problematic entity*. However, additional problems prohibit relying upon them to explain the prophetic psalms. Specifically, the prophetic passages of the second group (apart from the liturgies) concern speech forms which belong to the judgment prophets who were "free of the cult" and whom it can be shown do *not presuppose the holy site*. These prophetic portions of psalms, in every case, signify something new for cultic poetry (even if there were such a thing as cult prophecy as Mowinckel outlines it). Their speech forms are not those of the ancient prophets of judgment.

Based upon the suggested rationale, one would do well not to bother with the cult prophets whose existence, at the very least, seems highly debatable when considering the question of the cultic situation of the prophetic psalms. Rather, one should consider the influence of cult-free prophecy on the worship service.

44. Quite probably, even the *cult took notice* of ancient prophetic proclamation after history vindicated and confirmed them, even though the cult had not considered them correct. *Prophetic contents and forms* were then open to the cult. One can thus observe that prophetic ideas were far easier to adapt when removed from their prophetic forms than when they were formed in prophetic modes of speech.[434] The forms of prophecy and those of the worship poetry have only a few points in common with one another.

---

[432]Isa 28:7; Jer 4:9; 6:13; 14:18; Mic 3:11; Zech 7:3.
[433]Mowinckel, *Psalmenstudien*, vol. 3, p. 17.
[434]Cf. section VII.

With the exception of the *priestly torah*, which the *prophetic torah* was able to adopt, there is really only one place within cultic poetry into which prophetic forms could be incorporated—namely, the *liturgy*—with its combination of worship singing and divine speech.[435] The possibilities of this form were not so narrowly limited as those of the more rigorous genres. In this form, psalmody reproduced the powerful impression called forth by the red-hot words of the prophets which they hurled into the happy festival jubilation.[436] Here was the place where the prophetic rebuke, threat, judgment speech, and admonition would be adopted by psalmody.

The adoption of these speech forms into the liturgies suggests that one accept that the prophetic words were spoken by the same persons who would otherwise have proclaimed the *oracle* in the liturgy. One should thus think of a priest[437] or a temple singer,[438] but not a prophet. A prophet's essence includes "the free inspiration of the moment"[439] and the excited, ecstatic appearance. It would be difficult to conceive how such a person would have spoken in the cult which urged "ritual" forms, seeing in them a "guarantee of its own holiness and effectiveness."[440] This consideration gains weight when one realizes that these prophetic psalms were designed for *repeated performances*, requiring that their content be fixed. However, as Mowinckel himself concedes,[441] if only the (first) *formulation of the wording* was left for the prophet, then one must say that the speaker in these liturgies scarcely has anything in common with a prophet.

However, a *priest* or *singer* would very well speak the prophetic words because he would not require any special prophetic inspiration for doing so. His proclamation reveals nothing which had not already been heard. Rather, it depends upon prophetic ideas which were recognized as truth.

VII. The Purely Intellectual Influence of the Prophets on the Psalms

45. The influence of *prophetic ideas* upon psalmody reaches further than just the *prophetic forms*.[442] It is not always easy to prove them clearly because the characteristic signs of the prophetic linguistic forms are lacking. We arrange the ideas that can be traced back to prophetic influence according to the amount of probability which is valid for them.

One may certainly speak of prophetic influence when one encounters ideas which rely most closely upon characteristic thoughts of the prophets. The utterances which are hostile to sacrifice are foremost among these.[443] Mowinckel is not correct when he traces them back to the conditions of the exile when they were forced by circumstances to do without the cult.[444] Denying the cult because of external relationships explains *none* of the *basic*

---

[435]§11, section III.

[436]Pss 81; 95.

[437]See the commentary to Pss 12:6 and 15.

[438]See the commentary to Ps 20, p. 83, where one also finds references to Pss 75:3f; 81:7ff; 95:8ff.

[439]Mowinckel, *Psalmenstudien*, vol 3, p. 40.

[440]Mowinckel himself, *Psalmenstudien*, vol 3, p. 7; cf. Jer 29:26ff.

[441]Mowinckel, *Psalmenstudien*, vol 3, p. 7.

[442]See above, p. 286.

[443]Pss 40:7ff; 50:8ff; 51:18-19; 69:32.

[444]Mowinckel, *Psalmenstudien*, vol 1, p. 144.

formulations like those which say that YHWH desires no partial sacrifice nor grain offering, or has not demanded a whole offering and a sin offering.[445] It also does not explain statements that YHWH does not need the steer or the goat.[446] However, we still need to show how the words of the psalms should be seen in relationship to the *anti-sacrificial utterances of the prophets*,[447] and to notice their after-effect. Moreover, in the psalms, and among the prophets, sacrifice is refused not *for its own sake*. It is not validated for higher reasons. The fact that this higher element appears somewhat differently in the psalms than in the prophets is grounded in the character of the lyric genres. It shows the limits of adopting prophetic material. In the psalms this higher element specifically appears as the complaint song[448] and especially the thanksgiving song.[449] The higher element replaces the command for justice or the demand for grace and recognition from God.[450] A counterargument against prophetic influence cannot be deduced from this difference.[451] It may otherwise be noted as striking that Mowinckel recognizes the aftereffect of the great prophets in the refusal of the sacrifice in Ps 50, where *prophetic form* is combined with *prophetic content*.[452]

In addition, the *mocking of foreign gods* should *certainly* be seen as *prophetic material*.[453] The manner in which foreign gods are discussed relies most closely upon prophetic passages.[454] The heathen idol is silver and gold.[455] They are the product of human hands.[456] They have a mouth, eyes, ears, nose, feet, and hands, but cannot even begin to do anything.[457] Also, prophetic parallels can be found for the idea that the one making the image is the same as the image, and that the one worshiping the idol is the same as the idol.[458] One can observe how these ideas arose among the prophets, specifically in Deutero-Isaiah. They grow from the discussion of the meaning of world events in which the prophet recognizes the hand of his great God, the lord of the world. They express the contrast to the greatness, power, and wisdom of YHWH which the prophet is endeavoring to bring to light. Doubt can scarcely prevail after this blow that the mockery of foreign gods from from prophetic soil, and was transferred from there into psalmody. The *hymn* was the *place* where this occurred. The prophets contrast the futility of the idols with the overwhelming power and eternity of YHWH. The contrast makes the idea suitable for the glorification of the God of Israel: How great is he; how unbelievably limited are heathen gods.

---

[445]Pss 40:7; see 51:18.

[446]Ps 50:8ff.

[447]Cf. Amos 5:21; Hos 6:6; Isa 1:10ff; 66:1-4; Jer 7:21ff.

[448]Ps 50:15.

[449]Pss 50:14, 23; 40:10; 69:32.

[450]Amos 5:24; Isa 1:17; Hos 6:6.

[451]Cf. Mowinckel, *Psalmenstudien*, vol. 3, p. 42.

[452]¶¶33, 34, 36, 37, 38.

[453]Pss 115:3-4; 135:15-18.

[454]Jer 10:3ff; Isa 40:19-20; 41:6-7, 29; 44:9ff; Hab 2:18; cf. Isa 46:1-2.

[455]Pss 115:4; 135:15; parallels Jer 10:4; Isa 40:19.

[456]Pss 115:4; 135:15; parallels Jer 10:3ff; Isa 40:19-20; 41:6-7; 44:9ff; Hab 2:18.

[457]Pss 115:5-7; 135:16-17 parallels Isa 44:18ff; Jer 10:5-6; Hab 2:18; see also Isa 41:29.

[458]Pss 115:8; 135:18; Isa 41:24; 44:9, 11; Hab 2:18.

Further, one may argue for prophetic influence upon those psalm passages which emphatically raise moral commands. The clearest place is the torah liturgy,[459] a form which evidently served prophecy as well.[460] From the outset, the torah places demands which primarily relate to the administration of the cult.[461] Since *cultic demands* are then lacking in the psalms mentioned here, and since, instead, only *moral demands* are raised which *agree with the prophets*, then one can hardly doubt prophetic influence. They demand that one walk blamelessly and practice righteousness.[462] Speaking about truth has its parallel in the censure of untruth.[463] Proper behavior toward one's neighbor has its counterpart in the lament over the destruction of this relationship.[464] Refusal of the defiled gift is a frequently recurring prophetic demand.[465] Even the judgment against taking the census can be found.[466] Certainly none of these cases contain ideas which were first expressed by prophets. They are already found as demands in the Book of the Covenant.[467] The prophetic element lies in the *relentless emphasis* with which these ideas are pushed into the foreground. Thus, moral commands that agree with commands which the prophets champion, are encountered in a priestly torah, a place which would otherwise be occupied with cultic prescriptions. One thus finds another good reason confirming the effect of the great prophets.

Their influence goes even deeper. The wonderful word of Ps 51:19 rests upon a prophetic foundation when it says that the offering pleasing God is a broken spirit and a shattered heart.[468] It expresses the powerful and simultaneously comforting idea that YHWH lives as a holy one in the heights but also among those who are crushed and discouraged in heart.[469] It also states that YHWH pays attention to the pious one who is suffering and shattered in spirit, and that he rejects the sacrifice.[470] We recognize prophetic words which were known to the singer of Ps 51 (from hearing or reading them), which he brought to life in the depth of his painful self-confession.

The same holds true for another passage of this psalm. The singer recognizes in 51:12ff that by himself he has no power to do good, and that God must create anew a pure heart in him. He then harmlessly adopts an idea using his own peculiar expression, an idea which already appears more clearly in Jeremiah,[471] though it is more similar in wording to Ezekiel.[472] "I will give you a new heart and a new spirit within you. I will

---

[459]Pss 15; 24.

[460]Isa 33:14-16.

[461]Cf. §8, ¶44.

[462]Ps 15:2; see also Amos 5:24; Isa 1:16f; Mic 6:8; and further Jer 6:16; 7:3, 23; etc.

[463]Ps 15:2; Isa 32:7; 59:3; Jer 8:8; 9:4; Ezek 22:12.

[464]Ps 15:3; Jer 9:3.

[465]Ps 15:5; cf. Amos 2:6; 8:6; Isa 1:23; 5:23; 33:15; Mic 3:11.

[466]Ps 15:5; Ezek 18:7-8, 12-13; 22:12.

[467]Cf. Exod 22:24 for the command against taking the census and Exod 23:8 for the command about accepting defiled gifts.

[468]One should contrast it with Isa 57:15 and 66:2. These passages rely, in part, upon the vocabulary of Ps 51:19.

[469]Isa 57:15.

[470]Isa 66:2ff.

[471]Jer 32:39; 24:7; 31:33.

[472]Ezek 11:19; 36:26-27.

remove your stone heart from your flesh and will give you a heart of flesh ' . . . ', so that you walk in my commands and keep my laws, and do accordingly."

46. One would gladly show further lines like these which lead from prophecy into the center of the piety of the psalms. However, one can hardly say anything more with the certainty attained to this point.

One can certainly find individual sayings in the psalms which rely upon the most beautiful sayings and the proclamation of salvation in the prophets. One can compare Ps 103:9 ("He does not quarrel forever, and does not bear a grudge continually.") with a prophetic saying: "I will not quarrel forever, and am not angry forever."[473] The words of Ps 103:15ff compare the transitory nature of humanity with the grass and the flowers of the field, and contrast it to the eternal, lasting benevolence of YHWH. One recalls Isa 40:6ff: "All flesh is grass. All his 'elegance' is like the flower of the field. The grass withers. The flower fades. But the word of our God endures forever." The contact is less close between Pss 36:6; 57:11; 103:11 on the one hand and Isa 55:9 on the other. They all compare the height of the heavens, but the passages diverge when one examines them. The relationship appears rather superficial and formal. Certainly the possibility exists that, in these cases, the psalmic poets brought prophetic words to life. However, it is not completely certain. Experiences such as these could well have occurred to the one complaining or offering thanks from his own experience, thereby belonging to the particular ideas of the genres. Likewise, one can consider that the correspondences encountered among the prophets, specifically Deutero-Isaiah, can trace their wording to the *far-reaching influence of psalmody*. One could just as well argue that the prophetic passages related to the psalm sayings were evoked by psalmody.

Finally, one can suppose that the *ideas of God in the hymns* are influenced by the prophets. We expressed this in §2, ¶52. As far as the eschatological conceptualizations come into question, this influence can certainly be maintained. After that, caution should be exercised. Terror and power concerning God was already a subject of hymnic praise from antiquity.[474] Concerning the hymnic descriptions of the compassion and goodness of God which find prophetic counterparts,[475] the source for these is perhaps more likely to be sought in the experiences of the communal and individual thanksgiving songs than with a prophet who experienced the influence of the poetry of psalms. One must perhaps say more cautiously that psalmody and prophecy are encountered in cases like these.

VIII. The Time of the Prophetic Psalms

47. For the *question of the chronological placement* of the prophetic psalms, it is especially important to confirm the time after which we can account for prophetic influence upon psalmody. In so doing, we can achieve a fixed *terminus a quo*. Closer determination must yield more precisely datable details.

Since the various prophetic influences could have been operative from *very different time points*, it is recommended that we divide the eschatological psalms from the treatment of the others which reveal the effect of the judgment prophets.

---

[473]Jer 3:5, 12; Isa 57:16.
[474]Cf. the ancient psalms in 19; 29; 89:1-2, 6-19.
[475]Ps 30:6 parallels Isa 54:7-8; Ps 34:19 parallels Isa 57:15.

The ground was really well prepared for the influence of eschatological ideas *from the beginning of the exile*. With the exile, conditions arose which formed the psychological presupposition for adopting the prophetic proclamation about the future.[476] In addition, the possibility exists, maybe even the probability, that *individual ideas* of the ultimate hope were already adopted in the preexilic period, perhaps after Isaiah.[477] These ideas include the nations' attack against Zion, and the demolition of its walls. At any rate, the deliverance of Jerusalem in 734 and 701 was quite suitable for creating the recognition of these ideas in a broad circle. And in the unsettled times which lasted until the exile, one may have always hoped that the assembly of the nations who threatened to overcome Judah, or who really did pass through, might be destroyed on Zion. But then a psalm like Ps 48 appears among the Zion songs but speaks differently than others. It speaks about the nations being destroyed by YHWH under the walls of Jerusalem, and enthusiastically commands one to watch the *strong wall*, count the *towers*, and march through the *bastions*. Thus, one would most readily derive it from a time which had not yet experienced the destruction of the defense works, and had not yet seen the error of trusting in the protection of the strong walls. Comparably, Pss 46 and 76 do not speak about the strength of the walls, and are perhaps postexilic. They give the future expectation of Ps 48 in a correspondingly altered form when they only speak of divine action before the city.

In contrast to these psalms, the vast majority of eschatological psalms are certainly *postexilic*. See §3, ¶11, pp. 79, 80, for discussion of the eschatological enthronement songs. Among other reasons,[478] dependence upon Deutero-Isaiah in Pss 68 and 98 argues for a postexilic setting for eschatological songs. The approach of Galilean tribes toward Jerusalem presumed in Ps 68:28, like the hostility of Egypt in 68:31, point to the 4th century for a more specific time for the psalm.[479] The postexilic origin of Ps 149 is clear from the fact that it presumes foreign rule and refers to prophetic statements, as though referring to a holy scripture.

Among *prophetic liturgies*, consider the placement of Ps 75. The concept of the cup of the wrath of YHWH in 75:9 appears to be dependent upon Jer 25:15ff; 49:12; 51:39; Isa 51:17ff; and Ezek 23:31. Ps 85 presumes the conditions of the postexilic period when it longingly expects the change of destiny and YHWH's help and majesty.[480] The same is true for Ps 126:4.[481]

We reach the same conclusion for the psalms which have only adopted *individual eschatological ideas*. Of course, we cannot present this idea for every individual psalm. See the commentary for this information. We cite only a particularly clear example. When various texts[482] hope for the reconstruction of the walls of Jerusalem, they undoubtedly belong in the time which is bounded by the return of the exiles and Nehemiah's reconstruction of the wall. In a psalm which clearly presupposes the existence of the

---

[476]See section IV.
[477]Jer 10:12; 14:24ff, 29ff; 17:12; 31:4-9; 30:27-33.
[478]See the commentary, p. 287.
[479]See the commentary, p. 287.
[480]See the commentary, pp. 373ff.
[481]See the commentary, p. 551.
[482]Pss 51:20f; 69:36; 102:14ff; 147:2.

temple service along with the distress of the returnees, one may even deduce the fifth century more specifically.

48. Concerning the time of origin for the psalms influenced by the great prophets of judgment, one may begin by saying that prophetic influence upon psalmody first appears possible after their predictions were *believed* and given *authority*. Their predictions about the fall of Judah, the destruction of Zion, and the transportation into banishment were fulfilled in surprising way. Only after this time would one expect the appearance of their speech forms and their ideas.

This presumption is confirmed by more precisely datable references in those psalms in question. Ps 53 imitates the rebuke and threat. Ps 53:5-6 confront the priests who are similarly reproached in *postexilic* prophecy.[483] The judgment speech of Ps 82 which concerns the gods coincides with the corresponding judgment speeches in *Deutero-Isaiah*.[484] Moreover, a psalm proves itself to be late by *mixing* the judgment speech and admonition, signifying the dissolution of the strict style. It is first observed at the end of the history of the genres. Ps 95, which preserves a prophetic admonition, presupposes a time when the community that returned from exile has not seen YHWH's action for some time. As a result, the community begins to quarrel with him.[485] A similar time should be considered for Ps 81. The fact that the people longingly wait for the arrival of the time of salvation argues for this time frame. The *developed form* of the psalm and the mixing of rebuke and admonition points in the same direction.[486] For Ps 50, the *mixing* of judgment speech, prophetic torah, and admonition also offer substantiation, as well as *strong words* against the sacrifice. Finally, in the torah liturgies of Pss 15 and 24, one can cite the postexilic *prophetic parallel* of Isa 33:14ff in addition to the replacement of cultic stipulations with moral stipulations.

Also, among the psalms which only show contact with the prophets in *individual ideas*, various indications allow one to deduce postexilic origin. The evidence cannot be presented here because it falls too much into disconnected individual observations that would divert us from the main ideas. One does better to compare the reasons for chronological placement compiled in the commentary for the psalms treated under section VII. Anyone who examines them will be convinced of the postexilic origin of these prophetic psalms.

---

[483]Mal 1:6–2:9.
[484]Isa 41:21ff; 43:8ff.
[485]See the commentary, p. 420.
[486]See ¶33.

§10 Wisdom Poetry in the Psalms[1]

RGG article, "Weisheitsdichtung." — W. Staerk, *Lyrik in den 'Schriften des AT in Auswahl,'* vol. 3/1,[2] pp. 256ff. — E. Balla, *Das Ich der Psalmen*, 1912, pp. 39ff, 62ff. — W. Baumgartner, *ZAW* 34 (1914): 161ff. — H. Greßmann, *ZAW* n.s. 1 (1924): 272ff.; and *Die Spruchweisheit Israels*, 1925. (The last work conceives the word in a wider sense and speaks extensively about proverbs, riddles, fables, parables, etc. and their foreign origins.)

1. At approximately the same time that psalmody blossomed, "wisdom" was also cultivated in Israel, as it was among other peoples, especially the Egyptians and Babylonians.[2] Wisdom appears in various great books (Proverbs, Job, Ecclesiastes) and in the apocrypha (Sirach, Wisdom of Solomon). The finds at Elephantine show that narrative of Ahikar, with its wisdom proverbs, was read among the Jews.[3] Seen as a whole, wisdom represents a type of poetry that was far reaching, took multiple shapes, and was dominant for a long time. First, we will speak here of the "wisdom" of Israel *outside the psalter*, but only to the extent it is necessary for understanding its properties that are not very extensive in Psalms.

Wisdom's *subject* is *human life*. Someone is "wise" if they organize their life so that it leads to a good end (*ahărît*). Wisdom will teach one how to behave in every situation in order to reach this goal. According to H. Greßmann,[4] the *life setting* was originally very exclusive. Wise teaching was given to the "vizier," and to those who would become "scribes," in other words the young officials. This exclusivity was especially the case in Egypt, but many traces of this setting can also be found on Israelite soil.[5] The "scribe" did not play as decisive a role in other cultures as in the culture of Egypt. In other cultures, "wisdom" came to a certain middle group. Elders who were experienced in the ways of the world sat together in the gate or at street corners where they exchanged proverbs with one another.[6] The unexperienced young man was admonished to go there and learn wisdom.[7] This situation explains the tone of many proverbs. One who is knowledgeable of the world speaks to the one who is growing up.[8] It provides the young man with sound teaching in awareness of the elder's superior knowledge. With respect to form in Egypt,

---

[1]By Gunkel.

[2]A. Erman, *Literatur der Ägypter*, 1923, pp. 86ff, 242ff; H. Zimmern, *Babylonische Hymnen und Gebete*, vol. 2, pp. 27ff; H. Ranke and E. Ebeling in H. Greßmann, *Altoritetalische Texte*,[2] 1926, pp. 33ff, 291ff.

[3]*ZAW*, n.s. 1 (1924): 292ff; and *Die Spruchweisheit Israels*, pp. 47ff.

[4]H. Greßmann, *Altorientalische Texte*,[2] pp. 454ff.

[5]Cf. Prov 8:15f; 14:35; 16:12-14; 17:26; 20:18b; 21:22; 22:29; 23:1-3; 25:6f; Sir 7:4-6, 14; 8:8; 11:1; 13:9-13; 20:24f; 34:2; 38:33; 39:4; etc.

[6]Cf. Prov 1:20f; 8:2f.

[7]Cf. Prov 15:31; Sir 6:34; 8:8. See additional material in the *RGG* article "Weisheitsdichtung," 2; and in W. Baumgartner, *ZAW* 34 (1914): 162.

[8]Prov 1:4.

Babylon, and Israel, this wisdom was originally spoken in more or less short "proverbs" (*mešālîm*) that were often very cleverly phrased.

A further step occurs when men arose who created *more extensive poetry* on the basis of the older type of poetry. We designate this more extensive poetry, marked by vitality and power, as wisdom poetry to distinguish it from the older "wisdom proverbs." The beginning of this process is already found in the "Proverbs of Solomon."[9] One cannot deny that other sections[10] still exhibit the prototypical speech of single lines and groupings arising from them. Thus, it is no accident that the superficial adornment of alphabetic order appears in passages that have been pieced together like mosaics.[11] By contrast, the wisdom poem rises to its full height and splendor in the book of Job, where the subcategory of individual wisdom poem takes precedence.[12] This kind of poetry even existed in Egyptian and Babylonian poetry where questions of world view were treated in grand style.[13]

The international origin of the entire type of poetry makes it understandable that the earliest layer contained a *common human* and *almost universal character*. To the degree that religion was even mentioned, there is a certain "enlightened" attitude operating "which is raised above cult-friendly piety." H. Greßmann observed this tendency in the Egyptian proverbs,[14] and one even finds several indications of this attitude in the Old Testament.[15] The God who is revealed in wisdom is the "teacher of the nations."[16] In the book of Job, the name "YHWH" is apparently intentionally avoided since the heathen do not know it.

At a later stage, *moral and religious meditation* penetrates this literature. This happened already on Egyptian soil. "The teaching of Merikare and the wisdom of Amenemope are completely religious."[17] The doctrine of retribution even took over these proverbs in Egypt.[18] In the Israelite arena, both occurred and both were given prominence. Rules regarding the astuteness of the wise and moral commands permeated and were closely related. The doctrine of retribution was added. Both the wise and the pious were convinced that whoever followed their words would succeed in the desired goal. The wise recognized by observing the world that his counsel was useful, and the pious believed the just would not lack divine reward. Thus, the doctrine of retribution became the shining star of Israelite wisdom, and the general "maxim" appeared alongside the concrete rules of astuteness of the ancient period.

---

[9]Especially in the introductory chapters, 1–9. See also a passage like 23:29-35.

[10]Prov 31:10-31; Sir 2:1-18; 3:1-16; 6:7-17.

[11]Prov 31:10-21.

[12]Cf. Job 3.; 4:12-21; 5:17-26; 8:8-22; 15:17-33; 18; 20:5-29; 21:7-26; 24; 25; 27:11-23; 28; 33:14-33.

[13]Cf. H. Ranke in H. Greßmann, *Altorientalische Texte*,[2] pp. 25-29 and E. Ebeling in H. Greßmann, *Altorientalische Texte*,[2] 1926, pp. 284-91.

[14]*Vossische Zeitung* 23/6 (1924), and *Die Spruchweisheit Israels*, pp. 44; 53.

[15]Cf. the proverbs about sacrifice: Prov 15:8; 21:3, 27; Sir 7:9; 31:21-24; 32:1-5, 8f. See the commentary to Ps 112. Or see proverbs about prayer (Sir 15:9; 32:20ff) or dreams (Qoh 5:6; Sir 31:1f, 5).

[16]Ps 94:10.

[17]H. Greßmann, *Die Spruchweisheit Israels*, p. 52; cf. ZAW n.s. 1 (1924): 287.

[18]H. Greßmann, ZAW n.s. 1 (1924): 288.

In a third period, *doubt* was awakened against this foundational thought of the wise. A generation appeared whose own experience stood in painful contrast to this doctrine. The powerful poet of Job raised the shocking question of theodicy and turned his terrible attack against the dogma of God's righteous judgment. The author of "the Preacher" sorrowfully renounced the idea that one could find rational meaning in the confusing course of this world. Jer 12:1f already raises this type of question. However, similar kinds of doubt and soul distress appeared long ago on Egyptian and, especially on Babylonian soil (albeit in other forms).[19]

Even though witnesses to "wisdom" are manifold, one can nevertheless show a relationship of forms and of content[20] which belongs to the history of a genre.

2. *In the psalter* we find several poems which should be considered as wisdom poetry. It is significant that one can also recognize the *main stages* which we observed outside the psalter.

There we can observe several short *wisdom sayings* which delve into the midst of life, speaking with impressive words about the foolishness of human endeavor, the blessing of offspring, and the beauty of brotherly tolerance.[21]

The purely worldly poem of Ps 49 still belongs to the older poetry of the *wisdom poems* because its content treats the futility of possessions. It maintains that the fate of death even awaits the wealthy, whereby all possession lose their value.[22] This content is expressly designated as "wisdom" and *māšāl* ("proverb").[23] The linguistic form of wisdom appears in the celebratory introduction which turns toward all humanity,[24] addresses the students as "you,"[25] and delivers a warning in the form of "why will you. . . ."[26] The description of the wealthy corresponds to the typical wisdom portrayal of the corruption of the godless.[27] It compares humans who lack understanding to a "cow," a comparison which occurs frequently in *wisdom*.[28] Other ideas also typical of wisdom include the idea that human beings cannot save themselves from death,[29] and the idea that the one who

---

[19]See H. Ranke in H. Greßmann, *Altorientalische Texte,*[2] pp. 27-29, and E. Ebeling, in H. Greß-mann, *Altorientalische Texte,*[2] pp. 275, 284-87, 287-91.

[20]Cf. ¶¶4-6.

[21]Pss 127:1f, 3-5; 133. Counterparts from other wisdom poetry to the first saying are: Prov 10:22; Sir 11:10-13. See also Prov 21:31; Pss 33:16-18; (147:10). Counterparts to the form of an address can be found in Ps 127:2; cf. ¶4. Cf. The "woe sayings" to the beginning, "it is nothing for you, that you . . . " (see ¶6). The second saying is related to Prov 17:6. See also the "Wisdom of Ani" (A. Erman, *Literatur der Ägypter*, 1923, p. 295). See Ps 127:3 for counterparts to the form of the beginning, "behold" (see ¶6). The third saying carries the following forms of "wisdom:" "behold" (133:1 and 127:3), and "how beautiful it is" (cf. ¶6). Cf. ¶6 for the amassing of images in the following material.

[22]Counterparts from wisdom are found in Qoh 5:14f; 8:8; Sir 14:15; see also Ps 39:6c, 7.

[23]Ps 49:4, 5; cf. ¶4.

[24]Ps 49:2-5; cf. ¶1, 4.

[25]Ps 49:6, 17; cf. ¶4.

[26]Ps 49:6, cf. 49:17; ¶5.

[27]Ps 49:8ff; cf. ¶5.

[28]Ps 49:13; cf. Pss 73:22; 92:7; 94:8; Prov 30:2f.

[29]Ps 49:8; cf. Prov 11:4.

dies must leave his treasure to others.[30] Based on the style, this completely unified, magnificently lofty poem belongs to a more developed stage.

Even the age of the *doctrine of retribution* can be recognized in the wisdom poems of the psalter. Several psalms (Pss 1, 91,[31] 112, 128) express this doctrine in a form typical of wisdom poetry when they proclaim a blessing for the righteous.[32] They portray the virtue of the pious relatively briefly,[33] or more extensively,[34] and then pour out an abundance of divine grace over him.[35] Or, the psalms loftily proclaim God's protection from all evil.[36] The fate of the wicked is contrasted.[37] In the particularly stirring poems of 91 and 128, the righteous person, about whom one otherwise speaks in the third person, is even addressed directly, recalling the beautiful words of the priestly blessing.[38] Ps 91 is the most magnificent. It rejoices like a unified river, while the alphabetically arranged Ps 112 sounds more sober. Ps 112 uses the old style of individual proverbs and places the virtues and the rewards of the pious alongside one another without further context. The poet of Ps 1 has in mind a wisdom poem preserved in the book of Jeremiah (Jer 17:5-8), which he adopts with a legal spirit. Both poems recall a saying from the book of Amenemope.[39] One also sees the influence of the law in Ps 112:1.[40]

Occasionally, a powerful individualism appears in these poems. The individual stands out from the mass of humanity and knows he is gifted with a completely unique destiny.[41]

However, the psalter also transcribes the antithesis that should follow from this exuberant faith. The difficult question of *theodicy*, the beginning of all theology, has also fallen upon the soul of the poet. In Ps 37, the wise one, who is pious and experienced, warns the young man, who is angered over the good fortune of the wicked. The wise one warns him to keep faith in the patient trust of YHWH. He says that the humble will remain in possession of the soil while the wicked will disappear without a trace.[42] The standpoint of the poem is somewhat similar to that of Job's friends.[43] By form, the poem exists according to the old style of individual proverbs, with every second line being bound to the alphabet. In many cases the details also show how the psalms belong to wisdom poetry. See the admonitions and warnings in ¶5, the portrayals of the pious and the godless and their destiny in ¶6, and the speeches about YHWH's righteous retribution in ¶6. Sometimes, the poet relates experiences about his own life (37:25,35f). See ¶6. In

---

[30]Pss 49:11; Sir 14:15; Jer 17:11.

[31]See the commentary to 91:1.

[32]Cf. ¶6.

[33]Pss 91:2; 128:1.

[34]Pss 1:1f; 112.

[35]Pss 1:3; 112; 128:2ff.

[36]Ps 91:3ff.

[37]Pss 1:4f; 91:7; 112:10; cf. ¶6.

[38]Cf. ¶3.

[39]Cf. ¶3.

[40]Cf. ¶8.

[41]Ps 91; Job 5:17-26 is closely related.

[42]Cf. Prov 2:11f; 10:3; Ps 25:13.

[43]See the commentary. Counterparts to the whole are found in Prov 3:31; 23:17; 24:1, 19; Sir 11:12ff; cf. Pss 49:6; 73:3; Jer 12:1f; Mal 2:17ff.

addition, the psalm also compares the value of two things (37:16; see ¶6).[44] At several places older linguistic material clearly appears.[45] Ps 37 does not fill the space provided by the alphabet with by a strict progression of thought, or with particularly personal distress of suitable breadth, but it does repeat itself.

By contrast, in Ps 73 the inner life of the poet breaks out horrifically in a magnificently unified stream. He explains how the same experience presupposed by the young man from Ps 37 incited him to wrath. It angered him so that it almost led him into error concerning the rule of God. Finally, he concluded that the godless must finally fall, and he found inner peace. He realized that the nearness of God is the most costly possession of the pious. He experiences an inner wrestling which is comparable to that of Job. Indeed, the last words even surpass Job. One can deduce that Ps 73 also belongs to wisdom poetry from its mood. The connection of personal experience with the originally objective doctrine is not uncommon in the later wisdom literature.[46] Like Job, Ps 37, and Jer 12:1f, Psalm 73 treats the battle over the doctrine of retribution and the shock over the fate of the godless. One can note the details in the comparison between unfaithful and irrational animals,[47] and in the consideration of "the end" that is characteristic of "wisdom."[48] The dream as an image of futility shows an enlightenment already attested in Egyptian material.[49]

One may conclude from these observations that *wisdom sayings* and *wisdom poetry* are so different in tone that one would almost be inclined to call them different genres. However, contrary to this argument stands the fact that they treat the same subjects as a whole, as well as the fact that they often use the same forms.[50]

3. The thoughts and forms of wisdom literature even penetrated the characteristically lyric genres. This fact shows how popular wisdom literature was, especially in the later period.[51] The confession of the *thanksgiving song* expresses the experiences of the one who has been delivered for the benefit of the community offering sacrifice. The thanksgiving song thereby approaches wisdom teaching. The thanksgiving song borrows from wisdom, including its forms of address (such as "my son," or "sons"),[52] the form of the beatitude,[53] the expression "teach the path of YHWH,"[54] the image of the stubborn animal,[55]

---

[44]See the commentary.
[45]Cf. Ps 37:16, 25ab, 35f.
[46]See ¶6.
[47]Ps 73:22. See above concerning Ps 49:13.
[48]Ps 73:17. Cf. ¶1.
[49]Ps 73:20; cf. Sir 31:1f. See H. Grapow, *Bildliche Ausdrücke des Ägyptischen*, p. 140; cf. ¶1.
[50]See additional discussion at the end of ¶6 and ¶7.
[51]Pss 25:12f; 31:24f; 32:6f, 8-10; 33:16-18; 34:12-22; 39:6c, 7; 51:15; 62:9-11; 73:1f; 92:7; 94:8-11, 12f; 97:10; 107:43; 111:10ab; 119:1-3, 21, 118, 119a; Deut 32:1f; Lam 3:26-29; Sir 2:12-14; 32:22-25; Pss Sol 3:3ff; 15:2ff, 7ff.
[52]Ps 34:12.
[53]Ps 32:1f.
[54]Ps 51:15; cf. 32:8.
[55]Ps 32:9.

characteristic forms of wisdom (admonition and instruction),[56] and the content of wisdom (observing the essence of the fate of the godless).[57]

The same is true for the hymn when, in the later period, it moves into a more settled tone of pious observation and adopts components of wisdom. As a result, thoughts about retribution appear in a manner characteristic of wisdom.[58] Humans are designated over against God's unfathomable wisdom as "animal-like" and "foolish."[59] Also, the wisdom saying,[60] the admonition,[61] and the introduction of the wisdom speech penetrate the hymn.[62] Wisdom's influence upon the hymn continues into the postcanonical period, and finally transform the hymn into something sober.[63]

Wisdom poetry penetrates the *individual complaint song* in the *thoughts of comfort*,[64] where it speaks to the pious ones[65] about the rule of YHWH or about the futility of humanity and its wealth.[66] Formally, the influence is perhaps shown in the combination of question and answer that is characteristic of wisdom.[67]

The incorporation of wisdom can be seen formally in *mixed poetry* which use beatitudes about the righteous,[68] admonitions to confession, or admonitions for insight.[69] Regarding content, wisdom is perhaps recognizable in the designation of the godless as "animals" and "fools,"[70] in the idea that YHWH is the teacher and tutor of the people,[71] or in the idea that wisdom stems from YHWH himself.[72]

In general, even if not in every particular case, wisdom components (mostly sayings) stand out in the particular psalms by the fact that they speak about YHWH in the third person, and thus do not exhibit the form of a prayer.

From the opposite perspective, *lyric poetry* also influenced *wisdom*. In the book of Job, hymns and individual complaint songs in particular are woven into the composition.[73] And the book of Jesus ben Sirach exhibits an abundance of diverse lyric pieces in distinction to the proverbs preserved in the older style.[74]

---

[56]Pss 32:6f, 8-10; 34:12-22; 31:24-25.

[57]Pss 32:10ff; 34:12ff; Pss. Sol. 15:7ff.

[58]Ps 97:10.

[59]Pss 92:7; see 49:13; 73:22.

[60]Ps 107:43 as well as 34:13ff. See ¶6.

[61]Ps 33:16-18. See Prov 21:31; also Ps 34:17; Sir 31:19; Ps 111, which concludes with a praise of wisdom, borrowed literally from wisdom (Ps 111:10a = Prov 1:7; cf. 9:10).

[62]Ps 78:12.

[63]Sir 39:21-30; 42:23-24; Pss. Sol. 3.

[64]§6, ¶20.

[65]Ps 25:12f; cf. ¶6, Ps 25:13b.

[66]Pss 39:6c, 7; 62:9-11; cf. Ps 49; ¶6.

[67]Ps 25:12; see ¶6.

[68]Pss 94:12; 119:1-3; ¶6.

[69]Lam 3:39; ¶5; Ps 94:8; cf. Prov 8:5; Sir 16:24.

[70]Pss 94:8; cf. 49:13; 73:22; 92:7.

[71]Ps 94:10. The terms *limmed* and *yāsar* point to a wisdom origin.

[72]Ps 94:12. See ¶4.

[73]§1, ¶2; §2, ¶60; §6, ¶1.

[74]§2, ¶1; §4, ¶1; §6, ¶1; §7, ¶1. See W. Baumgartner, *ZAW* 34 (1914): 169ff. Regarding details, see Job 5:9-16; 36:22–37:13; Sir 10:14-1; 16:18f.

Even in the wisdom poetry of the psalter, traces of lyric genres are occasionally observed. The portrayal of the godless in Ps 73 sounds like the complaint of the complaint songs.[75] Ps 73:13 reads like a protestation of innocence,[76] and the conclusion in which the poet expresses his unshakeable hope in YHWH, offers the well-known assurances of confidence and the expressions of certainty.[77] In Ps 49, a later hand inserted a very personal motif of confidence into the didactic poem,[78] which can be demonstrated as not belonging to the whole by its deviation of style.[79]

This penetration of lyric components into wisdom poetry loans the latter a more personal dynamic, as one recognizes in Ps 73 and Job. It is no accident that the personal element appears most forcefully precisely in the poetic works that treat *theodicy*. There is nothing else which affected the heart and soul of persons of that time so deeply.

Prophecy and wisdom have generally not influenced one another. The sober spirit of the wisdom sayings and the ecstatic enthusiasm of the powerful men of God stand far apart from one another. Both the wise and the prophets have very different themes as a rule. The one speaks of the future of Israel, the other speaks of the relationships of the individual in the present. For example, when wisdom mentions the spirit of YHWH who will separate the pious and the godless from one another,[80] it does not mean the final judgment as in the prophets.[81] Rather, it means the continual rule of God.[82] Nevertheless, several influences of wisdom poetry can be confirmed within the prophetic message.[83]

4. The most important expressions and forms which appear in the "wisdom sayings" and the "wisdom poetry" of the psalter, as well as in the psalms influenced by wisdom, are the following: The poet calls his speech "wisdom,"[84] "instruction" (*tōrāh*),[85] "riddle" (*ḥîdāh*),[86] or "proverb" (*māšāl*).[87] The content of teaching is called "the fear of YHWH," meaning the manner in which one should fear and honor YHWH.[88] By form, the *direct address* which sometimes dominates the entire poem is particularly characteristic.[89] This direct address presupposes a situation in which the father speaks to the son,[90] the elder to

---

[75]§4, ¶7; §6, ¶8.

[76]§6, ¶21.

[77]§6, ¶19, 23.

[78]§6, ¶19.

[79]See the commentary.

[80]Pss 1:5; cf. 25:13; 37:13.

[81]Mal 3:18ff.

[82]See the counterpart in Qoh 2:14.

[83]Isa 3:10; Jer 17:5-8, 9f, 11; see also 12:1f. With several passages one should ask whether they are really of prophetic origin.

[84]Pss 49:4; 37:30; 111:10.

[85]Pss 78:1; 94:12; cf. Prov 1:8; 3:1; 4:2; 6:23; 7:2; 13:14; 28:4, 7, 9; 31:26; Job 22:22.

[86]Pss 49:5; 78:2; cf. Prov 1:6; Sir 8:8.

[87]Pss 49:5; 78:2.

[88]Pss 34:12; 110:10; cf. Prov 1:7; 2:5; 8:13; 9:10.

[89]Pss 32:8f; 34:12, 14f; 37; 49:2f, 5, 17; 62:9, 11; 78:1; 91:1-13; 94:8; 115:9-11; 127:2; 128:2f, 5f. The same thing occurs in Egyptian (see A. Erman and H. Ranke, *Ägypten*,[2] pp. 193f, 447f; H. Ranke, in H. Greßmann, *Altorientalische Texte*,[2] pp. 33ff) and in Babylonian didactic poetry (see H. Zimmern, *Babylonische Hymnen und Gebete*, vol. 2, pp. 27ff and E. Ebeling in H. Greßmann, *Altorientalische Texte*,[2] pp. 291ff), as well as in part of the biblical Proverbs (esp. 1–7).

[90]Tob 4.

the younger person, giving him sound teaching for life's path. Thus, one finds the frequent expression, "my son."[91] In addition, one finds the plural address "my sons,"[92] with commands. "Come, sons."[93] "Hear."[94] "Incline your ear,"[95] and "I will teach you."[96] It is quite clear from Pss 119:9 and 32:8 that the young and inexperienced are addressed.[97] The Babylonian teacher speaks to his student: "Come, my son, sit at my feet while I speak to you."[98]

Freer introductions appear in several passages[99] where the poet turns to the whole world,[100] and calls upon a *revelation* which he has received.[101] One can observe the high self-esteem for the wise breaks forth in these often strong words.[102] The Babylonian materials also know the pride of the teacher: "What is there which I do not know?"[103] The Syriac Ahikar says the youth should hear the word of the teacher like a "divine speech."[104]

5. The content of wisdom poetry comprises *admonitions* and *instruction*. There are *positive admonitions*, such as the admonitions to trust in YHWH, to fear YHWH,[105] to do good,[106] to avoid sin,[107] to confess at the proper time,[108] or to watch one's tongue.[109] Quite typically, a beautiful *promise* is added to these admonitions, sometimes introduced with "for."[110] Alongside these positive admonitions, one finds *negative warnings* (with אל and the jussive) against becoming disgruntled by misfortune,[111] provoked by the wealthy godless ones,[112] marveling too much over riches, or trusting in them.[113] A word concerning

---

[91]Ps 32:8 (see the passage); cf. Prov 1:8, 10, 15; 2:1; 3:1, 11, 21; 4:10, 20; Sir 2:1; 3:12, 17; 4:1; etc. The same thing occurs in the Aramaic Ahikar speeches (Pap. 56/I:2, 4; 56/II8; 53:4) and the sayings of the Syriac Ahikar in which the quote is continuously the same at the beginning. See Th. Nöldeke, "Abh. der Kgl." *Geschichte der Wissenschaften zu Göttingen*. Phil.=hist. Kl. New Series, 14/4 (1913): 34ff.

[92]Ps 34:12; see Prov 4:1; Sir 3:1; 23:7; 41:14.

[93]Ps 34:12; see Prov 1:23; 9:5; Sir 51:23.

[94]Pss 34:12; 49:2; 78:1; cf. Prov 1:8; 4:1; 5:1, 7; 8:6, 32; Sir 3:1; 23:7; 41:14.

[95]Pss 78:1; 49:5; cf. Prov 2:2; 4:20; 5:1.

[96]Pss 34:12; 32:8; cf. Prov 1:23; 4:2,11; 8:6; Job 15:17.

[97]Cf. Prov 1:4.

[98]See B. Meißner, *Babylonien und Assyrien*, vol. 2, 1925, p. 326.

[99]Pss 49:2ff; 62:2ff; 78:1f.

[100]See Job 15:17ff; 34:2, 10; Sir 16:24f; 24:32ff; 30:27; 39:12ff; see Deut 32:1f; Pss 34:10; 62:9; 115:9-11; 131:3; Wis 6:1.

[101]Pss 62:12f; 51:8; see Job 4:12f.

[102]See also Sir 51:29 and the parody to Prov 30:1-3.

[103]B. Meißner, *Babylonien und Assyrien*, vol. 2, p. 327.

[104]Th. Nöldeke, *Geschichte der Wissenschaften zu Göttingen* n.s. 14/4 (1913): 35.

[105]Pss 34:10; 37:5, 7, 34; 62:9; cf. Prov 3:5; 16:3; Sir 2:6ff; 11:21.

[106]Ps 37:3, 27, 37.

[107]Ps 37:27; cf. Sir 38:10.

[108]Ps 32:6f, 8f; Lam 3:26; cf. Job 5:8; 8:5; 11:13ff; 22:21ff.

[109]Ps 34:14; cf. Prov 4:23f.

[110]Ps 37:3f, 5f, 27, 34, 37; Lam 3:31ff; cf. Prov 3:5f, 7f, 9f, 21ff; 4:6ff, 10, 13, 23; Sir 4:10; 7:32; Wis 1:2.

[111]Ps 32:8; Job 5:17.

[112]Ps 37:1, 7, 8; cf. Prov 3:31; 23:17; 24:1, 19; Qoh 8:14; Sir 11:21f.

[113]Pss 49:17; 62:11; cf. Sir 9:11.

the *terrible fate of the godless* then follows these warnings, often introduced with "then."[114] In these admonitions and warnings, the seriousness of the moral challenges of the religion stand out powerfully. This manner of speech also appears in Babylonian and, especially, Egyptian materials.[115] Sometimes the warning is clothed in an *interrogative sentence* ("Why will you?").[116]

6. Concerning *the instruction*. The short sayings are sometimes introduced with "behold" (*hinnê*),[117] as are the religious didactic sentences.[118] Another introduction of the speeches is the sentence: "It is good,"[119] or "How good it is."[120] The opposite also appear as introductions: "It is bad;" "It is difficult;" "how great."[121] The poet of Proverbs begins with "better than . . . is . . . " In so doing, he compares two things with one another and expresses something entirely different than that which would generally be expressed.[122] The sayings of Amenemope[123] and the Syriac Ahikar also know this beginning.[124]

Characteristic for Proverbs is also the preference for *impressive comparisons*[125] and for *the piling of images*.[126] The later poetry gladly took the images from the area of the holy.[127] The combination of question and answer is also preferred. It is a form which is explained by the instruction.[128] One also finds a question with a subsequent admonition,[129] and the "numerical saying" appears at times.[130]

"Wisdom" treats the doctrine of retribution with numerous variations. When it does so, it usually describes the *pious* according to his behavior, the reward granted to him, or

---

[114]Ps 37:1f, 8f, 27f; cf. Prov 3:1f, 11ff, 31f; 4:14ff; 6:20ff, 25f; 7:25f; 22:22f; 23:10f, 17f, 20f; 24:15f, 19f, 21f; Sir 3:10, 23f; 4:23f; 5:6f, 8; 7:1f; 8:14ff; 9:10, 11; 18:30f; 19:8f; 32:14f; 38:9; 40:28ff; 41:3ff; Wisd 1:3ff.

[115]Cf. E. Ebeling and H. Ranke in H. Greßmann, *Altoritetalische Texte,*[2] pp. 33ff, 291ff.

[116]Ps 49:6; Lam 3:39; cf. Prov 5:20; Sir 13:17; cf. ("How long?") Prov 1:22; 6:9; Sir 51:24; ("When were you smart?") 94:8.

[117]Pss 127:5; 133:1.

[118]Pss 33:18; cf. 73:27; 92:10; 121:4; 128:4.

[119]Lam 3:26f; cf. Tob 12:6f,11.

[120]Ps 133:1; cf. Sir 25:4f. The latter also appears in Egyptian sayings. See H. Ranke in H. Greßmann, *Altoritetalische Texte,*[2] p. 33, chap. 16, ¶5.

[121]Sir 25:10; 28:21; 29:28.

[122]Ps 37:16; cf. Prov 3:14f; 12:9; 15:16f; 16:8, 16, 19, 32; 17:1; 19:1; 21:19; 25:7, 24; 27:5, 10; 28:6; Sir 10:27; 20:18, 25, 31; 25:16; 29:22; 30:14, 17, 30; 40:19-26; 41:14; Qoh 4:6, 9, 13; 5:4; 6:3, 9; 7:1, 2, 3, 5, 8, 18; Tob 12:8; Wisd 4:1.

[123]H. Ranke in H. Greßmann, *Altoritetalische Texte,*[2] p. 40, chap. 6.

[124]Th. Nöldeke, *Geschichte der Wissenschaften zu Göttingen* n.s. 14/4 (1913): 42; ¶51, 53.

[125]Pss 127:4f; 128:3; 133:2f; Jer 17:6, 8, 11; cf. Prov 10:26; 11:22; 12:4; 15:19; 16:24; 18:8; 25:12ff; Sir 20:19; 35:5f.

[126]Ps 132:2-3; cf. Sir 24:13ff; 26:16ff; 50:6ff.

[127]Ps 133:2cd, 3; Sir 24:15f; 26:17; 50:9a.

[128]B. Meißner, *Babylonien und Assyrien,* vol. 2, 1925, p. 327. Pss 25:12f; 34:13ff; 107:43; 119:9; Lam 3:39; Prov 23:29f; Sir 1:6ff; 10:19; 22:14; 34:9ff.

[129]Pss 34:13ff; 107:43.

[130]Ps 62:12f; cf. Prov 6:16ff; 30:15f, 18f, 21f, 24ff, 29ff; Job 5:19; 33:14; Sir 23:16ff; 25:1, 2, 7-11; 26:5f, 28; 50:25f; Ahikar Sayings Pap. 53:14, 15a; *Pîrkê Abôth* I/2.18; III/1; IV/13 and esp. V.

both.[131] Also, the *godless* is shown by his evil deeds and his terrible fate.[132] Frequently, the *righteous and the wicked* are very impressively contrasted with one another.[133]

One of the surest signs of "wisdom" is that the reward and the virtue of the righteous are praised in the form of a "beatitude" ("happy is the one who . . . " [*ašrê* is used, seldom *tob* or *bārūk*. Sometimes it is followed by "for."]).[134] When "for" appears, it is followed by beautiful promises. Ps 91 is filled with these promises. The *curse* and *woe saying* are less common,[135] while the same thing occurs in Egyptian wisdom ("Woe to his children").[136]

It is natural that wisdom usually describes YHWH's *action* as often as it proclaims retribution.[137]

Originally, the person speaking in this poetry receded completely into the background. Sometimes, however, the proverbial poet reports about personal experiences.[138] The same thing occurs in the sayings of Ptah-hotep,[139] and in the instruction of Duauf,[140] as well as in the Syriac Ahikar.[141] Later poems provide objective material in subjective clothing. In other words, the poets expressly relate their personal experiences through which they have come to their convictions. This combination of the two types of material is quite impressive and represents the highpoint of wisdom.[142] The *question of theodicy* was particularly well contested in this personal manner.

This combination shows that "wisdom sayings" and "wisdom poems" agree in the most significant forms. At the same time, it is also clear that all of the main forms of this wisdom poetry, as well as the related psalmic pieces, recur in the remaining wisdom writings.

7. The *overview* thus depicts a *very comprehensive genre* which is found on foreign and Israelite soil, in the canon and in the apocrypha, in the form of shorter "speeches" and

---

[131]Pss 1:1-3; 25:12f; 32:10; 37:6, 9, 11, 18f, 21f, 23f, 28, 30, 39; 91; 112; 128; cf. Prov 2:5ff; Sir 1:13, 16ff; 2:15ff; 21:11; etc.

[132]Pss 1:4f; 32:10; 37:2, 9, 10, 12f, 14f, 17, 21, 22, 28, 32f, 38; 73:4ff, 18ff; 112:10; 119:21, 118f; cf. Prov 1:29ff; 4:16ff; Sir 1:22; 21:25ff; 23:16ff; 28:1; Job 5:2ff; 15:20ff; 18:5ff; 20:5ff; 24:2ff; 27:13ff; etc.

[133]Pss 1:1-3,4f; 32:10; 34:17f; 37:9, 10f, 17, 21, 22, 28f; 112:1-9, 10; Isa 3:10f; cf. Prov 10:3, 6, 7, 11, 16, 20, 24,25, 27, 29, 31, 32; 11:3, 5, 6; etc. Sir 16:13; Pss. Sol. 3:5ff, 9ff.

[134]Pss 1:1-3; 32:1f; 34:9b; 91:1ff (cf. the commentary for this passage); 94:12; 112:1ff, 5f; 119:1f; 127:5; 128:1, 2; cf. Prov 3:13ff; 8:32ff; 14:21; 16:20; 28:14; 29:18; Job 5:17; Isa 3:10; Jer 17:7f; Sir 14:1, 2, 20ff; 25:7ff; 26:1; 28:19f; 31:17; 34:8ff; 50:28; Wisd 3:13.

[135]Pss 1:4f; 127:2; cf. Isa 3:11; Jer 17:5f; Sir 2:12ff; 28:13; 41:8.

[136]Sayings of Amenemope in H. Greßmann, *Altorientalische Texte*,[2] p. 41, chap. 9.

[137]Pss 1:6; 25:12; 32:10; 33:18; 34:16-21; 37:5, 13, 17, 18, 28, 33, 39, 40; 62:13; 73:1, 18, 27; 91:3f, 11; 94:9-11; 97:10; 119:21a; 127:1f, 3; 133:3; 136:13, 16; cf. Prov 3:6, 12, 33; 6:16ff; 10:3, 29; 15:29; 22:11; 30:5; Job 5:18ff; 34:20ff; 36:5ff; Sir 2:6, 11; 6:37; 10:14ff; 16:7ff; etc.

[138]"What I have seen I will tell" (Job 15:17; 37:25, 35f; Ps 73; cf. Prov 4:3f; 7:6ff; 24:30ff; Job 5:3; Sir 16:5; 31:12f; 51:13ff; Wisd 7:1ff; 8:2ff.

[139]H. Ranke, in H. Greßmann, *Altorientalische Texte*,[2] 1926, p. 33, §19, ¶7.

[140]Erman, *Literatur der Ägypter*, 101f.

[141]In Th. Nöldeke, *Geschichte der Wissenschaften zu Göttingen*. n.s. 14/4 (1913): 49 ("I have seen.") ¶32, 33.

[142]The following belong to this category: Ps 73; Sir 51:13; Wisd. Sol. 7:1ff; 8:2ff; and especially Job and Qohelet.

longer "poems," even in entire books. Within the psalter, one finds this genre within these poems, but also in diverse sayings which have been placed into other genres. The oldest element of this poetry would have been the "sayings." However, the poets (some of them very great poets) have strengthened the older form by powerfully expressing their personal encounters and experiences in detailed poems.[143] Several of the outstanding poems of the psalter are wisdom songs.[144] Thus, we can observe the same entry of personality into the psalmic poetry which we have seen in other genres.[145] In the *form of performance*, both stages can be distinguished. The short "sayings" were certainly spoken, while in Ps 49:5, we still find a clue that one sang "the wisdom poetry" to the accompaniment of "the zither." It is noteworthy that a divine response has been added to the wisdom poem of Ps 91 in 91:14-16. Thus, the first part may have been expressed as a priestly blessing for the people. This leads to the conclusion that the poem was performed *in the worship service*. The same is true in the superscriptions[146] (even if only for the latest period) which show that these poems arose in the early collections which stemmed from the worship services.

There is little doubt that wisdom poems did not originally have their place in the worship service. Rather, they were at home elsewhere.[147] Such is more than apparent for examples such as Pss 49; 127:3-5; and 133 whose contents are overwhelmingly secular (see ¶2, pp. 295f). Later, wisdom poems must have been adopted by those who had to care for the worship service, that is the *priests and singers*. Wisdom poems were apparently adopted because they were so loved by the laity that they could not do without them in cultic performances. The same thing is true to an even greater extent for the examples of the prophetic spirit.[148] One cannot determine at *which occasion* these wisdom poems would have been performed in the worship service.

W. Caspari presumes that Ps 91 would have been sung at the holy act of bringing an amulet to the body of one who was in some kind of danger or when holding a festival for someone like this (such as before war, a dangerous trip, etc.).[149] However, psalms of the type he mentions, and the form of performance itself, cannot be proven elsewhere. It is, however, the task of genre research to place the explanation of psalms on a firm foundation by indicating clear counterparts.

8. Finally, concerning how to *calculate the time*. The royal sayings in Proverbs are at least partially related to the native king (especially 16:10). This observation points to the preexilic period, even if not for the entire book. In addition, the explicit designation that the collection of Prov 25–29 was "compiled by the men of Hezekiah" has some credibility. The speeches which explored life so powerfully can be placed in the earlier period, since the prophets had not yet conquered the folk life and Israel was still naively open to foreign influence. Within the psalter, the freshness of Ps 127:3-5 and the generally humanistic mood of Ps 49 can be related to this period by content.[150]

---

[143]¶1.
[144]Pss 49; 73.
[145]§1,¶8; §2, ¶44; §6, ¶4, 28; §7, ¶8.
[146]Pss 37; 49; 73; 112; 127; 128; 133.
[147]Cf. §1, ¶4.
[148]See ¶9, p. 282ff.
[149]W. Caspari, *ZAW* n.s. 4 (1927): 254.
[150]See ¶2, 295f.

A new period follows in which a *religioethical tone* entered the wisdom poetry. This occurs in Ps 127:1ff with its strong confidence in God. It also occurs in Ps 133 which places value on Zion. One can recognize the antiquity of this change from Jer 18:18, where the "wise" with their "counsel" are mentioned as the pillars of Israelite life alongside the priests with their "torah" and the prophets with their "word." What this passage means by the wise is certainly not secular counsel, but a pious and moral counsel. At that time, the *doctrine of retribution*, applied to the individual, strengthened the wisdom teaching. This doctrine was certainly not entirely new at this point, but it increasingly became the central point of the religion of the time.[151] Among the psalms, only Pss 1, 91, 112, and 128 express themselves in this direction.

A later stage turned toward the doubt of this doctrine.[152]

One can also say something about the age of this change. Jeremiah had already expressed thoughts against the doctrine of retribution,[153] and the saying which could often be heard in his time: "The fathers have eaten sour grapes, and the sons' teeth are set on edge."[154] He mocks this belief. It bears the form of "wisdom poetry." It imitates a realistic observation of life as in Prov 14:20; 20:14; 27:10c.

From this determination of an internal history, one has only provided a possible beginning point for the individual psalms, not the actual time of composition. The older material does not tend to disappear with these developmental stages when the newer material enters. The different positions can exist alongside one another for a long time. This observation is all the more true for "wisdom" since we can determine that "wisdom" was nurtured for many centuries on Israelite-Judean soil. One can observe the end of the whole history of the genre in Sirach and the Psalms of Solomon.

Besides the beginning and end points just mentioned, one cannot say all that much about the *individual psalms*, nor can one speak too specifically. There is no reason to object to the early placement of Ps 49 and 127:3-5.

The influence of the prophetic spirit is especially clear from the powerful individual-ism in Ps 91. It appears that one should not move too far away from these great heroes. However, determining when the poem was performed for the worship service indicates a much later time, when wisdom poetry entered the cult.[155]

The artistic *alphabetic form* of many wisdom poems,[156] or poems influenced by wisdom,[157] suggests a relatively late period. However, even here we cannot provide a specific number, and Lam 3, which still belongs in the exile, warns us against assigning every example to the latest period without further information. Similar things could be said for *wisdom's entry into lyric poetry* and the *mixed poems* which resulted.[158] We can also recognize the sign of a more recent period when the religious powers abated and their immediate expression was increasingly pushed into the background by growing amounts

---

[151] See the *RGG* article, "Individualismus und Sozialismus im AT," ¶3, 5.
[152] ¶2, p. 296.
[153] Jer 12:1f; cf. ¶3, pp. 297f.
[154] Jer 31:29; Ezek 18:2.
[155] ¶7, p. 303.
[156] Pss 37; 112.
[157] Pss 25; 34; 119; Lam 3.
[158] See ¶3, p. 298.

of reflection. We also do not doubt that a piece like Ps 119 belongs at the end of the history. It is an alphabetic poem and therefore an overly artistic poem in which the process of mixing reaches its height. All of the genres are confusingly mixed together and among the numerous observations stand those which are taken from "wisdom." This recognition is also strengthened by Sirach, where the mixture reaches a particularly high degree, as well as in the Psalms of Solomon, where the ancient lyric retreats behind all kinds of observations. Of course, many of these do not have the precise form of "wisdom," but they approach it because of the domination of the doctrine of retribution and theodicy. Nevertheless, Lam 3 shows how early this development had already occurred. In Lam 3 one already finds the penetration of wisdom teaching into lyric poetry, even if only in its beginning stage.

We achieve a solid measuring rod from the relationship of *legal piety* to these psalms. Originally, wisdom poetry had no relationship at all to legal piety. In fact, it is not uncommon for the wisdom sayings to speak of "torah." However, this word does not designate the "law of Moses." Rather, "torah" almost exclusively designates "instruction," the teaching of the wise.[159] Later, however, the legal spirit enters lyric poetry as well as "wisdom." Thus, several passages describe the pious one as the true disciple of the law.[160] It is significant that this mixture also appears in Ps 119 where it is characteristic that a concern for the law has penetrated the transmitted lyric forms.[161] It is also noteworthy that we can observe how the legal spirit which had risen to prominence at the time felt itself superior to the older, more worldly wisdom poetry.[162] Those psalms which speak about the law in forms of wisdom thus belong to the latest period of the entire development, although not from the time of the Pharisees since there is no talk about "discussion" of the legal regulations.

In the book of Sirach, the law of Moses finally rises to the completely dominant position. He speaks about it in very many passages,[163] and compares it to "wisdom."[164]

Several *less significant signs* of the time of composition can also be addressed. Ps 128, which refers to the pitiful situation of the Israelite walls following the overthrow of the state, certainly stems from the postexilic period. Ps 112 points to an even later period since it appears to presuppose later commercial and economic activity instead of the older agricultural system. The language of Ps 73 points to a late period.[165]

In several psalms, signals of the time of origin are multiplied. These signals are attained from different perspectives, so that when this happens we obtain a very reliable final conclusion. This is especially true for Ps 119.

---

[159] See ¶4, p. 300.

[160] Cf. 1:2; 37:31; 112:1.

[161] Cf. Ps 119:1-3, 9 and 21.

[162] See Ps 119:98a, 99a, 100a, 104a; see the commentary.

[163] Pss 28:6f; 45:5, 17; etc.

[164] Pss 119:20; 24:23; 31:8; cf. Bar 4:1.

[165] Cf. the commentary.

§11 Mixtures, Antiphonal Poems, and Liturgies

I. Mixtures

E. Balla, *Das Ich der Psalmen*, 1912, pp. 110ff. — *RGG*[2] Article, "Klagelieder Jeremia," 3. — "Psalmen," 16. — H. Gunkel, "Die Psalmen," in *Reden und Aufsätze*, pp. 121f.

1. Over the course of history, the various psalm genres have adopted manifold relationships with one another. Tracing these relationships and investigating their causes constitutes the task of this chapter. In the first place, those psalms will be treated which can be designated *mixtures* of genres.

In history, one can observe that almost every psalm genre has incorporated ideas and forms from other genres in the endeavor to find a richer and more appropriate expression for the life in which it makes itself felt. In contrast to other mixtures discussed below, this process does not signify the disintegration of the adopting genre. It remains preserved completely intact. Clearly, as long as no dissolution occurs, the genre can only adopt those components whose material will accommodate to the mood or form. The identity of these components and the reasons they were adopted will be presented comprehensively in the specific paragraphs for the passages in question. In this regard, it is satisfactory to provide a brief overview of the foundational passages in the introduction: §2, ¶¶32, 54-60; §4, ¶¶4, 8, 12; §6, ¶¶10, 15, 19, 20, 24, 28; §7, ¶¶1, 5, 8; §8, ¶¶12, 13, 19, 22, 26, 27, 32, 37; §10, ¶¶3, 5, 6.

2. One must first fundamentally distinguish this type of mixture from those which presuppose the *dissolution* and *disintegration* of the genres. Along with the *penetration of reflection*, one can mention in particular the *separation of the genres from their original concrete situation* as the cause of dissolution. In other words, the poetry changed from poetry bound to the cult to spiritual poetry which was free of the cult. As long as a genre, such as the individual thanksgiving song, stands in a dynamic context with the celebratory event which finds appropriate expression in that genre, then its structure and its forms are protected from changes that do not coincide with the event. Material and ideas are kept away which would be perceived as foreign to the cause of that celebration. Once the genre becomes separated from the soil of the cult, the power of the genre's fixed style can even preserve the unity of the genre for a while longer when combined with the dynamic actualization of the celebration from which it started. However, the genre will gradually fall apart, thereby opening itself to forms and materials which would have been impossible in the time of the rigid style. In this case, the combination of various components from different genres no longer results from a fixed, concrete basis. Rather, it results form *associations* which the individual poet of the psalm controls.

The *mixed poetry* that has been preserved allows one to recognize clearly the various stages of this development. First, larger sections of one genre appear in a loose connection to others. Gradually, the penetrating sections become smaller and the mixtures more numerous, ultimately resulting in a mosaic of the smallest genre components, Ps 119.

3. One encounters the first traces of this mixing only with keen observation in the *hymn*,[1] and the *individual thanksgiving song*,[2] where a petition taken from the *individual complaint song* forms the conclusion. This kind of anti-climax cannot be understood from the strict genre since it demands a rejoining of the poem to the festal event or, with the thanksgiving song, the continuation in hymnic form of the enthusiasm of those who have been saved. However, it becomes understandable for the poet of a spiritual song, who no longer thinks about a worship performance. The perspective of the singer in Ps 104 immerses itself reverently in the miraculous words of YHWH. While scrutinizing the regions of the world, including those of the godless, the psalm also encounters those which offend the pious. He thus mentions his opposition to them and demands their destruction, even though these feelings are quite removed from the hymnic mood. Pursuing these feelings, he inserts a petition for their extermination, one which would be quite common in the complaint song.

Things are similar for the thanksgiving songs which were cited. When the poet attaches a petition to his confession after expressing his good fortune in having been delivered, he does so because the remaining troubles which still create problems for him force their way into the foreground despite everything. These troubles would not be expressed in connection with the happy celebration of the festival. However, where these troubles present no obstacle, they come to the lips of the poet. The fact that one of the two psalm passages, Ps 138:8c, presupposes cultic performance does not negate this understanding. Instead, we have to consider the impact of poetry free of the cult upon poetry which is cultically bound.

4. That which can only be seen here dimly becomes much clearer in other poems. Ps 33 is typical. The hymn appears in 33:19 with the praise of YHWH's action for the pious. This idea is common as a comforting idea in the complaint songs. This idea brings the troubles of his people to mind for the poet, troubles which are also causing him to suffer. His poem thus transitions into a *communal complaint song*. That which follows takes the hymnic statements as ideas of comfort: the portrayal of the longing for YHWH which is well-known in the complaint song (33:20a); the expression of confidence (33:20, 21); and finally the petitions preserved in the form of the wish (33:22a), followed by a concluding motif of confidence (33:22b).

The mixture in Ps 19 is even stronger. The ever recurring mention of the commands are praised more highly than all creation, including the sun. This recurring mention awakens ideas about how the pious person stands in relation to these commands. Since he follows these commands, he turns to the individual complaint song. He asserts that he walks in the commands (19:12, innocence motif). He confesses unknown transgressions (19:13a, confession of sin). He asks for forgiveness, protection, and the gracious acceptance of his words (19:14b-15, petition). The mixtures in Pss 90 and 139 are similar (refer to the commentary for details).

Ps 129 and Pss. Sol. 16 essentially correspond to the mixture treated here. In the style of the *communal thanksgiving song*, the poet of Ps 129 speaks about hostilities to which

---

[1]Ps 104:35; §2, ¶36, p. 40.
[2]Pss 40:12; 138:8c; §7, ¶8, p. 207.

Israel was exposed from the beginning of its history. It also speaks about the help Israel experienced from YHWH. However, at the point when consideration of history turns to the present, thereby awakening the poet's recollection of the suffering of his days, his poem turns to the *communal complaint song*. It concludes with a passionate petition, using the form of the wish, for the humiliation and destruction of all Zion's enemies.

Pss. Sol. 16 begins as an individual thanksgiving song. The poet is thankful that YHWH did not allow him to fall into sin and corruption, although he almost succumbed. Confronted with the danger which had almost slain him, he requests further gracious protection from guilt and a change of life which pleases God (16:6-12). Ideas undergirding the petition form the conclusion which should be perceived as a motif (16:13-15). It is characteristic of all of the psalms that ideas and forms arising from the individual complaint song appear about twice as often as the thanksgiving song. As a result, the accent of the poetry ultimately falls on those components which are foreign to the thanksgiving song and inorganically bound to it.

5. Other mixtures proceed from the *complaint songs*. Lam 3 is characteristic of these. The poem begins without direct address with a broad complaint preserved (3:1-18) in the tone of the monologue. Only after the monologue concludes does the poem achieve a personal relationship with YHWH by directing a petition to him (3:19-20). All kinds of *petitions* carrying comforting ideas are then attached. The space which they occupy, in comparison to the strict genre, is unusually large (3:20-39). Alongside the *assertion of confidence* (3:21,24), one encounters the comforting idea that YHWH's grace and faithfulness have no end (3:22-23). One also finds another comforting idea, that YHWH is good to those who long for him and seek him (3:25). In addition, thoughts are expressed which do not emerge from the genre. Instead, they stem from *wisdom poetry* (§10, ¶3). The poet maintains that it is good to suffer patiently, because the suffering means there might still be hope (3:26ff). He comforts himself with the knowledge that YHWH does not enjoy torment. Using rhetorical questions, he admonishes himself to hold fast to the beliefs that YHWH will not overlook any human injustice, that nothing happens with YHWH, and that evil and good stem from YHWH (3:33ff). In this context, he finally admonishes himself to recognize that it is pointless for humans to be completely rid of sins attracting YHWH's punishment (3:39). This idea drives him to further *admonition* that also arises from the forms of wisdom poetry. He includes himself in this admonition to examine his ways and his heart, to repent to YHWH, and to flee to YHWH for forgiveness (3:40-41). In so doing, the poem transition into the *communal complaint song* actually causing the inclusion of the *confession of sin* (3:42) and the moving *complaint* designed to stir YHWH's heart (3:43-47). Almost imperceptibly, the poem transitions into the *individual complaint song* as the poet describes how the distress of his people causes him pain personally (3:48-51). From there, the psalmist returns to the very tribulations that almost killed him. In the context of this complaint, he recalls how YHWH has saved him from mortal distress. That recollection leads him further into the *narrative* of the *individual thanksgiving song* (3:55). It unfolds by introducing the complaint song which had been sung (3:56). This experience gives him the confidence to face his current suffering. He thus concludes with a confidence-filled petition for the destruction of his enemies (3:59ff).

We can treat similar mixed poems more briefly following this extensive example. Ps 94 begins as a *communal complaint song* about insolent godless persons who knowingly act nefariously by saying YHWH does not see and that Jacob's God has no understanding.

This recollection leads the poet to indignant interaction with them. In so doing, he moves completely into the forms and ideas of *wisdom poetry* (§10, ¶3). It also leads him to the *blessing saying* about the man whom YHWH instructs, which is quite understandable for wisdom poetry with its contrast of the wicked and the pious (see the commentary for details). Finally, one should mention the alphabetic hymn of Pss 9/10 in this context. It mixes the *individual thanksgiving song* (Ps 9:1-5,14-15) and the *eschatological hymn* (9:6-17) with the *individual complaint song*: the wish and petition (9:18,21), the *confidence motif* (9:14), *petition* (9:20), the complaint about the wicked (10:1-11), petition (10:12f), confidence motif (10:14), petition (10:15), prayer motif (10:16), and the certainty of having been heard (10:17-18). The restriction of the alphabet also determined the mixing of genres in addition to the idea associations (see the commentary).

6. Finally, one should consider the mixture which took place between the *hymn* and the *thanksgiving song* on the one hand and *wisdom poetry* on the other. Mixtures between the hymn and wisdom poetry[3] became possible when the hymn began considering the works and deeds of YHWH reflectively instead of relying on immediate enthusiasm. As a result, the hymn can flow into a word of wisdom which considers the content of hymnic statements.[4] In this manner, however, the *ideas* of wisdom poetry also enter the hymn itself,[5] ideas which perceive the purpose of things. Or, the hymnic poetry becomes didactic when it provides the purpose the creator pursued with all of his works.[6] Hymnic forms also become permeated with forms of wisdom poetry. Thus, in Sir 39:12ff the introduction proceeds from the speaker's remark that he wants to be filled with wisdom, to speak of wisdom, and to listen to wisdom where the *warning* is directed to children of the pious (cf. §10, ¶4, p. 299). One encounters *wisdom forms* where the poet of the hymn praises the appropriateness of YHWH's works. Here one finds forms characteristic of wisdom poetry: *comparatives*,[7] and the *question and answer*.[8]

From the other side, *hymnic material* and *forms* penetrate the *admonition* of the wisdom poetry when the wisdom teacher grounds his words with reference to YHWH's incomparable greatness, his fearfulness, or his compassion.[9] Even the blessing saying which became the form of wisdom poetry, is connected with the *hymn*.[10] The connection was formed by the conclusion of the blessing saying. It concludes with the friendly lot which the Lord has prepared for the pious ones. This idea elicits the praise of God whose essence is goodness and compassion.

Pss. Sol. 3, 13, and 15 present a mixture of *thanksgiving song* and *wisdom poetry* that is not conceived from the rigid genre. The first example provides the call to thanksgiving (3:2), with the rationale included that a psalm from a pious heart might please YHWH. Verse 3 continues, however, that the righteous should think on the Lord at all times. Then the psalm glides into a description of the essence and fate of the one who fears God (3:4-

---

[3]Pss 107:43; 111:10; Sir 39:12-35; 42:15-43:33; 50:22; Pss. Sol. 6; 10.
[4]Pss 107:43; 111:10.
[5]Sir 39:17a, 21-30; 42:22-24; 50:22.
[6]Sir 16:26ff.
[7]§10, ¶6; Sir 39:21, 34.
[8]§10, ¶5, p. 301; Sir 39:21; 42:25.
[9]Sir 10:14-17; 16:18f; 17:29-32.
[10]Pss. Sol. 6:6b; 10:5-8.

8), as is typical of wisdom poetry. It also contrasts the image of the godless and his destruction (3:9ff), which is again typical of wisdom.

In Pss. Sol. 15, following the confession of the thanksgiving song (15:2), the deliberation is attached claiming that a person can do nothing more than praise the name of YHWH. If this idea can be perceived as indirect praise, then the reflective mood of the idea, as well as the self-evident nature of the answer to the interrogative form which is attached, point in the direction of wisdom poetry. Verse 3 points completely in this direction formally and materially. Whoever sings a new psalm with a happy and righteous heart will not be shattered by misfortune (15:3-7). That section is undeniably a description of the essence and fate of the pious, and it is easily understood when 15:8-13 follows by presenting the godless.

Pss. Sol. 13 is not immediately clear for the context. The thanksgiving song and the consideration of the pious and the godless appear quite distinctly from one another. The connecting idea, however, is expressed in 13:7-9. The distress of those fearing God, from which YHWH then delivers them, is nothing more than a salvific correction that will help place them on the right path. The suffering of the godless, however, is punishment and ends in ruin.

7. The mixing of genres is the most extensive in Ps 119. The poet, who wants to write his song to praise the law, could only fill the expansive framework by including every idea and form which could possibly allow a connection to the law. Since he also obligates himself to begin eight lines in succession with the same letter, it becomes necessary to alternate genres from line to line where possible. Otherwise, it would not have been possible to find the corresponding initial word according to the alphabetic principle. In this way, a colorful mosaic arose whose components can be studied from section to section in the commentary. Here we can only bring to one's attention the reasons for the mixture. Most of the forms and material are borrowed from the individual complaint song, where primarily the *complaint, petitions, wishes, assertions of one's own piety*, and all kinds of *comforting ideas* appear. Alongside these elements one can find motifs from the *hymn*, the *thanksgiving song*, and *wisdom poetry*. Almost all of the lyric genres are represented. The only genres not present are those dealing with the state of the community. In this psalm, the boundaries of almost all the genres are completely blurred, and it becomes clear what the loose mixing of genres means for the literary development. The development which originated and evolved from the simple, pure genres reaches the end from which there is no exit. The mixing of genres necessarily leads to the death of psalmody in general.

II. Antiphonal Poetry

8. Another possibility exists in psalmody for the way the various genres can appear in relationship to one another along with the *mixture*. In this case, the genres remain preserved as independent entities, but are combined into a higher unity: the liturgy.

The *alternation of voices* is characteristic of the performance of the liturgy. The performance shares this characteristic with psalm poetry, and this common characteristic may have been essential for pooling various genres in the form of the liturgy. It is therefore recommended that we preface the treatment of the liturgy by considering psalms performed with alternating voices. It can be called *antiphonal poetry*.

9. Antiphonal singing is not abundantly attested in Old Testament transmission. However, that which does appear suffices to provide a relatively clear picture.

First, one should recognize that psalmody knew antiphonal singing in every period. Exod 15:20f is the oldest witness: "Then Miriam, the prophetess, the sister of Moses, took the drum in her hand, and all the women marched behind her with drums while dancing. Then Miriam sang to them: Sing to YHWH, for he has raised himself high. He has thrown horse and chariot into the sea." This passage should be contrasted with the latest example, Jdt 15:14. Here, it appears in the context of a narrative treating a victory festival and this festival's performance of the holy dance by the women of the city and the victorious army: "And Judith raised the following song of praise before all Israel, *and all the people sang this praise song to her.*" Neh 12:27ff offers further witness from the fifth century. During the dedication, two choirs circle the new walls from a common starting point in opposite directions while singing, until they meet and their song blends together. 1 Chr 16:36 and Ezra 3:11 can also be cited as passages in which the people respond to the singing of the choir with "amen" and "hallelujah."

Further examples can be ascertained by allusions in Isaiah and in several psalms. The hymn of the seraphs in Isa 6:3 is sung in such a way that one sings to the other. The singing of the hymn in Ps 19 is presented so that it is transmitted to some by day and to others by night (19:3). Quite similarly, Ps 65:9,14c also speaks of antiphonal singing, if this text has been correctly restored: "the 'rising' of the morning 'and' the evening rejoice and sing." Finally, one should reference Ps 42:8 where the poet, in a gruesome reversal of the happy singing of the worship service, depicts how one *tehôm* sings to another accompanied by the music of the *ṣinnôr* (lyre) which has replaced the *kinnôr* (pipe).

10. The various passages mentioned provide several clues as to how the antiphonal singing should be conceived. They also allow one to recognize those presuppositions which shaped it. Undoubtedly, they do not exhaust the available possibilities, but they at least provide a desirable starting point for understanding the antiphonal poetry of the psalter.

It is recommended that we begin with passages like 1 Chr 16:36 and Ezra 3:11. A trained choir sings the hymn. The large festal community listens reverently to the praise song, and appropriates the hymn for themselves when all of them say the word, *'āmēn.* Or they join when the choir sings in loud rejoicing, using the well-known hymnic call, *hallelū 'et yahweh.* On the one hand, this dividing of the hymnic text is certainly stipulated by the community's insistence on participating in the enthusiastic singing of the praise song itself. On the other hand, it presumes the difficulty that the pious laity do not know the text and the manner of performance, and are not able to replace the trained choir. Both interests are done justice by dividing the text between the choir and the laity. The type of performance described in Exod 15:21 and Jdt 15:14 apparently derives from the same presuppositions. Here the lead singer sings the song to the choir (or the community) and this group sings after him, apparently line by line. It is improbable to think they sang entire psalm, especially since the Hebrews were not able to survey and to maintain larger units. The following speak of the antiphonal singing of the choirs: Pss 19:3; 42:8; 65:9,14c; cf. Isa 6:3. According to Ps 19:3 and Isa 6:3, it appears as though one choir throws a ball to the other, so to speak, and the other catches it in order to return it to the first. Pss 115:9-11, 118:1-4, and 135:19f afford another possibility. The same lofty words are sung in succession by different, closely designated groups, thereby attaining a particular nuance and an escalation of the impression.

11. If one applies these observations to the songs of the psalter, then those *choral songs* show themselves as a first group of antiphonal songs whose individual sections conclude with a *refrain*: Pss 46 (eschatological Zion song), 67 (communal thanksgiving song), 80 (communal complaint), and 99 (eschatological enthronement song). One should conceive their performance in such a way that the alternating psalm text falls to the choir and that the community took up and appropriated its song from strophe to strophe with the short, repeating refrain. The same idea underlies this division of the text as in 1 Chr 16:36 and Ezra 3:11. The refrain was used as a stylistic art form because of the particular effect and the concise uniformity it provides to the poem.[11] Occasionally, the origin becomes clear from the antiphonal singing, as in Ps 42/43, where the refrain belongs to the poet as the alternating text of his soul. Clearly, it imitates the assignation of the text to different persons.

Antiphonal poetry in which the choirs change from line to line, or even bi-cola to bi-cola, can be found in Ps 136 and the Prayer of Azariah. The text of a hymn falls to the one choir, while the other response in its alternating lines with an unchanging repeating word. This word is either taken from the introduction or represents an idea of the main hymnic portion. One cannot divide these psalms from the poems with refrains by explaining their form because of their close relationship. One can scarcely think of these psalms as a more abundant participation of the laity in the cultic singing. Rather, one should think of a conscious art form that was determined to introduce the aesthetic affect deriving from the refrain by using the alternating singing of the choir.

Also, as with the refrain, psalmody consciously raised the alternation of solo voices and choral singing to an artistic form of expression. Sir 51:12ff stands closest to the original relationships. At the end of his thanksgiving song, the one offering thanks sings a hymn to those gathered at the thanksgiving festival. They answer every line, as in Ps 136, with the same words of a hymnic corpus: "for his goodness endures forever." By contrast, Ps 8 uses the changes from solo to choir consciously as an art form. It begins with the hymnic praise of the choir (8:2). An individual voice then follows, which speaks of God's wonderful power and his incomprehensible conduct toward humanity. The choir takes up its words by repeating the words of his praise in reverential awe: YHWH, our Lord, how majestic is your name.

Each of the antiphonal poems cited is a pure example of its genre. It is differentiated from these genres only by the division of its text into alternating voices. Those few examples that have been preserved show what this stylistic treatment signified for the life and effect of the psalms. Is it any wonder that one did not limit the principle of antiphonal singing to the pure genres? One learned to recognize the particular effect. Instead, with the help of antiphonal singing, they sought to conjoin pieces of different genres into a new, higher unity. Thus, we come to the presentation of the *liturgy*.

---

[11]Isa 9:7-10:4; 5:24-30; Amos 1:3–2:16; 4:6-12.

III. Liturgies

H. Gunkel, "Der Micha-Schluß," *Zur Einführung in die literaturgeschichtliche Arbeit am Alten Testament*, 1923, pp. 145-78. — E. Balla, *Das Ich der Psalmen*, pp. 96ff. — K. Galling, "Der Beichtspiegel, eine gattungsgeschichtliche Studie," *ZAW*, n.s. 6 (1929): 125-30.

12. One should speak of a liturgy where elements of various genres are brought together in performance by alternating voices with the intention of a creating unified effect. The arrangement of the various components is thus not arbitrary. Rather, it depends upon specific rules provided by the character of the cultic process to which it belongs. The researcher must therefore attempt to achieve an image of the worship activity if he does not want to fall prey to caprice and error when determining a text as a liturgy. He must attempt to find the role of the cultic activity, or at least, if available reports are lacking, to bring together parallels of the same type of construction, so that the regularity of the liturgy he accepts can be raised beyond all doubt.

13. The Israelite worship service contains different moments which recognize a change of speech, and thereby can serve as the starting point for the art form of the liturgy. The laity are perhaps in doubt about particular purity prescriptions or specific festival days. They direct a related question to the priest and receive from him the requested torah response under God's mandate.[12] One can consider the *oracle* alongside the *promulgation of the torah* for cultic change of speech. The individual lay person searches for something of this type when he is indecisive regarding which of two possibilities he should choose,[13] or when he cannot fathom the cause of distress.[14] The one praying a complaint song also quite probably received an oracle between the petition and the certainty of having been heard. This oracle assures him that his desire has been heard (cf. §6, ¶23). The same change occurs between the petition and oracle in the *communal complaint song* (§4, ¶14).

14. It is quite understandable, given the significance the torah and the oracle, that the place of these alternating actions became liturgically shaped.

Let us first examine the *torah liturgy*.[15] It begins with the question from those seeking instruction. "Who may ascend YHWH's mountain? Who may enter the holy places? (Ps 24:3)." The *response* follows which we think must come from the mouth of the priest: "Anyone having pure hands and an innocent heart, 'whose' soul 'does not lead him' astray, and who does not swear deceitfully (24:4)." A *blessing* forms the conclusion. To bless is, of course, the privilege of the priest and only he could do that in the worship service. "He will receive a blessing from YHWH, and a just reward from the God of his salvation. Such is the generation of those who ask about 'YHWH,' who seek your 'redeemer,' Jacob (24:5-6)." Ps 15 and Isa 33:14-16 have precisely the same construction. The torah question stands at the beginning, followed by the priestly response, the promulgation of the torah. The blessing concludes for those satisfying the demands of the torah.

---

[12]Hag 2:10ff; Zech 7:1ff.

[13]1 Sam 23:2, 4, 10, 12; 30:7f; 2 Sam 5:19.

[14]2 Sam 21:1ff.

[15]Pss 15; 24:3-6. Prophetic imitations appear in Isa 33:14-16 and Mic 6:6-8.

The type that Mic 6:6-8 imitates differs just a little. Here the question is addressed about the possibilities of appeasing God's wrath. It wants an answer regarding how God will decide: "With what shall I appear before YHWH, and bow before the high God? Shall I appear before him with burnt offerings, or with year old calves? Do thousands of rams please YHWH or ten thousand rivers of oil? Shall I give my first-born for my guilt, the fruit of my body for my own sin offering?" The *torah* answers: "It has been told (*huggad*) to you, man, what is good and what YHWH requires of you. Do justice. Practice love and walk humbly (*hikkānēă'*) before your God." A concluding word of blessing is lacking here because there is no place for it in this matter.

15. Other liturgies proceed from the connection between the communal and individual complaint songs and the oracle.[16] In most cases, the genres are not transmitted with them. Apart from those cases where the developed genre no longer presupposes an oracle,[17] the reason may perhaps lie in the fact that one did not receive the oracle as a component of the complaint song.[18] Also, a text of this type could have been used over and over in the sanctuary, but not the oracle whose wording could not always be the same because it depended upon the changing result of the source of the oracle. One could also accept that one person praying could hardly repeat a complaint song, and that this genre as a whole lacked a place for an artistic expansion. If so, then one could understand that, with one exception, no liturgy is encountered[19] which would have emerged from an individual complaint song. Prophetic individual complaint songs, with a subsequent oracle of having been heard (which one could label *prophetic liturgy*),[20] should thus not be seen as an imitation of the complaint song liturgies. Rather, should be seen as a new creation by the prophets for which the change from complaint song to salvation oracle, well-known from the cult, served as the model.

Ps 121 shows us how a liturgy looks which developed from the individual complaint song. It begins with the words of those seeking help, whose origin one notices immediately: "From whence does my help come? (121:1)." The voice of the priest responds: "Help comes 'from you,' YHWH, the one who made heaven and earth (121:2)." Now the one seeking help begins again and turns to the *petition*. "Do not let 'my' foot falter, nor 'my' protector sleep (121:3)." The priest's voice then reassures: "No. The protector of Israel neither sleeps nor slumbers (121:4)." He adds the *salvation oracle*: "YHWH is your protector. YHWH is your shade going to your right so that the sun does not strike you by day or the moon by night." He concludes with the words of *blessing* (different in the commentary): "May YHWH protect you from all evil; May he protect your life. May YHWH guard your coming and going from now until eternity (121:7-8)." It is difficult to determine whether Ps 121 reflects poetry specifically designed for performance or a spiritual song which takes the forms of a liturgy as its model. In either case, one can deduce the characteristic lines of this kind of worship service liturgy from it. Oracle and complaint are bound together closely, and with every performance, they are thus constantly repeated together. It thus becomes possible that the complaint song requests

---

[16]Cf. §4, ¶14 and §6, ¶23, p. 182.
[17]Cf. the end of §6, ¶23.
[18]Cf. §6, ¶23, p. 183.
[19]See below.
[20]Jer 11:18-23; 15:15-21.

help and protection in very general terms, and that the oracle does not need to consider changing personal relationships. Positively, however, its continual repeatability provides the assurance of YHWH's help based upon his gracious essence which remains consistent. Perhaps one performed this liturgy when several persons in need, for various reasons, found their way to the temple (cf. Ps 107 as counterpart). Also, one could easily conceive these celebratory liturgical developments during a larger cultic activity.

Liturgies which developed from the *communal complaint song* are found more frequently.[21] This increase can be explained by the fact that the community's distress and its condition essentially remain the same. The repetition of the oracle which refers to the distress is not threatened from this point. In addition, the affirmation of help for Israel has an unchanging, fixed basis in the special relationship which existed between YHWH and his people, even in those times when the people either called upon its innocence or penitently confessed its sins.

One can clearly recognize the origin from the structure of the liturgy. It began with a communal complaint which was performed to the point of the *petition*.[22] The salvation oracle is consistently attached, which promises YHWH's hearing and help.[23] The conclusion allows various possibilities. Either the liturgy concludes with the oracle,[24] or it concludes with another petition,[25] or it ends with the certainty of being heard.[26]

In this context, one should also mention the liturgy which was performed before the king of Judah went to battle (Ps 20). It begins with a communal complaint song which prays for the gracious acceptance of the king's sacrifice and for the victory of his weapons (20:2-6). The response of the oracle follows. The response promises victory to the king because Israel is strengthened by the name of its God and will conquer its enemies (20:7-9). A brief petition for hearing and help for the king forms the conclusion (20:10). Even in this liturgy, the repeatability of the oracle rests in the enduring relationship of YHWH to Israel.

16. The conclusion of the festal celebration at day's end is developed liturgically in Ps 134. At the point of leaving the sanctuary, the festal gathering sings a hymn to the priests. It commands them to praise YHWH even at night according to their obligation (134:1-2, different in the commentary). The priests respond by offering YHWH's blessing to those departing (134:3).

17. Other liturgies were sung at recurring festivals in which the holy ark was the center (Pss 132; 24:7-10; see the commentary, p. 103f). Ps 132 was perhaps performed annually to recall the transport of the ark from Kiriath-Jearim to Zion. The event may have been symbolized by a processional. The liturgy begins like Ps 20 with the people's petition to YHWH to credit David's own castigation graciously (132:1-2). This petition becomes clear by introducing the words of David's vow (132:3-5). In 132:6-7, a group

---

[21]Pss 12; 60; 85.

[22]In Ps 12: call for help (12:2a), complaint (12:2b-3), petition (12:4-5); in Ps 60: address (60:3), complaint (60:3-5), and petition (60:6-7). Ps 85:5ff is a special case, a petition with a complaint included.

[23]Pss 12:6; 60:8-10; 85:9-14.

[24]Ps 85:14.

[25]Ps 60:11-14.

[26]Ps 12:7-9.

(perhaps a second choir which represents David's men) announces that since the ark of YHWH has been found, they should go to YHWH's dwelling place. Then one should conceptualize both choirs addressing a petition to YHWH, to let them make their way to his resting place. They adopt the forms of the ancient ark speech (cf. Num 10:35). They conclude with the petition for the anointed one, not to abandon him for David's sake (132:8-10). A voice then proclaims YHWH's response. It accepts the people's petition and praises David's endeavors. It speaks of David's dynasty enduring and the enduring majesty of Zion (132:11-18). Both contain material which requires no special revelation. Rather, the material rests upon a strong belief in the word of YHWH to David given in 2 Sam 7.

Ps 24:7-10 was sung by two choirs when the ark entered the temple. The scene plays out before the closed gates. Outside the choir waits with the ark upon which YHWH is invisibly enthroned. Inside, the other choir stands in the courtyard. One should conceptualize it as consisting of priests. The first choir, hindered from entering the sanctuary, demands a reason and begins: "O gates, raise your heads. Raise yourself, you ancient portals so that the king of glory might enter." Then, because not everyone is allowed entry, the choir of priests then responds from within with the question: "Who is the king of glory?" The first choir then responds triumphantly: "YHWH, a valiant warrior and hero. YHWH, a hero in battle." The alternating speech of both choirs is repeated once again, but this time the question about the king of glory echoes with the answer which contains the cult name of God: YHWH Sebaoth, the king of glory, is there. Then one should conceive that the closed gates are opened and the ark makes its entry.[27]

18. Liturgies developing from individual thanksgiving songs also demonstrate the alternation of two voices without sharing a divine speech like those in the beginning of Pss 132 and 24:7-10. The origin of these liturgies was noted in the group thanksgiving songs (cf. §7, ¶7). Pss 66 and 118 illustrate these liturgies. Both clearly presuppose the situation of a thanksgiving song.

Ps 66 opens with a hymn from the community at the thanksgiving festival which demands that they look at, listen to, and rejoice about YHWH's works in general terms, but not without giving attention to the particular situation. Gradually, it transitions to the material originating from the individual thanksgiving song. In this material, the community offers praise for that which the individual members have experienced from YHWH's gracious help (66:1-12). As the choir becomes silent, an individual voice is raised to sing a thanksgiving song for the deliverance to which the choir's song alluded (66:13-20). The performance makes one consider how YHWH's goodness, which the community praises, is reconfirmed in every individual case.

Ps 118 is constructed quite similarly. It begins with a hymn, which should perhaps be considered as having been sung by alternating voices (cf. ¶10, p. 311). The individual thanksgiving song follows (118:5-21). In contrast to Ps 66, the choir in this poem, perhaps quite late (see the commentary, p. 509), renews their speech. It rejoices over the help which the one offering thanks has experienced. It speaks in a style as though conducting the happy festival it now wants to celebrate. It closes with the petition for more help (118:22-25). One enters the sanctuary. The words of the thanksgiving song in 118:19-21 announcing the priest's blessing echo over those entering (118:26-27). The entire thing concludes with the word of thanksgiving from the one who has been saved. This con-

---

[27]See the details in the commentary.

clusion was formed in the style of the thanksgiving song which returns to the opening words of its introductory hymn by the singing of the choir.

19. The overview of the liturgies shows the effective possibilities of expression they provided for the worship service and how fully diverse this style is. The two liturgies that were bound to the holy ark with processions are undoubtedly preexilic and apparently belong to the middle of the monarchic period. In these circumstances, it is understandable that the *prophets* strengthened the liturgy, like the lyrical genres, in order to be able to express their ideas effectively in a manner that was reliable to the people. Hos 5:15–6:6 and 14:3-9 provide the oldest examples where the people's song of confession is combined with YHWH's oracle of response. In Mic 6:6-8, the prophet took up the torah liturgy. Nevertheless, this line of development can only be cited briefly here. Another line of development leading from the prophets to the worship liturgy is more important for psalmody.

20. The prophets influence more than the ideas of the liturgies (cf. §9, ¶47, p. 291). They also provided psalmody with the stimulus for the *development of new liturgical forms*. Postexilic priesthood, like the entire people, stood under the impression of the verification of the ancient prophets. The priesthood endeavored to reproduce liturgically the powerful impression of the prophets' appearance. They also provided for the entry into the cult of the prophets' particular forms of expression. Judgment prophets had frequently cast their gloomy, threatening speeches into the happy words of an enthusiastic hymn in order to shock all those who were present. The cult reproduced this event liturgically. The entire joy of the festal moment exists in a festal hymn, e.g. Ps 81:1-6; 95:1-7. The somber prophetic voice follows these passages with a warning not to forget the seriousness of the demands beyond the festal joy (Ps 81:6c-17). Or, the prophetic voice admonishes the participants to believe in the miraculous power of YHWH. This belief is easy during the festal days, but should also be maintained in the daily grind of a small and suffering present time (Ps 95:7-11). Both liturgies conclude with a threatening tone. In Ps 95, a conditional threat stands unexpressed, though clearly in the background. Ps 81 recognizes the threat in the conditional nature of the promise.

One finds another liturgical usage of prophetic forms in Ps 53. An angry prophetic rebuke and threat stand at the core of this psalm (53:1-6). The entire community stands under the impression of this word, and turns to YHWH with the petition for redemption from all evil (53:7). Or, a prophetic judgment speech against all the heathen gods stands in the center of the liturgy (Ps 82:1-7) like the judgment speeches in Deutero-Isaiah. The community takes up the words of the speaker which proclaimed certain destruction of the gods under whose authority they still suffer. The community besieges YHWH with the petition to bring about judgment (82:8). This liturgy would have arisen and been performed in times when the arrogance of the heathen gods could be noted clearly in the world events of the postexilic period. We can conceptualize the effect of this liturgy as powerful, captivating, and capable of strengthening confidence.

The liturgy also adopted and imitated the *forms of salvation prophecy*. Ps 85 and 126 offer examples. They furnish the impression which the prophetic message of salvation awakened in the heart of the people. They were performed in order to recall it continually and to keep it alive. Ps 126 is particularly clear. Using the effusive tone of salvation prophecy, an individual voice announces the majestic salvation of Zion, which he has seen as having already occurred with his enraptured eye (126:1-3). The community, however, is not gifted with this vision. It still suffers bitterly under the oppression of the present time. It responds to the prophetic messages with the petition of the complaint song. They petition YHWH to fulfill that which he has promised (126:4-6). The liturgy in Ps 85 begins similarly. A portion of this psalm was already observed in ¶15. Ps 85 begins with a salvation oracle of a certain tone in 85:2-4, followed by the communal complaint (85:5-8). The unusual part of this liturgy lies in the fact that this liturgy concludes with the oracle of having been heard (85:9-14). It uses the style of the complaint song liturgy, providing a peculiar mixture of two forms of liturgies.

21. In conclusion, we will attempt to present the *history of the liturgy* as briefly as possible. It proceeds from cultic soil. Specific changing cultic activities form a presupposition of its origin, including the promulgation of the torah, pronouncement of the oracle, and the individual and communal complaint celebrations. In addition, singing with alternating voices also appears, though this had been known for a long time in the performance of songs with a pure genre. These liturgies were perhaps authored by priests as songs of the cult, and are already encountered in the preexilic period. Pss 24 and 132 provide direct evidence for this preexilic period. Since Hosea and Micah imitate these liturgies one can deduce the preexilic period.

Further development occurred when the prophets took up the liturgy as a particularly appropriate means of expressing their ideas. By adopting it, the liturgy preserved the character of a scribal form.

The prophetic liturgy then affected the worship liturgy. The cult attempted to keep alive and to incorporate the impression and the effect of the prophetic appearance. This attempt lead to the origin of the final developmental step of the liturgy, the formation of forms described in ¶20.

§12 The History of Psalmody

H. Gunkel, "Die alttestamentliche Literaturgeschichte und die Ansetzung der Psalmen," *Theologische Blätter* 7 (1928): 85ff. — W. Baumgartner, *Die Klagegedichte des Jeremia*, BZAW 32, 1917.

1. Having described the individual manifestations, the presentation of the various psalm genres now requires that we determine the chronological relationship of the various forms and contents to one another, as far as the transmission allows it. One could thus grasp the historical development of each particular genre. The investigation cannot stop at this point, however. The individual study has succeeded in differentiating the genre's earlier and later material from one another, and in writing the genre's internal history. Now, the researcher faces another challenge, extracting this knowledge from its isolated state by placing it in the broader framework of a history of psalmody and simultaneously arranging it in the larger context of the history of Israel in general.

The presupposition for the solution to this task is that the various stages of development of the individual genres can be somewhat more precisely fixed chronologically. This presupposition holds up well enough to gain a relatively clear picture, even if it is not true or not uniformly consistent for every genre. In order to make sure every step is secure, one should proceed from those poems whose time of origin can be provided with relative certainty, or which allow one to deduce the earliest possible date available. Of course, the psalms of the psalter only meet these requirements minimally. However, this deficiency can be compared satisfactorily to the fact that the prophets have adopted the various genres and the forms of their speech. We can provide the time period of the prophets relatively well. We encounter numerous individual motifs which the prophets have borrowed and imitated, including a series of complete psalms which are traced to the prophets as authors. From these examples, we first attempt to ascertain the stages of literary development chronologically for the individual genres in the order of the introduction. From there, we will proceed to a history of psalmody.

2. The following hymns provide the basis for the chronological determination of the *history of the hymn*: Isa 6:3; Zeph 3:14-15; Isa 42:10-13; 44:23; 49:13; 52:9-10. In addition, one can include an example from the psalter, Ps 89:2-3, 6-19. In a second line, one should mention a series of prophetic speeches which have adopted an individual motif, generally the hymnic body.[1] The time is self-evident, as far as the prophetic speeches come into the question. The following considerations yield the time among the psalms. Ps 89:2-3, 6-19 stems from Northern Israel, and even more precisely from the monarchic period before 721.[2] 1 Sam 2:1-10 was available before 587 because it concludes with a

---

[1] Jer 5:22, 24; 20:13; Isa 40:22-24, 26b, 28b-31; 44:25-28; 45:18; 46:10-11; Jdt 5:3-5; 1 Sam 2:2ff.

[2] See the commentary to 89:13, 19.

brief wish for the king, a wish which could only stem from the Judean monarchic period.[3] The antiquity of the song of Deborah from the Northern Kingdom is uncontested.

These datable examples teach us, first, with full clarity that the genre of the hymn arose in the *preexilic period*. Isa 6:3 attests to its availability in 740. Ps 89 points to 721 as the latest date. The song of Deborah is even older, even if an exact date is not possible. In addition, the same can be said of entire manner in which Isaiah speaks of the seraphim in the antiphonal hymn. One can deduce from these examples that the hymn was not something unusual and new. Rather, it was something trusted and old. Further, these examples allow one to recognize that the singing of hymns was known in *Israel as well as Judah*.

One can continue by asking *what stages* can be perceived in the history of the hymn from the datable poems. If one proceeds from the complete hymns first, it appears as if the genre remained essentially in its original, very simple stage until the time of Deutero-Isaiah, that is until the end of the sixth century. It appears that only after 500 does the hymn develop further (in terms of larger size and more abundant content) and blossom fully. The examples of the hymn preserved from the time of the song of Deborah through Deutero-Isaiah (apart from Ps 89) are consistently shown to be quite small in size.[4] They exemplify simplicity of form. Here, the hymn consists only of a brief introduction and a brief hymnic body. These motifs are as simple as possible. The introduction knows only one form,[5] a form which appears to be somewhat revived in the later period by helping to provide three-fold variation to the basic ideas.[6] Isa 42:10ff offers the most developed form of the introduction in which imperative and jussive introductions are combined, with the latter escalating to a four-fold expression. The bodies are similarly simple. YHWH is consistently the subject. No variation occurs. It usually touches upon only *one* hymnic matter. The combination of various material is not found. Also, there is only direct praise, with no indirect praise. A hymn in Deutero-Isaiah (52:9-10) again shows the most advanced form. It speaks of YHWH's compassion to Zion and sings of the revelation of his majesty. It places mediated praise alongside direct praise.

It would be false to conclude from these examples that they represented the hymn until 500. Rather, they teach us only that the old, simple form of the genre was preserved alongside more extensive development with great tenacity. The fact that the prophets did not compose any extensive hymns does not prove they were unknown in the prophets' time. It also does not justify doubt about the antiquity of Ps 89. Instead, it only shows that the old, simple form sufficed as an expression of their message.

3. If one wishes to get to know the more extensive developments of the genre before 587 and 721, one should proceed from Ps 89 and the passages mentioned above in the second position. Excluding the hymnically expanded *confession of the thanksgiving song* in 1 Sam 2:3bff (§7, ¶¶5, 8), one should primarily consider the *discussion words of Deutero-Isaiah*, because they point to a much earlier time than the time of the prophet. Deutero-Isaiah prefers to make his case by starting with ideas about God. He therefore

---

[3]Cf. Gunkel. *Ausgewählte Psalmen*,[4] p. 208.

[4]Isa 6:3; 49:13 have two lines; 44:23 has three; 52:9-10 and Zeph 3:14-15 has four; Judg 3:3-5 has five; and Isa 42:10-13 has seven.

[5]Judg 5:3; Isa 52:9.

[6]Zeph 3:14; Isa 44:23; 49:13.

draws upon hymnic material well known to his contemporaries. He even uses this material in hymnic form which was familiar to his people and which suited his intentions.

These examples concur in showing the *completely developed hymnic style*. One cannot precisely evaluate the introductions because of the fortuity of the transmission. Nevertheless, in Ps 89:2 one encounters the *singular form* in the *first person* (§2, ¶11), and in 89:6 the *third person plural jussive* (§2, ¶3). The situation is even clearer with the main part of the hymn where one encounters all the forms that are developed in the hymn. Most importantly, various connections occur within the same poem. The hymnic *participle*[7] alternates with the *tempus historicum*[8] or the imperfect.[9] Direct praise is relieved by mediated praise.[10] Ps 89 already knows the *marveling question*[11] and the blessing saying for those worshiping God.[12] The typical active statement alternates with the *passive statement*.[13] YHWH as the hymnic subject varies.[14] In 1 Sam 2:8; Isa 40:22d; and 45:18, one encounters the continuation of the main clause by the *infinitive clause* using *le* (§2, ¶36).

The growth in terms of size corresponds to this richness of forms. In Isa 40:22ff, the main part of the hymn alone constitutes five lines and six lines in 40:28bff. The hymnic expansion of the thanksgiving song confession in 1 Sam 2:3ff offers at least twelve lines. The oldest example available, Ps 89:2-3, 6-19, goes even further.

Observations concerning the growth in size and in richness of form agree with observations about the *content*. While the hymn from the oldest time knows only *one* subject that elicits praise of God,[15] the examples treated here already show the combination of hymnic material characteristic of the expanded genre. Ps 89 praises YHWH's *essence*, his *grace* and *faithfulness* (89:3), his *fertility* and *incomparability* (89:8f), and his *righteousness and goodness* (89:15). In addition, the praise of the creator God appears, who overthrew the dragon, created the world, and assumed kingship over them (89:10ff). Finally, its praise of this God as the helper of Israel is the highest praise (89:16ff). In 1 Sam 2:3ff we encounter the following hymnic material: YHWH's *knowledge*, his *righteousness*, his *power* over the high and the lowly, the living and dead, his *wrath* concerning the wicked, and his *grace* toward those fearing God. One can also compare Isa 40:28ff, where one finds the praise of YHWH, the *eternal one*, the *creator*, the *all-knowing*, the one who is *able to give superhuman power* to the pious.

4. It is not necessary to take these observations further. They suffice well to confirm significant conclusions. They not only teach that one must come to terms with a *preexilic higher development of the genre*, they also confirm beyond any doubt that the hymn already *attained* its complete development and its complete flowering in the *preexilic period*. Ps 89 is extremely important for showing that the genre was completely developed and available not just before 587, but prior to 721. Its rise from the simplest forms to the

---

[7]Ps 89:8, 10; 1 Sam 2:6, 7, 8; Isa 40:22ac, 23; 45:18 (§2, ¶21).
[8]Ps 89:10, 11, 13; 1 Sam 2:6, 9a; Isa 40:22d, 23, 24; 45:18 (§2, ¶28).
[9]1 Sam 2:8b,c; Isa 40:26, 29; 44:25, 26, 27, 28 (§2, ¶27).
[10]Ps 89:13, 15, 16ff; 1 Sam 2:3b-5, 9, 10; Isa 40:22, 26, 28ff (§2, ¶29).
[11]Ps 89:7, 9 (§2, ¶31).
[12]Ps 89:16ff (§2, ¶32).
[13]Ps 89:3; 1 Sam 2:3b, 5a, Isa 40:26 (§2, ¶29).
[14]Ps 89:3, 14, 15 (§2, ¶26).
[15]See the examples mentioned in ¶2.

form represented by Ps 89 should accordingly be placed in the time between the song of Deborah and the year 721 as the latest point.

The *Israelite/Judean monarchic period* thus proves to be the *time of flowering* for hymnic poetry. The same conclusion can be derived from the observation that Deutero-Isaiah delivers his introductions using ideas borrowed from the hymn which presuppose these hymns were known for a long time: "Was it not proclaimed to you from the beginning?" (Isa 40:21); "Do you not know? Have you not heard?" (Isa 40:28).

The flowering of the genre reached during the monarchic period outlasted the overthrow of the national states and was preserved into the beginning of the postexilic period. The attraction which the hymn exerted upon Deutero-Isaiah shows this endurance, as does the appearance of hymns in postexilic works.[16] In fact, the hymn first rose to complete acceptance among the people in the postexilic period (§2, ¶64, p. 63). In essence, however, the hymn of the early postexilic period lived from that which the preexilic period had created. One can thus recognize that the legal piety did not influence the hymn as a whole. One encounters traces in Pss 111:7f; and 147:19. Ps 19:8-11 is the first and only hymn to the law.

These poems which were first possible from the beginning of the fifth century show undeniably that the genre was already in *decline* during this period. The hymns of this period only imitate the great patterns. They make use of the preformulated linguistic forms. They utilize derived and known expressions, but they completely lack the power and energy of the older poetry which they cannot attain (§2, ¶66). The cultic song used in the worship service of the Chronicler's time presupposes Pss 96, 105, and 106, which allows one to recognize how early in the postexilic period this change in the history of the hymn began (see 1 Chr 16:8ff). If 1 Chr 16:7ff is an addition to the work of the Chronicler, during the second half of the fourth century, then one may not date the origin of those psalms in that time. The probable time of origin of the psalter leads in this direction as well (see §13, ¶7).

5. Isa 52:7ff teaches undeniably that the genre of the *songs of YHWH's enthronement* were already available in the middle of the sixth century. In other words, they were available in the *exilic period*. They did not first arise in the time of the second temple. Deutero-Isaiah's song also makes clear, however, that the genre is older than that prophet. The victorious God returns from the battle field in triumph, entering his *city which lays in ruins*. On the walls where breaches had been made, lookouts stand, keeping watch for the victory messenger. These images can only be understood as a deviation of a well-known older type that was altered during the time of Deutero-Isaiah. If the prophet himself had first created it, these objectionable ideas would not be understandable. Rather, the genre would have would have spoken more originally about the *victorious return of God into his city which had never been conquered by enemies*. It would have spoken about the *valiant walls* where the guards kept watch for the messenger of God's victory. However, this imagery implies that the genre was available before the destruction of Jerusalem in 587.

The brief enthronement song, preserved in five lines in Zeph 3:14-15 leads to the same conclusion, though neither Mowinckel nor Gunkel recognized its character. "Rejoice, Daughter Zion. Shout for joy, Israel. Be happy. Rejoice in your heart, Daughter Jerusalem.

---

[16]Cf. the examples given in §2, ¶1.

YHWH has removed your tyrants (*mešōpetayik*). He has defeated your enemy (*'ōyebayik*). YHWH has become king in your midst. You will see no more suffering." It is contested whether this song belonged to Zephaniah. It should not be doubted that it stems from the preexilic period, because it presupposes the undamaged state of the city, and because the oppression of foreign rule during the later Judean monarchic period is quite recognizable.

However, if Zeph 3:14-15 is preexilic, then one can be assured that the genre already had an eschatological character before 587. However, if so, then Deutero-Isaiah cannot be seen as the creator of the eschatological enthronement song (deviating from §3, ¶11d, p. 80). Rather, the turn toward the eschatological would be *ascribed to preexilic salvation prophecy*. Unfortunately, nothing is preserved which bears directly. However, *preexilic salvation prophecy* certainly promised liberation from enemies, the continuation of the state, good fortune, and peace.[17] These promises differentiate it from the judgment prophets, and make the conclusion probable that Deutero-Isaiah adopted the form created by the preexilic salvation prophecy.

Whether extensive examples of the genre were known in the preexilic period alongside these brief examples cannot be decided due to the lack of firmly dateable texts. Also, the older stages deduced in §3, ¶11, p. 80, cannot be traced further chronologically, if they prove adequate otherwise. One can only say so much. The origin of the genre and its history until it took an eschatological turn in the latter Judean monarchic period must take precedence.

The genre's postexilic development is recognizable by Pss 97 and 99. Ps 97 presupposes Deutero-Isaiah (see the commentary). Ps 99 appears to contemplate the priestly writing. The postexilic regard for the law is also clear in Ps 99. These examples should not be divorced from the type in Ps 96 (and 98). They show a picture of the genre which bears a striking resemblance to that of the hymn. The old forms were nurtured further. Derived expressions and ideas appear. Literal borrowings from other psalms are encountered (see the commentary). The original, very concrete, ideas are toned down, while foreign ideas penetrate. Ps 99:6-8 borrows from the legends. Ps 99:40,7 treasure the law. But the old power and momentum are lacking. It is characteristic of the flat and completely apolitical spirit of the postexilic descendants that Ps 97 only knows to offer praise as the result of YHWH's enthronement because YHWH has delivered the life of his pious ones from the hand of the wicked, and given delight to the humble heart (Ps 97:10-12).

Similarly to the hymn, this development should be considered as completed in the early postexilic period, as proved by Ps 99, the latest of our examples, which shows itself to be taken with legal piety. It can only have arisen after the second half of the fifth century.

Ps 99 taught us that by this time the genre was already in decline. Its original lines of thought (enthronement and the establishment of a just government) are only still encountered at the beginning of the poem (99:1-4). Nevertheless, they are no longer very concrete, especially the second idea. The idea of a universal kingdom can no longer be recognized, and it speaks rather apolitically about the just government. The psalm says that YHWH will establish a just order in Jacob and that YHWH has created justice and righteousness. Ps 99:6ff completely leaves the genre since the material of the legends pushes it way into the foreground. One can barely recognize that Moses, Aaron, and Samuel,

---

[17]Cf. Jer 6:14; 14:13ff; 23:17; 27:9ff, 14f, 16ff; 28:2ff; 29:8f.

stand at the point where homage to the royal household had been expressed (cf. Ps 47:10). The scene has nothing more to do with what is said about them.

The decay noted here makes it understandable that in the later period, as in the Psalms of Solomon, no example of the genre appears. One could hardly expect anything else. Eschatological hope was only expressed by that time in the eschatological hymn preserved essentially in general terms.

6. We are essentially directed to examples from the prophets for determining the development of the *communal complaint songs*.[18] None of these examples present a complete complaint song. Only individual motifs of the genre are found. However, the adoption of the motif still teaches us that the prophets presupposed the genre as a known entity. The following can be clearly noted among the prophets: the *complaint*,[19] *petition*,[20] *confidence motif*,[21] *confession of sin*,[22] *honor motif*,[23] *possession motif*,[24] *confession motif*,[25] and *words of comfort*[26] spoken in the third person.

These witnesses lead with certainty to the conclusion that by the time of Jeremiah, before 600, the genre already existed. Accordingly, its origins lay further back in the preexilic period.

Characteristics of the formal style are already available in the time of Jeremiah and Deutero-Isaiah. This observation is also of fundamental significance for the history of the genre. Examples include: the *hymnic arrangement of the address*;[27] the *introduction of the passionate complaint and petition* with *lāmmah* ("Why?" Jer 14:8b,9), *maddūa'* (Jer 14:19b), or the simple question (Jer 14:19a; §4, ¶7, p. 89), and the literal introduction of the words of the enemies.[28] They also know the material (*natural catastrophes*[29] and *political distress*).[30] Significantly, in the days of Jeremiah the genre had already drawn close to the individual complaint song. It had borrowed the style of the complaint and petition from the individual complaint song.[31] The frequency of the examples shows how common and how old this borrowing is. Finally, around this time the genre becomes longer. One may conclude this fact with relative certainty on the basis of Lam 5, a communal complaint song that arose shortly after Jerusalem's destruction (cf. §4, ¶15, p. 98). With respect to the dating which is less certain, nothing more can be ascertained. Ps 144:1-10 leads to the same conclusion.

---

[18]Isa 40:27cd; 49:14, 24; 51:9ff; Jer 3:22b-25; 4:10; 14:2-6, 7-9, 19-22; 31:18ff; and Hos 6:1-3. Finally, one should note the materially and thematically related royal complaint song in Ps 144:1-10.

[19]Jer 3:24, 25a; 4:10b; 14:3-6, 19; 31:18b, 19b; Isa 40:27b; 49:14 (§4, ¶7).

[20]Jer 14:7a, 9c, 21; 31:18c; Isa 51:9 (§4, ¶8).

[21]Jer 3:22b, 23a; 31:18c (§4, ¶10, p. 92).

[22]Jer 3:23a, 25b; 14:7b; 31:19a (§4, ¶10, p. 92).

[23]Jer 14:9b; Isa 51:10, 11 (§4, ¶9).

[24]Jer 14:21 (§4, ¶9).

[25]Jer 31:18cd (§4, ¶10, p. 92).

[26]Hos 6:1-3 (§4, ¶10, p. 92).

[27]Jer 14:8; Ps 144:1 (§4, ¶4, p. 86).

[28]Jer 4:10 (§4, ¶7, p. 88).

[29]Jer 14:2-6, 8f, 19.

[30]Jer 3:24c-25a; 4:10; 10:19ff, 25; cf. also Ps 144 (§4, ¶4, p. 86).

[31]Jer 3:4; 10:19-22; 31:18f; Isa 40:27; 49:14.

These observations teach us with certainty, that the genre existed in completely developed form in the late Judean monarchic period. Accordingly, its beginnings and its rise to full blossoming belong to the older and middle monarchic period.

7. The exile also had no epoch-making significance for the *communal complaint song*. The genre first reaches its climax in the preexilic period. Poems like Isa 59:9-15b and 63:11–64:11 allow one to recognize this observation. However, in contrast to other genres one can observe in the communal complaint song that it preserved a dynamic character even into the latest periods, conceivably because the postexilic period contained abundant causes for the communal complaint.[32] This fact deserves to be explored before one investigates the manifestations which undoubtedly point to a decline sometime after 500. A certain muffling of the tone can be consistently observed. Also, the communal complaint song of the later period moves only among previously developed forms and ideas. It even borrows literally from older poems (see the commentary to Ps 79). It is also characteristic that the confession of sin takes a rather large amount of space as the motif bearing the petition.[33] Reflection about the cause of the misfortune penetrate. Israel is guilty. YHWH had to punish.[34] Significantly, most examples of the genre in the psalter resist these ideas, and accordingly must be older (§4, ¶10, p. 92). In addition, since the end of the fifth century, one finds the influence of legal piety which sees the breaking of the law as the cause of all distress (Pr Azar 6-7), the influence of the legends (Pr Azar 12ff), and reference to fixed, written transmission.[35] All of these examples attest to the fact that since the year 500, the genre forfeited its ancient freshness and immediacy and entered the age of its decline.

8. We will pass over the *royal psalms* because there is nothing more to say than that they belong to the preexilic period because they are so few in number and because they are also divided among various genres. We thus come to the *individual complaint song*. Two songs from the psalter are important for its early history, Pss 61 and 63. These psalms were available before 587 based on the additions related to the ruling king.[36] In addi-tion, the royal complaint song in Ps 144:1-11 must also be ascribed to the preexilic period.[37] Finally, one must mention the complaint songs of Jeremiah.[38]

Altogether, these passages illustrate that the individual complaint song also did not first arise in the period of Judaism. Rather, its origins lie in the preexilic period. In addition the observable usage of this genre in the communal complaint songs of the monarchic period also point in this direction (see ¶6, p. 324).

Upon closer inspection, these examples show that the genre was completely developed by the time of Jerusalem's overthrow, around 600. Known motifs are encountered, including: the introductory *cry for help*,[39] *complaint*,[40] *petition*,[41] the combination of the impera-

---

[32]One may compare Ps 79; Sir 33:1-13a; 36:16b-22; Pr Azar 3-22; Pss. Sol. 7.

[33]Isa 59:12ff; 64:4-6; Ps 79:8-9; Pr Azar 6-7; Pss. Sol. 7:3, 5.

[34]Pr. Azar 4,5,16; Pss. Sol. 7:3ff (§4, ¶10, 92.).

[35]Cf. Pr Azar 12f; Sir 33:6, 10; 36:16, 18, 21.

[36]See the commentary to Pss 61:7-8 and 63:12.

[37]See the commentary, p. 605.

[38]Jer 11:18-20; 15:15-21; 17:12-18; 18:18-23; 20:10-13; see also 12:1-6; 15:10-12; 20:7-9, 14-18. Regarding their genuineness, see Baumgartner, *Die Klagegedichte des Jeremia*, pp. 68ff.

[39]Ps 61:2-3 (§6, ¶12, p. 161).

tive petition with the petition preserved in the wish form,[42] the *confidence motif*,[43] the *innocence motif*,[44] the *honor motif*,[45] the *humility motif*,[46] the *certainty of being heard*,[47] and the *vow*.[48]

Frequently, the motifs are longer. This tendency corresponds to the fact that the poems themselves are relatively large (cf. specifically Jer 18:18-23; Pss 61; 63; 144:1-11). It is most important, however, that the individual motifs manifest a developed style. The introduction of the words of the enemy is quite common in the context of the complaint.[49] At the end, the vocabulary of the offering of the thanksgiving song appears instead of the vow.[50] The comfort idea is spoken in vivid and appropriate images from the personal experience of the one praying. It rises above the typically general nature of the statements.[51] The simple, unadorned form has further developed the "description of praying" to a lyrical expression whose fantasy and feeling are as deeply moving as the original form of lyrical expression.[52]

The *richness of material* demonstrates the genre's complete development. Enemy persecution[53] and the enemies' painful mockery[54] dominate the complaint. The complaint knows loneliness and sorrow,[55] discouragement, disappointment, and abandonment by YHWH.[56] In the petition, one encounters the demand for vengeance upon the enemies,[57] for their annihilation,[58] and their shame.[59] One encounters the demand for salvation,[60] help,[61] for deliverance from the violent waters, from the sword, for liberation from the hand of foreigners, and protection from lying mouths.[62] In addition, one should mention the petition for certainty in Ps 61:2 and for the justification of one's own action.[63]

Further, in this context, one should refer to the fact that the eldest stage, the complaint song of one who is ill (§6, ¶6, p. 137) lies in the distant past by the time of Jere-

---

[40] Jer 11:19; 15:17-18; 18:18, 21; 20:10; Ps 61:3 (§6, ¶11, p. 155).

[41] Jer 15:15; 17:14, 17; 18:19, 21-22; Pss 61:3b; 63:10-12; 144:5-11 (§6, ¶12, pp. 157ff).

[42] Jer 17:18; 18:21, 22, 23; cf. Ps 63:10-12 (§6, ¶14, 15, p. 165).

[43] Jer 17:14; Ps 61:4-5; 144:2 (§6, ¶19, p. 172).

[44] Jer 17:16 (§6, ¶21).

[45] Jer 15:15; 18:20 (§6, ¶20, p. 175).

[46] Ps 144:3-4 (§6, ¶20, p. 175).

[47] Jer 11:20; 20:11; Ps 61:6 (§6, ¶23, pp. 180ff).

[48] Jer 20:13; Pss 61:9; 63:5-7; 144:9-10 (§6, ¶24, pp. 184ff).

[49] Jer 11:19; 17:15f; 18:18; 20:10 (§6, ¶11, 156).

[50] Jer 20:13; Ps 144:9-10 (§6, ¶8, 186).

[51] Ps 63:7-9 (§6, ¶20, pp. 175f).

[52] Ps 62:2-3 (§6, ¶12, p. 161).

[53] Jer 11:18-19; 15:15; 18:18; 20:10 (§6, ¶8).

[54] Jer 11:18; 15:15; 17:15f; 18:18; 20:10 (§6, ¶8, p. ?).

[55] Jer 15:16b, 18 (§6, ¶7, p. 138).

[56] Jer 18:18; Ps 61:3 (§6, ¶7, p. 137).

[57] Jer 15:15; 17:18; Ps 63:10-12 (§6, ¶12, p. 161, §6, ¶15, p. 165).

[58] Jer 17:18; 18:20-22; Ps 63:11.

[59] Jer 17:18 (§6, ¶12, 14).

[60] Jer 17:14 (§6, ¶12, p. 164).

[61] Jer 17:14 (§6, ¶12, p. 164).

[62] Ps 144:7-11b (§6, ¶12, p. 164).

[63] Jer 17:17 (§6, ¶13, p. 162).

miah. He already uses the statements of this stage of the genre metaphorically in Jer 17:14. The complaint song has already become an expression of inner personal distress and tormenting religious questions.[64] The style appears loose. The complaint and the petition can recede into the background even though they are the most important motifs for the genre. Others appear in the foreground: the portrayal of praying with the expression of the desire for YHWH in Ps 62:2-3 (different in the commentary); the comfort idea by observing one's own life (Ps 63:7-9); and the expanded vow (Ps 63:4-6). Only then, in contrast to the usual style, does a petition directed against the enemy appear (Ps 63:10-12).

Finally, the important step of the dissolution from the cult and the turn to a spiritual poetry occurs in the preexilic period. This change can be deduced with certainly from Jer 11:18ff; 15:15ff; 18:18ff; 20:10ff; 12:1ff; 20:7ff. Ps 61 can be mentioned from the examples in the psalter. It was prayed at a considerable distance from the sanctuary (see the commentary to Ps 61:3). All of these observations lead to the conclusion that the genre had already reached its climax by 600.

9. Our transmission allows us to recognize easily that the genre was preserved was preserved at this height beyond the time of banishment into the postexilic period. Ps 51 demonstrates this fact since it relies on the ideas of the great prophets, and presupposes the postexilic period (§9, ¶45, p. 289). Pss 61 and 102 show the same thing when they look back at the catastrophe of 587 (see the commentary). One may also cite Pss 42/43 in this context because of its treasury of the temple at least postdates the Deuteronomist. These psalms count as outstanding creations of their genre, and they know the full development of all the stylistic methods. This fact requires no special evidence at this point (see the commentary).

It is more difficult to determine how long the flowering lasted. At this point statements which narrow the range will have to suffice. Pss 51, 69, and 102 cannot be placed too late because of the great distance between these psalms and those of the Maccabean period which show the genre has completely dissolved (§6, ¶30, p. 197). However, the allusions in Ps 51:20 (in the supplement) and 102:14,15 should be understood before the time of Nehemiah because they lament the destruction of the walls. One may place Ps 69 in the same period because it recognizes the postexilic cult, and it presupposes the continuing wailing of Zion (see the commentary to this passage). The fact that these psalms do not yet manifest concern for the legal piety of the later period also argues for this placement. From these observations, we may accept that the flowering of the genre was preserved until the beginning of the fifth century.

This placement can be confirmed by the fact that one can observe the decline of the genre from that point onward. Pss 19:12-15 and 119 serve as starting points. Ps 19:12-15 can be dated to the end of the fifth century at the earliest because of its high evaluation of the law. Ps 119, which is utterly filled with legal piety, must be placed even later because of its size and completely disintegrated form. Both show how reflection has penetrated,[65] and becomes even more strongly accentuated.[66] The original liveliness has disappeared. An undeniable impoverishment of the material and the forms of expression

---

[64]Jer 15:15-18; 17:15f; 18:19ff; 20:7ff; cf. 12:1bff.

[65]Pss 19:12b, 13a; 119:23, 24, 27, 35, 39, etc.

[66]Pss. Sol. 5:5-6, 15, 19f; 16:1-4, 9, 11b, 12-14 (§6, ¶30, p. 197).

enters. The complaint continues to recede into the background, disappearing almost completely. In addition to the use of derived material, expressions, and images, the literal borrowing of older poetry characterizes the poetry belonging specifically to this period.[67] The decomposition of the genre announced in the previously mentioned examples is then completed in the first century, B.C.E. The Solomonic psalter no longer contains a single pure example of the individual complaint song. Rather, that genre is only mixed with others (cf. §6, ¶30, p. 197).

10. Relatively few examples of the *individual thanksgiving song* have come to us (§7, ¶1). The number of thanksgiving songs is even smaller which can be dated with certainty, and from which the history of the genre can be ascertained chronologically. Only Jer 20:13 and 33:11 can be considered from the time before 587, as well as Ps 18 and 1 Sam 2:1-10. Determination of the time of the first two examples is given by the fact that they are words of Jeremiah. The time of the other two examples concurs in that they presuppose the Judean monarchic period. Ps 18 is a royal thanksgiving song (cf. the commentary) and 1 Sam 2:1-10 concludes with a wish for the reigning ruler (cf. *Ausgewählter Psalmen*,[4] p. 209).

One may thus confirm with certainty that the origins of this genre lie in the preexilic period, and should not be sought in the era of Judaism. The small, very simple thanksgiving songs in Jeremiah demonstrate the original form. However, they do not lead to the state of the genre for the time of this prophet. Rather, they only make clear that the simple style is demonstrable until this time. Ps 18 and 1 Sam 2:1-10 show how far back chronologically this stage of the genre goes. These passages show that the completely developed form of the individual thanksgiving song was available before 587. The size already achieves the mass of the later thanksgiving songs. All of the motifs that are characteristic of the genre can be demonstrated: the *introduction*,[68] the *narrative of distress*,[69] the *narrative of the petition*,[70] the *narrative of having been heard and of deliverance*,[71] the *confession*,[72] and the *pronouncement of thanksgiving*.[73] Throughout, these motifs are not encountered in a concise form. To the contrary, they are generally preserved in extensive form. Further, one finds the brief summary of the main contents in a concise narrative which immediately follows the introduction.[74] The custom of allowing the thanksgiving song to traverse the same path twice is already known.[75] The didactic turn of the confession appears in 1 Sam 2:3.

It is particularly instructive that the individual thanksgiving song and the hymn have grown closer. The thanksgiving song has borrowed from the hymn. The confession in 1 Sam 2:3-10a undeniably offers hymnic material (also Ps 18:26-28, 31). One can even demonstrate the development of the narrative of deliverance in Ps 18:8ff by the lines of

---

[67]See the commentary to Ps 38 and esp. 119.

[68]Ps 18:1-3; 1 Sam 2:1.

[69]Ps 18:5-6.

[70]Ps 18:7-8.

[71]Ps 18:8-20, 33ff; 1 Sam 2:1bd.

[72]Ps 18:26-31; cf. 18:47-49; 1 Sam 2:2ff.

[73]Ps 18:50-51.

[74]Ps 18:4.

[75]Ps 18:1-31, 32-51.

thought of the theophany. Hymnic forms are also adopted with the hymnic material: the hymnic participle (1 Sam 2:6-8), indirect praise (1 Sam 2:4-5), the praise of YHWH's incomparability in the form of the negative sentence (1 Sam 2:2; §2, ¶31, p. 38), and the amazed questions (Ps 18:32; §2, ¶31, p. 38). In fact, the change belongs to the preexilic history of the genre. The thanksgiving song does not return to the announcement of thanksgiving in the festal situation. Instead, it concludes with a confession climaxing in a hymn (cf. 1 Sam 2:3ff). Finally, it appears as if the change to spiritual poetry and the dissolution from the cultic soil had already occurred in this period. One may perhaps conclude that 1 Sam 2:1-10 betrays absolutely no internal relationship to temple service.

These observations show the genre in the stage of its flowering. It is accidental that we cannot prove the thanksgiving song to be an extension of the individual complaint song in this period. The examples at our disposal also do not contain an introduction of the complaint song in the narration of the distress. We are left to wonder whether the wisdom saying had already become a form of expression for the confession. Caution should rule on this point, but this reservation does not preclude the conclusion that we encounter the individual thanksgiving song in its full extent in the latter part of the Judean monarchic period.

11. Ps 40 seems important for dating the later history of the poetry. It stands under the influence of the prophetic polemic against sacrifice and simultaneously betrays an esteem for the law (see the commentary to 40:7-9). It thus stems from the time after the middle of the fifth century.

The example also shows that in this genre the catastrophe of the exile had no epoch-making significance from a history of literature perspective. It also demonstrates that this genre continued to bloom, at least into the latter fifth century. The example does make clear, however, how the sharp boundaries between the individual genres begin to blur. It also shows the first sign that this genre begins to disintegrate. The pronouncement of thanksgiving lost the well-known form. The poet alludes to what he has *done*, but nothing more. He does not mention what he *will do*. At the same time, his thanksgiving song concludes with a petition borrowed from the individual complaint song (40:12). In the course of history, this development led to a point in which a thanksgiving song could flow into a long complaint song, thereby shifting the accent from the former to the latter. An example is preserved from the Maccabean period with Pss. Sol. 16 (cf. §7, ¶8, p. 207; §11, ¶4, p. 308).

Accordingly, the decline and disintegration of the genre (the details of which can be seen in §7, ¶13, p. 221), must have taken place in the time between 500 and the first century B.C.E. One can add that thanksgiving songs which certainly stem from the later postexilic period illustrate this disintegration, specifically Sir 51 (around 200 B.C.E.) and Pss. Sol. 15 and 16 (cf. §7, ¶13, p. 221).

12. Only one of the smaller genres treated in §8 can be more closely determined chronologically, and that one represents one of the smallest genres in the psalter, the *pilgrimage song*. We know that this genre had already arisen in the preexilic period in Israel and Judah, based upon the prophetic imitation of it.[76] Beyond that, however, one can also confirm that its escalation to its highest form belongs to the time before 587. Ps 84

---

[76]Hos 6:1ff and Jer 31:6.

provides the evidence. It has received an addition which itself belongs to the time of the monarchy, a petition for the ruling king.[77]

Ps 84 teaches us that, by the latter period of the Judean monarchy, the pilgrimage song was connected with the Zion song (§8, ¶22, p. 237) which, for its part, had already adopted the blessing saying (§8, ¶6, p. 225f). Also, the pilgrimage song had by that time already experienced the influence of the individual complaint song. The description of the singer's desire stems from this influence (§6, ¶12, p. 161f). Thus, the pilgrimage song expressed the personal feelings of an individual before 587. Finally, the influence of wisdom is not lacking in Ps 84:11 (see §8, ¶22, p. 237).

Even though we know little else about the pilgrimage song, we can recognize from Ps 84 that its beginnings lie far back in the period before 587. From there, Ps 84 shows us more than the preexilic existence of genres, like the Zion song, whose chronology is otherwise not comprehensible. It also graphically illustrates how early the psalm genres appear in relationship to one another. Also, Ps 84 indirectly demonstrates that the genres it adopted had already reached their high point by the end of the Judean monarchic period since this process could only begin at the stage when the genre appeared in complete form.

13. The result is quite similar for the *liturgies*. The *torah liturgy* (§11, ¶14, p. 313) is presumed to be well known and imitated by Micah at the end of the 8th century.[78] The liturgy consisting of complaint song and oracle is also preexilic.[79] Even the special dramatic form which combines the communal song of confession with the responsive oracle is preexilic. It is imitated by Hosea.[80] The liturgy belonging to the procession with the holy ark also belongs to the monarchic period.[81]

Nevertheless, the characteristic period of the flowering of the liturgy can first be placed in the reestablishment of the temple service in the post-exilic period. The fact that we possess extensive prophetic liturgies from the later period points in this direction,[82] as does the fact that the combination of components of various genres caters to the dissolution and mixing of genres that is also characteristic for the postexilic period. Liturgies such as Pss 81, 82, 95, 118, and 126 argue this case since they are certainly dated to the postexilic period, although a more specific date is generally not possible.

14. In all probability, the *mixed poem* is scarcely older than the time around 500. The fundamental requirement for its origin is the dissolution of the genres and the blurring of their boundaries in connection to one another, which first occurred around 500. In addition, an abundance of mixed poems are transmitted precisely from this period. Among the Psalms, the entire composition of Pss 19 and 119 belong to this period with certainty, as does an alphabetic psalm like Pss 9/10. The following come from the time around 200: Sir 10:14-17; 16:18ff; 17:29-32; 39:12-35; 42:15–43:33; 50:22. The Solomonic psalter is characteristic of the first century.

---

[77]See the commentary to Ps 84:9-10.

[78]Mic 6:6-8.

[79]Pss 20; 132 (preexilic because they are royal songs). See also Jer 3:22b–4:2; 14:2-9, 10, 19-22; 15:1.

[80]Hos 5:15–6:6; 14:3-9.

[81]Ps 24:7-10.

[82]Isa 26:8-21; 33:1-13; 63:7–65:25; Hab 1–3.

15. The observations which could be made for the individual genres lead essentially to the same conclusion. It thus becomes possible to make relatively justifiable conclusions for those genres which cannot be immediately ascertained because of the random lack of datable examples. In this context it one can ascertain their main developmental stages chronologically within the history of psalmody. One may believe the following based upon the observations of those genres which were investigated.

The beginnings of Hebrew psalmody belong to the earliest time of Israel. The earliest example of a hymn, Judg 5:3-5, reaches into the days before the kings. One may also place the origin of other genres belonging closely with the cult. At any rate, one may go back to the first part of the monarchic period. It is not wise to place the beginnings later because then the time would be too short for the complete development of the genres under consideration. Psalmody climbed to its high point around the middle of the eighth century. The hymn in its fully developed form can also be referenced in Israel before 721 by Ps 89. One may accept similar things for the other genres. We must generally be satisfied with the affirmation that its complete formulation is demonstrable before 587. This number only signifies the latest time period which we can assign, and it should not be doubted that the high point was reached earlier. At any rate, one may accept that the literary development in Israel possessed a certain chronological head start in comparison to that of Judah.

Psalmody entered the period of its flowering in the eighth century, which was also the time in which the great prophets of Israel seized the forms of psalmody in order to express their own particular ideas. This relationship had an impact upon psalmody and provided new stimuli and content (cf. §9). This age of flowering reaches into the fifth century B.C.E. according to our investigation. The exile set aside the national states of Israel and Judah and decisively altered the people's form of existence, but did not usher in a new epoch in psalmody. That which the preexilic period had created was so dynamically powerful and so assuredly valid, the exilic and early postexilic period sang and spoke like the preexilic period.

The beginning of the dissolution from the cult and the change to cult-free spiritual poetry begins during this time. One can illustrate these changes from the time around 600 with the individual complaint song and the individual thanksgiving song (cf. ¶8, p. 327, and ¶10, p. 329). Individual genres turn to eschatological elements during this time. The eschatologization of the enthronement psalm can be demonstrated before 587, and quite probably the Zion songs if ideas considered in §9, ¶47, p. 291 prove correct.

Around 500, the power of psalmody begins to deteriorate. Around this time, they generally begin to value the available psalms highly. In fact, psalmody remained aloof toward legal piety in general. The style of the flowering period continued to have an effect until this time. However, it increasingly moved only in the transmitted ideas, forms, and images. The lyrical richness gives way to an undeniable poverty of content. A discernible dampening of tone, and ultimately even a dampening of understandable ideas, replaces the lively, fresh mood. Reflection establishes itself in psalmody and stimulates the disintegration of the genres which had been rising since 500. In this period, the mixed poem and the liturgy blossom. In this time, one scarcely encounters songs in the old, pure style any longer, nor genuinely lyrical contents. Essentially, Sirach typifies this period. This age ends with the complete dissolution of the genres and the expulsion of feelings by reflection, as encountered in the Psalms of Solomon. However, the purity of the genre represents the most essential element of existence for Hebrew lyric poetry in the period when it began and flowered. However, for this reason the disintegration of the genres signifies the end of the religious poetry as it had been known. Thus, the history of psalmody reached its clearly recognizable end point in the Maccabean period.

§13 The Collection of Psalms

1. We encounter the earliest recorded name for the collection in which the psalms of the canon are combined among Jews writing in Greek and the people in the Ancient Near East whose origins emanate from Judaism. The name is ψαλμοί according to the superscription of codex B of the LXX and Luke 24:44, or βίβλος ψαλμῶν according to the subscription of codex B; Luke 20:42; and Acts 1:20. Additionally attested are the names ψαλτήριον (codex A) or ψαλτήριον τῷ Δαυίδ (codex R).

Apparently, ψαλμοί reflects the Hebrew *mizmôr*. At least, this possibility is suggested by the twelve words from which to choose, and the one which is most frequently attested. It appears fifty-seven times in the superscriptions of the individual psalms.

Hebrew and Aramaic speaking Jews generally adopted another term for the collection of psalms: *tehillîm* and *sefer tehillîm* or relatedly *tillîm, tillîn, and sefar tillîn*. This terminology can also be found among the church fathers (see the details in Steuernagel, *Einleitung in das Alten Testament*, §152, ¶1).

In the Old Testament, *tehillāh* is known as a *terminus technicus* for the hymns described in §2. The notable masculine plural form is not yet utilized in the Old Testament, but was chosen with the intention of expressing the idea of "song book." Deviating from other witnesses, the Masorah prefers the feminine plural *tehillôt* (see Steuernagel, *Einleitung in das Alten Testament*, §152, ¶1).

Undoubtedly, the expression is used here in a more generalized sense than in the Old Testament. Only a fraction of the collection consists of hymns. The collection received the name of these hymns because they were considered the most important part of the collection.

2. The entire textual transmission agrees that the collection contained 150 songs. LXX manuscripts recognize a 151st psalm which is transmitted differently.[1] At the same time, however, they designate it as one which stands ἔξωθεν τοῦ ἀριθμοῦ, thus not really belonging to the collection.

In the numbering, however, MT and the LXX differ. The LXX counts the Masoretic psalms 9 and 10 as a single psalm, and also 114 and 115. However, since the Masoretic psalms 116 and 147 are each divided into two psalms, the LXX also reaches the number 150. The result is different numbering for MT and the LXX. The following table allows one to recognize the relationship of both numbering systems to one another.

---

[1]Cf. M. Noth, "Die fünf syrisch überlieferten apokryphen Psalmen," *ZAW* n.s. 7 (1930): 1ff.

MT		LXX	MT		LXX
1–8	=	1–8	116:10-19	=	115
9–10	=	9	117–146	=	116–145
11–113	=	10–112	147:1-11	=	146
114–115	=	113	147:12-20	=	147
116:1-9	=	114	148–150	=	148–150

The entire transmission divides the collection into five books, whose conclusions are made recognizable by doxologies. The last book lacks this concluding formula. Most agree Ps 150 replaced this concluding formula. The individual books comprise the following range: Pss 1–41 (I); 42–72 (II); 73–89 (III); 90–106 (IV); 107–150 (V). The reason and origin of this division will be treated elsewhere (cf. ¶17).

3. One can easily recognize that the reason for dividing the *arrangement of the psalms* does not result from the content. They are also not combined on the basis of individual genres. For example, the hymns in the first book (Pss 8; 19; 24:1-2; 29; 33) do not appear next to one another. The royal psalms (Pss 2; 18; 20; 21) do not form a group which belongs together. Even when we mention the individual complaint songs, these are scattered (3; 5; 6; 7; 13; 17; 22; etc.). The remaining books yield the same results.

The entirety is also not arranged according to the names of the authors mentioned in the superscriptions. Davidic psalms are found in Pss 3–32; 34–41; 51–65; 68–70; 86; 101; 103; 108–110; (122); 131; 133; 138–145. In between, one finds other songs which are also separated from one another: the Korahites (Pss 42–49; 84–85; 87–88); Asaph psalms (Pss 50; 3–83); the Solomonic psalms (72; 127). We have not even mentioned the scattering of anonymous poems.

To be sure, one also finds the grouping together of psalms with the *same superscription*. In addition to the continuous examples of Davidic psalms already cited, see the *ma'ălôt* songs (Pss 120–134), the hallelujah psalms (146–150), the *miktam* psalms (56–60). However, not all of the psalms belonging to these groups stand together. One finds a *miktam* psalm by itself in Ps 16 and psalms superscripted with hallelujah are found, for example, in Pss 106; 111–113.

Also, even the most cursory glance will show that the poetry is not arranged according to the external *criterion of size*.

Simple, clear reasons for the arrangement of the psalms cannot be demonstrated. For this reason, scholarship has endeavored to derive causes for the sequence of the individual psalms, some of which are quite complicated.

Fr. Delitzsch (Symbolae, etc., *Psalmen Kommentar*), attempts to show that the combination of the psalms depends upon the relationship of prominent external and internal markers. Ps 51 follows Ps 50 because both accentuate views against sacrifice. Ps 35 is placed after Ps 34 because these two psalms are the only ones in which angels appear (Pss 34:8; 35:5, 6). The order of Pss 5 and 56 was determined through the catchword "dove" (55:7; 56:1). Thus, the psalms are chained to one another in series according to different criteria.

In cases such as those cited, one cannot fail to recognize the correctness and the convincing power of these arguments. One can only question whether the principle continues throughout the psalter. The danger of arbitrariness is suggested by the exposition of a thoughtful relationship as when seeking the alleged connecting catchwords. Take the idea, for example, that Ps 86 was inserted between Pss 85 and 87 because, on the one hand, its petition ("Show me your way, Lord," and "grant your servant your protection.") alludes to Ps 85:8. On the other hand, the perspective of the repentance of the heathen suggested in Ps 86:9 approaches Ps 87. These ideas can hardly be designated as unforced, and they are certainly not convincing. Connections by catchwords and similarities can therefore perhaps be recognized in individual cases, but the principle fails in relation to the whole psalter.

Recently, R. *Hallo* attempted to show that the psalter was arranged according to a psychological principle.[2] He takes the path of prayer, which the author suggests with the following questions: "Do we not all begin with childish obstinacy because of and based upon our own limits? Should we not all end singing praise in unison? Should we not force everything, the evil and the good, the lifeless and the living, to kneel with us between rest and conquest?" (p. 35) Contrary to this presumption, one should fundamentally object from the outset that the path of prayer he presupposes has nothing to do with the path of prayer operating in the time under consideration when the collection of psalms arose. (Cf. §5 and §6, as well as Dan 9; 2 Chr 6:14ff; Tob 3:2ff, 11ff; Jdt 9:2ff; 13:5; Wisd Sol 9:1-4; the Prayer of Manasseh; and Additions to Esther 3:1-4, 14ff.) Thus, Hallo's thesis is pulled to the ground, leaving only the task of demonstrating in detail the amount of violence connected with the execution of his supposition.

The idea of *J. Dahle* is just as unsatisfying. He thinks that the order of the psalms follows the sequence of the material in the Pentateuch,[3] so that during the reading in the worship service songs suitable for the Pentateuchal passage would be available. Apart from the question of whether he can transplant evangelical worship service's practice of alternating scripture and song to the Israelite-Judean worship, demonstrating the relationship between psalm passages and Pentateuchal passages proves tiresome, forced, and quite unconvincing. A more detailed interaction with this effort for introduction in the psalms is not worth the effort.

4. One cannot recognize a unifying principle for the transmitted sequence, although perhaps various viewpoints are demonstrable for the combination of individual psalms (similarities of specific ideas, agreement of particular catchwords, common author, equivalent superscriptions). This result forces one to conclude that the book of Psalms owes its current state to a complicated process of origin. In this process, one must not only consider the combination of various small collections, but one must also consider rearrangements which took place without paying attention to the boundaries of the old small collections. A remark in Midrash Tillim points in this direction. It allows one to recognize the recollection of a the complicated history of origin of the collection. When Rabbi Joshua ben Levi thought of changing the order of the psalms, a hymnic voice warned him with the words, "Do not disturb that which is old."[4]

5. The question of the *time of origin of the collection* is more important than the question of its name and arrangement principle. Unfortunately, one can only answer this question approximately. We must be satisfied with designating an *upper and lower limit* from the broader time period during which the collection must have arisen.

---

[2]*Der Morgen*, Jahrgang 33, vol. 1, pp. 23-36.
[3]J. Dahle, *Das Rätsel des Psalters gelöst*, 1927.
[4]Cf. J. Fürst, *Der Kanon des Alten Testament*, p. 68.

In order *to determine the lower limit*, one should proceed from the prologue of the Greek translation of Sirach. Its author already knows the three-part Old Testament canon. He knows that his grandfather ardently studied this canon. He also presumes that this canon was available in Greek during his time. Since the grandson came to Egypt in the 38th year of Euergetes (II), 132 B.C.E., according to his own assertion, the approximate time of his grandfather can be placed around 190. The prologue's reference to the availability of the three-part canon should also be considered from this time.

Since the third part of the canon was not yet complete at that point, one must raise the question whether the psalm collection already belonged to the canon. One should affirm such is the case with attention to the tradition which sees the psalter as the most important, or second most important book in the *ketūbîm*.[5] One may conclude from this high evaluation that the psalter belonged to the oldest components of the third part of the canon. The first citation of a psalm as holy scripture is found around 100 B.C.E. in 1 Macc 7:17, citing Ps 79:2-3.

These confirmations, however, leave open the question whether the psalm collection already had reached the size of the current psalter. Anyone who believes that individual canonical psalms could only have arisen in the Maccabean period, i.e., after 165 B.C.E., will deny that the previously mentioned references could refer to smaller collections. They must also think that the entire collection first occurred in the first century B.C.E. Meanwhile, no real reason exists for this conclusion. First, the explanations of the psalms showed that none of those psalms which could be conceived as Maccabean contain completely unambiguous allusions to the Maccabean period.[6] Thus, they must not be derived from that period. Comparison with genuine Maccabean psalms, the Psalms of Solomon, shows that the canonical psalms are so distinct stylistically and by content (cf. §12, ¶15, p. 331), that one has every reason for accepting a long time span between the earlier canonical psalms and the later Psalms of Solomon. In addition, the existence of the collection of the Psalms of Solomon argues against the end of the collection in the first century and against accepting psalms first deriving from this time. The collection of the Psalms of Solomon presupposes the canonical psalter as a complete entity, which is traced back to David.[7] Otherwise, one cannot explain why a particular collection of compiled poems bearing Solomon's name would not have been adopted into the psalter. Finally, one should point to the precise agreement of the LXX psalter with the Masoretic psalter with respect to size and order. The simplest explanation for this agreement comes by accepting that the completely closed psalter already lay before the translator. The supposition that a smaller LXX psalter was later completed according to the Hebrew is less probable. In addition, this argument derives from the viewpoint of making the Maccabean dating of certain psalms conceivable. According to p. 336, the Greek translation of the psalms had been available long before 132. As such, it corresponds with the fact that Chronicles,

---

[5]For citations, see the details in H. B. Swete, *An Introduction to the Old Testament in Greek*, pp. 200ff.

[6]Pss 2; 12; 16; 17; 18; 19; 20; 21; 30; 33; 44; 45; 51:20f; 53; 56; 58; 59; 60; 68; 72; 74; 76; 79; 80; 83; 89; 94; 99; 102; 110; 113; 116; 118; 124; 132; 137; 140; 141; 143; 149.

[7]See Sir 47:8-10.

which also belongs to the *ketūbîm*, can be shown to exist in Greek translation around 157 B.C.E., and Job in the second century.[8]

Based upon the considerations cited, one may name 200 B.C.E. as the *lower limit for the time of origin for the psalter.*

6. It is harder to determine the upper limit. Setting the upper limit essentially depends upon the following questions: How does Ps 106:48 relate to 1 Chr 16:36, and how do the *benê qōraḥ* in the psalter relate to the Chronicler's singer guilds?

Ps 106:48 and 1 Chr 16:36, two frequently discussed passages, correspond literally at the beginning, and are essentially differentiated only in tense at the end. One recognizes that in 1 Chr 16:8ff a poem appears which had Pss 96, 105, and 106 at its disposal and used them. Proceeding from this recognition one may suppose the following reason for the close connection between the two passages. The author of 1 Chr 16:8ff found Ps 106:48 available before him and transferred it as a component of the psalm he used, but changed the tense based upon the connecting narrative since that verse, as in Ps 106, stood at the end. However, since Ps 106:48 is also the concluding doxology of the fourth book of Psalms, one may consider the most far reaching conclusion that 1 Chr 16:36 presupposes the five-part division of the psalter. Anyone wishing to evade this conclusion may hardly conclude with Kittel from 1 Chr 16:36 that Ps 106:48 once formed the conclusion of a single psalm collection (*Die Psalmen*,[3 and 4] p. 348). Despite many differences in wording, one cannot overlook strong literal connections with the other concluding doxologies (Pss 41:14; 72:18-19; 89:53). Rather, there is only one other possible explanation, specifically that one should see 1 Chr 16:8-36 as a later insertion and continue from that point with this insertion placed in an appropriate time.

First, however, this line of thought overlooks the relationship of the concluding doxologies, and one can hardly deny that these doxologies belong together. Second, it overlooks the fact that the text which appears before the other three words in Ps 106:48 ("and let all the people say") falls outside the frame of the common items and is hardly justified materially. Finally, this line of thought does not consider that the text in 1 Chr 16:36 ("and all the people said, 'amen and hallelujah'") is quite appropriate to the situation in which the Chronicler's narrative places it. Given this condition, the argument that the Chronicler simply changed the tense of Ps 106:48 is not convincing. Thus, one is continually, and correctly, faced with the originality of 1 Chr 16:36 over against Ps 106:48.[9]

How should one explain this situation? 1 Chr 16 describes a worship service in the form of the later postexilic period. The custom of the people responding to a praise of YHWH with the words *'āmēn ū'āmēn* is also encountered in Neh 8:6 and was adopted by Christianity (cf. 1 Cor 14:16; 2 Cor 1:20). Accordingly, it argues for Steuernagel's conclusion that 1 Chr 16:36 found a doxology before him that was quite appropriate for concluding the psalm reading (cf. Steuernagel, §156, ¶8).

One can understand the transposition of the doxology to the conclusion of the psalm books because the form and position were based upon this worship practice. With regard to the relationship of Ps 106:48 to 1 Chr 16:36, one may accept that 1 Chr 16:8-36 was a well-known liturgical composition of the later postexilic period. It was a song which

---

[8]Cf. Steuernagel, *Einleitung in das Alten Testament*, §10, ¶3.

[9]J. Wellhausen, in Bleek, *Einleitung*,[4] p. 506n.1; C. H. Cornill, *Einleitung*, p. 252; K. Steuernagel, *Einleitung*, §156, ¶8; Briggs, *Psalmes*, vol. 1, p. lxxxviii; B. Jakob, *ZAW*, 1896, 152.

David had entrusted to Asaph and his brothers at the institution of the holy service. If this is true, then it is understandable why the redactors of the psalter placed Ps 106 at the end of a book. Its last verse was connected with the doxology by transmission of the worship service. Quite probably, it did not yet possess the words, "so the people said," and "hallelujah," along with the first three words. They would have entered via a later correction based upon the passage in Chronicles.

If Rothstein-Hänel are correct in assuming that the Chronicler's work belongs to the period around 400, and that the insertion of 1 Chr 16:6ff belongs not too much later, then the influence of the Chronicler's text on Ps 106:48 would have taken place around 350. However, as presented above, since Ps 106:48 was related to the entire psalter, then the *earliest possibility for the time of this collection would thus be between 400 and 350.* Apparently, the boundary lies a little bit lower, as the discussion of the second point made clear.

7. In the superscriptions to 42–49, 84–85, and 87–88 we encounter the *benê qōrah*, a singers' guild which possessed the right to perform in the worship service according to the above mentioned psalms. They also joined these songs into a special collection belonging to them. The parallels of the Asaph psalms argue for this interpretation. They are also combined with the well-known singers, the sons of Asaph regardless of whether one sees the *le* in the superscription as collectively designating the singers's guild with Asaph, or whether the superscription intends that they be perceived as stemming from Asaph as the author. Finally, 2 Chr 20:19 expressly attests the Korahites as a singers' guild.

In the psalter, the Korahites rank equally with the Asaphites. By contrast, in Chronicles (taking the work as a whole), the significance of the Korahites recedes considerably behind the Asaphites. The Korahites are overwhelmingly portrayed as threshold guards, not singers. Clearly a historical development lies between the stages designated in the psalter and in Chronicles. One can only ask whether it concerns an escalating or a descending development.

R. Smith, in his book, *Das Alte Testament: Seine Entstehung und Überlieferung* (1894), decides in favor of the second possibility for the following reasons. The time of Chronicles knows three singers' guilds, Asaph, Heman, and Ethan-Jedutun, which are counted with the three Levitical families of Gershom, Kahat, and Merari. The psalter knows only two guilds, Asaph and the Korahites. The latter was a threshold guard in the time of Chronicles. On the other hand, according to Ezra 2:41 and Neh 7:44, only the Asaphites were temple singers at the time of the return from exile. Based upon this information, one concludes that at the time of Nehemiah the Korahites were *not yet* temple singers and at the time of Chronicles they were *no longer* temple singers.

This decision has correctly raised misgivings. People have objected that it hardly coincides with the rise of the lower temple officials which can be seen in Chronicles. They object that one would hardly have allowed the names to have remained with the psalms if the guild was demoted.

But what argues positively for the rise of the Korahites? A decision is not easy since the various references of the Chronicler's work which contradict one another are difficult to arrange in historical sequence. Nevertheless, one may consider the following as certain.

According to Ezra 2:40ff (=Neh 7:43ff), which is a list that predated the Chronicler, the temple personnel were divided into Levites, singers, and gatekeepers. Only the

Asaphites were singers. The first family of gatekeepers are the *benê Šallūm*. 1 Chr 9:17 explicitly accents their significance as "head of the threshold guards." One must consider this position as original, since they appear in this function elsewhere in 1 Chr 9:17,19,31, as well as in 26:14 (*šelemyāh*), 1 Chr 9:21; 26:1 (*mešelemyāh*), and Neh 12:25 (*mešullām*). From the significance which came to this family as the head of the threshold guards, one can assume that the family attempted to rise higher. Indications for this attempt are available in the Chronicler's work. While the ancient list simply introduced the family as *benê Šallūm*, its derivation from Korah comes with the *claim of Levitical rank* in the insertion in 1 Chr 9:19-21. The family believed it possessed gatekeeper status in the tent of revelation during the wilderness period. *Šallūm* and his brothers are here designated as Korahites. The various genealogies, as well as the various Korahite officials who were elevated can only be understood as attestations of a rise which was not yet complete at the time of Chronicles. The different lines are placed alongside one another in their incompatibility.

The Korahites are sharply separated from the Levites and the singers in Ezra 2:42 (=Neh 7:45); Ezra 10:24; and Neh 12:5. By contrast, they were specifically numbered among the Levites in 1 Chr 9:19,31; 2 Chr 20:19. In addition, one has the evidence of the family tree in 1 Chr 6:18ff. 1 Chr 15:17 should be mentioned in the context of the last passage. The fact that Levitical rank appears so late proves the uncertainty of the derivation from Levi. According to 2 Chr 20:19, the Korahites were not traced back to Kohath, since they are named alongside the Kohathites. By contrast, for example, 1 Chr 6:18ff counts them among this family. Their higher employment vacillates in contrast to their unmistakable position as gatekeepers in older times. In 1 Chr 26:12 official functions in service of the house of YHWH are assigned to them as well as other gatekeepers. According to 1 Chr 9:31, *Mattitiah ben Šallūm* controlled the bakery as a Levite. They appear as singers in 1 Chr 10:19. According to 1 Chr 6:18ff, they accept the claim that the highest ranking singer of David, Heman, was their ancestral father and tribe member. Perhaps one should also presume the Korahite claim to be singers in 1 Chr 15:18 and 16:5 if the Zechariah standing at the top of the singers of the second order is identical with Zechariah, the first son of *Šallūm-mešelemhāh* (1 Chr 26:1). The appearance of other gatekeepers among the singers in 1 Chr 15:18 and 16:5, specifically *'ōbēd 'edōm* and *ye'î'ēl* (1 Chr 15:18, 24), encourages this conclusion. According to the first of the passages mentioned the Korahites only claim the rank of the head of the singers of the second rank. However, according to 16:5 they claim the second position behind the chief singer Asaph.

In our opinion, all the observations of this type only allow the conclusion that the gatekeeper family of the Korahites sought to elevate its status in the Chronicler's time. However, at this point, its claim to the office of singer and its rank among the singers had not yet attained complete acceptance. The singers' guild of the Korahites must therefore be later than the conclusion of the Chronicler's history. Chronicles was completed around 400 (the commentary of Rothstein-Hänel contributes noteworthy reasons for this date, see volume 1, p. xlivff.). Thus, the collection of the Korahite psalms comes later chronologically, after which comes the collection of the current psalter. Thus, one may consider the time between *350 and 300 as the upper limit*.

8. For what purpose was the psalter combined? This question has increased significance currently over against earlier times because in his psalm studies S. Mowinckel

establishes a specific purpose for the psalter and from that purpose draws far-reaching conclusions for the poetry it contains.

> One may proceed from Gunkel's foundational recognition (that the origin of psalmody should be sought in the cult), and give satisfactory attention to the fact that the psalter was transmitted as the songbook of the second temple, and was unquestionably used as such. If so, then the obligation grows for the researcher to investigate whether the majority of psalms can best be explained as genuine cult songs, composed from the beginning for the cult" (*Psalmenstudien* 6:27).

Mowinckel thus adopts the view presented by Wellhausen, Stade, Cornill, Briggs, Baethgen and others as his own, unfortunately without ever asking whether the opinion they express could be understood the same way he means that the psalter was compiled exclusively for worship purposes. It is regrettable that Mowinckel assumes this idea without ever renewing an examination of its correctness. It is even more regrettable, since strong objections have been leveled against them, like the objections of B. Duhm and W. Staerk.

Concerning the argument that the psalter was compiled for the purpose of the cult, one can deduce the following reasons from the psalter itself. Individual psalms were sung at particular worship occasions according to evidence of their tradition. Thus, Ps 30 belongs to the temple dedication service, Ps 92 to the sabbath, and Ps 29 (according to the LXX) to the final day of the festival of booths. The LXX further indicates that Ps 24 (23) was used on Sunday, Ps 48 (47) on Monday, Ps 94 (93) on Wednesday, and Ps 93 (92) on Friday. Italian and Armenian translations claim Ps 81 (80) for Thursday. According to their superscriptions, other psalms appear to have been sung at particular sacrifices. It is worth considering that Pss 38 and 70, and certainly Ps 100, belonged to the thanksgiving sacrifice.

Of course, these traditions are very sparse, and, in part, attested late. By themselves, these traditions hardly justify a specific view about the purpose of the collection. Even more importantly, they are expanded by a rich transmission of another type. One encounters the term *lammnaṣṣēǎh*. Whatever this *terminus technicus* might have meant in particular, it is certain that it cannot be separated from the *naṣṣaḥ* below,[10] and that it relates to the performance of psalms in the temple service. One also may refer to the tradition ascribing a number of psalms to the singers' guilds of Asaph and the sons of Korah.

Even these reasons, however, do not guarantee the cultic purpose of the collection. The entire collection of psalms arose from small individual collections (cf. ¶11, pp. 343f). For this reason, one must consider whether the liturgical-musical notations arose from the individual collections that were partially determined by the worship service. If so, then it is not wise to draw a conclusion for the entire psalter based upon psalms bearing these superscriptions.

Drawing conclusions from the genre of the individual psalm and thus multiplying the material evidence is completely unallowed. It is undeniable for many psalms that they were composed for the worship service, but it does not follow that the poet's intention was the same as the collector's intention. Take a case like Ps 30 where an individual thanksgiving song was used for the temple dedication ceremony, a completely foreign celebration for the genre. In another case, Jonah 2:2ff, undoubtedly a cultic thanksgiving

---

[10]Ezra 3:8f; 1 Chr 23:4; 2 Chr 2:1, 17; 34:12, 13.

song, is transferred to a completely noncultic situation. These examples show that one must distinguish between original intention and later usage, and they admonish us to use extreme caution. Therefore, one must functionally exclude conclusions based upon psalm genres in the question of the intention of the collection.

In this situation, the reason why the collection was named *sefer tehillîm* cannot lead to the goal. Even if the masculine form was chosen in order to form a comprehensive expression for the various poems of the collection, and could thus be translated Ꞌcordingly as "songbook," it is still not possible to deduce an exclusively cultic purpose ꞌn this term. This is even more true since the superscription is probably not simulta- ꞌ with the collection (cf. ¶1, p. 333).

The power of these reasons to convince is further limited by the argument that the Ꞌꞏr of the noncultic purpose of the collection of psalms puts forward. Numerous show no trace of tradition tying them to the worship service. If one omits all the s which possibly have a cultic notation, 40 psalms still remain. Of course, ꞌ of a cultic purpose can object that the abundance of psalms with notations refer- worship service may also stem from smaller collections. However, in compari- Ꞌꞌaller number of other psalms take on greater importance. One may not con- Ꞌꞌꞏꞌꞏ ꞏꞏꞌuꞏn concerning cultic practice based upon the lack of thoroughgoing tradition. One cannot deny the propriety of this counter argument. However, it leads to nothing more than the affirmation of a possibility, because one may not draw conclusions from the genre of psalms without notations (see above, 340).

This possibility appears to be called into question again by the particular reasons which Duhm, especially, validated for the noncultic character of the psalter. It is difficult to conceptualize that a psalm like 119 could ever have been sung in a worship service, with its 176 lines and its cumbersome, unmoving, and unlyrical manner. More likely, it was determined for edifying reading. The same holds true for psalms whose lines or strophes begin with the subsequent letter of the alphabet.[11] This embellishment can only be appreciated by the eye, not the ear. From this point, the conclusion seems unavoidable that the psalter was composed with the intention of creating a religious book for the people. This book was designed for the edification and devotions of the laity. This collection combined more recent poems designed only for devotional reading with older poetry that arose in the cult, and songs that the cult still used.

However, this interpretation is just as impossible to prove beyond all doubt as the first. The fact that it appears impossible to those of us living today to see Ps 119 as a cult song does not prove that ancient persons would have felt the same way. One cannot state that it is impossible that an alphabetic psalm composed for the laity could not later have been used in the worship service. As with psalms composed for the cult, one must distinguish between the intention of the author and later usage. In fact, three of the alpha- betic psalms contain liturgical-musical notations according to which the psalms were used in the worship service. This development is not without counterpart. One can recall the acrostic songs encountered in the evangelical songbook, or consider that in the early middle ages, the *Symbolum Quicumque*, the most theological of the old church confessions was sung audibly like a psalm in worship.[12]

---

[11]Pss 9/10; 25; 34; 37; 111; 112; 119; 145.
[12]Cf. H. Mulert, *Konfessionskunde*, 1927, pp. 68f.

If one considers these counter arguments, then one ultimately has to doubt the view of Duhm and Staerk, that was as first so illuminating. One must agree, that even this view cannot be affirmed with certainty. Each of the theses that were contrasted with one another can cite a certain degree of probability, but they do not suffice to disprove the other. One can understand, given this condition, how various researchers have responded to the question of the purpose with an answer between the two answers already discussed, including: R. Smith, (*Das Alte Testament: Seine Entstehung und Überlieferung*, 1894, p. 176), Cornill (*Einleitung*, p. 247), J. Meinhold (*Einführung in das Alten Testament*,[3] p. 329), and with more reservation K. Budde (*Geschichte der althebräischen Literatur*, pp. 248ff). They believe that the collection was primarily concerned with the temple cult, but secondarily concerned with worshipful edification. Therefore, they describe the psalter as the "songbook and the book of edification for the Jewish community" (Meinhold, *Einführung in das Alten Testament*,[3] p. 329).

It is questionable whether the reasons taken from the psalter justify this designation. Given the equal weight with which the various reasons for contrasting conceptions of the purpose of the psalter exist, both appear open to criticism. In our opinion, only one conclusion seems possible. Since the reasons taken from the psalter itself invalidate one another, one cannot decide about the purpose from this perspective. It is recommended that one leave the question open as *non liquet* (impossible to decide) and attempt to find the answer from another angle.

10. One can make substantial progress if one gathers the witnesses for the use of psalms in the time period in which the psalter arose. Undoubtedly, psalmody held significance for the temple service. This usage hardly needs proof.[13] But what is the situation with respect to cult-free poetry and with respect to the noncultic use of psalms originally composed for the cult (which should be the same for our purposes)?

One can draw a line which runs from the prophets to the Maccabean period. One can recall the complaint poetry of Jeremiah, the complaint song motifs of the book of Job, and the hymns of Deutero-Isaiah, as well as individual hymnic elements (Isa 42:10ff; 44:23). One can recall the psalms and psalm pieces in Sirach (hymns in 42:15-43:33; individual thanksgiving song in 51:1-12; individual complaint song in 51:10; and communal complaint song in 33:1-13a; 36:16b-22). In addition, one can refer to Daniel's thanksgiving song (2:20ff), the song of the three men in the fiery oven, the prayer of Manasseh, and the Prayer of Azariah. Neither Jeremiah nor Job show connection with the temple service. Connection to the temple was not possible for Deutero-Isaiah, and not a consideration for Sirach. The situations in which several narratives have placed particular songs leads powerfully to the use of psalms independent of the worship service. Hezekiah sings his psalm on the sickbed (Isa 38:9). Jonah sings from the belly of the fish (Jonah 2:2), and Daniel sings his thanksgiving song in his house in Babylon (Dan 2). The narrative places the song of the three men in the fiery oven (Add. To Dan 1:23 [46]ff). Tobit inscribes his praise for God at home (Tob 13:1). The pious one of the Maccabean period praises and sings hymns when he awakes from sleep in the morning (Pss. Sol. 6:6). The fact that the songs in Sirach are intended for the edification of the reader, can be seen clearly from its context with the wisdom book. Everything that stands in this book is "insightful and understandable teaching" (50:27).

---

[13]See 1 and 2 Chronicles; Sir 32:20; 38:9-11; 47:9; 50:18f; 1 Macc 4:24, 54; 13:51; etc.

One can thus demonstrate that cult-free poetry and the nonworship use of originally cultic songs existed from Jeremiah until the Maccabean period. As a result, one is perhaps justified in accepting that the concluding collection of psalms be considered cultic and spiritual psalmody. Of course, one cannot prove this idea conclusively, but one can raise the level of probability beyond the unsatisfying conclusions from the notes of the psalter. In fact, even more is achieved from this result than is visible at first glance. It shatters the certainty of the views that the psalter was collected exclusively to serve a cultic purpose. It thereby removes the most important presupposition for Mowinckel's one-sided cultic understanding of Psalms.

11. Deriving an incontrovertible verdict concerning the goal of the psalter is thus so difficult because it was not compiled in a single act according the plans of a single collector. Instead it derives from partial collections (cf. ¶4).

One has observed for a long time that the group of Psalms in 42-83 are differentiated from all other poems by a conspicuous, one-sided preference for the name *'elōhîm* over YHWH. This characteristic can only be traced to the work of the collector who changed them. One can recognize numerous places in these psalms which escaped the attentiveness of the collector where they originally used the name YHWH (e.g., Pss 42:9; 46:8, 9, 12; 47:3; 48:1; etc). In addition, an expression such as *'elōhîm 'elōhāy* (43:4) or a comparison of Ps 53 with Ps 14.

The fact that the collector of Pss 42-83 should be distinguished from the collector of the whole is also evident from the fact that the other psalms are not subjected to an *'elōhîm* recension. In addition, individual songs collected in 42-83 occur outside this framework.[14] If the psalter was only compiled from individual psalms rather than the use of smaller collections, then the appearance of doublets could not be explained.

The Elohistic Psalter (42-83) thus once existed as an independent entity. It also presupposes three different psalm collections as its sources. In the Elohistic Psalter, they form three groups clearly separated from one another.

The first group extends from Pss 42 to 49. They take their character from the fact that each individual psalm bears the title: "belonging to the sons of Korah." This group is also arranged according to a clearly recognizable principle. At the beginning stand psalms with the notation *maśkîl* (Pss 42-45), followed by Ps 46 with the notation *šîr*, and finally Pss 47-49 with the notation *mizmôr*. This songbook of the Korahites, as the supplements in Pss 84-88 show, was only partially incorporated into the Elohistic Psalter. Or should one consider that the Korahite Psalter only included Pss 42-49 at the time of the Elohistic Psalter?

A second collection traced back to David is just as clear. It encompasses Psalms 51-65 (67), 68-70 (71), and is also arranged according to a plan. Pss 52-55 bear the notation *maśkîl*. Pss 56-60 have *miktām*. Pss 62-65 and 67-68 have *mizmôr*. In Pss 69-71 the psalms without notation are placed together. Ps 72 is a supplement, a Psalm of Solomon, which was added later. The current disruptions of the planned order are caused by later rearrangements, which occurred during or after the conclusion of the psalter. For example: *mizmôr* stands at the beginning of Ps 51; one encounters a psalm without superscription (61) between the *miktāmîm* and the *mizmôrîm*; or that someone has placed a nameless

---

[14]Pss 53 = 14; 70 = 40:14-18; 58:8-12 + 60:7-14 = 108.

mizmôr among the *mizmôrîm* in Ps 66. The subscription of Ps 72 also argues for the original independence of the Davidic Psalter: "the end of the prayers of David, the son of Jesse." It can only stem from the collector of the Elohistic Psalter who wanted to mark the end of the Davidic collection he had incorporated. It does not account for the Davidic psalms which appear subsequently in the Psalter. It also does not fit for the Davidic psalms in the first book of Psalms. These psalms represent an independent collection as shown by the doublets to the Elohistic David collection (Ps 14=53; and 40:14-18 = 70).

Pss 73–83 stand at the end of the Elohistic Psalter as a group which are unified by the superscription, "by Asaph." It must remain open whether this collection of songs of the Asaphites was adopted entirely or only partially. In contrast to the first two collections, a corresponding lack of material order to the Asaph psalms is lacking. One cannot determine whether the current order of these poems already existed or whether the current order rests upon later transposition. One may perhaps ascribe the separation of Ps 50 from the group of Asaph psalms, and its insertion between the Korahite and Davidic songs, to a transposition which presumes the entire psalter.

12. The question of the purpose of the individual collections is easy to answer for the Korahite and Asaph psalter. It is apparent that the songbooks of the temple singer guilds were compiled for and determined by temple service. Individual observations lead to the same result. With the exception of Pss 48 and 87, the songs of the Korahites inside and outside the Elohistic Psalter consistently bear the notation *lammnaṣṣēăh*, which relates to worship performance. This notation is only encountered five times in the Asaph psalms (Pss 75, 76, 77, 80, 81). However, both the Asaph and Korahite psalms agree in another respect. The majority of the songs united in the temple song books were composed for the cult. In the Korahite Psalter, only Pss 42/43, 49, and 88 were not cultic and in the Asaph Psalter only 73, 77, and perhaps 78 were not cultic. This situation should be interpreted to mean that the temple singers have incorporated half of the individual spiritual songs for their character and beauty. They combined them with the main body of their cult songs. One should add that in the Korahite and Asaph psalms, one finds references to the musical performance (Pss 45; 46; 84, 88, 75, 76, 77, 80, 81). Thus, one may deduce that the worship aims of both collections can be assumed.

The Davidic Psalter was also a songbook of the temples service. All of its songs, with the exception of 63 and 71, bear the notation *lammnaṣṣēăh*. However, since Ps 71, which has no superscription, should probably be viewed as a continuation of Ps 70, only one exception remains that could have been inserted. In addition, the majority of the Davidic psalms bear musical technical notations.[15] The fact that this notation belongs to the Davidic collection and was not first added by the collector of the Elohistic Psalter may be derived from *lammnaṣṣēăh*. These notations appear consistently in the Davidic Psalter, but not in the Elohistic Psalter. One could not understand why the collector only places his remarks randomly elsewhere, but uses them with more consistent regularity in the Davidic psalms, or at least has shows a one-sided preference for them in the Davidic psalms.

If it cannot be doubted that the Davidic Psalter was a worship songbook, one may still not overlook the other side, namely that a number of noncultic psalms have been incorporated into it (Pss 51, [52], 54, 55, 56, 57, 58, 59, 61, 62, 63, 64, 69, 70, 71). One

---

[15]Pss 53, 54, 55, 56, 57, 58, 59, 60, 61, 62, 67, 69.

thus observes the same process as with the other collections. The temple worship service later sought to make this psalm poetry suitable which had been free of the cult.

A number of these psalms that originally had not been determined for the worship service bear a short biographical notice which provides the situation in David's life for which he had supposedly composed the psalm.[16] Characteristically, they all represent noncultic situations in which the psalm in question was supposed to have been sung. One feels tempted to conclude that every superscription was older than the Davidic Psalter, and that that they point to a psalm collection that was designed to be used at home by the laity. In a situation similar to those situations stated by David (these are consistently complaint songs), the lay person could pray the psalm and gain comfort from it. One may not object to the supposition that Pss 52 and 60 also offer a biographical note in the superscription, and that the second one, at least, is a cultic psalm. Psalms designed for the worship service had been used in situations outside the worship service. See Isa 38 and Jonah 2 (the psalms of Hezekiah and Jonah respectively). However, the situation becomes quite complicated by the fact that one encounters Davidic psalms with a biographical notation outside of our Davidic Psalter. The situation becomes so complicated that one should only suggest a possibility (and its likelihood) and be satisfied with the lack of unambiguous references.

This condition is recommended over against striving to trace additional collections which served as sources for the Davidic Psalter. As the example of Briggs shows, this attempt yields highly questionable results. In order to accept that there was earlier a collection of *miktāmîm*, *mizmôrîm*, *maśkîlîm*, etc., or whether the psalms of different authors had been unified in this earlier collection, one would first have to know what the expression in question means. In addition, another possibility remains. A collector himself could have arranged the various psalms of David which he found in material groups.

The question of the goal of the Elohistic Psalter which compiled the various smaller collections seems more important. Since it unified the three worship service song collections, it must also be evaluated as a worship songbook. The Elohistic recension also agrees. As the books of Chronicles allow one to recognize, the cult of that time preferred the name Elohim to the older name YHWH.

13. A supplement has been added to the Elohistic Psalter which no longer experienced changes to the divine name. It consists of four Korahite psalms (84, 85, 87, 88), one of which (Ps 88) is supposed to have belonged to the ancestor Heman (1 Chr 6:18), and a psalm from the singer Ethan (89) known from 1 Chr 6:29; 15:17, 19. Currently, a Davidic psalm disturbs the context of the Korahite psalms. Suppositions about the time and the reason for its placement are precarious. It could have received its current placement as a result of transpositions within the whole psalter. The time of the supplement cannot be established, nor can one establish whether it presumes the Elohistic Psalter, knows the combination of Pss 3–83, or stands in connection with the whole collection. It remains uncertain whether Ps 89:27 really wants to correspond with Ps 2:7, as Driver/Rothstein (*Einleitung*, p. 399) argue.

14. One should distinguish another Davidic psalter as a source of the entire collection from the Davidic Psalter of the Elohistic collection. It comprises Pss 3–41. The anonymous Ps 33 certainly entered this context secondarily. The collection reaches its conclu-

---

[16]Pss 51, (52), 54, 56, 57, 59, 63.

sion in Ps 41. One can observe that the conclusion of the Elohistic Davidic collection was marked by a doxology (Ps 72:18) like the end of the supplement expanding the Elohistic Psalter in general (Ps 89:53). The same thing happens with the doxology (Ps 41:14) standing at an original conclusion.

In its current state the collection does not exhibit a material arrangement corresponding to the Elohistic Davidic Psalter. Psalms with notices of *mizmôr, šiggayôn, miktām,* and *tefillāh* stand alongside one another, and regularly alternate with psalms that have no notation. The attempt to create order by accepting three subordinate collections arranged by their song types (Steuernagel, §156, ¶4b) is unsatisfactory because even such an accepted original order breaks down in places. It is recommended that one exercise caution with this question rather than lose oneself in relatively uncertain presuppositions.

The answer to the goal of the Davidic collection appears to suggest itself. One encounters the notation *lammnaṣṣēăh* in the superscription related to the cult 19 times.[17] If *mizmôr* can also be perceived as an expression pointing to the cult because of *zimmer* (to play an instrument), then there are 26 psalms in all which tradition associates with the worship service.[18] Eight of the psalms designated with *lammnaṣṣēăh* also bear technical musical notations.[19] It thus appears as though this Davidic Psalter was also collected for worship use.

This conclusion may nevertheless be too hasty. In contrast to the other song collections we have observed to this point, this collection contains 12 poems completely lacking any notation directed to the worship service (Pss 7, 16, 17, 25, 26, 27, 28, 32, [33], 34, 35, 37). With the lack of any tradition, one cannot simply claim that they were designed for worship use. Such a claim would be even less convincing since nine of them (7, 16, 17, 25, 27 [as a whole], 32, [33], 35, 37) recognize no relationship to the worship service.

If these considerations are true, then the goal of the collection must be determined for these poems. It was then compiled with the intention of creating a *devotional and home book* for the pious laity. The details of the process should be conceptualized as follows. A group of songs known and trusted from the worship service were bound with spiritual, cult-free psalms.

The examples compiled in ¶10 concerning the non-cultic use of spiritual and worship songs add probability to this supposition. The following observations also argue for the same conclusion. The spiritual songs offer comforting words about YHWH's action toward his pious ones, especially at the conclusion.[20] These songs thus inspire the god-fearing reader and encourage him. The didactic conclusion of the thanksgiving songs in Pss 32 and 34 (as well as 37 in its entirety) specifically seek to elicit the idea that YHWH does not forget his pious ones. Instead YHWH sends them help. Also, almost all of the psalms are suitable for private use because they consist of genres for the individual.[21] These

---

[17]Pss 4, 5, 6, 8, 9, 11, 12, 13, 14, 18, 19, 20, 21, 22, 31, 36, 39, 40, 41.
[18]Pss 3, 4, 5, 6, 8, 9, (11), 12, 13, 15, 19, 20, 21, 22, 23, 24, 29, 30, 31, 38, 39, 40, 41.
[19]Pss 4, 5, 6, 8, 9, 12, 22, 39.
[20]Pss 7:11-12; 16:10; 32:10-11; 33:18ff; 34:16ff; 35:26f; 37.
[21]Individual complaint songs: Pss 3, 5, 6, 7, 9/10, 12, 13, 17, 22, 25, 26, 27, 28, 31, 35, 36, 38, 39, and Ps 19 taken as a whole. Songs of confidence: 4, 11, 16, 23. Individual thanksgiving songs: 18, 30; 32; 34; 40; 41. And an individual hymn: Ps 8.

observations really strengthen the presumption already expressed and do not validate the acceptance of a cultic purpose.

15. Within Pss 90–150, one can easily recognize Pss 120-134 were once an independent collection. Each of these psalms bears the superscription *šîr hamma'ălôt*, though one (Ps 121) has *šîr lamma'ălôt*. Pss 122, 124, 131, and 133 are ascribed to David, and Ps 127 to Solomon. Nevertheless, the transmission is very contested.

The small collection's goal is not clearly recognizable because the meaning of the expression *ma'ălôt* is not certain. If it should mean "pilgrimage," as we accept in the commentary, then we have a psalter before us which unites a number of songs that were designed to be sung by pious laity marching on the annual pilgrimage to Jerusalem. In addition, this interpretation would coincide with the fact that none of these songs contains any type of notice which relates to the performance in the temple service. Accordingly, the purpose of the collection would fall between a devotional and prayer book on the one hand and a cultic psalter on the other. However, since the expression *ma'ălôt* is still contested, one cannot advance beyond suppositions at this point.

Among the psalms joined in Pss 120–134, only one, Ps 122, is really a pilgrimage song according to its genre, designed to be sung when the pilgrim enters Jerusalem (see §8, ¶21). Certainly, Pss 121, 126, 132, and 134, as liturgies (see §11, ¶¶15, 16, 17, 20), were designed for performance in the cult. Pss 120, 130, and 131 are cult-free (individual complaint song, §6, ¶¶4, 5). Ps 123 is mixed between the individual and communal complaint song (§4, ¶12). Ps 125 is a communal song of confidence (§4, ¶10, p. 92). Pss 124 and 129 are communal thanksgiving songs (§8, ¶38, p. 246). Pss 127:1-2, 3-5; 128; and 133 are wisdom songs (§10, ¶2).

The collection offers no linchpins concerning the time it arose.

16. No ordering principle can be discovered among the remaining psalms that would indicate a smaller collection. The majority of the psalms are nameless. Pss 101, 103, 108–110, and 138–145 are traced to David, while Ps 90 is traced to Moses. Most of the psalms also bear no superscriptions. Superscriptions are found only in the following: *mizmôr* in Pss 92, 98, 100, 101, 108–110, 139–141; *lammnasṣēăh* in Pss 109, 139; 140; *maśkîl* in Ps 142; *hallelūyāh* in Pss 106, 111–113, (114), (116–118), 135, (136), 146–150. The superscription of the psalms enclosed in parentheses have erroneously been moved to the end of the previous psalm. It is questionable whether one can deduce a smaller collection from this condition. One could certainly form four groups, each of which conclude with hallelujah psalms. However, Pss 119 and 137 must then be added, and one must make allowances for the separation of Davidic psalms from one another.

It must thus remain uncertain whether Pss 90–150 preserve other collections, apart from the *ma'ălôt* psalter. This uncertainty is underscored by the doxology in Ps 106:48. In contrast to the other doxologies, one cannot recognize that Ps 106:48 stands at the end of a group that belongs together. It must also remain uncertain whether Pss 90–150 could ever have been formed as an independent collection. It is quite conceivable that the core (Pss 3–89) consisted of known smaller collections, and that when the whole psalter was combined, Pss 90–150 were attached as a particular group even though, for the most part, they had been transmitted individually.

17. The origin of the entire psalter is mentioned with these last ideas. Its gradual growth can best be illustrated in a chart:

David 1	Korahite	David 2	Asaph		
Pss 3-41	Pss 42-49	Pss 51-72	Pss 50, 73-83		
	84-85			*ma'ălôt songs*	Individual psalms
	87-88				
	Elohistic Psalter			Pss 120-134	
Elohistic Psalter with Supplement					
[Collection of Pss 3-89 (?)]					
Psalter					
Transpositions in the Psalter					

Only a few words need to be added to this chart.

One can hardly deduce convincing conclusions about the chronological order from the sequence in which the smaller collections were adopted into the psalter. This statement is especially true for the relationship of the first Davidic Psalter to the Elohistic Psalter. One can only say with certainty that the more recent collection process was attached to the older collection. The possibility exists that the first Davidic collection was placed at the front for the same purpose which the entire psalter pursues. Specifically, one can observe that the first Davidic collection represents a devotional book and a prayer book. If one makes this observation then perhaps it was placed at the beginning because the collector wanted the entire psalter to be perceived as a devotional book and a prayer book. Perhaps from this point, one can move beyond the cautious decision on p. 343. In any case, this possibility shatters the certainty of chronological conclusions for the individual smaller collections.

The psalter was divided into five books, separated from one another by concluding doxologies. We would like to presume that the number five was no accident, but was chosen by the collector himself. The number five is found elsewhere as an ordering principle (five visions of Amos, five books of the Pentateuch, etc.). He apparently adopted three doxologies with the smaller collections. He added the fourth himself to the end of Ps 106, thus completing the division of the entire psalter into five sections. This psalm offered itself, so to speak, because its final words were connected with the doxology of the community in worship practice (cf. ¶6, p. 337).

§14 The Superscriptions of the Psalms

As a supplement we would like to pursue several notes concerning the superscriptions of the Psalms to the degree that they allow us to say something new and perhaps more certain. A complete treatment would essentially repeat what has already been said, and will thus not be attempted. The notes that are provided here relate exclusively to the musical additions of the superscriptions. They should be perceived as the substitution for the treatment anticipated in the commentary (p. 1), which the author was unable to bring at the end of the commentary.

One finds brief notes in the superscriptions that are characterized by the following common traits. They are introduced with *'al*.[1] In the overwhelming number of cases, the substantive which depends upon the preposition ends with a feminine *t*.[2] Finally, the prepositional phrases consistently follow the word *lammnaṣṣēăh*.[3] Generally, the name of the author follows the prepositional phrases with the exception of Pss 46, 49, and 88.

These commonalities point to the fact that the notes should be treated together when explaining them. If one succeeds in extrapolating the meaning of several of them, then one can only suppose that the remainder have a similar meaning.

The notations certainly relate to musical performance, by providing special instructions. In the first place, this conclusion can be deduced from the superscription "With stringed instruments" (*bingînôt*). Its meaning is completely clear and it stands in the same place.[4] This conclusion can also be seen by the fact that two of the expressions occurring in the superscriptions (*'al 'almūt* and *'al haššemînît*) appear in 1 Chr 15:20,21 in a context where one cannot doubt its character. Both stand in close proximity to instruments: the first with *nebālîm* and the second with *kinnôrôt*. The latter also has a close connection with *naṣṣēăh*, a word that, no matter what its precise meaning, has to do with leading temple music and temple singing. From the context, one deduces that the expressions combined with *'al* cannot relate to the use of specific instruments. This idea would be expressed with *be*. Rather, these expressions must relate to the manner in which the instruments should be played or in which the song should be performed.

1. When interpreting the individual expressions, it is recommended that we begin with *'al haggittît* in Pss 8:1; 81:1; and 84:1. The closest possibility for translating this expression can only be "according to the Gathites." *Gittî* is the very common *nomen*

---

[1]Pss 6:1; 8:1; 9:1 (LXX, Aquila, Theodotian; 12:1; 22:1; 45:1; 46:1; 53:1; 56:1; 60:1; 62:1; 69:1; 77:1; 81:1; 84:1; 88:1. Relatedly, *'el* should be corrected to *'al* in Pss 5:1; 57:1; 58:1; 59:1; 75:1; 80:1. In addition, the *le* in Ps 39:1 should be expanded to *'al* as in Pss 62:1 and 77:1. An *'al* should also be added before *'almūt* in Ps 48:15 which has erroneously been attached to Ps 48.

[2]Only Pss 57:1; 58:1; 59:1; and 75:1 offer exceptions where the words are not vocalized as feminine today, but do end in *t*. The only examples having masculine forms are Pss 39:1; 45:1; 60:1; 62:1; 77:1; 80:1.

[3]Only the corrupted superscription of Ps 49:1 offers an exception.

[4]Cf. Pss 4:1; 54:1; 55:1; (61:1); 67:1; 76:1.

gentilicum for the name of the well-known Philistine city of Gath. The word has nothing to do with *gat* (winepress). By way of expansion, one can only wonder whether it is a tonal type, a particular development of singing, or a special way of playing instruments.

From this point, it becomes apparent that the other substantives ending with *t* should also be conceived as *nomina gentilicia*. The text transmission creates no difficulties since one can consistently recognize that they forgot the expressions quickly and then attempted to explain them via all types of attempts to vocalize them.

2. The superscriptions to Pss 9:1; 46:1; and 49:1 (cf. 1 Chr 15:20) have *'al 'ǎlmūt*. In Pss 9:1 and 48:15, the text is divided into two words in part of the transmission and read *'ǎl mūt*. The preposition is thus lost. In the first case, the LXX reads *'ǎlūmôt* ("that which is hidden") and in the second case it reads *'ôlāmôt* (eternity). In Ps 46:1 four attempted solutions have been transmitted: in the MT, *'ǎlāmôt* ("virgin"); as in 1 Chr 15:20 several mss have *'ǎlmūt* ; the LXX read *'ǎlūmôt* ; and Symmachus has *'ôlāmôt*. The correct reading, as Graetz (*Psalmen*, p. 71) already suggested, is *'al 'ēlāmît* ("according to the Elamite" [manner], or something similar).

3. In Ps 56:1, "according to the dove of the distant gods" stands in the place where one would expect the musical expression. It is undoubtedly correct, with Perles (*Analekta*, vol. 2, p. 64), that it should be read *'al yewānît* ("according to the Greek [manner]). In the continuation, one should read *'iyyîm* instead of *'elem* or *'ēlîm* (with the LXX). One should thus translate the entire expression, "according to the Greek manner of the distant Islands)." One encounters the "distant islands" alongside *yāwān* in Isa 66:19.

4. Similarly, a *gentilicum* is hidden behind the meaningless *'al taḥšet* ("do not corrupt") in Pss 57:1; 58:1; 59:1; and 75:1. One must read *'al taḥšît* ("according to the Taha-shites"), thereby connecting it with the Aramean tribe *taḥaš* well-known from Gen 22:24. This tribe's land would have been identical with the country located in the Lebanon region, known as *tḥš* in Egypt and *taḥši* in the Amarna-letters (cf. O. Procksch, *Genesis*,[2,3] p. 143).

5. In Pss 6:1; 12:1; and 1 Chr 15:21, one should seek a *gentilicum* behind *'al haššemînît* which is usually translated "according to the eight" and related to the octave. It could perhaps be *'al haššimrônît* (according to the Shimronites). Shimron was a Canaanite royal city known from Josh 11:1 and 19:15. The LXX consistently reflects the name with Sumown, and the Talmud identifies it with *Simonîyāh* (see the examples in Gesenius-Buhl, *Hebräisches und Aramäisches Handwörterbuch*). One must thus consider that the name was pronounced as *šimyôn* following the loss of the *r*, or that someone erroneously equated *šimyôn* for the older *šimrôn*. If either the first or the second possibility took place, then one could explain the consonantal text without changing it, reading simply *'al haššimiyônît*.

6. With the expression *'al mhlt* in Pss 53:1 and 88:1 (to which one should add *'al nhlt* in Ps 5:1), one may perhaps think of a tribe *mahǎlat* which is the name of Esau's wife in Gen 28:9. If that appears uncertain, one should consider the possibility that the *gentilicum* should be derived from *'ābēl meḥôlāh* in Issachar (cf. Judg 7:22; 1 Sam 18:19; 1 Kgs 4:12; 19:16). Both cases have to account for a slight corruption of the consonantal text. Both cases involve one *t* too few. The first case would have read *'al mahǎlātît* and in the second case *'al meḥôlātît*.

7. One must also reckon with the same erroneous omission of the second *t* at the end in Ps 22:1. One does not expect "according to the hind of the sunrise" (as it was still

translated in the commentary) at this point in the superscription. Apparently, one should read 'al 'ēlātît ("according to the Elathites), deriving the *gentilicum* from the well-known harbor city Elath on the Red Sea. It cannot be determined what *šhr* means and whether one should consider it dependent upon the preceding.

8. Now we come to the prepositional expressions with masculine substantives. In the superscriptions of Pss 45:1; 60:1 (LXX); 69:1; and 80:1, one finds 'al *šôšnîm* (Ps 60:1 mangles this to *šušn*). In the context of the examples already treated, it became probable (following the supposition expressed by Perles, *Analekta*, vol. 2, p. 64), that one must consider a slight displacement at the end. One should thus correct the text to 'al *šûšānît* ("according to the Shushites"). See Fr. Delitzsch, *Die Lese- und Schreibfehler im Alten Testament*, §129b. The displacement was required so that the one transmitting the text, who did not know anything beginning with *šûšānît*, thought of the form of *šûšan* ("lily").

9. Finally, the expression 'al *yedûtûn* in Pss 62:1 and 77:1. No one can doubt that it represents a notice related to the musical performance, and that it has nothing to do with the singer Jedutun in Chronicles. The erroneous superscription in Ps 39:1 came about by recalling that person. The formation of the expression with 'al prevents one from thinking of an author, as well as the observation that with the remaining superscriptions we have seen, the indication of the author follows. Unfortunately, one cannot say what the expression means positively.

The understanding of the musical notations discussed here does not claim to have found the ultimate correct reading in every case. However, we certainly feel assured in accepting that the key to understanding the musical notes lies here. One must still wonder how to deal with the expansion of the *nomen gentilicum*. However, apart from this question, one must recognize that the Israelite-Judean temple singing was not afraid to make use of tonal types and methods of singing stemming from foreign lands if it elevated the beauty of the holy song and holy music.

Index of Scripture References

Psalms

The Psalms and Other Scriptures indexes were compiled with the aid of Melanie Greer Nogalski.

Other Scriptures

To facilitate location, these canonical, deuterocanonical, and noncanonical texts appear here in alphanumeric order. Texts with ordinals (first, second, etc.) are of course in alphabetic order by title and numeric order by ordinal.

Printed in Great Britain
by Amazon